Historical Agency and the 'Great Man' in Classical Greece

The 'great man' of later Greek historical thought is the long product of traceable changes in ancient ideas about the meaning and impact of an individual life. At least as early as the birth of the Athenian democracy, questions about the ownership of the motion of history were being publicly posed and publicly challenged. The responses to these questions, however, gradually shifted over time, in reaction to historical and political developments during the fifth and fourth centuries BC. These ideological changes are illuminated by portrayals of the roles played by individuals and groups in significant historical events, as depicted in historiography, funerary monuments, and inscriptions. The emergence in these media of the individual as an indispensable agent of history provides an additional explanation for the reception of Alexander 'the Great': the Greek world had long since been prepared to understand him as it did.

SARAH BROWN FERRARIO is Associate Professor of Greek and Latin at The Catholic University of America. She is a specialist in Greek history and literature, particularly of the fifth and fourth centuries BC.

Historical Agency and the 'Great Man' in Classical Greece

SARAH BROWN FERRARIO

CAMBRIDGE
UNIVERSITY PRESS

CAMBRIDGE
UNIVERSITY PRESS

University Printing House, Cambridge CB2 8BS, United Kingdom

Cambridge University Press is part of the University of Cambridge.

It furthers the University's mission by disseminating knowledge in the pursuit of education, learning, and research at the highest international levels of excellence.

www.cambridge.org
Information on this title: www.cambridge.org/9781107037342

First published 2014

Printed in the United Kingdom by Clays, St Ives plc

A catalog record for this publication is available from the British Library

Library of Congress Cataloging in Publication data
Ferrario, Sarah Brown, 1974–
Historical agency and the 'great man' in classical Greece / Sarah Brown Ferrario.
    pages   cm
Includes bibliographical references and index.
ISBN 978-1-107-03734-2
1. Greece – History – To 146 B.C. – Historiography.   I. Title.
DF211.F47   2014
938.0072 – dc23   2014007600

ISBN 978-1-107-03734-2 Hardback

For Ollie, the greatest little *man I know.*

Contents

Tables

Acknowledgements

I am most fortunate to be able to acknowledge here a great number of debts. This book began as a dissertation entitled *Towards the 'Great Man': Individuals and Groups as Agents of Historical Change in Classical Greece*, submitted to the Department of Classics at Princeton University in 2006 and now expanded and changed both in organization and in some detail, although the central arguments remain. To my supervisor, Josiah Ober, and my first reader, Michael Flower, I owe many points, both large and small, that helped me to develop and sustain this project, and the recurrences of their names in the notes and the bibliography form only the smallest recompense for the support and assistance they have given me. I also remain very grateful to my second dissertation reader, Christian Wildberg, and to others whose mentorship has shaped my work over the years, most notably Froma Zeitlin and Andrew Feldherr at Princeton, and Tim Long, Matthew Christ, and Cynthia Bannon at Indiana University, Bloomington.

The dissertation phase of this project was funded by a Graduate Prize Fellowship from the Center for the Study of Human Values at Princeton University (2003–04) and by a Fellowship from the Dolores Zohrab Liebmann Fund (2004–05); it also benefited indirectly from a Fulbright Scholarship to Greece (2001–02), a Princeton University Graduate Fellowship (1998–2003), a Marshall Scholarship from the Marshall Aid Commemoration Commission (1996–98), and a Herman B. Wells Scholarship from Indiana University (1992–96). Its transformation into a monograph was assisted by a Summer Stipend from the National Endowment for the Humanities (2008) and, most importantly, by a residential Junior Fellowship at the Center for Hellenic Studies in Washington, DC, under the directorship of Gregory Nagy (2009–10), where the leadership, staff, and fellows combined to make my year there an inordinately pleasant and profitable one.

Portions of this monograph in the same or similar form appear in the following locations:

- Material now in Chapters 5 and 6: "The Tools of Memory: Crafting Historical Legacy in Fourth-Century Greece," in Giovanni Parmeggiani, ed., *Between Thucydides and Polybius: The Golden Age of Greek Historiography*

(Washington, DC: Center for Hellenic Studies, Hellenic Studies Series 64, 2014), 263–88.
- Material now in Chapters 5 and 6: "Historical Agency and Self-Awareness in Xenophon's *Hellenica* and *Anabasis*," in Fiona Hobden and Christopher Tuplin, eds., *Xenophon: Ethical Principle and Historical Enquiry* (Leiden: Brill, 2012), 341–76.
- Material now in Chapters 2, 4, and 5: "Replaying *Antigone*: Changing Patterns of Public and Private Commemoration at Athens *c.* 440–350," in Cynthia Patterson, ed., *Antigone's Answer: Essays on Death and Burial, Family and State in Classical Athens = Helios* 33 S (2006), 79–117.

I am grateful to all of these editors and publishers for permission to reprint, and also to the presiders, presenters, and audiences at the following conferences who offered comments on oral papers that have also contributed to the finished product:

- "Xenophon: Ethical Principle and Historical Enquiry," University of Liverpool, England (2009).
- American Philological Association (APA) Annual Meeting, Chicago, IL (2008).
- "Greek Historiography in the Fourth Century BCE: Problems and Perspectives," Università degli Studi di Bologna and Harvard University, Bologna (2007).

Those who read chapters (or the conference papers that helped to work them out), answered questions, provided advice on individual details, recommended bibliography, and advanced my thinking in conversation include, but are by no means limited to, the editors of my published pieces listed above, as well as Emily Baragwanath, Nino Luraghi, John Marincola, William McCarthy, Gregory Nagy, Ivana Petrovic, Tim Rood, Gunnar Seelentag, Melina Tamiolaki, Tarik Wareh, and Xiaoqun Wu. Special thanks go to Andrej Petrovic, who provided significant epigraphical assistance, although I of course wish to emphasize that any errors that remain – whether in that area or elsewhere – are entirely my own. I am also deeply grateful to Lilla Kopár and Leonora Neville for their ongoing wisdom and encouragement, both as colleagues and as friends.

 The library staff at The Catholic University of America (CUA), especially Kevin Gunn, and the librarians of the Center for Hellenic Studies, Erica Bainbridge, Sophie Boisseau, Lanah Koelle, and Temple Wright, provided essential resources for what has proven to be a very long and wide-ranging project, and Beth Newman Ooi, Benjamin Lewis, and Andrew

Hagstrom stepped in as research assistants to check references and Greek texts in the near-final versions of the manuscript. Throughout its preparation, my colleagues in the Department of Greek and Latin at CUA, Frank Mantello, William Klingshirn, William McCarthy, and John Petruccione, have supported my work with patient mentoring, sage advice, and the judicious parceling of teaching and professional responsibilities. And at Cambridge University Press, Michael Sharp, Elizabeth Hanlon, and Gaia Poggiogalli have been invariably generous in their editorial guidance. Sincere thanks are also due to Nina Marcel for her careful copy-editing, and to Roger Bennett for the subject index.

My remaining obligations are both personal and numerous, but I will confine them here to two expressions of profound gratitude: firstly, to the members of my family, especially my most important teachers, Joseph and Nancy Ferrario, *optimis parentibus*; and lastly, to my husband Andrew Simpson and our young son Oliver, *sine quibus nihil*.

Notes on translations, abbreviations, and transliterations

Translations of ancient texts and inscriptions not otherwise acknowledged are my own; all others are cited individually as they are quoted.

Ancient Greek and Roman authors and their works are abbreviated throughout as in the *LSJ* and the *OLD*. Names of journals and periodicals are abbreviated as in *L'année philologique*. The most important exception to the standard bibliographic conventions is Christoph W. Clairmont, *Classical Attic Tombstones*, 8 vols. (Kilchberg, 1993), which is cited as "Clairmont 1993" with page numbers when reference is made to essays and introductory material, and as *CAT* with entry numbers when individual tombstones or their records are cited.

Greek names of both people and places are most often Latinized, with some exceptions where a Hellenizing transcription is in more common use, and with one particular personal indulgence ("Kerameikos" rather than "Ceramicus"). Original spellings have also been preserved in quotations from other sources.

1 | The search for the 'great man'

1.1 Who 'owns' history?

In 352 BC, an Athenian man named Euthycles went to court to prosecute a charge of *graphê paranomôn*, or the proposing of an illegal governmental decree. Like many citizens of his day, he engaged a *logographos*, a speechwriter, and the arguments that he delivered at the trial were therefore composed by Demosthenes. Since the case centered upon the award of potentially undeserved privileges to a mercenary who was at best only a dubious friend of Athens,[1] Demosthenes scripted for his speaker a penetrating reading of the attitude of the Athenian *dêmos* towards the roles of eminent individuals in the motion of history:

> οὐδ' ἔστ' οὐδεὶς ὅστις ἂν εἴποι τὴν ἐν Σαλαμῖνι ναυμαχίαν Θεμιστοκλέους, ἀλλ' Ἀθηναίων, οὐδὲ τὴν Μαραθῶνι μάχην Μιλτιάδου, ἀλλὰ τῆς πόλεως. νῦν δ', ὦ ἄνδρες Ἀθηναῖοι, πολλοὶ τοῦτο λέγουσιν, ὡς Κέρκυραν εἷλε Τιμόθεος καὶ τὴν μόραν κατέκοψεν Ἰφικράτης καὶ τὴν περὶ Νάξον ἐνίκα ναυμαχίαν Χαβρίας· δοκεῖτε γὰρ αὐτοὶ τῶν ἔργων τούτων παραχωρεῖν τῶν τιμῶν ταῖς ὑπερβολαῖς αἷς δεδώκατ' ἐπ' αὐτοῖς ἑκάστῳ τούτων. (D. 23.198)

> There is no one who would claim that the naval battle at Salamis was the possession of Themistocles; rather, it was that of the Athenians. Nor [would anyone claim] that the battle of Marathon was the possession of Miltiades; rather, it was that of the polis. But now, men of Athens, many people say just this: that Timotheus took Corcyra, that Iphicrates massacred a Spartan division, that Chabrias won the naval battle at Naxos. You yourselves, then, seem to concede ownership of these deeds through the excesses of honors that you have given for them to each of these men.

Demosthenes' condemnation is not merely a semantic one. Instead, he is posing very serious questions about both popular sentiment and popular

---

[1] For more detailed information on the historical context, including ancient citations and a description of the major arguments of D. 23 (the prosecution speech), see Sealey 1993: 130–1; cf. also the introduction to D. 23 in Vince 1935.

government. Does the Athenian *dêmos* now depend, whether functionally or cognitively, upon its leaders in ways that it once did not? Who ultimately creates the history of Athens, the group or the individual?

In this section of the speech against Aristocrates, Demosthenes draws his images from the familiar tropes of Marathon and Salamis.[2] Reaching back to the glorious victories of the Persian Wars, he claims that the Athenians conceptualize their past very differently from the way that they view their present. The *dêmos*, though it may believe that it was once the chief agent of its own history, now looks in its critical moments to the direction of important individuals instead. These men, whether political leaders, military commanders, or even foreign potentates, have therefore become de facto indispensable – with the result that (for Demosthenes) the efficacy of the democracy is compromised. Read in this context, the issues at hand become emblematic of much larger questions not only about the operation of the Athenian government, but about the very mindset of the Athenian people.

How did the Athenians arrive at this point? As Demosthenes' examples suggest, the process has had a long gestation. As early as the end of the sixth century BC, a discernible debate is underway at Athens over the ownership of pivotal historical moments. This symbolic 'conversation,' manifested in literature, epigraphy, monuments, art, and even popular song, questions the role of the Tyrannicides (as opposed to the roles of the Spartans, the Alcmeonids, or the Athenian populace)[3] in the establishment of the Athenian democracy. It represents a first point of entry into an extended dialogue that reveals changing perceptions, throughout the classical period, of the roles of individuals and groups in the motion of history.

These changes are of particular interest because they are not confined to the literary sphere. Tracing the 'rise of the individual' in Greek literature has long been a rich and productive pursuit in modern scholarship on ancient biography and ancient characterization.[4] Such work has shown that Greek authors in general, despite differences in geographical origin, political affiliation, or literary genre, appear over time to have focused with increasing intensity upon eminent men. The extent to which this

---

[2] On the use of these battles as traditional themes in oratory, see Nouhaud 1982: 147–61.

[3] For a reading of the relationship between the agency of the *dêmos* and that of Cleisthenes in the 'Athenian Revolution,' see Ober 1996a: 32–52.

[4] For varied approaches, e.g. Edwards and Swain 1997; Gill 1996; Bulloch et al. 1993; Pelling 1990; Gentili and Cerri 1988; Momigliano 1971; Dihle 1956; Misch 1950; Stuart 1928; Leo 1901; Bruns 1896; the latter two works remain influential and are still frequently cited. A brief retrospective of work on this general topic during the first half of the twentieth century appears in Homeyer 1962.

choice is representative – or formative – of wider popular thought, however, has been less frequently explored. It may be plausible, for example, to try to access broader sentiment by suggesting that Demosthenes would not select examples or craft generalizations wholly unlikely to resonate with the Athenian citizen body. But such an argument necessarily remains incomplete, because it is still dependent upon the content of the literature alone.

A similar problem is evident in the years intervening between the Tyrannicides and Demosthenes' own day. Close readings of the texts of Herodotus, Thucydides, and Xenophon do reveal that the kinds of questions Demosthenes poses about perceptions of historical agency were energetically examined in historiography during the fifth and earlier fourth centuries. The historical writers, however, focus most significantly upon members of the socio-political elite, while the experiences of the more ordinary people, or even of those just outside the upper echelon of political or military power, receive much less attention. The perceptions of the members of Demosthenes' audience (and of the members of the *dêmos* before them), therefore, must be sought in other media.

Particularly at Athens, commemorative efforts from the classical period support more comprehensive interpretations of popular sentiment. The accumulated activities of non-elites,[5] which permit the study of the spread of ideas on a wider scale, emerge from a comparatively abundant body of material evidence. Funerary monuments reveal how Athenians thought about individuals, about their roles in the community, and about the value and consequences of their actions. The commemoration of a life with a tombstone was a visible, memory-making act: Athenian burial plots were located along the sides of the main roads entering and exiting the city, so travelers and citizens alike passed by the monuments daily. In this context, a tombstone represents the deliberate choices of those who erected it. It not only indicates how the dedicators believed that the dedicatee should be remembered by his community, but also reveals how the dedicators interpreted, and perhaps also challenged, that community's cultural dictates and expectations. In contrast, public inscriptions express the official position of the state regarding the historical contributions and the memorialization of both groups and individuals – and the public and private viewpoints do not always align. Indeed, it is where they compete, or even conflict, that the richest and most complex readings emerge.

---

[5] I am influenced in my thoughts about 'elites' and 'non-elites,' and in my use of associated terminology, by Ober 1989.

This material evidence suggests that members of the wider Athenian populace were also thinking about the historical roles of individuals and groups in the course of the fifth and fourth centuries BC. Although they were doing so under terms that differed from those of the historiographers, traces of the same issues emerge in funerary iconography and epitaphs, and in the language of public commemoration. Over time, the Athenians seem to acknowledge in their own monuments not only the fundamental dependence – whether perceived or real – of the *dêmos* upon eminent individuals, but also a growing gap between those individuals who are positioned to 'make history' and those who are not. The literary and popular discourse about individual historical agency becomes so well developed, in fact, that those acquainted with its priorities can deliberately present themselves as exemplars.

To what extent can what is true for Athens be applied to the rest of the Greek world?[6] Admittedly, Athens does supply a dominant proportion of Greek funerary and epigraphical remains,[7] particularly from the classical period. Athenian intellectual influences and historical experiences also played an important role in the development of historiography.[8] But Athens itself was still a Greek polis, and many of its cultural priorities and civic behaviors were therefore held in common with other Greeks.[9] Access to popular discourse outside of Athens is sometimes affected by more limited corpora of localized evidence, but the self-presentation and reception of some well-known non-Athenians, such as Lysander[10] and Agesilaus of Sparta, Epaminondas of Thebes, and Philip II of Macedon, suggest that some of the same issues about individual and group historical agency that were under discussion at Athens were also receiving consideration elsewhere.

Tracing the development of the eminent individual in Greek thought down to the later fourth century will therefore contextualize the sentiments of Demosthenes quoted at the opening of this chapter. But it will also help to illuminate the remarkable reception of Alexander 'the Great' by showing

---

[6] On Athenocentrism in modern classical scholarship, see e.g. the references collected by Hedrick 1999: 390 n. 11; an example of a recent methodological discussion is Vlassopoulos 2007.

[7] See e.g. Morris 1987 and Hedrick 1999, respectively.

[8] E.g. Seager 2001; Hornblower 1995; Murray 1972. Thomas 2000 highlights many of the non-Athenian influences upon Herodotus, but Fowler 2003; Moles 2002; Blösel 2001; Forsdyke 2001; Raaflaub 1987; et al. explore Herodotus' interest in Athens.

[9] As C. Morgan 2003: 5–6 suggests, the publications of the Copenhagen Polis Centre provide an important way of helping to contextualize Athens within a much larger world of other Greek city-states. A partial bibliography of Polis Centre materials, compiled by F. Naerebout, can be found at http://www.teachtext.net/bn/cpc/ (last accessed September 10, 2011).

[10] I remain indebted to M. Flower for initially connecting the career of Lysander to my wider argument.

that his effect is deeply rooted in well over a century of ancient Greek experience and imagination. The magnitude of his impact, ironically, is perhaps most vividly displayed at the point where his image passed beyond his own control: at his death.

1.2 The alchemy of Alexander

Whether it was malaria, or alcohol poisoning, or even strychnine, Alexander was dying in Babylon.[11] The feverish, weakened king had been sinking for several days. Now he asked his senior generals to remain in attendance at the Babylonian palace, and his lesser officers to keep vigil outside. The *Ephemerides*, the 'royal diaries,'[12] assert that shortly thereafter the king lost his ability to speak,[13] and so it is perhaps at this point that the following anecdote must be understood:

> ἐπειδὴ τὸ ζῆν ἀπέγνω, περιελόμενος τὸν δακτύλιον, ἔδωκε Περδίκκᾳ. τῶν δὲ φίλων ἐπερωτώντων, Τίνι τὴν βασιλείαν ἀπολείπεις; εἶπεν, Τῷ κρατίστῳ, καὶ προσεφθέγξατο, ταύτην τελευταίαν φωνὴν προέμενος, ὅτι μέγαν ἀγῶνα αὐτῷ ἐπιτάφιον συστήσονται πάντες οἱ πρωτεύοντες τῶν φίλων. οὗτος μὲν οὖν τὸν προειρημένον τρόπον ἐτελεύτησε. (D.S. 17.117.3–5)

> When he had abandoned hope of survival, then, removing his ring, he gave it to Perdiccas. His Companions asked him, "To whom are you bequeathing the empire?" and he said, "To the strongest." And he made his final utterance by saying that all those who were foremost amongst his Companions would engage in a great funerary contest on his behalf. And in this way he ended his life.

Diodorus, the earliest extant continuous account of the life and campaigns of Alexander, has this story of the ring in common with both Curtius and Justin,[14] the other members of the Alexander 'Vulgate' tradition.[15] The other

---

[11] Bosworth 1988b: 173, with references (esp. n. 460); see also Green 1991: 476–7.

[12] *FGrH* 117; also Robinson 1932. Bosworth 1971: 117–23 argues that the *Ephemerides* were assembled in the months following Alexander's death in order to thwart rumors of poisoning. *Contra*: Hammond 1989.

[13] *FGrH* 117 F 3a–b.

[14] 'Curtius' is here taken to be [Quintus] Curtius Rufus (first century AD), on whom see e.g. Kraus and Woodman 1997: 84–7. On the identity of Marcus Iunian[i]us Iustinus, the epitomizer of the lost *Philippica* of Pompeius Trogus, see Develin's introduction to Yardley 1994, where it is noted that 'Justin' may have been active in the late second century AD, or may have written as late as *c.* AD 395.

[15] The passing of the ring is mentioned in these sources at D.S. 17.117.3–4, 18.2.4; Curt. 10.5.4, 10.6.4; Just. 12.15.12–13 (these represent only slight changes from the Perdiccas-related

two extant Alexander historians, Arrian[16] and Plutarch, omit the ring, likely because they are less immediately interested in the *Diadochoi*, the military leaders, court officials, and personal friends who became the immediate 'Successors' of Alexander.[17] All of the Vulgate writers, however, do provide some treatment of the wars of the *Diadochoi*, and the ring anecdote therefore helps them to explain the political ambitions of Perdiccas and the vengeful jealousy of Ptolemy.[18] Whether or not there ever really *was* a ring,[19] then, a major segment of the historiographic tradition has employed it as a strong symbolic link between the fact of Alexander's death and its historical consequences.

Other 'Alexander objects' achieved similar status in the historical accounts. The lack of a clear successor meant that a vicious struggle ensued amongst the *Diadochoi* almost immediately upon the loss of their king, and the historians focus their accounts of the opening conflicts around the personal effects – and even the body – of Alexander himself.

At the 'settlement' taken by the *Diadochoi* at Babylon shortly after Alexander's death, Perdiccas is said to have sought regency over Alexander's unborn child by his Bactrian wife Rhoxane.[20] In Curtius' sketch, the initial

references collected by Bosworth 1971: 128 n. 7, who also adds *Metz Epitome* 112). The 'Vulgate' is likely derived primarily from the account of Cleitarchus (scanty fragments at *FGrH* 137), who probably wrote *c.* 310 BC (Baynham 2003: 10 n. 31). The Vulgate category also traditionally includes the *Metz Epitome*, save for its last section, the independent *Liber de morte testamentumque Alexandri*: see Baynham 2003 esp. 10–11, 15–16 for a discussion of all of these texts and their transmission.

[16] On Lucius Flavius Arrianus (early second century AD) and his work, see Bosworth 1980. Arrian, like Diodorus, mentions the bequest of the empire τῷ κρατίστῳ and the expectation of a μέγαν ἐπιτάφιον ἀγῶνα (Arr. 7.26.3).

[17] Both Arrian and Plutarch conclude their accounts almost immediately upon Alexander's death and reserve discussion of later events for other projects. Plutarch's coverage of the *Diadochoi* and the subsequent Hellenistic dynasties is contained in other *Lives* (see esp. *Eum.*, *Phoc.*, *Demetr.*). Arrian's fragmentary *Ta meta tou Alexandrou* ("Events after Alexander" = *Succ.*) is accessible in two major editions, *FGrH* 156 and Roos and Wirth 2002. Bosworth 2002: 22 n. 55 offers some reasons to prefer the latter.

[18] Bosworth 1971: 128 n. 7 suggests that Arrian may have omitted the ring because Ptolemy, one of Arrian's favored literary sources, did the same, given that the story would have reflected badly upon Ptolemy's own aspirations for legitimate power; see also Roisman 1984: 374–5 and n. 10, who agrees and collects references to this interpretation. Hammond 1989: 159–60 holds that Arrian did not himself trust the authenticity of the ring anecdote.

[19] The anecdote's relationship to historical reality is debated: see Bosworth 1971 with Hammond 1989.

[20] See Bosworth 1993 on this phase of the 'Settlement of Babylon.' The long negotiations and their immediate aftermath are treated in detail amongst the major sources only in Curtius (10.6.1–10.8), which poses particular problems of bias (e.g. Bosworth 1971: 128 on the potential influence of Roman themes in Curtius' account). For additional analysis of both text and historical events, see Errington 1970 and Schachermeyr 1970.

negotiations are 'attended' by Alexander's former royal insignia: his *regia sella*, "royal seat," or "throne," is brought in, decorated with his *diadema vestisque . . . cum armis*, "crown, robe, and arms," and Perdiccas adds the ring to the display (Curt. 10.6.4). Ptolemy, while disagreeing with Perdiccas' larger proposals, argues that the throne itself should be used as a physical and symbolic nexus around which future political meetings should take place (Curt. 10.6.15).[21] As the settlement discussions continue, Meleager, a phalanx commander in Alexander's army, begins to agitate against Perdiccas (Curt. 10.6.20–4). A faction supports the accession of Arrhidaeus, Alexander's half-brother by their mutual father Philip II. Arrhidaeus is fetched and saluted by the military mob as king 'Philip' (Curt. 10.7.6–7), and, as tensions mount, he, too, is forced to enter into the competition of Alexander symbols:

> Cesserat ex contione Arrhidaeus, principum auctoritate conterritus, et, abeunte illo, conticuerat magis quam elanguerat militaris favor. Itaque revocatus vestem fratris (eam ipsam, quae in sella posita fuerat) induitur. Et Meleager, thorace sumpto, capit arma, novi regis satelles. Sequitur phalanx, hastis clipeos quatiens, expletura se sanguine illorum, qui adfectaverant nihil ad ipsos pertinens regnum. In eadem domo familiaque imperii vires remansuras esse gaudebant: hereditarium imperium stirpem regiam vindicaturam: adsuetos esse nomen ipsum colere venerarique nec quemquam id capere nisi genitum, ut regnaret. (Curt. 10.7.13–15)

> Arrhidaeus had withdrawn from the session in terror at the strength of the leaders, and with his departure the good will of the troops had not slackened, but rather grown quiet. And so [Arrhidaeus] was summoned back and dressed himself in his brother's robe (the very one that had been laid on the throne). And Meleager, clad in his thorax, took up his arms as a companion to the new king. The phalanx followed, striking their shields with their spears, ready to glut themselves on the blood of those who had attempted to control royal power that bore no connection to them. They were overjoyed that the imperial authority would remain in the same clan and house; that kingly lineage would justify hereditary reign; and that they were already used to revering and paying homage to that very name, and no one took it unless he were born for sovereignty.

---

[21] Eumenes, who inherited Alexander's elite military unit of *Argyaspides* ("Silver Shields"), was also said to have convened their leaders in front of a vacant royal throne graced by the royal insignia to emphasize that they were still under the symbolic command of the long-deceased Alexander: see Stewart 1993: 216 n. 75; Smith 1988: 37 n. 50, both with ancient references.

The robe of Alexander thus serves different symbolic functions for each of its interpreters. For Arrhidaeus, it is the visible sign of the royal power that his supporters claim as his birthright. It is also a guarantee of his safety: his perceived right to assume the robe makes him valuable to a volatile and potentially violent military mob (see also Curt. 10.7.1–7). For Meleager, the robe is the mark of a metaphorical ascent into the elite ranks of the king's *Sômatophylakes*, "Bodyguards," as evidenced by his assumption of the ceremonial and protective role of armed escort. For the soldiers, the robe makes Arrhidaeus, for the moment, interchangeable with Alexander: the phalanx even forms up behind him as if ready for battle. The ensuing action is perhaps predictable: *igitur Perdicca territus conclave, in quo Alexandri corpus iacebat, obser[v]ari iubet*, "and so Perdiccas, frightened, commanded that the chamber where Alexander's corpse lay should be locked" (Curt. 10.7.16).[22] With the most potent 'Alexander objects' now divided amongst several individuals, the struggle for Alexander *himself* began.

After the defeat and death of Meleager at the hands of Perdiccas, the assignment of the Macedonian kingship to Arrhidaeus and the infant Alexander IV with Perdiccas as regent, and the division of the Eastern conquests into a series of satrapies to be governed by the *Diadochoi* and others, armed conflict temporarily cooled.[23] At last, probably late in the year 322 or early in 321,[24] attention could be paid to Alexander's belated funeral. The body, which had been kept at Babylon, was placed in a richly decorated golden sarcophagus set on a golden wagon.[25] The destination of the elaborate funeral cortege, accompanied by ceremonial military units with cavalry and elephants, was to be the Egyptian oracle of Ammon at Siwah that had established Alexander's 'divine' connections during his lifetime.[26] No sooner had the spectacular procession, escorted by Arrhidaeus, reached Damascus, however, than it was met by Ptolemy, now satrap of Egypt and accompanied by an army. Diodorus provides the most detailed account of the events that followed,[27] recording that Ptolemy, under the guise of

---

[22]   There is a textual problem at the word *obser[v]ari* (see Lucarini 2009 *ad loc.*); I have followed Rolfe 1946 in translating *obserari* here.

[23]   See Bosworth 2002: 54–63 for a narrative of this period.

[24]   The year 322: e.g. Bosworth 2002: 12; the year 321: e.g. Errington 1970: 64.

[25]   The assemblage is described in detail at D.S. 18.26.3–28.1.

[26]   Relevant references and bibliography are collected by e.g. Bosworth 2002: 13 n. 30; Stewart 1993: 221, 369, 374, (both citing D.S. 18.3.5; Curt. 10.5.4; Just. 12.15.7, 13.4.6), Stewart further noting that the latter two authors represent this location as Alexander's own choice.

[27]   D.S. 18.28.2–6; cf. the narrative account of Erskine 2002: 167–71, citing (169 n. 26, as do Bosworth 2002: 13 n. 31 and Stewart 1993: 221 n. 88) Badian 1968.

honoring the dead king, brought Alexander's body to Alexandria instead, where it was placed in a magnificent precinct and celebrated with games. In return, Ptolemy is said to have received the devotion of his people and the blessings of the gods.[28]

The standoff had surely been risky, but Ptolemy's bid for the body of Alexander was a spectacular success. By hijacking the funerary cortege, he gained control of a unique work of art – the sarcophagus itself – and of an elaborate procession whose display value would guarantee both an audience for his newly acquired authority and a long, glorious memory of the results of his daring act.[29] Additionally, the triumphal quality of the procession may have suggested to viewers that Alexander himself was approving Ptolemy and deliberately moving to Alexandria.[30] The results, in Diodorus' reading, were incontestable: the honors that Alexander 'paid' to Ptolemy, and that Ptolemy returned, were understood by the public as signs of the gods' favorable disposure towards the new satrap and of Ptolemy's personal worthiness to rule.[31]

Such arrangements accorded poorly with the plans of Perdiccas, who had now lost control of a most important sign of his legitimacy,[32] and so he set out against Ptolemy.[33] There can be little doubt that, had he been successful on his Egyptian expedition, the first piece of booty he would have seized would have been the gold-enshrined body of Alexander. But Perdiccas did not survive the campaign: after a series of unsuccessful operations, he was assassinated by his own troops.[34] The long wars that followed[35] could not unseat Ptolemy, and in 304, his power secure, he took for himself in Egypt the title of 'King.'[36] Blessed with a fertile and wealthy country, protected from without by comparative geographic isolation and from within by a Hellenized aristocracy, the dynasty Ptolemy founded with the help of his precious prize ultimately endured unbroken far beyond the lifespans of

---

[28] D.S. 18.28.4–6.   [29] Kuttner 1999: 102.   [30] Ibid.

[31] Erskine 2002: 173–4 reaches a similar conclusion.   [32] See e.g. Erskine 2002: 170–1.

[33] See Badian 1968: 186–9 on the possibility that Arrhidaeus was cooperating with Ptolemy by this point.

[34] In 320 BC.

[35] The most extensive continuous ancient account of the wars of the *Diadochoi* is D.S. books 18–20, probably substantially dependent upon the (lost) history of Hieronymus of Cardia (*FGrH* 154: see Hornblower 1981), the latter an acquaintance of Alexander's former secretary Eumenes. Useful surveys of the era include Bosworth 2002; Green 1990: 3–134.

[36] Ptolemy was not alone in the timing of his decision to formally accept a crown. On the 'Year of the Kings' between 306 and 304, see, amongst the works cited by Bosworth 2002: 246–7, esp. Gruen 1985; Müller 1973: 78–107; and add Ritter 1965: 79–108 (dealing particularly with the assumption of the highly symbolic diadem).

the other Hellenistic kingdoms. Its last queen, Cleopatra VII, was finally defeated by Caius Iulius Caesar Octavianus, the future Roman emperor Augustus, at the battle of Actium in 31 BC.

Never before in Greek history had an individual been treated quite like this, and the phenomenon therefore begs some explanation. It has sometimes been claimed that Alexander, and even his father, Philip II, demonstrated through their conquests that one man could change the known world. In this view, the Hellenistic Greek historians and artists – and their Roman heirs – who depict 'great men' are subscribing to a new vision of history, one that was born in the later fourth century BC of the mating of large-scale political changes with larger-than-life personalities.[37] Filtered through the interests of Renaissance humanism, what came to be seen as the ancient 'great man' paradigm helped to lay foundations for historical and political thought in the early modern West,[38] and Alexander remained of central interest for both positive and negative reasons.[39] Modern discussions, too, frequently invoke the same selections of ancient individuals in thinking about 'great men' (the preferred examples from Greco-Roman antiquity being Alexander and Julius Caesar), but they do not always reflect in more detail upon the earlier political and social factors that provided the necessary and sufficient conditions for this 'greatness.'

The Greek historical writers of the Hellenistic and Roman eras, however, saw themselves as heirs to an intellectual inheritance that began, in many cases, with Herodotus.[40] They also owed significant debts to rhetoric, ethnography, genealogy, and even travel literature stretching back into the

---

[37] On such readings explicitly of Alexander e.g. the references collected by Fredricksmeyer 1982: 86.

[38] Southgate 2001: 30–61 *passim*, esp. 40–1 on Plutarch's biographies as literary, historical, and moral exempla. For more on Plutarch's *Lives* during the Renaissance, see e.g. Pade 2007; for a more detailed treatment of the reception of the past (including the ancient past) in the Renaissance era, see Hampton 1990; on the relationship of Renaissance concepts of 'great men' to ancient biographical interests, see Joost-Gaugier 1982.

[39] A bibliographic sketch can only provide points of entry on this subject. Beginning from antiquity, a useful survey of Alexander's *Nachleben* in the Hellenistic period is Errington 1975; on the Roman period, see Wirth 1975, in the same volume; on the art works, see Stewart 1993 and Bieber 1964. On the *Alexander Romance* and its effects upon the later literary reception of Alexander, see Cary 1956; on Alexander in the Middle Ages, see Aerts, Hermans, and Visser 1978. For a more general survey stretching from the Hellenistic period through medieval Islam, see di Vita and Alfano 1995: 153–91, and for one on Alexander legends, see Stoneman 2008; on a particular Renaissance treatment of Alexander (in Italian verse), e.g. Tordi 2004; on the early modern era, e.g. Brauer 1980 (focusing specifically on England, but with broader bibliographic references as well).

[40] E.g. Flower 1997 *passim*; Marincola 1997 *passim*; Christ 1993; Gray 1986; Fornara 1983a *passim*; Murray 1972; Bruce 1970; Connor 1968; Pearson 1960; Keller 1910–11.

fifth century.[41] It is likely, therefore, that their views about the influence of individuals upon history were shaped by their relationships to this tradition. It is also difficult to posit that the popular reception that Philip and (especially) Alexander enjoyed, and upon which their successors constructed the concept of Hellenistic kingship, was solely the result of their immediate programs of self-presentation. Successful promotion requires sophisticated interaction with the expectations of one's audience, and the perception of individual historical significance is as intimately dependent upon context as it is upon content. The public image that Alexander created for himself was likely the combined product of what his Hellenizing literary education, his upper-class Greco-Macedonian social circle, and his diverse experiences as prince, king, and general suggested to him would captivate the collective imagination.[42]

Evolving conceptions of individual historical potential during the classical period, then, comprise the central subject of this study. The results show that although Alexander's career had an enduring future, the factors that produced that effect were the products of a long past. The 'great man' as interpreted by the Hellenistic age and beyond was neither the cultural result of an isolated, striking biography nor the literary invention of a single intellectual. Rather, he was the evolutionary product of complex historical and social developments during the late archaic and classical periods. His story can be told in particular detail at Athens, but it was by no means confined there.

1.3 'Great men' and the motion of history

I have already begun to deploy terms that will recur throughout this project, and to introduce important concepts that require definition before the main body of evidence is treated in the chapters that follow. What constitutes a 'great man' in ancient Greek terms is the subject of this book, but the ideas of 'historical agency' and 'historical consequence' require more immediate explication.

---

[41] See Fornara 1983a: 1–29, and recently the survey by Oliver 2006, esp. 113–14. For general information on the intellectual content of Hellenistic historiography, see e.g. the papers collected in Verdin, Schepens, and de Keyser 1990; on the 'Atthidographers,' whose varied approaches represent diverse influences in microcosm, see Harding 2008, esp. the introduction at 1–12, citing, with many others, the foundations laid by Jacoby 1949.

[42] See Stewart 1993 on the impact of Alexander's 'program' upon the next generation of rulers. Stewart emphasizes iconography, but the scope of his discussion ranges much more broadly.

What does it mean for an individual or a group to be a 'historical agent'? The *reductio ad absurdum* would hold that every event in the past is in some way contributory to every event in the present (albeit, perhaps, at varying levels of direct and indirect causation),[43] and therefore all people may legitimately be viewed as agents of all history. In practice, however, the assignment of historical agency or responsibility rests significantly upon interpreters' evaluations of event outcomes:[44] in one reading, the motion of economic forces may 'start' a revolution; in another, it may be the collective sense of oppression on the part of the disenfranchised poor; in still another, the same revolution may be ascribed to the man who incites the opening riot.[45] Because this is a project about perceptions, the choice amongst factors such as these is left here to the ancients' interpretations. Historical agency in the ancient evidence may be claimed by individuals or groups through iconography, open statement, or the evocative use of language; it may be bestowed upon one individual or group by another; it may also be implicitly or explicitly assigned by historiographers.

What historical agency *looks* like in ancient Greek terms, however, varies in both degree and kind. Connections such as those discussed by Demosthenes at the opening of this introduction – of Themistocles with Salamis and Miltiades with Marathon – represent widely understood interpretations developed over time in a variety of literary and material contexts. The Athenian *dêmos* as a whole makes overt claims about its sovereignty (and therefore about its determination of its own history) through, amongst other forms of discourse, its commemorative and honorific inscriptions. The historiographers offer judgments upon the positions and contributions of eminent leaders. Further down the political and social ladder, however, the historical impact of less highly positioned individuals is most often invoked by associating them with specific historical events or heroic imagery, by noting their lasting contributions to the polis, or by highlighting their separate roles in smaller events that were still held worthy of commemoration, such as legal proposals or embassies.[46] While these figures would hardly qualify as 'great men' by modern standards, their depictions often use the same methods as those of their more famous leaders, and may therefore be read as claims to historical agency on a more limited scale.

---

[43] See Carr 1969: 122–39, discussing determinism and chance in the interpretation of historical causality.

[44] My articulation of this situation derives from the lucid summary of Southgate 2001: xi et al.

[45] Carr 1969: 116–17, 139; cf. also Pomper 1996; Aron 1958: 17–27; and the discussion of the Athenian Tyrannicides at the opening of Chapter 2, below.

[46] See the examples discussed in Chapters 2, 4, 5, and 6, below.

In ancient Greek terms, historical consequence is an outgrowth of the assignment of historical agency: an individual or group held even partially responsible for an event may be considered historically consequent as a result of the event's acknowledged impact. It apparently did not take long after the conclusion of the Persian Wars, for example, for the Athenians to believe in the existence of a 'Themistocles decree' advocating the momentous (in retrospect) decision to evacuate Attica. Such an important event, the thought seems to be, should have been recorded and commemorated with a stone inscription – and so it shortly was, even if only as a retroactive 'copy' of a nonexistent original.[47] The converse is also true: certain individuals seem to have received popular acclaim for historical consequence far beyond their actual achievements, due to their ability to attract notice and claim exaggerated responsibility for the motion of events. The most egregious example of this phenomenon during the classical period, as will be discussed in due course, is Alcibiades.[48]

Responsibility for history-making events in ancient Greece tends to be ascribed to highly visible participants, typically those in influential political or military positions, rather than to those who offer advice, who unwittingly create coincidences, or who act on a moment to tip a balance. The outcome of the Trojan War, for example, both for good and for ill, is laid in fifth-century Greek thought squarely at the feet of Agamemnon, not Epeius, the legendary architect of the Trojan horse.[49] There is much concern at Athens as to how the glory affixed to the memory of Marathon is to be apportioned, but the leading candidates are Miltiades, Callimachus, the *Marathonomachoi*, and the Athenian *dêmos*. No real account is taken of the fortunate turn (again in retrospect) that the Persians landed their ships on this particular patch of shore. Herodotus' narrative is frequently enriched by the predictions of 'wise advisers' or 'tragic warners,'[50] but emphasis is more often maintained in his text upon kings' ownership of the decisions they make, whether in accordance with or in spite of the advice given by their counselors. There are, of course, exceptions (one fourth-century inscription, for example, honors an individual for military advice which, if taken, "would have" resulted in the capture of enemy ships),[51] but credit

---

[47] On the inscription itself, see Jameson 1962 and 1960; for interpretation of its potential position in ancient thought, see Robertson 1982 and 1976. A more detailed reading of the decree's implications also appears below at the opening of Chapter 9.

[48] See Bloedow 1973 and Chapters 4 and 5, below.

[49] E.g. A. *Ag.*; Thuc. 1.9.1–10.1. On Epeius, e.g. Franko 2005/2006.

[50] Lattimore 1939 has served as the basis for many subsequent discussions of these traditional figures.

[51] *IG* ii/iii² 29, on which see Chapter 5, below.

and consequence are so often linked that it is sometimes even possible to see, as in the case of Alcibiades, the former actually preceding the latter in popular thought, as if the result of collective wishful thinking.

The effects of these conceptions of the motion of history upon commemorative efforts of the classical era can be read, analyzed, and in certain cases even quantified. While the evidence is complex, the generally externalized discourse makes it possible to trace shifts in historiographic thought, elite behaviors, and wider popular sentiment over time, and to examine the reception of individual people and events.

This focus upon the processes and the mechanisms of change means that the organization of this book is essentially chronological, beginning in the spring of 514 BC with the Tyrannicides. The dramatic stroke of the sword is a memorable starting point (as it seems to have been for the ancient Athenians, as well), but there are more practical reasons for this choice.[52] The study of ancient Greek characterization, biography, or 'the rise of the individual,' as others have shown, may legitimately commence as early as Homeric epic.[53] But ideas about the potential historical agency of groups cannot be examined as effectively at that early date: the necessary variety of literary and material evidence is simply not available. The fifth century witnesses a number of important changes that make this study possible. The engagement with the tension between individual and group in the rhetoric of the Athenian democracy,[54] coupled with the sheer size of the Athenian polis, generates a great deal of material for discussion. Also of central importance are the coalescence of historical writing into a way of discussing the past in prose; and the gradual increase in the number of extant public inscriptions, private tombstones, and other commemorative monuments throughout Greece. None of this is to claim that there was no interest in historical agency before the late sixth century BC, only to observe that wider popular sentiment can be far more broadly documented after that time, and so it is the most productive place to begin.

1.4 Structure and summary

Below, Chapter 2, "Man, myth, and memory under the early Athenian democracy," returns to the time of the 'Athenian Revolution' and studies

---

[52] I remain grateful to J. Ober for convincing me that this was the appropriate point of departure for this project.

[53] Cf. note 4, above; see also Starr 1968 for an analysis of the development over time of a 'historical sensibility' in Greek culture, climaxing in the work of Herodotus.

[54] On this subject in general, see esp. Ober 1989.

shifting Athenian understandings of the historical roles played by individuals and groups down through the earlier fifth century (*c.* 514–440 BC). The chapter begins by discussing the reception of the Tyrannicides and their memorialization as democratic 'heroes.' Major topics then treated include funerary practices (particularly changes in grave monuments over time and the tradition of civic burial known as the *patrios nomos*), the varied commemorations of the battle of Marathon, the institution of ostracism, and the acknowledgement of individuals and groups in public inscriptions.

Chapter 3, "Culture clash? Individuals and groups in the *Histories* of Herodotus," explores patterns in Herodotus' presentations of historical agency. Although his work is frequently understood in terms of binary oppositions between Greeks and barbarians, Herodotus actually has three different ways of reading the history-making deeds of human actors: he observes individual agency on the part of barbarians (generally foreign kings), group agency on the part of Greeks (most frequently acting in polis divisions), and individual agency on the part of Greeks. The tension between these latter two categories is associated with the material evidence treated in Chapter 2: eminent Greeks such as Solon, Hippias, Aristagoras, Miltiades, Demaratus, and Themistocles are problematic figures in Herodotus, often conflicting with the very polis groups that they aspire to lead.

Chapter 4, "Claims to immortality: Memories of the Peloponnesian War," focuses upon individuals and groups as cooperating and (especially) competing historical agents from just before the outbreak of the Peloponnesian War in 431 BC down to the 390s. In this turbulent era, tensions between leaders and led spawn not only a new entry in the intellectual debate on historical causality (Thucydides), but also a series of challenges to the equalizing rituals of democratic commemoration. Thucydides' openness about the illusory independence of the Athenian democracy and its reliance on its political leaders represents a more complicated reading of the problems articulated by Herodotus. Pericles, Cleon, Nicias, and Alcibiades, in particular, are depicted by Thucydides as participating in delicate symbolic negotiations with the Athenian *dêmos* over historical agency. This era also witnesses a number of developments in material commemoration at Athens that imply a growing emphasis on the historical relevance of the individual. These changes include the appearance of document reliefs honoring the benefactions of outstanding persons, the increase in epitaphs providing specific details about individual lives, and the re-emergence of figured relief sculpture used to adorn tombstones – including tombstones that challenge the rights of the *dêmos* to the exclusive commemoration of its war dead.

Chapter 5, "Into the fourth century: Learning one's limits, knowing one's place," concentrates upon the period from the outbreak of the Corinthian War in 395 BC to the middle of the fourth century. During the post-Peloponnesian War era, new currents of thought are at work at Athens, as the ability of the *ordinary* individual to make history seems to come under question. The *Anabasis* and *Hellenica* of Xenophon emphasize individual agency as a central factor in the motion of history. The same preoccupation is evident in remarks made by the fourth-century orators, who contend that the Athenian *dêmos* believes itself to be functionally and symbolically dependent upon its outstanding leaders. Individual-centered literary and public discourse is well paralleled in the notable increase in extant honorific inscriptions and document reliefs dedicated to individuals, both foreign and Athenian, during the first half of the fourth century. In what may be a deliberate contrast to these public trends, however, even the most descriptive funerary monuments of this era shift their collective focus away from historical contributions and political experiences towards more intimate relationships, especially the family.

Chapter 6, "Out beyond Athens: Historical agency in Sparta and Thebes," examines evolving conceptions of historical agency elsewhere in fourth-century Greece. It uses monuments, inscriptions, and historiographic and biographical texts to study *perceptions* of Lysander and Agesilaus of Sparta and Epaminondas of Thebes, amongst others, as agents of history. The evidence suggests that deliberate 'performance' towards historical memorialization was a known behavior for eminent Greek leaders of this period, and that questions about individual agency in cooperation or competition with the authority of the polis were being actively posed outside of Athens. While Athenian democracy seems to have provided sufficient conditions for this debate's arousal, it does not appear to have been necessary for its continuance.

Chapter 7, "A 'new world order'? Philip II of Macedon," opens with a discussion of the Lion of Chaeronea, a monument whose unanswered questions about individual and group commemoration further suggest that the tensions over agency and memorialization were comprehensible to a broad Greek audience. The chapter as a whole then focuses on Philip II of Macedon, highlighting Theopompus' *Philippica* as a significant point in the orientation of Greek historiography towards the 'great man.' It also studies Philip's efforts to control his image through (amongst other techniques) monuments and coinage as a paradigmatic large-scale attempt to exploit established Greek ways of thinking about history-making leaders.

Chapter 8, "Alexander 'the Great,'" reads Alexander's image as the culmination of evolving individual-centered theories of history in classical Greece, and suggests that the long gestation of these ideas helps to account for the unique vitality of Alexander's impact and legacy. Evidence from the extant Alexander historians (Diodorus, Curtius, Plutarch, Arrian, and Justin), from fragmentary Hellenistic historiography, and from the material record characterizes Alexander's self-presentation and reception. A brief conclusion, as Chapter 9, presents a reading of the 'Themistocles decree,' inscribed in the fourth or third century BC almost as a recovered memory of the era of the Persian Wars.

2 | Man, myth, and memory under the early Athenian democracy

2.1 The Tyrannicides and the symbolic vocabulary of 'greatness'

Just outside of Athens' Dipylon Gate in the spring of 514 BC, Hippias, the elder son of the deceased tyrant Pisistratus, was marshaling a grand festival parade in honor of the goddess Athena. There is no evidence that he knew anything of the conspiracy that was about to attack his family, assassinate his brother, and reshape the way the Athenians viewed their history.

Harmodius and Aristogeiton struck down Hipparchus, Pisistratus' younger son, there in the Kerameikos as the Panathenaic procession prepared to start for the Acropolis. Although they were killed almost immediately as they fled, the actions of these 'Tyrannicides' marked the beginning of a rapid sequence of transformative events.[1] Hippias, already unpopular, maintained his grip on power for less than four more years before he was forced to flee the city;[2] two years later, following a popular uprising and an external military intervention, the Athenian democracy was established.[3] Popular thought seems to have interpreted this series of incidents as links in a causal chain, thereby assigning historical agency for the foundation of the new government – and the 'freedom' that was understood as accompanying it[4] – to Harmodius and Aristogeiton. This embrace likely depended upon cycles of advertisement and reception[5] in a variety of forms, both public and

---

[1] Testimonia of the Tyrannicides in ancient literature, inscriptions, and iconography are collected and discussed by Taylor 1981: 198–209 and *passim*, to whose thorough efforts, catalogs, and bibliography many subsequent analyses, including my own, are indebted.

[2] See e.g. Hdt 5.55.1, 5.65.1–5; Thuc. 6.55.3, 6.59.2–4.

[3] On this sequence of events, see Ober 1996a: 32–52.

[4] On the development of this concept, see Raaflaub 1983 and esp. Raaflaub 2004.

[5] Fornara 1970 analyzes one particular aspect of this reception – the development of a cult of the Tyrannicides – in detail. Amongst the earlier arguments that he reviews, the most important are Jacoby 1949: 158–66 (arguing that the cult of the Tyrannicides was created by anti-Alcmeonid factions in an effort to disparage the powerful clan and its contributions to the expulsion of Hippias in 511/10) and Ehrenberg 1956 (contending that the cult was quickly adopted by the Alcmeonids themselves and turned into a symbol of the new democracy, a perspective with which Fornara [170] agrees).

private.[6] The symbolic vocabulary that was employed in this exchange and the responses of the ancient historians to it[7] provide a foundational model for exploring the contestation of historical agency in Greece throughout the fifth century and into the fourth.

It is likely that some of the most important Tyrannicides evidence, due in part to its high visibility, helped to codify new ways of making claims about history in democratic Athens even as it drew upon certain aspects of pre-existing discourse.[8] Such a mechanism is not necessarily new at this point in Greek history, but the 'documentation' for it is significantly richer than ever before. Public, private or popular, and literary perspectives on this single event are all available, and certain of the media[9] and ideas that they represent endure as important resources for the expression and understanding of history-making 'greatness' down to the time of Alexander and beyond. Throughout the classical period in ancient Greece, heroism (Homeric, athletic, and even that of the *ktistês*, the colonial founder), the relationship of the individual to the citizen group, and the ability to provide a definitive interpretation of the past recur as important themes in litera-ture, inscriptions, and monuments that invoke historical agency both for people and for poleis. Amongst the body of evidence for the Tyrannicides, these patterns are most clearly visible in the *skolia*, the Agora statues of Har-modius and Aristogeiton and the epigram that probably comes from their base, the mode of the two men's funerary commemoration, their apparent reception of cult, and the accounts of their deeds in Thucydides and (especially) Herodotus.

A group of *skolia* (drinking-songs) about the Tyrannicides was probably already in circulation during the early decades of the fifth century.[10] Three of the four extant versions name Harmodius and Aristogeiton together; the remaining one imagines Harmodius dwelling in the νήσοις . . . μακάρων, the "islands of the blessed," along with Achilles and Diomedes, the Iliadic

---

[6] The explication of these cycles is the central goal of Taylor 1981 (see esp. 1–5).

[7] See e.g. Raaflaub 2003: 63–9; Taylor 1981: 3; Fornara 1970: 155–6, all noting the same conflict of the historians with popular sentiment, but for somewhat different reasons than I do.

[8] This pattern was suggested to me by the symbolic role that Whitley observes for the *soros* of Marathon: see note 55, below.

[9] Most importantly, poetry, public inscriptions, statuary, funerary commemoration, and historiography.

[10] Texts: Page 1962: 474–5 nos. 893–6. The dates of composition and circulation of these brief songs have been much debated: see Taylor 1981: 52–4 for a summary of the arguments in favor of the early fifth century. The *skolia* were certainly in existence, as Taylor 1981: 52–3 and many others have pointed out, by the year 425, when they are first referred to – incompletely, implying close audience familiarity – by Aristophanes (first at Ar. *Ach.* 980, 1093; for additional fifth-century testimonia, see Taylor 1981: 206).

heroes.[11] Beyond this overt Homeric reference, epic and other high poetic diction and imagery can be found throughout the poems, where they were used to project magnified honor upon the verses' subjects – and probably also upon their performers.[12] But the historic action for which Harmodius and Aristogeiton are being praised and their impact as individuals upon the polis are also carefully recorded:[13] the same three epigrams that name both Tyrannicides also note their killing of a τύραννον ("tyrant"), and nos. 893 and 896 conclude with the same line, ἰσονόμους τ᾿ Ἀθήνας ἐποιησάτην, "and they made Athens [a city of] equal rights under the law."[14]

Literary evidence indicates that statues of the Tyrannicides were twice raised in the Athenian Agora. The original bronze group sculpted by Antenor was presumably erected at some point between the expulsion of Hippias from Athens in 511/10 and the Persian invasion of Greece in 480/79,[15] as the ancient testimonia record the statues' removal by Xerxes during the sack of Athens.[16] The lost figures had apparently acquired sufficient importance to be missed upon the reoccupation of the city;[17] soon thereafter, a replacement pair of bronzes was commissioned, this one sculpted by Critius and Nesiotes.[18] In this group (known from Roman marble copies),[19] Harmodius and Aristogeiton are depicted nude, evoking connotations of the athletic, the heroic, and even the divine.[20] But they have been captured in the moment of

---

[11] Page 1962: 474–5 nos. 893, 895, 896 name both of the Tyrannicides; the Achilles and Diomedes references are in no. 894.

[12] Taylor 1981: 64–70 analyzes the Homeric and other poetic resonances in the *skolia*, and suggests that these songs would have been performed at a symposium of like-minded men as "a way of justifying the events of the recent past and of placing themselves and their accomplishments with a heroic framework" (69). On the symposium as a forum for self-conscious reflection and social instruction through performance, see e.g. Hobden 2009; Kurke 2000b *passim*; Stehle 1997: 213–61; Rösler 1995; Murray 1990 *passim* (esp. Pellizer 1990).

[13] Derderian 2001: 97–102 finds the roots of this blending of the heroic and the historical in archaic funerary epigrams dedicated to warriors, and reads as pivotal its continuation in the Persian War epigrams (102–10). This combination of poetical language and historical context becomes an extremely important thematic element in commemoration throughout the classical period and beyond.

[14] On the fifth-century concept of ἰσονομία, see the references in note 30, below.

[15] Fornara 1970: 157–8 provides a summary, with references, of the argument for following Pliny the Elder's date of 510/09 (*NH* 34.9.17) for the Antenor statues.

[16] See Brunnsåker 1971: 39–41 for a complete list of these Antenor group testimonia and a summary of the evidence they provide.

[17] Taylor 1981: 46.

[18] Collected testimonia on the identity of the Critius–Nesiotes group may be found at Taylor 1981: 47 n. 1, 202.

[19] These are catalogued by Brunnsåker 1971: 45–83.

[20] On the symbolic meaning of the Greek nude, see Bonfante 1989, with references to earlier scholarship. On the athletic resonances of the statues' poses, see e.g. Keesling 2003: 173–5.

their perceived historical – and historic – agency,[21] with Harmodius' sword dramatically raised over his head to strike and Aristogeiton's arm, shielded by his cloak, extended as he advances forward. Like mythological heroes, the Tyrannicides were shown in the eternal re-enactment of a famous deed, but their statues were also surrounded by what the Athenians of the classical era viewed as the consequences of that deed: the daily functioning of the democracy as it went about its institutional business in the Agora.[22] That location was a special one: even in the fourth century BC, the Tyrannicide statues were recalled as being the first ones set up within the bounded civic space.[23] Ajootian has further suggested that their specific placement, likely close to the racetrack where the Panathenaic games were held, would have invoked heroic associations by symbolizing a connection with elite athletics and funeral games.[24]

An inscription found in the Agora during the early years of the American excavations there[25] contains part of what is probably the epigram from the base of the Critius–Nesiotes monument.[26] If it represents the same text quoted by Hephaestion, *Enchiridion* 4.6 (where it is attributed to Simonides),[27] then the epigram reads:[28]

⌊ἒ μέγ' Ἀθεναίοισι φόος γένε<θ>' ενίκ' Ἀριστο-⌋
⌊γείτον hίππαρχον κτẽνε καὶ⌋ hαρμόδιο ⌊ς⌋ ⌊
[−⏗−⏗−⏗−⏗−⏑−−]
⌊−⏗−⏗− πα⌋τρίδα γẽν ἐθέτεν.

[A great light was born for the Athenians when Aristogeiton
and] Harmodius [killed Hipparchus].
. . . they two made their ancestral land . . .

[21] Ajootian 1998: 1–3, with additional references.   [22] Ibid. 9.
[23] Keesling 2003: 174 cites Arist. *Rh.* 1.1368a18 on this subject; Ajootian 1998: 1 n. 4 adds Plin. *NH* 34.9.17. D. 20.70 is frequently cited on this point, as well, but Demosthenes is actually talking about the uniqueness of the Tyrannicide statues *after* their erection (saying that they were the only ones there until the statue of Conon was set up: see Chapter 6, below), not before. Collections of these and other testimonia include Brunnsåker 1971: 33–40; Wycherley 1957: 93–8 (with translations).
[24] Ajootian 1998.   [25] Meritt 1936: 355–8.
[26] As opposed to the earlier Antenor one. Meritt 1936: 357 presents some comparanda for letter-forms in favor of the later monument, but also suggests (358) that the epigram itself may be older than the inscription. Page 1981: 187–8, however, points out that the years intervening between the assassination and the erection of the Critius–Nesiotes Tyrannicides group would have allowed the 'myth' of Harmodius and Aristogeiton as liberators "time to grow," and permitted the development of the sentiment expressed in the extant epigram.
[27] In favor of the two texts' being identical, in addition to Meritt 1936, e.g. Page 1981: 188 n. 1 (with additional references). *Contra*: Day 1985: 31–4.
[28] Edition from Hansen 1983: 237 = *CEG* 1.430 (cf. Meritt 1936: 355).

The inscription as restored, like the *skolia*, claims high status for Harmodius and Aristogeiton through its use of poetic form and epic-style language.[29] Again like the *skolia*, it also represents its subjects as history-making agents who changed the condition of their homeland, an interpretation that can stand even if the Hephaestion restorations are discarded.[30]

The public perception of Harmodius and Aristogeiton as historical agents was also demonstrated – or perhaps reified – by the location of their burial. Pausanias (1.29.15) reports seeing their tomb along the road to the Academy, where, in the fifth century, Athens' most eminent citizens were interred alongside group burials of battle casualties subjected to the rites of the *patrios nomos*.[31] Harmodius' and Aristogeiton's funerary monument may have represented a later democratic rehabilitation of an initial disposal of criminals; it may even have been a cenotaph. But the final outcome was that the Tyrannicides were memorialized amongst the later Athenians whose deeds were claimed to have shaped the history of their city. As fellow occupants (even if only by extension or imagination) of this space,[32] they symbolically became honorary and honored citizen-members of the Athenian democracy that was born after their deaths.

But Harmodius and Aristogeiton were not only understood as *members* of the democracy: they also came to be acknowledged as its "founders," or *ktistai*. The figure of the *ktistês* occupied a significant position in Greek

---

[29] The image of a new light being born, for example, φόος γένε<θ>, evokes, amongst other phrases, the Homeric refrain ἦμος δ᾽ ἠριγένεια φάνη ῥοδοδάκτυλος Ἠώς, "when the morning-born Dawn came forth, rosy-fingered," which occurs twice in *Il.* (1.477, 24.788) and twenty-one times in *Od.* (first at 2.1). Other Homeric resonances are discussed in detail by Taylor 1981: 73.

[30] There has been abundant speculation about the missing adjective once applied to the word πατρίδα, "ancestral land," in the statue-base epigram. Page 1981: 189 favors a form of ἰσόνομος, which would match the *skolia*. On that word in those poems, see the review by Taylor 1981: 55–60; on the fifth-century concept of ἰσονομία, see e.g. Raaflaub 1996 esp. 134–50; Vlastos 1953.

[31] Literally, "ancestral tradition," a term taken from Thuc. 2.34.1 and referring to collective burial and commemoration of fallen warriors undertaken by the Athenian government and supported by public funds, as described by Thuc. 2.34.1–7. See Clairmont 1983 as a point of entry into the bibliography.

[32] Patterson 2006a esp. 53–6 argues that the phrase *dêmosion sêma* ("public memorial ground"), employed by Thucydides (2.34.5) in apparent reference to this general area, is an exceptionally rare verbal usage and not likely a meaningful way of denoting the actual use of this or other Athenian burial space, which could and did admit both citizens and foreigners (but see the response by Arrington 2010: 500 n. 4). Clairmont 1983: 29–45 examines the testimonia and archaeological evidence from the Academy road area in detail, and does not see the area as being reserved either for state tombs or for Athenian citizens (44). Here, I recommend only that the close presence over time of *polyandria* (group tombs) for the war dead and tombs for individual members of the Athenian elite would have been suggestive for the interpretation of the memorial of Harmodius and Aristogeiton.

thought, often as the creator of a new colony. The leader of a colonial expedition is typically recalled as being an aristocrat, often one distinguished from his populace by nonconformist behavior or beliefs. Once he and his colonists have separated from their mother-city, the *ktistês* functions as a political and religious leader. In addition to establishing the new city he also traditionally selects or creates its laws and other institutions; after his death, he is often heroized and receives cult.[33] In the case of Harmodius and Aristogeiton, such cult is not mentioned until well over a century after their deaths, but it may already have been active long before that time.[34] For these men to be treated, even if only by a segment of the population,[35] as the *ktistai* of the democracy both contextualized their contribution to their polis and insisted upon their lasting importance: for those who subscribed to the cult, Athens had effectively become a different city through the agency of the Tyrannicides, who remained active as the protectors of their new creation.

But historical agency was not viewed in fifth-century Greece as being irretrievably objective. Thucydides, for example, takes issue with the ascription of the 'liberation' of Athens to the Tyrannicides, emphasizing Harmodius' and Aristogeiton's involvement in a lovers' quarrel and the removal of Hippias by the Spartans and the Alcmeonids.[36] It has been correctly pointed out that Thucydides acknowledges that his version of the story was already in active circulation.[37] But the historian nevertheless saw fit to offer a very detailed new narrative (the passage is several sections in length), and, further, to highlight the problems with the transmission of the story during the first-person methodological discussion in his preface.[38] The fact that the preface passage attempts to correct such an elemental error as the true identity of the ruling tyrant suggests not only, as Taylor recommends, that a popular version of the Tyrannicides legend was still quite strong,[39] but also

---

[33] Dalby 1992: 23 n. 50, citing Graham 1964: 29–39. The summary here of the significance of the *ktistês* is based upon the points iterated by Osborne 1996: 8–17, 115–29, 202–7, 232–42; and Murray 1993: 102–23; for sample narratives, see e.g. Hdt. 4.150.1–159.6, on Cyrene, and Thuc. 6.2.1–5.3, on Sicily.

[34] The earliest testimonium that refers to sacrifices for Harmodius and Aristogeiton, as cited by Taylor 1981: 20 and others (see e.g. Kearns 1989: 55 n. 53, noting further testimonia at Wycherley 1957: 93–8), is *Ath. Pol.* 58.1. It is uncertain, however, how early such sacrifices may have begun: see Fornara 1970, with detailed summaries of earlier arguments and an exploration of how various political factions could have exploited the potential cult.

[35] See Fornara 1970, note 34, above.   [36] Thuc. 6.53.3–59.4.

[37] E.g. Raaflaub 2003: 66–7; Taylor 1981: 2–3.   [38] Taylor 1981: 2–3, citing Thuc. 1.20.2.

[39] Taylor 1981: 3. Fornara 1968: 402–6 argues that Thucydides' suggestion that the Tyrannicides ought to have been driven by "political and ideological considerations" (405) lay in contrast to an earlier "vulgate" tradition, which focused more centrally upon Harmodius' and Aristogeiton's 'vengeance' upon the tyrants and their 'heroic' deaths.

that such a defining event as the foundation of the democracy was actually still available for discussion and debate,[40] in spite of Thucydides' own later claims that a general appreciation of the 'truth' was already in existence. This internal narrative conflict reveals the writer of history at deliberate pains to reify his interpretation of historical agency even as he demonstrates that he, too, is potentially subject to others' counter-claims.

The same set of issues emerges even more clearly in Herodotus. Taylor correctly notes that there is a conflict between the sentiments expressed by Miltiades before the battle of Marathon (promising Callimachus the potential for lasting fame that will surpass even that of Harmodius and Aristogeiton, Hdt. 6.109.3) and those of Herodotus himself.[41] The historian provides a narrative of the entire 'Athenian Revolution' and ultimately attributes the ousting of the tyrants to the clan of the Alcmeonids.[42] He presents the information in both of these passages in his own narrative voice, which lends additional rhetorical strength to his version,[43] and provides his interpretation of the role of the Alcmeonids immediately following his account of the battle of Marathon.[44] In effect, then, the historian shows himself taking control of the narrative back from his own characters, who have attempted to inscribe their version of the past by invoking the 'wrong' agents of Athenian democracy. Again, Taylor is right to suggest that popular tradition may have created something for the historian to work against,[45] but in *demonstrating* that work so deliberately, Herodotus is also making very strong implicit claims about the ability of his own narrative to assign historical agency – and therefore to create lasting memory.[46]

---

[40] On pro- and anti-Alcmeonid responses to the events surrounding the foundation of the democracy, for example, see Podlecki 1966, with detailed treatments of earlier arguments.

[41] Taylor 1981: 3.   [42] Hdt. 5.55.1–65.5, 6.123.1–2.

[43] On the rhetorical authority created by the use of first-person interjections in Herodotus, see e.g. Dewald 1987; on the evidence that the sentiment expressed at 6.123.1–2 is indeed Herodotus' own judgment, see Develin 1985. On the Alcmeonids' larger role in the expulsion of the Pisistratids, see the continuous account at Hdt. 5.62.1–65.5, as well as the analysis and bibliography in Camp 1994.

[44] The Marathon sequence effectively concludes at 6.120, with the digression on the Alcmeonids and their status as "haters of tyrants" (μισοτύραννοι, 6.121.1, 123.1; only here in all of Herodotus) following immediately at 6.121–31.

[45] Taylor 1981: 3.

[46] There is a rich scholarly tradition on the connections in general between writing and the creation of memory (or of history) in ancient Greece. On a variety of issues (some of which would agree with my general interpretation here and some not), e.g. Derderian 2001; Shrimpton 1997; Thomas 1992; Thomas 1989; Starr 1968; see also Robertson 1976; Finley 1965.

The ancient debate manifested in the body of Tyrannicides evidence is therefore a theoretical one, taking place not over the reality of the Tyrannicides' act, but over its meaning and the right to assign it. The democracy that had probably twice commissioned the Tyrannicides' statues and seen to the erection of their funerary monument, and the singers of the 'Harmodius song,' represented particular points of view about the two men's impact upon Athenian history. The perspectives of Herodotus and Thucydides represented quite another.[47]

The case of the Tyrannicides, however, was not unique. The invocation and disputation of historical agency seem in fact to have been important concerns in Athenian habits of commemoration, both public and private, throughout the classical period. This ongoing 'conversation' as it is manifested during the earlier years of the democracy, down through the 440s BC, is the subject of the remainder of this chapter. I argue here that the issue of "who moves history?" was a comprehensible and meaningful question for both elites and non-elites, who not only witnessed the debate in progress over the memorialization of large-scale events (most notably the battle of Marathon), but also submitted their own entries to it through their funerary monuments and through their active participation in certain features of Athenian civic life. It is notable that the rhetoric of Athenian collective commemoration, even in its most official, public forms, seems not actually to have confined the ascription of historical agency to the Athenian *dêmos*, and in fact seems to have maintained many of the same inherent symbolic conflicts as are represented in the body of evidence surrounding Harmodius and Aristogeiton.

2.2 Marathon and the *patrios nomos*

Who won Marathon?

The acknowledgement of the history-making battle of Marathon (490 BC) called for a delicate balancing act, particularly on the part of the Athenian state. Individual men had given their leadership and their lives, but the achievement had also earned lasting fame for the entire city. Athens was now confirmed in an indisputable position of primacy amongst the other Greek

---

[47] Both Herodotus and Thucydides assert (Hdt. 5.62.2; Thuc. 6.59.2) that the increasing violence and paranoia of Hippias' last years in power were motivated by the assassination of Hipparchus. This 'reign of terror' is not, however, assigned by either historian as a primary motivating factor for the Athenian Revolution of 508/7.

states, and its young democracy had therefore to arrive at an appropriate commemorative response. Marathon undoubtedly had profound significance for Athens, but how was its meaning to be assigned historically? Should it be connected to the efforts of living individuals (whose continued guidance was essential) and to the deceased, whose memories their families undoubtedly wished to honor? Or should it be assigned to the collective will of a still-new government that could benefit immensely from the legitimization?

In the end, both perspectives received attention. The burial of the dead from the battle; the commemorations at Athens, at Delphi, and at Marathon itself; and even the later cultural reception of the Marathon experience[48] all indicate that the meaning of Marathon during the first half of the fifth century could be deliberately and explicitly located at some point between individual and group historical agency. The position of a single effort between these two poles depended upon the driver of the acknowledgement and the context in which it was made: amongst the most important pieces of material evidence established nearly within the lifetime of the combatants are the Marathon *soros* beneath which the Athenian battle casualties were buried, the 'Persian War epigrams' set up at Athens, the varied memorials established at Delphi, the trophy and the potential Miltiades monument from the battlefield, the Callimachus monument on the Acropolis, and the paintings in the Stoa Poikilê in the Agora.[49]

The *soros* of Marathon is a large earthen mound, currently about 50 m in diameter and 9 m high, located on the plain where the battle took place. When excavated,[50] it was found to contain a layer of charred wood, ash, and burnt human bones accompanied by unburnt Attic black-figure *lekythoi*.[51] Modern scholars generally concur that this tumulus was the burial site of the 192 Athenians who fell in the battle of Marathon, in keeping with

[48] The question as to whether the honor of Marathon was to be assigned to groups (e.g. *Marathonomachoi*, Athenian citizens, Greeks in general, or still others) or individuals resurfaces repeatedly over time in Greek literature: see the references collected by Loraux 1986: 155–70 *passim*. Jung 2006, an analysis of the reception of the battles of Marathon and Plataea, was released too late to play a role in the original development of these arguments.

[49] Testimonia and archaeological evidence for the material commemoration of Marathon are collected and summarized, with modern bibliography, by Petrakos 1996: 18–49, to whose efforts and resources my analysis is indebted.

[50] On Schliemann's early explorations of the site, see Petrakos 1996: 22, who also records that the documented excavations upon which modern scholarship bases most of its conclusions were carried out by Staïs in 1890–1 and published as Staïs 1890 (note that there are two reports in the volume, the first collaborative and the second, by Staïs alone, more extensive) and 1893.

[51] My brief description of the *soros* here is indebted to Petrakos 1996: 18–24; see also Whitley 1994: 215–16; Hammond 1968: 14–18.

Thucydides' notice that these men were interred at the site as a special honor.[52] The decision to bury the Marathon dead on the battlefield was likely not motivated by expediency; rather, this seems to have been a custom in the earlier fifth century, regardless of convenience,[53] and indeed the *soros* was probably a very labor-intensive choice.[54]

The symbolic meaning of the tomb is rich. As Whitley demonstrates, the *soros* invokes older forms and older meanings even as it helps to legitimize certain aspects of a new type of memorialization that will soon become standard under the new democracy, the *patrios nomos* (see below).[55] In its format as a mound covering cremations, it recalls individual Homeric heroism even as it usurps traditional methods of individual and clan memorialization from the archaic period.[56] In so doing, it effectively creates an entirely new social unit consisting of the 192 members of the Athenian democracy who share it as a resting-place, the fallen *Marathonomachoi* ("Marathon-fighters"). It therefore transforms individual action into group historical agency by symbolically re-enacting – and legitimizing, as a monument of victory – the Cleisthenic reassignment of Athenian citizens from the old clans to the new tribes under the democracy.[57] This function may also have been emphasized through the listing of the dead *by tribes* on the stelai that Pausanias claims crowned the mound.[58] As a further sign of the

---

[52] Thuc. 2.34.5.

[53] Jacoby 1944: 42–7; see also Gomme 1945–56: vol. II, 94 *ad* Thuc. 2.34.1. The Athenians seem to have expected later in the fifth century that casualties could be conveyed home from locations far more distant than Marathon: note the public outcry over the failure of the commanders to retrieve their dead from Arginousae in 406 (X. *HG* 1.6.35, 7.1–35).

[54] Putative late archaic or early classical Athenian sumptuary legislation recorded by Cicero (see note 152, below) was remembered as having decreed *ne quis sepulcrum faceret operosius quam quod decem homines effecerint triduo*, "that no one should build [a tomb] that required more than three days' work for ten men" (Cic. *de leg.* 2.64). This restriction was supposed to have been applied in the Kerameikos cemetery, where space even by the later sixth century was already at a premium (a fact frequently noted in the scholarship that can be appreciated from the density of the graves presented in the original publication, Kübler 1976). If anything like thirty man-days was later understood as an estimated construction outlay for a burial mound in the cramped Kerameikos, the effort expended upon the Marathon *soros* must have been extraordinary.

[55] Whitley 1994: 213, 227.

[56] Ibid. 213, 227–8. See also note 158, below, on heroic mound burials in Homeric epic.

[57] These points are developed from, though not precisely identical to, the observations made by Whitley 1994: 227, 230.

[58] Paus. 1.32.3. This would only have been the case, of course, if the stelai were at least nearly contemporary to the burials. The Athenian democratic "tribes" (*phylai*) were artificial civic divisions established by law, designed to limit the power of older aristocratic alliances. They were intended, amongst other purposes, to ensure fairness and equity in access to governmental offices and to promote a sense of corporate identity that transcended the geographic divisions of Attica: see note 151, below.

special qualities of the battle, its dead probably received heroic cult there at the *soros*.[59] It was likely not long after the battle that the *patrios nomos* was instituted at Athens: the recognition given to the *Marathonomachoi* likely provided appealing precedent.[60]

Another Athenian state memorial was probably represented by the monument that originally bore the 'Persian War' epigrams. As currently known, these consist of four separate pairs of elegiac couplets inscribed on three stones, in three different hands.[61] The first stone was found in two separated pieces, for a total of four fragments, all discovered out of archaeological context and published over a period of some 130 years in the course of the nineteenth and twentieth centuries.[62] Epigrams 1 and 2 have survived in better condition, been longer known, and received more scholarly attention than have epigrams 3 and 4.[63]

[59] Hero-cult was being formally paid to the *Marathonomachoi* by at least the late second century BC: see Whitley 1994: 216 n. 13; Kearns 1989: 55 and n. 50; Clairmont 1983: 97 and 286 n. 5, all citing Paus. 1.32.4–5. Whitley 1994, Kearns 1989, and Loraux 1986: 35 n. 71 also add *IG* ii² 1006. Kearns (citing Thuc. 3.58.4) would like to push the cult of the Marathon dead back into at least the early fifth century, on analogy with the Plataea casualties; Clairmont 1983: 97 and Jacoby 1944 esp. 47 n. 49 would place the foundation of the cult immediately after the battle, but Loraux 1986: 29–30 and esp. 39–41 examines the difficulties associated with determining its date. Festivals involving games (which could have had rich Homeric-heroic associations: see *Il.* 23 *passim* on the elaborate funeral games for Patroclus), were apparently also held at Marathon (Clairmont 1983: 23, with references). The main body of evidence for these is late, but there are earlier analogs attested at Athens (Clairmont 1983: 24–5, with references). McCauley 1993: 151–5 suggests that the cult of the *Marathonomachoi* may have represented a rare occurrence, and that not all of the war dead buried in accordance with the *patrios nomos* during the fifth century were truly heroized.

[60] Whitley 1994: 230 and n. 106, with references; Jacoby 1944; cf. also Loraux 1986 esp. 39–41. It is worth noting that there is no evidence as to precisely who authorized and oversaw the construction of the *soros*. Thuc. 2.34.1–5, however, represents the agents of its creation as "the Athenians"; he frequently uses the same phrase elsewhere to refer to official decisions taken by the democracy.

[61] See recently the edition and detailed commentary by Petrovic 2007: 158–77; and the summary by Keesling 2010: 117–18.

[62] Convenient sources for the major bibliography on all four epigrams and the monument as a whole include the *IG* entry for the epigrams (i.e. *IG* i³ 503/504); Barron 1990; Clairmont 1983: 106–11; Meiggs and Lewis 1969: 54–7 no. 26; Jacoby 1945: 161 nn. 19–20 and *passim*; and the references in note 61, above. Amongst their collective citations, Oliver 1933 is the initial publication of the most critical fragment (the second piece of stone A, bearing epigrams 1 and 2) and reviews past discussions in detail at 480 n. 1. An important fourth-century copy of epigram 1 (*SEG* 28.29: see Meritt 1956) allows the restoration of nearly half of the extant text of that poem. It should be noted that as of Barron 1990 the full texts of epigrams 3 and 4, now printed in the newest edition of *IG*, were not yet available for general consultation. The most significant recent update, as will be discussed below, is Matthaiou 2003 (see the comments by Arrington 2010: 505 and Keesling 2010: 117).

[63] Editions of all four epigrams from *IG* i³ 503/504. Translations of epigrams 1 and 2 from Fornara 1983b: 51 no. 51; translations of epigrams 3 and 4 my own.

Epigram 1 (*IG* i³ stone A)

ἀνδρõν τõνδ' ἀρετε[....⁹..... ος ἄφθιτον] αἰεί [⋮] / ⊢ [....⁸....]ν[.]ρ
[– – – ⁹ – – – νέμοσι θεοί⋮]

ἔσχον γὰρ πεζοί τε [καὶ ὀκυπόρον ἐπὶ νεõ]ν⋮ / hελλά[δα μ]ὲ πᾶσαν δούλιο[ν
ἔμαρ ἰδε̃ν ⋮].

These men's courage [– 9 – imperishable] forever, / | [– – gods grant] / |
For they checked, as footsoldiers [and on swift-faring ships], / | all of
Hellas from [witnessing the day] of slavery.

Epigram 2 (*IG* i³ stone A)

ε̃ν ἄρα τοῖσζ' ἀδαμ[α‿–‿–‿] ηότ' αἰχμὲν / στε̃σαμ πρόσθε πυλõν
ἀγ‿–‿–

ἀγχίαλομ πρε̃σαι ρ‿–‿–‿–‿/ ἄστυ βίαι Περσõν κλινάμενο[ι‿–].

They truly possessed an *adamantine* [- - -] when the spear / | was poised
in front of the gates *in the face of* [- - -] / | [who wished] to burn the
sea-girt [- - -] / | city, turning back by force the Persian [power.]

Epigram 3 (*IG* i³ stone B)

[–‿–‿–‿–πε]ζοί τε καὶ ⊢ –‿/–‿–‿––‿‿–‿‿–
–‿–‿–‿–‿–‿ ο νέσοι / [–‿–‿––‿‿–έ]βαλον.

... both men on foot and ...
... islands ... they threw.

Epigram 4 (*IG* i³ stone C)

ηέρκος γὰρ προπάροιθεν ‿–‿–‿–‿ν / ΤΕΣ ‿–‿ μεμ Παλλάδος
ηιπο|‿–/

οὔθαρ δ' ἀπείρο πορτιτρόφο ἄκρον ἔχοντες ᵛ / τοῖσιμ πανθαλὲς ὄλβος
ἐπιστρέ||[φεται].

A defense in front ... the horse[men?] of Athena ...
holding the fertile promontory of the boundless, all-nourishing ...
All-blooming happiness turns towards them.

The subject matter of these brief poems has been diagnosed at a minimum as
dealing with various aspects of the Persian Wars. Epigram 1, in its reference
to ships, has in the past invited recollections of Salamis;[64] Epigram 2 has
more often been taken as a reference to Marathon.[65] Epigram 3 appears to

---

[64] Although this recommendation should likely be changed in light of newer arguments by
Matthaiou 2003; these are discussed below.
[65] With Athens being construed as the "sea-girt city" in the second couplet. Matthaiou 2003: 200,
however, has recommended that the word printed in the above edition as ἀγχίαλομ should be

tell of a large-scale military struggle, perhaps involving both infantry and cavalry;[66] Epigram 4 provides another account of the defense of Athens.

The intent of all of the epigrams, insofar as the extant texts can demonstrate, is the memorialization and glorification of group effort, rather than of the accomplishments of individuals.[67] As Derderian has shown, epic and other poetical language is employed to invoke the magnitude and the lasting importance of the achievements described,[68] but these achievements are placed within a specific historical context and related both to the polis and to the whole of Greece.[69] From the standpoint of group historical agency, the texts further reveal some potential socio-political elisions that may add to the universalizing stance of the monument. For example, in Epigram 1, the potental sharing of the honors by "footsoldiers" and those "on swift-faring ships," may represent not just multi-force fighting, but two very different financial and social classes within the Athenian democracy, the marginal *thetes* who rowed in the fleet[70] and the wealthier hoplites, joined together in common effort and common glory.[71] The cavalry, whose ranks included the

taken as ἀγχιάλο̅μ (different accentuation) and construed as modifying πυλο̅ν to mention "gates near the sea," thereby describing the topography of Marathon, and indeed that for a variety of reasons the monument as a whole is specific to that particular conflict (see below). The earlier debate over the identifications of these epigrams with the individual battles is summarized by Clairmont 1983: 107 and by Meiggs and Lewis 1969: 54–7, with references; see also Barron 1990: 137–8. Derderian 2001: 105 (also with collected references at 104 n. 150) refutes Barron's argument (139–40) that Epigram 2 commemorates Salamis.

[66] A possible heta has been read near the end of the first line of the first couplet of Epigram 3, which might permit the restoration of cavalry (h[ιππεῖς]) to accompany the infantry, as suggested by Peek and Hansen (see *IG* i³ 503/504 in the apparatus *ad loc.*).

[67] From both temporal ends of the scholarly tradition, e.g. Derderian 2001: 107–8 (correctly emphasizing the tendencies within the poems of plural agents to produce singular, collective outcomes); Oliver 1935: 200; cf. Oliver 1933: 487 (arguing that the collective references at the beginning of Epigram 1 indicate casualty lists mounted in the upper part of the monument).

[68] The high style of the poetry has frequently been noted in the scholarship, but Derderian 2001: 102–3 presents an edition of the epigrams that marks out and cross-references specific resonances of Homeric and other poetic phraseology, concentrating most significantly upon Epigram 1. To these references should also be added the resonances in Epigram 4 recorded in the commentary at *IG* i³ 503/504.

[69] Derderian 2001: 106–7. Derderian would relate these developments to archaic warrior epigrams and in particular to the development of writing as a means of encoding real, specific information beyond oral tradition: see also 109–10.

[70] On the complicated position of the *thetes* (the lowest economic citizen class, who seem to have provided the majority of the oar-power in the Athenian navy) within the military, social, and political structures of the democracy, see Strauss 1996.

[71] The vagueness of the category of those "on swift-faring ships" would likely have left this interpretation available to those who wanted to read it as such, even if the original intent might have been e.g. the commemoration of the hoplites who served upon each ship as marines (I am grateful to M. Flower for this point). On these *epibatai* (who might under extraordinary circumstances even be *thetes* themselves), see e.g. Thuc. 6.43.1, 8.24.2; Jordan 1975: 195–8; Gomme, Andrewes, and Dover 1970: vol. IV, 310 *ad* Thuc. 6.43.

noblest citizens, may be named in Epigram 4 – and perhaps were mentioned directly alongside the hoplites in Epigram 3.[72]

The location and the form of the monument are an equally important part of its participation in the ongoing Athenian 'discussion' of historical agency. Most of the stones on which the inscriptions appear were found in the area of the Agora, which suggested to many scholars that the original stood in or near the public center,[73] but the most recent discovery, stone C,[74] was located in "the retaining wall of the ancient road which led from the Kerameikos to the ancient [Academy]."[75] This has helped to recommend to Matthaiou that the original monument may have been located in the Kerameikos, and indeed that it may have been a cenotaph specifically for the dead of Marathon, a landmark that is also mentioned in a second-century inscription as the site of memorial games.[76]

The physical configuration of the memorial is also an important issue. Matthaiou and Korres have shown that cuttings in the extant blocks allow the restoration of sockets that would likely have held stelai.[77] This in turn suggests that the epigrams may have served as collective honorific inscriptions for what would then become perhaps the earliest known casualty lists at Athens, their inscribed names functioning as the antecedents of the demonstrative pronouns in the poems.[78] The monument as a whole might therefore have provided, as did so many other commemorative efforts from the Persian Wars in general and Marathon in particular, a functional precedent for later democratic practices, in this case the setting-up of stelai bearing the names of the war dead during the ritual of the *patrios nomos* (see below).

What of the broader context in which this monument might have appeared? If, as Matthaiou suggests, it stood in the area of the Kerameikos later represented by Thucydides' *dêmosion sêma*,[79] where the war dead and

---

[72] See note 66, above.   [73] See Barron 1990: 133 n. 1, 134–5 n. 10.

[74] Matthaiou 1988.   [75] Matthaiou 2003: 198.

[76] Ibid. 197–200, with discussion of the inscription at 197, citing *Agora* I 7529, an "unpublished decree from the Agora of Athens." Matthaiou further bolsters his argument for this interpretation by suggesting that the phrase that concludes the second couplet of Epigram 4, τοῖσιμ πανθαλὲς ὄλβος ἐπιστρέ|[φεται], "all-blooming happiness turns towards them," is a reference to the deceased (196–7).

[77] Barron 1990: 134–6 summarizes the argument by Matthaiou 1988: 119 and Korres (who provided the diagrams in Matthaiou 1988: 121–2), and also reviews earlier discussions. Matthaiou 2003: 105–6 provides a briefer recapitulation.

[78] First argued from the newest evidence by Matthaiou (note 77, above), but other scholars earlier suggested casualty-list stelai: see most notably Oliver 1936: 225, 227 (diagram); Oliver 1935: 194–5; Oliver 1933: 487–8.

[79] Matthaiou 2003: 198–200, also suggesting that the "operation of the Demosion Sema began" with this particular memorial. On Thucydides' use of this term, see note 32, above.

the most eminent figures were buried later in the fifth century, it might have had some good company: the tomb of Harmodius and Aristogeiton. If the two were close enough together to invite comparison, rich parallels and contrasts might have emerged.[80] If Harmodius and Aristogeiton could be construed as the founders of the Athenian democracy, the men who fought and died at Marathon, as the epigrams themselves suggest, could be thought of as its saviors, and both contingents likely received heroic cult.[81] But Harmodius and Aristogeiton were represented both here and elsewhere as significant *individuals*, with portrait-statues in the Agora and an epigram there that likely also contained their names. Their tomb would probably have depicted them in the same way. The Persian War monument was very different, in that it seems to have minimized individuality not only by (probably) employing generalizing discourse in the epigrams, but also by commemorating separate warriors at most only in collective casualty lists. In the openness of many of its sentiments, it may have implicitly praised the polis at large,[82] even as it lionized the dead in particular.[83]

Another recently published inscription, a brief epigram in early-looking script that mentions "the Medes" and heads a casualty list from the Athenian tribe Erechtheis, further suggests that the Persian War monument was not alone in either its sentiments or its mode of their commemoration. This new piece seems to have originally formed part of another collective monument for the Athenians lost at Marathon, this one erected at the site of the battle and probably including casualty-list sections for each of the ten tribes of the democracy.[84] Assuming that the archaic appearance of the lettering indicates a primary production rather than a later facsimile,[85] the epigram

---

[80] Clairmont 1983: 110 suggests that the Persian War monument, if located in the Agora, might have been near the statues of the Tyrannicides, and this idea invited my reflections upon the potential juxtaposition of these same memorial themes in the Kerameikos.

[81] See notes 34 and 59, above, respectively.

[82] Derderian 2001: 107 n. 157 notes that Peek 1960: 495–7 sees the function of the monument as being "encomiastic, with paradigmatic significance for the reader." I would recommend that this be pushed still further, to suggest that the reader is not only implicitly encouraged to emulate the individuals and the values that are explicitly invoked by the monument, but is also invited, through its 'open' language, to participate actively in the pride that the monument both commemorates and inspires. That is, all Athenians are intended to have some share in the monument.

[83] Such glorification of the entire city through the honored fallen, according to Loraux 1986, was an essential goal of the *patrios nomos*.

[84] Steinhauer 2004–09 esp. 684–6; see the summary by Hartnett 2010.

[85] In favor of an archaic date for the inscription is most notably Steinhauer 2004–09 (cf. also Steinhauer 2010 [*non vidi*], as reviewed by Proietti 2011, who outlines there the reasons for her own skepticism), followed by e.g. Arrington 2011 esp. 185 n. 42 (with additional bibliographic references, including the *SEG* entries for the inscription, 49.370, 51.425, 53.354, 55.413) and

was certainly removed from its original context, since it was discovered in a Roman-era villa in Arcadia belonging to Herodes Atticus.[86] Like the Persian War epigrams already known from Athens itself, this new poem employs heroic language and style to glorify its collective subjects,[87] but in this case the accompanying tribal casualty list is not a hypothesis, but a reality,[88] following directly after the verses (although not reprinted here):[89]

> Φε̃μις ἄρ' | hος κιχ[ά|ν]<ει> αἰεὶ ‖ εὐφαο̃ς | hέσσχατα | γαί[ες]
> Το̃νδ' ἀνδ|ρο̃ν ἀρε|τὲν ‖ πεύσεται, | hος ἔθανον
> [μ]αρνάμε|νοι Μέ|δοισι ‖ καὶ ἐσστεφά|νοσαν Ἀ|θένα[ς]
> [π]αυρότε|ροι πο|λλο̃ν ‖ δεχσάμε|νοι πόλε|μον.

> Good report indeed, as it reaches always the furthest ends of
> well-lit earth, will learn of the *aretê* of these men, how
> they died fighting against Medes and crowned
> Athens, a few having awaited the attack of many.

The various pieces of evidence discussed in this chapter thus far, then, while they share certain literary and symbolic qualities (most notably their connections with heroic themes), demonstrate two radically different ways of interpreting the motion of history, one centered upon individuals and the other upon groups. The fact that the visible, monumental constructions amongst these items – the Tyrannicides statues, the tomb of Harmodius and Aristogeiton, the Marathon *soros* and the Persian War and Erechtheid epigrams – likely either originated with or were permitted by the Athenian government would likely have created a strong composite message that the Athenian *dêmos* was the arbiter of its own history.[90] That individual events within that larger narrative might be recalled in such diverse fashion (one thinks again, for example, of the re-interpretations of the Tyrannicides episode by Herodotus and Thucydides) further suggests a sophisticated engagement with the concept of historical agency, but it also highlights a significant tension between the historical roles ascribed to individuals and

---

Hartnett 2010. Cf. also MacKay 2011. I do not here engage with the suggestions of the excavator, Spyropoulos, regarding the relationship between this monument, Herodes Atticus (cf. below), and the Marathon *soros*: Proietti 2011 provides a good summary of these arguments, with bibliography.

[86] Specifically at Kynouria: Morgan, Pitt, and Whitelaw 2008–09: 26.

[87] Olson 2012; Hartnett 2010; Steinhauer 2004–09: 681–2, all of whom offer specific observations.

[88] See Steinhauer 2004–09: 689.

[89] Edition from Steinhauer 2004–09: 680. Translation from Hartnett 2010 with a suggestion adopted from MacKay 2011 ("learn"). MacKay 2011 further discusses potential textual changes that might be desirable in later editions.

[90] This is a perspective that Forsdyke 2000 sees as emerging from the institution of ostracism, as well: cf. below.

to groups under the Athenian democracy that seems never to have been resolved.[91]

This tension emerges again when we consider some of the other monuments deriving from Marathon, both at Delphi and in Attica. The most important panhellenic monument at Delphi to the wars as a whole was the Serpent Column,[92] but the Athenians also ventured some grandiose claims there specifically relating to the battle of Marathon. Most notably, the Athenian Treasury and a large statuary monument (now lost) described by Pausanias represent very different perspectives on the historical agency of individuals and groups.[93] The first version of the Treasury itself may date to shortly after the battle.[94] An inscription on a base "built against the front of the south wall"[95] explicitly asserts the collective, group agency of the Athenian citizen body in both the achievement of Marathon and the consequent dedication, thereby expanding the credit for the victory to encompass the entire populace:[96]

> Ἀθεναῖοι τ[õ]ι Ἀπόλλον[ι ἀπὸ Μέδ]ον ἀκ[ροθ]ίνια τε͂ς Μαραθ[õ]νι
> μ[άχες].
>
> The Athenians [give] to Apollo the choice spoils from the Medes, from the battle at Marathon.

The lost sculptural monument is attested only by Pausanias (10.10.1–2), whose description suggests that this monument likely represented a very different perspective on the Marathon experience:

---

[91] Ober 1989 is important on this general problem; for more specific discussion of the relationship between this tension and evolving concepts of the motion of history at Athens, see esp. Chapters 4–5 below.

[92] See e.g. Meiggs and Lewis 1969: 57–60 no. 27.

[93] Walsh 1986 has argued that a third major Delphic monument, the Stoa of the Athenians, should be downdated from the 470s to the 450s, and should therefore be associated with the First Peloponnesian War, rather than with the Persian Wars.

[94] At least according to Paus. 10.11.5. Modern scholars continue to debate whether the Treasury was actually constructed before or after Marathon: see e.g. Bommelaer and Laroche 1991: 135–6, with additional references; the bibliography collected by Meiggs and Lewis 1969: 35 no. 19; and esp. La Coste-Messelière 1957: vol. I, app. 2, 259–67. Cf. also note 100, below.

[95] Quote from Meiggs and Lewis 1969: 35 no. 19. A number of scholars have asserted that this inscription is not intended to refer to the Treasury itself, but rather to another sculptural monument memorializing Marathon: see e.g. Petrakos 1996: 32–3. Concerns expressed with this interpretation have included the fact that this putative sculptural group is unattested either in Pausanias or elsewhere, as well as the fact that the statuary monument incorporating Miltiades and actually mentioned by Pausanias (see below) would then be largely redundant: see the summary and references in Meiggs and Lewis 1969: 35 no. 19.

[96] Edition from *IG* i³ 1463 B.

Τῶι βάθρωι δὲ τῶι ὑπὸ τὸν ἵππον {τὸν δούρειον δὴ} ἐπίγραμμα μέν ἐστιν
ἀπὸ δεκάτης τοῦ Μαραθωνίου ἔργου τεθῆναι τὰς εἰκόνας· εἰσὶ δὲ Ἀθηνᾶ
τε καὶ Ἀπόλλων καὶ ἀνὴρ τῶν στρατηγησάντων Μιλτιάδης· ἐκ δὲ τῶν
ἡρώων καλουμένων <ἐπωνύμων> Ἐρεχθεὺς καὶ Κέκροψ καὶ <Παν>δίων,
{οὗτοι μὲν δὴ} καὶ Λεώς τε καὶ Ἀντίοχος ὁ ἐκ Μήδας Ἡρακλεῖ γενόμενος
τῆς Φύλαντος, ἔτι δὲ Αἰγεύς τε καὶ παίδων τῶν Θησέως Ἀκάμας, οὗτοι
μὲν καὶ φυλαῖς Ἀθήνησιν ὀνόματα κατὰ μάντευμα ἔδοσαν τὸ ἐκ Δελφῶν·
ὁ δὲ Μελάνθου Κόδρος καὶ Θησεὺς καὶ Φιλαιός ἐστιν, οὗτοι δὲ οὐκέτι τῶν
ἐπωνύμων εἰσί. τοὺς μὲν δὴ κατειλεγμένους Φειδίας ἐποίησε, καὶ ἀληθεῖ
λόγωι δεκάτη καὶ οὗτοι τῆς μάχης εἰσίν. (Paus. 10.10.1–2)

On the pedestal below the horse is an epigram [saying that] the statues
were funded by a tenth part of the spoils from the battle at Marathon. They
include Athena and Apollo and one of the men who was in command,
Miltiades. And out of the [group of] so-called <eponymous> heroes are
Erechtheus, Cecrops, <Pan>dion, Leus, Antiochus (fathered from Meda,
daughter of Phylas, by Heracles), and then Aegeus and Acamas, one of
the children of Theseus. These gave their names to the Athenian tribes in
accordance with an oracle from Delphi. And Codrus the son of Melanthus
and Theseus and Philaeus are there, as well, but they are not amongst the
eponymous [heroes]. Phidias fashioned the images described here, and it
is true that they are funded by the one-tenth share of the battle [proceeds].

Conventionally dated to *c.* 465,[97] this dedication seems to have assigned
extraordinary agency, value, and memory to an *individual*. Representing
Miltiades alongside the eponymous heroes of Athens would have connected
him iconographically with the establishment of the democracy,[98] again
constructing Marathon and the Persian Wars as a time of Athenian rebirth,
and perhaps even inviting the contemplation of Miltiades as a founder
figure. Placing him beside the gods would have suggested divine approval
of his deeds, particularly since (as Pausanias recalls) Apollo's oracle had
named the *eponymoi*, and would also have symbolized his recompense
and gratitude for their patronage. And the presence of this monument to
a military triumph in a sanctuary would likely also have resonated with
traditional ways of commemorating athletic victors that had their roots in
the archaic period.[99]

This dedication therefore reveals a distinct vision of history: even if Miltiades could in some sense be construed as a metonym for his polis, the statue

---

[97] Bommelaer and Laroche 1991: 110–11, with additional references.
[98] On the eponymous heroes and their relationship in thought to the foundation of the
Cleisthenic democracy, see Kearns 1989: 80–92.
[99] Keesling 2003: 178, citing Kurke 1993, 1992, and 1991; see also note 110, below.

group, in its representation of an identifiable person amongst the heroes, would have drawn a sharp distinction between individual commemoration and the collective ideology of, for example, the *soros* and the Persian War epigrams. The Athenian Treasury inscription, at a minimum located nearby, would have participated in this same contrast.[100] If the inscription was connected by viewers in any way (whether it was the original intention of its builders or not) with the Miltiades monument, the central event at hand would have been essentially ascribed to an individual by the iconography and to a group by the nearby text.[101] The case is not dissimilar to the potential relationship discussed above between the Tyrannicides' tomb and the Persian War epigrams, which showed that the Athenian *dêmos* was quite capable of creating complex and sometimes conflicting messages about historical agency. There is no need, therefore, to assume that the Miltiades monument must necessarily be a private one, even though the general had perished in disgrace not many years after his most famous battle.[102] It has been suggested that his son Cimon, one of the leading politicians at Athens, may have been the donor of a private dedication, elevating Miltiades at last to his due place and thereby claiming enhanced status for himself and his family. But Cimon may also have wielded sufficient political influence to advocate for a public project.[103] In either case, the Miltiades monument again participates in the close juxtaposition of different ways of interpreting the same historical event, perhaps advocated by an individual or a faction within the *dêmos*,[104] but nevertheless showing that agency itself could be publicly debated.

---

[100] I was pleased to discover after the fact that my interpretation here aligns with the arguments of Neer 2004, who does connect the inscription directly with the Treasury (thereby reading the Treasury itself as a civic dedication resulting from Persian spoils) and suggests as one of the results of that association that the Miltiades monument "is a *response* to the Treasury. It allows Miltiades to take his place amongst the heroes as a quasi-divine victor . . . [it] reclaims Marathon – and indeed, the whole Cleisthenic tribal structure – from the collectivity of the *polis*" (82–3).

[101] Krumeich 1997: 95 correctly notes that Pausanias seems to be "paraphrasing" the Treasury inscription at the beginning of his description of the Miltiades monument and using the mention of the *akrothinia* (the god's share of the spoils) to argue that a tithe paid for the statues.

[102] On the fall from public esteem and death of Miltiades, see Hdt. 6.132.1–136.3.

[103] There is no general agreement amongst scholars as to whether this monument might have been the result of public action (and public funds) or whether it was a private dedication: see e.g. Keesling 2003: 177, 192; Krumeich 1997: 94–6 (with detailed references and reviews of earlier scholarship, esp. 95 n. 363, 96 n. 364, noting the importance of D. and E. Kluwe in reading the monument as being a private one); Mattusch 1994: 73–4; Castriota 1992: 81.

[104] On the possibility that the Tyrannicides statues in the Agora or the growth of their cult may have been part of a larger program of factional (whether pro- or anti-Alcmeonid) propaganda, see e.g. Fornara 1970; Podlecki 1966.

A similar contrast may have been created on the battlefield itself. A trophy, erected some time after the battle, likely represented a memorial of group achievement. Once a single Ionic column in white marble, the trophy is now extremely fragmentary: at some point its remains were employed in the construction of a medieval tower near the church of Panaghia Mesosporitissa, over 3 km northeast of the *soros* on what was probably the opposite side of the battlefield.[105] The battered column capital and two drums are now in the Marathon Museum. Its very fixture in stone appears to have been an innovation at this point in Greek history, which would again recommend the importance of the memory of Marathon for Athens as a whole.[106] Although no inscription from this particular monument survives, the Spartan regent and general Pausanias is said to have severely damaged his reputation by having an elegiac couplet in honor of himself inscribed upon the golden tripod that once crowned the Serpent Column at Delphi.[107] This would help to suggest that battle-monuments of this period were generally oriented towards collective commemoration.[108] A localized challenge to that ideological stance, however, may have been represented by a monument erected on the battlefield in honor of Miltiades, cited by Pausanias the traveler as he toured the field of Marathon.[109] Without additional evidence, it is not possible to determine whether Pausanias' identification of this unknown memorial is correct or how long after the battle it might have been established. For such commemorative competition to take place on the battlefield during this period would have been especially venturesome,[110] but if genuine and (roughly) contemporary, it would again have invoked agency for an individual in very close physical proximity to similar claims made for his

[105] Vanderpool 1966 is the first publication of the trophy (noting earlier speculation about its identity at 102 n. 17); he believes that it was erected some thirty years after the battle, *c.* 460 BC. See Vanderpool's description of the trophy remains and the medieval structure into which they were built at 93–101, and the briefer summary of Petrakos 1996: 27.

[106] West 1969 esp. 18–19.

[107] Thuc. 1.132.2–3; cf. note 92, above. I am grateful to A. Petrovic for calling my attention to the fact that Pausanias did ultimately succeed, however, in commemorating himself at Byzantium: see Petrovic 2010: 202–5 and the comments by Loomis 1990: 491 n. 24 on Hdt. 4.81.3.

[108] West 1969: 11, 14, also citing (14 n. 36) the Pausanias example (note 107, above).

[109] Paus. 1.32.4, referring to ἀνδρός... ἰδίαι μνῆμα, "a private monument of a man." It may originally have been located somewhere in the area of the *soros*, as Pausanias notes it immediately after the τάφος... Ἀθηναίων, the "tomb of the Athenians" and ἕτερος Πλαταιεῦσι... καὶ δούλοις, "another [tomb] for the Plataians and the slaves" (1.32.3). Petrakos 1996: 44 calls attention to the testimonium but refutes previous attempts to identify material remains of this monument.

[110] West 1969: 11, noting that at this time "proper commemoration of a battle was ordinarily by votive offerings made to a deity in his sanctuary." See also Krentz 2007: 737 n. 12, with ancient and modern references.

citizen group. The other evidence surrounding Marathon and the Tyrannicides at least suggests that this is possible.

   An individual monument was also established in connection with Callimachus, the polemarch for the year 490/489 BC. He was killed at
Marathon[111] and was presumably buried with the other casualties in the
soros, but he was also commemorated in Athens on the Acropolis. The
inscription on the broken shaft of an Ionic column, though extremely fragmentary, has been generally acknowledged as mentioning the polemarch
by title (most scholars also believe that there is at least one position for his
name), the battle itself, the identity of the statue that once stood atop the
column, the dedication of the offering to Athena, and the deme of Aphidna,
to which Callimachus belonged. Because the text presents so many possibilities for restoration,[112] it is impossible to establish with certainty precisely
who planned, funded, and erected the monument, whether it was Callimachus himself (in which case others would have completed the project
on his behalf), or others, perhaps even the state, who were interested in
giving permanent form to his memory.[113] But in either case, this monument seems to have been somewhat less audacious in its message than the
Miltiades group at Delphi and the possible memorial to the same man on
the battlefield.[114] Callimachus' dedication was established in the familiar
context of the sanctuary,[115] but its honorand (or donor) was not recollected
with a portrait statue, a more venturesome form of individual commemoration that during this period was largely confined to a long tradition of
honoring athletes.[116] Instead, the monument was crowned with a draped

---

[111] Hdt. 6.114.1.

[112] Petrakos 1996: 47–9 conveniently presents six proposed restorations side by side for
       comparison (including that of the current *IG* entry for the inscription, *IG* i³ 784) and provides
       (47 n. 98) additional references. Cf. now also the textual discussion by Keesling 2010: 101–13.

[113] Keesling 2010: 115 suggests that "Callimachus had vowed a dedication to Athens before the
       battle that could be made only after his death . . . [and] it might have seemed acceptable to
       inscribe the name of Callimachus on an Acropolis dedication precisely *because* he was already
       dead." See also ibid. 116, 118 on the possibility that in its finished form this memorial of
       Callimachus was a civic monument.

[114] Neer 2004: 80–1 sees the Callimachus monument as being more civically oriented than I do:
       in my reading, while there were certainly negotiative aspects to the monument's context and
       imagery, it still represented a dramatic claim to the agency of an individual in the course of
       the city's most famous battle.

[115] See note 110, above, on dedications resulting from warfare.

[116] Keesling 2003: 29–30, 66–9, 89, 170–80, 195–8, with references, discussing the
       commemoration of individuals, especially athletes and warriors, in sanctuaries; cf. also
       Keesling 2010: 130.

female figure, likely a demigoddess, whose presence may have symbolized Callimachus' piety – and even his participation in a historic victory.[117]

Based upon the evidence examined thus far, it might be appealing at this point to suggest that during this early period of the Athenian democracy individuals could potentially be memorialized in sanctuaries, but that acknowledgement elsewhere in the city, especially in the Agora, was largely reserved for the *dêmos* as a whole, with the Tyrannicides serving as a natural exception.[118] The Stoa Poikilê within the Agora, however, complicates that view. It displayed on one of its walls a large mural of the battle of Marathon[119] that, as described by Pausanias, hovered itself between assigning glory to individuals, to the group of fighters, or to the Athenian citizen body:

> τελευταῖον δὲ τῆς γραφῆς εἰσιν οἱ μαχεσάμενοι Μαραθῶνι· Βοιωτῶν δὲ
> οἱ Πλάταιαν ἔχοντες καὶ ὅσον ἦν Ἀττικὸν ἴασιν ἐς χεῖρας τοῖς βαρβάροις.
> καὶ ταύτηι μέν ἐστιν ἴσα <τὰ> παρ᾽ ἀμφοτέρων ἐς τὸ ἔργον· τὸ δὲ ἔσω
> τῆς μάχης φεύγοντές εἰσιν οἱ βάρβαροι καὶ ἐς τὸ ἕλος ὠθοῦντες ἀλλήλους,
> ἔσχαται δὲ τῆς γραφῆς νῆές τε αἱ Φοίνισσαι καὶ τῶν βαρβάρων τοὺς ἐσπίπ-
> τοντας ἐς ταύτας φονεύοντες οἱ Ἕλληνες. ἐνταῦθα καὶ Μαραθὼν γεγραμ-
> μένος ἐστὶν ἥρως, ἀφ᾽ οὗ τὸ πεδίον ὠνόμασται, καὶ Θησεὺς ἀνιόντι ἐκ γῆς
> εἰκασμένος Ἀθηνᾶ τε καὶ Ἡρακλῆς· Μαραθωνίοις γάρ, ὡς αὐτοὶ λέγουσιν,
> Ἡρακλῆς ἐνομίσθη θεὸς πρώτοις. τῶν μαχομένων δὲ δῆλοι μάλιστά εἰσιν ἐν
> τῆι γραφῆι Καλλίμαχός τε, ὃς Ἀθηναίοις πολεμαρχεῖν ἥιρητο, καὶ Μιλτιάδης
> τῶν στρατηγούντων, ἥρως τε Ἔχετλος καλούμενος, οὗ καὶ ὕστερον ποιή-
> σομαι μνήμην. (Paus. 1.15.3)

> In the last place in the painting are the men who contended at Marathon. The Boeotians who inhabit Plataea and the Attic part [of the fighting force] are struggling directly with the barbarians. And at this location the progress of both sides is equal. But on the inside of the battle there are barbarians fleeing and shoving one another into the marsh, and at the edge of the battle there are Phoenician ships and Greeks slaughtering the barbarians who are rushing towards them. Here the hero Marathon, after whom the plain is named, is depicted, and Theseus, who looks as if he is rising from the earth, and Athena and Heracles. For Heracles was first a

---

[117] Petrakos 1996: 47 identifies this fragmentary draped female figure as Iris; Raubitschek 1940: 52 calls it a Nike.

[118] See Shear 2007: 106. Shear's project postdates the original development of these arguments, but she also notes, as I do, a change in general habits of commemoration at Athens over time, with the *dêmos* gradually yielding pride of place to individuals (see esp. 91, 105–15, with Shear's interpretation of the Stoa Poikilê differing from mine).

[119] Wycherley 1957: 31–45 assembles literary testimonia regarding the Stoa and its paintings.

god amongst the people of Marathon, as they themselves say. Amongst the combatants, those most clearly [visible] in the painting are Callimachus, who was chosen as polemarch for the Athenians, and Miltiades, [one] of those who were in command, and the hero called Echetlus, whom I will describe later.

Although Athenians, Plataeans, and Persians were apparently identifiable throughout, with the Greeks clearly engaged in various deeds of valor, the only human beings whom Pausanias as viewer singles out by name are, again, Callimachus and Miltiades.[120] The fact that the other outstanding figures are all gods and heroes implicitly but effectively assimilates the two generals to the ranks of the (semi-)divine, just as the Delphi sculptural monument apparently did for Miltiades. But the overall meaning of the painting points towards a divinely ordained victory for all of Athens, as embodied by the sanctioning presence of the local heroes, Marathon, Echetlus, and especially Theseus, and of the patron goddess Athena.[121]

Who won Marathon, therefore, seems to have remained a question to which different answers were given in different contexts. An important issue, however, is the extent to which the Athenian *dêmos* is presented as an agent, even a shared one, of this history-making event. Towards this end, selected pieces of the evidence may be reviewed from Athens outwards. The Marathon painting in the Agora's Stoa Poikilê participated in the lionization of the citizen group, demonstrating in its iconography that the cause of Athens itself was favored by the gods – except that the picture additionally featured the contributions of two special individuals, Callimachus and Miltiades. The fact that the two men's names were apparently not inscribed near their likenesses may later have been intentionally interpreted as a democratizing gesture,[122] but the multiple representations of agency in the painting would have remained recognizable to its audiences as long as the separate figures of the generals could be identified. Again, even in the Agora itself, different ascriptions of agency could be made regarding the same historical narrative, here even within the same public monument. In the Kerameikos,

---

[120] Aeschin. 3.186 suggests that in the fourth century, at least, these figures were recognizable by their stances and positions, but were not labeled.

[121] Harrison 1972 assembles numerous ancient testimonia and iconographic comparands to attempt a tentative reconstruction of various details of this painting. She also calls attention to the connections drawn between Callimachus and the Tyrannicides by Hdt. 6.109.3; by Plu. *Mor.* 628D-E; and quite possibly by the artists of the Nike Temple frieze (see esp. 355 n. 22).

[122] See note 120, above.

the Persian War epigrams seem to have expanded the scope for the acknowledgement of the Marathon victory. Clairmont's suggestion that Epigram 2
"addressed itself to those who had survived as well as to the memory of the
192 who fell in battle"[123] might well be enlarged to embrace the ethos of the
monument as a whole, as its location further enhanced the many universalizing messages of its texts to reach beyond the casualty lists it likely displayed.

When the comparisons are extended to include evidence outside of
Athens, the invocations of agency become even more complex. The battlefield trophy was likely a realization in stone of an original temporary commemoration; the customary construction of wood and arms would have
immediately claimed the victory at Marathon for those who had participated
in the event directly, but the final marble monument would perhaps have
contributed a broader sense of universality.[124] The *soros* (and now, perhaps,
the epigram monument that may have accompanied it) seems to have been
exclusive in some ways and inclusive in others. The fallen *Marathonomachoi*,
given their likely reception of heroic cult and their collective burial, were
probably viewed as a discrete group – but one whose sacrifice brought lasting
glory to their *polis*. The *dêmos* therefore, if not an explicit agent of the victory
on those terms, might at least be seen as a partaker in it, particularly as it
renewed its kinship with the *Marathonomachoi* every time rites and games
were performed on their behalf. That same message is represented even
more strongly by the Athenian Treasury inscription at Delphi that notes the
collective dedication of the Marathon spoils to Apollo. In contrast to these
invocations of group historical agency, however, stand the two most secure
individual-oriented monuments, to Callimachus on the Acropolis and to
Miltiades at Delphi. The Callimachus monument seems moderate in its
tone, combining its treatment of an individual's military achievement with
an impersonal image as a victory-offering. But the Miltiades monument,
with its bronze portrait-statue standing amongst the heroes of Athens and
the patron deities of both city and sanctuary, claims unique, history-making
status for its single human subject. Athens itself is acknowledged only in the
form of its superhuman protectors. If Marathon was the will of the gods,
this monument suggests, then Miltiades was their agent, and in response to
his success they have now virtually assumed him into their midst.

---

[123] Clairmont 1983: 108.
[124] West 1969 esp. 11–12, 14, 19, noting (19): "In turning an impermanent marker of victory into
       a permanent commemorative monument, Athens reveals the enduring significance with
       which she endowed Marathon and Salamis in the years of the *Pentecontaetia*."

The place of the patrios nomos

It is uncertain precisely when the Athenian state instituted the rites collectively known as the *patrios nomos*,[125] appropriating the right to memorialize the war dead as a group in lieu of private, individual family funerals. But the treatment of the fallen *Marathonomachoi* strongly suggests that certain aspects of the later formal public burial – collective interment, the acknowledgement of citizens by given name and tribe, and (perhaps) funerary games and heroization – were already legitimate symbolic currency before the first generation of the democracy had passed away, either because these traditions were meaningful before Marathon or because they were created or validated by it.[126] In its fullest form, however, the *patrios nomos* also involved the conveyance of the deceased home to Athens and the pronunciation of an oration over the tribal *larnakes*,[127] the boxes that held the cremated remains, before they were moved to their final, collective resting-place. It is likely that these arguably most characteristic and most democratic parts of the tradition were added to the ceremonies during the second quarter of the fifth century BC.[128] This is not far removed in time from a discernible simplification in the styles of private funerary monuments at Athens,[129] and given the generally equalizing tone both of the corpus of tombstones and of the contents of the *patrios nomos*, the civic ritual as a whole is often acknowledged as having essentially taken over for the private burials of warriors known from earlier periods.[130]

Although the Athenian state did not arrogate to itself the privilege of burying all of its citizens, its appropriation of funerals and monuments for the war dead served as a vivid demonstration of socially and politically acceptable 'democratic' and group-oriented ideals of funerary commemoration. The *patrios nomos* probably at least discouraged the

---

[125] On this term and its usage, see note 31, above.

[126] Whitley 1994 *passim*, esp. 213, 227, 230; Loraux 1986: 30; Jacoby 1945: 174–7.

[127] Thuc. 2.34.3.

[128] *Contra* Thuc. 2.34.5 (cf. also notes 52–53, above). The precise date of the introduction of this tradition to Athens has been much discussed: see e.g. Clairmont 1983 esp. 7–15 and Jacoby 1944 for the details of many of the arguments.

[129] Discussed in the next section of this chapter.

[130] Esp. Stupperich 1977, although see the thoughtful reservations of Parker 1996: 132–5, with additional references. While I agree with Parker that it is difficult to posit a strict one-to-one correspondence between the development of the public burial of warriors and the limitation or demise of the private one early in the fifth century, iconographic relationships between the two types of tombs that begin in the material record later in the fifth century (see Stupperich 1994; Morris 1992: 143–4) suggest that the Athenians themselves may have connected them in thought, at least with the passage of time.

separate memorialization of war casualties,[131] preventing the erection of an individual monument to the deceased and suppressing the unique claims that his survivors might have made thereby.[132] A warrior buried by the state could not use his tomb to describe his own particular place either in the public history of his polis or in the private history of his *oikos*.[133] In the lavish ascription of group historical agency that was the *patrios nomos*, then, the possibility to claim individual agency was effectively denied. On the casualty lists that took the place of private tombstones, nearly all of the fallen citizens were listed only by battle, given name, and tribe,[134] distinguished solely by the unique and arbitrary division of the *polis* to which they belonged[135] and which had assumed not only the right to bury them, but also the privilege of assigning their historical relevance, just as it had done with the fighters of the Persian Wars and even with the Tyrannicides.

The imposition of democratic equality under these circumstances demanded a focus not upon individual achievement, or upon private loss and grief, or upon the relationship between survivors and deceased, but upon the relationship between deceased and city.[136] The funerary oration, or *epitaphios logos*, that was part of the ceremony of the *patrios nomos* articulated this relationship by providing a universalizing story of Athens that now included the actions of the recent war dead.[137] In so doing, it appropriated not only the tradition of ritual lament[138] (an activity that could have evoked in fifth-century Athens uncomfortable associations with Homeric royalty

---

[131] Loraux 1986: 37 suggests that two literary testimonia recommend against the existence of a formal law: Thuc. 2.34.7; Pl. *Mx.* 234b, 235c, "unless Plato is deliberately misstating the facts in order to strengthen beforehand his criticism of the topos of improvisation." Morris 1994: 72–3 contrasts Loraux's tendency to see the *patrios nomos* as restrictive (a perspective with which I agree here) with the views of Humphreys 1980.

[132] Under these circumstances, families would also have been denied the opportunity to pay ongoing ritual or material attentions to private tombs. On the significance of tomb-visitation in classical Athens, see Garland 1985: 104–20, with ancient and modern references.

[133] The term *oikos* is understood as referring to a related, multigenerational kin group, loosely construed as a 'household,' incorporating both living and deceased members, but nowhere near so extensive or extended as an archaic 'clan.' On the determinative role of the *oikos* in Greek (and particularly Athenian) civic life and personal identity, see Patterson 1998; on *oikos*-centered memorialization, see Closterman 1999.

[134] Bradeen 1969 surveys and summarizes the characteristics of the casualty lists; so does Clairmont 1983: 46–69. Both point out that the lists also included some non-Athenians (Bradeen at 149–51; Clairmont at 50–1; see also Loraux 1986: 32–5) and occasionally listed some Athenian citizens with their military ranks and titles (Bradeen at 147; Clairmont at 51–2).

[135] Loraux 1986: 23, with references.   [136] This is the central theme of Loraux 1986.

[137] Loraux 1986 esp. 132–71; cf. Derderian 2001: 175, 178.

[138] Derderian 2001: 164–88; Loraux 1986: 44–7; cf. Alexiou 1974: 19–23.

and other ancient hierarchies,[139] as well as with ostentatious private funerals), but also, again, the right to ascribe historical agency. The speaker of the *epitaphios logos*, as representative of the city,[140] supplied a narrative that in the end, even if over separate objections, had to be taken to apply to all.[141]

The *patrios nomos*, however, could not provide appropriately for *individuals* whom the state wanted or needed to honor in a distinctive way. It created some symbolic conflicts on both small levels[142] and large ones, especially when men like Harmodius and Aristogeiton lay buried at public expense in close proximity to the collective monuments to fallen warriors.[143] An uncomfortable sense of hierarchy was therefore likely created in the neighborhood of the Kerameikos. Democratic equality hallmarked by near-anonymity, implicitly (by the monuments) and explicitly (during the funeral ceremonies) claimed as the highest dignity that the state could bestow upon its dead, was effectively undermined by the even 'higher' honors granted to eminent figures.[144] If all were in theory equal, some – those whose achievements apparently earned them individual memorials – were evidently more equal than others.[145] This juxtaposition implied to a potentially resentful viewing public that some men were 'special' enough to have the best of both worlds: an individual tomb constructed with public sanction and even perhaps at public expense. And it also likely invited a questioning of the effectiveness and value of the democratic group as opposed to the outstanding individual.

2.3 Historical agency and the dead: Memory and the polis in the Athenian cemeteries

Concern about the assignment of permanent memory to groups or to individuals also emerges in the wider body of Athenian funerary evidence from the earlier fifth century. In most cases, it takes the form of agreement

---

[139] Loraux 1986: 44–7.   [140] Thuc. 2.34.6.

[141] See Thuc. 2.35.2, where Pericles admits that ὅ τε γὰρ ξυνειδὼς καὶ εὔνους ἀκροατὴς τάχ᾽ ἄν τι ἐνδεεστέρως πρὸς ἃ βούλεταί τε καὶ ἐπίσταται νομίσειε δηλοῦσθαι, "a listener who is fully knowledgeable and well disposed could well think that something is presented in a manner rather inferior to what he prefers and knows."

[142] As, for example, when some Athenians were separately acknowledged within the casualty lists as having been military officers: see note 134, above.

[143] See notes 31 and 32, above.

[144] The most detailed (so claimed) iteration of both individual and collective burials in the Kerameikos is Paus. 1.29.3–16, who mentions Pericles' tomb at 1.29.3.

[145] This would likely have remained the case even if the literal reason why an individual like Pericles was buried separately was that he was not a war casualty. I am grateful to M. Flower for pointing out the possibility that this is why such distinctions might have been made.

(or not) with what seem to be equalizing norms for the structure of grave monuments. Two epitaphs from the middle years of the fifth century, however, both for foreigners, furnish a clear connection between funerary commemoration and the invocation of historical agency. They offer a reminder that for many individuals, the tombstone was an important way (and sometimes the only way) to inscribe one's place in history, and they demonstrate the endurance of the vocabulary of agency first visible in the evidence surrounding the Tyrannicides. They also serve as points of entry to some additional trends in Athenian public memorialization that become increasingly pronounced in the later fifth and earlier fourth centuries.

As has been widely noted, habits of commemoration in general seem to shift at Athens between the foundation of the democracy and the conclusion of the Persian Wars. In particular, between *c.* 510 and 480, Athenian funerary monuments as a corpus become very different.[146] Before this period, archaic practices are in full evidence, with figured-relief stelai, sculpture in the round, and other large, showy monuments marking the graves of the elite.[147] The symbolism employed by these memorials suggests a closed class of aristocrats, using images with heroic overtones, like lions, horsemen, athletes, or chariots, to advertise their elite status.[148] When they carry epitaphs, the inscriptions tend to focus upon exemplars rather than distinct personal qualities, recalling the deceased according to a fixed set of accepted elite values.[149] The archaic monuments therefore functioned in part as an eternally cycling claim to elite authority, effectively re-creating it by prescribing its future even as they memorialized its past.[150]

[146] A useful summary of this process is Stears 2000b: 27–37. Parker 1996: 133 is correct in noting that *c.* 500 is a frequently cited date for the disappearance of archaic styles, "but some would put a few survivors as late as *c.* 480." Stears is one of the latter, and her case is convincing. See also note 152, below.

[147] On the stelai, see Richter 1961. Amongst the other types of grave markers available to elites in the archaic period were (inventory by Kurtz and Boardman 1971: 79–89) large vases; 'built tombs' (the term used by Kurtz and Boardman 1971: 81–3 and others), i.e. stuccoed blocks of bricks that may have been decorated with painted terracotta plaques (Kurtz and Boardman 1971: 83; Boardman 1955); and sculpture in the round, generally *kouroi* and *korai* (youths and maidens). On *kouroi* and *korai*, see Keesling 2003 *passim* (focused most substantially upon *korai* dedicated on the Athenian Acropolis, but with some attention to funerary contexts as well); Osborne 1998: 28–32 (*kouroi* only); Stewart 1990: 109–12, 120 (specifically on funerary function and meaning); Ridgway 1977: 149–51 (brief summary); Richter 1960 and 1942 *passim* (a foundational study).

[148] Kosmopoulou 2002: 44–50, 54 (discussing the use and interpretation of these images on the carved-relief bases of funerary stelai); Day 1989 esp. 20–2.

[149] Day 1989; cf. also Osborne 1998; Humphreys 1980: 114, 123, *et passim*; Jeffery 1947: 129–30.

[150] On archaic funerary monuments as creators and maintainers of the memory of the deceased, see the references collected by Kosmopoulou 2002: 63 n. 130.

The post-Revolutionary Athenian democracy, however, worked to impose nominal (if artificial) equality upon all citizens, including the descendants of the leading archaic clans.[151] This pressure, whether legal or social,[152] likely created an atmosphere in which ostentatious funerary monuments were an uncomfortable fit. Although they did not disappear immediately, the figured stelai and other archaic memorial styles are generally not represented after the Persian Wars.[153] The earlier classical monuments that replaced them and endured down even into the 430s, as Morris has observed, tend to avoid display rather than embracing it.[154] Most notably, with few exceptions, figured reliefs are almost entirely absent during this period. The most common grave markers recorded are small, flat, rectangular stone 'slab stelai.'[155] Frequently, the only adornment upon their plain faces is the inscribed given name of the deceased, occasionally made more specific with a patronymic or (much more rarely) a demotic.[156]

There are, however, some exceptions to this homogeneity. As Morris has demonstrated, interest in individual funerary display, broadly defined, seems never to have entirely vanished from Athens. This is witnessed, for example, by his analysis of the sequences of tombs established over and around large mounds in the Kerameikos and in Piraeus Street.[157] These structures, with their Homeric overtones,[158] labor-intensive format, and

[151] On particular aspects of the Cleisthenic reforms designed to break down or channel the power of the archaic clans, see e.g. Traill 1975 *passim*; Bradeen 1955, with additional references.

[152] The possible sumptuary legislation mentioned by Cicero, who claims (*de leg.* 2.59–60, 64–5) that archaic and classical Athens was twice subjected to such regulations, once under Solon (cf. also Plu. *Sol.* 21.5–7) and once *post aliquanto* ("rather later," Cic. *de leg.* 2.64; this would be the ostensible law that, for some scholars, curbed the archaic tombstones and whose effects lasted into the 430s) has been abundantly treated in the critical literature. The arguments and bibliography summarized by Stears 2000b: 42–3 and Clairmont 1970: 11 permit rapid acquaintance with the various approaches and problems. Perhaps the most serious argument *against* sumptuary legislation has been the observation that, even given the vagaries of preservation and excavation, archaic-style memorials appear to decline gradually in the archaeological record rather than suddenly disappearing.

[153] Stears 2000a: 29; see also the references collected by Meyer 1993: 107 n. 16 and Morris 1992: 128–9 esp. n. 1, and cf. notes 146 and 152, above.

[154] See Morris 1994 *passim*; Morris 1992: 108–55, both with references. On the cultural milieu of mid fifth-century Athens and the general currents of democratic thought during this time, see e.g. Loraux 1986: 57–72.

[155] I adopt here the term employed for such monuments by Kurtz and Boardman 1971: 123–4 *et passim*.

[156] See the distribution graph in Meyer 1993: 100 fig. 2.

[157] Both Mound G (in the Kerameikos) and the Piraeus Street mound are thoroughly treated by Morris 1992: 132–6 (cited in Stears 2000b: 33 n. 4), with additional references. Morris' interpretations are followed here, *contra* e.g. Knigge 1991: 32.

[158] Morris 1992: 134, with modern references; cf. *Il.* 23.136, 245–8, 255–7 (the mound over the tomb of Patroclus). On the literary evidence for Homeric-style burial, see Mylonas 1948.

impressive appearance (they often seem to have served as exaggerated bases for florid stelai or other finials)[159] would have presented a symbolic challenge to the modest markers that were their contemporaries, particularly during the first two-thirds or so of the fifth century. Their now-anachronistic invocations of archaic forms could potentially be taken as overt references to the archaic (and patently non-democratic) values espoused by the sixth-century funerary monuments.[160] The monuments depicted on Attic white-ground *lekythoi*, which were popular as gifts to the dead both above and below ground[161] during the latter two-thirds of the fifth century,[162] may also refer, whether in the positive or the negative, to the same archaizing style of funerary commemoration.[163] The pictures of tombs on the vases look very much like the mound burials, topped by elaborate stelai with vegetal ornamentation,[164] but excavation has yielded almost no parallels for the stelai, and the precise reasons for this gap remain unknown.[165] The inherent flexibility of these images, however, as Morris shows, meant that the pictures on the *lekythoi* could potentially function as either an invocation or a rejection of archaic ways of thinking about and memorializing the individual.[166]

The epitaphs of Pythagoras of Selymbria and Pythion of Megara were likely set up near the midpoint of the fifth century. Both were found at Athens, and both are dedicated to foreigners, not citizens. But they provide an essential link that both recalls the acknowledgements of the Tyrannicides and presages certain commemorative habits of the later fifth and earlier fourth centuries. In their utilization of high poetical language, their attention to historical agency, and their careful relation of their subjects to the Athenian citizen group, these epitaphs employ discourse that is also evident

---

[159] Kurtz and Boardman 1971: 80–1, 353 (numerous archaic examples listed); cf. also 105–6, 356, on the classical period.

[160] Morris 1992: 133–4; cf. note 147, above.

[161] Images on the *lekythoi* themselves frequently suggest this, with clearly drawn *lekythoi* silhouetted against tombstones or sitting on their stepped bases, sometimes in groups, and ranging in contextual size from tiny to quite large (depicted as being perhaps three-quarters life-size): e.g. Kurtz 1975: 65–6.

[162] The predominance of funerary iconography on many fifth-century white *lekythoi*, coupled with the fragility of their finish (see Morris 1994: 78) and their comparatively frequent appearance in graves (see Morris 1992: 111–16), has led most scholars to conclude that they were nearly always destined for burial.

[163] Morris 1994: 78–9 and esp. 80, 90, with additional references, esp. Shapiro 1991: 649–55.

[164] Morris 1994: 78; cf. also note 157, above.

[165] Stears 2000b: 33; Shapiro 1991: 655. Many possible archaeological explanations for this phenomenon have been proposed: these are summarized effectively by Stears 2000b: 33–5, with references.

[166] Morris 1994: 80.

not only in some later tombstones for Athenian citizens, but also in the honorific decrees that become increasingly common at Athens during and (especially) after the Peloponnesian War.[167]

The epitaph for Pythagoras proclaims the honor of a public burial conferred upon a *proxenos*, a foreign 'friend' of the city who served as an informal ambassador.[168] The stoichedon inscription in elegiacs appears upon a marble base (which originally would have supported a stele) found in the Kerameikos:[169]

Πυθαγόρο.

προξενίας ἀρετῆς τε χάριμ προ<γ>όνων τε καὶ αὐτõ/
ἐνθάδ᾽ Ἀθηναῖοι Πυθαγόρην ἔθεσαν /
υἱὸν δημοσίαι Διονυσίο, ἱππόβοτον δὲ /
πατρίδα Σαλυβρίαν ἵκετ᾽ ἄχος φθιμένο.

Of Pythagoras
Because of the virtue of his proxeny, his and that of his ancestors,
the Athenians buried Pythagoras here,
the son of Dionysus, at public cost, and grief for the dead
came to his homeland, Selymbria, where horses graze.

Dated by *IG* to *c.* 460–50, the epitaph displays a blend of older traditions with newer ideas. In its form (elegiac couplets), in its mention of honor linked with ancestry (line 2), and in its use of elevated poetic language, evoking both epic and lyric,[170] this brief funerary poem looks backwards to the commemorative techniques of the archaic age.[171] Other features of the epitaph, however, seem to respond to political conditions under the young Athenian democracy. The factually prosaic, if rhythmic, line 3 contains a concept that would have had no home in archaic Attica: as a single, united populace, *the Athenians* buried Pythagoras, not a kinsman or fellow countryman of the deceased, which would have been the expected

---

[167] Discussed in Chapters 4 and 5, below.
[168] On the evolution of proxeny as a Greek institution down to the mid fifth century, see Wallace 1970.
[169] *IG* i³ 1154 = Pfohl 1967: 29–30 no. 88; cf. *SEG* 10.408. Edition here from *IG*.
[170] ἀρετή, line 2, is a central virtue of the Homeric heroes and beyond; ἱππόβοτος, line 4, is first employed in the Homeric poems (e.g. *Il.* 2.287; *Od.* 4.606), but its rich potential for elite associations is even more clearly evident in Sappho (e.g. Sapph. 2.9 L.-P.); the phrase ἵκετ᾽ ἄχος in the final line finds near parallels in Homeric poetry, ἄχος being a favored epic word for sorrow or grief, rather than physical pain (*Il.* 2.171, 23.47; see also *h. H. Cer.* 90).
[171] See Derderian 2001: 87–94, with references, on the relationship between the archaic epigram and traditional modes of poetical expression.

acknowledgement in the archaic period.[172] The sense of democratic agency is reiterated in line 4, with the word δημοσίαι interrupting the more traditional identification by patronymic. Finally, the opening word of the very first metrical couplet, προξενίας, suggests that what was most significant about Pythagoras the individual was his position as *proxenos*, whose duties he is represented as executing with high, even heroic, skill (ἀρετή, line 2). Pythagoras, this memorial implicitly declares, affected Athens for the better. His epitaph invokes traditional archaic models to elevate – and perhaps even to justify – his public esteem, even as it assigns him a permanent place in the city's history.[173]

The extended epitaph for Pythion of Megara, found near the Acharnian Gate of Athens, is carved on a marble block that was likely part of a larger grave monument. Rather than the more familiar elegiac couplets, this one is composed in dactylic hexameters:[174]

> μνῆμα τ[όδ' ἐστ' ἐ]πὶ σάματι κείμενον ἀνδρὸς ἀρίστο. / Πυθίων
> ἐγ Μεγάρω<ν> δαιώσας ἑπτὰ μ<ὲ>ν ἄνδρας, / ἑπτὰ δὲ ἀπορρήξας λ-
> όγχας ἐνὶ σώματι ἐκείνων / εἵλετο τὰν ἀρετὰν πατέρα εὐκ-
> λείζων ἐνὶ δήμωι. / οὗτος ἀνήρ, ὃς ἔ<σ>ωισεν Ἀθηναίων τρ-
> 5   ῆς φυλὰς / ἐκ Παγᾶν ἀγαγὼν διὰ Βοιωτῶν ἐς Ἀθήνας, / εὔκλ-
> εισε Ἀνδοκίδαν δισχίλοις ἀνδραπόδοισιν. / οὐδέ{δε}να
> πημάνας ἐπιχθονίων ἀνθρώπων / ἐς Ἀίδα κατέβα πᾶσιν μα-
> καριστὸς ἰδέσθαι. / φυλαὶ αἵδ' εἰσίν· Πανδιονίς, Κεκρ-
> οπίς, Ἀντιοχίς.

> [This] memorial [is] set over the grave of the bravest of men. / Pythion | of Megara slew seven men / and broke seven s|pears in their bodies. / He chose the path of bravery, bri|nging honor to his father among his
> 5   people. // This man, who rescued thr||ee Athenian tribes / by leading them from Pagae through Boeotia to Athens, / brought | honor to Andokides with his two thousand prisoners. / No | mortal man suffered improper injury at his hands / and he went down to Hades most bl|essed in the eyes of all. The tribes are these: Pandionis, Kekr|opis, Antiochis.

[172] On archaic epigrammatic formulae in general, e.g. Day 1989 and 1985; Jeffery 1947; see also note 171, above.
[173] Derderian 2001: 97–101 (cf. also 92–3) sees the epigrams of warriors, in particular, from the archaic period as negotiating between individual and collective interests and memory, a reading that harmonizes well with the features of Pythagoras' epitaph analyzed here and suggests that Pythagoras' monument emerges naturally out of a broader expressive context.
[174] *IG* i³ 1353 = Pfohl 1967: 31 no. 91; cf. *SEG* 10.411. Edition here from *IG*; translation from Fornara 1983b: 112 no. 101.

This inscription is probably to be dated from its content to 446/5 (the year of the revolt of Megara).[175] As in the epitaph of Pythagoras, poetic and historical elements are combined. Two particular incidents provide vivid witness to Pythion's contribution to Athenian history: his slaying of seven men in battle (lines 2–3) and his securing of safe conduct for a large number of men on their way home to Athens from Pagae (lines 4–5). Although the first incident has good parallels in the archaic commemoration of warriors and in heroic memorialization,[176] the second act is recollected as having directly benefited a subset of the Athenian democratic populace.

The first line of the text finds many near parallels in epitaphs of the archaic period.[177] Its mention of a μνῆμα ἐπὶ σάματι, a "memorial over a grave," too, would likely have been read three generations earlier as a reference to an archaic-style mound burial.[178] Pythion's deeds are praised in traditional epic-formulaic language as a gesture of elevation; the abundance of Homeric resonances in particular is doubtless assisted by the hexameter rhythm chosen for the epitaph. Although some of the Homeric echoes are straightforward,[179] the phrases πατέρα εὐκλείζων and εὔκλεισε Ἀνδοκίδαν (lines 3–4 and 5–6, respectively) may subtly represent the surpassing of a scene from heroic poetry. At *Il.* 8.285, the word ἐϋκλείης occurs as part of an admonition from Agamemnon to Teucer to do honor in battle to his father Telemon, even though Teucer was born a νόθος, a "bastard." Pythion has here answered the same call, but as (presumably) a legitimate son, the glory he has brought to his own father in war is ostensibly unqualified.

The last epic-style phrase in the epitaph, ἐς Ἀΐδα κατέβα πᾶσιν μακαριστὸς ἰδέσθαι, "he went down to Hades most blessed in the eyes of all," is likely where a reader would expect the epitaph to conclude; similar expressions often heralded the conclusions of individual death-vignettes in

---

[175]   *IG* i³ 1353, citing Thuc. 1.114.1–3. The *IG* entry also provides additional references to disputes over the dating.

[176]   See Derderian 2001: 92, 97–8.   [177]   See note 172, above.

[178]   See notes 157, 158, and 159, above. This suggestion is, of course, premised on the printed reading: Bekker read σώματι (apparatus, *IG ad loc.*).

[179]   E.g. δαΐζω (line 2): passive, describing Patroclus' mangled body: *Il.* 18.236, 19.211, 283, 319; active, describing heroic attack: e.g. *Il.* 7.247, 11.497. ἀπορρήγνυμι (line 2): later, particularly in tragedy, in metaphorical statements about dying (e.g. A. *Pers.* 507, πνεῦμ' ἀπέρρηξεν βίου, "broke off the spirit of life"); in epic, however, used physically: of a horse's tack in a recurring simile (*Il.* 6.507, 15.264) and of the mountain-top hurled at Odysseus' fleeing ship by the Cyclops (*Od.* 9.481). Its employ in this epitaph is appropriate to the associations with death that the verb had acquired by this time, but the concrete usage preserves what would have been expected in epic. A person functioning as a πῆμα, "misery" (as a participle, line 7) to others: first mention at *Il.* 3.50, with Helen as πῆμα for the Trojans.

epic.[180] But a final tag provides the most important historical information of all: the identities of the tribes who benefited directly from Pythion's
bravery. This 'signature,' which likely also identifies the donors of the tomb
and the inscription, links Pythion directly to an enduring reality in the physical and historical world: the tribes of Athens.[181] Like the *epitaphios logos*,
the "speech over the tomb," of the *patrios nomos*, the epigram creates new
significance for a single historical act – in this case, Pythion's conduct of the
troops through Boeotia – by connecting it directly back to the polis.[182]

    While these two epitaphs claim historical agency for foreigners rather than
for citizens, they demonstrate some essential continuities in their language
and symbolism with the evidence surrounding the Tyrannicides. They also
work, like the *patrios nomos* does, to relate the productive honorand to the
city, but they do so on the level of the individual, rather than that of the
group. Why might this be? It is possible that any social or legal limitations
that affected the acknowledgement of Athenian citizens at this time applied
somewhat more lightly to foreigners. Stears points out that a few of the slab
stelai from the period between *c.* 480 and 440 are modestly adorned with
carving or painting (one even has a relief), and most or all of these were
dedicated to non-citizens.[183] More detailed epitaphs in verse from roughly
the same period at Athens tend to be for group burials of Athenian war
casualties; similar memorials for individuals are much rarer, particularly
until around the time of the Peloponnesian War.[184] When honors for living
individuals enter the epigraphical record at Athens, these, too, tend to be
for foreigners first and Athenians only slightly later on.[185] This is not to
suggest that Athenian citizens were ineligible for special honors in the fifth
century (the literary testimonia, in fact, provide evidence that they were,

[180]   E.g. *Il.* 13.415, 16.856 (the death of Patroclus) = 22.362 (the death of Hector); *Od.* 3.410 (a
       remembrance), 11.277 (a transformation of what is more normally a heroic usage to describe
       the death of Iocasta).
[181]   See Derderian, note 182, below.
[182]   For this concept see Loraux 1986: 132–55 and *passim*; and Derderian 2001: 106–8 on the
       special meaning conveyed by the invocation of historical context rather than only the poetical
       "referential tradition."
[183]   Stears 2000b: 31. A few of the examples listed there are dated by *IG* to ranges that may extend
       down into the time of the Peloponnesian War (*IG* i³ 1343, 1356, 1361).
[184]   Drawing from the examples collected by Pfohl 1967 (examples marked * are known from
       literature but not from material evidence): known or likely for Athenian war dead: nos. *84 =
       Peek 1955 no. 12, *85 = Peek 1955 no. 13, 86 = *IG* i² 946, *89 = Peek 1955 no. 16, 90 = Peek
       1955 no. 17, 92 = *IG* i² 943, perhaps 93 = *IG* i² 935. Individuals: nos. 82 = *IG* i² 979, 88 = *IG*
       i² 1034 (Pythagoras), 91 = *IG* i² 1085 (Pythion), and likely also 96 = *IG* i² 1084 (although the
       date is unclear). A group of foreigners: 87 = *IG* i² 932. Unknown: nos. 83 = Peek 1955 no. 2,
       95 = *IG* i² 962.
[185]   See Chapters 4 and 5, below.

and increasingly so with the passage of time).[186] Rather, it is to suggest that the symbolic language for such awards may have first been established in dealings with outsiders, which might have provided a 'safer' place to work out a discourse of productive cooperation with the democracy.[187]

2.4 Historical agency and the living: Ostracism and public decrees

Ostracism

Though it seems to arise in the earlier years of the democracy, the date of the introduction of ostracism at Athens remains unclear.[188] In essence, it seems to have permitted the *dêmos* to exile a politically suspect citizen for a period of ten years, after which time he was permitted to return to the polis and resume his former place in civic life; he was never deprived of property or income.[189] The institution may have been intended as a check on the development of excessive individual power or on any plans for renewed 'tyranny.'[190] It also, however, de facto promoted the formation of subgroups within the voting citizenry that could band together to intimidate or oust an opponent. These cliques, ironically, threatened the very ideology of purified democratic equality that ostracism theoretically sought to protect.

On a conceptual level, ostracism in fifth-century Athens may be read as a symbolic reversal of the *patrios nomos*. Rather than being publicly creative of the past historical significance of the group, ostracism was publicly destructive of the future historical significance of the individual.[191] Rather

---

[186] Domingo Gygax 2006: 490–6.

[187] The bodies of work done by Morris and by Kurke (individual contributions collected in my bibliography) regarding the relationship of the outstanding individual to the polis have helped to shape my general thinking on this problem.

[188] On the archaeological evidence, see Lang 1990: 7–8, who provides a publication list of Athenian ostraka; see also the references in Vanderpool 1970: 5–16. On the dating, see the review of literature by Thomsen 1972: 11–60, adding Rhodes 1981: 268–9 *ad Ath. Pol.* 22.3–4; Keaney and Raubitschek 1972 (responses to the latter are collected at Lang 1990: 3 n. 11). Many of the testimonia ascribe ostracism to Cleisthenes: see Kagan 1961: 393–6 on the arguments.

[189] Lang 1990: 1–3 collects translated literary evidence; see also Kagan 1961: 393–5 and the analysis by Brenne 1994.

[190] See the arguments collected by Forsdyke 2000: 255 n. 88.

[191] The analogy may be carried one step further: rather than being creative of the past historical significance of the group through the performance of an individual (i.e. the speaker of the *epitaphios*, who was at once, paradoxically, honoree and anonymous voice of the polis), ostracism was destructive of the future historical significance of the individual through the performance of the (voting) group.

than inspiring citizens to sanctioned action in service to the state, ostracism was designed to check the selfish or un-democratic impulses of an individual – not only practically but also morally, for its open proceedings were probably intended as a deterrent.[192] In theory, ostracism would emphasize the sovereignty of the *dêmos* by making the voting populace the collective agents of change for the betterment of the polis. By engaging in tightly controlled democratic ritual, the citizens of Athens would band together to protect their city from obvious threats to the democracy, just as the fallen warriors memorialized in the *patrios nomos* had done. The weapons in this case, however, would be ballots, designed to ward off enemies from within, rather than from without. And rather than producing eternal memory and honor as the *patrios nomos* did, ostracism would instead generate a functional scapegoat[193] whose long absence from Athens would ideally both eradicate recollection of his deeds in the past and limit his efficacy in the future.

But ostracism does not seem to have accomplished what it set out to do. Again like the *patrios nomos*, ostracism required a series of individual acts that were theoretically in keeping with democratic ideology, but created problematic side effects. The *patrios nomos*, aside from suppressing the funerary privileges of the families of the war dead, could not provide for individuals whose unique historical actions had merited separate memorialization from the state. Ostracism was inherently unable to check factionalism, which saw unofficial groups join together for the effacement of individuals,[194] and which probably contributed to the de facto demise of the institution before the end of the Peloponnesian War.[195]

Well into the fourth century, however, the possibility of ostracism was consistently raised in the form of an "annual question in the [Athenian A]ssembly."[196] That the citizenry repeatedly voted 'no' may be an indicator

---

[192] Forsdyke 2000, recommending that ostracism represented the democratic usurpation and formalization of archaic "aristocratic politics of exile" (232), and that much of its power was symbolic and perceptual, rather than practical.

[193] On ostracism as scapegoating, see Sagan 1991 esp. 170–6.

[194] Factionalism is evident in small handfuls of ostraka directed against less-prominent individuals, which may indicate personal enmity rather than widespread political action (see Rhodes 1981: 271 on the concept, and Lang 1990 *passim* and Thomsen 1972: 68–108 on the evidence). A unique find of some 191 Themistocles ostraka lettered in only 14 different hands may imply the same instincts: Broneer 1938: 228–43.

[195] It is likely that the Hyperbolus episode (see Lang 1990: 64 on the date, sometime between 417 and 415, with bibliography) helped to motivate the virtual abandonment of ostracism: Roberts 1982: 152–3, with additional references. *Contra*: Christ 1992: 338. The ostracism law itself was apparently not formally repealed: Rhodes 1981: 526 *ad Ath. Pol.* 43.5.

[196] Forsdyke 2000: 255, citing (n. 89, with others) *Ath. Pol.* 43.5.

that the institution was perceived as having little practical value. It has been suggested that such authority as ostracism possessed had by this time passed over to the more easily enacted charge of *graphê paranomôn* (the proposing of an illegal decree, which usually came with a fine but not exile) and even to *eisangelia* (a more serious accusation for, most notably, bribery or treason, whose penalty was usually death).[197] Why, then, was the offer of ostracism still made? It may have been a ritualized but meaningful check upon the ambitions of the elite.[198] But it may also have represented an entry into the ongoing negotiations at Athens about individual and group historical agency, which at that time were growing increasingly complex. Read in this way, the ostracism invitations of the fourth century become a form of tacit cooperation between the *dêmos* and its elites: a performed acknowledgement of the (nominally regrettable) necessity of allowing powerful leaders to emerge as *prostatai tou dêmou,* "guardians of the populace."[199]

Public decrees

During the first generations of the democracy, the 'epigraphical habit'[200] at Athens becomes far more pronounced.[201] Decree inscriptions, in particular, proliferate as the government establishes laws and uses the written word both to reify and to memorialize its actions. The general presentation of these inscriptions is highly formulaic,[202] especially in their identifying 'prescripts,'[203] but their structure recalls the tension between individual and group historical agency so prominent across other commemorative media during the earlier fifth century. A nameless democratic body, generally the *boulê* or the *dêmos,* whose assent both formalizes and activates the new

---

[197] See Sagan 1991: 176, citing (n. 16) Roberts 1982: 153; and Hansen 1975.

[198] Forsdyke 2000: 233, 255, also citing (n. 91) Christ 1992 (see esp. 340) and Rosivach 1987: 163.

[199] E.g. *Ath. Pol.* 2.2 et al. On the role of eminent individual politicians in the government of fourth-century Athens, see Ober 1998 and 1989; Connor 1971. Connor's model is helpful in understanding fourth-century democratic processes as well as the fifth-century ones upon which his work focuses.

[200] The term is borrowed from the title of Hedrick 1999, who adopts it in turn from MacMullen 1982.

[201] The number of preserved Athenian inscriptions rises in the course of the fifth century and peaks during the fourth: Hedrick 1999: 390–5, 399, 404–6; see particularly the graphs (= figs. 1–2) at 392.

[202] On the limited flexibility of the formulae over time, see Henry 1977: 104–5; Henry 1977: 4 outlines the two most common fifth-century patterns.

[203] Henry 1977: xi. Some early prescript examples down to *c.* 430–15 are collected at 5.

decree, leads the inscription; this acknowledgement is followed *pro forma* by the names of certain officers.[204] Individual citizen actors, however, are generally given credit by name when they propose a decree or amendment, or otherwise bring an important motion. The democracy itself therefore enacts a decree or law, but it does so in explicit partnership with a citizen from within the group.

The agency of individuals receives even more emphasis in honorific decrees,[205] where the *dêmos* acknowledges positive disposition or good work done on its behalf and offers benefits in return.[206] During the earlier years of the democracy, these tend to be issued not for Athenian citizens, but rather for foreigners, often involving grants of *proxenia*.[207] This trend in the public-epigraphical record is very similar to that observed in the tombstones, where non-Athenians seem to have enjoyed greater access to more individualized memorials.[208] Both the private and the public discourse during this period, then, suggest that the reinforcement of 'democratic' ideologies was a more important consideration for members of the Athenian citizen group than it was for foreigners,[209] even for foreign friends who were buried at Athens. This distinction could have worked in two different directions, extending unusual individuation as a privilege – but by that very privilege also pointing out that the recipient of such 'honors' was not, after all, a full member of the exclusive body of Athenian citizens. The extension of Athenian citizenship as an honor in itself, which seems to have begun slightly later in the fifth century, was therefore a logical next step in the navigation between the elevation of the individual and the invocation of the authority of the group.[210]

---

[204] Henry 1977: 4.

[205] Examples of these are collected in chronological order by Henry 1983: 333–54.

[206] While the contributions of the honorands are sometimes expressed only in the abstract (Henry 1983: 1, 4–6, table at 9–14 listing whether or not the services are specified), the rewards to be given to them are usually meticulously recorded (Henry 1983, with each chapter dedicated to a different type of "privilege," and exceptions listed at 311).

[207] See Walbank 1978: 63–146, collecting both inscriptions and testimonia of twenty-three proxenies of Athens that he accepts as potentially dating to the year 440 or earlier.

[208] See notes 183 through 187, above.

[209] Morris 1992 esp. 149–55 suggests, amongst other things, that trends in "moderation" vs. "display" or in (149, citing Renfrew) "group-oriented" vs. "individualizing" behavior are likely to be visible in the archaeological record beyond the funerary practices upon which he focuses, and my analysis here provides further support for these recommendations. Cf. also Morris 1994 on "good taste" (his term, referring in part to the appropriate degree of moderation) in Athenian funerary commemoration of the fifth century BC.

[210] See Chapter 4, below.

2.5 Conclusion: Ancient and modern ascriptions of agency

Cleisthenes is the acknowledged 'mastermind' behind the Athenian
democratic system in nearly all *modern* accounts of the classical age. His
reception during the fifth and fourth centuries BC, however, was moderate
at best. No known inscriptions or artifacts bear Cleisthenes' name, and his
major appearances in the extant literature,[211] while respectful, are brief and
rather flat. Although Pausanias does claim (1.29.6) to have seen a funerary
monument for him in the Kerameikos, far higher honors were accorded to
the Tyrannicides. That the Athenians likely did not glorify Cleisthenes to the
same degree does not necessarily diminish his historical significance in
the long view,[212] but it does offer an object lesson in Athenian concepts
of history that may serve as a summary of the developments explored in
this chapter. During the earlier portion of the fifth century, the murderers
of a tyrant's brother could be recollected as the founding heroes of a
government whose creation dated to nearly a decade after their act. Neither
the individual (Cleisthenes, the inventor of the democracy's organizational
systems) nor the group (the populace that rioted in the streets) directly
involved in the Athenian Revolution[213] ever acquired places in the imagination of Athens quite so prominent as those of Harmodius and Aristogeiton.
In the very shadow of their statues, however, the Athenian *dêmos* continued
to assert its agency and authority both in the commemoration of its past
and in the decrees it passed to shape its future. Whether there was still room
for other democratic heroes remained to be seen, but in the meantime the
vocabulary that would later be employed to elevate eminent individuals
was being quietly developed in the safe and acceptable commemoration of
the foreigners who did not need to conform too precisely to the story the
dêmos had begun to tell about itself.

[211] Hdt. 5.66.1–2, 69.1–73.1, with the 'Athenian Revolution' continuing to 5.78.1; cf. also 6.131.1;
Ath. Pol. 20–2.
[212] It does suggest, however, that recent scholarly re-evaluations of Cleisthenes' position and
activities were very much in order. Ober 1996a: 32–52, in particular, espouses the sentiments
expressed here and offers an interpretation of Cleisthenes in his historical context.
[213] Ober 1996a: 32–52.

3 | Culture clash?

Individuals and groups in the *Histories* of Herodotus

3.1 Creating history

The news that trickled down from the paths above Trachis in August of the year 480 BC was not good. Megistias, the soothsayer traveling with the Greek army, had predicted it, and it had shortly been confirmed both by runaways and by scouts: the Persians had encircled the Thermopylae pass.[1] The narrow confines that had for two days prevented the massacre of the small allied Greek force would soon fall to the enemy, opening a pathway towards the south.

As far back as the legends of the Trojan War, Greek military operations had often involved multiple commanders from a variety of city-states, and this one was no exception. Contingents from Tegea, Mantinea, Arcadian Orchomenus, Arcadia itself, Corinth, Phlius, Mycenae, Thespiae, Thebes, Opuntian Locris, and Phocis represented the Peloponnese and central Greece (7.202.1–203.1). In high command was Leonidas, one of the two kings of Sparta, at the head of a handpicked force of three hundred Spartan hoplites. Now, with the garrison's destruction certain, Leonidas stood at both a physical and a metaphorical crossroads. The choices he made would determine not only the fates of his own men and their allies, but also the way that the events about to unfold would be remembered.

Herodotus initially presents the dissolution of the Greek forces as the result of collective decision-making (7.219.2), but it soon emerges (by 7.222.1) that Leonidas himself has chosen to send most of the troops home. The character's own convictions become clearer in the course of this passage. Initially, the general impression, reported neutrally as a rumor (7.220.1), is that the king does not wish to force a massacre, but thinks it "fitting" or "appropriate" (εὐπρεπέως, ibid.) that he and the Spartans, at least, should stay. Herodotus suggests, however, that Leonidas' true motivations are far more direct: an oracle has foretold destruction, and Leonidas

---

[1] Hdt. 7.219.1. In the remainder of this chapter, all passages from Herodotus are cited by number only.

is determined to at least salvage heroic κλέος[2] for his doomed expedition, so
he dismisses the allies whose reliability is in doubt (7.220.2, 4). Herodotus'
Leonidas therefore exploits his position of leadership to ensure that the
history-making agency will belong centrally to himself and his own citizen
group.

This section further reveals overlapping negotiations of historical agency
both inside and outside the world of the text. Herodotus shows his character
thinking through the assignment of the responsibility for a history-making
event – but due to the omniscience of the historian's external perspective
and his extensive treatment of the incident, the character seems to have
already apprehended the magnitude of a battle that has not yet taken place.
Leonidas' decision-making process prior to the action becomes a projection
of the historian's own assessment afterwards, and the literary character is
consequently gifted with foresight that reaches beyond his own position in
the narrative.[3] This intimate connection between character and narrator
further invokes the memory-making qualities of Herodotus' own literary
genre,[4] for his presentation of Leonidas' motivations recalls the wording
and content of his own preface: μένοντι δὲ αὐτοῦ <u>κλέος μέγα</u> ἐλείπετο, καὶ
ἡ Σπάρτης εὐδαιμονίη οὐκ <u>ἐξηλείφετο</u>, "great fame would be left him if he
stayed, and the good fortune of Sparta would not be erased" (7.220.2);
ὡς μήτε τὰ γενόμενα ἐξ ἀνθρώπων τῷ χρόνῳ <u>ἐξίτηλα γένηται</u>, μήτε ἔργα
<u>μεγάλα τε καὶ θωμαστά</u>, τὰ μὲν Ἕλλησι, τὰ δὲ βαρβάροισι ἀποδεχθέντα,
<u>ἀκλεᾶ</u> γένηται, "so that what has happened amongst men may not fade with
time, and that acts both great and amazing, some accomplished by Greeks
and others by barbarians, may not lack fame" (praef.).[5] In short, Herodotus'
Leonidas is deliberately acting towards history – and, as Herodotus implies,
towards historiography.

---

[2] The term is Homeric and deeply charged, referring to the honor, reputation, and memory
    sought by the epic heroes. On Herodotus' relationship to Homeric epic and other poetry, see
    Marincola 2006 (including discussion of κλέος and related matters at 17–19); Pelling 2006;
    Boedeker 2002.
[3] Herodotus' Leonidas here may therefore presage Thucydides' Pericles. See, most notably, the
    direct assessment at Thuc. 2.65.6–7.
[4] See Luraghi 2006 esp. 87.
[5] Others have also noted this echo and its function: e.g. Baragwanath 2008: 68–70 and nn. 41–2
    (reading a connection between Leonidas and Herodotus himself in thought as well as in words);
    Pelling 2006: 93–4 and n. 51 (noting the performative qualities of the behavior of Leonidas and
    his Spartan warriors), both with additional references. Baragwanath 2008 was released too late
    to play a role in the original development of these arguments, but occasional points of contact
    have been noted.

"Who lost Thermopylae?" therefore seems to be as important a question to Herodotus in this portion of his narrative as "Who won Marathon?" was to the Athenians in the earlier fifth century. Leonidas, whose fallen body provokes a struggle as if over a Homeric hero,[6] eventually receives his own commemorative monument (7.225.2), while the Spartans collectively share in both the epitaph attributed to Simonides and the poem dedicated to all of the Greeks who set out to hold the pass (7.228.1–2).[7] The glory of the sacrifice has been assumed by the leader – but also shared with his citizens. And all of those participants are in turn memorialized by Herodotus.[8] In the end, then, it is the collaboration between the warriors and their king, between leader and led, that has brought about their distinction, their κλέος, and their memory.[9]

As suggested by his account of Thermopylae, Herodotus' work reveals an energetic interest in exploring the roles of individual and group agency in the motion of history, in many ways addressing issues that were also being examined in Athens during the same period.[10] The most conservative interpretation might ascribe this connection to Herodotus' known interest in Athenian affairs:[11] as a reader of Athens and perhaps even a reader *in* Athens,[12] he may have been influenced in his thinking by the cultural debate[13] in progress there. But Herodotus' interpretive choices also suggest that he believed questions about historical agency would be

---

[6] See note 2, above; Pelling 2006: 92–3 and n. 48 notes some of the particular details in this scene.

[7] Megistias, the Acarnanian soothsayer who served at Thermopylae (cf. above), is also recorded by Herodotus as having received a private epitaph there (7.228.3–4). The historian adds, however, that the memorial was a private gift of friendship from Simonides, rather than one of the (apparently) official monuments set up by the Amphictyons.

[8] It might be argued that Herodotus implies *individualized* memorialization for all of the Spartans who fell at Thermopylae when he says that he knows all of their names (7.224.1), but he chooses not to record them in his final medium of arbitration, his own text.

[9] See Low 2006 on the various memorials for Thermopylae, discussed in more detail in Chapter 6, below.

[10] See Chapter 2, above.

[11] On Herodotus' close study of Athens, see e.g. Fowler 2003; Moles 2002, with extensive references; Blösel 2001; Forsdyke 2001; Ostwald 1991; Raaflaub 1987.

[12] There is limited evidence that Herodotus may actually have visited Athens: see Ostwald 1991: 138. Herodotus' own travels both within and outside of Greece are debated: see most notably Podlecki 1977; Fehling 1971 (English version 1989; Fehling's arguments are countered in greatest detail by Pritchett 1993); see also Shrimpton and Gillis in Shrimpton 1997: 229–65; Armayor 1985, 1978a, 1978b, 1978c.

[13] I am indebted to J. Ober for the descriptive phrase "cultural debate," and for his suggesting the overall structure for the arguments in this chapter.

comprehensible to and relevant for non-Athenian listeners and readers, as well.

The *Histories* are frequently (and productively) interpreted as being centrally defined by the division between the Greek and non-Greek, 'barbarian' worlds,[14] but Herodotus' construction of historical agency, in particular, defies classification in terms of binary oppositions. Instead, he offers at least three distinct ways of understanding the historical contributions of human actors: he depicts non-Greeks (most notably Croesus, Cyrus, Darius, and Xerxes) as individual agents, Greeks as group agents, and, most importantly, individual agency on the part of a select few Greek leaders who are often involved in problematic relationships with their respective citizen bodies – and whose behavior is not always entirely distinct from that of their barbarian counterparts. Herodotus returns to the issue of individual–group associations amongst the Greeks throughout his narrative, and the increasing complexity of such analyses as the text progresses suggests the gradual complication of what may have been a rather schematic (and ultimately, in Herodotus' final view, inadequate) starting point: the idea that foreign rulers act as individuals, but Greeks tend to work collectively, generally by polis.[15] Herodotus' treatment of historical agency, then, represents not only an entry into the same kind of larger intellectual and social 'conversation' that is already visible at Athens,[16] but also an increasingly subtle attempt to understand and describe the roles of individuals in history.[17]

This chapter, then, examines agency in Herodotus by looking at the roles played both by individuals and by groups in the motion of events. It begins by differentiating between autocracy and historical agency: the former depends

---

[14] E.g. Gould 1994; Redfield 1985; and esp. Hartog 1988, all of whom suggest in various ways that Herodotus uses the ethnic 'other' as a means or a "mirror" (Hartog) for examining and thinking about Greek culture. Pelling 1997c, however, highlights the need to account for significant slippage between these categories.

[15] I am grateful to J. Ober for an email communication of January 3, 2005, that suggested this point.

[16] And, as Chapter 6 will show, elsewhere in Greece, as well.

[17] It has frequently been acknowledged that events in the *Histories* are not always driven exclusively by human design. Causality may be assigned in whole or in part, for example, to "the divine" (ὁ θεός) or to fate. Even these, however, may under certain circumstances be coupled in thought with human responsibility: e.g. Munson 2001. Harrison 2000 considers religion as being central to Herodotus' thought in general and to his models of historical causality in particular, but see Lateiner 2002 and 1989, and esp. Immerwahr 1954. Particularly as Herodotus' subject matter progresses forward in time, an increasing emphasis is placed upon human beings as the drivers of historically significant action, and likely related to this tendency is the gradual reduction of authorial interjections and apologiae as the text progresses: see Marincola 1987.

upon social and political station, the latter upon action and its consequences as assigned by the narrative, and the second does not necessarily proceed naturally from the first. Next, some paradigmatic individual agents from early in the *Histories* (Croesus, Solon, and Cyrus) not only reveal some of Herodotus' narrative methods for contextualizing his most important figures, but also show the historian thinking through the measures by which individuals can or should be considered to be historically consequent, a question addressed in particular detail by the meeting between Solon and Croesus. After a consideration of Cyrus as an individual agent, a reading of the Persian 'Constitutional Debate' further suggests that Herodotus' Persians tend not to interpret history as being driven by the actions of groups, which in turn implicitly supports the historian's subsequent individual-centered presentation of Darius' expeditions. This pattern finally culminates in Herodotus' treatment of Xerxes, whose personal ownership of his invasion of Greece is invoked and reiterated by both the character and the historian on multiple occasions.

An examination of agency by Greeks, however, yields rather more complex findings. Leonidas provides an immediate contrast to Xerxes in that he creates history and memory through productive collaboration with his people. Greek groups, too, can serve as historical agents in Herodotus (most notably "the Athenians," e.g. 7.139.1–6), but the largest unit in which they are consistently capable of productive action is the polis: neither "the Ionians" (during their revolt from Persia) nor "the Greeks" are able to sustain cooperation to the degree that Herodotus would see them as making history together, whether for good or for ill. Similar problems are also visible in the attempts of several eminent individual leaders to work together with their respective poleis: Hippias, Aristagoras, and especially Miltiades and Themistocles prove unable to reconcile their own interests and their desires for individual agency with the expectations of their cities. In narrating their experiences, Herodotus ultimately demonstrates his own authority: the characters invoke or invite certain kinds of agency for themselves, but the historian's text can provoke other associations.

The clearest productive individual historical agents in Herodotus' text, in the end, are Leonidas and Solon, both of whom are able to work together with their poleis to achieve history-making results, one in war and the other in peace. The fact that one of these 'collaborative' leaders is Spartan and the other Athenian invites further reflection upon the applicability of Herodotus' models – and the questions he raises – to the debate over historical agency as it was enacted outside of Athens, an issue that will be further explored in Chapter 6.

3.2 Historical agents from Solon to Cyrus

Autocracy vs. agency in Herodotus

The autocrat in Herodotus, most clearly embodied by the barbarian ruler,[18] is generally also construed as a military and political leader, regardless of intervening chains of command. He himself determines upon a given course of action, often with – or despite – the assistance of oracles, portents, and advisers, and therefore bears personal responsibility for both success and disaster. Within the sphere of the activities that he designs and motivates, the autocrat, especially the barbarian ruler, often becomes the narrative metonym for his people, to the degree that their collective name within the text is frequently replaced by his own.[19] In these respects, autocracy and historical agency may initially appear to be very near to one another. Comparatively few of the autocrats in Herodotus, however, whether Greek or non-Greek, are actually depicted as agents of large-scale historical change. Many of them instead receive only very limited treatment in the *Histories*, particularly if their reigns have little contact with the history-making events of the Persian Wars. Within the world of the text, such individuals are most often insular figures, though the reasons for these limitations vary.[20] Sometimes they are little more than links in a chain of traditional chronography,[21] or they are preoccupied with comparatively minor internal affairs. Some are recalled mainly through colorful anecdotes; others are only tangentially involved in events driven by forces – or men – much larger and more powerful than themselves.[22] Two autocrats who do *not* function as agents of history in Herodotus, Cambyses of Persia and Polycrates of Samos, are representative of this type.

Dewald has shown that Herodotus' treatment of Cambyses' reign presents patterns of autocracy, imperialism, and even misjudgment that are shared

---

[18] But not exclusively: Dewald 2003: 33, 36–40 shows that Greek tyrants often share character and behavioral traits with Eastern rulers in Herodotus: in other words, they, too participate to a certain extent in the "despotic template" established centrally by the barbarian kings (cf. also note 23, below).

[19] See Chapters 4 and 5, below, on 'commander narrative,' a similar feature that appears in Thucydides and Xenophon.

[20] Dewald 2003: 40–4, 48–9 emphasizes the "idiosyncratic" qualities of the stories of the Greek tyrants, highlighting that they do participate in the patterns of tyranny centrally modeled by the stories of the Eastern kings (see note 23, below), but that the specific features of their treatments differ from one another.

[21] As is the case with nearly all of the Egyptian rulers at 2.99.1–182.2, and particularly those who predate Amasis (the treatment of the latter's reign begins at 2.172.1).

[22] Dewald 2003: 43–8, on the Greek tyrants.

most notably with Croesus, Cyrus, Darius, and Xerxes.[23] An important
distinction, however, is that Cambyses is not depicted *within the narrative* as achieving a historical impact comparable to those of the other four
kings. Cambyses' conquest of Egypt was in reality a significant event in the
regional history of the Near East.[24] Herodotus, however, focuses his treatment of Cambyses much more significantly upon sensational anecdotes: the
intrigues over the daughter of the Egyptian pharaoh Amasis (3.1.1–5), the
demeaning and bloody treatment of the family and friends of the pharaoh
Psammenitus (3.14.1–15.1), the desecration of Amasis' mummy (3.16.1–7),
the ill-provisioned chase into Ethiopia after the 'Table of the Sun' (3.18.1–
25.7), the destruction of the Apis calf (3.27.1–29.3), the bizarre acts of Cambyses after he is driven 'mad' (3.30.1–38.1), the flaying of a judge to make
a courtroom-seat of human skin (5.25.1–2). Even the Persian occupation
and administration of Egypt after Cambyses' conquests receives only the
barest attention, and then most significantly when an Egyptian revolt temporarily distracts Darius and Xerxes from their plans against Greece (7.1.3,
7.1–8.1).[25] The lasting impact of Cambyses upon the Persian monarchy, too,
is deliberately minimized by the historian. Instead, at the moment of the
king's obituary, Herodotus emphasizes both his lack of direct descendants
to succeed him and his almost pathetic inability to convince the distrustful
Persians that the Smerdis who is about to ascend the throne is actually a
usurper (3.65.1–66.3).

   A similar lack of impact is visible in the case of Polycrates of Samos: there
is a striking gap between his direct characterization by Herodotus and his
actions within the narrative. The introduction he receives seems at first to
promise great things (3.39.3–4).[26] A tone of wonder highlights an impressive
figure: the geographic extent of Polycrates' fame, the pat exaggeration of
his initial successes, the ascription of his accomplishments to him alone
(rather than to his people), the vast and conveniently round numbers of
his military forces, and the anecdotal account of his imperial philosophy

---

[23] Ibid. 33–5; Dewald also classes Cambyses (along with these four latter kings) as one of the "five
      major monarchs in the *Histories*" (33).

[24] Ray 1988 *passim*; see also ibid. 254–62 and Young 1988: 47–52 on the historical reign of
      Cambyses.

[25] Tangential mention is made at 4.39.1 of a canal built by Darius, at 4.43.1–7 of the exploration
      of Africa from Egypt under Xerxes, and at 7.34.1, 89.2–3; 8.68.γ1, 100.4; 9.32.1 of Egyptians in
      the Persian military, but this slight material represents nearly the entire extent of Herodotus'
      coverage of Persian involvement in Egypt after the death of Cambyses.

[26] The first mention of Polycrates in Herodotus actually occurs at 2.182.2, but it is only a passing
      reference to the tyrant's friendship with Amasis.

combine to create not only the impression of an autocrat[27] but also the sense of a legend or folk-tale. The latter impression, too, is immediately borne out by Herodotus' presentation of the story about Polycrates' ring (3.40.1–43.2).

But Polycrates, contrary to these initial expectations, has little historical impact upon the larger Herodotean world. His war against the Spartans is the only interstate conflict that Herodotus treats in real time (as opposed to summary backward references), and it climaxes in a defensive battle as Polycrates, listed by Herodotus as the actual commander, must struggle to break the siege upon his own polis (3.54.1–56.2). While this conflict receives somewhat extended treatment – mainly because it prompts a number of anecdotal digressions about past animosities between Samos and Sparta, Corinth, and Corcyra (3.44.1–56.2, *passim*) – it concludes with an oddly anticlimactic retreat by the Spartan forces (3.56.1–2) and no apparent lasting effect. When Polycrates next resurfaces, it is because he is about to become the victim of Oroetes, the Persian hyparch of Sardis. Like many quarrels (whether petty or international) in Herodotus, this one arises in reaction to a perceived personal slight (3.120.1–122.1), and Oroetes sets a trap baited with sufficient wealth and power to tempt Polycrates' greed against the warnings of his friends, advisers, and daughter (3.122.1–125.4). Upon arriving at Magnesia to meet Oroetes, Polycrates is quickly dispatched, and Herodotus' final summation of the tyrant of Samos again contains strong and promising generalizations that have not been borne out by the intervening narrative (3.125.2).[28]

Herodotus' paradigmatic agents: Solon and Croesus

Croesus of Lydia, like Polycrates, is introduced in dramatic fashion (οὗτος ὁ Κροῖσος βαρβάρων πρῶτος τῶν ἡμεῖς ἴδμεν τοὺς μὲν κατεστρέψατο Ἑλλήνων ἐς φόρου ἀπαγωγήν ... πρὸ δὲ τῆς Κροίσου ἀρχῆς πάντες Ἕλληνες ἦσαν ἐλεύθεροι, "this Croesus was the first of the barbarians of whom we are aware to subject Greeks to the payment of tribute ... before the sovereignty of Croesus all Greeks were free," 1.6.2–3), but Croesus' historical importance, in contrast, is emphasized and proven throughout the narrative that follows.

---

[27] See note 18, above.

[28] Dewald 2003: 38 observes a pattern here: "from book 3 [of the *Histories*] onward, tyrants in the Greek world have been increasingly portrayed as looking to the Persian king to establish, maintain, or reestablish their power and as being unscrupulous about asking for Persian military support if necessary. Polycrates is the first intimation of this new trend: he dies because he has become embroiled in the ambitions of Persian satraps."

After a brief digression on the history of Lydian power, Herodotus returns to Croesus' ascendancy and his subjection of the Greeks and other peoples of Asia Minor (1.26.1–28.1). The events of these two passages presage significant developments to come. The Asian Greeks will pass from the sphere of Lydia into that of Persia (1.141.1–169.2), and play a pivotal role in drawing mainland Greece into the Persian Wars when they attempt a major revolt (5.28.1–6.32.1 *passim*). Croesus' initial actions upon his ascent to the Lydian throne will have well-known repercussions that will echo throughout the *Histories*.[29]

The tale of "Solon and Croesus" follows immediately upon the treatment of Croesus' early conquests in Asia.[30] This rich anecdote, in addition to the other productive interpretations it has received,[31] can be read as an inquiry on Herodotus' part into the ways in which individuals are acknowledged as shaping the course of history. Three of its characters – Croesus, Solon, and Tellus, the otherwise unknown Athenian credited by Solon as being ἀνθρώπων ὀλβιώτατος, "happiest amongst men" (1.30.3)[32] – represent a trio of different perspectives on the potential consequences generated by an individual human life, and the diverse ways in which historical agency can be invoked and remembered.

---

[29] The passage at 1.6.2–3 may evoke thoughts of the Athenian Empire, given Herodotus' use of the word φόρος to describe the tribute exacted from the Asiatic Greeks by Croesus: φόρος was also the term applied to the 'contributions' demanded from its imperial allies by Athens during the fifth century, e.g. Thuc. 1.96.2; for the Athenian tribute lists themselves, see Meritt, Wade-Gery, and McGregor 1939–53. On likely resonances of contemporary (i.e. before and during the early part of the Archidamian War) Athenian politics and culture in Herodotus' *Histories*, see the references in note 11, above.

[30] Solon and Croesus would likely not have encountered one another under the circumstances that Herodotus describes, given the temporal gap between their approximate periods of authority: Croesus' reign is believed to have lasted *c.* 560–46, and Solon's reforms are conventionally dated to his archonship *c.* 594/3. This would not, as M. Flower has pointed out to me in correspondence, preclude the possibility of a historical meeting between the two at some point near the estimated end of Solon's lifetime.

[31] Shapiro 1996, with selected prior bibliography collected at n. 1, observes that "it has traditionally been seen as programmatic, i.e., as expressing Herodotus' own views about the gods and human happiness and as providing a philosophical framework for the *Histories* as a whole" (338). Flory 1987: 151–6 discusses the literary anecdote as an inheritance of oral culture's moralizing stories (especially those about kings and rulers) and as a possible reflection of the organizing principles of early prose; cf. also Gray 1986; Lang 1944.

[32] The phrase is used in this location to indicate how Croesus hopes that he himself will be described; Solon's narrative about Tellus catches Croesus by surprise. Although Solon subsequently awards the second place of happiness to Cleobis and Biton (1.31.1), their quasi-mythical anecdote functions as a thematic introduction to Solon's own philosophical stance on the unpredictability of human existence, rather than focusing, as Tellus' tale does, upon the accomplishment of historical action.

Croesus' historical impact is measured here by Herodotus (and by the character himself) in terms of his conquests. During his encounter with Solon, he expresses his own value in terms that derive directly from his success in war and empire: his wealth (1.30.1–3). Elsewhere in the narrative, too – including at the very point of Solon's arrival (1.28.1–29.1) – Herodotus depicts both Croesus' imperialistic success and his storied riches in sufficient detail[33] to employ them as a convincing metonym for their king's historical significance.

The history-making actions of Solon are depicted in a less direct way. While Croesus' activities are presented on a broad scale and iterated in comparative detail, Solon's historical role at Athens is acknowledged in a single clause, Σόλων ἀνὴρ Ἀθηναῖος, ὃς Ἀθηναίοισι *νόμους κελεύσασι ποιήσας*..., "Solon, a man of Athens who established laws for the Athenians when they appealed [for them]..." (1.29.1). The subsequent information provided about Solon's ten years of travel is anecdotal in both nature and tone (1.29.1–2), and likely participates in a folkloric model for the life of a legendary wise man or lawgiver.[34] In so doing, however, it also invokes common contemporary audience knowledge about Solon,[35] employing traditional references to offer implicit reminders of a wholly different type of historical impact: one created through the reification of wisdom, rather than through conquest.

A third depiction of history-making action within this anecdote is represented by the account Solon provides of Tellus the Athenian:

> ἀποθωμάσας δὲ Κροῖσος τὸ λεχθὲν εἴρετο ἐπιστρεφέως· Κοίη δὴ κρίνεις Τέλλον εἶναι ὀλβιώτατον; ὁ [Σόλων] δὲ εἶπε· Τέλλῳ τοῦτο μὲν τῆς πόλιος εὖ ἡκούσης παῖδες ἦσαν καλοί τε κἀγαθοί, καί σφι εἶδε ἅπασι τέκνα ἐκγενόμενα καὶ πάντα παραμείναντα, τοῦτο δὲ τοῦ βίου εὖ ἥκοντι, ὡς τὰ παρ' ἡμῖν, τελευτὴ τοῦ βίου λαμπροτάτη ἐπεγένετο· γενομένης γὰρ Ἀθηναίοισι μάχης πρὸς τοὺς ἀστυγείτονας ἐν Ἐλευσῖνι βοηθήσας καὶ τροπὴν ποιήσας τῶν πολεμίων ἀπέθανε κάλλιστα, καί μιν Ἀθηναῖοι δημοσίη τε ἔθαψαν αὐτοῦ τῇ περ ἔπεσε καὶ ἐτίμησαν μεγάλως. (1.30.4–5)

Croesus, stricken by this account, asked harshly, "In what way do you determine that Tellus is the happiest?" Solon said, "Tellus had good and

---

[33] E.g. especially the gifts deposited at Delphi (1.50.1–51.5) and the gold-dust given as a gift to Alcmeon (6.125.2–5).

[34] Szegedy-Maszak 1978, examining the narrative trope of the lawgiver figure and comparing Solon to other individuals whose life stories follow similar patterns.

[35] See the references on Solon's biography collected by Szegedy-Maszak 1993: 205 n. 29, and the same essay as a whole for a way of 'reading' the reception of Solon in fifth-century Athens, specifically in the work of Thucydides.

beautiful children at a time when his city was flourishing, and he saw children come to all of them, all of whom survived. And while he was doing well in his own life, as such is [acknowledged] amongst us, a most noble end came upon him. For as a battle was taking place between the Athenians and their neighbors in Eleusis, after bringing help and turning the enemy back he died most gloriously, and the Athenians buried him at public cost there where he perished and honored him greatly.

Herodotus does not suggest when Tellus lived, or what particular battle took his life.[36] Whether he was real, legendary, or utterly fictional, however, Tellus would have to have been understood by Herodotus' audience as dying before the 540s, when Croesus' empire fell to Cyrus II of Persia.[37]

As was discussed in Chapter 2, the memorialization of outstanding individuals at Athens (and elsewhere) during the sixth century tended to focus upon the commemoration of generic qualities, emphasizing the participation of the deceased in a cycle of validation that served to perpetuate the continuing authority of elites.[38] Deceased adult or subadult males might be described in their traditional verse epitaphs as "beautiful" (καλός) or "good," (ἀγαθός), but they were generally presented as fleeting examples of a continuing standard, not unlike the Homeric heroes.[39] Tellus, however, is not treated in this manner; in fact, his recollection by Solon is anachronistic for the era of the narrative. Firstly, Tellus is considered fortunate for having lived into comparative old age amongst his descendants, a sharp contrast to the archaic period's apparent fascination with early death and its tendency to raise elaborate funerary monuments to noble adolescents who died unmarried.[40] Secondly, Tellus' material prosperity is downplayed, its oblique mention devoid of any of the evocative language employed here and elsewhere to describe the wealth of Croesus.[41] This not only allows Solon – and therefore Herodotus – to contrast Tellus' way of life with that of the Lydian king, but also distances Tellus from the values expressed in archaic Greek poetry, where references to luxury and precious metals often occur in close proximity to claims to nobility and happiness.[42]

---

[36] How and Wells 1912: 67 *ad loc.* hold that the struggle in question was actually a conflict between Athens and Megara that happened to take place at Eleusis, during the wars in which Pisistratus is supposed to have distinguished himself, *c.* 570–565 BC.

[37] On the modern understanding of this sequence of historical events, see Young 1988.

[38] On the formulaic qualities of archaic-era memorialization, see Chapter 2, above.

[39] On features of archaic epitaphs, see Chapter 2, above.

[40] See e.g. Day 1989 esp. 18; Jeffery 1947 esp. 128–30; and Chapter 2, above.

[41] See note 33, above.

[42] Kurke 1999; see also Morris 1996 and cf. Page 1968: 240 no. 444, a *skolion* possibly by Simonides or Epicharmus that offers a concise encapsulation of this worldview.

Further, Tellus' obituary, rather than focusing upon eternal heroic values, is explicitly set in a historical context.[43] Just as the economic circumstances of Sardis are used by Herodotus as a situational marker to place the arrival of Solon at a specific time (1.29.1), so does Solon in turn locate Tellus in time by the condition of Athens (1.30.4). That the circumstantial participles (Σάρδις ἀκμαζούσας, "Sardis at its zenith"; τῆς πόλιος εὖ ἡκούσης, "the city [sc. Athens] flourishing") are to be read as temporal in both cases is strongly suggested by the employ of the phrase τοῦτον τὸν χρόνον, "then," perhaps best translated as "at that time," in 1.29.1. Tellus is also recollected as a participant in a historical event, the battle at Eleusis that cost him his life. By Solon's account, this very event inspired his memorialization in a most un-archaic manner, i.e. δημοσίῃ.[44] Tellus receives here the same honor that was accorded to the Athenian dead of Marathon, who were buried (probably by the state) where they fell.[45] But Tellus is eulogized by Solon as an individual, rather than as a member of his citizen group. In a sense, Solon's narrative functions as an epitaph or even as an *epitaphios*, which further complicates Tellus' potential impact upon an Athenian audience acclimated to the collectivizing rituals of the *patrios nomos*.[46] The politics of Tellus' death and burial, then, place him in a social and temporal position that is unclear. In an Athenian reading, at least, he is neither a heroized archaic noble nor a properly equalized democratic citizen: he fits neither the era of the narrative nor the world of its immediate audience. His position in history is determined by a smaller and ostensibly simpler set of factors than would affect an individual of the stature of Solon or Croesus, but the historian's picture of his reception and memory betrays the same unresolved tensions between individual and group agency that the Athenians had been questioning since the days of the Tyrannicides.

The story of Tellus (and that of the "second happiest" amongst men, Cleobis and Biton) and the extended speech on the fragility of human prosperity (1.32.1–9) demonstrate Solon's position within Herodotus' text as a foil to Croesus. Amongst other contrasts, Croesus and Solon represent two distinctly different views of the way that an individual may make a historical impact upon the world. Croesus' stance, as noted above, emphasizes his immediate imperial successes as represented by his vast wealth (1.30.1–3), and Herodotus calls attention to this by focusing up to this

[43] On the increasing involvement of historical context in funerary memorialization during the fifth century, see Derderian 2001 esp. 102–11, 161–88, 192–4.
[44] Cf. the epitaphs of Pythagoras and Pythion discussed in Chapter 2, above.
[45] How and Wells 1912: 68 *ad loc.*
[46] On the *patrios nomos* and the *epitaphios logos*, see Chapter 2, above.

point upon the king's acts of subjection and destruction. The violent verbs that describe these activities in the active and middle voices (e.g. ἐπεθήκατο, 1.26.1; ἐπεχείρησε, 1.26.3; κατεστράφατο, 1.27.1) are almost inevitably in the third person singular, presenting Croesus as a sole individual agent in direct conflict with a series of groups that are represented by their ethnic or geographical origins (1.26.1–28.1), most notably the Greek poleis of Ionia (1.6.2–3, 26.1–3). Croesus is also depicted as a sole agent in the series of events that depose him. The decision to move against the encroaching Persians is verbally assigned to him alone (1.46.1–3). Croesus himself designs his grandiose experiment to test the efficacy of the leading Greek and Libyan oracles (1.47.1–49.1), creates the bizarre stew that he expects the distant seers to identify (1.48.2),[47] and takes individual responsibility for the history-making decision to go to war against Persia (1.71.1). His later implication of the Delphic oracle and the god Apollo in his losses (1.87.1–2, 90.1–91.6) is personal, and even when he is at the final mercy of Cyrus, he does not absolve himself of responsibility for his own actions and their effects (1.87.3).

Solon's perspective, in contrast, while best known for its philosophical emphasis upon man's unpredictable condition, also takes the positive exchange between the individual and his polis as a central theme. Solon's lawgiving is said to have taken place at the Athenians' bidding; in return for his efforts, they are bound by oath to obey his enactments for a decade (1.29.1–2). In Solon's description, Tellus distinguishes himself in the defense of his city; the crowning honor of his life's story is the city's expression of gratitude through his burial at public expense (1.30.5). Even Cleobis and Biton perform their acts of piety at a pan-Argive festival, are acclaimed there, and are then commemorated by their fellow citizens at Delphi (1.31.1–5). Where Croesus' perspective emphasizes simultaneously the destructive and self-aggrandizing abilities of the individual at the expense of groups (including, as emerges later, his own people, the Lydians), Solon's model is both collaborative and constructive: the individual and the polis, in Solon's view, are capable of a productive relationship with one another. And at life's end, Solon's ideal individuals are left not with wealth or imperial power, but with recollection and lasting memory amongst their fellow citizens.

Solon himself, however, having collaborated with his own city to produce a new law code, is now effectively in self-imposed exile while that code is tested, separated from his people and his polis. One might ascribe this

---

[47] As shown by Christ 1994, Croesus' experiment is only the first in an extended sequence of tests and trials personally carried out by barbarian kings in Herodotus, and the use of such activity as a motif within the *Histories* "not only explores the character of autocrats, but also holds up a mirror to [Herodotus'] own activity as inquirer" (167).

narrative curve to folk motifs: lawgivers often undergo a period of estrange-
ment in the traditional stories about them.[48] It might also be suggested that
Herodotus needs to highlight Solon's travels in order to 'stage' a meeting
with Croesus. But the placement of this important anecdote so near the
beginning of the *Histories*, at the start of the first substantial *logos*, also recommends, as has been suggested by Shapiro, a "programmatic" reading.[49]
Croesus models for Herodotus' audience patterns of behavior that come
to be expected of autocrats later in the narrative.[50] Solon, however, also
introduces a set of important typologies: not only is he an example of the
traveling sage and the 'wise adviser,'[51] but he is also the first Greek leader to
undergo separation, both cognitive and physical, from his city and his people. This particular pattern will recur throughout the *Histories* as Herodotus'
Greeks struggle to discover a model for productive action, and as Herodotus
himself works to discover a way of understanding the historical impact of
individuals. But the examination of other eminent Greek individuals will
also reveal the specialness of Solon's case: his separation from Athens has
been peaceful and productive, done as much for his people's good as for his
own. In this, he will prove unique – and be remembered for it.

Herodotus' paradigmatic agents: Cyrus

As an individual agent, Cyrus is the ruler whose imperial aspirations may
initially appear to have had the least immediate consequences for the Greeks,
and this may be why Herodotus is so explicit in defending both the relevance and the content of his account at 1.95.1.[52] The structural relationships
between this latter passage and the preface to the *Histories* suggest that the
Cyrus segment is to be understood as an important part of the larger narrative. Both sections open with a reference to the historian and to the work at
hand, intensified by an adjective or adverb that provides a sense of imme-
diacy, and introduce the subject of the coming discussion with a promised
emphasis on the study of processes. Finally, the transition made back into
the stream of the main narrative by both passages involves the acknowledgement of multiple stories told by Persian sources. These resonances lend
significance to the Cyrus *logos* before it has even begun.

---

[48] Szegedy-Maszak 1978: 205–6.   [49] See note 31, above.

[50] Dewald 2003 esp. 26, 32–5, 43, discussing throughout a pattern of behavior amongst
Herodotean autocrats, both Greek and non-Greek, that she terms the "despotic template."

[51] Sage: Szegedy-Maszak 1978: 202–4; 'wise adviser': Lattimore 1939.

[52] On non-Herodotean views of Cyrus, e.g. Drews 1974, who contends that many elements of
Cyrus' 'biography' derive from Near Eastern legends.

Cyrus' first act as a historical agent is to bring about the revolt of the Persians from the Medes (1.125.1–127.1). Although within the narrative he is pressed on by Harpagus (1.123.1–124.3), the Herodotean Cyrus is nevertheless depicted as the prime mover of the uprising. He has himself falsely designated as the sole commander of the Persian military, creates his own method for testing the soldiery (1.125.1), personally carries out the demonstration he has devised (1.125.2–126.4), and finally assumes leadership over the victorious revolutionary army (1.126.5–128.3). Cyrus' successes mean in turn that "the Persians" can now be considered as a distinct people, and the question of group agency on their part therefore surfaces for the first time. Although both Herodotus' preface and the early emphasis upon Persian stories (e.g. 1.4.1) have suggested that Persian agency will play a significant role in the text, this expectation is not actually borne out.[53] "The Persians" are sometimes listed as the performers of a given action in the narrative, often in comparison or contrast with other national groups.[54] But they are almost inevitably depicted as the arm of the autocrat or of his general, and his responsibility for their activities is generally asserted nearby.[55]

This pattern emerges in the Cyrus *logos* almost immediately after the capture of Sardis, when Cyrus turns his attention to Ionia (1.141.1–4). Here, although "the Persians" are initially mentioned as the victors over "the Lydians," Cyrus and Croesus are quickly taken up as metonyms for their respective peoples, and verbally represented as sole individual agents.[56] Cyrus is the recipient of the various Greek messengers, and Cyrus is said to have asked the Ionians to revolt from Croesus. In contrast, the Greeks are represented not by named individuals, but by ethnic, local, or regional collectives: "the Ionians," "the Aeolians," and "the Milesians." This distinction is further emphasized by the description of the Ionian determination to send for Spartan help as a κοινῷ λόγῳ, a "decision [made] in common" (1.141.4). This essential contrast between individual barbarian agents and Greek group agents will be sustained throughout the *Histories*, although it will be complicated by Herodotus' increasingly detailed attempts to grapple with the historical roles of certain individual Greek leaders.

---

[53]　I am grateful to J. Ober for an email communication of January 3, 2005, that suggested this point.

[54]　I am grateful to M. Flower for raising this point and citing as examples 8.100.1–5, 9.59.1–2, 62.1–63.2, 67.1–68.1.

[55]　E.g. 6.9.1, 18.1 with 20.1, 33.3; 7.210.1–213.1; 8.16.1–17.1, 51.1–54.1, 84.1–89.2 (esp. 86.1, 89.2), 130.1–4; 9.62.1–63.2.

[56]　The reference near the end of the passage to ὁ Λυδός, "the Lydian" (1.141.4), in the masculine singular, a usage that might otherwise have been understood in isolation as indicating the anonymous Lydian populace as a whole, may also evoke the memory of Croesus.

Temperamental behavior and decision-making based upon emotion are established hallmarks of nearly all Herodotean autocrats,[57] but for Croesus, Cyrus, Darius, and Xerxes, in particular, such conduct tends to generate palpable historical consequences. Cyrus' attack on the Massagetae, for example, causes his own death (1.212.1–3, 214.1–5). Just before his final campaign, however, the narrative recalls his prophetic dream of the young Darius (1.209.1–210.1).[58] Herodotus' immediate correction here of the king's misinterpretation of the omen (1.210.1)[59] suggests that Cyrus' death is actually to be understood as an important link in a larger historical-causal chain. The dream not only foreshadows the transfer of Persian sovereignty to the Achaemenid line that will eventually attack the Greeks, but it also suggests that Darius, not the intervening ruler Cambyses, is Cyrus' true successor in the making of Persian history.

Darius returns to prominence during the conspiracy of the Persian nobles against Smerdis the Magus (3.70.1–71.1),[60] where he quickly emerges as the leading planner and literal executor of the successful coup (3.71.1–73.3, 76.1–78.5). But before Darius is crowned king, Herodotus takes a dramatic pause to build his significance by implication, centrally through the staging of the Persian 'Constitutional Debate' (3.80.1–82.5).[61]

3.3 The Persian 'Constitutional Debate' and the kingship of Darius

Positioned at a critical point both in Herodotus' narrative and in the histories of Greece and Persia, the debate may be read as a meta-argument about control, power, and historical consequence.[62] Its three component speeches,

---

[57] Dewald 2003: 26–35; cf. also Gammie 1986.

[58] Dreams are a common motif throughout the *Histories*, though their functions in context vary widely: see e.g. the collection and discussion by Frisch 1968.

[59] Κῦρος μὲν δοκέων οἱ Δαρεῖον ἐπιβουλεύειν ἔλεγε τάδε· τῷ δὲ ὁ δαίμων προέφαινε ὡς αὐτὸς μὲν τελευτήσειν αὐτοῦ ταύτῃ μέλλοι, ἡ δὲ βασιληίη αὐτοῦ περιχωρέοι ἐς Δαρεῖον, "Cyrus said these things in the belief that Darius was forming plans against him, but this was the way divine power was revealing that he was about to end his life there in that place, and that his royal power would pass to Darius" (1.210.1).

[60] There are minor, almost conversational references in the meantime to Darius' construction of a canal in Egypt (2.158.1) and to his famous experiment of asking Greeks and Indians to exchange their funerary *nomoi* (3.38.3–4).

[61] In spite of Herodotus' firm contention that ἐλέχθησαν λόγοι ἄπιστοι μὲν ἐνίοισι Ἑλλήνων, ἐλέχθησαν δ' ὦν, "speeches were delivered that are suspicious to some of the Greeks, but they were certainly delivered" (3.80.1), the debate is likely fictional, but this places no limit upon the insights it offers into Herodotus' vision of the motion of history.

[62] This conversation has also been productively read as a front for the discussion of Greek political systems: Forsdyke 2001: 329–30 n. 3 collects some references to this

focusing respectively upon democracy, oligarchy, and monarchy, initially explore ways of understanding human action that might verge closer to the Solonian model than to those of Croesus and Cyrus. The first two speakers, however, do not frame comprehensive depictions of the alternative forms of government that they advocate, and this allows both the conversation and the 'constitution' to return to the status quo.[63] Nevertheless, an important result of the digression is a much clearer picture of the ways in which Herodotus' Persians tend to conceptualize the role of the individual in history as the wars with Greece draw closer.

Otanes' opening speech (3.80.2–6) in favor of government by "the masses" (τὸ πλῆθος, 3.80.6) devotes approximately three-quarters of its text to the evils of monarchy. Claims are made as to the abstract virtue of group decision-making, but no consideration is applied to the historical consequences of collective action. Otanes' discussion does not treat the long-term impact of the governmental system that he proposes; he does not even commit to the logical next declaration that decisions taken in common are better decisions. Further, his employment of technical terminology is sufficiently inconsistent that it may invite the audience to question his characterization of democracy, at least in the Athenian sense. Certain words associated with the Athenian democracy do occur, in particular ἰσονομία ("equal rights under the law," 3.80.6, in the form ἰσονομίην),[64] and εὔθυνα (a post-term inquiry into the conduct of an official while in office, ibid., in the form ὑπεύθυνον).[65] But most notably, the actual word δῆμος and its derivatives are curiously absent – and Otanes' substitution, τὸ πλῆθος, is a more problematic word that does not always bear positive connotations.[66] In contrast, Otanes does seem to have a longer and better-grounded view of the potential historical impact of monarchy, and this interest serves here as a prescient signal of the political system with which he is in the end most familiar. Otanes' problems with monarchy are based largely upon what he views as the endemic personal failings of kings (their privileges lead to *hubris*), but he does explicitly found his arguments upon tangible historical evidence from living memory (referring both to Cambyses and to

interpretation. Although my reading was developed independently of his, Pelling 2002 represents a very useful resource for additional bibliography on the debate.

[63] I am grateful to J. Ober for assistance in articulating the ideas represented in this and the preceding sentence.

[64] On the concept of ἰσονομία, see the discussion of the Tyrannicides in Chapter 2, above.

[65] See Hansen 1975 on impeachment proceedings in late classical Athens, and for a fuller discussion of terminology.

[66] See Ober 1989: 11 n. 15, with references.

"the Magian") and upon his opposition to the violation of traditions that have been established by historical precedent.[67]

The speech of Megabazus (3.81.1–3) in favor of oligarchy (here referenced by its established technical term, ὀλιγαρχίη), like the speech of Otanes, devotes the major part of its argument to refutation, in this case attacking the concept of democracy that Otanes has supported. But the colorful language that Megabazus employs to portray the potential difficulties of mob rule[68] has its impact weakened by the fact that, unlike Otanes' arguments against monarchy, this critique is not based upon historical experience. This may be why Megabazus reverts to argument from natural likelihood ("good men will make good laws") in the single sentence that states his proposal (3.81.3). This methodology is well in keeping with the Greek rhetorical fashions of Herodotus' day, and particularly with the techniques of the sophistic movement.[69] By casting Megabazus as a pseudo-sophist, Herodotus can subtly suggest that his speaker's content might be suspect,[70] or that at the very least Megabazus has limited substantive material available with which to make his case. In any case, like Otanes, Megabazus does not consider the potential historical consequences of his chosen form of government. His speech has proposed two possible strong incentives for the adoption of oligarchy: not only will good men make good laws, but ἐν γὰρ δὴ τούτοισι καὶ αὐτοὶ ἐνεσόμεθα, "we ourselves will be amongst these men [sc. the good ones]" (3.81.3), i.e. the seven conspirators against the Magus will find themselves in power. The appeal here is essentially a selfish one: let us establish an oligarchy so that we ourselves may retain a favorable position. It may be intended to resonate with some of the moments of self-indulgent behavior demonstrated by barbarian autocrats within the narrative thus far,[71] again subtly suggesting that the status quo dominates Megabazus' thoughts even as he advocates innovation.

The debate concludes with Darius' speech in support of monarchy (3.82.1–5). Here, Herodotus suggests through both content and argument not only that this speaker's view will ultimately win out, but also that it is actually the most informed voice in the debate. This, in turn, permits

---

[67] νόμαιά τε κινέει πάτρια, "[the king] undermines the traditional laws," 3.80.5. Evidence for the use of the adjective νόμαιος to refer to formal laws is generally post-classical: see *LSJ ad loc.*

[68] His term for the general populace, [ὁ] ὅμιλος, is probably more derogatory than Otanes' τὸ πλῆθος: see *LSJ ad loca* and esp. Ober 1989: 92, 112, 114 on Thucydides' use of ὅμιλος.

[69] On the sophists and their rhetoric, e.g. Poulakos 2008; de Romilly 1992; Kerferd 1981; Kennedy 1963: 26–70 (revised and abridged by Kennedy 1994: 11–29).

[70] Critics of the sophists in the later fifth century particularly feared that slippery rhetoric could successfully 'sell' poor or invalid ideas: see the references in note 69, above.

[71] See note 57, above.

Herodotus to make some implicit but important claims about his own readings of historical agency amongst the Persians. Darius' speech, unlike the two that preceded it, consistently and strongly reiterates his assertion that monarchy is the best form of government. This claim both opens and closes his argument, and both intermediary points (about the degeneration of oligarchy and democracy) conclude with it. Darius also employs descriptive technical terminology, referring to democracy as δήμου . . . ἄρχοντος, "the leadership of the *dêmos*" (3.82.4), or more literally, "with the *dêmos* ruling." Far more importantly, however, Darius' proofs against the other two proposed forms of government are argued from a *historical* perspective. Trends are studied, their outcomes projected, and their connections with one another established (3.82.3–4). Neither Otanes nor Megabazus has demonstrated such a wide-ranging interest in the motion of history. Even if Darius' analysis is inaccurate from either an ancient or a modern point of view, it is significant in that it presents a future Persian king reading a 'cycle of constitutions'[72] as leading eternally back to monarchy. This argument may be seen, therefore, as simultaneously foreshadowing and validating Darius' approaching ambition for the throne. It also represents an opportunity for Herodotus to present his views about historical agency through the speech of one of his most important agents. Herodotus' implicit claim (as established thus far in the course of the narrative) that barbarians who significantly affect the larger course of history tend to do so as individuals, not as groups, is here 'proven' correct, as Darius demonstrates that the barbarians themselves, whether intentionally or through cultural conditioning, tend to perceive history operating in this way, too.

Not long after his accession to the kingship, Darius' control of his vast territories is compromised by a difficult revolt in Babylon (3.150.1–152.1),[73] and the noble Zopyrus devises an elaborate, violent ruse to recapture the city (3.154.1–155.6). After mutilating himself, he cuts down thousands of Darius' disarmed soldiers at the head of the rebellious Babylonians (3.157.1–4) – and then throws open the city to the Persians (3.158.1–159.1). Is the capture of Babylon, then, to be attributed to Zopyrus or to Darius? Is Zopyrus portrayed as the king's deputy, or as a separate, distinct historical agent?[74]

---

[72] *Pace* Plb. 6.5.1–9.11, and see the connections drawn between Herodotus and Polybius by von Fritz 1954: 60–3, with references.

[73] Godley 1921 vol. III: 185 n. 1: *ad* 3.150 notes: "According to the course of Herodotus' narrative, this revolt would seem to have taken place some considerable time after Darius' accession (521 BC). But the Behistun inscription apparently makes it one of the earliest events of his reign."

[74] I am grateful to M. Flower for pointing out the importance of this question.

Two passages are relevant, bracketing the narrative at its beginning and end (3.153–4, 3.160).

In Zopyrus' decision to embark upon his plot (3.153.1–154.2), he wishes the capture of Babylon to be ἑωυτοῦ τὸ ἔργον, "his own accomplishment" (3.154.1) – and yet he seeks the king's charge for the plan so that he may be eligible for reward (3.154.1, 155.1–6). The capture of the city, then, is to be a mutually beneficial transaction. That Darius fully appreciates the terms of this exchange is underscored by the vocabulary that the end of this tale shares with its beginning (αἱ ἀγαθοεργίαι ἐς τὸ πρόσω μεγάθεος τιμῶνται, "outstanding deeds [amongst the Persians] are valued for the status [they convey] in the future," 3.154.1; ἀγαθοεργίην . . . ἐτίμησε δέ μιν μεγάλως· καὶ γὰρ δῶρά οἱ . . . ἐδίδου . . . τιμιώτατα, "[sc. for his] outstanding deed [the king] valued him highly [and] he gave [him] . . . most worthy gifts," 3.160.1–2). The anticipated benefactions are duly provided in return for services rendered, as a master to a servant. And Zopyrus' symbolic debasement at the outset (mutilation was considered a shameful punishment by the Persians)[75] highlights his subordinate position. He may have conceived and initiated the plan himself, but his success was dependent upon Darius' cooperation and his ensuing good fortune upon Darius' generosity. While Darius may not perhaps himself be credited with the capture of Babylon, he maintains in his behavior throughout this episode that he has in effect commissioned it.

Darius' individual agency is also firmly maintained in Herodotus' treatment of the failed Persian expedition against the Scythians in book 4. The extended Scythian ethnography (4.1.1–82.1) is prefaced and followed by expressions that name Darius as the leader of both army and campaign (4.1.1, 83.2), and on the march towards Scythia, Darius' name and identity are sometimes used as a metonym for his army (e.g. 4.89.1, 89.3, 92.1, 124.1, 124.2, 125.2). Still more striking, however, are the physical monuments created to provide tangible reminders of Darius' personal ownership of the vast expedition: the bilingual pillars at the Bosporus iterating the extent of both his rule and his command through their lists of conscript nations (4.87.1–2); the painting and inscription commissioned by Mandrocles to commemorate his work on Darius' pontoon bridge (4.88.1–2); the inscribed pillar at the Tearus river that Herodotus says explicitly noted Darius' personal command of the army (4.91.1–2); the stones at the Artescus river, each added to the impressive piles by a single soldier (4.92.1). All of these

---

[75] See Desmond 2004 esp. 31 n. 24 (for the typographical error "Zosimus" in this location read "Zopyrus"); West 2003: 433; cf. also the references collected by Stern 1991: 307–8 n. 19.

objects represent physical realizations of a version of history sanctioned or created by Darius himself. And Herodotus' careful iteration of them (down to a claimed quotation of the Tearus inscription) accepts and reinscribes their message in his own medium, historiography.

The responses of the Scythians and their allies to the invasion provide an effective rhetorical contrast. While the neighboring kings consistently refer to the enemy as "the Persians" (4.119.1–4), the Scythians often employ the singular instead (e.g. 4.118.1–4, 120.2), a hint that is finally made more explicit when "the Scythians" first come out against "the army of Darius" (4.121.1). Although "the Persians" do appear as named actors during the conflict phase of the campaign, the narrative still emphasizes Darius himself, who echoes his former architectural commemorations by starting construction on several fortresses deep inside Scythian territory (4.124.1); demands the surrender of the Scythian king to himself as δεσπότῃ τῷ σῷ, "your lord" (4.126.1); and devises his own interpretation of the objects that the Scythians send to him (4.132.1), refusing to adopt the (ultimately correct) plan of his adviser Gobryas until he has seen the Scythians' confidence with his own eyes (4.134.1–3). Even the Scythians themselves, attempting to convince the Ionians to withdraw from the Bosporus bridge, depict Darius as their mutual, individual enemy (4.136.4). And the Ionians' rejection of the Scythian plan is finally presaged upon that same individual relationship: the tyrants of the Ionian cities owe their positions to Darius (4.137.2–138.2).[76] The king's personal control over his subjects has therefore made him the individual agent of a disastrous expedition, but it has also guaranteed his passage home. The commander left behind in Europe, Megabazus, is to serve as his arm instead,[77] and Darius' wish that he had a pomegranate's worth of such men (4.143.2–3) should perhaps be aligned with his valuation of Zopyrus after Babylon:[78] the king's ability to count such individuals as his personal resources emphasizes his ownership of their activities.

Book 5 and the earlier part of book 6 (through 6.32.1) focus centrally upon the Ionian Revolt of 499–494 BC. In the larger arc of Herodotus' analysis, this event, and particularly the involvement of the Athenians in it, provides a highly personal motivation for Darius' attack upon the

---

[76] Cf. note 28, above.

[77] This is shown most clearly not long thereafter, at 5.2.2: ἤλαυνε τὸν στρατὸν ὁ Μεγάβαζος διὰ τῆς Θρηίκης, πᾶσαν πόλιν καὶ πᾶν ἔθνος τῶν ταύτῃ οἰκημένων ἡμερούμενος βασιλέϊ· ταῦτα γάρ οἱ ἐνετέταλτο ἐκ Δαρείου, Θρηίκην καταστρέφεσθαι, "Megabazus drove his forces through Thrace, conquering every city and every tribe of those who dwelt there, on behalf of the king. For the command to make Thrace subject had been issued him by Darius."

[78] See West 2003: 428.

Greek mainland (5.105.1–2, 6.94.1). Although the Persian campaign that concludes at Marathon is led by Datis and Artaphrenes, the narrative makes clear, as it did in the cases of Zopyrus and Megabazus, that these commanders are following Darius' direct orders (6.94.1–2, 6.101.3), and Darius indeed reacts to the loss by immediately initiating preparations for a fresh attack on Greece (7.1.1–2.1, 4.1). Although he dies before he is able to exact his planned vengeance (7.4.1, cf. 7.8.β2), his impulse helps motivate his son Xerxes to plan an expedition of his own.

3.4 Xerxes' war

Xerxes in many ways represents the culmination of Herodotus' explorations of individual agency. This emerges immediately upon his accession to the throne, when he announces in a dramatic speech his intention to attack Greece:

> ὡρᾶτε μέν νυν καὶ Δαρεῖον ἰθύοντα στρατεύεσθαι ἐπὶ τοὺς ἄνδρας τούτους. ἀλλ' ὁ μὲν τετελεύτηκε καὶ οὐκ ἐξεγένετό οἱ τιμωρήσασθαι· ἐγὼ δὲ ὑπέρ τε ἐκείνου καὶ τῶν ἄλλων Περσέων οὐ πρότερον παύσομαι πρὶν ἢ ἕλω τε καὶ πυρώσω τὰς Ἀθήνας, οἵ γε ἐμὲ καὶ πατέρα τὸν ἐμὸν ὑπῆρξαν ἄδικα ποιεῦντες. πρῶτα μὲν ἐς Σάρδις ἐλθόντες ἅμα Ἀρισταγόρῃ τῷ Μιλησίῳ, δούλῳ δὲ ἡμετέρῳ, [ἀπικόμενοι] ἐνέπρησαν τά τε ἄλσεα καὶ τὰ ἱρά· δεύτερα δὲ ἡμέας οἷα ἔρξαν ἐς τὴν σφετέρην ἀποβάντας, ὅτε Δᾶτίς τε καὶ Ἀρταφρένης ἐστρατήγεον, [τὰ] ἐπίστασθέ κου πάντες. τούτων μέντοι εἵνεκα ἀνάρτημαι ἐπ' αὐτοὺς στρατεύεσθαι. (7.8.β2–γ1)

You saw that Darius was eager to campaign against these people. But he died and was not able to take his vengeance. For his sake and for the rest of the Persians I will not stop before I capture and burn Athens, whose people were the initiators in perpetrating injustice towards my father and me. Firstly, when they approached Sardis together with Aristagoras of Miletus, my subject, they set fire to the groves and shrines. Secondly, you all know the things they did to us when we came to their country, when Datis and Artaphrenes were in command. For these reasons I am ready to wage war against them.

The deployment in this section of the forms of the first-person pronoun and its corresponding pronominal adjective, of the word πατήρ ("father"), and of Darius' name,[79] suggest an intensely personal investment in this

---

[79] Though only presented once in this excerpt, it also occurs earlier in the same chapter, as part of the phrase, "Darius my father."

plan, and Xerxes further bears this out by assessing the motion of history from the Persian point of view, centered upon the individual. The passage connects the Ionian Revolt with the expedition to Marathon (πρῶτα . . . δεύτερα) in the same way as Darius explicitly linked the two events during his own reign. In a further Herodotean acknowledgement of the Persian concept of individualized historical causality, Xerxes relates the major phases of the prior conflict to the names of those who brought ignominy upon the Persian cause: Aristagoras in the Ionian Revolt (cf. 5.105.1) and Datis and Artaphrenes at Marathon. Finally, Xerxes announces his plans for a second invasion of Greece, and the emphatic repetition of the first-person verbs shows that he sees the forthcoming attack as his very own.

The scene that follows is familiar: a Herodotean autocrat with grandiose plans receives counsel from a 'wise adviser' or 'tragic warner' (in this case, Artabanus),[80] and performs a test of a religious or occult institution (in this case, a dream) in order to decide whether to trust its messages (7.10.1–19.2).[81] There are clear connections here back to the Croesus *logos* in book 1,[82] but there are also some telling differences that highlight some of the more complicated historical factors at work in the later books of the *Histories*. Most importantly, the adviser's position has shifted substantially from book 1 to book 7. Croesus received enjoinders from Solon that were largely gnomic and philosophical in nature (see especially 1.32.1–9). Artabanus, however, first confronts Xerxes not with maxims, but with arguments bolstered by historical evidence from the recent past (7.10.α2–δ1). He recalls his former advice to Darius not to undertake the expedition against the Scythians, and perceptively connects the near-betrayal of Darius' bridge over the Thracian Bosporus with Xerxes' proposal to transit the Hellespont.

Artabanus also seems concerned about the very patterns of individual historical agency amongst the Persians that the narrative has by now established. In his speech against Xerxes' expedition, he expresses trepidation about situations where one man's will is capable of causing widespread destruction (7.10.1–δ1). This initially appears to question the wisdom of the Persian tendency to yield to the resolve of individuals, but as the passage continues, so does the emphasis upon the agency of the king. What is truly terrible, as Artabanus puts it while reviewing a crisis from the Scythian

---

[80] On the trope of the 'wise adviser' or 'tragic warner' in Herodotus (the two classifications have much in common), see the seminal treatment by Lattimore 1939; cf. also the numerous studies of the individual figures who fit this model, e.g. Munson 1988, on Artemisia; Boedeker 1987, on Demaratus.

[81] See note 47, above.   [82] See e.g. Dewald 2003: 43, with references.

expedition, is that a mere human being (ἀνδρί γε ἑνί; the γε provides the disparaging tone) should bear responsibility for the designs – or the fate – of the more-than-mortal βασιλεύς (7.10.γ2).[83]

When Xerxes approaches Artabanus about his recent dreams and asks his uncle to pose as himself to see if the apparitions will recur (7.15.1–3), Artabanus' reply once more seems to question the rationale of the narrative's pattern, but then again quickly retreats (7.16.1–γ3). Although much notice is granted to dreams and portents throughout the *Histories*,[84] Artabanus offers a 'scientific' explanation that discounts the possible mystical or religious validity of these experiences. It appears, at least initially, that a significant motivating factor for the Herodotean ruler is about to be rejected. Artabanus' interpretation, however, merely provides a psychologically based explanation for the phenomenon – and this explanation is still centered upon Xerxes. The historical action will still hinge upon the king's individual feelings, judgment, and agency, and the results will ultimately be the same.

As Xerxes plans and executes his march, Herodotus inserts textual and structural markers that foreshadow the wide-ranging historical impact that the king's individual decisions will create. At 7.20.1–21.2, the historian summarizes the vast scale of Xerxes' expedition. He begins by comparing it to prior military efforts, two of which hold special meaning: the force recently brought by Darius against the Scythians, and the Greek army believed to have once attacked Troy. The note that Xerxes has intentionally outstripped his father's unsuccessful preparations is a sign that the new king has attempted to correct for recent history, but the reference to the Trojan War suggests that the struggle to come may generate both myth and memory.[85] There follows an abundance of passages designed to magnify and personalize Xerxes' project. Lists of place-names contacted and passed[86] serve as a virtual refrain between anecdotal episodes, and collections of evocative appellations form an impressive metonym for both the volume and the diversity of the foreign army.[87] The two catalogs of Xerxes' forces, one brief (7.40.1–41.2), the other extensive (7.61.1–99.3), continue the effect of potentially epic scale

---

[83] On the traditional quasi-divine status of the Persian king see e.g. Sancisi-Weerdenburg 2002: 589–90.

[84] See note 58, above.

[85] See note 2, above. Haubold 2007 further recommends that the relationship between Xerxes' expedition and the Trojan War was not merely a connection made by Herodotus, but one deliberately invited and performed by Xerxes.

[86] E.g. most notably 7.26.1–3, 30.1–32.1, 42.1–43.2, 58.1–3, 108.1–116.1, 121.1–124.1.

[87] Cf. note 95, below.

and impact.[88] As has often been appreciated, sight and the act of viewing become increasingly important themes.[89] The gaze upon the Persian host is almost inevitably focalized upon the Persian king,[90] and Xerxes' ownership of this force and of its future activities is both personal and personalized,[91] as revealed through his constant desire to look upon it.[92] Finally, Xerxes' autocratic behaviors and experiences are presented throughout book 7 as magnified versions of those of his predecessors.[93] Darius' catalog of tribute nations (3.89.1–97.5) is outstripped by Xerxes' catalog of his military forces (7.61.1–99.3). Cyrus and Darius were addressed by 'wise advisers' and 'tragic warners,' but Xerxes' are both more vocal (in both the length and the frequency of their interjections) and more numerous.[94] And while Cyrus conducted invasions by crossing rivers (1.189–91, 202, 205–11), Xerxes famously bridges the entire Hellespont (7.33.1–37.3, 54.1–56.2).[95]

As the confrontation between invaders and defenders draws closer, Herodotus highlights the opposition between the individual Persian king on the one hand and the several Greek collectives on the other (7.138.1–139.6): "Xerxes" or "the king" is repeatedly depicted as the enemy of "the Athenians," "the Spartans," and "the Greeks." At last, on the final approach to Thermopylae (7.196.1–201.1),[96] the scene for the battle is set with another explicit opposition of Xerxes the individual to the Greeks as a whole and in subgroups. This time, however, the confrontation is physical, and mirrored

---

[88] Especially, as has been frequently noted, through their invocation of the Homeric 'Catalog of Ships' (*Il.* 2.484–877): see e.g. Boedeker 2002: 103. A similar effect is further generated by Herodotus' calculations of Xerxes' land and sea forces at 7.184.1–187.2.

[89] Konstan 1987 esp. 62–9.

[90] On the rhetorical power of the focalized gaze in ancient Greek historiography, see Walker 1993.

[91] On Xerxes' gaze as a sign of his "mastery" over his army, more so than any of the other kings, see Immerwahr 1966: 182, cited by Konstan 1987: 63 and n. 8.

[92] At least four times during the approach to Thermopylae alone: 7.44.1–45.1, 56.1, 59.2–60.3, 100.1–3.

[93] See Dewald 2003: 32–5, 43.

[94] E.g. Artabanus, 7.46.1–52.2; Artemisia, 7.99.1–3, with additional evidence to come at 8.68.1–69.2 and 8.101.1–103.1; Demaratus, 7.101.1–104.5, again with additional evidence to come at 7.208.1–209.5, 234.1–235.4. Cf. also note 80, above.

[95] On "human dominion over nature" in Herodotus, see Romm 2006: 186–91; on the symbolic dangers associated in the Herodotean world with the violation of established divisions, whether political, physical, or purely natural, see Lateiner 1989: 126–35.

[96] Xerxes the character has essentially been held in dramatic reserve from 7.139 up to this point, save for one brief retrospective anecdote about Greek agents visiting the massive barbarian force at Sardis (7.146.1–148.1) and, of course, references and implications in the fears expressed by the Greek combatants. In the interim, the Persian fleet – not surprisingly introduced back into the narrative by Herodotus as ὁ . . . ναυτικὸς Ξέρξεω, "the navy of Xerxes" (7.179.1) – has made initial contact with the Greeks (7.179.1–182.1) and also sustained significant damage in a heavy storm (7.188.2–191.2).

by the landscape on each side, with Xerxes in control of the north and the
Greeks of the south (7.201.1). After the introduction of the Greek forces
(7.202.1–203.2), the presentation of a brief biographical sketch marks the
entry of a new and important figure into the narrative: Leonidas (7.204.1–
205.2).

Herodotus' treatment of Leonidas is unique: alone amongst the individual
Greek agents in the *Histories*, Leonidas provides an untroubled model for
productive leadership and collaboration with his citizen group.[97] During
the account of Thermopylae, he is presented as a foil to Xerxes, and the
contrasts between them suggest that Herodotus is crafting in Leonidas an
alternative view of the individual leader's potential to contribute to the
motion of history. An important distinction lies in the relationship of each
man to his people. Whereas Xerxes' command of his forces is possessive,
Leonidas' generalship is essentially collaborative. To an extent this is due
to the multistate makeup of the Greek opposition (7.205.3–206.2), but it
is also related to Herodotus' larger ideas about historical agency: Greeks
in Herodotus tend to act in collectivities, and Leonidas is set apart by his
ability to work with and even within these groups.

At 7.207.1, Leonidas casts a personal, individual vote at a meeting also
attended by "the Peloponnesians," "the Phocians," and "the Locrians," as a
decision is made to hold the Thermopylae pass and send out requests for
aid. The fact that he is singled out as a leader, however, in no way hinders the
presentation of "the Spartans" as a defined group with the potential to have
a significant effect in the battle.[98] Once the fighting commences, Xerxes is
credited with deciding upon the Persian course of action (often determined
by his own emotional responses, e.g. 7.210.1, 215.1; cf. 212.1), while "the
Greeks" and "the Spartans" repulse the Persian attack and "the Phocians"
stand guard (7.211.1–212.2). Although Leonidas is the commander of the
Greek operations, the placement of the Phocians is attributed not to orders,
but rather to a mutual understanding (7.217.2).

As the final assault on the pass begins, Herodotus balances Xerxes and
Leonidas against one another by assigning them to corresponding grammatical positions in the same sentence, despite the fact that their physical positions are in fact very different. The text reads οἵ τε δὴ βάρβαροι οἱ ἀμφὶ Ξέρξην
προσήισαν καὶ οἱ ἀμφὶ Λεωνίδην Ἕλληνες . . . ἐπεξήισαν (7.223.2), "the barbarians about Xerxes approached, and the Greeks about Leonidas . . . went

---

[97] I am grateful to J. Ober for clarifying this point for me.

[98] Demaratus describes the Spartan opposition to Xerxes at 7.209.1–5, for example, without once
mentioning Leonidas' name.

out against [them]." The verbal and syntactical parallels between the two clauses are very strong – but Leonidas is, as he has always been, in the pass with his troops, whereas the forces with Xerxes are only "with" him in the sense that he is their operator, for Xerxes himself does not fight. In fact, Xerxes temporarily exits the narrative at this point. Until the battle is over[99] he is neither seen nor discussed, except in tangential references. Historical agency and relevance at this point are thus ceded to the Greeks as Herodotus, in the manner of a Homer or a Pindar, provides Leonidas and his Spartans with the very κλέος that he claims the king desired (7.223.2–228.4; cf. 7.220.1–4).[100]

But the war is not yet over. Xerxes is again absent from the main stream of the narrative during the buildup to Salamis, as Herodotus concentrates upon the Greek preparations. Reminders of Xerxes' personal ownership of his expedition, however, are almost constant, as the king's shadow hovers over every activity in which his forces engage. The Persian armament is referred to as specifically belonging to its king.[101] The Persian fleet joins battle off Artemisium because its admirals worry about retribution from Xerxes if they do not (8.15.1); there is expectation amongst the Greeks that if Xerxes can be brought to personal, emotional suspicion of the Ionians he will expel them from his naval forces (8.22.3). Xerxes is individually credited with the failed ruse to conceal the numbers of his own dead at Thermopylae (8.24.1–25.2). The Boeotians try to demonstrate their Medism in a manner that will convince the king himself (8.34.1); and the goal of the Persian violation of Delphi is summarized as ὅκως συλήσαντες τὸ ἱρὸν τὸ ἐν Δελφοῖσι βασιλέϊ Ξέρξῃ ἀποδέξαιεν τὰ χρήματα, "so that after despoiling the shrine in Delphi they might deliver its riches to Xerxes the king" (8.35.2). When Xerxes himself at last reappears, the siege of the Athenian Acropolis has begun, and the Persian king is represented as personally owning not only the ἀπορίη (lack of a clear course of action) on the Persian side during the battle (8.52.2), but the very city of Athens once it is over (8.54.1).

Xerxes' history-making decision to offer naval battle at Salamis is pre-ceded by a scene of counsel. Asked for their opinions as to the advisability of a sea fight, the Persian admirals support the idea to a man; only Artemisia, here in the role of the tragic warner,[102] dissents (8.67.1–69.2). What appears to be a vote is taken (8.67.2–68.1) and Xerxes sides with the opinion of

---

[99] When he debriefs Demaratus, receives advice from Achaemenes, and then severs his symbolic ties to Leonidas by having his opponent's body desecrated, 7.234.1–238.2.

[100] See notes 2 and 5, above. For a reading of the connections between Pindar and Herodotus, see Nagy 1990: 215–381 *passim*.

[101] 8.10.1, 16.1, 16.2, 17.1, 25.3, 65.1, 65.6, 66.1, 81.1; cf. 50.2.   [102] See note 80, above.

the majority. He does so, however, for his own reasons, believing that the determining factor in the conflict to come will be not the military strength he can bring to bear, but rather his personal presence (8.69.2). Collective dread of the watching king (8.86.1), however, is not enough. Xerxes, who has functioned as the driving agent of Persian affairs from the start of the invasion, is finally unable to affect what happens before his very eyes.

The Xerxes *logos* also magnifies and complicates the pattern of the despot's subordinate leader. Zopyrus, Megabazus, Datis, and Artaphrenes represented Darius' interests and acted, both physically and symbolically, in his stead. In a similar way, Mardonius now accepts command of the newly defeated expedition and functions as Xerxes' arm in Greece.[103] The transfer of nominal authority is dwelt upon at greater length than any previously (8.100.1–107.1), and Xerxes' withdrawal from the narrative is equally gradual, as he exits from mainland Greece back the way he came, losing additional portions of his forces along the route (8.115.1–120.1, 129.1–130.1). By 8.126.3, Mardonius is firmly in charge and has even acquired a subordinate of his own in Artabazus. Although reminders that Mardonius acts under charge from Xerxes and on the king's behalf are comparatively frequent, they do grow more widely spaced with the passage of text and time, as both the Greeks and, ostensibly, Herodotus' audience grow accustomed to physical and logistical agency resting with Mardonius, rather than nominal agency being tied to Xerxes.[104] The first half of book 9, then, is preoccupied with Mardonius' command in Greece, until he is finally killed during the Persian rout at the battle of Plataea (9.63.2). Recollection is again made at this highly strategic point, however, of Xerxes' ownership of the entire enterprise (9.68.1), and Pausanias of Sparta finally claims, in a final unifying statement, that Leonidas and the other dead of Thermopylae have now been avenged – upon both Mardonius and Xerxes (9.78.3).

3.5 Greeks and "the Greeks" in Herodotus

In contrast to the strongly individual sense of historical agency observed and enacted by Herodotus' Persians, agency amongst the Greeks is essentially divided, and at times negotiated, between individuals and groups. "The Athenians," "the Spartans," and even "the Ionians" can all be acknowledged as group historical agents. At the same time, however, their leaders also

---

[103] See Flower and Marincola 2002: 8–11.
[104] E.g. 8.140.α1–β4, 143.2–144.3; 9.3.2, 7.α1–2, 11.2, 24.1, 41.1.

receive Herodotus' close scrutiny as individual agents: a number of the most successful individual Greeks become alienated from, or even come into conflict with, their home poleis and people.

Greek agency by poleis

It is productive to begin at the climactic confrontation between Xerxes and the Greeks at Salamis. The romanticized perspective on this battle presented by Aeschylus in 472 (A. *Pers.* 249–514) was patently not adopted by Herodotus in the next generation.[105] Herodotus' Greeks at this point in his narrative (8.40.1–100.5) are far from unified. Their tortuous negotiations over which lands and cities are to be abandoned to the invading Persians are dwelt upon for some time (8.49.1–74.2) before an admittedly selfish ruse by Themistocles traps the allied fleet into fighting at Salamis (8.75.1–76.1, 78.1–83.2). The dark characterization of the days before the battle may be a deliberate rhetorical choice on Herodotus' part, designed both to magnify the surprising totality of the ensuing triumph and to demonstrate the gap between perceptions and realities. The emphases placed upon Themistocles' persistent advocacy, upon the Athenians' stubborn reluctance to abandon their territory and their dependants, and upon the contributions of the Athenian commanders and their fleet may also be intended as proof for the sentiments Herodotus expresses at 7.139.1–6, namely that the victory over the Persians would have been impossible but for the intervention of Athens. As these sections suggest, Herodotus' Greeks, with or without the explicit guidance of their leaders, tend to think and move in polis groups, and even a moment of high crisis cannot eradicate these essential divisions.

There is an important distinction to be drawn, however, between group *action* and group *historical agency*. Herodotus conditions his audience to think in terms of group action from the very beginning of the *Histories* (praef., 1.1.1–5.4), where, as briefly mentioned above in the discussion of group agency amongst the Persians, he examines stories of the origins of the conflict between Europe and Asia. After a single reference to a particular sub-group (Περσέων . . . οἱ λόγιοι, "the Persian chroniclers," 1.1.1), Herodotus completes the remainder of his preamble by crediting exclusively generic group performers with the repeated kidnappings (save the Trojan prince Paris, 1.3.1) and with the stories from which he draws his source material:

---

[105]   See Pelling 1997a: 1–19 for a discussion of the relationships between Aeschylus' drama, Herodotus' account, and the historical battle itself.

"the Phoenicians," "the Greeks," "the Persians." Herodotus himself, however, refuses to acknowledge these tales either as demonstrably historical or as causative of the later events he plans to treat (1.5.3), and the divisions he employs in the preface (particularly "the Persians," and to an extent "the Greeks" as well) are generally *not* those most frequently credited with historical agency later in the narrative. Similarly, the collectives so frequently named in the ethnographic passages of the *Histories* (e.g. "the Egyptians" in book 2, or "the Scythians" in book 4) are not depicted as historical agents. Although they might participate in characteristic activities in a corporate fashion, or be credited with shared sentiment, they generally do not shape the progression of world affairs – or even of local affairs – by their actions, and they seem to exist outside of time, with their *nomoi* depicted as eternal and virtually unchanging.[106]

Group historical *agency* in Herodotus is a very different matter: the historically significant actions of Greek corporate groups are depicted as real events, recoverable by evidence or inquiry, that have been performed in a specific temporal context and that affect the course of subsequent activities. Such agency on the part of Greek groups (outside of Athens and Sparta, which merit separate examination) is best observed in Herodotus' large-scale narrative of the Ionian Revolt (5.28.1–6.32.1). Although the collective citizenries of individual states are occasionally depicted as giving outstanding service (e.g. Herodotus' coverage of the partnership of the Cyprians, 5.104.1–116.1, or his tragic account of the valiant Chians and their accidental massacre, 6.15.1–16.2), the most historically prominent and effective group throughout the earlier portion of the episode is called simply "the Ionians."

Perhaps because the later group agency of the Greeks during the Persian Wars is so fragmented by contrast, the temporary corporate agency of the Ionians during the Revolt is striking. "The Ionians" achieve the most spectacular act of vengeance upon the Persians when they manage to burn Sardis

---

[106] Herodotus claims to have had some access, whether oral or otherwise, to Egyptian king-lists or chronographies. What he calls "Egyptian *logoi*" are recorded beginning at 2.99.1, at and after which point the historian repeatedly issues the caveat, both implicit and explicit, that he has gathered most of the earlier portion of his information from the Egyptian priests and therefore cannot personally vouch for its accuracy: e.g. 2.99.1, 100.1, 101.1–2, 102.3, 103.2, 107.1, etc., with the summation ἐς μὲν τοσόνδε τοῦ λόγου Αἰγύπτιοί τε καὶ οἱ ἱρέες ἔλεγον, "the Egyptians and their priests provided the narrative up to this point," coming at 2.142.1. For his later material, he claims to have acquired ὅσα δὲ οἵ τε ἄλλοι ἄνθρωποι καὶ Αἰγύπτιοι λέγουσι ὁμολογέοντες τοῖσι ἄλλοισι κατὰ ταύτην τὴν χώρην γενέσθαι, "the things that Egyptians and other people concur took place in that country," 2.147.1. Herodotus does not, however, connect these numerous rulers and the genealogical accounts of their reigns to any changes in the apparently static Egyptian way of life he describes at 2.35.1–98.2.

(5.100.1–102.1); "the Ionians" conduct planning sessions with the Cypriots when battle looms (5.109.1–3); and "the Ionians" muster together for the final defense of Miletus (6.7.1). The quasi-Homeric catalog of ships that then iterates their complement (6.8.1–2) serves a dual purpose: while it initially appears to paint an impressive culminating picture of the united front that the Ionians have shown to date,[107] it also foreshadows the separation of the coalition when the tide of battle turns against them (6.13.1–14.3). Chiefly fingered amongst these deserters during the final conflict are "the Samians" and "the Lesbians," but Herodotus further notes that the Ionians "all blame each other" (6.14.1) for the fragmentation. Under pressure, then, just as will happen again before the battle of Salamis, the potential agency of the larger, coalition Greek group gives way to individual poleis, as the prior entrants in the 'heroic' catalog of ships flee for their separate homes.

Herodotus' concept of Greek collective historical agency organized by polis is represented most fully in his treatments of the Spartans and the Athenians, who are consistently depicted as distinct and very different groups, sometimes with conflicting ideologies and goals.[108] The historian details the separate backgrounds and cultural characteristics of both peoples before the major conflicts of the first Persian War take place (e.g. most notably the large-scale digression on Athenian history at 5.55.1–95.2, and the description of the Spartan kingship at 6.51.1–59.1). He also presents vivid portraits of leaders from both states whose dealings with the Persians emphasize selected national characteristics of their respective homes, and whose depictions essentially 'prove' that Herodotus' treatments of their poleis elsewhere are accurate: Themistocles, the clever Athenian general so bent upon action that he will even resort to treachery to induce it (8.75.1–80.2); Hippias, the deposed but ambitious Athenian tyrant who colludes with the Persians in hopes of reinstatement (5.96.1–2; 6.102.1, 107.1–2);[109] Demaratus, the exiled Spartan king who describes the unflinching will of the Spartan warrior (7.101.1–104.5, 208.1–209.5).[110] Finally, Herodotus emphasizes the central roles of both Athens and Sparta in history-making conflicts during the

---

[107] Cf. note 88, above.

[108] The political divisions depicted between Athens and Sparta in the *Histories* are occasionally anachronistic (Fowler 2003: 309–10), likely due in part to Herodotus' desire to contrast and balance, to the extent that it was possible, their contributions to the Persian Wars, and perhaps also due to the two states' increasingly antagonistic relationship later in the fifth century: see Fowler 2003: 305–6, 311–12, with references; Raaflaub 1987 *passim*.

[109] Cf. also the self-aggrandizing behavior of his father Pisistratus, 1.59.1–64.3.

[110] On the loyalty of Demaratus to Sparta despite his relationship with Xerxes, see Boedeker 1987: 192–3.

Persian Wars, Athens at Marathon and Salamis (6.108.1–117.3 and 8.40.1–100.5, respectively), Sparta at Thermopylae and Plataea (7.201.1–234.1 and 9.19.1–3, 25.2–85.3). In each of these cases, the other state's fighting contingent is either not present[111] or its role is minimized in order to maintain historiographic focus on the leading group of the moment, whose agency is frequently emphasized through the repetition of its collective name.

The balance of Herodotus' focus, however, eventually tips towards Athens: for him, "the Athenians" ultimately determine the motion of history and the fate of Greece. The extended diagnosis that the Athenians saved Greece from Persia (7.139.1–6)[112] offers surface-level representation of the contrasts that Herodotus has maintained throughout between his two chief Greek group historical agents, Athens and Sparta. The steady valor of the Spartans, the historian claims, would have fallen noble victim to a characteristically static and inherently flawed defensive policy, while instead Athenian daring and flexibility (particularly emphasized in their refusal to yield to the dire warnings of the Delphic oracle) ultimately won the day.[113] There is, however, an even more significant contrast here, between the group historical agency of the Athenians[114] and their apparent rescue of all of Greece. Consistent with Herodotus' depiction of the crisis before the battle of Salamis and of the fragmentation of the Ionian Revolt, this division between separate state and larger ethnic entity once again makes the claim that at pivotal historical moments, Greeks ultimately move in poleis. Greece as a whole would have been unable to save itself from Persian domination had Athens as a polis not maintained its own identity and defended what were admittedly its own interests throughout the wars. This reading is mirrored by Herodotus' speculations about the potential fate of the Peloponnesians had they chosen to stake their futures on the fortification of the Isthmus: this artificial corporate geographic entity, too, would have become fragmented (in this case, due to anticipated Persian city-by-city attacks), until only the Spartans were left to face the invaders, once again polis against Persians.

---

[111] The Spartans are recorded as having missed the battle of Marathon (6.106.1–107.1, 120.1), and there are no Athenians stationed at Thermopylae during the account of the final struggle there (7.222.1).

[112] This passage is especially striking given the relative infrequency of authorial interjections later in the *Histories*: on this, see Marincola 1987.

[113] Cf. Thuc. 1.70.1–9, where the Corinthian ambassadors to Sparta emphasize similar cultural features of both poleis.

[114] It is worth noting that none of the individual Athenian leaders is mentioned here, an omission that is clearly representative of the type of historical agency Herodotus wishes to emphasize in this passage (cf. below on eminent Greek individuals in Herodotus). Themistocles will be introduced into the narrative shortly after the passage under discussion here, at 7.143.1.

But an interesting question yet remains.[115] It is evident that the names of autocrats in Herodotus can be taken in many cases to stand for their respective peoples, armies, or even actions (to give the most reductive example possible, "Darius" certainly did not attack the Scythians single-handedly). But what about the reverse? In other words, to what extent might a reference to a polis implicitly include its eminent leaders, whom Herodotus frequently portrays – particularly in the cases of Athens and Sparta – as embodiments of the characters of their respective peoples? Should "the Athenians," for example, particularly in situations involving decision-making, really be construed as a stand-in for "the leading politicians of Athens, in particular Themistocles"?

Two responses to this issue are relevant here. The first, as has been demonstrated by the analytical methods employed throughout this chapter, is that the representation of agency by a historian involves a series of deliberate rhetorical choices. To attribute history-making action to "the Athenians," as opposed to (e.g.) "the Athenians led by Miltiades" or "Miltiades and Callimachus," is to maintain literary emphasis upon the corporate identity of the polis and what is to be construed in context as the collective, if not unanimous, activity of its citizens. Under many circumstances, representations of those citizen groups are likely intended to include – but not to highlight – the political and military elite. This observation leads naturally to the second response: Herodotus does take significant interest in the relationships between leaders and their people, particularly amongst the Greeks, and he explores both their productive collaborations and their conflicts, a subject that is treated in more detail later in this chapter. Further, when a populace takes action that is explicitly *not* indebted or obedient to its political leaders, Herodotus does sometimes choose to highlight that distinction, particularly at Athens.[116]

Certain activities like trials or the enactment of exile (or at Athens, ostracism) can be ascribed to the typical political operations of popular assemblies, but even granted that they may be motivated by factionalism or personal attacks, they do nevertheless demonstrate the ability of a citizenry to take consequent action on its own authority. The trial of Miltiades at Athens (6.136.1–3; cf. below) provides an example: as is the usual procedure for public cases under Athenian law, the prosecution is brought by an individual, one Xanthippus (no relative of Pericles, 6.136.1), but the

[115] I am grateful to an anonymous reader for suggesting the importance of this issue for my larger discussion.

[116] The helpful indices in Strassler 2007 (s.v. esp. "people" and "Athenians") pointed me towards most of the examples discussed in this paragraph and the next.

responsibility for the verdict is characterized as resting with the *dêmos* (6.136.3), which is the source for the citizen jury. There are also situations where Herodotus records action taken (or not) by a citizenry that is apparently independent of established political and legal frameworks. The most famous and historically significant instance of this, as demonstrated by Ober, is the historian's treatment of the 'Athenian Revolution' in 508/7,[117] but one might also note uprisings where popular parties or "the masses" are the protagonists, as for example at Syracuse (7.155.2), and the Spartan refusal to assist the Ionians and Aeolians against Cyrus when an improvised plea is individually staged out in public (1.152.1–2).[118]

An interesting mirror image of this latter scene, however, is worth noting for the serious consequences of what appears on the surface to be ordinary political action. It takes place much later in the narrative, when Aristagoras of Miletus comes to Athens to ask the Assembly to support the Ionian Revolt (5.97.1–3) – and succeeds. Despite the fact that this incident occurs in the context of normal Athenian political procedures, Herodotus makes a special point of commenting upon the long-term results of this particular choice:

καὶ οὐδὲν ὅ τι οὐκ ὑπίσχετο οἷα κάρτα δεόμενος, ἐς ὃ ἀνέπεισέ σφεας. πολλοὺς γὰρ οἶκε εἶναι εὐπετέστερον διαβάλλειν ἢ ἕνα, εἰ Κλεομένεα μὲν τὸν Λακεδαιμόνιον μοῦνον οὐκ οἷός τε ἐγένετο διαβάλλειν, τρεῖς δὲ μυριάδας Ἀθηναίων ἐποίησε τοῦτο. Ἀθηναῖοι μὲν δὴ ἀναπεισθέντες ἐψηφίσαντο εἴκοσι νέας ἀποστεῖλαι βοηθοὺς Ἴωσι . . . αὗται δὲ αἱ νέες ἀρχὴ κακῶν ἐγένοντο Ἕλλησί τε καὶ βαρβάροισι. (5.97.2–3)

And because [Aristagoras] was begging energetically for [this assistance], he promised everything, until he convinced them. For it appears to be less trouble to mislead many people than [to mislead] one, given that he was unable to sway Cleomenes of Sparta alone, but accomplished it in the case of thirty thousand Athenians. So the Athenians thus convinced voted to dispatch twenty ships to help the Ionians . . . but these very ships were the start of the problems for the Greeks and the barbarians.

This is a highly significant moment in Herodotus' narrative, since these twenty ships will mark the intervention of Athens in the Ionian Revolt and ultimately incur the dangerous enmity of Darius (5.105.1–2, 6.94.1). Nowhere are the Athenians' political leaders mentioned: the historian's

---

[117] Ober 1996a esp. 44–6, for which reference I am indebted to the same anonymous reader acknowledged in note 115, above.

[118] How and Wells 1912: 125 *ad loc.* call this episode "unhistorical" precisely because it occurs outside of the usual structures of Spartan politics, but this does not detract from its rhetorical function.

disparagement is directed towards the Assembly itself. The meaning here is complex. Without this event, the Athens that emerged from the Persian Wars transformed and worthy of admiration (see especially 7.139.1–6) would never have come into being, but the Ionian Revolt itself was not only a failure but also a bait for years of destructive foreign invasion. Herodotus' criticism in this passage might at one extreme represent a wholesale indictment of democratic decision-making, at the other an apologia for the handful of experienced elites who might have been expected to advocate a more prudent course of action.[119] But I would suggest instead that it demonstrates a profound need for the kind of productive collaboration between leaders and led that is sketched elsewhere in the narrative (see below) through Herodotus' treatments of Leonidas and Solon.

"The Greeks" in Herodotus

As a collective, "the Greeks" are occasionally accorded credit within Herodotus' narrative for historically consequent action at meaningful moments. Such examples are concentrated in books 7–9, and occur most often when Herodotus is exploring the gap between the illusion of pan-hellenic unity and the reality of polis-centered division. In keeping with this demarcation, Herodotus may temporarily assign to "the Greeks" some kind of corporate action or sentiment, but the identities of the various poleis and ethnic groups soon reassert themselves as separate opinions are expressed and separate actions taken.

One of the most illustrative passages in this regard is, again, 7.138.1–139.6. Here Xerxes' pretense of attacking Athens alone is contrasted with his true intention to turn his forces against "all Hellas," i.e. the whole of Greece. Although "the Greeks" are collectively aware of the threat, they do not react as a unified group; instead, some of the states immediately surrender, while others are eventually tempted to Medize. Still a third perspective is represented by the Athenians, whose direct resistance to Xerxes, Herodotus claims, saved Greece. The attitude of "the Greeks" is contrasted with that of "the Athenians": "the Greeks" cannot agree on a single course of action, and the leadership of a polis group is therefore required.[120]

---

[119] Cf. e.g. the Athenian debate over the meaning of the oracles before the battle of Salamis (7.141.3–143.3), where after much popular discussion and dissent the opinion of Themistocles is accepted.

[120] The Athenians' motivations, even for Herodotus, do not appear to have been wholly altruistic, but this does not alter the historical outcome.

This pattern of temporary unification followed by fragmentation is repeated as the Persian march continues southward towards central Greece. The resisting Greek states seek external support by appealing to panhellenism (7.145.1–2). This plan, however, bears no fruit: the requests of the envoys are rebuffed at Argos (7.148.1–149.3), in Sicily (7.153.1–162.2), at Corcyra (7.168.1–4), and on Crete (7.169.1–2). An allied attempt to protect the Thessalian passes quickly fails when the force is warned off by the king of Macedon (although Herodotus suggests that the motive for the withdrawal may have been trepidation at the route of the Persian approach, 7.172.1–173.4). The once patriotic-sounding Thessalians, who had claimed that holding Thessaly would shelter "all Hellas" from war (7.172.2), now Medize to protect themselves. Herodotus adds, perhaps with a note of bitterness, that they "zealously" (προθύμως) became "of great service" (χρησιμώτατοι) to Xerxes (7.174.1).

Although it is again "the Greeks" who determine to hold Thermopylae against the invaders (7.175.1), this force (detailed at 7.201.1–204.1), too, gradually fragments. Dissenting opinions surface as the Persians approach (7.207.1); after the initial conflicts at the pass, the lack of cohesion gives rise to physical separation, and either under orders or of their own accord most of the Greek troops depart (7.219.1–220.4; cf. above). At Artemisium, too, there is friction within the allied fleet over which polis contingent should be in command (8.3.1–2). Herodotus initially presents the Athenians as wise and self-sacrificing, sensitive to both the greater good and the longer view. Just as quickly, however, he revises his claim: the Athenians cultivated this attitude (or this pretense) only μέχρι ὅσου κάρτα ἐδέοντο αὐτῶν, "while they acutely needed the other [poleis]" (8.3.2). This fragile and even specious understanding between Athens and Sparta will also soon fragment, once the Delian League is formed after the war. It may have begun under the aegis of panhellenism, but much of its true motivation likely derives from self-interest.

Dissent continues amongst "the Greeks" as the determination is made to fight at Salamis (8.49.1–2, 56.1–64.2, 74.1–2, 78.1) and an act of pure deceit by Themistocles (8.75.1–76.3, 79.1–80.2) forces the allies to make their stand at a location favorable to Athens. The combat narrative opens with descriptions of the actions of "the Greeks" (8.83.1–84.1), but Herodotus soon admits that even "the Greeks" themselves cannot agree upon how the battle began: both Athens and Aegina claim credit for the first attack (8.84.2). The Ionians fighting on behalf of the Persians do not appear to be holding back, despite Themistocles' prior appeal to their panhellenic sentiments (8.85.1, cf. 8.22.1–3). By the time Herodotus reports the outcome of the battle, he is already once again acknowledging the contributions of separate states (Athens and Aegina: 8.86.1, 91.1–93.2).

The same shift in emphasis from the larger group to the individual poleis reappears in high relief when "the Greeks" dedicate thank-offerings for the battle at Salamis and at Delphi. At the sanctuary, they make inquiry of Apollo κοινῇ, as a community, to discover whether the god is satisfied with their gifts – and the oracle demands a separate offering from the Aeginetans (8.122.1). Another attempt at corporate celebration and acknowledgement fails immediately thereafter, at the Isthmus: when the time arrives to award the prize to the ablest commander, each leader casts his vote for himself, leaving the honor to pass to the collective second choice, Themistocles (8.123.1–2; cf. above).

Pausanias' call for Athenian assistance before the battle of Plataea appeals to panhellenic sentiment, calling the upcoming struggle a contest ἐλευθέρην εἶναι ἢ δεδουλωμένην τὴν Ἑλλάδα (9.60.1), "over whether Greece is free or in servitude." He makes his case, however, in the face of the recent desertion of allied troops (9.52.1) and a lack of cooperation from the Athenians them-selves (9.55.1–56.2). The Athenians do hasten to the rescue, but are stopped in their tracks by Medized Greeks (9.61.1–3) – and the battle of Plataea de facto becomes a Spartan story, not a panhellenic one. Herodotus does temporarily return his verbal emphasis to "the Greeks" in describing the rout of the Persians (especially at 9.69.1), but he appears to be contrasting the allied fighters and "the rest of the Greeks," the deserters whose flight and slaughter is recorded in the same location (9.69.1–70.1, cf. 9.52). The casualties for Plataea are listed by polis (9.70.5); the state burials are sepa-rately conducted and separately iterated (9.85.1–3); and the next activity in which "the Greeks" participate together is the vengeful ravaging of Thebes (9.86.1–88.1).

Even the erection of the Serpent Column at Delphi (9.81.1) to celebrate the achievements of the allied Greek states against the Persians does not disguise the deep divisions between them. To Herodotus, as to themselves, the separate poleis had largely separate histories, and their ability to achieve history-making action as a multi-city group is as limited within the nar-rative as it seems to have been in reality. By the time of the last major battle, the seeds of mistrust between Athens and Sparta are already evident. The victory of "the Greeks" (e.g. 9.90.1, 92.2, 96.1, 98.1–101.3, 103.1) over the Persians at Mycale is assisted, in Herodotus' account, by the open desire of the Athenians to claim the honor of the battle for themselves, rather than leaving it for the Spartans (9.102.2; cf. 9.105.1). After the conflict is over, Athens and Sparta find themselves again at odds over the disposition of

Ionia (9.106.2–4). The agreement that emerges from this dispute lays some of the groundwork for the later Athenian Empire, ultimately steering the course towards the Peloponnesian War.

Individual Greek leaders

Even though Herodotus' Greeks do tend to act in polis units, a polis is not only a group entity, even if the artificial imposition of a high degree of nominal sameness, such as that of the Spartan state military system or the Athenian democratic government, would have it appear so. A polis is also comprised of individuals, and certain of these, for Herodotus, defy classification amongst their peers. Whether because they are exceptionally gifted, because they have access to positions of extraordinary power, or both, these figures complicate the historian's perspective on the large-scale motion of events. Their individual actions can potentially be seen as history-making in their own right, but despite sharing in some distinctive autocratic character traits, such as self-centeredness,[121] they lack the exclusive, determinative control of the foreign kings. Instead, these Greek individuals are involved in complex and often tumultuous relationships with the groups from which they come. Within the world of the narrative, their decision-making and the realizations of their plans are often met by negotiation or resistance. Many, even most, of these figures experience sufficient opposition to drive them from their homes. A number of them, ironically, find a better 'fit' in Persia, where their marked status earns them credibility.[122] Nearly all of the most prominent Greek leaders in Herodotus, especially the Athenians, conform to this pattern to some degree: of particular note are the treatments of Hippias, Aristagoras, and especially Miltiades and Themistocles.

Hippias' reign as tyrant of Athens is discussed during the digression on Athenian history in book 5,[123] but he also makes a brief appearance in book 1. Pisistratus, having already twice gained and lost the Athenian sovereignty, removes himself from Attica to Eretria, and seeks the advice of

---

[121] See note 18, above.

[122] Boedeker 1987: 191–2 describes a "[familiar] narrative pattern" in Herodotus "of the exiled or alienated Greek who, for his or her own purposes, induces Persian incursions against fellow citizens," and cites seven examples in addition to Demaratus (the latter being the central focus of her argument). Boedeker's reading of this pattern, however, has different qualifying parameters, and does not involve precisely the same group of figures that I treat here. Individual points of contact are separately acknowledged below.

[123] 5.55.1 marks the beginning of the episode of the Tyrannicides (cf. Chapter 2, above), and 5.65.1–5 the expulsion of the Pisistratids from Athens; thereafter Hippias generally appears in exile.

his sons as to whether he should press once more for supremacy. Ἱππίεω
δὲ γνώμη νικήσαντος ἀνακτᾶσθαι ὀπίσω τὴν τυραννίδα (1.61.3), "since the
conviction of Hippas, that they should take hold of the tyranny again, won
out," the family swings into action and, ten years after their departure, eventually succeeds in a military capture of Athens (1.62.1–64.3). By this early
association with his father's illegitimate bid for power, Hippias is already
represented as an outsider to his people. In addition, his recommendations
for reconquest are made while he is sharing his father's exile from their home
polis, a physical separation that in the world of the *Histories* emphasizes his
difficult status, both current and future.

The culmination of Hippias' poor relationship with the people of his polis
(5.55.1, 62.1–2) is the downfall of his dynasty (5.65.1–5). There is no longer
any place for this problematic individual within his native citizen group.
As did Solon, Hippias travels eastward, and is ultimately received in Persia,
where he continues machinations to re-establish his power at Athens (e.g.
5.96.1–2). Like his father Pisistratus, Hippias too makes a historic return to
Attica, but his attempts to have himself reinstated as tyrant fail utterly. In
the end, even his guidance of the Persian expedition to Marathon (6.102.1,
107.1) concludes in dramatic defeat (6.113.1–2).[124]

The experiences of Aristagoras of Miletus during the Ionian Revolt also
reveal Herodotus' interests in the tensions between individual and group
historical agency. "The Ionians" and the individual poleis are not the only
drivers of events during the episode. Aristagoras and his cousin Histiaeus
(the tyrant of Miletus, in reluctant residence with Darius at Susa), are represented by Herodotus as planning the Revolt in the first place to serve their
individual purposes: Aristagoras is unable to deliver Naxos to the Persian
governor Artaphrenes as promised, and Histiaeus is dissatisfied with his de
facto exile from his powerful position in his home polis (5.35.1–36.2). In
response to these personal difficulties, Aristagoras begins his machinations.
He first attempts to enlist the interest of several collectives, ranging from
his own supporters at Miletus (who join him almost immediately, 5.36.1),
to the Spartans (amongst whom Cleomenes rebuffs him, 5.49.1–51.3), to
the Athenians (who agree to send ships, 5.55.1, 5.97.3). The united contingents achieve dramatic success in the burning of Sardis (5.99.1–102.1),
but after a defeat at Ephesus (5.102.2–3), Aristagoras is no longer able to

---

[124] Hippias apparently never ceased to press for the Persian conquest of the Greek mainland
(Boedeker 1987: 192–3, for example, sees Hippias as providing a foil to Demaratus in terms of
the threat that each represents to his home polis: cf. note 122, above): 7.6.2–5 may refer to
Hippias as part of "the Pisistratids," although he is not explicitly mentioned by name. He was
probably dead, however, by the time of the same mention at 8.52.2.

hold his allies together, and the Athenians and Cypriots abandon the cause (5.103.1–104.1). The Persians quickly take Cyprus (5.108.1–116.1), make a strong attempt upon Caria (5.117.1–121.1), and move upon Ionia and Aeolia, beginning with Clazomenae and Cyme (5.123.1).

Herodotus' summation of the situation at this point is damning, and points towards Aristagoras' impending physical separation from his people and his country (5.124.1–2). Concerned that he and those who have revolted alongside him may be removed from Miletus if the Persians retake the city, Aristagoras seeks the advice of his co-conspirators and plans to resettle elsewhere. The language of his indirect speech is that typically used of the foundation of a colony: εἴτε . . . ἐς Σαρδὼ ἐκ τοῦ τόπου τούτου ἄγοι ἐς ἀποικίην, "whether he should conduct [them] from that place to Sardo, to a colony" (5.124.2).[125] The colonial founder in Greek thought is often a liminal figure, chosen, invited, or forced to leave his home polis,[126] which here suggests that Aristagoras sees himself as a prospective outcast, without support either from the broader coalition he has tried to forge or from "the Ionians." His new polis, then, may potentially consist only of the subset of his fellow Milesians who have remained loyal to him.

But Aristagoras actually refuses to collaborate with even this much smaller body of supporters: he rejects the very advice he has sought (5.125.1–126.1), cleaves to his own opinion, and departs with what willing followers he has to Myrcinus, in Thrace (5.126.1). Once there, he becomes a renegade and suffers an ignoble death in offensive operations against a city that had volunteered to surrender (5.126.2). In the end, without the backing of the wider group of allies, of the Ionians themselves, or even of the other Milesians, Aristagoras' historical impact, like that of Hippias, is a negative one. Not only does he fail to free Ionia from the Persian sway,[127] but his actions in raising the Revolt help to motivate the Persian attacks upon mainland Greece (5.105.1, cf. 6.94.1; in both places the hostility of Darius is directed against the Athenians for their part in the rebellion).

Within Herodotus' coverage of the first Persian invasion of Greece, the depiction of Miltiades also allows the re-examination of the reception of Marathon (cf. Chapter 2, above). Miltiades, though of Athenian descent, is a ruler in the Thracian Chersonese (the result of his father's exile from

---

[125] The ἀποικ- word root is employed in the classical period and beyond to refer to the process and the products of colonization: see *LSJ ad* ἀποικία et al.

[126] See Chapter 2, above, and Chapter 4, below.

[127] The Hippias-pattern is also repeated in miniature by the Ionian tyrants whom Aristagoras helped to topple during the Revolt. Like Hippias, they, too, escape to Persia and return, as Hippias to Marathon, to provide leadership against their own poleis (6.9.2).

Athens by Pisistratus, 6.103.1), until his anti-Persian activities and problems with the Phoenicians (4.137.1–139.1, 6.39.1–41.4) arouse sufficient
trouble that he flees to Athens (6.41.4). Once arrived, he is quickly cleared
of legal problems remaining from his time in the north and chosen *strategos*
(6.104.1–2). Although Herodotus provides no speculation as to how Miltiades might have risen so rapidly, the new general clearly has the support of
his polis group for the actions he is about to undertake. This relationship
with "the Athenians," while it lasts, will empower Miltiades to heights of
positive historical impact such as neither Hippias nor Aristagoras was able
to effect.

Herodotus opens his treatment of Miltiades' most famous battle at a
moment of crisis: the ten Athenian generals are uncertain as to whether
they should engage the superior Persian numbers at Marathon. The tie-
breaking vote falls to the polemarch Callimachus, and Miltiades, effectively
taking matters into his own hands, delivers an impassioned, fictive speech
that advocates confronting the enemy (6.109.3–6). Continuous speeches,
even ones of moderate length such as this, are comparatively rare in the
earlier books of Herodotus,[128] which makes Miltiades' performance at this
point especially striking. The rhetoric is strong, sprinkled with references to
the possible outcomes of the war – slavery or freedom – and to the prospect
that Marathon may unify the *dêmos* and ultimately help to make Athens
the leading city in Greece. Most significantly, Miltiades promises in his very
first sentence that Callimachus' choice to fight will allow him to μνημόσυνον
λιπέσθαι ἐς τὸν ἅπαντα ἀνθρώπων βίον οἷον οὐδὲ Ἁρμόδιός τε καὶ Ἀρισ-
τογείτων, "bequeath a remembrance to all generations of men surpassing
even Harmodius and Aristogeiton" (6.109.3). Herodotus elsewhere decon-
structs his character's use of the Tyrannicides analogy as a representation of
the liberation of Athens,[129] but its employ here suggests that the character
Miltiades is at this moment imagining himself and Callimachus as potential
individual agents of history.

Miltiades is credited by Herodotus not only with securing the polemarch's
deciding vote to meet the Persians, but also with supreme command on
the day of the actual conflict (6.110.1–111.1). This would ostensibly cast
him as the individual representative of Athenian heroism at Marathon –
but Herodotus reclaims control of the right to assign the agency that the
character seems to have assumed during his speech. Miltiades is never

---

[128] See e.g. Solmsen 1944: 194, 1943: 241 and *passim*. On speeches in Herodotus in general, see
      Hohti 1976; cf. also Flower and Marincola 2002: 7–8, with updated references.
[129] See Chapter 2, above.

actually mentioned during the narrative of the battle, where pride of place is reserved exclusively for "the Athenians" (6.112.1–113.2), and proper names are omitted until Herodotus begins to tally up the dead (6.114.1). Again, then, as was observed in the monuments erected after Marathon, historical agency for the victory can be disputed, and here the rhetoric of the historian claims primacy for the version of events presented by his text.

Success and pre-eminence can provoke difficulties in a Herodotean leader's relationship with his polis group, and Miltiades is no exception. Fresh from his experiences at Marathon, he asks for a military force for what is essentially a personal punitive expedition. Without even stating his destination, he promises riches to the Athenians if they will support him, and they agree (6.132.1). Miltiades' month-long siege of Paros, however, motivated by a private quarrel rather than by strategic considerations, fails miserably (6.133.1–135.1). The Athenians are so incensed that the former hero, dying of a gangrenous wound sustained during the ludicrous 'campaign,' is put on trial before the Assembly for having deceived the *dêmos*. Narrowly avoiding the death penalty, he is fined a small fortune (50 talents) and dies in disgrace (6.136.1–3), alienated from his polis as the result of his selfish abuse of power.

The most complex Greek leader represented in the *Histories* is Themistocles, whose character and whose relationship with the Athenian populace are both depicted as somewhat suspect.[130] On the one hand, Themistocles was recalled in the later fifth century as a pivotal figure in the events leading up to the history-making battle of Salamis.[131] Not only had he advocated the construction of major additions to the Athenian fleet after a new vein of silver was discovered at Laurion (7.144.1–2),[132] but he was also credited with the plan to evacuate the city upon the approach of the Persians, leaving the democracy to stake its all on the sea (7.143.1–144.3).[133] Herodotus' character, however, is at times almost disturbingly self-assured and self-aggrandizing, particularly after the success at Salamis is past. Buoyed by

---

[130] Despite the fact that Herodotus does not explicitly mention Themistocles' later ostracism, which, like the exile and death of Pausanias, lies outside the main temporal scope of the *Histories*' narrative, he does hint at some of the arrogance, double-dealing, and fiscal corruption that apparently helped to motivate some of the later charges against the statesman: see immediately below, and cf. note 138, below, on the problems with Pausanias.

[131] See Chapter 5 and Chapter 9, below.

[132] Though the new vessels were intended to press Athens' advantage in its ongoing war with Aegina, the city's increased naval power, Herodotus asserts, played an important role in Athens' struggle against the Persians.

[133] Cf. also the discussion of the 'Themistocles decree' in Chapter 9, below.

his new authority after the battle, Themistocles begins dallying in personal *rapprochement* with Persia (8.109.5–110.3) and indulges in such ferocious blackmail of the 'Medizing' islanders of Andros that other island polities, terrified at the possibility of attack by the Athenian fleet, dispatch payments for protection (8.111.1–112.3). Much of this wealth, Herodotus strongly suggests, found its clandestine way into Themistocles' own pocket (8.112.1, 3).

The diverse problems Themistocles causes with Greek groups are not confined merely to his own citizenry. His troubled associations surface quite early in his career in the *Histories*, when he accepts inducements from the Euboeans to advocate a line of defense against the Persians that will protect Euboean territory, and quickly skims off most of the funds for himself (8.4.2–5.3). The outcome of this transaction is a negative one. Themistocles advocates the useless mass butchering of the Euboeans' flocks (ostensibly to keep them from falling into the hands of the enemy, 8.19.1–2),[134] and the Greek fleet eventually withdraws from Artemisium, leaving the coastal regions of northern Euboea to the Persians (8.23.1). Later, with the allied naval forces assembled at Salamis and aware of the Persian sack of Athens (8.40.1–56.1), Themistocles again opposes the interests of a larger Greek group, this time the Peloponnesians and their fellow supporters of the plan to make a stand at the Isthmus (8.49.1–2, 56.1, 59.1–62.2). Although the choice is indeed made to fight at Salamis (8.63.1–64.1), the allied fleet soon grows nervous and hesitant, especially the membership from the Peloponnese (8.70.2), and a significant contingent determines to withdraw (8.74.1–2). At this point, Themistocles takes matters into his own hands: He sends a deceptive message to the Persian forces in order to entrap the Greek fleet and force the decisive battle to take place immediately (8.75.1–80.2).

As the conflict is about to begin, Herodotus offers a reminder that however fragmented the contributing contingents may really be, the achievement of Salamis is understood within the world of the narrative as a joint venture between individuals and groups (8.83.1). On the verge of the fighting, the Greeks assemble a group of *epibatai* (marines, or shipboard hoplites) for the customary pre-battle speeches. Themistocles' address is the only one memorialized by both name and content, for Herodotus provides a

---

[134] For Blösel 2001: 184–5, Herodotus uses the slaughter of the flocks to "whitewash Themistocles," i.e. to demonstrate Themistocles' single-minded devotion to the welfare of the fleet and to its mission, but it seems more likely that this is an early and vivid representation of Themistocles' individual decision-making coming into conflict with the interests and preferences of a group.

brief summary (8.83.1). The battle joined, Greek groups receive the central focus, with occasional breaks for anecdotes about incidents involving individuals (e.g. the insults of Polycritus to Themistocles, 8.92.1–2). In the end, "the Aeginetans" and "the Athenians" are awarded most coverage of and credit for their actions (8.86.1, 91.1, 93.1–2), more so than any one commander or soldier on the Greek side. The men most spoken about after the battle, according to Herodotus, are Polycritus of Aegina, Eumenes of Anagyrus, and Ameinias of Pallene, but, as noted above, when "the Greeks" meet at the Isthmus to award the commander's prize, each leader votes for himself, leaving a disgruntled Themistocles the universal second (8.123.1–2).[135]

Themistocles after Salamis, like Miltiades after Marathon, attempts to use Athens' strength to further his personal agenda – and enhance his personal fortune (8.111.1–112.3). He also, according to Herodotus, opens another dialogue with the Persians, taking personal credit for restraining the Greek forces from the crucial Hellespontine bridges that would let the barbarian army escape back to the East (8.109.1–110.3). Themistocles' true motivation for convincing the Athenians not to pursue their defeated foes, in Herodotus' account, was to prepare the way for asylum in case the Athenians were to turn on him (8.109.5). The historian's summation that τά περ ὦν καὶ ἐγένετο (8.109.5), "and those things actually took place," seems to confirm not only Themistocles' suspicions, but also the paradigm of the Greek individual unable to reconcile with his polis that Herodotus has been constructing throughout his narrative.[136]

For those members of Herodotus' audience who were aware of the experiences of Themistocles and Pausanias (the Spartan general who was the victor at Plataea) after the conclusion of the *Histories*, this model of problematic Greek leadership might have held still greater significance. Both of these individuals, after stunning achievements,[137] were mistrusted by their respective peoples and discredited; both left their poleis within a decade after their triumphant commands during the Persian Wars. Themistocles, ostracized, took up residence at Argos (Thuc. 1.135.3); Pausanias lived for a time at both Byzantium and Colonae, allegedly adopting an increasingly Eastern lifestyle, before being recalled for judicial inquiry at Sparta, then being betrayed and starved to death at Taenarum (Thuc.

---

[135] Themistocles also encourages his own acclaim: for example, at 8.124.1–125.2, he travels to enjoy what honors the Spartans will give him.

[136] See note 122, above.

[137] Herodotus calls Pausanias' triumph at Plataea νίκην . . . καλλίστην ἁπασέων τῶν ἡμεῖς ἴδμεν (9.64.1), "the most beautiful victory of all those I know."

1.130.1–134.3).[138] Themistocles eventually fled to Persia, where he was said to have been well received by the king, Artaxerxes son of Xerxes (Thuc. 1.138.1–2), and to have lived there until his death.[139]

Herodotus' coverage of these Greek leaders examines the ways individuals can invoke agency for themselves by the kinds of attentions they invite: his Aristagoras compares himself to a colonial founder, his Miltiades refers openly to Harmodius and Aristogeiton, his Themistocles deliberately seeks after rewards for his military service. In his detailed coverage of both the positive and negative outcomes of their choices, however, Herodotus also demonstrates that the permanent memory that individuals like these tend to seek out is ultimately arbitrated by the historian. It is the writer of history who can perceive and reveal the patterns at work over longer periods of time, and who can therefore rescript the meaning of his characters' individual performances by selecting the details that he reports or by offering his own interpretations.

3.6 Conclusion: Collaborative agency in Herodotus: Leonidas and Solon

Notably absent from the list of eminent Greek leaders who have troubled relationships with their citizen groups are Leonidas and Solon.[140] Both of these individuals are closely compared by Herodotus with their barbarian counterparts, Xerxes and Croesus, and this parallel structure invites their consideration together, a process that illuminates Herodotus' ideas about historical causation and calls attention to his interpretations of the events of the fifth century that postdate the contents of his written narrative.

Leonidas is killed in the very action that secures his place in history (7.224.1) and is therefore never forced to face the potentially divisive consequences of his new pre-eminence.[141] But the fact that he also receives

---

[138] Herodotus does also make some tangential references to Pausanias' hubristic conduct after the Persian conflicts were concluded, e.g. 5.32.1, 8.3.2.

[139] Thucydides offers several anecdotes about Themistocles' rumored suicide in Persia and his family's secret burial of him in Attic soil (Thuc. 1.138.4, 6); he also mentions a Themistocles monument standing in the agora of 'Asiatic' Magnesia[-upon-the-Maeander] (Thuc. 1.138.5).

[140] I am grateful to J. Ober for suggesting the synkrisis in this section, for calling to my attention the productive qualities shared by both characters, and for contextualizing his recommendations within my larger argument (email correspondence of January 3, 2005).

[141] In addition to the experiences of the other Greek leaders discussed above, cf. 7.229.1–233.2, for example, on the difficulties experienced by the other (very few) surviving veterans of the Thermopylae campaign.

the most overtly Homeric treatment of any Greek leader in the *Histories*[142] marks him as distinctive within Herodotus' text, and, indeed, he is different in a number of important ways. Leonidas, as discussed above, is a productive leader who works *with* his citizen group to accomplish history-making goals. The character is also prescient far beyond his position in the narrative, capable of thinking ahead to – and attempting to control – how he and his Spartans will be remembered for their actions. Solon, too, appears to have established a cooperative relationship with his fellow citizens, in light of the solemn agreements struck over his new law-code. But the meaning of his ten-year absence from Athens afterwards is potentially much more interesting at the conclusion of the *Histories* than it was at the beginning. The "leaving one's polis" paradigm that Solon established is re-enacted throughout the text,[143] but Solon is the only Greek leader who is portrayed as having undertaken that departure for peaceful, productive, and altruistic reasons. His self-imposed exile both binds and releases his fellow citizens: They are held by oath to follow Solon's laws, but are challenged to do so on their own, in the deliberate absence of a leader who even by simply answering appeals might have exercised control to rival a monarch.

Leonidas, then, represents a positive way of entering into the individual-Greek leadership paradigm; Solon offers a model for its safe conclusion, along with a reading of the human condition that would suggest that Leonidas actually achieves true happiness, by living a comfortable life, benefiting his people, and dying well. In Solon's interpretation, then, Leonidas might be placed beside the examples of Tellus and Cleobis and Biton: The details are different, but the story is very much the same.

The versions of Solon and Leonidas presented by Herodotus have particular resonance when potential connections to events of Herodotus' own day are taken into account. Regardless of the precise date of the text's compilation or circulation,[144] much of Herodotus' adult life and working years would have been passed under the cloud of escalating tensions between Athens and Sparta leading up to the Peloponnesian War.[145] The detailed, positive engagement that the historian shows with these very different monumental figures from each side may signal a reaction to, or at least a consciousness of, the rapidly changing shape of the Greek world. While viewing these exempla

---

[142] See notes 2 and 5, above, esp. Pelling 2006: 93–4 and n. 51.   [143] See note 122, above.

[144] An economical review of selected references on this problem may be found in the notes to Evans 1987.

[145] On the relationship between Herodotus' text and the Peloponnesian War, see the references collected in note 11, above.

as prescriptive would likely be overreaching, it is perhaps not too much to see them as diagnostic: As the next chapter will demonstrate, Herodotus' successor, Thucydides, saw the relationship between eminent individuals and the citizen group, and particularly between the Athenian leaders and the *dêmos*, as critical to understanding the motion of history.

4 | Claims to immortality

Memories of the Peloponnesian War

4.1 The indispensable individual

In 425 BC a typical early-summer Mediterranean squall forced an Athenian fleet to complete a planned landing at the isolated Peloponnesian headland of Pylos, against the objections of its commanders. Demosthenes,[1] general-elect and acting as guide,[2] alone contended that Pylos was an ideal base for Athenian operations in the area; Eurymedon, Sophocles,[3] and the men of the fleet remained unconvinced. As the ships could not be re-launched until the weather cleared, however, the soldiers were left to their own devices, and Thucydides reports that in order to pass the time they decided to fortify the site, using improvised construction methods to accommodate their lack of appropriate tools and equipment (4.4.1–3).

This is an unusual moment for a number of reasons. The fortification of Pylos would shortly prove to be a history-making choice. From this makeshift base, the Athenians would gain control of the island of Sphacteria and of the handful of valuable Spartan *homoioi* (full fighting members of the Spartan warrior class) who would be trapped there. Spartan desire to exchange these prisoners would in turn prompt them to negotiate towards the Peace of Nicias,[4] the most extensive reduction in hostilities of the entire war. But the actual acquisition of the highly strategic site, however, is treated by Thucydides almost as an accident wrought by sheer boredom. Further, the Pylos sequence, which is otherwise carefully balanced in Thucydides' narrative against Athens' disastrous Sicilian expedition in books 6–7,[5] opens with an ideal opportunity to present Demosthenes at a pivotal moment of good judgment, to contrast with his later defeat and execution by the Syracusans. Yet Thucydides chooses not to do this: Demosthenes is correct

---

[1] Son of Alcisthenes, and not the fourth-century orator. He was *strategos* in the following year: Pritchett 1940: 472.

[2] Thuc. 4.3.1–4.1. In the remainder of this chapter, all passages from Thucydides are cited by number only.

[3] Son of Sostratidas, and not the fifth-century tragedian.   [4] E.g. esp. 5.15.1.

[5] Hornblower 1996: 16, 120–1, 164 *ad* 4.10.5, 166–7 *ad* 4.12.3, 184 *ad* 4.26.4, 228 *ad* 4.65.4, all with references.

in calling for the occupation of Pylos, but only once the men take action on their own does the work of fortification actually begin, and their future general is not acknowledged as having motivated it.

The discussion of Herodotus in Chapter 3 (above) shows that group action with history-making consequences is not new in Greek historiography, but this incident in Thucydides reveals a fresh perspective. By the conclusion of his account of the incident, it becomes clear that the fortifications at Pylos are at least partially intended for self-defense (4.4.3). The notice that αὐτοῖς τοῖς στρατιώταις . . . ὁρμὴ ἐνέπεσε, "a compulsion came over the soldiers themselves" (4.4.1), therefore takes on military overtones in retrospect, since a ὁρμή can also be an "attack."[6] At the opening of the passage, however, the ὁρμή appears to be simply a spontaneous idea to improvise a fort. The nameless Athenian soldiers seem unaware of the potential consequences of their choice, while their leader and guide, who can well foresee the outcome, has the capacity to think, speak, and advise, but he cannot act alone. Each party requires the cooperation of the other, however indirectly and however misunderstood, in order to accomplish its history-making task.

This anecdote also introduces some important features of Thucydides' larger views on historical agency. For Thucydides, group agency cannot account completely for the movement of history, or even for the history of the Athenian democracy alone. Collective character, common decision-making, and corporate action may be significant factors, but, as witnessed by the inability of the soldiers at Pylos to predict the actual impact of their actions, they represent only one side of a more complex equation. Individual leaders are essential catalysts for, and at least partial agents of, nearly all history-making action in Thucydides, as witnessed here by the fact that it is Demosthenes who insists upon the unpopular landing at Pylos, and whose plan is vindicated by the action that follows.

Throughout Thucydides' text, the roles of individuals like Demosthenes are frequently represented at the surface level: Nearly all routine dispatches of military forces by both sides in the war are noted as being personally led by a particular commander.[7] This leader in turn receives individual 'credit' for his men's activities in much the same way as did the foreign autocrats (but, significantly, often not the Greek leaders) in Herodotus. Far beyond these indicators, however, the complexities of the relationships between eminent individuals and their respective groups, and the ways in which

---

[6] *LSJ ad* ὁρμή.

[7] As Dillery 1998: 14 and n. 13 points out, Connor 1984: 54–5 calls this literary mode 'commander narrative,' noting (55 n. 7) a change to it at 4.2.4, "when the account of Pylos' campaign begins."

these associations affect decision-making processes and produce history-making action, are deeply explored in Thucydides' text. Four large sections centered upon Athens demonstrate the complications of individual and group agency with particular effectiveness: the leadership of Pericles from the time of the outbreak of the war in book 1 to his death in book 2; the Pylos–Sphacteria narrative in book 4; the Sicilian expedition in books 6 and 7; and the oligarchic coup in book 8.

As this chapter will demonstrate, Thucydides' views about the complex, sometimes troubling, relationship between the Athenian *dêmos* and the men who lead it resonate strongly with evidence from beyond the literary sphere. During the later fifth century, similar perspectives are reflected in Athenian political monuments, which reveal delicate negotiations between the acknowledgement of individual and group agency in the context of the democratic government. These issues are also revealed in habits of funerary commemoration, where an increasing prioritization of the individual becomes apparent in the course of the Peloponnesian War, and certain grave monuments even seem to directly challenge the ideal of democratic sameness promoted by the *patrios nomos*. In both public and private discourse, then, late fifth-century Athens seems to have been an active locus for the continuing debate about the role of the individual in the motion of history.

4.2 Individual and group agency in Thucydides

Thucydides presents eminent Athenian leaders as pivotal historical figures and as individual personalities, but he also closely examines their relationships with Athens. 'Athens' in this case is a wide-ranging metonym, encompassing variously the Assembly, the *dêmos*, or even the entire populace; but if 'Athens' is to accomplish history-making action in Thucydides, it must do so by working with or by delegating to its leaders. These individuals function not only as Athens' agents, but also as historical agents: within the narrative, they are assigned ownership of individual events both by the *dêmos* and by Thucydides himself.

Athens under Pericles

Pericles is quietly introduced into Thucydides' narrative at 1.111.2, where he is listed as the commander of a failed expedition to capture Acarnanian Oeniadae during the first Peloponnesian war, perhaps in the year 454. Although he enjoys a series of military successes on campaign for the Athenian Empire during the 440s (e.g. 1.114.1–3, 116.1–117.3), it is not

until fresh hostilities develop between Athens and Sparta that Pericles' special status and unique value to his city are described (1.127.1–3). Pericles is
said (in the voice of the historiographic narrator)[8] to be δυνατώτατος τῶν
καθ' ἑαυτὸν καὶ ἄγων τὴν πολιτείαν, "most influential amongst the men
of his time and the leader of the government," and is represented by the
Spartans as an individual whose removal might affect the balance of power
between the two leading states of Greece:

> τοῦτο δὴ τὸ ἄγος οἱ Λακεδαιμόνιοι ἐκέλευον ἐλαύνειν δῆθεν τοῖς θεοῖς πρῶ-
> τον τιμωροῦντες, εἰδότες δὲ Περικλέα τὸν Ξανθίππου προσεχόμενον αὐτῷ
> κατὰ τὴν μητέρα καὶ νομίζοντες ἐκπεσόντος αὐτοῦ ῥᾷον <ἂν> σφίσι προ-
> χωρεῖν τὰ ἀπὸ τῶν Ἀθηναίων. οὐ μέντοι τοσοῦτον ἤλπιζον παθεῖν ἂν αὐτὸν
> τοῦτο ὅσον διαβολὴν οἴσειν αὐτῷ πρὸς τὴν πόλιν ὡς καὶ διὰ τὴν ἐκείνου
> ξυμφορὰν τὸ μέρος ἔσται ὁ πόλεμος. ὢν γὰρ δυνατώτατος τῶν καθ' ἑαυτὸν
> καὶ ἄγων τὴν πολιτείαν ἠναντιοῦτο πάντα τοῖς Λακεδαιμονίοις, καὶ οὐκ εἴα
> ὑπείκειν, ἀλλ' ἐς τὸν πόλεμον ὥρμα τοὺς Ἀθηναίους. (1.127.1–3)

> This, then, was the pollution that the Spartans were commanding the
> Athenians to expel, as if they were exacting punishment on behalf of the
> gods, but aware that Pericles, son of Xanthippus, was a sharer in that
> [guilt] through his mother's family, and thinking that if he were gone it
> would be easier for them to gain the advantage from the Athenians. They
> did not so much hope that he would actually suffer this [exile] as that they
> would bring slander against him in the eyes of the polis, with the result
> that a share of the war would be [thought] derived from his troubles. For
> he was the most influential amongst the men of his time and as the leader
> of the government he opposed the Spartans at every turn, not allowing
> the Athenians to pull back, but rather pressing them for war.

Eminent Greek leaders played significant history-making roles at critical
moments in Herodotus, but they generally made their greatest impact at
moments of productive cooperation with their citizen groups (e.g. Leonidas
at Thermopylae, or Themistocles at Salamis). The case of Pericles already
looks very different. He is depicted here not merely as a leader of his people,
but as the sole instigator of their foreign policy; he does not collaborate with
his citizen group, but instead imposes his own will upon them. In short,
Pericles' capacity for historical agency is presented as a limiting factor upon
the *dêmos*' access to it.

At Pericles' next major appearance, a Spartan embassy has arrived at
Athens to seek the revocation of the 'Megarian decree' (the sanction banning

---

[8] Badian 1993a: 152–3 calls attention to the change in focalization between 1.127.2 and 3: 1.127.2
is focalized upon the Spartans, 1.127.3 upon the historiographic narrator.

Megarians from Athenian ports and markets), and the Athenian Assembly convenes to consider the question.

> καὶ παριόντες ἄλλοι τε πολλοὶ ἔλεγον ἐπ᾽ ἀμφότερα γιγνόμενοι ταῖς γνώμαις καὶ ὡς χρὴ πολεμεῖν καὶ ὡς μὴ ἐμπόδιον εἶναι τὸ ψήφισμα εἰρήνης, ἀλλὰ καθελεῖν, καὶ παρελθὼν Περικλῆς ὁ Ξανθίππου, ἀνὴρ κατ᾽ ἐκεῖνον τὸν χρόνον πρῶτος Ἀθηναίων, λέγειν τε καὶ πράσσειν δυνατώτατος, παρῄνει τοιάδε. (1.139.4)

> And many others stepped forward and spoke, representing both sides of the issue: that it was necessary to go to war, or that the decree should not be an obstacle to reconciliation, but should rather be repealed. And then there presented himself Pericles the son of Xanthippus, the leading man of that time amongst the Athenians, most influential both in words and in deeds, and he delivered the following recommendations.

Here, the same contrast is sustained. The opinion opposed to that of "the Spartans" is not that of "the Athenians," but rather that of Pericles, about to be presented in a powerful speech (1.140.1–144.4) that will help to sway the Athenian populace to war (1.145.1–146.1) – perhaps Pericles' most historically significant act. The speech itself prepares the declaration of hostilities and at last justifies the claims to Pericles' importance made at 1.127.1–3 and 1.139.4. Thucydides, however, furnishes additional preparatory material first: the ends of the careers of Pausanias and Themistocles. Far from being a digression, this passage (1.128.1–138.6) provides both a series of connections to Herodotus' ideas about individual historical agency and a template for interpreting the presentation of Pericles that follows it.

While Herodotus did not present the conclusions of Pausanias' and Themistocles' respective 'stories,' Thucydides addresses them in detail. By this point, however, his narrative has already suggested that comparisons with Herodotus should be made in the consideration of these two figures. Firstly, Thucydides introduced earlier in book 1 two casual references to pivotal moments of Themistocles' career that were narrated by Herodotus: the construction of the Athenian fleet from the revenues of the silver strike at Laurion (1.114.3, in the midst of a discussion about naval armaments, cf. Hdt. 7.144.1–3); and the command of the Athenian forces in the battle of Salamis (1.74.1, cf. Hdt. 8.57.1–125.2 *passim*). Secondly, the 'Pentecontaetia' (1.89.1–118.3), the section of Thucydides' narrative that fills in the temporal gap between the Persian and the Peloponnesian Wars and begins almost precisely where Herodotus concluded his own narrative (after the siege of Sestos in 479/8 BC, Hdt. 9.121.1), focuses at its outset upon the activities of Themistocles and Pausanias (1.90.1–95.7): Themistocles' suspicious diplomacy during the rebuilding of the Athenian fortifications causes suppressed frustration amongst the Spartans (1.92.2), and Pausanias' hubristic offenses as admiral of the allied Greek fleet are causally connected to Athenian leadership over the Delian League (1.95.7–96.2), the future Athenian Empire. Thucydides has thus established a chain linking the events of two generations past to the attitudes and conditions that stimulated the outbreak of the Peloponnesian War – and the connection rests in significant part upon the dubious activities of the leading Spartan and Athenian generals. This link is underscored again after the Pentecontaetia concludes, when a brief return to the present time in the main narrative shows the Peloponnesian forces gathered at Sparta and voting for war (1.122.1). A "pretense" (πρό-φασις, 1.126.1) employed by the Spartans to arouse hostilities, the demand that the Athenians expiate the curse of the Alcmeonids, ultimately prompts another narrative departure back into the past – and once again, the focus falls upon Pausanias and Themistocles (1.128.1–138.6).

What is gained by this close association of the earlier generals with their treatments in Herodotus, and how is this intended to reflect upon Thucydides' depiction of Pericles? Pericles dies of plague during the third year of the Peloponnesian War (2.65.6). Although the shadow of his abandoned policies hangs heavy over the remainder of Thucydides' narrative,[9] his historical impact later in the war is perceived largely through his absence. This is one possible explanation for the connection with Pausanias and Themistocles: the earlier generals, in their Herodotean manifestations, led their respective peoples into triumphant battles that changed the course of Greek history, and had Pericles lived, he might have been expected to do the same. Cut off in the prime of his leadership, however, Pericles generally avoids in Thucydides' analysis the kinds of problems that tarnished the later careers of his predecessors. In this particular regard he resembles Herodotus' Leonidas, who distinguished himself immeasurably, but who also did not live long enough in a time of crisis for substantial difficulties to develop in his relationship to his citizen group.

For Thucydides' Pericles, however, there is more at work in his immortalization than the timing of his loss: Precisely the qualities that he *does not* share with Pausanias and Themistocles are the ones that set Pericles apart. Unlike the earlier generals, Thucydides claims, Pericles is never dominated by desire for self-aggrandizement (2.65.7), and cannot be bribed (2.65.8). He leads not by deception (2.65.8; contrast most notably Herodotus' Themistocles at Hdt. 8.75.1–76.3, 78.1–83.2), but by example and argument (2.65.8–9). He

---

[9] See e.g. Hornblower 1991: 226 *ad* 1.140, with references.

has therefore crafted for himself, by the time of his death, a unique position in the context of his polis, so that ἐγίγνετό τε λόγῳ μὲν δημοκρατία, ἔργῳ δὲ ὑπὸ τοῦ πρώτου ἀνδρὸς ἀρχή, "[what was] called democracy evolved in effect into the sovereignty of its leading citizen" (2.65.9). What this citizen might have accomplished in the course of the Peloponnesian War, however, and what historical impact he might have made thereby, is left to analogy with the earlier figures. The conclusion that Thucydides seems to invite is that Pericles would have been all that Pausanias and Themistocles were to their respective peoples in their days of glory, and more besides, as he lacked some of his predecessors' best-known flaws.

Pericles' relationship with the Athenian *dêmos* therefore establishes a paradigm against which Thucydides states that all others are to be judged (2.65.7, 10–13). An especially effective way to assess it is through Pericles' three direct speeches (the recommendation for war at 1.140.1–144.4, the Funeral Oration at 2.35.1–46.2, and the justification of policy during the plague at 2.60.1–64.6) and his one extended symbouleutic prescription in indirect discourse (2.13.1–9). Unlike many of the other major addresses in Thucydides, Pericles' three Assembly speeches are never paired with any others, which confers a sense of natural authority not only upon his point of view, but also upon his character.[10] In these Thucydidean Assemblies, therefore, there is no presence of note save that of Pericles on the one hand and the *dêmos* on the other, and the *dêmos* inevitably yields to Pericles' recommendations (1.145.1, 2.14.1, 2.65.1–4).[11] The Funeral Oration, too, is set apart by both content and context. Although Pericles is one of the elected *strategoi* ("generals") of Athens and does campaign during the war (e.g. 2.56.1–6), he is never seen addressing his troops prior to battle, as most other Thucydidean leaders do.[12] Instead, perhaps precisely because his wartime career is truncated so early, Pericles is given an expansive speech over the first year's war dead. In a universalizing gesture that emphasizes his central position within the polis, his audience consists of the entire Athenian populace, the voting portion of which has appointed him to this position of honor (2.34.8).

From these details, it might be expected that historical agency in Thucydides' earlier books would often reside with the "leading citizen" alone. The actual picture, however, is more complex. As witnessed by the section

---

[10] De Romilly 1992: 88; and see the listing in West 1973.

[11] In the last of these examples, the *dêmos* immediately takes Pericles' advice on political matters, but fines him as a form of blame for the war's impact on private life – before renewing its loyalty later on.

[12] See, again, the listing in West 1973.

of the Pylos narrative that opened this chapter, individuals and groups – or, more particularly, Athenian leaders and the Athenian people – in Thucydides are often presented as joint parties to an inextricable relationship. Group historical agency therefore frequently depends upon the involvement and leadership of an eminent individual. In the case of Pericles, it is *because* of Pericles that the Athenian *dêmos* engages in history-making acts, and *through* the actions of the *dêmos* that Pericles himself affects the course of history. The contents of Pericles' speeches therefore provide important insights into Thucydides' understanding of the complex relationship between Pericles and Athens.

Pericles' first speech, the Assembly argument for the declaration of war against Sparta and her Peloponnesian allies (1.140.1–144.4), opens with a detailed and delicate negotiation between individual and collective responsibility for the action to come:

> Τῆς μὲν γνώμης, ὦ Ἀθηναῖοι, αἰεὶ τῆς αὐτῆς ἔχομαι, μὴ εἴκειν Πελοποννησίοις, καίπερ εἰδὼς τοὺς ἀνθρώπους οὐ τῇ αὐτῇ ὀργῇ ἀναπειθομένους τε πολεμεῖν καὶ ἐν τῷ ἔργῳ πράσσοντας, πρὸς δὲ τὰς ξυμφορὰς καὶ τὰς γνώμας τρεπομένους. ὁρῶ δὲ καὶ νῦν ὁμοῖα καὶ παραπλήσια ξυμβουλευτέα μοι ὄντα, καὶ τοὺς ἀναπειθομένους ὑμῶν δικαιῶ τοῖς κοινῇ δόξασιν, ἢν ἄρα τι καὶ σφαλλώμεθα, βοηθεῖν, ἢ μηδὲ κατορθοῦντας τῆς ξυνέσεως μεταποιεῖσθαι. (1.140.1)

> Men of Athens, I cling unswervingly to the same conviction, that we must not give in to the Peloponnesians, even though I am well aware that people are not driven by the same passion in fighting a war as they are in being urged to its declaration, since they alter their opinions in light of the situation. But I see that I must offer the same or similar recommendations even now, and I deem it right for those of you who are convinced to support the general opinion, even if we fall short in some respect, or to invoke no part in our wisdom if we do well.

After a clear statement of his case that acknowledges his personal opinion, Pericles offers a common rhetorical pose, that of the speaker well acquainted with the foibles of human nature.[13] This particular *gnomê* ("saying") is structurally appropriate, in that it contrasts the changeable mood of members of pluralities with the unswerving conviction that Pericles himself has just expressed. But it is also prophetic. This sentiment both foreshadows the general course of the war for Athens and prefigures the attitudinal shift in the Athenian populace during the plague and the first invasion of Attica that

---

[13] E.g. de Romilly 1992: 91; Kennedy 1963: 30–1.

will motivate the delivery of Pericles' final speech in the narrative before his death (2.59.1–3).

The next thought group in the passage again has Pericles advocating his own opinion before the *dêmos* (ὁρῶ δὲ καὶ νῦν ὁμοῖα καὶ παραπλήσια ξυμβουλευτέα μοι ὄντα, "I see that I must offer the same or similar recommendations even now"), but here the grammatical construction is much stronger. The use of the verbal adjective ξυμβουλευτέα to express obligation shows the speaker depicting himself as an essential counselor of his people. In the clause that follows, however, Pericles begins to create an assumed share in his unchanging opinion for the members of the *dêmos*, shifting away from the opposition of the first-person singular and second-person plural pronouns μοι and ὑμῶν to a call for the support of collective decisions (τοῖς κοινῇ δόξασιν), and finally to a collective first-person plural verb, σφαλλώμεθα, ironically when he is admitting the possibility of failure. Pericles and the Athenians, as is indicated by both grammar and content, must agree to work in concert, and will share the outcome of their actions both for good and for ill.

At this point in the speech (1.140.2), Pericles begins to present justifications for war with the Peloponnesians, and the first-person singular pronouns give way entirely to first-person plural verbs and occasional addresses to the audience as the collective "you." Pericles has smoothly blended his own particular recommendations into a representation of the general interests of his citizen group, and the remainder of this section (1.140.2–141.1) constructs an opposition between the Spartans on the one hand and the Athenians on the other. An illusory potential for independent historical agency is crafted for the *dêmos*: As it is the *dêmos* that has suffered wrongs at the hands of the Spartans (1.140.2) and the *dêmos* that is being wrongly asked to take actions to avoid conflict (1.140.3), it is the *dêmos* that must maintain its authority and power by upholding the Megarian decree and embracing the possibility of war (1.140.4–141.1). That this interpretation is Pericles' own – and, more importantly, that the *dêmos*, if it acts as recommended, will really function as the executing arm of Periclean policy – is almost wholly minimized. Only a passing rhetorical formula, ὥσπερ ἔμοιγε ἄμεινον δοκεῖ εἶναι, "as I believe is the best course" (1.141.1), refers back to the speaker himself, as he restates his call for war at the close of the section.

The opposition constructed between the Athenians and the Spartans is extended to "the Peloponnesians" in the next, longest subdivision of the speech (1.141.2–143.5), as Pericles enumerates the specific weaknesses of the enemy in contrast to the strengths of the Athenians. There are no individuals treated here at all, only the dichotomy of "us" vs. "them." The routine first-person singular usages, as before, return near the end of the section (ἔμοιγε τοιαῦτα καὶ παραπλήσια δοκεῖ εἶναι, "this is how things seem to me, or nearly so," 1.143.3, and ἐκείνοις ἐμεμψάμην, "I censured them," ibid.) as the argument is restated to conclude the segment. A coda follows, speculating on the possible outcomes of mutual devastation of territory and capped by an emotional flourish:

> τήν τε ὀλόφυρσιν μὴ οἰκιῶν καὶ γῆς ποιεῖσθαι . . . καὶ εἰ ᾤμην πείσειν ὑμᾶς, αὐτοὺς ἂν ἐξελθόντας ἐκέλευον αὐτὰ δῃῶσαι καὶ δεῖξαι Πελοποννησίοις ὅτι τούτων γε ἕνεκα οὐχ ὑπακούσεσθε. (1.143.5)

> [It is necessary] not to grieve over your houses and land . . . if I believed that I could have convinced you, I would have ordered you to go out and burn them and thus show the Peloponnesians that you will not give in to them because of things like those.

Defensive destruction of property and resources was a known tactic in ancient warfare,[14] but Pericles here constructs a *reductio ad absurdum*. As a rhetorical device, however, this statement is highly effective. It places imaginary limits on the speaker's ability to bend the *dêmos* to his own will, and also projects onto the *dêmos* a flattering image of corporate strength in difficult times. Thucydides' Pericles is shaping the sentiments of his audience while simultaneously denying his ability to do so.

The final section of the speech returns to Pericles' indispensable leadership, focusing not only upon the speaker's own opinions, but also upon the need for his guidance in the future:

> Πολλὰ δὲ καὶ ἄλλα ἔχω ἐς ἐλπίδα τοῦ περιέσεσθαι, ἢν ἐθέλητε ἀρχήν τε μὴ ἐπικτᾶσθαι ἅμα πολεμοῦντες καὶ κινδύνους αὐθαιρέτους μὴ προστίθεσθαι· μᾶλλον γὰρ πεφόβημαι τὰς οἰκείας ἡμῶν ἁμαρτίας ἢ τὰς τῶν ἐναντίων διανοίας. ἀλλ᾽ ἐκεῖνα μὲν καὶ ἐν ἄλλῳ λόγῳ ἅμα τοῖς ἔργοις δηλωθήσεται. (1.144.1–2)

> I have many other reasons to hope for our success if you are willing to avoid growing the empire while we are at war and taking on additional freely chosen dangers. For I am more afraid of our own faults than of the intelligence of our enemies. But those things will be disclosed in another speech as events unfold.

In order to preserve the delicate illusion of corporate agency on the part of the *dêmos*, Pericles casts the remainder of his speech in the

---

[14] E.g. Hanson 1983: 3–107, who discusses the strategy (and defenses against it) as part of a larger argument.

first-person plural, offering his recommendations in the guise of a hor-
tatory subjunctive (ἀποκρινάμενοι ἀποπέμψωμεν, "let us dispatch this reply
[sc. to the Peloponnesians]," 1.144.2) and concluding with a stirring call
to equal οἱ γοῦν πατέρες ἡμῶν ὑποστάντες Μήδους, "our forebears [who]
resisted the Persians" (1.144.4). The most telling remark in the closing
section, however, summarizes the tension between the individual and the
group that Pericles has maintained throughout the speech:

> εἰδέναι δὲ χρὴ ὅτι ἀνάγκη πολεμεῖν . . . ἔκ τε τῶν μεγίστων κινδύνων ὅτι καὶ
> πόλει καὶ ἰδιώτῃ μέγισται τιμαὶ περιγίγνονται. (1.144.3)
>
> It is essential to understand that going to war is a necessity . . . and that
> out of the greatest dangers the greatest honors arise both for the polis and
> for the private citizen.

The generic quality of this statement lends itself well not only to Pericles'
current purposes, but also to the larger concept of historical agency that
Thucydides is constructing. The polis here is, of course, Athens, but the
identity of the "private citizen" is deliberately unclear. The audience within
the narrative might be expected to think of Pericles, but there is nothing here
to hinder any other citizen's picturing himself as the recipient of wartime
honors; in fact, the proverbial tone might invite precisely this interpretation.
Both the city and the individual, here members of an equally balanced
grammatical pair, καὶ πόλει καὶ ἰδιώτῃ, will face danger in time of war; both
will have the opportunity to be remembered for great deeds. The ordinary
individual, the separate, non-eminent member of a Greek group, is here
potentially elevated to a status from which he was essentially barred in
Herodotus: he may be imagined as an agent of history.

The context of Pericles' next speech, his only one presented in indirect
discourse, is as significant as the speech itself. The Spartans are preparing
to invade Attica, and Pericles realizes that his personal prominence may
create public difficulties (2.13.1). Many residents and landowners of rural
Attica will likely lose their estates to Spartan ravaging expeditions, and so
Pericles' voluntary surrender of his own land, recorded in this passage, may
appear to be an attempt to share in the experiences of his citizen group. But
it also, ironically, underscores his separateness from the other members of
the *dêmos*: Pericles is possessed of connections to one of the hereditary royal
families of Sparta, and also of property sufficiently valuable that its survival
through an enemy raid would be a source of potential enmity from his own
people. By gifting his lands to the Athenian state, Pericles sets himself apart
as a benefactor even as he is ostensibly attempting to even his 'losses' with
those of his fellow citizens.

The indirect speech that follows (2.13.1–9) contains a reiteration of Pericles' recommended strategies for the war, with much of the substance repeated from his first speech.[15] Now, however, the collection of evidence and arguments is denser, devoid of extensive rhetorical decoration and replete with inventories of money, precious metals, men, and fortifications. The impact is made through the content, which itself demonstrates Pericles' unique status: he has access to highly specific information about the resources of Athens. His command of numbers and his emphasis upon facts lend him a level of credibility that helps to justify Thucydides' bald presentation of the Athenians' immediate obedience (2.14.1). Just as Pericles himself had predicted at the opening of his first speech (1.140.1), matters look very different to the *dêmos* now that conflict is imminent. The litany of resources may seem to focus upon the affairs of the city, but its presentation and reception demonstrate instead the vast influence enjoyed by its "leading citizen."

In the context of the current argument, the Funeral Oration is best examined in the light of the material evidence from this period, and so it will be treated near the conclusion of this chapter. Following closely upon it, however, comes Pericles' justification of his war policy during the plague, a performance before the Assembly traditionally known as his "second speech" (2.60.1–64.6). Again, the immediate context is significant. Pericles is under personal attack, and the *dêmos* attempts for the first time in the narrative to act independently of his strategies:

> καὶ τὸν μὲν Περικλέα ἐν αἰτίᾳ εἶχον ὡς πείσαντα σφᾶς πολεμεῖν καὶ δι' ἐκεῖνον ταῖς ξυμφοραῖς περιπεπτωκότες, πρὸς δὲ τοὺς Λακεδαιμονίους ὥρμηντο ξυγχωρεῖν· καὶ πρέσβεις τινὰς πέμψαντες ὡς αὐτοὺς ἄπρακτοι ἐγένοντο. πανταχόθεν τε τῇ γνώμῃ ἄποροι καθεστηκότες ἐνέκειντο τῷ Περικλεῖ. (2.59.2)

> And they were holding Pericles at fault, [believing that] he had swayed them to go to war, and that because of him they had met with hardships. And they wanted badly to settle matters with the Spartans. But even after dispatching some emissaries to them, they remained unsuccessful. So being at a loss on every side, they raged at Pericles.

Having suffered during the plague, the *dêmos* scapegoats the creator of its war strategy and tries a new approach, but ends up flailing. The two alpha privatives in this passage emphasize the inability of the Athenians either

---

[15] This repetition is openly acknowledged by Thucydides: παρῄνει δὲ καὶ περὶ τῶν παρόντων ἅπερ καὶ πρότερον, "and he offered the same recommendations regarding current affairs as [he had] in the past," 2.13.2.

to halt the course upon which Pericles has steered them (ἄπρακτοι, in the sense of being unable to act productively) or to design a new one (ἄποροι, in the sense of being unable to plan).[16] In their moment of vulnerability, they turn, as so often before, to Pericles, not now to seek his guidance, but to blame him for the design of the city's recent policies. The *dêmos* understands Pericles as an individual apart, but is apparently unable to make the causative connection between its rejection of his leadership and its inability to act. Like Demosthenes' soldiers at Pylos, the members of the Athenian Assembly seem to lack a fuller understanding of the relationships between individuals and groups that are such a central part of Thucydides' conception of the movement of history.

Pericles, however, like Demosthenes, is possessed of a wider view: the character has anticipated his citizens' discontent and plans to use his speech to render their collective temperament ἠπιώτερον καὶ ἀδεέστερον, "less intense and less anxious" (2.59.3). This emphasis on the foresight of Pericles continues into the beginning of the speech, where the same sentiments are expressed in direct discourse (2.60.1). The theme not only foreshadows the Athenians' positive reaction to the speech itself (2.65.1–4) and anticipates the obituary of Pericles that follows (2.65.5–13), but also creates a strong sense of credibility. Thucydides can therefore employ this suggestion of his character's good judgment to flag as especially significant the message that Pericles is about to deliver.

The first section of Pericles' second speech (2.60.2–6) emphasizes the dichotomies between public and private, state and citizen, collective and individual. In its acknowledgement of these divisions as fundamental for the understanding of the motion of Athenian history, this passage functions as a symbolic recapitulation of Pericles' career shortly before the report of his death (2.65.6) and highlights central themes that require observation throughout the remainder of Thucydides' text. Several significant concepts receive treatment: the indissoluble link between the fortunes of the individual and the fate of his city (2.60.2–3); the selfishness of those who would place their own sufferings ahead of the safety of the state (2.60.4); and the contention that skill and talent, when supported by patriotism and incorruptibility, confer upon a given man the right to advocate a particular course of action to his polis (2.60.5–6). In this opening segment, then, Thucydides' Pericles sketches out both sides of the relationship between the eminent individual and his city, emphasizing that just as it is not in the best interest of any man, however prominent or successful, to make choices that will

---

[16] The adjective ἄπορος, in particular, carries with it a sense of futility (*LSJ ad loc.*).

injure his polis, it is not in the best interest of the polis to reject the advice of a man whose talents and personal qualities set him apart.[17] Such open assertion of the value of the individual in the political life of his city represents a change from Herodotus, where the history-making productivity of Greek leaders in concert with their respective citizen groups was demonstrated, but not explicitly discussed, much less analyzed by such a central figure as Pericles.

As the speech proceeds, the conceptual division between the eminent individual and his city receives continued emphasis. In the second section of the speech, Pericles contrasts his own opinions with those of his fellow citizens (ἐγὼ μὲν ὁ αὐτός εἰμι καὶ οὐκ ἐξίσταμαι· ὑμεῖς δὲ μεταβάλλετε, "I myself am the same and I am not retreating, but you are changing your minds," 2.61.2), and claims that the flaw in their point of view is that they are fragmented due to their focus on private sorrow (τὸ μὲν λυποῦν ἔχει ἤδη τὴν αἴσθησιν ἑκάστῳ, τῆς δὲ ὠφελίας ἄπεστιν ἔτι ἡ δήλωσις ἅπασι, "the suffering is making an impression on each of you, but the explanation of the benefits is yet wanting for everyone," 2.61.2). For Pericles, a key justification for the cognitive separation of self from city is, ironically, altruism. Because Pericles has the larger concerns of the city in mind, his individual opinion should, he argues, carry greater weight than those of other individual citizens, who are thinking primarily of themselves even as they are collectively opposing him. Again, the *dêmos*' understanding of the situation is depicted as being incomplete, and Pericles' broader view is required to fill out the picture.

The third section (2.62.1–5) employs a technique also used in Pericles' first speech: it explicitly turns away from the voice of the individual (2.62.1) in order to emphasize the collective power and potential agency of the *dêmos*. The goal is to inspire confidence in the imperial capability of Athens, whose citizens are here contrasted with the Great King of Persia in terms of their control of the sea (2.62.2). The juxtaposition places an individual in opposition to a group, and an enemy whose predecessor was conquered in the past[18] against the strength of the *dêmos* in the present (cf. also 2.62.3). It may also, however, acknowledge a central contrast of historical agency constructed by Herodotus: that of the sole barbarian potentate versus

---

[17] Note especially in this context Pericles' comment that closes this section of the speech, ὥστ᾽ εἴ μοι καὶ μέσως ἡγούμενοι μᾶλλον ἑτέρων προσεῖναι αὐτὰ πολεμεῖν ἐπείσθητε, οὐκ ἂν εἰκότως νῦν τοῦ γε ἀδικεῖν αἰτίαν φεροίμην, "so that if you complied in going to war while deeming me to be even somewhat more notable than others with regard to these abilities, it would not be right for me to take on the blame for causing harm," 2.60.7.

[18] On the cognitive 'interchangeability' of successive Persian kings, with the office meaning more than its holder, see Sancisi-Weerdenburg 2002.

(generally) polis-based Greek groups. Read in this way, the text suggests that this particular scheme is a simplified way of understanding the movement of history, delivered to the *dêmos* at large by a leader whose unique foresight provides him with a more complex understanding of the true situation.

The memorable warning in the next thematic section of the speech (ὡς τυραννίδα γὰρ ἤδη ἔχετε αὐτήν, ἣν λαβεῖν μὲν ἄδικον δοκεῖ εἶναι, ἀφεῖναι δὲ ἐπικίνδυνον, "for you have [an empire] that by now is like a tyranny. To possess it may be unjust, but to liberate it is hazardous," 2.63.2) therefore takes on fresh meaning. In an era when the figure of the tyrant played such a significant role in Athenian political imagination,[19] the depiction here of the *polis* or *dêmos tyrannos* (the "tyrannical city" or "tyrannical populace," also known elsewhere in fifth-century literature)[20] is an especially clever turn. If the *dêmos* is construed as the tyrant in this situation, then Pericles cannot occupy that role; if individual self-centered opinions are harming the *dêmos* at large, then Pericles, opposing current popular views, may represent the better interests of the group. Indeed, the character argues precisely this at the close of the section: those who would fragment the *dêmos* for private concerns are dangerous (2.63.3).

The final section of the speech recapitulates a number of Pericles' earlier rhetorical techniques. Like the opening of the first speech, this closing portion of the second speech explicitly acknowledges the differing perspectives of Pericles and the *dêmos* (2.64.1) and then works to integrate their concerns. Here, the common cause is the polis itself (2.64.2–4), with the brief sketch of glorious Athenian achievements echoing both the themes and the attitudes of the Funeral Oration (see below). Gnomic statements, too, are once more employed as universalizing exempla (2.64.5). The speech concludes, at last, with a general statement that embodies the very dichotomy under examination here:

> ... ὡς οἵτινες πρὸς τὰς ξυμφορὰς γνώμῃ μὲν ἥκιστα λυποῦνται, ἔργῳ δὲ μάλιστα ἀντέχουσιν, οὗτοι καὶ πόλεων καὶ ἰδιωτῶν κράτιστοί εἰσιν. (2.64.6)
>
> ... as those whose dispositions are least grieved in times of suffering and who endure it through their actions are the strongest ones, both poleis and private citizens.

[19] Raaflaub 2003 surveys the evidence and argues that tyranny was largely a negative theme in fifth-century Athenian politics: it was what the *dêmos*, collectively, did not want to be, and what it measured itself against. This essay appears in a volume (Morgan 2003) whose other contributions are also relevant to this issue.

[20] See note 19, above, and Scanlon 1987 on Thucydides in particular, with references to other, more general studies as well at 286 n. 1.

Like the remark at the closing section of Pericles' first speech (1.144.3), this statement acknowledges the potential historical agency of both groups and individuals. But because the wartime situation at Athens has now grown more difficult, this statement invites more complicated conclusions. The individuals referenced here appear to be the separate members of the Athenian *dêmos*, but Pericles claims to be demonstrating himself the same attitude he requires from them, and so he, too, likely belongs in this category. The state under discussion is Athens, but the speech has already acknowledged that Athens is comprised of individuals whose separate dispositions can affect its course.[21] The message with which Pericles leaves the scene, then, is that *individuals* can move history through the choices they make, even if those choices are expressed collectively, and their consequences shared, through membership in a polis.

This emphasis on the individual is further highlighted in Thucydides' obituary of Pericles.[22] In at least three separate places (2.65.4–5, 6–7, 9–11), Pericles is presented as a unifying force, preventing through his individual effort the varied private interests of citizens from hindering the corporate progress of the polis. This summary message further refines the concept that closed Pericles' final speech. Individuals can indeed affect the course of history, but if ordinary citizens wish to participate in positive progress, they are best advised to do so as a group. That group, in turn, is ideally to be guided by a leader like Pericles.

That Thucydides' text questions both implicitly and explicitly the ability of the Athenian *dêmos* to make productive decisions without the advice of a powerful figure like Pericles is well known.[23] But the text also implies an awareness of the separability of the *dêmos* that Herodotus' *Histories* did not acknowledge. The Thucydidean *dêmos*, unlike the Herodotean one, is composed of individuals who may possess dissenting opinions and competing claims.[24] These individuals are all *theoretically* capable of history-making action, just as a leader like Pericles is – or at least they are conditioned to think that this is the case. Whether this is a credulous belief on the part of Thucydides' *dêmos*, a deliberately shared fiction between leaders and led,[25] or something in between, this conditioning may represent Thucydides' attempt to capture a snapshot of Athenian democratic *mentalité*. The

---

[21] Cf. note 24, below.

[22] 2.65.5–13; 2.65.1–4 shows the Athenians reacting to Pericles' second speech.

[23] E.g. Gomme 1945–56: vol. II, 125–6 *ad* 2.41.1; see also Yunis 1991, with additional references.

[24] I am grateful to J. Ober for calling this important distinction to my attention. See also Gribble 2006: 453–5.

[25] As ostracism may have been in the fourth century: see Chapter 2, above.

delicate negotiation between individual and group historical agency revealed in Pericles' rhetoric therefore has wider-reaching implications: in its efforts to craft a productive relationship between the speaker and the *dêmos*, it may provide a paradigm for the unification of the separate views of that *dêmos*' individual members.[26]

The Pylos narrative and Cleon

Demosthenes directs the Athenians to Pylos and commands the first phase of their operations there; Nicias apparently supervises the succeeding activities.[27] But it is Cleon who finally captures Sphacteria and accomplishes what Thucydides calls παρὰ γνώμην τε δὴ μάλιστα τῶν κατὰ τὸν πόλεμον τοῦτο, "the most surprising thing [that happened] during the war" (4.40.1). The historian's depiction of Cleon's role in the Pylos campaign offers a striking contrast to the leadership styles and methods of Pericles.[28] But it also represents a consistent and coherent reiteration of Thucydides' views on individual historical agency. Though Cleon is certainly no Pericles, he occupies in this context the position of the individual leader without whom the *dêmos* cannot act effectively.

Up until the point of Cleon's intervention (4.27.5), Thucydides' treatment of the Pylos campaign foregrounds Demosthenes, dwelling upon his careful preparations for the first major attack by the Spartans (4.9.1–4), his pre-battle speech to his soldiers (4.10.1–5), and the positive effects of his actions (4.11.1–2). Demosthenes' accurate perception of the Athenian situation,[29] his exhortations to his men to cast aside their individual views in favor of corporate action (4.10.1), and his detailed proofs of a likely Athenian victory (4.10.2–4), all evoke the methods and the speeches of Pericles, and imbue Demosthenes' literary character with a sense of significant promise. Once the Spartan assault begins, however, Demosthenes disappears from the scene (4.11.2).[30] The descriptive emphasis shifts over to "the Athenians" in battle (4.11.3), just as happened so frequently in Herodotus.

---

[26] I am grateful to J. Ober for this point.

[27] Demosthenes receives his official appointment to oversee Pylos at 4.5.2. He probably remains in command until at least the entrapment of the Spartan *homoioi* on the island of Sphacteria (Thucydides' account of the battle concludes at 4.14.5). At some point before 4.27.5, Nicias seems to have been placed in charge, though no reference is made in the interim to the change.

[28] Cleon's general depiction in Thucydides as a foil to Pericles has been frequently noted: see e.g. Cairns 1982: 203; Connor 1971: 120, with references.

[29] Cf. the discussion at the opening of this chapter, and see also his assessment of the most likely location for a Spartan landing at 4.9.2–4, borne out at 4.11.2.

[30] The comparatively limited treatment or even underestimation of Demosthenes in Thucydides' narrative has long been a point of discussion: see e.g. Woodcock 1928.

At this stage, a different Greek leader, Brasidas of Sparta, is singled out for his actions in battle against "the Athenians" (4.11.3–12.1, especially 4.12.1). In Herodotus, the individual in conflict against a group was almost inevitably a foreign autocrat; here in Thucydides, however, a Greek may also play this role. Brasidas is introduced as being πάντων δὲ φανερώτατος ("most notable of all," 4.11.4). He is able to compel his ships and those of his allies to land by shouting from a distance (ibid.), and he himself then rushes for the shore against a throng of enemies, only to suffer wounds that remove him from the action (4.12.1).[31] Rather like Herodotus' Leonidas or Thucydides' Pericles, Brasidas demonstrates qualities that the immediate narrative context will not let him bear out in full. He will eventually return, however, to demonstrate his historical significance on a major campaign in the north.[32]

Despite the actions of two Greek leaders who have both shown some of the skills of Pericles, the situation at Pylos reaches a stalemate. A brief skirmish initiated by the Athenians strands the Spartan troops on Sphacteria (4.13.3–14.5), and fruitless negotiations ensue (4.15.1–21.1). At this point, Cleon makes his second major appearance. His first, during the Mytilenean debate, was accompanied by a brief characterization (ὢν καὶ ἐς τὰ ἄλλα βιαιότατος τῶν πολιτῶν τῷ τε δήμῳ παρὰ πολὺ ἐν τῷ τότε πιθανώτατος, "both the most ferocious amongst the citizens and by far the most persuasive of the *dêmos* at that time," 3.36.6) that is echoed, as is well appreciated, by his re-introduction here: . . . ἀνὴρ δημαγωγὸς κατ᾽ ἐκεῖνον τὸν χρόνον ὢν καὶ τῷ πλήθει πιθανώτατος, ". . . a demagogue at that time who was most persuasive of the masses" (4.21.3). The vocabulary actually degenerates between the first passage and the second. Earlier on, Cleon is extremely violent (*LSJ ad* βιαιός), but in the second passage he becomes a δημαγωγός, "demagogue," a much more dangerous term.[33] In the first passage, Cleon's audience is the *dêmos*, but in the second it has become a πλῆθος, a much more ambiguous word.[34] These two Cleon passages are also likely intended to contrast with two earlier ones that characterize Pericles, 1.127.3 and 1.139.4.[35] Whereas Cleon here is twice πιθανώτατος, "most persuasive,"

---

[31] There are Homeric resonances here: Gomme 1945–56: vol. III, 448 *ad* 4.11.4 points out that Brasidas was compared to Achilles as early as Plat. *Symp.* 221c.

[32] 4.81.1–135 *passim*. See Chapter 6, below, for a fuller discussion of Brasidas.

[33] Connor 1971: 109–10, 143–4.

[34] See the discussion of negative terminology during the treatment of Herodotus' Persian 'Constitutional Debate' in Chapter 3, above.

[35] Cf. note 28, above. Cairns 1982: 203 (with references at nn. 2–5) notes that the passages most often exercised in examining Cleon as a contrast to Pericles are not those presented here, but rather the three apparent echoes of Pericles' second speech that appear in Cleon's contribution to the Mytilenean debate.

Pericles was twice δυνατώτατος, "most influential," in action as well as in speech (λέγειν τε καὶ πράσσειν), and a "leader of the government" (ἄγων τὴν πολιτείαν).[36] In contrast, Cleon's main skill is the art of rhetorical influence, potentially dangerous in the era of sophistic education.[37] And Cleon has most recently been using this speaking ability to press the Athenians so that, dangerously, πλέονος ὠρέγοντο, "they were grasping for more" (4.21.2).[38]

Cleon, indeed, is no Pericles. Two other men with clearly Periclean qualities, Demosthenes and Brasidas, have already failed to bring the Pylos situation to a conclusive close, and the likelihood that Cleon will make history here therefore appears to be slight. But the lesson that Thucydides is constructing will be of primary importance for understanding the remainder of his narrative: history can indeed be affected, even for the better, by individuals who patently do not display 'Periclean' virtues.

The anti-Periclean characterization of Cleon continues as the episode develops. His harshness towards the Spartan envoys (4.22.2)[39] earns him the distrust of the Athenians (4.27.1–2), much as Pericles was criticized during the plague (2.59.1–2). But although Cleon, like Pericles, perceives what is happening and why (4.27.3, cf. 2.59.3), his reactions are very different. Whereas Pericles successfully turned the *dêmos* back to his point of view with a speech that carefully negotiated between individual and group responsibility, Cleon hurls groundless accusations (4.27.3) that backfire miserably (4.27.4). Trapped in his own lies, he attempts to redirect the ire of his audience from himself to Nicias (4.27.5). This gesture, above all, contrasts with Pericles' actions. During the plague, Pericles summoned the Assembly and focused attention on himself and his policies (2.59.3); Cleon, now in the spotlight, cannot sustain or defend his point of view (4.28.1–3). In the end, Cleon is forced to yield to the *dêmos* rather than molding it to his will (as Pericles was so adept at doing), and he then presents a brief outline, in indirect discourse, of his plan for Pylos.

This small indirect speech (4.28.4), too, contrasts Cleon with Pericles, because it is utterly self-focused. There is no room for delicate negotiation

---

[36] The verb ἄγω can bear indications of political guidance as well as physical leadership, and the noun πολιτεία carries connotations of citizenship, membership in a civilized state, and constitutional government (*LSJ ad loca*).

[37] On the sophistic movement and its general social context, see the references during the discussion of Herodotus' Persian 'Constitutional Debate' in Chapter 3, above.

[38] πλεονεξία, loosely speaking, "greed," is a highly problematic emotion in Greek literature, even during the classical period: see Balot 2001.

[39] The passage is highlighted by the evocative verb νεικέω, a word for quarreling or strife that finds its earliest usages in the *Iliad* (*LSJ ad loc.*; see also Martin 1989: 67–76).

between the individual and the group, no attempt to characterize "the Athenians" as the agents of the speaker's proposed policies, no call for the unification of the diverse potential views within the *dêmos*. Instead, the audience of the speech is explicitly excluded from Cleon's plans (ἔφη ... πλεύσεσθαί τε λαβὼν ἐκ μὲν τῆς πόλεως οὐδένα, "he said that he would sail taking [along] no one from the city"), as he opens by emphasizing his own emotions (παρελθὼν οὔτε φοβεῖσθαι ἔφη Λακεδαιμονίους, "stepping forward, he said that he was not afraid of the Spartans") and closes by venturing grandiose claims with himself as the understood subject of every verb: ἔφη ... ἐντὸς ἡμερῶν εἴκοσιν ἢ ἄξειν Λακεδαιμονίους ζῶντας ἢ αὐτοῦ ἀποκτενεῖν, "he said that inside of twenty days he would either bring in the Spartans alive or kill them there").

Despite Cleon's lofty promises, the narrative focus now returns to Demosthenes, whom Cleon has selected as his colleague because Demosthenes is already about to storm Sphacteria. Once again, Demosthenes' astute and careful plans are detailed (4.29.2–30.3), suggesting that he may play a significant personal role in the fight to come. After Cleon's arrival (4.30.4), however, with conflict nearing, both generals are relegated to the background,[40] and "the Athenians"[41] are the ones who attack the island. The narrative emphasizes collective Athenian activity throughout,[42] and when the generals finally take action in their own right, it is only to halt the battle for negotiations so that the Spartan *homoioi* may be taken alive (4.37.1–38.1). If either of the Athenian commanders, in the end, has distinguished himself at Pylos, it is Demosthenes, but Thucydides still claims, though with some effort, that the agent of Athens' victory is Cleon (4.39.3–40.1).

If Cleon's promise to the clamoring Athenian Assembly was "crazy" (μανιώδης, 4.39.3), his success was certainly unexpected. Although Thucydides suggests that the true surprise was that the Spartans on Sphacteria did not fight to the death (cf. 4.40.2), Cleon's return of the prisoners from Pylos within his own deadline also provokes notice. It is Cleon whose interaction with the Athenian *dêmos* has set these events in motion, and while he is clearly incapable of guiding the populace in the manner of a Pericles, his historical agency at the conclusion of the episode is not left open for debate.

---

[40] As is in keeping with the narrative patterns observed thus far in both Herodotus and Thucydides; note particularly the slippage of the verbal subjects in 4.31.1, where the understood agents could be either the commanders or their entire 'side.'

[41] E.g. 4.32.1, 33.1, 35.3, 36.3.

[42] Save for an acknowledgement of the success of Demosthenes' strategies for the amphibious assault (4.32.3–4) and a brief notice of a flanking maneuver by the Messenian general approved by Cleon and Demosthenes (4.36.1).

History can be made in Thucydides by individuals who seem singularly undeserving of the memorialization: good actions are not always driven by good men.

Athens' Sicilian expedition and Nicias

Of all of Nicias' projects during the war,[43] the one treated in the greatest depth is his command of the Athenian expedition to Sicily. The entire endeavor is cast by Thucydides as a spectacular failure,[44] but Nicias' leadership role merits particular attention, as his relationship with the Athenian *dêmos* in Thucydides differs significantly from those of Pericles and Cleon. Although Thucydides' Nicias possesses superior moral qualities and at least passable military and oratorical skill, he is unable to direct the Assembly in accordance with his own foresight, and is therefore trapped into becoming part of the mechanism of Athens' self-destruction. In the context of the Sicilian expedition, Nicias functions both as an individual historical agent (in the sense that he is explicitly held responsible for certain actions he takes) and as an enacting arm of Athens' collective, group historical agency. But Thucydides emphasizes the gap between Nicias' strategic intentions and Athens' actions, which effectively shifts most responsibility for the Sicilian disaster away from the reluctant general and onto the *dêmos*. This in turn implicitly questions whether democratic decision-making and group historical agency can yield effective action when they become essentially independent of the guidance of an individual leader.[45]

The importance of this issue emerges from the structure of the earliest portion of the Sicilian episode (6.8.3–32.2). Here, Thucydides simply summarizes the background negotiations and the naïvely optimistic Assembly meeting at which the expedition is approved[46] (6.6.1–3, 6.8.1–2) and concentrates instead upon the allocation of supplies by the Assembly some five days later (6.8.3). At this session, Nicias and Alcibiades, both assigned to Sicily, present their opposing viewpoints about the project.[47] Nicias is

---

[43] Summarized with citations by Westlake 1968: 86–96, 169–71.

[44] Or, more particularly, a tragedy: Cornford 1907 is a classic reading of tragic influences in Thucydides' thought and text.

[45] This is an important issue for Thucydides in general: see Ober 1998: 52–121, with earlier bibliography collected at 52 n. 1.

[46] The event itself is only briefly acknowledged, but the tone is condemnatory: καὶ οἱ Ἀθηναῖοι ἐκκλησίαν ποιήσαντες καὶ ἀκούσαντες τῶν τε Ἐγεσταίων . . . τά τε ἄλλα ἐπαγωγὰ καὶ οὐκ ἀληθῆ . . . ἐψηφίσαντο ναῦς ἑξήκοντα πέμπειν ἐς Σικελίαν, "And the Athenians, after convening an assembly and hearing from the Egestaeans . . . other things that were both attractive and untrue . . . voted to dispatch sixty ships to Sicily," 6.8.2.

[47] Nicias' two speeches occur at 6.9.1–14.1, 6.20.1–23.4; Alcibiades' speech is at 6.16.1–18.7.

reluctant but powerless to check the unbridled optimism of his audience, while Alcibiades is infectiously enthusiastic and quickly energizes the *dêmos* to validate his point of view (6.19.1, cf. 6.26.1). The motion of past events would suggest that it is Alcibiades who will function in this context as the catalyst, the individual whose leadership will allow the Athenian *dêmos* to make history.[48]

But Alcibiades is quickly removed from the picture by the incidents of the Hermocopidae and the profanation of the Eleusinian Mysteries (6.27.1–28.2). Though he embarks with the expedition, his recall to Athens to stand trial (6.53.1, prepared at 6.29.1–3) is brought about so quickly that he essentially does not participate in the Sicilian campaign at all. The *dêmos* is therefore left with Nicias by default.[49] The case of Pericles showed that an effective leader who can sway the *dêmos* to his will can both produce historical impact and project a share of it upon the city. The experiences of Cleon during the Pylos campaign revealed that even a less talented individual may serve as the partner of the *dêmos* in the making of history. But Nicias has been cornered into his command, questions the entire endeavor, and is unwilling to project even false confidence, and so he and the *dêmos* are essentially at cross-purposes from the start. This lack of collaboration bodes ill for the expedition. It also raises questions about whether the group or the individual will actually 'own' the historical impact of this large-scale failure.

Closer examination of the direct Assembly speeches of Nicias early in book 6 supports these interpretations and defines both the characterization and the role of Nicias in greater detail. The introduction to Nicias' first speech (6.8.4) suggests through context and content that he is to be compared with both Pericles and Cleon. Like Cleon before Pylos, Nicias has reluctantly assumed command of a challenging enterprise: during the Pylos narrative, ironically, Nicias resigned from the mission and spurred the

---

[48] If the personal description that Thucydides provides for the charismatic young general (6.15.2–4) is problematic, so was the description of Cleon (see above), and Cleon was, after all, surprisingly successful at Pylos.

[49] Lamachus, the third general initially assigned to the Sicilian expedition (6.8.2), will essentially prove a non-factor. Thucydides indicates this in several ways: firstly, Lamachus is given no role in the Assembly meeting that witnesses the debate between Nicias and Alcibiades (6.8.3–26.1), and in fact delivers no direct speeches at all during his limited tenure in the Sicilian narrative; secondly, when opinions about the proper course of action are expressed upon arrival in Sicily, he briefly voices a distinct point of view (6.49.1–4), but then gives his support to the opinion of Alcibiades (6.50.1); finally, even when he is a participant in the action in Sicily, Lamachus receives almost no direct mention by name, instead being classed under the rubric "the Athenian generals." He is killed in battle just as the crisis at Epipolae is beginning to develop (6.101.6), and the focus returns immediately thereafter to the actions of Nicias instead (6.102.1–2).

dêmos to demand that Cleon take it over (4.28.1–3). Now Nicias himself is trapped instead. Like Pericles during the plague (cf. 2.59.2–3), Nicias here approaches the Assembly with the goal of turning it away from an irrational desire for immediate action.[50]

Nicias' two speeches during the Sicilian debate suggest that he is not prepared to function as the *dêmos'* leader. Although he does employ some of the same rhetorical techniques that Pericles used to negotiate between individual and group agency,[51] they do not extend beyond the surface level of his meaning and his tone is far from conciliatory. In his first speech (6.9.1–14.1), Nicias emphasizes the divide between his own perspective and that of his audience (e.g. 6.9.1, 10.1–3,[52] 11.2, 13.1), employs sarcasm that belittles the decisions of the *dêmos* (6.10.5), and directly attacks his popular opponent (6.12.2, cf. 6.16.1). Nicias' second speech (6.20.1–23.4) opens with a bald acknowledgement that he has lost the vote (6.20.1), and then tries to undermine the confidence of the *dêmos* by exaggerating the armaments and supplies required for the expedition (cf. 6.19.2). The attempt at psychological manipulation is ill-timed, and it backfires (6.24.2).

The closing remarks of the two speeches, in particular, show Nicias trying to separate his own individual role in the expedition from the role taken by the Athenians. The first, unique in Thucydides, is a rhetorical address to the *prytanis*, the presiding officer of the Athenian Assembly, requesting a second vote on the question of attacking Sicily (6.14.1). In isolation, this passage might suggest that Nicias is presenting himself, obliquely, as the state's potential savior; after all, he is the one calling for the change in the vote. In the larger context, however, this section also removes Nicias by one level from responsibility for the action in progress. It emphasizes the ownership of the decision-making by the Athenians, and explicitly declines to claim even the most positive characterization – that of the individual who wishes only to benefit his country – for Nicias himself. This distancing effect is heightened by the conclusion of Nicias' second speech: after a series of hyperbolic prescriptions, the general ends by volunteering to relinquish

---

[50] It is also possible to recall here the position of Cleon during the Mytilenean debate. After a prior Assembly meeting at which a decision was reached, a second meeting was held to reconsider the choice, and Cleon spoke out strongly in favor of upholding the original action of the Assembly (3.36.5–40.8). Here, the second Assembly meeting is held to detail support for the prior decision, and Nicias speaks in favor of reversal.

[51] Including verbally incorporating himself with his audience through the use of the collective "we," *passim*, and acknowledging that individual listeners may possess independent and differing points of view, 6.13.1.

[52] Nicias' correction here of the general Athenian perspective on the existing treaties is lent greater weight by his direct participation in their foundation, recently treated at 5.23.1–24.2.

his position: εἰ δέ τῳ ἄλλως δοκεῖ, παρίημι αὐτῷ τὴν ἀρχήν, "but if different [plans] seem good to anyone else, I give up my leadership to him" (6.23.3). This offer parallels the one that Nicias made during the Pylos debate (cf. 4.28.1–3), and, given the context, it is likely that the character here hopes for the same effect as before. The *dêmos* sought a new, more impetuous leader for Pylos; perhaps they will do the same for Sicily and spare Nicias the leadership of an expedition that he believes is doomed.

But the *dêmos* will have nothing of it. The ἔρως ἐκπλεῦσαι, the "passion to sail" (6.24.3) that has come over the Athenian Assembly is a stronger and still less rational impulse than the ὁρμή that gripped the soldiers of Demosthenes at Pylos.[53] Like the men who decided to fortify the headland overlooking Sphacteria, the Athenian *dêmos* lacks a full understanding of the situation at hand. Further, the general from whose foresight they might have benefited has failed to restrain his listeners and has obscured the facts in a failed attempt to capitalize on rhetorical exaggeration. The Sicilian debate scene therefore downplays the individual agency of Nicias, who despite his foresight has effected no change in the situation, and highlights the misinformed collective agency of the *dêmos* (see especially 6.24.1–4). Bolstered by Alcibiades, the group has essentially trapped an individual into doing its bidding and serving as its functional arm, no matter how reluctant he may be. The history-making act that follows, the departure of the grand expedition (6.30.1–32.2), thus belongs to Athens itself.

Even en route to Sicily, Nicias' potential for historical agency – indeed, his very opportunity to make large command decisions – is deliberately minimized. All activities at this point are ascribed not to named leaders, but to "the Athenians,"[54] or to "the [Athenian] generals" (6.42.1–2; 44.4, likely understood; 46.2). Once the news reaches the Athenian forces at Rhegium that the Egestaeans do not have the promised capital, Nicias reappears to have his foresight confirmed (6.46.2) and his conservative response rejected (6.47.1 with 6.50.1). He has again been trapped into a course of action that he would not recommend for the *dêmos*, this time by the very individual who had courted the *dêmos*' favor at Nicias' expense: Alcibiades.[55]

The historical agency of the *dêmos* in the Sicilian affair is implicitly criticized by Thucydides' brief account of the next major event, the recall of

---

[53] The word ἔρως carries with it physical and sexual connotations that imply it is more primal than ὁρμή (see *LSJ ad loca*).

[54] E.g. 6.30.1; 31.2, where present generals are not mentioned even when past generals are; 32.1–2, emphasizing the unity of the military force, the Athenian citizen body, and its allies; 43.1.

[55] Λάμαχος . . . προσέθετο καὶ αὐτὸς τῇ Ἀλκιβιάδου γνώμῃ, "Lamachus . . . sided with the proposal of Alcibiades," 6.50.1.

Alcibiades (6.53.2–3). "The Athenians" in this passage are presented as the paranoid and credulous agents of their own destruction. The city has pulled out the general who encouraged its military aspirations,[56] and left in place another who has been struggling throughout *not* to represent the *dêmos*. The mention of the fear of tyranny[57] (6.53.3, echoed at 6.60.1–2), while variously interpreted,[58] seems to invite serious reservations about the willingness of the *dêmos* to collaborate with a strong leader. This reluctance to be guided, manifested here in an apparent aversion to the prominence of Alcibiades (cf. 6.51.1), has already surfaced in the Assembly's chronic unwillingness to heed the farsighted warnings of Nicias. It will endure throughout the remainder of Thucydides' account of the Sicilian expedition.

Coverage of the first season of the Sicilian campaign and the early part of the second shows Nicias credited by name in only two situations: once for ambassadorial activities (e.g. 6.52.4), and once addressing his troops before battle (6.62.3–69.1). In operations against the Syracusans, the invading combatants are almost inevitably represented, particularly once battle is joined, as "the Athenians,"[59] with no mention made of their leaders. The emphasis of Thucydides' coverage begins to shift, however, with the death of Lamachus (6.106.6). Nicias now remains in sole command, and his difficult relationships with the expedition and with the Athenian *dêmos* begin to receive closer attention.

Almost immediately following the loss of Lamachus, Thucydides relates a brief anecdote: Nicias, confined by sickness to the Athenian fortifications at Epipolae, orders desperate fires set to avert a Syracusan attack (6.102.1–2). Rather than emphasizing Nicias' heroism or cleverness, Thucydides focuses upon the general's infirmity, upon the coincidence of his presence at the beleaguered fort, and upon the danger of the situation. The burning missiles save the stronghold, but the Athenian outworks are destroyed. Nicias is now physically trapped upon this campaign, just as he was figuratively trapped into it from the outset, and his one gesture of individual agency apart from the commands issued by the *dêmos* has been a barely productive accident.

Nicias' role as an enacter of Athens' collective historical agency is further clarified in the episode surrounding his letter to the *dêmos* from Sicily

---

[56] Regardless of whether the *dêmos* intended to return Alcibiades to Sicily afterwards (6.61.5 is not clear), the recall removes him from the expedition by prompting his escape (6.51.6–7).

[57] See notes 19 and 20, above.

[58] This part of the passage has traditionally been taken as being especially difficult in terms of the cognitive flow of the narrative: see the references and arguments collected in Gomme, Andrewes, and Dover 1970: vol. IV, 325–9, *ad* 6.54–9.

[59] E.g. 6.63.1–2, 66.1, 67.1, 69.1–71.2 *passim*, 88.1–5, 94.1–4, 96.1–101.5 *passim*.

(7.8.1–16.2). The very fact of the correspondence emphasizes that he views himself as Athens' representative at Syracuse, rather than as an independent operator, and Thucydides' introduction (7.8.1–3), cast as if it represents a window into Nicias' own thoughts, supports this interpretation. The opening of this brief passage has Nicias connecting σωτηρία, "security," or even "salvation," with the decisions of the *dêmos* back in Athens. His evident desire is to caretake the Sicilian situation until an answer is forthcoming from "the Athenians," as he is now paralyzed by τὴν σφετέραν ἀπορίαν ("his state of not knowing what to do," 7.8.1). For Nicias, the responsibility for the rest of the Sicilian story now rests with his citizens, and his use of the unflattering word ὄχλος[60] to refer to them is suggestive of the problematic relationship with them that the letter will further reveal.

Thucydides next presents the letter's text as if verbatim. The grimness of the tactical situation (7.11.1–13.2) naturally invites some speculation as to the wisdom of recent command decisions, but Nicias focuses instead upon a cascade of circumstances that have conspired against the Athenian cause.[61] Even more importantly, *Thucydides* does not seem to assign responsibility or historical agency to Nicias, either. Thus far the historian has highlighted surprisingly few of the general's activities and has emphasized instead the actions of the *dêmos*; he has also refrained from external commentary. Now, he gives Nicias the opportunity to vent his frustrations at the *dêmos* in terms that seem to recall the character's difficulties with the Assembly near the beginning of book 6: μὴ οἷόν τε εἶναι ταῦτα ἐμοὶ κωλῦσαι τῷ στρατηγῷ (χαλεπαὶ γὰρ αἱ ὑμέτεραι φύσεις ἄρξαι), "It is impossible for me, the commander, to avert these [problems], for your natural character is difficult to lead" (7.14.2). The comment is likely also applicable to Nicias' broader relationship with the *dêmos*, as suggested by his depiction of the general mood (using the same word as before, φύσις) of the Assembly just three sentences later (7.14.4).

The final section of the letter (7.15.1–2) contains repeated abdications of Nicias' responsibility: troops and leaders alike have carried out the mission of the *dêmos* as intended, but circumstances have hindered their success; the response now lies in the hands of the *dêmos*, which must vote for withdrawal or reinforcement; Nicias is physically unable to continue the campaign

---

[60] See the references during the discussion of Herodotus' Persian 'Constitutional Debate' in Chapter 3, above.

[61] See the introduction to Nicias' letter in Gomme, Andrewes, and Dover 1970: vol. IV, 386–7, *ad* 7.10–15, particularly the comment (387) that Nicias "was temperamentally inclined to blame anyone and anything except himself."

(cf. 6.102.2); he has done the *dêmos*' bidding and deserves its indulgence in considering his recall. The closing sentence caps the case:

> ὅτι δὲ μέλλετε, ἅμα τῷ ἦρι εὐθὺς καὶ μὴ ἐς ἀναβολὰς πράσσετε, ὡς τῶν
> πολεμίων τὰ μὲν ἐν Σικελίᾳ δι᾽ ὀλίγου ποριουμένων, τὰ δ᾽ ἐκ Πελοποννήσου
> σχολαίτερον μέν, ὅμως δ᾽, ἢν μὴ προσέχητε τὴν γνώμην, τὰ μὲν λήσουσιν
> ὑμᾶς, ὥσπερ καὶ πρότερον, τὰ δὲ φθήσονται. (7.15.2)

> Whatever you are anticipating, act right away at the beginning of spring, and without delay, since our enemies will soon acquire [support] in Sicily, and then later from the Peloponnese. And if you do not focus upon your purpose, the latter will slip away from you just as in the past, and the former will act before you do.

The letter's intended audience, the listeners in the Assembly, are here cast as direct opponents of the enemies who are now closing in around the troops in Sicily. The categories of "we" (i.e. the Athenian forces encamped with Nicias above Syracuse) and "you" have been rhetorically broken down to demonstrate that the Sicilian expedition, too, is part of the *dêmos*. In deciding the fate of the distant forces, then, the *dêmos* is determining direct consequences for itself. Nicias has in effect erased himself from the picture.

The *dêmos* responds by offering further support for the expedition and two new colleagues for Nicias (7.16.1–2), but it has failed once more to appreciate Nicias' foresight. The general has tried to recuse himself, but rather than remove such a pessimistic and apparently ineffective leader, the Assembly has kept him in place. A study in contrasts quickly emerges: while Demosthenes and Eurymedon, the newly appointed generals for Sicily, cross one another's paths at sea and busy themselves with domestic campaigns, supply lines, and the transport of reinforcements,[62] the besieged Nicias lies passively in wait at Syracuse.[63] Once the generals finally meet, the differences between them are strongly underscored by the observations that Thucydides places in the mind of Demosthenes:

> ὁ δὲ Δημοσθένης ἰδὼν ὡς εἶχε τὰ πράγματα καὶ νομίσας οὐχ οἷόν τε εἶναι
> διατρίβειν οὐδὲ παθεῖν ὅπερ ὁ Νικίας ἔπαθεν (ἀφικόμενος γὰρ τὸ πρῶ-
> τον ὁ Νικίας φοβερός, ὡς οὐκ εὐθὺς προσέκειτο ταῖς Συρακούσαις, ἀλλ᾽ ἐν
> Κατάνῃ διεχείμαζεν, ὑπερώφθη τε καὶ ἔφθασεν αὐτὸν ἐκ τῆς Πελοποννήσου

---

[62] 7.26.1–3, 31.1–5, 33.3–6, 35.1–2.

[63] There is little narrative treatment of Nicias' activities during this time. He passes some information to the Sicels that leads to a successful surprise attack at 7.32.1–2, and at 7.38.2–3 he stations some merchant ships before the Athenian harbor barricade, but those are the only actions with which he is credited by name. The remainder of the military activity around Syracuse is ascribed to "the Athenians."

στρατιᾷ ὁ Γύλιππος ἀφικόμενος, ἣν οὐδ' ἂν μετέπεμψαν οἱ Συρακόσιοι, εἰ ἐκεῖνος εὐθὺς ἐπέκειτο. (7.42.3)

Demosthenes, perceiving the state of affairs, thought that he was not in a position to delay or to withstand what Nicias had suffered – for Nicias when he arrived at first was a source of fear, but since he did not straight away fall upon Syracuse, but instead stayed for the winter in Catana, he was discounted, and Gylippus, approaching from the Peloponnese, got ahead of him with his forces, which the Syracusans would not have summoned if [Nicias] had invested immediately.

This is the strongest criticism of Nicias' lack of initiative thus far, but it is not presented by the historian's persona; rather, it is cast in the sentiments of Demosthenes, a fellow officer with a very different opinion as to how the war should be conducted (cf. 7.42.4–5). Demosthenes, however, is also thwarted. His hasty attack brings on the disastrous night battle for Epipolae, and "the Athenians," to whom the combat is exclusively ascribed once battle is joined, suffer a terrible defeat (7.43.3–46.1). Thucydides' construction of the entire sequence strongly implies that if Nicias does not have the right solution, neither does Demosthenes. The *dêmos* cannot appreciate either the scope of the larger endeavor it has undertaken (cf. 6.1.1–32.2 *passim*) or the immediate situation, and the expedition is foundering.

Nicias' difficult relationship with the *dêmos* is highlighted again as he and Demosthenes discuss withdrawing the Athenian forces. Demosthenes' arguments are purely strategic and practical: escape and travel are currently still possible; Athens needs to concentrate upon Decelea; the Syracusans are no longer easy prey; the expedition is creating a financial drain (7.47.3–4). But Nicias' concerns are very different: although he is weighing intelligence information (7.48.1–2) and "still wavering between the two alternatives" (7.48.3), he refuses to withdraw. He cites his fear of the Assembly, including the concern that the personal safety and even the lives of the generals may be in jeopardy if they pull back without permission (7.48.3–4). His interpretation once again assigns the responsibility for the expedition, and even for its possible destruction, to the *dêmos*; and yet, his regard for his own well-being informs his choice to stay.

This very choice, more than any other, might invite the understanding of Nicias as a historical agent. Had he not been so careful in referring all action to the *dêmos*, had he not been able to convince Demosthenes and Eurymedon to remain at Syracuse (7.49.3–4), had he not surrendered to scruple after the eclipse of the moon (7.50.3–4), the Athenian forces might have been able to attempt an earlier escape. But even now Thucydides does not assign responsibility for the situation to Nicias alone. Demosthenes and Eurymedon are said to suspect that Nicias' commitment is actually due to secret intelligence (7.49.4), and Nicias' discomfort with the lunar omens is shared by the majority of the soldiers (7.50.4). The historian is again working to shift responsibility and historical agency towards the Athenian populace, and away from its problematic general.

As the final battle in the Great Harbor of Syracuse draws near, Thucydides pauses to review the combatants (7.57.1–59.1). Such an iteration was estab-lished as a paradigm by the Homeric 'Catalog of Ships' (*Il.* 2.484–877), and was employed at various points in Herodotus.[64] Thucydides' list, however, does not reflect the complex role played by individual historical agents in his text: it mentions none of the generals by name.[65] There would have been good precedent for the naming of commanders: Thucydides has by now made the mention of leaders on campaigns almost routine[66] (at least prior to the joining of battle), and the Homeric catalog dwells luxuriantly upon the names of kings and warriors. Thucydides' decision here may pos-sibly be attributed to the influence of Herodotus, who tends to cast both combatants and catalogs either in ethnic plurals or in poleis groups. But Thucydides has been working throughout to place responsibility for the Sicilian expedition squarely upon the Athenian *dêmos*, and naming "the Athenians" as chief combatants on the eve of the battle reinforces that interpretation.

Thucydides does give Nicias the expected speech (7.61.1–64.2) before the final struggle in the Great Harbor begins. But it is followed by a narrative that produces a certain sense of irony. After Nicias orders the ships to be boarded, (7.65.1), attention shifts to Gylippus and his Syracusan allies (7.65.1–69.1). Nicias reappears to offer one more word to the trierarchs (7.69.2), then stations the infantry along the beach as a show of support (7.69.3). Only then is the command structure for the Athenian side outlined: Demosthenes, Menander, and Euthydemus will be on board the ships to serve as admirals (7.69.4); Nicias will literally be watching from the sidelines.

The battle is a disaster for the Athenians. The naval combatants are driven back to shore and retreat in chaos towards their damaged fortifications; there is no mention of any guidance from their commanders (7.71.5–7). When Demosthenes and Nicias attempt to regroup for a dawn escape by

---

[64] See Chapter 3, above.

[65] This pose is maintained through what appears to be a deliberate circumlocution once the Peloponnesian contingent is listed: Λακεδαιμόνιοι μὲν ἡγεμόνα Σπαρτιάτην παρεχόμενοι (7.58.3), "the Lacedaemonians, who provided a Spartan leader" (referring to Gylippus).

[66] See note 7, above.

sea, the stricken troops will not obey them (7.72.4–5). For Thucydides, the massed, anonymous force of "the Athenians" on the Sicilian expedition functions as an effective extension of the power, authority, and activity of the Athenian *dêmos*, and he intentionally limits the individual agency of Nicias in order to highlight the collective agency of the Athenian citizenry. The sailors' refusal to fight is therefore pivotal: it 'proves' that the generals, and particularly Nicias, are not solely responsible for the disastrous decision to retreat overland. The troops have forced the issue, and the *dêmos*, by extension, has pulled *itself* still closer to its own destruction.

The connection between the army trapped in Sicily and the *dêmos* back in Athens is reiterated as the retreat begins (7.75.2).[67] Thucydides emphasizes the link by recollecting (ibid.) the "hope" once explicitly shared by the *dêmos* and the military forces,[68] and by comparing the army on the march to a defeated polis driven from its home (7.75.5, cf. also 7.77.4, by Nicias). Adding to the pathos is the futile encouragement offered by one of the only individuals who remains to lead this lost 'city': Nicias presents one final speech (7.77.1–7). After Thucydides' detailed efforts to portray Nicias as no more than a performer of the flawed decisions of the Athenian *dêmos*, this speech is ironic in several ways. Firstly, its content is largely speculative and empty: perhaps it is time for fortune to turn (7.77.3); any envy from the gods has likely been satisfied by Athenian sufferings (7.77.3); there is some safety in numbers (7.77.4–5); the Sicels are sufficiently afraid of the Syracusans to assist the Athenians (7.77.6). Of particular note, however, is Nicias' admission that his own condition has reversed:

> κἀγώ τοι . . . οὔτ᾽ εὐτυχίᾳ δοκῶν που ὕστερός του εἶναι κατά τε τὸν ἴδιον βίον καὶ ἐς τὰ ἄλλα, νῦν ἐν τῷ αὐτῷ κινδύνῳ τοῖς φαυλοτάτοις αἰωροῦμαι. (7.77.2)

> And even I, who seem, I think, to rank below no one else's good luck in my private life or in any other respect, am now caught up in the same peril as the most ordinary [soldiers].

The rhetorical pose is likely intended as that of the general who experiences hardships alongside his men, but in context it means something different. Nicias has throughout the Sicilian expedition functioned not as a self-sufficient leader, but rather as an extension of the will of the *dêmos*.

---

[67] This is later the perception of the *dêmos* as well: 8.1.1–2.

[68] Particularly as the expedition was organized and departed: see 6.24.3, 30.2, 31.6, in all instances incorporating forms of the same word, ἐλπίς. Cf. also the explicit contrast of the mood of the retreat with the mood of the departure at 7.75.7.

Now he has been absorbed into what remains of the *dêmos* in Sicily. There essentially never was an individual historical agent present on this journey to work in concert with "the Athenians," and Nicias has at last acknowledged the situation openly.

Nicias' last speech also explicitly disavows an important model of individual historical agency known from other cultural contexts: that of the colonial founder.[69] While colonial expeditions typically sought divine sanction, particularly from Delphi, Nicias suggests that divine hostility has affected the Athenian forces in Sicily (7.77.3). His idea, noted above, that the army on the march could potentially become a polis if it were to settle down (7.77.4) is cast entirely in the second-person plural, with no hint that he himself would volunteer as the leader of such a polis. He closes this part of his speech by explicitly placing responsibility for their progress upon the men themselves, both individually and as a group (7.77.5), adding that a successful battle will provide them with both πατρίδα καὶ τεῖχος, "fatherland and refuge," there in Sicily (7.77.5). But their potential new πατρίς, their imagined colony, has no leader named, either for its moment of immediate crisis or for its future. Nicias, in fact, makes no reference to himself for the remainder of his speech, save his use of two first-person plurals to discuss the army's lack of resources and the possibility of its moving to a safer area (7.77.6).

It is perhaps not surprising, then, that in the end, during the final struggle at the Assinaurus, a breakdown in discipline ensures the massacre of Nicias' army. With some of the men desperate for water and others attempting to ford the crossing too quickly, the lines collapse, and the slaughter commences (7.84.3–5). Nicias surrenders his command and relinquishes any possibility of heroic individual action. Even his final attempt to sacrifice himself to save the lives of his men (7.85.1–2) is unsuccessful: the prisoners, rather than being ransomed, are subjected to fearful suffering in the quarries of Syracuse, where many of them perish and the remainder are enslaved (7.87.1–4). Nicias' own end is quick and without ceremony (7.86.2–4), but Thucydides provides a particularly telling closing comment:

> καὶ ὁ μὲν [Νικίας] . . . ἐτεθνήκει, ἥκιστα δὴ ἄξιος ὢν τῶν γε ἐπ' ἐμοῦ Ἑλλήνων ἐς τοῦτο δυστυχίας ἀφικέσθαι διὰ τὴν πᾶσαν ἐς ἀρετὴν νενομισμένην ἐπιτήδευσιν. (7.86.5)

> And so Nicias . . . died. Indeed, he was the least worthy of the Greeks of my time to experience such misfortune, because of his consistent dedication to virtue.

---

[69] On the typical features of the colonial foundation experience, see Chapter 2, above.

The reader, whether ancient or modern, has likely been tempted by the sequence of events to place at least some of the blame for the Sicilian disaster upon Nicias.[70] Thucydides, however, here suggests once more in the emphatic voice of the historian[71] that one should not. The Athenian *dêmos* has been the true agent of this history-making event, and Nicias has served almost exclusively as its messenger.

πρῶτον μὲν οὖν περὶ Ἀλκιβιάδου τίν' ἔχετον γνώμην ἑκάτερος;[72]

Alcibiades makes his initial appearance in Thucydides' narrative at 5.43.1. He is prominently featured in the diplomatic maneuvers in the Peloponnese throughout the remainder of book 5,[73] and in the events surrounding the launch of the Sicilian expedition in book 6 (6.12.2–61.7, *passim*).[74] Despite the amount of attention he receives earlier in the war, however, the first time Alcibiades is actually presented in a history-making role that involves his extended interaction with the group agency of the Athenian *dêmos* is during the oligarchic coup in book 8.[75] At the climactic moment, while still technically in exile himself, he is able to prevent the democratically inclined navy at Samos from attacking its own home city:

> καὶ δοκεῖ Ἀλκιβιάδης πρῶτον[76] τότε καὶ οὐδενὸς ἔλασσον τὴν πόλιν ὠφελῆ-
> σαι· ὡρμημένων γὰρ τῶν ἐν Σάμῳ Ἀθηναίων πλεῖν ἐπὶ σφᾶς αὐτούς, ἐν

---

[70] Gomme, Andrewes, and Dover, for example, do wish to assign some of this blame to Nicias: see note 61, above.

[71] First-person interjections in the voice of the historian, such as this one, are much rarer in Thucydides than they are, for example, in Herodotus (e.g. Marincola 1987), but see Gribble 1998, who contends that the historian's voice can be accessed within Thucydides' text in spite of the general third-person presentation.

[72] "So first, regarding Alcibiades, what opinion does each of you have?" (Ar. *Ran.* 1422–3).

[73] On the general historical ineffectiveness of Alcibiades' machinations during this time, see Bloedow 1973: 3–8, 12, with references.

[74] The history-making impact of Alcibiades upon the Sicilian expedition, *as implied by Thucydides* (the distinction is important in the context of the current argument), is essentially that created by his absence from it: cf. the treatment of his role in the debate and in the earliest days of the expedition covered in the discussion of Nicias, above, and the reading of Gomme, Andrewes, and Dover 1981: vol. V, 423–5, 427. Bloedow 1973: 11–13 maintains that in the 'real' world Alcibiades' prospects for history-making success in Sicily were slim in any case.

[75] Bloedow 1973: 18–19, with references, argues that Alcibiades should not be accorded sole credit (or blame) for the Spartans' sending Gylippus to Sicily. Gomme 1945–56: vol. 3, 680 *ad* 5.19.2 points out that it may be significant that Alcibiades' name is omitted from Thucydides' list of Athenian witnesses to the Peace of Nicias (5.18.1–19.2) and wonders, "Had he been passed over as delegate, as too young or too irresponsible? Had he refused? Or was he busy with some private and lawless affair of his own?" In any case, the net effect is to minimize Alcibiades' position at a moment of high interest.

[76] πρῶτον in MS B as here, πρῶτος in others; on this textual problem, see Gomme, Andrewes, and Dover 1981: vol. V, 286–7 *ad* 8.86.4. I am grateful to M. Flower for calling this issue to my attention.

ᾧ σαφέστατα Ἰωνίαν καὶ Ἑλλήσποντον εὐθὺς εἶχον οἱ πολέμιοι, κωλυτὴς γενέσθαι. καὶ ἐν τῷ τότε ἄλλος μὲν οὐδ’ ἂν εἷς ἱκανὸς ἐγένετο κατασχεῖν τὸν ὄχλον, ἐκεῖνος δὲ τοῦ τ’ ἐπίπλου ἔπαυσε καὶ τοὺς ἰδίᾳ τοῖς πρέσβεσιν ὀργιζομένους λοιδορῶν ἀπέτρεπεν. (8.86.4–5)

And Alcibiades seems to have first assisted the polis at that time, in a manner second to none. For when the Athenians in Samos were eager to sail against their own [fellow citizens], under which circumstances the enemy would straight away have seized Ionia and the Hellespont, [Alcibiades] stopped them. At a time when no one else would have been able to hold back the throng, he prevented their attack and, reprimanding them, directed away their personal anger at the emissaries.

How does Alcibiades' changing relationship with the *dêmos* in book 8 eventually allow him to assume the essential leadership position in which he clearly functions here?

At the point where the text previously took leave of Alcibiades, he was a fugitive from an Athenian death sentence (6.61.7) urging the Spartans to invade Attica and establish a base for their operations at Decelea (6.93.1). When he reappears at 8.6.3, he is still cooperating with the Spartans, negotiating for the Peloponnesian cause with the Persian satrap Tissaphernes and urging enemy operations against Athenian interests in the eastern Aegean. The narrative of these activities continues *passim* to 8.26.3, and is followed by coverage of military operations that do not explicitly involve Alcibiades. It is only after 8.45.1, therefore, when he once more switches allegiances and decides to support the Athenian cause again,[77] that Alcibiades' associations with the various subdivisions of the Athenian *dêmos* during the oligarchic coup[78] can be examined.

Here, for the first time in Thucydides' narrative, a prominent individual is observed reconstructing his relationship with his polis from the outside. Given Alcibiades' precarious personal and diplomatic position, it might be anticipated that any performance of history-making action in conjunction with his citizen group would be postponed until he could consolidate his authority with a formal recall and pardon. But Thucydides shows Alcibiades machinating for oligarchy precisely in order to facilitate his restoration (8.47.1–2), and then emphasizes that the coup is also the result of deeply scored divisions within the Athenian *dêmos* (8.47.2–48.1). The momentous

---

[77] Cf. also Alcibiades' advice to Tissaphernes at 8.46.3, i.e. that the Athenians would make more palatable – and pliable – partners for the Persians than would the Peloponnesians.

[78] Ending at 8.98.4 with the words καὶ ἡ ἐν ταῖς Ἀθήναις ὀλιγαρχία καὶ στάσις ἐπαύσατο, "and the oligarchy and the civil strife at Athens concluded."

suspension of the Athenian democracy will therefore be a significant historical event brought about, again, by the joint activities of individual and
group agents.

The assertion of shared individual and group responsibility for the coup,
coupled with the nature of the governmental change, prompts recollection
of the Athenian Revolution that originally brought the now-endangered
democracy to power. Thucydides himself draws the parallel at the moment
of the changeover to the oligarchic constitution:

> χαλεπὸν γὰρ ἦν τὸν Ἀθηναίων δῆμον ἐπ’ ἔτει ἑκατοστῷ μάλιστα ἐπειδὴ οἱ
> τύραννοι κατελύθησαν ἐλευθερίας παῦσαι, καὶ οὐ μόνον μὴ ὑπήκοον ὄντα,
> ἀλλὰ καὶ ὑπὲρ ἥμισυ τοῦ χρόνου τούτου αὐτὸν ἄλλων ἄρχειν εἰωθότα.
> (8.68.4)

> For [here] in the hundredth year or so since the tyrants had been expelled,
> it was challenging to take freedom away from the Athenian *dêmos*, not
> only because it had been sovereign [at home], but also because for half of
> this period it had grown used to having authority over others.

The famous act of the Tyrannicides, so closely associated in Athenian
thinking with the foundation of the democracy, had its meaning constantly
re-negotiated in art and literature throughout the fifth century. Ownership
of the history-making foundation of the democracy could be awarded to
Harmodius and Aristogeiton, but it could also be assigned to the Alcmeonids and the Spartans (as in Thucydides’ own view, 6.59.4), or even represented as the triumph of the collective will of the Athenian *dêmos*.[79] Like
the episode of the Tyrannicides, the story of the oligarchic coup, as Thucydides presents it, also pivots around an indispensable individual whose
role appears essential to the other players in the narrative: Alcibiades. What
he actually accomplishes, however, is not so significant as what others do
based upon their perceptions of him. The structure and content of Thucydides’ narrative reveal that the *reception* of an individual can be of even
greater historical moment than his own activities.

Alcibiades begins working for a coup by approaching the Athenians
posted at Samos, paying special attention to reaching a carefully chosen
audience of elites. He claims to possess influence with Tissaphernes, the
Persian satrap of Lydia and Caria – and, by spectacularly exaggerated extension, with the Persian king, who just might favor an Athenian oligarchy
(8.47.1–48.1). The prospect of oligarchic government is attractive to a certain sector of the military officers (8.48.2), and the potential support of

---

[79] See Ober 1996a esp. 40–6, 50–2.

Persian gold appeals to the rank and file (8.48.3). Both strata are apparently sufficiently charmed by the possibilities to lay aside the immense grounds they possess at this time for mistrusting Alcibiades.[80] Thucydides, perhaps by way of a reminder, casts the logical objections to both the plan and its designer in the skeptical mind of the Athenian general Phrynichus (8.48.4–7).

Phrynichus, however, is swiftly outmaneuvered by the pro-oligarchic contingent at Samos (8.49.1). His attempts to denounce Alcibiades to the Peloponnesians as a double agent backfire when the Peloponnesian general Astyochus himself becomes an informer in turn (8.50.1–51.3). At this point, Thucydides reports, μετὰ δὲ τοῦτο Ἀλκιβιάδης μὲν Τισσαφέρνην παρεσκεύαζε καὶ ἀνέπειθεν ὅπως φίλος ἔσται τοῖς Ἀθηναίοις, "After this Alcibiades was grooming Tissaphernes and convincing him to become friendly towards the Athenians" (8.52.1). The sense of the passage of time within the narrative has been enhanced by Thucydides' detailed coverage of the elaborate trap set for Phrynichus, and Alcibiades now appears somewhat late in his attempts. He may have to deliver upon at least certain of his exaggerated promises to the Athenians, and there is a new urgency to his negotiations: ἄτε περὶ μεγάλων ἀγωνιζόμενος, προθύμως τὸν Τισσαφέρνην θεραπεύων προσέκειτο, "as if in a contest over great things, [Alcibiades] was eagerly dedicating his attentions to Tissaphernes" (8.52.1). The vocabulary here is rich with associations:[81] the verb ἀγωνίζομαι is associated not merely with competition, but even with hard physical effort; the adverb προθύμως carries hints of energetic dedication; the verb θεραπεύω, whose root bears connotations of servitude, is also negatively associated with sycophancy in Attic prose; and the verb form προσέκειτο might perhaps even remind the reader's eye, particularly in this context, of the verb προσκυνέω, already used in both Aeschylus and Herodotus to depict the fawning *proskynesis* (ritual prostration) practiced by Persians, a behavior abhorrent to Greeks.

Even though Alcibiades has overstated his influence with the Persians, his plan for the coup moves forward. When Peisander's delegation from Samos reaches Athens, the same chain of argument based upon the same false premise is used to overcome objections both by enemies of oligarchy and by enemies of Alcibiades: the Athenians are outarmed, outmanned, and underfunded in the Aegean; only Persian money can provide the needed support; only Alcibiades can provide the Persians; and only a changeover to

---

[80] Alcibiades' escape and defection to the enemy during the Sicilian expedition (6.53.1–2, 61.1–7) would ostensibly have left him terribly suspect; see, however, Ar. *Ran.* 1422–32 on the love–hate relationship that Athens seems to have maintained with him.

[81] *LSJ ad loca.*

oligarchic government will enable him to do it (8.53.1–54.2). The latter two points have already been shown by Thucydides to be highly suspect, but the *dêmos* acquiesces nevertheless (8.54.1). Although Thucydides does not explicitly condemn the *dêmos* for yielding to Peisander on the diplomatic negotiations, the Assembly appears rather credulous just a single sentence later, when it falls easy prey to groundless charges against Phrynichus and abruptly removes him from his position as general (8.54.3). Phrynichus had served as Thucydides' mouthpiece (in indirect discourse) for the obvious initial objections to Alcibiades' plans (8.48.4–7). With him deposed, however, that strand of thought is symbolically silenced, and a lie is employed to clear the path for 'progress' based upon Alcibiades' misrepresentations and double-dealing.

Once the Athenian delegation returns to Tissaphernes, Alcibiades endeavors not to bring the two sides together, as he has been promising throughout, but to divide them in their interests (8.56.1–4). Afraid that he cannot persuade Tissaphernes to support the Athenians on rational terms, Alcibiades sabotages the negotiations by voicing absurd demands on behalf of the Persian side. At long last, the Athenians withdraw νομίσαντες ... ὑπὸ τοῦ Ἀλκιβιάδου ἐξηπατῆσθαι, "thinking ... that they had been misled by Alcibiades" (8.56.4).

Two narrative patterns are relevant here. Firstly, the Thucydidean model of the individual leader functioning as an essential catalyst (or at least as an agent) for the activities of the *dêmos* appears at this point to be broken down. Alcibiades' interests and those of the *dêmos* are not only different in scope and nature but also functionally independent (Alcibiades is neither an officer nor a delegate of the Athenians at this stage). Secondly, on a closer level of detail, Thucydides again (as in the account of the Assembly meeting with Peisander, 8.54.1–3) affixes to the conclusion of this passage a detail that casts what has preceded it in a negative light. As soon as the negotiations with the Athenians fail (as Alcibiades had ensured that they would), Tissaphernes returns to the Peloponnesians and concludes another treaty with them promising continued support for their naval operations in the Aegean (8.57.1–59.1). This event is in almost literal keeping with the advice that Thucydides earlier showed Alcibiades dispensing to Tissaphernes.[82] Its notice at this point shows, once again, that Alcibiades is untrustworthy in his claims to represent Athenian interests; it implies that the Athenians are unable to grasp the true complexities of the diplomatic situation; and

---

[82] 8.46.1–5, where Alcibiades proposed that it was in the Persians' best interests to ensure that the Greek belligerents on both sides continued to wear one another down.

it demonstrates the vast consequences that attach to the Athenian *dêmos'* perceptions of its relationship with a highly questionable individual.

Coverage of the oligarchic coup itself commences at 8.63.3, and Alcibiades is temporarily thrust aside. Still holding his native polis at arm's length, he refuses to join the oligarchic faction of Athenians at Samos, which comforts itself with the notion that Alcibiades οὐκ ἐπιτήδειον αὐτὸν εἶναι ἐς ὀλιγαρχίαν ἐλθεῖν, "was not an appropriate entrant into an oligarchy" (8.63.4). The treatment of the progress of the coup at Athens, however, also considers the interactions between individual and group historical agency. Even the oligarchs, it seems, recognize that the essential key to effective group action is collaboration with an eminent individual:

> καὶ καταλαμβάνουσι τὰ πλεῖστα τοῖς ἑταίροις προειργασμένα. καὶ γὰρ Ἀνδροκλέα τέ τινα τοῦ δήμου μάλιστα προεστῶτα ξυστάντες τινὲς τῶν νεωτέρων κρύφα ἀποκτείνουσιν, ὅσπερ καὶ τὸν Ἀλκιβιάδην οὐχ ἥκιστα ἐξήλασε, καὶ αὐτὸν κατ' ἀμφότερα, τῆς τε δημαγωγίας ἕνεκα καὶ οἰόμενοι τῷ Ἀλκιβιάδῃ ὡς κατιόντι καὶ τὸν Τισσαφέρνην φίλον ποιήσοντι χαριεῖσθαι, μᾶλλόν τι διέφθειραν. (8.65.2)

> And [at Athens the oligarchs traveling with Peisander] discovered that most things had been completed ahead of time by their comrades. After organizing, some of the younger men had secretly murdered Androcles, the most eminent leader of the *dêmos*, who was also the most responsible for the expulsion of Alcibiades. There were two reasons why they killed him: [firstly,] because of his demagoguery, and [secondly,] anticipating that it would please Alcibiades, since he was about to return and make Tissaphernes their ally.

The assassination of Androcles is supposed to fetter potential retaliation by the *dêmos*, but it is also intended to curry favor with Alcibiades, whom the oligarchs perceive to be essential to their long-term projects.

The fragmentation of the *dêmos*, a problem against which Pericles once warned (particularly in his final speech during the plague in book 2), now paralyzes it as the oligarchic coup progresses. The democratic leaders of the Assembly can no longer assist in converting scattered private sentiment into unified public discourse. Individuals hold personal opinions that their neighbors are unable to read, and the people are afraid to move on matters not previously approved by the oligarchs (8.66.1–5). On the opposite side, several men have already emerged to advance the oligarchic cause:

> ἦν δὲ ὁ μὲν τὴν γνώμην ταύτην εἰπὼν Πείσανδρος, καὶ τἄλλα ἐκ τοῦ προφανοῦς προθυμότατα ξυγκαταλύσας τὸν δῆμον· ὁ μέντοι ἅπαν τὸ πρᾶγμα ξυνθεὶς ὅτῳ τρόπῳ κατέστη ἐς τοῦτο καὶ ἐκ πλείστου ἐπιμεληθεὶς Ἀντιφῶν

ἦν ἀνὴρ Ἀθηναίων τῶν καθ᾽ ἑαυτὸν ἀρετῇ τε οὐδενὸς ὕστερος καὶ κράτιστος
ἐνθυμηθῆναι γενόμενος καὶ ἃ γνοίη εἰπεῖν. (8.68.1)

> Peisander was the one who made this motion, having been in other ways as
> well apparently the most eager to dissolve the democracy. But the one who,
> after figuring out how to do it, established the entire project towards this
> end and had the closest charge of it was Antiphon, a man in virtue second
> to none of the Athenians of his time, formidable both in his thinking and
> in speaking what he thought.

Phrynichus and Theramenes are mentioned elsewhere in this section as
prominent oligarchs (cf. 8.68.3–4), but Antiphon in particular is sketched
here in a manner that recalls the introductions of other significant Thucydidean characters.[83] The suggestion is that Athens' new government has
features in common with its old one, especially in that individual leaders are
essential for guiding the progress of the wider group at a time of significant
historical change. Thucydides' view of the motion of history, therefore,
does not appear to be confined to a particular constitutional framework; it
remains consistent even when the surface details shift.

When the Samian democrats learn that their government is also under
threat by a conspiracy of oligarchs, they, too, explicitly seek out individuals
who will provide leadership in their defense. Leon and Diomedon, both
Athenian generals, and Thrasybulus and Thrasyllus, Athenian naval and
infantry officers respectively, quickly organize a resistance movement that
not only preserves the Samians' democratic constitution, but also prefigures
events to come: the Athenian army at Samos will seek to maintain an
Athenian democracy in exile (8.73.1–75.3). In its need for the guidance of
individual leaders, however, the democratized army does not stop at electing
new officers (8.76.2); its members remind one another that Ἀλκιβιάδην τε,
ἢν αὐτῷ ἄδειάν τε καὶ κάθοδον ποιήσωσιν, ἄσμενον τὴν παρὰ βασιλέως
ξυμμαχίαν παρέξειν, "if they would provide him with amnesty and the
opportunity to return, Alcibiades would be pleased to furnish alliance with
the king" (8.76.7). No matter how empty the hope or how tendentious
the expectations, the perception of the power of Alcibiades still lingers on
amongst the democrats – just as it endured amongst the oligarchs.[84]

At 8.81.1, Alcibiades is at last granted some semblance of what he has
long been working for: The Athenian democracy-in-exile at Samos, tempted
by the prospect of Persian alliances and Persian money, finally votes for

---

[83] E.g. 1.139.4 (and cf. 1.127.3), on Pericles; 3.36.6, 4.22.3, on Cleon; cf. also Nicias at 7.77.2,
reflecting back upon his former status in a manner that recalls these kinds of introductions.

[84] Cf. the discussion of 8.65.2, above.

his recall. Brought to Samos, Alcibiades addresses the democratic assembly (8.81.2–3) in terms that differ very little from his speech prior to the Sicilian expedition in book 6. Like the earlier speech, this passage, cast in indirect discourse, indicates Alcibiades' preoccupation with his personal affairs (cf. 6.16.1–5), encourages unrealistic expectations (cf. especially 6.17.2–8, 18.4–5), and inspires emotional fervor (cf. 6.19.1). Its effect, too, is similar, for the aroused and credulous audience hastens to charge Alcibiades with the current enterprise (8.82.1); all too familiar, however, is Alcibiades' choice to place his private interests first. Once again he physically abandons the Athenians (if only for the time being) to seek his advantage with the Persians (8.82.2).

Shortly following his return from his visit to Tissaphernes, Alcibiades does Athens a service: When envoys from the oligarchs at Athens arrive at Samos, the angry democratic army wishes to immediately attack the Piraeus (8.86.1–4). Alcibiades calms the storm and dismisses the oligarchs without incident by voicing moderate hopes of eventual reconciliation (8.86.4–7). The larger coup narrative thus far does suggest some grounds for Thucydides' assertion that ἐν τῷ ... ἄλλος μὲν οὐδ' ἂν εἷς ἱκανὸς ἐγένετο κατασχεῖν τὸν ὄχλον, "at [that] time no one else would have been able to hold back the throng" (8.86.5). Thucydides has constructed throughout a coherent historiographic role for Alcibiades: whether or not his consequent actions appear to merit the position, he is now, as he was early in book 6, established in the role of the essential individual leader. The way in which he is *perceived* determines certain historically significant actions taken by the groups with which he interacts. He can now control the exiled portion of the Athenian *dêmos* that has both created and validated his leadership role by electing him general. His authority derives almost exclusively, as it has always done, from his image, and this image has gradually accumulated significant force.

While Alcibiades indulges in further empty negotiations with Tissaphernes (8.88.1), the power of the oligarchy at Athens begins to dissolve. Lingering fear of the democracy-in-exile and its maverick general leads a number of the oligarchs to plan a different path. As if they themselves have read the text in which they are appearing, these renegade oligarchs seek out the position of the leader supported by his citizen group that Thucydides has been depicting in various guises throughout the narrative:

> σαφέστατα δ' αὐτοὺς ἐπῆρε τὰ ἐν τῇ Σάμῳ τοῦ Ἀλκιβιάδου ἰσχυρὰ ὄντα
> καὶ ὅτι αὐτοῖς οὐκ ἐδόκει μόνιμον τὸ τῆς ὀλιγαρχίας ἔσεσθαι· ἠγωνίζετο οὖν
> εἷς ἕκαστος αὐτὸς πρῶτος προστάτης τοῦ δήμου γενέσθαι. (8.89.4)

> The strength that Alcibiades possessed at Samos in particular stirred them up – along with the fact that the oligarchy did not seem as if it would be permanent. And so each one of them struggled in competition to become the leading guardian of the *dêmos*.

The leadership model, like the coup itself, has now come full circle. Thucydides does not explicitly acknowledge a 'cycle of constitutions,' but he does imply some belief in constitutional patterning (see 8.89.3), foreshadowing the fall of the oligarchy and the effective re-establishment of the democracy with the rule of the Five Thousand (8.97.1–2, cf. 98.1–3). Likewise, the oligarchs who can foresee the destruction of their government are here seeking to occupy positions within the democracy similar to that once enjoyed by Pericles. That particular place, however, is apparently already reserved for the individual who has managed in the course of the coup to reinvent his relationship with his citizen group. In the sharpest possible contrast to Pericles, this leader has essentially managed to make history merely by making images, and in whatever form his government still believes him essential to its success. One of the first actions of the new government of the Five Thousand, therefore, is to formally recall Alcibiades to Athens.

Thucydides' indispensable individuals in their wider cultural context

Westlake has shown that Thucydides' portrait-studies of individual political and military figures are of key importance for unveiling general meaning and structure within his text.[85] The *relationships* between eminent individuals and the Athenian *dêmos*, however, allow exploration of Thucydidean conceptions of historical agency in greater detail. From the guiding hand of Pericles to the distanced performance of Nicias; from the unsupported Cleon, dispatched to Pylos almost as a joke, to the mythologized Alcibiades, credited with power (and altruism) that he does not actually possess, these four men represent a spectrum of ways in which leaders can interact with the Athenian *dêmos* to make history. The Greek individual is foregrounded in Thucydides in a way that he was not in Herodotus: within the world of historiography, at least, "the Athenians" cannot function without him.

This growing concern for the discussion, accreditation, and memorialization of the individual is also discernible at Athens outside of historical writing. During the last third of the fifth century BC, the commemorative vocabulary of the polis witnesses a notable growth in both the

---

[85] Westlake 1968.

public and the private spheres.[86] The artificial sense of equality visible in certain funerary and other monuments of the earlier generations of the democracy is now significantly challenged by efforts to acknowledge the lifetime contributions, on both larger and smaller scales, of individual Athenians.

4.3 Individuals and groups in the commemorative vocabulary of late fifth-century Athens (*c.* 440–396)

Following the Persian Wars, as discussed in Chapter 2, above, Athenian funerary commemoration seems to have maintained for several decades a general façade of democratic sameness.[87] Most individual Athenian tombstones between *c.* 480 and 440 BC lack significant decorative elements: in particular, unlike their archaic predecessors, they do not employ figured relief sculpture. Probably near the end of the 430s,[88] however, figured reliefs reappear in comparative abundance.[89] Their proliferation suggests an increasing emphasis on the memorialization of the individual, and their epitaphs sometimes indicate active contemplation of the historical impact of an individual life.[90] These same tendencies are also visible in other Athenian commemorative efforts, particularly in certain types of public inscriptions.[91] In their breadth and their variety, then, the civic and the private monuments suggest that active appeals for particular kinds of memorialization were understood widely enough to make them worth, at least for the time being,

---

[86] The distinction drawn here between "public" and "private" is generally intended to represent commemoration at state, tribe, or deme expense on the one hand vs. clan, family, or friend expense on the other.

[87] See Chapter 2, above.

[88] Perhaps coincidental with or even because of the outbreak of the Peloponnesian War: Clairmont 1993: intro. 13 and n. 4.

[89] E.g. Clairmont 1993: 12–13; Stupperich 1977: 71–87; Clairmont 1970: 41–5; Friis Johansen 1951: 146.

[90] The distinction between the 'timeless' attitudes represented by archaic funerary monuments and epitaphs as opposed to the historically grounded memorials that appear in the fifth and fourth centuries is important: see the discussion in Chapter 2, above.

[91] Morris 1994 suggests (at 67) that "[in] the whole Greek world, a generally egalitarian fifth-century ideology began to break up" after about 430, and that this is significantly reflected in changes in funerary commemoration. Morris 1992: 149–53 proposes thinking about these processes as representing a complex and not always linear evolution from a group-centered to an individual-centered ethos, and I think that Morris is quite correct about this broader pattern: the distinction that I make here is to read certain of these funerary changes, both at Athens and elsewhere (see esp. Chapter 6, below) for reflections upon historical agency, and to consider how ideas about history may have affected – and been affected by – habits of memorialization, both funerary and otherwise.

the social, economic, and political currency that was expended upon them. They also provide evidence that the tension between individual and group agency and authority at Athens was showing no signs of resolution during the Peloponnesian War.

Public inscriptions and honorific decrees

The epigraphical prescript formulae of the Athenian democratic government do not change significantly in the course of the fifth century: The solo voice of the proposer of the decree is still juxtaposed with the unified chorus of the ratifying democracy. The general content of the Athenian public epigraphical corpus, however, does shift somewhat before and during the Peloponnesian War. Inscriptions dealing with the business and administration of the Athenian Empire are naturally more common in the archaeological record after the 450s.[92] A possible corollary to this development, however, is the increase over time of expressions of official gratitude to individuals who have performed useful economic, political, or even religious service for the *dêmos* and its subjects. The extant examples of such inscriptions from the fifth century are offered to foreigners, especially *proxenoi*,[93] but by the fourth century there are also examples of honors to Athenian citizens.[94]

A metaphorical intermediary between the honors awarded to foreigners and those awarded to citizens is the official grant of Athenian citizenship, presented by the state to outsiders as an act of appreciation in return for benefaction to the *dêmos*. The earliest securely known and dated decree of this type whose inscription survives is from 410/9;[95] though fragmentary, it records the extension of citizenship to Thrasybulus of Calydon:[96]

---

[92] Hedrick 1999: 399–400, esp. nn. 54–5, 59.

[93] Walbank 1978: ix–xiv lists sixteen possible proxenies of Athens whose earliest likely dates fall before 450, and seventy-eight whose likely dates fall between 450 and 400 (sixty-eight of these proxenies were attested by inscriptions, nine by literary testimonia, and seventeen by next-generation documentation, ibid. vi). Cf. also below on the prominence of *proxenoi* in the corpus of Attic document reliefs, particularly during the fifth century.

[94] These first appear in the archaeological record after the Peloponnesian War and continue to proliferate during the first three quarters of the fourth century: Henry 1983: 13, 22–3; cf. also Chapters 5 and 6, below.

[95] Walbank 1978: 487–8 cites two possible citizenship grants that may be earlier: one to Corinthi[acus?] and his sons (*IG* i³ 158), and one to Evagoras, king of Salamis in Cyprus (*IG* i³ 113), but the former is too badly damaged to offer a complete guarantee of its content (see Walbank 2008: 137 n. 30, noting that Corinthi[acus?] is "apparently granted citizenship") and the latter's date can only be approximated to *c*. 411/10.

[96] Edition from *IG* i³ 102 (cf. the comments of Henry 1983: 64 on the restorations); translation from Fornara 1983b: 183–5 no. 155. Meiggs and Lewis 1969: 261–2 no. 85 present a slightly different version of the text.

[ἐπὶ Γλαυκί]π π ο ἄ [ρ] χ ο ν [τ] ο ς.
[Λ ό β ο ν ἐ κ] Κ ε δ ῶ ν ἐ γ ρ α μ μ ά τ ε υ ε.
[ἔδοχσεν τῖ] βολῖ καὶ τῖι δέμοι· hιπποθοντὶ-
[ς ἐπρυτάνε]υε, Λόβον ἐγραμμάτευε, Φιλιστίδε-
5   [ς ἐπεστάτε,] Γλαύκιππος ἔρχε : Ἐρασινίδες εἶπ-
[ε· ἐπαινέσα]ι Θρασύβολον ός ὄντα ἄνδρα ἀγαθὸ-
[ν περὶ τὸν δῖμ]ον τὸν Ἀθεναίον καὶ πρόθυμον π-
[οιῖν hό τι δύνα]ται ἀγαθόν· καὶ ἀντὶ ὅν εὖ πεπο-
[ίεκεν τέν τε πόλιν] καὶ τὸν δῖμ[ο]ν τὸν Ἀθεναίο-
10   [ν στεφανõσαι αὐτὸν χρυσõι στε]φάνοι, ποιῖσα-
[ι δὲ τὸν στέφανον ἀπὸ χιλίον δρ]αχμõν· hοι [δὲ h]-
[ελλενοταμίαι δόντον τὸ ἀργύρι]ον. καὶ [ἀνειπ]-
[ῖν τὸν κέρυκα Διονυσίον ἐν τõι] ἀγõνι hõν hέν-
[εκα αὐτὸν hο δῖμος ἐστεφάνοσ]ε ⁝ Διοκλῖς εἶπε·
15   [τὰ μὲν ἄλλα καθάπερ τῖ βολῖ·] εἶναι δὲ Θρασύ-
[βολον Ἀθεναῖον, καὶ φυλῖς τε κ]αὶ φρατρίας hõ-
[ν ἄν βόλεται γράφσασθαι αὐτό]ν· καὶ τἆλλα τὰ ἐ-
[φσεφισμένα τõι δέμοι κύρια ἔ]ναι Θρασυβόλο-
[ι· ἔναι δὲ αὐτõι εὑρίσκεσθαι π]αρὰ Ἀθεναίον κ-
20   [αὶ ἄλλο hό τι ἂν δοκῖ ἀγαθὸν π]ερὶ hõν εὐεργέ-
[τεκεν τὸν δῖμον τὸν Ἀθεναίον.] καὶ ἀναγραφσά-
[το hο γραμματεὺς τὰ ἐφσεφισμ]ένα· hελέσθαι δ-
[ὲ ἐγ βολῖς πέντε ἄνδρας αὐτί]κα μάλα, hοίτινε-
[ς] δι[κάσοσι Θρασυβόλοι τὸ μέ]ρος τὸ γιγνόμεν-
25   ον. τὸς [δὲ ἄλλος, hόσοι τότε εὖ ἐ]ποίεσαν τὸν δῖμον τὸν Ἀθε[ναίον,.....¹⁰.....]ιν καὶ Ἀγόρατο-
ν καὶ Κόμονα [καὶ...⁶...]ο[.]ο[....] καὶ Σῖμον κα-
ὶ Φιλῖνον κα[ὶ....⁸....]α, εὐεργέ[τα]ς [ἀ]ναγράφ-
σαι ἐμ πόλε[ι ἐν στέλει λ]ιθίνει τὸν γραμ[μα]τέ-
30   α τῖς βολῖς. [καὶ ἔγκτεσι]ν εἶναι αὐτοῖς õμπερ
Ἀθεναίοις, [καὶ γεπέδο]ν καὶ οἰκίας, καὶ οἴκεσ-
ιν Ἀθένεσι, [καὶ ἐπιμέλ]εσθαι αὐτõν τὲν βολὲν
τὲν αἰεὶ β[ολεύοσαν κα]ὶ τὸς πρυτάνες, hόπος ἄ-
ν μὲ ἀδι[κõνται. τὲν δὲ σ]τέλεν ἀπομισθοσάντο-
35   [ν hοι πολεταὶ ἐν τῖ βο]λῖ· τὸς δὲ hελλενοταμ-
[ίας δõναι τὸ ἀργύριον]. ἐὰν δὲ δοκῖ αὐτὸς καὶ
[ἄλλο εὑρίσκεσθαι, τὲν] βολὲν προβολεύσασαν
[ἐχσενεγκῖν ἐς τὸν δῖμ]ον : Εὔδικος εἶπε· τὰ μὲν
[ἄλλα καθάπερ Διοκλῖς· περὶ] δὲ τῶν δοροδοκεσ-
40   [άντον ἐπὶ τõι φσεφίσματι], ὃ ἐφσεφ[ί]σθε Ἀπολλ-
[οδόροι, τὲν βολὲν βολεῦσ]αι ἐν τῖ πρότει hέδ-
[ραι ἐν τõι βουλευτερί]οι, καὶ κολάζεν, τõν [δ]ορο-
[δοκεσάντον καταφσ]εφιζομένεν καὶ ἐς δικασ-

[τέριον παραδιδõσα]ν, καθότι ἂν δοκε̃ι αὐτε̃[ι]· τ-

45 [ὸς δὲ βολευτὰς τὸς] παρόντας ἀποφαίνεν ἡά[ττ᾽]

[ἂν εἰδõσιν, καὶ ἐάν] τίς τι ἄλλο εἰδε̃ι περὶ τ[ού]-

[τον· ἐχσε̃ναι δὲ καὶ] ἰδιότει, ἐάν τις βόλετα[ι ᵛ]

vacat

[In Glauki]ppos' *archonship* (410/9). | [Lobon of] Kedoi was Secre-
tary. | [Resolved by the] Boule and the People, Hippothonti|s *held the*

5 *prytany*, Lobon was Secretary, Philistide||s [presided], Glaukippos was
Archon. Erasinides made the motio|n: Thrasyboulos [shall be com-
mended] since he is a good man | [toward the] *People* of the Athen-
ians and zealous [t|o do whatever] good [he can]. In return for the

10 good he has d|one [to both the city] and the *People* of the Athenian||s,
[he shall be crowned with a golden] *crown*, [and] they *shall* mak|e [the
crown (at a cost of) one thousand] *drachmas*. The [H|ellenotamiai are
to provide the money. Proclamation shall be made by the herald, at
the Dionysia(?) during the] festival, of the *rea|sons* [why the People

15 [gave him a crown]. Diokles moved: || Let all the rest be as the Boule
(proposed)], but Thrasy|[boulos] shall be [an Athenian (citizen); and
in whatever tribe] *and* phratry | [he prefers, he shall be enrolled], and
the other things which [h|ave been voted by the People] *shall be* [valid]
for Thrasyboulo|s. [It shall be permissible for him to acquire] *from* the

20 Athenians || [in addition any other thing which seems good to them]
on account of his *good d|eeds* [toward the People of the Athenians].
And a record shall be set | up [by the Secretary of what has been de-
creed]. There shall be elected | [five men from among the Boule]
immediately, wh|o [are to] *determine* [what Thrasyboulos'] *portion*

25 shall b||e. The [others who at that time] *benefited* the Peo|ple of the
Athe[nians – 10 -]is and Agorato|s and Komon [and – 13 –] and Simon
an|d Philinos *and* [– 9 –], they shall as benefactors be record|ed on the
Akropolis [on a stele of] *marble* by the Secretar||y of the Boule. [The
(same) right of owning land] shall be theirs which | Athenians (pos-

sess), [both plots of land] and houses,[97] and a residen|ce in Athens, and
they shall be *entrusted to the care* of the Boule | at any given time *in
office, and* to the Prytaneis, so that they ma|y not *suffer harm*. [The]

35 stele shall be let out for contrac||t [by the Poletai in the] *Boule*. The
Hellenotam|iai [shall provide the money]. If it is decided that they are
also | [to receive other (benefits), the] Boule, after having formulated a
preliminary decree, | [shall bring it before the People]. Eudikos made
the motion: Let all the rest | [be as Diokles (moved), but as to] those

---

[97] See the difficulties regarding property-grants in this and other situations described by Meiggs
and Lewis 1969: 263, with bibliography.

40   who brib‖ed [for the sake of the degree] which was voted for Apol-
        l‖[odoros, the Boule shall deliberate in its first *sess*|*ion* [in the Bouleu-
        terion], and it shall exact punishment, with those who were *brib*|*ed*
        being condemned and [handed over] to a *cou*|*rt* in accordance with
45   what seems best to it. *T*‖ *he* [Bouleutai who] are present shall reveal
        what|*ever* [they know (about the affair) and (so shall)] anyone (else)
        who knows anything further about *i*|*t* [– 12 –] private person (to testify)
        if anyone wishes.

The precise service that Thrasybulus is believed to have provided to the
Athenian *dêmos*, while not mentioned in the decree, is the assassination
of Phrynichus during the oligarchic coup of 411.[98] As Meiggs and Lewis
explain, however, the fifth- and fourth-century testimonia about Thrasybulus that they have collected present variations on the events. Thucydides
attributes the murder of Phrynichus to a border guard, although he also
says that there were intimations of a larger plot (8.92.2). Lysias makes Apollodorus a conspirator but a bystander to the killing (Lys. 13.71); finally,
Lycurgus assigns Apollodorus a share in the actual assassination (Lycurg.
Leocr. 112).[99] The narrative of the death of Phrynichus, then, seems to have
been refined, corrected, and perhaps even massaged during the century that
followed it. Even as early as the inscription date of the second amendment
to the decree (lines 38–47), there are hints that credit may have been sought
where it was not unanimously perceived to be due. Lines 39–40 imply that
honors may have been sought for Apollodorus through corrupt means,[100]
and line 42 explicitly calls for punishment if it is needed. What rehabilitated
Apollodorus' reputation between the time of the decree and the time of
Lycurgus is unknown, but the total picture shows, significantly, that it is
the *memory* of an event, negotiated over time, that often determines its
long-term meaning.[101]

The citizenship decree as a general concept also represents elaborate
symbolic negotiation between the historical agency of the individual and
that of the group. The new citizen is elevated by both the fact and the content
of the decree as being separate from his peers, in that he has distinguished
himself both from the other members of his own polis or *ethnos*[102] and

---

[98] See above on Alcibiades for a discussion of the oligarchic coup and of Phrynichus.
[99] Meiggs and Lewis 1969: 262.   [100] Ibid. 263.
[101] Cf. Chapter 2, above, on the reception of the Tyrannicides. The historical significance of the
      assassination of Phrynichus, too, only gradually became clear, as his death intensified the call
      to abolish the government of the Four Hundred and permit the Five Thousand to rule: Thuc.
      8.92.2–11.
[102] "Tribe," "nation," or "group" (see *LSJ ad loc.*), understood by the Athenians as a non-polis
      form of local belonging.

from the Athenian *dêmos* that has chosen to honor him. The outstanding individual, however, is enrolled by the typical citizenship decree into a tribe, a deme, and a phratry,[103] and by this action is officially incorporated into the *dêmos*. He has thereby relinquished not only the status of 'other' but also the status of individual. His independent activities have benefited the *dêmos* in the past, and it has responded by offering its highest honor – full membership in its own body – but this very honor also represents a subtle claim to the *dêmos*' agency and authority. Even as it is becoming increasingly dependent upon the benefactions of individuals, the *dêmos* draws such men into itself, transforming their unusual distinction into a productive form of public service.[104] The foreigner's favor is returned to him in a most democratically acceptable guise, and his past assistance is even rewritten by the grant of citizenship into what may now be understood as a *leiturgia*.[105]

Attic document reliefs

'Document reliefs,' occasionally commissioned to record official governmental transactions, most frequently treaties or honorific decrees,[106] also increase in the archaeological record at Athens in the late fifth century. These monuments are flat, rectangular stone stelai that carry carved stone reliefs in their upper sections and inscriptions in their lower ones. The reliefs themselves are most frequently of deities (especially Athena), heroes (often the eponymous ones of the Athenian tribes), or personifications of concepts such as *Dêmos*, but some also depict the individuals whom they mention, usually the recipients of honors.[107]

The subject matter of the extant document reliefs diversifies over time. Many examples from the late fifth century are centrally concerned with the

---

[103] Henry 1983: 69 (with references) notes that two early examples of the citizenship grant, that made to Thrasybulus (*IG* i³ 102) and *IG* ii² 17, lack one of these enrollments; the former omits a deme and the latter a phratry (although there is space for the word itself in a lacuna, and Kirchner ventures the supplement).

[104] My thinking on this point has been influenced by Kurke's 1991 analysis of the negotiative and redemptive functions of Pindaric poetry. Kurke reads the poems, in part, as a means of symbolically reincorporating the elite (and potentially divisive) athletic victor into his household, social class, and polis as a source of productivity and civic pride.

[105] "Liturgy," a form of public service assigned to wealthy members of the Athenian *dêmos*.

[106] Lawton 1995: 5–10. Lawton further relates that other subjects represented much less frequently in the extant document reliefs include accounts and inventories (frequently of sacred treasury boards), cult administration, public dedications in thanks for victories, and a small handful of laws and oaths.

[107] Description summarized from ibid. 40–62.

business and the interests of the Athenian Empire:[108] of the fourteen (possibly fifteen) reliefs securely and the twenty-one reliefs approximately dated by Lawton to this period,[109] at least sixteen certainly or likely deal with imperial transactions or interstate relationships during the Peloponnesian War.[110] A handful, however, explicitly commemorate or honor individuals.[111] These special monuments all appear to have been dedicated to foreigners, specifically (where determinable) *proxenoi*.[112] As with the funerary monuments of the middle years of the fifth century, and with the honorific decrees during the Peloponnesian War, then, the most prominent exceptions to democratic sameness and equality seem to belong to non-citizens.[113]

Lawton's nos. 65 (= *IG* i³ 65, probably 427 BC), dedicated to Apollonophanes of Colophon, and 10 (= *IG* i³ 125, 405/4 BC), for Epicerdes of Cyrene, possess more extensive and better-preserved texts and reliefs than the other examples of their kind and era. Their prescripts and certain features of their contents are formulaic, but their emphasis upon the benefactions of individual agents recalls certain features of the mid fifth-century epitaphs for Pythagoras and Pythion (Chapter 2, above).

Lawton's no. 65 reads as follows:[114]

[Ἀ π ο λ λ] ο ν ο φ ά ν ο ς τ ὅ
[. . . ⁶ . . .] θ ο ς Κ ο λ ο φ ο ν [ί ο].

lacuna

[. . . . . ¹⁰ . . . . .]ν[. . . . . ¹⁹ . . . .]
[. . . . . . ¹¹ . . . . .]α[. . . . . ¹⁸ . . . .]
5   [. . . τὸ δὲ φσέ]φ[ι]σ[μα τό]δε ἀνα[γράφσαι τ]-
[ὸγ γραμματ]έα [τἒ]ς [βο]λἒς ἐν σ[τέ]λει λ[ίθ]-
[ίνει καὶ κα]τ[αθ]ἒγ[αι] ἐμ πόλ[ει]. ᵛ Ἀντικλ-

---

108 Ibid. 6, 19–21. I follow Lawton in accepting Mattingly's arguments (to Lawton's references add also Mattingly 1992) for the dating of the three earliest document reliefs, thereby placing the entire corpus (most likely) after *c.* 430. Lawton's comment upon the evolution of the genre is also well taken: "Overall, the context and the consistent emphasis upon diplomatic concord in early document reliefs indicates that their origin was political, and it appears that it was the coincidence of Athenian propagandistic concerns and the revival of relief sculpture in Athens that brought about the practice of putting reliefs on inscribed public documents" (21).

109 Ibid. 81–90, nos. 1–15, and 112–22, nos. 63–83. Lawton's numbering system for the document reliefs is here employed throughout, cross-referenced with *IG* when editions are printed.

110 Ibid. nos. 1–2, 5–12, 63, 66, 68–9, and 71–2.

111 Ibid. nos. 10, 11, 64, 65, 68, 72, and 79. Nos. 74, 77, 81, and 83 are also likely inclusions in this list, but their texts are far too fragmentary to determine their precise nature.

112 Ibid. 6 comments generally upon this situation.

113 During the fourth century, however, there are instances of Athenian citizens receiving individual honors from state, religious, and military organizations on document reliefs: see Chapter 5, below.

114 Edition from *IG* i³ 65 (see Lawton 1995: 113–14 for additional bibliography and references). Restorations are translated but not marked; no argument will be made from the restorations.

[ἐες (?) εἶπε· τὰ μὲ]ν ἄλ[λ]α καθ<ά>περ τε͂ι βολε͂-
[ι· Ἀπολλονοφ]άνε[ι δ]ὲ το͂ι Κολοφονίοι ἐ<πιγράφσαι „ἐ>-
10   [πειδὲ ἀνέρ] ἐστιν [ἀ]γαθὸς περὶ τὸν δε͂μ-
[ον τὸν Ἀθ]εναίον [κα]ὶ τὸς στρατιότας“· τ-
[ο͂ δὲ χορ]ίο Διὸς hι[ε]ρο͂ ἐπιμέλεσθαι αὐ-
[τὸν τε͂]ς φυλακε͂ς, hόπος ἂν σο͂ον ε͂ι Ἀθεν-
[αίοισ]ι· συνεπιμέ[λ]εσθαι δὲ αὐτο͂ι καὶ
15   [τὸς στ]ρατεγὸς τ[ὸς] ἀεὶ ἐόντας ὅτο ἂν δ-
[έεται] καὶ τὲν βολ[ὲ]ν τὲν βολεύοσαν κα-
[ὶ τὸς π]ρυτάνες, κα[ὶ] πρόσοδον ε͂ναι αὐ-
[το͂ι πρ]ός τε τὸς π[ρυ]τάνες καὶ τὲμ βολὲ-
[ν καὶ ἐ]ς τὸν δε͂μον [π]ρότοι μετὰ τὰ hιερ-
20   [ὰ ὅταν] τι δέεται· [καὶ] μὲ ἐχσε͂ναι αὐτὸν
[μεδεν]ὶ ζεμιο͂σα[ι ἂν]ευ το͂ δέμο το͂ Ἀθεν-
[αίον· ταὐ]τὰ δὲ ἐ[ᾶσαι καὶ] τοῖς ἐκγόνοι-
[ς τοῖς Ἀπ]ολλο[νοφάνος· κ]αὶ ἐάν τις τού-
[τον τι παρ]αβα[ίνει, ... ¹⁵ . . . .]

- -

Of Apollonophanes [son (?)] of
...thus of Colophon
5   ... for the secretary of the *boulê*
to have this decree inscribed on a stone stele
and have it set up in the city. Anticle-
es (?) proposed: other things in accordance with
the *boulê*,[115] but for Apollonophanes of Colophon to have inscribed,
10   "since he is a good man with regard to the
dêmos of Athens and its soldiers."
And let him have charge over the guard
for the territory of Dioseritae in order that it be safe for the Athenians.[116] And let the generals in office
15   collaborate with him whenever there is
need, and the *boulê* as it deliberates and
the *prytaneis*, and let him have the right of approach
to the *prytaneis* and the *boulê*
and the *dêmos* first after the sacrifices,
20   whenever there is need. And let no one seize him or
punish him without the consent of the Athenian *dêmos*.
These things are to be allowed to him and to the descendants
of Apollonophanes. And if anyone
transgresses against this...

---

[115]   Cf. note 119, below, and cf. the rendition of the amendment formula in Fornara's translation
     of l. 15 of *IG* i³ 102, for Thrasybulus, above.
[116]   Translation of this individual provision from Jansen 2007: 155, with light adaptation.

Apollonophanes' particular benefit to Athens was likely associated with the Athenian re-colonization of Notium, Colophon's port, in 427 BC.[117] Precisely what service Apollonophanes provided is lost in the lacuna between lines 2 and 3, but lines 10 and 11[118] represent the more general reason for his honor: it is because he is ἀνὲρ ἀγαθὸς περὶ τὸν δὲμον τὸν Ἀθεναίον καὶ τὸς στρατιότας.[119] Like Pythion, Apollonophanes has merited this commemoration for his active service towards the collective Athenian citizen body. The phrase ἀνὲρ ἀγαθός, which in earlier times would have recalled the timeless virtues espoused by archaic elites,[120] has here been co-opted to commemorate historical deeds.[121] Despite being a benefactor of the *dêmos*, however, Apollonophanes is explicitly not a member of it: he is still an independent agent who will henceforth enjoy a special level of interaction with the Athenian citizen group (lines 16–20). The grant of priority approach to the democratic governing bodies acknowledges Apollonophanes' potential value to Athens' future, but it also poses implicit counterclaims about how history is made at Athens, where the *dêmos* is often construed as a group agent of significant action.

This monument presented still more complex symbolic statements through its iconography and its (likely) location. The inscription was originally headed by a relief which, though badly damaged, still shows the outline of Athena crowning a man who lifts his right hand towards her.[122] The human figure is likely Apollonophanes, accepting praise from the city's patron. His gesture, a sign of acknowledgement and respect,[123] combines with the traditional reduced size of his mortal figure[124] to produce a visual impression of the natural superiority of Athena – and, by extension, her

---

[117]   Lawton 1995: 113, also collecting ancient and modern references for this interpretation.

[118]   Meritt 1945: 118 (cited by Lawton 1995: 113) points out that the text from line 9 onwards represents the content of an amendment or addition to the decree.

[119]   A. Petrovic highlights that the direct quotation in ll. 9–11 shows that this inscription is itself ordaining another honorific decree that will use this phraseology.

[120]   See Day 1989: 21.

[121]   Cf. the discussion of historical context in Chapter 2, above, and see Donlan 1978 esp. 99–100 on the changing usages of this kind of terminology over time.

[122]   Lawton 1995: 113, observing that the man has his right arm lifted; *IG* makes no mention of this detail.

[123]   Ibid. 60.

[124]   In relief scenes of the classical period, human beings were typically depicted at a smaller scale than deities. The most famous example is probably the Parthenon frieze, where the gods watching the procession are depicted seated to accommodate their greater size within a zone that also presents humans on horseback. These comparative proportions (large gods, small humans), however, are also observed in votive reliefs, document reliefs, and elsewhere: see Rauscher 1971, cited in Lawton 1995: 60 n. 142.

polis and her *dêmos*[125] – even as she thanks the human being for his service. The message is clear: the ideal channel of productivity for an outstanding individual is the service of the greater good of Athens.[126]

Lawton's no. 10 reads as follows:[127]

```
        Ἐπικέρ[δης Κυρηναῖος]  in taenia
              εὐερ[γέτης·]
        [ἔδο]ξεν τῆι [βολῆι καὶ τῶι δήμωι· ....]
        [.. ὶς ἐπ]ρυτ[άνευε, ..... 9 .... ἐγρ]αμ[μ]-
5       [άτευε, ..... 9 .... ἐπεστάτ]ε, Ἀλεξίας
        [ἦρχε, ..... 10 ..... εἶπε· ἐπ]αινέσαι Ἐπ-
        [ικέρδει τῶι Κυρηναί]ωι ὡς ὄντι ἀνδρ-
        [ὶ ἀγαθῶι καὶ .... αἰτ]ίωι γεγενημέν-
        [ωι ........ 15 ......]ας τὸς ἐξ Σικελ-
10      [ίας ....... 13 ..... ]ν τῶι πολέμωι· αὐ-
        [τὸς γὰρ μνᾶς ἑκατὸν] ἐθελοντὴς ἐς σω-
        [τηρίαν ..... 10 .....] \ωσιν Ἀθηναιοι
        [... 6 ... ἀτελείας δε]δομένης ὑπὸ τῶ δ-
        [ήμο ..... 10 ..... τάλ]αντον ἀργυρίο α-
15      [........ 15 .......] εὖ πεποίηκεν Ἀθη-
        [ναίων τὸν δῆμον κα]ὶ ἃ νῦν ἐπαγγειλά-
        [μενος ποιεῖ, στεφ]ανῶσαί τε αὐτ[ὸ]ν [..]
        [........ 15 .......]εκα[.]ε[..... 9 ....]
        [.... 7 ...]αν [......... 20 .........]
20      [....] τῆς ἐς Ἀθη[ναίος ..... 12 ......]
        [. κα]ὶ εἶναι καὶ [αὐτῶι τυχὲν ἄλλων ἀγ]-
        [αθ]ῶν Ἀθήνησιν κ[αθάπερ ἂν αἰτῆται Ἀ]-
        θηναίος. ἀνειπὲν [δὲ καὶ τὸν κήρυκα π]-
        [ρ]οσκηρύξαντα ἐ[ν τῶι ἀγῶνι τῶι αὐτί]-
25      κα μάλα ἐν ἄστει [ὅτι πρότερον Ἐπικέ]-
        ρδης ὁ Κυρηναῖο[ς μνᾶς ἑκατὸν ἐσήνε]-
        γκεν Ἀθηναίο[ις ἐς σωτηρίαν ἀνθ' ὧν κ]-
        αὶ αὐτὸν ἐστε[φάνωσαν ἀνδραγαθίας]
        [ἕ]νεκα καὶ εὐν[οίας τῆς ἐς Ἀθηναίος· τ]-
30      [ὸ] δὲ ψήφισμα τ[όδε ἀναγράψαι τὸν γρα]-
        [μ]ματέα τῆς βολ[ῆς ἐμ πόλει ἐν στήλη]
        [λι]θίνηι ⁿ Ἀρχε[.... εἶπε· τὰ μὲν ἄλλα]
        [καθάπερ τῆ]ι βο[λῆι - - - - - - - - - -]
              - - - - - - - - - - -
```

---

[125] On Athena as a metonym for Athens in the document reliefs, see Lawton 1995: 40–4 esp. 40.
[126] Hedrick 1999: 410.
[127] Edition from *IG* i³ 125 (see Lawton 1995: 87 for additional bibliography and references). Restorations are translated but not marked; no argument will be made from the restorations.

Of Epicerdes of Cyrene,
      benefactor
Resolved by the *boulê* and the *dêmos*...
... held the prytany, ... was the secre-
5   tary, ... presided, Alexias
was archon, ... proposed: that praise be given to Epicerdes of Cyrene because he is a good
man and ... has been responsible for
... those from Sicily
10   ... in the war. [For] he himself
willingly [contributed one hundred minas] for deliverance
... the Athenians ...
... given [exemption from liturgies] by the *dêmos*
... a talent of silver
15   ... he has been a benefactor of the Athenian
dêmos, and after making these things public,
to crown him ...
20   ... towards the Athenian people
... and for him to have a share in other
good things at Athens, just as
an Athenian would be entitled to. And for a herald
to make this proclamation at the current contest
25   in the city, that Epicerdes of Cyrene in the past
conveyed one hundred minas
to the Athenians for the sake of their deliverance, in return for which
they crowned him because of his virtue
and his good will towards the Athenian people.
30   And let the secretary of the *boulê* inscribe this decree
in the city on a stele
of stone. Arch ... proposed: other things
in accordance with the *boulê* ...

Despite damage, the surviving text provides an even clearer account of the specific historical service that Epicerdes provided to the Athenian *dêmos* than did the dedication to Apollonophanes. References to Sicily and to the Peloponnesian War (lines 9–10) locate Epicerdes and his benefaction firmly in their historical context; lines 10–11, 14, and 26–7 likely even acknowledge the exact amounts of his financial contributions to the waning Athenian cause. The iconography of this relief, too, is similar to that of Apollonophanes: here, a small Epicerdes lifts his right hand to

acknowledge a larger, draped (likely) Athena[128] near the center. The benefactor is again subordinated to the goddess, even as she in turn conveys
distinction upon him. In rewarding Epicerdes and others with public honors, the *dêmos* claims a productive, transactional relationship with an eminent individual. But it also, ironically, suggests that it cannot make history
alone.[129]

Funerary monuments (before c. 396): Growing claims for the individual

The commemorative funerary practices of classical Athens shift significantly
during the last third of the fifth century BC.[130] Most notably, figured reliefs
carved upon rectangular stone stelai or upon stone vases reappear as private
memorials,[131] following an almost total absence from the archaeological
record for some fifty years.[132] Although a few monumental burial structures
were employed during the earlier and middle years of the fifth century,[133]
the re-entry of the reliefs is striking. It may result from changes in sumptuary
laws,[134] from the relaxation of social compliance with unwritten tradition,[135]
or even from shifting perceptions of the accessibility or appropriateness of
funerary display for ordinary members of the *dêmos*.[136]

   These new grave markers may also be interpreted as claims to the significance of the individual *alongside* – in complement to or even in competition with – the significance of the group. Thucydides' Periclean speeches
and the honorific inscriptions of the late fifth century, for example, have
revealed negotiations of authority, power, and historical agency between the

---

[128] Lawton 1995: 87, with a fuller description of the relief and noting that "Athena . . . alone
bestows honours for Athens in this period."

[129] As Lawton 1995: 87 points out, the service of Epicerdes was still recalled more than fifty years
later by Demosthenes (citing D. 20.41–2, 355 BC).

[130] The rural demes of Attica are also considered in the following discussion to be part of
"Athens" unless otherwise stated.

[131] As opposed to state-sponsored monuments erected as part of the ritual of the *patrios nomos*:
see Stupperich 1994 on what these may have looked like.

[132] The date of the return of the figured reliefs is debated. Clairmont 1970: 42–3, and in
subsequent publications, believes that all extant examples must postdate the year 430, but
cites references to other perspectives. Other proposed *termini post quem* generally fall between
c. 440 (e.g. Friis Johansen 1951: 13) and *c.* 425 (e.g. Morris 1992: 134, 141–4; Kurtz and
Boardman 1971: 121). Clairmont 1993 (= *CAT*) strives to provide a complete catalog of
classical Athenian tombstones carved in figured relief, updating Conze 1893–1922.

[133] See the discussion of these in Chapter 2, above.   [134] See Chapter 2, above.

[135] E.g. Loraux 1986: 23, 28, 31.

[136] Humphreys 1980: 123. Morris 1994: 72–3 shows that Humphreys' and Loraux's (see note 135,
above) views are essentially opposites of one another.

eminent individual and the *dêmos*. In a similar way, the Athenian tombstones
of the late fifth and the earliest fourth centuries[137] can employ their epitaphs,
their iconography, and their physical settings to acknowledge membership
in the *dêmos* even as some of them may also question the primacy of the
citizen group. Certain monuments in particular seem to commemorate the
significance of an individual life: those with more extensive inscriptions;
those with personalized elements in their iconography (these are generally
reflections of life experience, e.g. occupation, rather than of physiognomy);
and a group belonging to warriors that appear to defy or compete with the
collectivizing ethos of the *patrios nomos*.

The quantitative evidence regarding the epitaphs presented here and in
Chapter 5, below,[138] involves a set of statistics derived from *IG* i³ and *IG*
ii/iii², the largest available centralized corpora of Attic funerary inscriptions.
There are some important caveats involved with the use of this data. Multiple
potential venues for epigraphical publication mean that *IG* cannot ever be
comprehensive, and ongoing progress of excavations in and around the
city of Athens (indeed, in the entire Attic territory) constantly reshapes in
reality a corpus that is de facto fixed when printed. In addition, nearly all
the dates suggested by *IG* are of necessity approximate, and in the case of the
fourth-century entries in particular, there are variations in the ways in which
the dates are labeled (see Chapter 5, below). Finally, the usual problems of
preservation mean that the numbers are at best incomplete. Given this,
all figures cited from *IG* should best be taken as broadly proportionate
estimates, rather than as exact counts. The analysis that I introduce here
and complete in Chapter 5 is based not upon absolute values, but rather
upon large-scale relationships within the data.

Excluding undated examples and inscriptions so poorly preserved that
conclusions cannot be confidently drawn about their content, *IG* i³ presents
at least 111 private epitaphs of both Athenians and foreigners excavated in
Attica and likely dating to approximately the last third of the fifth century

---

[137] Although the conclusion of the Peloponnesian War in 404 represents a historical break, there
are several important examples of funerary monuments aligned with the fifth century in their
typologies and ideology that are probably slightly later than that date. As such, it seems safest
to follow Meyer 1993: 121 and 'begin' the fourth century in the 390s. This chapter therefore
maintains a *terminus ante quem* of *c.* 396 – one of the traditional, if disputed, death-dates for
Thucydides and, more importantly, the year before the outbreak of the Corinthian War
(395–387/6). The ways in which this boundary has been employed are discussed in detail in
the notes to this chapter and to Chapter 5.

[138] I am grateful to the general comments of Stears 2000a: 212–14 about some of the dominant
features of fourth-century tombstones and epitaphs, which inspired me to study them more
closely from both quantitative and qualitative perspectives.

Table 4.3 *Approximate census of* IG i³ *and* IG ii/iii² *Attic epitaphs from the later fifth century BC (to c. 396), by type*

	Category 1: Name(s) ± identifiers only	Category 2: Name(s) + brief extension	Category 3: More extensive epitaphs
GRAND TOTALS	336	24	44

and before 403/2.[139] *IG* ii/iii² allows the addition of at least 293 more separate entries likely dating from after 403/2 down to the 390s.[140] Of these, eighty-three entries from *IG* i³ and 253 from *IG* ii/iii² (for a total of 336) display only a name or names, sometimes accompanied by patronymics, demotics, or, in the case of non-Athenians, national or *polis* identifiers. I refer to these in Table 4.3, above, as "Category 1" epitaphs. In contrast, twenty-eight *IG* i³ and forty *IG* ii/iii² entries (for a total of sixty-eight) are somehow extended beyond the name-label. Of these sixty-eight, twenty-four are inscriptions of the briefest and most generic type, which simply read e.g. (most commonly) "Thrason, a good man," or "Nicostratus lies here."[141] "Brief extension" epitaphs such as these are labeled as "Category 2" in Table 4.3, above. The remaining forty-four epitaphs, those of "Category 3," are more expansive, and certain of these endeavor to create some sense of unique identity for the deceased.[142]

---

[139] The earliest *IG* dating incorporated into this count is '450–425'; less specific dates such as 'mid-fifth century' or 'after the mid-fifth century' are not included in these figures, as they are more likely to be associated in time and concept with the material treated in Chapter 2, above.

[140] The latest *IG* datings incorporated into this count are '410–390' and 'beginning of the fourth century.' Less specific dates such as 'before the mid-fourth century' are not included in these figures, as they are more likely to be associated in time and concept with the material treated in Chapter 5, below. It should be noted that the conservative approach to these date ranges will have produced low estimates both here and in the various subcategories treated hereafter.

[141] *IG* i³ 1307, 1307 ter: these read, respectively, Θράσον | ἀνὴρ ἀγαθό[ς] and Νικόστρ|ατος ἐνθά|δε κεῖται, displaying the vocabulary ordinarily employed for such examples during this period. Of the twenty-eight *IG* i³ and forty *IG* ii/iii² entries extended beyond the name-label, eleven examples from *IG* i³ are of these or very similar 'generic' varieties (e.g. *IG* i³ 1376); thirteen from *IG* ii/iii² also fit the 'generic' category, although the most common elaboration in the latter corpus is the simple designation of familial relationships with words like θυγάτηρ, μήτηρ, and υἱός (at least six out of thirteen). One-word mentions of occupations, while they are known from this period (e.g. *IG* ii/iii² 11689, dated by *IG* to *c.* 400, which reads Θρᾶιξ | περσικ|οποιός, "Thraix, a maker of slippers") become more common in the earlier fourth century (see Chapter 5, below). These familial and occupation observations are also made generally by Stears 2000a: 212–14, who does not, however, explore them with detailed statistics.

[142] Subtracting the 'generic' epitaphs described in note 141, above, *IG* i³ provides seventeen more extensive examples and *IG* ii/iii² twenty-seven; it is out of this group of forty-four

Amongst the epitaphs of "Category 3" are, for example, that of Mnasagora and Nicochares (*IG* i³ 1315, dated by *IG* to '*c.* a. 420–10?'), a brother and sister whose inscription suggests that their monument is a cenotaph[143] and says that their deaths grieved their parents. The epitaph of Ampharete (*IG* i³ 1290, dated by *IG* to '*c.* a. 410–400?') notes her love for the deceased grandchild whose fate (and possibly tomb) she shares; that of Onesous (*IG* ii/iii² 12378, dated to the end of the fifth century) records his death in a fire. Foreigners are also represented: Pythocles' epitaph (*IG* ii/iii² 8523, dated by *IG* to the beginning of the fourth century) presents a careful iteration of the members of his family and notes his place of origin as Ephesus. Also specific about its subject, although in image rather than in words, is *CAT* 1.630, the stele of Xanthippus, likely dated to 430–420.[144] The inscription provides only his name, but the relief shows a seated, bearded man accompanied by two girls and holding a last,[145] a wooden model around which a cobbler molded leather to form shoes. From the identification of the deceased as a craftsman, the experienced viewer in ancient Athens is able to reconstruct an image of his training, apprenticeship, and daily work;[146] from the images of the children, the viewer may postulate a wife (whether living or dead); from the ages of all three figures, the viewer might conclude that a rather young family has been separated by death.[147] Finally, the unusual relationship between the expense of the high-quality art work and the working-class occupation of its beneficiary may have been intended to recommend Xanthippus' positive connections with other craftsmen, his prosperity at his own trade, or both.[148]

Details like these, whether expressed in word or image, are biographically specific: they emphasize individual sets of experiences rather than invoking

---

(approximately 13% of the total number of epitaphs of any type counted for the period currently under discussion) that the inscriptions selected for closer readings here were chosen.

[143] This interpretation is not unanimous: see the bibliography in *IG ad loc.* and more recently the bibliography collected by Clairmont at *CAT* 1.610.

[144] Perhaps nearer to the lower end of that range: *CAT ad loc.*

[145] *CAT ad loc.*, with collected references and bibliography; Clairmont notes that this is the interpretation favored by most archaeologists.

[146] On details of cobblers' products and their place within the "craft world" of classical Athens, see Sobak 2009 esp. 127–201 (on the term "craft world," see ibid. 154).

[147] Clairmont 1993: vol. I, 403 notes that this particular tombstone is usually taken to show a family group, and offers some relevant general observations, as well (at Clairmont 1993: intro. 27–9): although age seems often to have been only approximated on Athenian tombstones (particularly those whose iconography may not have been specifically commissioned), definite age-classes are discernible and, when prosopography can be determined, these age-classes appear to have been employed to depict relative generational relationships within family groups.

[148] Clairmont 1993: vol. I, 404 notes this gap but interprets it somewhat differently, saying that "neither the dignified representation of Xanthippos nor the accompanying two daughters

the general social values of archaic elites,[149] as was more common before the Persian Wars.[150] It is important, however, to distinguish between *identity* and *agency*.[151] The literary and material examples treated in Chapters 2 and 3 and in the discussion of Thucydides, above, generally took up the themes of heroism, the relationship of the individual to the citizen group, and the ability to provide a definitive interpretation of the past. Memorials like that of Xanthippus, however, address these issues in only the most tangential manner, if at all. If they are 'thinking' about history, the history that they construe is a very small one, confined to the *oikos* or at least not extended to the polis as a whole. There are some other monuments from this period, however, which reach beyond simply providing biographical detail or notice of occupation[152] and seem to deliberately contextualize their recipients within the larger world of the polis. In some cases, the subject of the memorial derives additional relevance (and perhaps meritorious memory) from active participation in the city's communal life, but in others, specifically those of several warriors, the tombstone appears to invoke agency for the individual beyond what the state would have granted through the *patrios nomos*.

The epitaph of Mannes (*IG* i³ 1361) is inscribed on a very small, otherwise undecorated stele that served as a funerary monument for a foreigner who probably perished during the Peloponnesian War:[153]

> Φρυγῶν ὃς ἄριστος ἐγένατ' ἐ-
> ν εὐ\<ρ\>υχόροισιν Ἀθήνα\<ι\>ς, Μάν-
> νης Ὀρύμαιος, ὃ μνῆμα τόδ' ἐσ-
> τὶ καλόν. 'καὶ μὰ Δί' οὐκ εἶδον
> 5   ἐμαυτõ ἀμείνω ὑλοτόμον.' *vv*
> ἐν τῶι πολέμ\<ω\>ι ἀπέθανεν.

> He who was the best of the Phrygians
> in wide-wayed Athens, Mannes

---

would ever suggest, had we not the cobbler's last, the humble trade in which Xanthippos was engaged."

[149] That this was a deliberate choice is suggested by *IG* ii/iii² 5768, the epitaph of Philetaerus, dated by *IG* to the beginning of the fourth century (the history of its monument is complex: see *CAT* 1.891), which does use archaizing themes and imagery such as that of the youthful death.

[150] See Chapter 2, above.

[151] I am grateful to J. Ober for sharpening my analysis of the monuments discussed here in these terms.

[152] A number of scholars have noted that mentions or depictions of professions (outside of warfare) increase on tombstones during the later fifth century and are also known in the fourth (see e.g. Stears 2000a: 212; Clairmont 1993: vol. I, 220–5; Clairmont 1970: 9–10, 57–8, 85–6, 97–8, 130–1, with references). However, possessing a profession and claiming historical agency cannot be automatically equated.

[153] Edition from *IG* i³ 1361.

the Orymaean,[154] this is his lovely
monument. 'And by Zeus, I did not know
5   a woodcutter better than myself.' ᵛ ᵛ
He died in the war.

Dated by *IG* to '*c*. a. 432–21?,' this epitaph communicates the name of the deceased, his ethnicity, the location of his current residence and therefore the implication that he relocated some time ago, either his locality of origin or his father's name, his occupation (or at least a skill at which he claimed to excel, i.e. the felling of wood), and the temporal and political circumstances of his death. The opening two lines offer a brief echo of heroic poetry (and therefore of generic archaic epigrammatic formulae)[155] in calling Mannes the "best of the Phrygians," but they are followed by a different kind of claim to lasting memory made in the 'voice' of the deceased himself: he wishes it to be known that he was not only the "best of the Phrygians," but also the best with an axe.

The final line of Mannes' epitaph reads ἐν τῶι πολέμ<ω>ι ἀπέθανεν, "he died in the war." Variations on the sentence "these died in the war" were part of the formulaic heading on Athenian casualty lists at least as early as *c.* 460, the approximate date of the (likely) earliest introduction preserved, at the opening of *IG* i³ 1147, which reads ḥοίδε ⋮ ἐν τõι ⋮ πολέμοι ⋮ ἀπέθανον.[156] Mannes himself was explicitly not an Athenian, as a number of items in the epitaph attest, and yet the inscription claims distinction of some sort for him at Athens (ἄριστος ἐγένατ' ἐν . . . Ἀθήνα<ι>ς); perhaps the meaning is that Mannes served or supported the Athenian cause in a military context,[157] and earned his honors (and lost his life) that way. If Mannes had fallen with a detachment of allies, he might have been considered eligible for inclusion in the burial of the *patrios nomos* alongside the Athenians: this practice is known from the foreigners included on some of the extant casualty lists.[158] The tone of the epitaph itself, however, suggests that perhaps this is not what happened. Rather, the inscription's explicit invocation of Mannes' relationship to Athens seems to highlight his status outside of a group to which he might have wanted very much to belong.

---

[154] The obscure Greek adjectival form Ὀρύμαιος (line 3) may refer either to a locality (Ruge) or stand for a patronymic (Wilhelm): see the apparatus in *IG ad loc.*

[155] See Chapter 2, above, and in particular Day 1989; Jeffery 1947.

[156] For additional commentary and bibliography on this particular casualty list, see Meiggs and Lewis 1969: 73–6 no. 33, highlighting amongst their references Bradeen 1964: there, see 23–4, 33–4, 45–8, and the reconstructed monument at 26.

[157] See Wilhelm's observation of the possibility of an appropriate conflict in the apparatus of *IG ad loc.*

[158] Bradeen 1969: 149–51; see also Clairmont 1983: 50–1 and cf. Loraux 1986: 32–5.

Nicomachus' epitaph (*IG* ii/iii² 7180) reads as follows:[159]

in lutrophoro:

Νικόμαχος Περαιεύς.

in latere stelae:

Λήμνο ἀπ' ἠγαθέας κεύθει τάφος ἐνθάδε γαίας
ἄνδρα φιλοπρόβατον· Νικόμαχος δ' ὄνομα.

Nicomachus of Piraeus
From the sacred land of Lemnos a tomb here covers
a man who loved his sheep. Nicomachus was his name.

Two words in the epitaph are of particular interest: ἠγαθέας, which contains hints of heroic poetry,[160] and the evocative and extremely rare φιλοπρόβατον.[161] From the latter, Nicomachus seems to have made some or all of his living by pasturing, whether on his own or through a network of others who worked for him.[162] Whether it is intended to address Nicomachus' affection for his animals or his dedication to his occupation, this word may be pointing out a sense of loss that extends beyond simply the departure of the deceased.[163] The epitaph demonstrates that Nicomachus was an Athenian citizen (his deme, Piraeus, is given), and that he was a returnee to Athens from Lemnos. As Clairmont notes, this has prompted the recommendation of *IG* that the monument be associated with the era in which Athenian cleruchies were withdrawn from the island (and therefore that it be dated roughly between the end of the Peloponnesian War and the beginning of the Corinthian one), although there is no explicit need to take Nicomachus' death as coincidental with his return to Athens.[164] The general circumstances, however, do suggest that Nicomachus may have himself been a cleruch or an employee of one, which could have intimately connected his life experiences to the fortunes of his city: the loss of Athens' overseas territory with the breakup of the empire may have been what removed Nicomachus from the life he had built on Lemnos as a representative and a dependent of his home polis.[165]

---

[159] *IG* ii/iii² 7180; edition here from *IG*.
[160] Clairmont 1970: 155 n. 213, with Homeric references.
[161] Beyond this inscription, PHI and *TLG* searches reveal the use of this root only five times, in Dorotheus, Hephaestion, and Palladius. None of these is earlier than the first century BC.
[162] Suggested by Clairmont 1970: 155.
[163] Clairmont 1970: 155 notes that the inscription suggests that "the memory of his years spent on Lemnos was vivid": I agree with this interpretation of the tone.
[164] *CAT* 1.303; Clairmont 1970: 155, recommending a date no more specific than "early fourth century," and n. 214.
[165] I am grateful to J. Ober for this point.

CAT 1.075, probably dating to around or shortly after 430 (*CAT ad loc.*), though broken below the neck of its single relief figure, shows a young man holding a female tragic mask. He is likely an artist in that most Athenian of performance genres, the theatre.[166] By the later fifth century, theatre offered varied opportunities for individual achievement in a highly visible and sanctioned civic context. Poets, *choregoi* (producers of choruses), and actors competed for prizes in the dramatic competitions,[167] and for the permanent memory that victory-monuments and inscriptions could secure for them. Their performances, however, especially at the City Dionysia,[168] were not only sanctioned by the state, but also embedded within a larger ritual context that celebrated the life of the polis.[169] This monument, then, potentially invokes meaning for its subject in terms of his relationship not only to his art, but to his city.[170] In its reference to tragic drama and in its creation of permanent memory, this tombstone now stands in place of the monuments that might have commemorated its subject's future victories.

CAT 5.150, the stone *lekythos* of Myrrhine, is decorated with five figures in relief: Myrrhine herself, clearly labeled with her name; Hermes *Psychopompos* ("escorter of souls"), who leads Myrrhine along;[171] and three other individuals, depicted slightly smaller in scale, whose identity and relationship to Myrrhine remains debated.[172] The monument may in fact be dedicated to an individual also known from an inscribed epitaph excavated in Zographou.[173] If the two Myrrhines are in fact one and the same person, then this is the *lekythos* of an Athenian priestess of Athena Nike.[174] The interpretation would accord well with the elevated status suggested by Myrrhine's idealized appearance, larger size (she is depicted at the same

---

[166] The iconography of this relief, particularly when compared to roughly contemporary vase-painting and to later sculptural types, suggests that the subject is represented as either a performer or a poet: *CAT ad loc.*, citing Slater 1985: 341–3, with references; cf. also Webster 1967.

[167] The *didaskaliai* (production notices) and other records of the ancient dramatic competitions are collected by Snell 1971 (= *TrGF* 1): 3–52; see also the testimonia in Csapo and Slater 1995.

[168] On the other Athenian festivals that included theatrical performances, see Pickard-Cambridge 1968.

[169] See esp. Goldhill 1990.   [170] I am grateful to J. Ober for this point.

[171] Clairmont 1993: vol. V, 162 suggests that Hermes is presumably directing Myrrhine towards the underworld, as on Attic white-ground *lekythoi* of the period.

[172] Clairmont 1993: vol. V, 161–2.

[173] Clairmont 1993: vol. V, 160–5 and 1979 calls the cut block of stone on which this inscription appears a "pillar" or a "pillar-stele." Lougovaya-Ast 2006 calls it a "stele," noting (222) that it is "tall, narrow, and thick."

[174] Clairmont 1979; see also Clairmont 1993: vol. V, 164–5. Rahn 1986 agrees with Clairmont that the *lekythos* and the inscription were dedicated to the same individual; Lougovaya-Ast 2006: 222 n. 32 (also citing Clairmont and Rahn) recommends caution.

scale as Hermes), and accompaniment by a god.[175] Addressing the written memorial first, the epitaph reads:[176]

```
        Καλλιμάχο θυγ-
        ατρὸς τηλαυγὲ-
        ς μνῆμα, / ἣ πρώτη
        Νίκης ἀμφεπόλ-
5       ευσε νεών. / εὐλο-
        γίαι δ᾽ ὄνομ᾽ ἔσχ-
        ε συνέμπορον, ὡ-
        ς ἀπὸ θείας / Μυρ-
        ρίν<η ἐ>κλήθη συ-
10      ντυχίας· ἐτύμω-
        ς ⋮ / πρώτε Ἀθηναί-
        ας Νίκες ἕδος ἀ-
        μφεπόλευσεν / ἐ-
        κ πάντων κλήρω-
15      ι Μυρρίνη εὐτυ-
        χίαι.
```

This is the conspicuous memorial of the daughter of Callimachus who was the first to serve as attendant at the temple of Nike. She had a name that was a companion to her good reputation, since she was aptly called Myrrhine by divine chance. Myrrhine was the first to serve the sanctuary of Athena Nike, and, out of all, she was chosen by the luck of the draw.

This epitaph displays some traditional, even archaizing features: it is composed in elegiac couplets (three in all), and it opens with a formulaic introduction of the physical monument.[177] Its vocabulary, too, is both elevated in tone and heroic in association.[178] But Myrrhine also is explicitly contextualized within her polis, particularly through the iteration of her positions as priestess[179] and through the acknowledgement that she was

---

[175] Clairmont 1993: vol. V, 162–5 and esp. Rahn 1986: 197, although Clairmont (esp. 163 n. 1) disagrees with the heroic overtones that Rahn reads in the iconography.

[176] Edition from *IG* i³ 1330; translation from Lougovaya-Ast 2006: 211–12. Lougovaya-Ast notes that "the [letter-]cutter . . . at the end of the first verse . . . omitted τόδ᾽ ἐστίν [after μνῆμα], which is required by both sense and meter," and which is re-introduced in the edition that she quotes, Hansen 1983: 54 = *CEG* 1.93.

[177] Such connection of the physical with the literary was especially common in the archaic era: Derderian 2001: 71–3, with references.

[178] Rahn 1986: 203 surveys the vocabulary of the epitaph in relation to Homeric and Pindaric poetry. Cf. the discussion of earlier epitaphs in Chapter 2, above.

[179] Lougovaya-Ast 2006: 213–18 reviews the history of scholarship on the epitaph and on Myrrhine's service, and concludes that "Our Myrrhine was chosen by lot in *c.* 450–445 to be an attendant at the sanctuary, which perhaps had a statue or other cult object of Athena Nike;

chosen for her position by lot (κλήρωι), a method that was not only "probably a significant democratic innovation" in terms of cult practice,[180] but was
also a common means of selection to political office under the democracy,
as well.[181]

Lougovaya-Ast, in discussing the date of the written memorial, points
out that Myrrhine's inscription has more in common physically, and her
epigram shares more in terms of content, with comparands from the mid-
to-later fifth century than it does with examples from the earlier fourth.[182]
The profile of the stone, she suggests, bears some resemblance to the simpler grave monuments of the middle years of the fifth century,[183] and the
epitaph, in its rare mention of the occupation of the deceased and its lack
of various verbal tropes (particularly those of formulaic mourning) that
became common in the fourth century, seems not to have settled into
generic conventions that are known later in time.[184] If the stone *lekythos*
and the inscription are indeed for the same individual, they may also be
examples of a practice first implied by other monuments, specifically those
of warriors, during the later fifth century:[185] that of multiple memorialization. The *lekythos* and the epigram were not found in the same location:
the former was excavated near the heart of the modern city, the latter in a
suburb, with no evidence of its having been re-purposed for later building
projects.[186] Rahn suggests that the inscription may have served as a local
memorial within the deme, the showier *lekythos* as a more prominent commemoration closer to the city, whether as the product of public admiration

once the temple was built in the mid-420s, Myrrhine, while currently serving as priestess of
Athena Nike, became the first priestess at the newly built temple." Cf. also the discussion of
the epitaph's level of detail at 220.

[180] Lougovaya-Ast 2006: at 212. See also Rahn 1986: 207 n. 65.

[181] I am grateful to J. Ober for highlighting the importance of this connection.

[182] Lougovaya-Ast 2006: 220–2.

[183] Ibid. 222; see also Rahn 1986: 204 on the simplicity of the written monument. The mid
fifth-century stelai are mentioned in Chapter 2, above; see esp. Stears 2000b: 31.

[184] Lougovaya-Ast 2006: 220–1, noting that (221) "references to particular details of the
deceased's life and lack of generalization seem to be characteristic of verse epitaphs in Athens
of the period when the tradition of inscribing grave epigrams for individuals had not fully
resumed." Fourth-century formulaic expressions of grief are discussed in Chapter 5, below.

[185] See the discussion of the epitaphs of Glauciades and -Ulus, below. This possibility continues
into the fourth century, for example, as witnessed by the multiple efforts made on behalf of
Dexileus: see Chapter 5, below.

[186] On the locations of the finds (the Diochares Gate area for the *lekythos*, Zographou for the
epigram) and the lack of evidence for re-use, see Rahn 1986: 195 nn. 1–2, 206 n. 64,
respectively. As Rahn (206 n. 64) points out, Clairmont 1979: 105 (see also Clairmont 1993:
vol. V, 164–5) suggests that both items were part of the same physical monument, but this
would admittedly require the inscription and the *lekythos* to have experienced separate
material histories after the monument's destruction.

or of familial pride.[187] But even if both items were part of the same physical display, they would together have employed a wider vocabulary of memorialization, combining both words and iconography and using what may be an older style of inscription alongside a more 'contemporary' work of art.[188] The epitaph specifically contextualizes Myrrhine within the polis, while the *lekythos* presents a more generalized visual narrative in terms familiar from funerary pottery of the era.[189] These may represent the complementary attempts of a family to memorialize a famous member in more than one way, in order to increase recognition and prestige at a time when commemoration was diversifying. Or one memorial may be private or personal, the other sponsored by (e.g.) the state, Myrrhine's deme, or even a religious organization, any of which might have preferred to recall Myrrhine in a different manner than her family did.[190]

The possibility of commemorative tension between the preferences of individual families and those of the state emerges more strongly in the cases of tombstones depicting warriors. At issue is the possible relationship of these memorials to the state-sponsored burials conducted in accordance with the *patrios nomos*. For the last third of the fifth century,[191] there are at least eighteen tombstones in *CAT*[192] of known, attributed, or likely Attic provenance[193] that certainly or probably belong to one or more warriors. There are three major ways that the warriors themselves are represented on

---

[187] Rahn 1986: 206–7.

[188] On the style of the *lekythos* and its reliefs, see Rahn 1986: 201.

[189] See note 171, above. Clairmont 1979: 109 (see also Clairmont 1993: vol. V, 162) believes that the other figures on the *lekythos* besides Myrrhine and Hermes are intended to represent "Athenian citizens" rather than family members. If this interpretation could be created by ancient viewers (even if unintended by the artist), the *lekythos* could be seen as invoking privatizing iconography in making a statement about Myrrhine's role in the city's public life.

[190] Rahn 1986: 206–7 offers the private and public possibilities for the *lekythos*, but it is also important to consider how the two memorials may have complemented one another's meaning.

[191] *CAT* provides estimated date-range classifications for its monuments that are consistently divided into the following spans: 430–420, 420–400, 400–375, 375–350, 350–300 (see Clairmont 1993: intro. 2–3). For the current analysis, only monuments assigned to the first two spans were employed. The periods 400–375 and 375–350 will be treated in Chapter 5, below.

[192] *CAT* 1.193, 1.194, 2.121, 2.130, 2.131, 2.155, 2.156, 2.189, 2.192, 2.197, 2.630, 3.171, 3.191, 3.192, 4.180, 4.650, 4.671, 4.690.

[193] Of these eighteen, provenance is unrecorded for four (*CAT* 3.191, 3.192, 4.650, 4.690), but they are all made of Pentelic marble and have been taken by scholars as being of Attic workmanship; a fifth member of this group of eighteen, 2.131, is the Villa Albani relief, found in modern times in the Gardens of Maecenas in Rome. A number of tombstones listed in Clairmont 1993: vol. VI (indexes [*sic*]), s.v. 'Warriors' are not included in this group of eighteen for various reasons: 1.153 and 2.180 may be from Megara; 2.178 was excavated at Kertch, in the former Soviet Union; 2.651 and 3.141, though they do display warriors in their

these tombstones:[194] they may be shown standing or shaking hands, with or without other soldiers;[195] in action, most often against an enemy;[196] or in 'domestic' scenes with what are likely to be family members.[197] Stupperich and Clairmont have both recommended that the scenes that are exclusively military may be intended to imitate the iconography of the Athenian *polyandria*,[198] but without additional information about them it is difficult to decide whether to view them as cooperative or competitive with the civic monuments.[199] Like the white-ground *lekythoi* that depicted archaic-style tombs,[200] it is possible that their individual messages may have been intentionally ambivalent. The 'domestic' warrior tombstones, however, might be seen as responding to state memorialization by answering it with a different kind of narrative.[201] In their iconographic emphasis upon familial, rather than civic, loss, they re-personalize the death of an individual whom the *patrios nomos* would seek to incorporate instead into a virtually anonymous group. The fallen warrior is memorialized as a lost member of a particular family (a separation that is emphasized by the stark contrast between his military equipment and the civilian dress of the figures that accompany him), rather than being symbolically subsumed into the history of his polis.[202]

---

figure groups, are likely intended to commemorate a non-warrior as the deceased (see *ad loc.*); 2.158 (as Clairmont suggests *ad loc.*) is probably a votive relief rather than a tombstone.

[194] This classification is derived from Clairmont 1993: vol. I, 223–4, vol. II, 78–9.

[195] *CAT* 1.193, 2.155, 2.156, 2.197, 3.192.   [196] *CAT* 1.194, 2.130, 2.131, 2.192.

[197] Whether with old men likely to be their fathers (*CAT* 2.189), women likely to be their wives (2.121), or probable family or household groups 2.630, 3.171, 3.191, 4.180, 4.671, 4.690 (4.650 is a unique example that displays three tableaux: a pair of warriors shaking hands, a seated woman with a child behind her, and a warrior on a horse).

[198] Stupperich 1994; Clairmont 1993: vol. II, 78–9, 89; Clairmont 1983: 67–73; Clairmont 1970: 100–2; see also notes 209, 219, 220, below.

[199] Clairmont 1993: vol. II, 79 seems to strike a middle course: "in considering the scarcity of private memorials with battle scenes I would suggest that the family members honoring the death of their casualty, by choosing the battle iconography, wished to reminisce with intent purpose the iconography of polyandria reliefs which were familiar to Athenians from the public monuments in the Demosion Sema. This, if anything, was another supplementary means of heroization of the deceased, all victims in warfare sharing heroization. However, in the still scenes with warriors amongst their families the very connotation of heroization is rather dim. Does the predominantly bourgeois attitude in the fourth century explain the preference for still scenes as it possibly explains the *quasi* total lack of polyandria in the same period?"

[200] See Chapter 2, above.

[201] Provided, of course, that the soldier is indeed the deceased: see the cautions expressed by Bergemann at note 213, below.

[202] Stupperich 1977: 199, noting that these monuments elevate the individual and prioritize his position in family funerary cult. See also the articulation of the views of Loraux 1986 by Morris 1994: 72–3.

Even clearer ambivalence towards the ideology of the *patrios nomos*, however, emerges from a handful of inscribed epitaphs, which seem to bear out even more strongly Morris' assertion that in the later fifth century "households began to reappropriate from the polis some of the honour and glory of their war dead."[203] There are at least seven epitaphs from this period listed in *IG* that make clear or probable references to warfare; four of these in particular, *IG* ii/iii² 7716, 10593, 10780, and 10998, are likely dedicated to Athenians and have texts that are sufficently preserved to permit closer analysis of their content and expression.[204] They are taken here in roughly chronological order.

IG ii/iii² 7716, dated by *IG* to the end of the fifth century, is inscribed upon a fragmentary relief, *CAT* 2.130. It is the epitaph of one -Ulus of the Attic deme of Phlia:[205]

> [−‿−‿− ἕταροι δέ τε πάντες ἴ]σασιν
> καὶ πατρὶς ὡς πολλὸς ὤλεσα δυσμεν[έων]. |
> 2   [ὑμεῖς δ', ὦ παριόντες, ἐνὶ ξείνοισι γένε]σθε
> μάρτυρες ὅσσ' ἀρετῆς <σ>τῆσα τρόπαια μά[χης]. |
>
> 3 - - ΥΛΟΣ ΦΛΥΕΥ΄Σ.

> [All my companions] and my fatherland know
> how many of the enemy I killed.
> 2   [You, O passers-by, be amongst foreigners]
> witnesses of how many trophies I set up to my virtue in battle.
>
> 3 - - ULUS OF PHLIA

What remains of the damaged relief shows the head and front portion of a horse riding down a fallen warrior. The individual mounted upon the horse, likely intended to represent -Ulus, is almost entirely missing.[206] Enough information is preserved, however, to note that this relief belongs

---

[203] Morris 1992: 143, citing in support (143–4) the iconography of the monuments of Dexileus and -Ulus, and that of the Villa Albani relief (on all of these connections, see Chapter 5, below), and -Ulus' epitaph (which I also analyze, below). The additional evidence presented here shows that these trends were still more widespread.

[204] The seven are *IG* i³ 1288, 1288 bis; *IG* ii/iii² 7716, 10593, 10780, 10998, and 11678. The last, part of the 'Tomb of the Lacedaemonians' in the Kerameikos, refers to two Spartan polemarchs who fell in the struggles between the Thirty and the democrats in 403 BC: see (as cited in *IG ad loc.*) X. *HG* 2.4.28–33. 10593, whose language is at first glance more general, is identified as referring to warfare in Clairmont 1993: vol. I, 255, who explains his reasons for refining his original views about the stele as expressed in Clairmont 1970: 76–7.

[205] Edition from *IG* ii/iii² 7716 (supp. Kaibel). Restorations are translated, but no argument will be made from them.

[206] See the more detailed description of this monument at *CAT ad loc.*, to which this summary is indebted.

to the group of 'military action scenes' referenced above. Its iconography may therefore have offered an echo of – whether in invocation, competition, or both – the state funerary monuments,[207] or it may simply have presented an arresting visual statement about individual military prowess, glory, and memorialization. In either case, it could have presented a significant symbolic challenge to the group-centered ideology of the *patrios nomos*.

The epitaph carries this possibility further. Firstly, it employs the word πατρίς to refer to -Ulus' native polis. The word πατρίς means "fatherland" or "homeland" in a wide variety of Greek literary genres from the eighth through the fifth centuries (it appears, for example, in Homer, the lyric poets, and the tragedians, as well as in the rhetoricians and the historians). But this same word appears to enjoy greater prominence in Thucydides at moments of dramatic military tension: its forms appear nearly twice as often in books 6 and 7 (i.e. during the larger narrative of the Sicilian expedition) as they do in the entire remainder of the *History*.[208] It therefore seems a particularly appropriate choice for this epitaph: a good fit with the high tone of the poetry, yet still useful for the description of 'real-life' military operations.

Further Thucydidean connections are also relevant: Pericles twice employs forms of the word πατρίς at significant points in his speeches (2.42.3, 60.3). The latter occurrence comes near the opening of his justification of policy during the plague (his second speech, 2.60.1–64.6), when Pericles offers the important suggestion that the fate of the individual is inextricably tied to the fate of his polis. The generalization is part of the very first argument Pericles makes after announcing why he has called this Assembly meeting. Prominently located and structured as an aphorism or a proverb, it harnesses the universalizing sense of the word πατρίς in order to apply it to a more specific, significant situation, just as the epitaph of -Ulus does. The other Periclean use of the word πατρίς in Thucydides occurs during the Funeral Oration:

> καὶ γὰρ τοῖς τἆλλα χείροσι δίκαιον τὴν ἐς τοὺς πολέμους ὑπὲρ τῆς πατρίδος ἀνδραγαθίαν προτίθεσθαι· ἀγαθῷ γὰρ κακὸν ἀφανίσαντες κοινῶς μᾶλλον ὠφέλησαν ἢ ἐκ τῶν ἰδίων ἔβλαψαν. (2.42.3)

> And it is right that courage in war on behalf of the fatherland should take pride of place even for those who were less worthy in other ways. For [these men], who erased their evil by their goodness, rendered greater service in common than they did injury in their personal lives.

---

[207] See note 198, above.   [208] This gap is easily revealed by e.g. a *TLG* search.

The memorial of -Ulus symbolically offers a distinct reinterpretation of this sentiment. The *patrios nomos* does elevate the fact of death in warfare for the polis above all other concerns, including – as Thucydides chooses to make explicit here – those of separate identity. -Ulus' tombstone attempts to reclaim the deceased's individuality instead.

The inscription further disagrees with the sentiments expressed in Thucydides by constructing Athens not as the inspiration for warfare, but rather as the audience of -Ulus' bold deeds. Other "witnesses" (μάρτυρες) are also called upon to see or testify to the other honors -Ulus has gained (or invoked) for himself. An elaborate network of viewers and objects is therefore constructed: working backwards, the trophies are visual manifestations of -Ulus' ἀρετή, which are themselves to be "witnessed" by unknown others and perhaps spoken about in turn to still further audiences; the πατρίς and the other subjects of the verb ἴ]σασιν are to be recipients of the knowledge of -Ulus' prowess at dispatching enemies; and the entire message is further publicized by the iconography and the text of the monument itself, which not only shows but also tells the immediate viewer how -Ulus is to be understood and remembered.[209] The demotic ΦΛΥΕΎΣ, featured so prominently at the conclusion of the epitaph, caps the challenge.[210] The *patrios nomos* memorialized fallen men by tribes, i.e. by artificially imposed civic divisions; -Ulus is recollected instead by his deme, i.e. the unit of local belonging that depended upon his legitimate membership in his *oikos*.[211]

A natural question is how this strongly confident monument might have been received by contemporary audiences. As an Athenian citizen, if he had perished in war, -Ulus would most likely have been entitled to burial at the state ceremonies. His survivors, however, may have chosen to erect a separate monument for him either instead of or along with the public privileges.[212]

[209] Clairmont 1993: vol. II, 89 and esp. 1970: 101–2 notes the close relationship between the thematic material of the epitaph and the relief, although he has seen this monument (1970: 101) as cooperating, rather than competing, with civic traditions, suggesting that "The family of the fallen soldier combined the epigram with the relief in such a way that the adoption of a public theme did not give offense when used for a private memorial," and reading the epitaph as invoking the positive contributions of -Ulus to the state.

[210] An observation made by J. Ober.

[211] See Meyer 1993, and cf. the changing emphases of epitaphs during the fourth century discussed in Chapter 5, below.

[212] Stupperich 1977: 194–9 (cited in Bergemann 1997: 43 n. 88) sees many tombstones that display images of warriors as potential cenotaphs for individuals otherwise buried in accordance with the *patrios nomos*; Bergemann 1997: 43, 63–4, discussing fourth-century tombstones in particular, notes that images of soldiers need not indicate death in battle, and need not even be automatically identified with the deceased, particularly when they occur as parts of family groups. The emphasis placed here upon epitaphs, as Bergemann notes, helps to

There is also the chance, however remote, that -Ulus, for all the claims of his prowess in warfare, perished by some other means[213] and was therefore ineligible for the *patrios nomos*; this memorial might then be read as an attempt at compensation, an invocation of honors that were perceived due but were denied on a 'technicality.' It is unlikely, though admittedly not impossible, that this tombstone stood in the Kerameikos; it was found in Chalandri, a modern suburb located north of the Athens city center. If it was not originally located in physical proximity to the civic burials the possibility of its making a hubristic or competitive visual impact might have been somewhat diminished, but given its text and iconography, probably not eliminated. -Ulus' name has frequently been restored as 'Aristob]ulus,' and there is an Aristobulus entered on the Athenian casualty lists for the tribe Pandionis in the year 409/8,[214] but he cannot be identified with the owner of this tombstone, as Phlia, -Ulus' deme, belonged to the tribe Cecropis.[215]

IG ii/iii² 10593 is dated by *IG* to "before the mid-fourth century," but Clairmont recommends that the relief that it accompanies should be dated to "about 400."[216] The epitaph, dedicated to one Athenocles, reads as follows:[217]

πόλλ' ἀρετῆς μνημεῖα λιπὼν ἔργοις δὲ κρατή[σας]
κεῖται Ἀθηνοκλῆς ἐνθάδε ἀνὴρ ἀγαθός.

Having left behind many reminders of his virtue after
        prevailing in his deeds,
Athenocles lies here, a good man.

The relief, which shows a bearded man in a *petasos* (traveler's hat) holding a long shaft,[218] does not immediately invite the interpretation of this memorial as belonging to a soldier.[219] But Clairmont has noted that the phrase

---

limit, but not to eliminate, the uncertainties (see note 213, below). Whether these individual monuments are graves or cenotaphs, for war dead or not, however, they claim status, agency, and memory for the individual in contrast with that accorded to the citizen group.

[213] Bergemann 1997: 63 recommends this kind of caution, pointing out that the epitaph does not preserve the cause of death.

[214] See *CAT ad loc.*; Clairmont 1983: vol. II, 329.

[215] My analyses of the monuments of -Ulus, Glauciades, and Dexileus (see Chapter 5, below) were completed before Hurwit 2007 became available: I was glad to see that we agree on some of the most important points (regarding the material discussed here, see esp. Hurwit 2007: 44 on -Ulus).

[216] Clairmont 1970: 77.   [217] Edition here from *IG* ii/iii² 10593.

[218] See the description in *CAT ad loc.*

[219] Stupperich 1977: 194 (cited in Clairmont 1993: vol. I, 255), for example, does not commit to this attribution, but Stupperich 1994: 95 is more certain, and believes the iconography was inspired by that of the *polyandria*; Clairmont 1970: 76 (also referenced by Clairmont 1993: vol. I, 255) originally thought of "warfare or trade?" as possible interpretations, calling the object depicted on the relief a "staff."

ἀνὴρ ἀγαθός tends to be applied to fallen warriors, and combines that with the reference to ἔργα and the image of what he now construes as a "lance" to recommend that this, too, is a warrior dedication, perhaps to a casualty buried in accordance with the *patrios nomos*.[220] Heroic language is evident in the reference to ἀρετή (a Homeric virtue), but the word μνημεῖα (singular μνημεῖον) does not occur in epic. Rather, it is strongly contextualized in the fifth and fourth centuries, both in prose and in poetry (especially tragedy) as being something that creates memory, including a funerary marker.[221] The closest parallels for the wording of the epitaph itself, in fact, occur in the earlier orators and in Xenophon's encomiastic biography of Agesilaus.[222] To generalize, then, the words and even the concepts may have a heroic feel to them, but the phraseology resonates with contemporary invocations of achievement, agency, and memory for exemplars both past and present.

IG ii/iii² 10780, dated by *IG* to the beginning of the fourth century, reads as follows:[223]

[εἰ] τοιῶνδε ἀνδρῶν ἔη πόλις, ὅποτ᾽ ἂν αὐτ[ῆς]

[ἐ]χθροὶ στήσαιεν Ζηνὶ τρόπαιον ἕδος.

in altero latere lapidis:

[κ]τ<ώμ>ενον εὔκλεα<ν> [δ]ορὶ καὶ χερὶ τόνδε πρὸς ἀ[νδ]ρὸς

[ἐχθροῦ Ἀρι]σ[τ]όκρ[ι]<τ>ον ὤλεσε θοῦρος Ἄρ<ης>.

5   [. . . . ἔ]ξοχα σ - -

If only there were a city of men of this kind, its
enemies would never have set up a trophy-place for Zeus.
Raging Ares felled this man Aristocritus, who procured glory with his
arm and spear, at the hands of his enemy.
. . . preeminence . . .

As other epitaphs have done, this one, too, employs language and imagery from high poetry: most notably, θοῦρος (line 4) is a Homeric epithet, as here, of the god Ares; ἔ]ξοχα is a Homeric word, as well. Although the word εὔκλεα<ν> in line 3 is also of good Homeric pedigree, Threatte points out that here it is used in an "unmetrical spelling," as is the ἔη in line 1.[224] The phrase [δ]ορὶ καὶ χερί clusters closely with a form of the root

---

[220] Clairmont 1993: vol. I, 255 (although cf. the slightly more cautious stance of Loraux 1986: 106–7); see also Stupperich 1994: 95 on the relationship of the iconography of this tombstone to the public *polyandria*.

[221] See *LSJ ad loc.*; a full-corpus search on the word-root in the *TLG* offers further support.

[222] As revealed by a *TLG* search: Isoc. *Bus.* 10, *Panegy.* 186, *Areop.* 38, *Philippus* 112; Isae. *Dicaeogene* 41; X. *Ag.* 6.2, 11.16; Lys. *Theomnest. I* 28, *Theomnest. II* 10.

[223] Edition here from *IG* ii/iii² 10780.

[224] Threatte 1977: 183–4. The Homeric usages (in the epics and the Hymns) of the ἐϋκλ- root employ diaeresis.

θουρ- in Aeschylus' *Agamemnon*, in a passage sufficiently famous that it was later mocked by Aristophanes.[225] Finally, the fact that [Aristocritus][226] is represented as receiving his death from the god of war creates further heroic associations.

If the poetical usages are concentrated in the second couplet, the first couplet contextualizes the epitaph and its honorand within contemporary civic and funerary traditions. The opening wish for a "city of men of this kind" invites a comparison between the subject of the epitaph and his fellow citizens, in which the larger group is somehow found lacking. This suggestion is borne out in the second line, when unnamed "enemies" are in fact depicted in victory, setting up a battle-trophy to Zeus.[227] The monument of [Aristocritus] therefore participates in several contrasts simultaneously. It is a memorial to one man that highlights his distinction from his community. In its physicality, his monument symbolically responds to the τρόπαιον established by the enemy, both providing a memorial and imagining a counter-narrative in which an army of warriors like [Aristocritus] is in fact victorious. As long as there are no other men who can match him, however, his tombstone suggests, he is deserving of separate memorialization, since his city cannot meet his standard.

IG ii/iii² 10998, dated by *IG* to the beginning of the fourth century and found in Menidi, Attica, is associated with a relief so fragmentary that its composition, which may have included a warrior, a woman, and a child, cannot be confidently reconstructed.[228] The inscription upon it, however, is well preserved. It represents an epitaph for one Glauciades.[229]

---

[225] A. *Ag.* 109–12: ὅπως Ἀχαιῶν δίθρονον κράτος, Ἑλλάδος ἥβας / ξύμφρονα ταγάν, / πέμπει ξὺν δορὶ καὶ χερὶ πράκτορι / θούριος ὄρνις Τευκρίδ᾽ ἐπ᾽ αἶαν, "how the raging bird-sign sent the double-throned power of the Achaeans, the single-minded leadership of the youth of Greece, against the land of Teucer with spear and hand that sought redress," transformed in a satirical context by the Euripides character at Ar. *Ran.* 1284–90 (1289 reads σὺν δορὶ καὶ χερὶ πράκτορι θούριος ὄρνις, "with spear and hand that sought redress, the raging bird-sign . . . ").

[226] Threatte 1977: 190 points out that the restoration of this individual's name is "by no means certain." He will therefore be referred to here as [Aristocritus].

[227] On battle-trophies as offerings to Zeus, see West 1969: 8 n. 8.

[228] See the summary of the relief's condition presented at *CAT* 2.768. Although Clairmont would date this tombstone to the second quarter of the fourth century (*CAT*'s 375–350 date range), the *CAT* entry is marked n.v., and the reported state of the fragments further suggests that caution is in order in any attempt to date this monument by sculptural style. The editors of *IG* ii/iii² prefer to place this tombstone at the beginning of the fourth century according to its lettering. Neither approach is conclusive, and it seems that a re-evaluation of the complete monument is in order.

[229] Edition from *IG* ii/iii² 10998.

τὸς ἀγαθὸς ἔστερξεν Ἄρης, ἐφίλησε δ᾽ ἔπαινος
καὶ γήραι νεότης οὐ παρέδωχ᾽ ὑβρίσαι·
ὧγ καὶ Γ[λ]αυκιάδης δηίος ἀπὸ πατρίδος ἔργων
ἦλθ᾽ ἐπὶ πάνδεκτον Φερσεφόνης θάλαμον.

Ares loved the good men, praise cherished them,
and early life did not give them over for the later years to despoil them.
Amongst them, warlike Glaukiades, because of the deeds [he performed]
    for his fatherland,
went to the bridal chamber of Persephone, which receives all.

The language of the first three lines of this epitaph is highly poetical: most notably, the mention of the god Ares as a metonym for warfare is a usage especially common in tragedy, and the adjective δηίος, describing a hostile fighter, is frequent in Homeric poetry (cf. *LSJ ad loca*). The pride in, praise of, and memorialization of the valiant youthful death finds good precedent not only in the story of Achilles, but also in the (likely connected) idealizing fascination with early decease during the archaic period.[230] The epitaph concludes, finally, with two of the generalizing tropes that become increasingly common in funerary inscriptions during the fourth century: the explicit reference to the mythological underworld and the reminder that death is universal.[231]

The language of the first three lines also highlights the potential relationship of this individual memorial to the generalizing tendencies of the *patrios nomos*: the inscription calls pointed attention to Glauciades, as a *specific* individual, out of the anonymous body of "good men" who have perished in war.[232] The deceased is not here explicitly named as an Athenian, but no other home is particularly likely for him. Menidi, where his tombstone was found, is a suburb only some 10 km north of modern Athens, situated in the ancient deme of Acharnae, and it is probable that he was indeed a citizen, perhaps from that very deme.[233] The word πατρίς, analyzed above in the discussion of the tombstone of -Ulus of Phlia, recurs here in the epitaph of Glauciades, as well. In the case of -Ulus, the "fatherland" was to witness -Ulus' deeds in war. Here in Glauciades' epitaph, however, the connection is made even more explicit: He received his death and deserves his honor because of what he did for his city. Again as in the cases of -Ulus, Athenocles, and [Aristocritus], this memorial may have been intended as a

[230] See Chapter 2, above.   [231] See Chapter 5, below.   [232] An observation made by J. Ober.
[233] As Meyer 1993 shows, demotics, which can function as confirmations of Athenian citizenship, become more common in funerary inscriptions in the course of the fourth century, but are not by any means the rule during this or any other period. See also Chapter 5, below.

response to the *patrios nomos*, reclaiming relevance, agency, and memory for the individual.

The funeral oration as verbal monument

It must be acknowledged that the yearly burial of fallen Athenian warriors according to the rituals of the *patrios nomos* was not entirely anonymous. At least as early as the 460s, the names of the deceased were listed, grouped by tribes, on stone stelai set up over their tomb.[234] No testimonia, however, suggest that these names were read as part of the funeral. Instead, the rituals included the delivery of a major laudatory speech, the *epitaphios logos*, that integrated the lost men and their achievements into the ongoing history of the city.[235] The *dêmos* and (especially) the polis were the focus throughout, with the polis functioning as the eternal goal that gave meaning, relevance, and collective fame to its lost men.[236] Loraux has analyzed in detail the many contradictions that the verbal and symbolic rhetoric of the *epitaphios* produced in its efforts to subsume and transform the glory of the dead for the good of the polis,[237] and so I will concentrate here upon relating the *epitaphios* as a genre and the circumstances of its delivery, together with Thucydides' particular composition for Pericles, to the issues raised by the tombstones discussed above.

Part of the honorific currency of the *epitaphios* seems to have derived from the stature of its speaker, typically an eminent political or military leader who would also have needed to be a talented orator (Thuc. 2.34.6). This individual was tacitly required by the expectations of both circumstances and genre to engage in a ritualized subordination of his own prestige to the (temporary) honor of the group of fallen soldiers, something that Thucydides has Pericles acknowledge at the opening of the Funeral Oration, when he disclaims his ability to appropriately eulogize the fallen and feigns reluctance to assume his role (2.35.1–3).[238] Like the *epitaphios* as a genre, then, and just as the character did in his other direct speeches, Thucydides' Pericles works to create an illusion of group sovereignty in a context where individual eminence and authority can never be entirely suppressed.

---

[234] See Chapter 2, above.   [235] Loraux 1986 esp. 132–71.

[236] Ibid. *passim*, esp. e.g. 27, 104–6 (at 106 noting "*There is no life but that of the city*" [emphasis *sic*]), 132–7, 238–41, 269–77.

[237] Ibid. *passim*.

[238] Ibid. esp. 233–8. Kennedy 1963 also offers some relevant comments: see 48–51 on the disclaimer of rhetorical skill in Thucydidean oratory, and 154–66 as a general discussion of the rhetoric of *epitaphioi*.

This is not to say, however, that the Periclean Funeral Oration, in its emphasis upon the collective, takes no account whatsoever of the separate citizens and soldiers who comprise the Athenian state. Indeed, it speaks in some detail about how such individual men are judged suitable for office and service (2.37.1) and are essentially expected to participate in politics (2.40.2). But 2.37.1, in particular, sketches a meritocratic system in which preference and honor are extended to those who can usefully contribute to civic life. This implicitly defends Pericles' position of prominence not only in the *patrios nomos* but in the Athenian government, and may further imply that those outside of such ranks have essentially been debarred from access by a kind of cultural peer review. Further, all of these imaginary individual Athenians remain nameless, abstract exemplars, distinguished rather by the use of the grammatical singular (e.g. "each man," "the one who") than by any true identity – and they are still discussed exclusively in terms of their relationship to the polis. Even at the moment of their deaths, their value is established by their military sacrifice for the good of the group (2.42.3–4), which is explicitly stated to be so much more important than their own personal affairs that even baser men can redeem themselves thereby: ἀγαθῷ γὰρ κακὸν ἀφανίσαντες κοινῶς μᾶλλον ὠφέλησαν ἢ ἐκ τῶν ἰδίων ἔβλαψαν, "For [these men], who erased their evil by their goodness, rendered greater service in common than they did injury in their personal lives" (2.42.3).

The *epitaphios* in Thucydides is a literary product rather than a transcript, but it nevertheless both discusses and embodies some of the tensions that the *patrios nomos* likely generated. Even in contexts where Thucydides' Pericles seems to be treating or celebrating the individual citizen, two particular problems emerge: the dominance (and, indeed, open acknowledgement) of methodologies for political and social valuation that essentially favor the existing elite; and the consistent subordination of the significance of all but the most eminent to the interests of the polis. These issues, however, are not confined to the historigraphic text: they are also represented in the material realities of the Athenian cemetery.

As discussed in Chapter 2, above, the *patrios nomos* was likely unable to resolve the inherent contrast created by the collective burial of the war dead beside individual memorials for eminent Athenians and foreign benefactors. The rhetoric of both speech and ceremony praised the *dêmos* and the entire polis through the medium of the fallen warriors, but audiences both present and future could immediately compare the relative 'greatness' of groups and individuals merely by observing the local monuments.[239] The tombstones

---

[239] See Chapter 2, above.

of -Ulus, Athenocles, [Aristocritus], and Glauciades seem to answer this challenge by employing an increasingly familiar symbolic vocabulary to claim agency and memory for their subjects. Not only may some of these monuments and others like them have responded visually to the memorials set up by the Athenian state,[240] but their texts employ ways of invoking a place in history that find precedents at least as early as the Tyrannicides. In their use of high, even heroic, poetical language, their careful relationship of the contribution of their subjects to the polis, and their bold assertions of a particular historical narrative, these epitaphs suggest that the alchemy of 'making history' was intelligible – and meaningful – even amongst the private citizens who created and viewed the memorials in the cemetery.

The tombstones for Mannes, Nicomachus, the anonymous young thespian, and the priestess Myrrhine discussed above do not make the same counter-claims as those of the warriors, but they do use many of the same techniques to elevate their subjects, contextualize them as specific individuals within the polis, and claim a place for them in memory. In their focus upon the loss of a distinct person, these monuments ironically display a more specific sense of historical positioning than does the *patrios nomos*, which in its attempts to 'eternalize' military sacrifice ultimately de-emphasizes its historical context.[241]

4.4 Conclusion: The Periclean citizenship law of 451/50 and the tombstones of Athens

During the last third of the fifth century BC, individual contributions to the motion of history gain prominence at Athens in historiography and in public and private commemoration. Not long before this time, the sources relate, Pericles proposed a new law decreeing that μὴ μετέχειν τῆς πόλεως ὃς ἂν μὴ ἐξ ἀμφοῖν ἀστοῖν ἦι γεγονώς, "no one should share in the polis who is not born of a pair of citizens" (*Ath. Pol.* 26.4).[242] Regardless of its motivation,[243]

---

[240] See notes 199, 219, and 220, above, and see Chapter 5, below, on the monument of Dexileus.

[241] See Loraux 1986: 118–31 and 478 s.v. "Time, temporality," on the temporal qualities of the *epitaphios logos*, and Derderian 2001: 97–110 on the development of historical context in written memorials during the earliest classical period; cf. also Chapter 2, above.

[242] Plutarch's version says that those only were to be Athenian citizens who were ἐκ δυεῖν Ἀθηναίων γεγονότας, i.e. "begotten of two Athenian citizen [parents]" (Plu. *Per.* 37.3). Boegehold 1994: 57 (citing both ancient sources) suggests that the earlier version in *Ath. Pol.* probably more closely resembles the original text, as it cites the law in the form of a prohibition, accompanied by references to the eponymous archon and the proposer of the decree.

[243] Boegehold 1994: 57–60 and *passim* speculates about the immediate circumstances that might have provoked the proposal, and summarizes a number of scholarly arguments.

this more restrictive law may have rendered Athenian citizenship a rarer and more ostensibly desirable commodity.[244] Such a development would correspond well with the extension of citizenship to foreign benefactors as a special honor, which, as noted above, is attested in the epigraphical record at least as early as 410 and may have begun still earlier.[245]

Might this law also have had something to do with the changes in commemorative practices for individuals observed at Athens during the later years of the fifth century? Meyer has noted that the demotic, the portion of an Athenian name that identifies the location of an individual's enrollment as a citizen, increases in frequency on extant Athenian tombstones after 403/2, the year in which the Periclean citizenship law was re-issued or reinforced.[246] This rise in demotics, which continues well into the fourth century, cannot be conclusively proved to be a direct outcome of the legislation of 403/2,[247] but both of these developments may suggest a fresh prioritization of the expression of democratic citizen status in a diversely populated polis recently rocked by a pair of serious oligarchic coups (411, 404/3).[248]

As will be discussed in the next chapter, however, these demotics are also accompanied by changes in funerary iconography and (especially) epitaphs that suggest a growing focus upon smaller units of local belonging, most notably the family.[249] Amongst the most notable of these changes is the increasing number of funerary monuments to females of all age groups surviving from the late fifth and fourth centuries. On the one hand, the citizenship status for Athenian women announced by the Periclean law and its reiteration[250] may have helped to motivate their more frequent representation – with their demotics – on tombstones.[251] But on the other,

[244] Patterson 1981 esp. 133, noting that the law was likely "both the result of the increasing consciousness of an *Athenian* identity and the cause of further development of the belief that being Athenian was a distinct and distinctly valuable status." Cf. also Osborne 1997 esp. 4–11 on the "exclusiveness" (10) of the sense of belonging in classical Athens.

[245] See note 95, above.

[246] Meyer 1993: 110 nn. 25–6, with references. Patterson 1981: 140–7 holds that while the law of 451/50 may have been only variously enforced, especially during the oligarchic upheavals of 411 and 404/3, it was never withdrawn or changed before its re-emphasis in 403/2.

[247] Meyer 1993: 110 n. 26 casts doubt upon Whitehead 1986: 71–2 on this point.

[248] This is a central argument of Meyer 1993.

[249] See Chapter 5, below, and Meyer 1993: 111–12 and *passim*, engaging in particular with the arguments of Humphreys 1983. Humphreys sees certain changes in Athenian funerary monuments during the fourth century as being primarily the consequence of familial interests; Meyer wishes to emphasize the extent to which civic concerns might also have played a role.

[250] Note in particular the use of duals in the testimonia discussed above, intended to refer specifically to pairs of citizen parents: ἐξ ἀμφοῖν ἀστοῖν in *Ath. Pol.* 26.4, ἐκ δυεῖν Ἀθηναίων in Plu. *Per.* 37.3.

[251] Osborne 1997.

the potential for non-elite individuals outside of obvious positions of political power to 'make history' seems to have been perceived less optimistically in the fourth century than it was in the fifth, and the monuments for women occur alongside tombstones for men that betray these sentiments. As Chapter 5 will show, these fourth-century monuments as a corpus seem to claim that the meaning of an individual life is significantly derived from personal membership in local and localized groups, rather than from membership in the polis as a whole, which is itself also more frequently acknowledged in the fifth century than it is in the fourth.

5 | Into the fourth century

Learning one's limits, knowing one's place

5.1 Individual commemoration in a postwar world

Dexileus of Thoricus was killed in battle in 394/3 BC, during the first season of the Corinthian War.[1] He was buried in accordance with the *patrios nomos*, along with the other Athenian citizens lost in war during that year, and his name was inscribed on a monument alongside those of the other fallen cavalry of his tribe, Acamantis.[2] His relatives, however, created what seems to have been a separate cenotaph for him in the family *peribolos* (walled grave plot) in the Kerameikos.[3] The tombstone survives nearly intact, and bears this epitaph:[4]

> Δεξίλεως Λυσανίο Θορίκιος.
> ἐγένετο ἐπὶ Τεισάνδρο ἄρχοντος,
> ἀπέθανε ἐπ' Εὐβολίδο
> ἐγ Κορίνθωι τῶν πέντε ἱππέων.

> Dexileus son of Lysanias of Thoricus. Born in
> the archonship of Tisandrus; died in
> that of Eubulides, at Corinth as one of
> the five cavalrymen.

The careful mentions of birth and death dates, along with both deme and patronymic and the circumstances of his service, ensure that Dexileus

---

[1] As noted in Chapter 4, above, my readings of the monuments of -Ulus, Glauciades, and Dexileus were completed before Hurwit 2007 became available: I was glad to see that we agree on some of the most important points, including most significantly the interpretation discussed at note 12, below.

[2] *IG* ii/iii² 5222. Dexileus is listed by his given name, along with nine others, after the heading οἵδε ἱππέης ἀπέθανον ἐν Κορίνθωι | φύλαρχος Ἀντιφάνης, "These horsemen perished at Corinth: Antiphanes the phylarch..." This grouping is followed by the entry of one other horseman, Neocleides, who is listed alone as having died "at Coronea."

[3] Four other inscribed monuments (besides that of Dexileus) dedicated to members of the same family have been found in and around the *peribolos*, *IG* ii/iii² 6226, 6227, 6230, 11817 (the latter now lost). D. 40.52 allows the addition of another member (Lysistratus) to the family tree. Sources for inscriptions and testimonia: stemma *ad IG* ii/iii² 6217; *CAT* 2.209; Closterman 1999: 227 fig. 2 (stemma), 323–4 (inventory and description of the entire *peribolos*).

[4] Edition from *IG* ii/iii² 6217; translation from Rhodes and Osborne 2003: 41 no. 7.

is precisely identified as a specific individual who attained military distinction,[5] a claim that is reiterated by the iconography of the relief. On it, Dexileus, atop a rearing horse, aims a bronze spear (now missing, implied by mounting holes) at an enemy lying on the ground.[6] The young cavalryman is depicted as a triumphant military victor,[7] but the monument's individuality and its location claim his sacrifice for his family, rather than for the state.[8]

Dexileus' tombstone, although it seems to share the attitudes and even the iconography of the monuments of -Ulus and Glauciades discussed in the previous chapter,[9] was displayed in a far more prominent location. Erected on the south side of the Street of the Tombs, close to the large intersection with the Sacred Way, it decorated what was probably one of the first *periboloi* installed in this section of the Kerameikos, and stood well above the level of the street.[10] It faced northeast, not only back towards the city, but also probably towards the area of the cemetery where the war casualties were buried.[11] Whether the intention was to amplify, compete with, or even defy the group memorialization Dexileus had received on the other side of the Kerameikos, his family had rescripted the symbolic narrative constructed by the polis during the rites of the *patrios nomos*.[12] Whatever Athens had allotted to Dexileus' memory, his survivors apparently felt that it was not enough.

The bid for the significance of the individual made by Dexileus' monument may be echoed in the grave-goods it housed. Though these were

---

[5] Although the editors of *IG* ii/iii[2], citing Pfuhl 1932: 4, caution against the easy acceptance of this connection, the "five cavalrymen" of the epitaph have been connected with the strategy recommended by X. *Eq. Mag.* 8.25.

[6] See the more detailed description of the relief at *CAT* 2.209, to which this summary is indebted.

[7] Knigge 1991: 111.   [8] Morris 1992: 143.

[9] See Chapter 4, above. These three tombstones are often connected to one another by scholars, though more often because of their iconography than their epitaphs: e.g. Hurwit 2007: 44; Low 2002: 112–15; Bergemann 1997: 63–4; Morris 1994: 81; Morris 1992: 143–4; *CAT* 2.130; Clairmont 1970: 100–2, all with additional references.

[10] Knigge 1991: 110. See also ibid. 112 fig. 107 for a possible reconstruction of the precinct.

[11] Ibid. 111, 113. The area that held the *patrios nomos* monuments is sometimes referred to in modern scholarship, as here in Knigge, as the *dêmosion sêma*, the "public memorial [ground]"; however, the distinction may not be appropriate to the ancient demarcations: see Patterson 2006b and the response to it by Arrington 2010: 500 n. 4.

[12] This interpretation is commonly shared: see the references collected in note 9, above. I myself tend to see the attitudes of monuments like this one as being more individualizing and more competitive than some others do: my views agree with those of Hurwit 2007: 44 (cf. note 1, above) and Morris 1992: 143–4. Low 2002: 113–14 observes "a tension . . . which it is not perhaps possible, or even necessary, to resolve" (114) between individualizing and group-oriented ideologies, but suggests that "by the time of Dexileos' death . . . when individual memorials were again more common, it was not necessarily a challenge to the dominant democratic ideology to erect an individual monument, even to a soldier who would already be commemorated on a state memorial."

inhumed, they would have been visible at the moment of their deposition, and may have played a part in any 'funerary' rituals the family performed outside of the *patrios nomos*. Amongst the pottery probably from this tomb is an *oinochoe* that depicts the Tyrannicides.[13] This item recollects the interpretation of the Athenian Revolution that lionized Harmodius and Aristogeiton. It may be intended to venture a similar claim to individual heroism for Dexileus,[14] who in reality probably shared little more with the Tyrannicides than Harmodius' youth and violent death.[15]

Dexileus' monument exemplifies some trends in the commemoration of the individual that developed in fifth-century Athens, especially in its invocation of separate, historically contextualized identity within the state.[16] But it also stands at an important turning point: in the course of the fourth century, the views about individuals and groups displayed by historiography and public inscriptions on the one hand, and by private funerary monuments on the other, diverge noticeably. During the first half of the fourth century, historiography, honorific inscriptions, and document reliefs continue in many cases to acknowledge the authority and historical agency of the collective citizen group. This stance, however, sometimes appears to be motivated by regard for traditional means of expression, rather than by a genuinely perceived need to assert the sovereignty of the Athenian *dêmos*. In general, there is now a markedly increased interest in the activities and contributions of individuals. Both literary and public-epigraphical discourse reveal a growing perception that the political, military, and social roles of eminent men are essential to the motion of history. Private Attic funerary memorials of the first half of the fourth century, however, seem in general to be shifting away from complex ideological expressions like those contained in the monument of Dexileus. During this time, comparatively fewer tombstones display expansive epitaphs or even qualitative adjectives than did so in the fifth century. While they do show new developments in both scale and decorative detail, their iconography grows increasingly standardized and tends towards domestic scenes. Overall, they tend to construct meaning not through claims of historical impact or beneficence to the polis, but rather

---

[13] Vermeule 1970: 103–7.

[14] Clairmont 1983: 220–1; see also Ajootian 1998: 8, on "the conjunction of the Tyrannicides with Agora athletics."

[15] For a more detailed political reading of the Tyrannicides iconography, see Vermeule 1970: 104–6; and now Hurwit 2007: 39–40. Low 2002: 114 n. 41 calls attention to a relationship "between the tyrannicides and the commemoration of the war dead" noted by Taylor 1981: 23–5.

[16] See Chapters 2 and 4, above.

through an individual's membership in a network of smaller 'belongings,' especially the family.[17]

The symbolic and literary discourse of Athens, which once described a charged debate over historical agency and meaning, is changing. Outstanding individuals increasingly attract the attention of fourth-century writers and orators; the wealthy and the powerful, both Athenian citizens and foreigners, are accorded public monuments in return for the tangible and intangible assets they bring to the citizen group. Whether or not the *dêmos* might actually have been able to function effectively without its eminent leaders, the inscriptions and the literature present outstanding individuals as possessing historical relevance and social value, thereby creating a feedback loop between perceptions and realities. More ordinary individuals seem to have responded by memorializing their lives in very different ways. Perhaps in part because the public discourse during this period makes increasingly obvious claims about "who makes history," the private discourse turns inward to embrace the smaller-scale connections that give distinct identity to an individual life. In short, the idea that any given member of the *dêmos* might "make history" seems to have enjoyed less credence, or at least less currency, in the fourth century than it might have in the fifth.

On the literary side, the major continuous, contemporary historiographic source for the first half of the fourth century is Xenophon (*c.* 430/25– 355/4 (?) BC).[18] Though Athenian-born and an intellectual disciple of Socrates,[19] Xenophon accumulated an array of experiences that crossed both polis divisions and national boundaries. His mercenary service in the failed coup of Cyrus of Persia and his command on the march of the Greek Ten Thousand back from Cunaxa in 401/0; his service with Agesilaus of Sparta from at least as early as 395/4; his exile from Athens; and his residence of some twenty years in the Peloponnese on his Spartan-donated estate at Scillus (concluding probably in 370, after which time he seems to have had

---

[17] These general observations are common in the scholarship, although explanations for them vary: I summarize mine in the next paragraph. For a variety of perspectives, including dissenting ones, see e.g. Tsagalis 2008 esp. 183–98; Stears 2000a: 210–13; Closterman 1999 *passim*; Bergemann 1997: 86–8; Osborne 1997 esp. 14–33; Hoffmann 1993 esp. 172–9; Meyer 1993 esp. 107–9; Ridgway 1997: 162; Humphreys 1980 esp. 112–21.

[18] Other significant sources for the era include Diodorus 13–15, possibly dependent via Ephorus on the Oxyrhynchus Historian (see Dillery 1995: 269–70 n. 10, 129–30, 258–9 n. 7, 269–70 n. 10, 277–8 n. 20, with bibliography); the Oxyrhynchus Historian ("P") himself (see e.g. McKechnie and Kern 1988); and Plutarch's *Lives* of Alcibiades, Lysander, Agesilaus, and Pelopidas (his *Life* of Epaminondas is lost).

[19] On Xenophon's relationship with Socrates and his teachings, see e.g. Anderson 1974: 20–33; on the nature of Xenophon's Socratic writings, see the bibliography collected by Morrison 1988.

access to Athens again) all appear to have left their mark on this thinking and on his literary output.

How may the writings of a long-term exile with such independent loyalties be compared with monuments shaped by explicitly Athenian political, social, and aesthetic concerns? One possible answer is that Xenophon was possessed of an Athenian aristocratic education and background:[20] he was an adult and nearly of marriageable age[21] by the time he undertook the journey to Persia. The significant impact of his early intellectual life emerges both implicitly and explicitly from the 'Socratic' literature within his corpus, and he continued, even during his period of service and residence with the Spartans, to read and study Athenian writers and to be shaped by their ideas.[22] Xenophon's *Hellenica*, for example, in a well-known departure from the historiographic practices of its predecessors, does not include a preface or introduction of any kind.[23] It begins instead *in medias res* with the words Μετὰ δὲ ταῦτα οὐ πολλαῖς ἡμέραις ὕστερον, "After these [events], a few days later…" (*HG* 1.1.1).[24] In presuming familiarity with the coverage of the Peloponnesian War by Thucydides, this opening constructs an audience versed in the traditions of specifically Athenian historiography.[25]

A more comprehensive response to the issue of "Xenophon the Athenian,"[26] however, emphasizes not Xenophon's Athenian roots, but rather his status as an outsider. Xenophon was forced by his exile to examine his native polis at a distance, and his corpus reveals an interpretation of Greek politics that reaches well beyond his home, paying special attention to Sparta in particular.[27] So while Xenophon's interest in the history-making ability of individuals may have been partially due to his experiences as an

---

[20] See Seager 2001 on resonances of Athenian democratic thought in Xenophon; Seager, however, correctly cautions that "a number of the basic principles involved … are not exclusive to Athens or to democracy" (385).

[21] On the age of maturity for men in classical Athens, see e.g. Roisman 2005: 11–12 and *passim*, with references.

[22] Any influence of Isocrates' *Evagoras* upon Xenophon's *Agesilaus*, however, may be the result not of distant intellectual contact between Athens and Scillus, but rather of Xenophon's redemption at Athens late in his life, since Isocrates' work was most likely composed sometime between 374 and 365: on the "intellectual context" that produced both of these encomia, see Pownall 2004: 5–37.

[23] Dillery 1995: 9–11 discusses the significance of this omission.

[24] In the remainder of this chapter, all passages from Xenophon are cited by title abbreviation and passage numbers only.

[25] The degree to which Xenophon's narrative of the final years of the Peloponnesian War (*HG* 1.1.1–2.3.10) was explicitly intended to imitate Thucydidean style is debated: see the bibliography collected by Dillery 1995: 9 nn. 10–11.

[26] This is the title of a book by Higgins 1977.

[27] Seager 2001 esp. 396–7; see also Proietti 1987: xi–xviii; Westlake 1969a: 203.

Athenian citizen, his writings, in which this problem is addressed in detail, likely presume a comprehension of and an interest in this issue outside of Athens, as well.[28]

This chapter and the next one, then, concentrate primarily upon the first half of the fourth century BC, examining the perceived roles of individuals and groups in the motion of history prior to the Macedonian ascendancy over mainland Greece. The subject matter of the examination, however, begins slightly earlier in time. Like Thucydides, Xenophon covered the Peloponnesian War (in his case the latter portion of it), and his portrayal of one of its central figures, Alcibiades, shows a shift in his thinking about the history-making individual away from the example set by his predecessor. Following the discussion of Alcibiades, this chapter treats the historical agency of arguably the most significant native-born Athenian in Xenophon's corpus: the character that represents the historian himself in the *Anabasis*. Xenophon's coverage of non-Athenian characters is reserved for the discussions of Sparta and Boeotia in Chapter 6.

5.2 Looking back on the Peloponnesian War: Xenophon's Alcibiades

As established in Chapter 4, interaction between the leaders and the *dêmos* is, for Thucydides, key to the performance of history-making action. Alcibiades' exploitation of that model leads to his projection of hollow (but effective) promises, and ultimately to the prospect for his restoration from exile. Thucydides' Alcibiades constructs his influence over his citizen group by advertising that he is indispensable to the *dêmos'* collective agency. Although he fled when summoned back from the Sicilian expedition to stand trial (Thuc. 6.61.6–7), by Thuc. 8.97.3, Alcibiades has been recalled by the Athenian government of the Five Thousand, and by 8.108.1–2, near the conclusion of Thucydides' text, the character himself is taking firm individual credit for what appear to be nearly independent operations in the eastern Aegean.

Thucydides' version of Alcibiades, then, constantly held out the promise, however illusory, that the Athenian *dêmos* could achieve its own ends with him or through him. But the assumption in Xenophon appears to be that the *dêmos* depends both functionally and cognitively upon its leaders, and

---

[28] Other epigraphical, literary, and material evidence for this situation will be discussed in Chapter 6.

that the leaders themselves are the ones who drive the accomplishment of history-making action. Xenophon's Alcibiades abandons the façade of leader–*dêmos* collaboration in historical action that Thucydides' character once (selectively) exploited: in effect, the veneer of agency ascribed to the *dêmos* in Thucydides has been stripped away.

Xenophon frequently sets the individual and his citizen group in contrast with one another, particularly in scenes involving military operations. Not only are the activities of his own forces often verbally assigned directly to Alcibiades in the *Hellenica* (e.g. *HG* 1.1.5, 15, 18, 2.16, 3.4–6), but "the Athenians" as a group are credited with almost no independent action in the narrative that does not involve the close collaboration – or at least the close mention – of an individual commander.[29] In the case of Alcibiades, his individual agency frequently removes "the Athenians" from dubious or even dangerous situations. The pattern occurs, for example, in the buildup to and the battles of Abydus (*HG* 1.1.4–6) and Cyzicus (*HG* 1.1.9–18), and in the approach to and the siege of Calchedon (*HG* 1.3.1–8), where "Alcibiades" is able to accomplish what the Athenian forces cannot do alone.

Xenophon also explores the political association between Alcibiades and the Athenian populace. Just as Demosthenes the orator accused the *dêmos* of doing in the speech against Aristocrates (quoted at the beginning of Chapter 1, above), Xenophon's Athenian populace in the *Hellenica* is openly willing to assign historical agency to its leaders, rather than to take it unto itself. Xenophon's *dêmos* is also fascinated, whether for good or for ill, with the activities and the behavior of individuals.[30] This is particularly witnessed by the narrative of Alcibiades' homecoming from exile (*HG* 1.4.12–21). The passage is likely intended to interact with Thucydides, and particularly with the departure of the Sicilian expedition in book 6.[31] More specifically, however, Xenophon appears here to be setting up a deliberate contrast with Thucydides' depiction of the relationship between leader and *dêmos*.

---

[29] As Dillery 1998: 14 and n. 13 points out, Connor 1984: 54–5 identifies this manner of portraying military operations in Thucydides, where individual leaders are often credited with the actions of their troops. Dillery correctly notes in examining the *Anabasis* that this mode of presentation is even more prevalent in Xenophon, preferencing the individual's actions, decision-making, and guidance almost to the point of the exclusion of the military group.

[30] On the preoccupation of the *Hellenica* in general with individuals, e.g. Westlake 1969a esp. 205.

[31] Soulis 1972, for example (cited and discussed by Rood 2004b: 344), notes specific points where Xenophon makes textual contact with Thucydides, including with this particular passage. More detailed comparisons, however, have also been made by Rood 2004b and Due 1991 (cited in Pownall 1998: 262 n. 74), both of whom illuminate resonances that range even more widely over Thucydides' text.

As Due suggests, "the episode ... can be seen as a conflict between the masses and the individual, represented by Alcibiades."[32] On the most elemental level, Xenophon maintains a distinct separation in both syntax and thought between the city or citizen group on the one hand and Alcibiades on the other. The return scene also contains a variety of deliberate verbal and physical oppositions between Alcibiades and the city. They show resonances of the public–private dichotomy familiar from Thucydides;[33] they contrast Alcibiades on the one hand with the state or the body of citizens on the other; and they even note the isolation of Alcibiades as the object of the collective gaze of the wondering crowd.[34]

The first sentence (*HG* 1.4.12) contains several small-scale verbal oppositions between leader and polis. The opening lines present three reasons in Alcibiades' own mind why he can return safely to Athens at last: the city is well disposed towards him; the people have elected him general; and his friends are offering encouragement. The similar (but not precisely parallel) opening phrases ἑαυτῷ εὔνουν οὖσαν, "being well disposed towards him" and στρατηγὸν αὐτὸν ᾑρημένον, "having been selected general" have as the understood subjects of their participles the polis itself on the one hand and Alcibiades on the other. The commander and the polis are next again noted separately, almost gratuitously so, in the report that "some people" believed that the date of the homecoming was ἀνεπιτήδειον εἶναι καὶ αὐτῷ καὶ τῇ πόλει, "problematic both for him and for the polis." The close mention thereafter that no Athenian would venture to engage in serious activities during the Plynteria not only casts an ominous tone over the scene, but also

32 Due 1991: 46.   33 Rood 2004b: 368.
34 Phrases of particular note on these latter two points include ἀνεπιτήδειον εἶναι καὶ αὐτῷ καὶ τῇ πόλει ("problematic both for him and for the polis," *HG* 1.4.12); θαυμάζοντες καὶ ἰδεῖν βουλόμενοι τὸν Ἀλκιβιάδην ("marveling and wanting to see Alcibiades," 13); κράτιστος εἴη τῶν πολιτῶν ("he was the most outstanding amongst the citizens," 13); ἐκείνου ἀεὶ τὸ κοινὸν αὔξοντος καὶ ἀπὸ τῶν αὐτοῦ καὶ ἀπὸ τοῦ τῆς πόλεως δυνατοῦ ("he worked constantly to strengthen the community, both through his personal resources and through those of the polis," 13); τῶν παροιχομένων αὐτοῖς κακῶν μόνος αἴτιος εἴη, τῶν τε φοβερῶν ὄντων τῇ πόλει γενέσθαι μόνος κινδυνεῦσαι ἡγεμὼν καταστῆναι ("He alone was to blame for the evils [that had afflicted] them before, and he was also in danger of becoming the sole agent of things that were sources of fear for the polis," 17); ἀναβαίνει εἰς τὴν πόλιν μετὰ τῶν παρεσκευασμένων, εἴ τις ἅπτοιτο, μὴ ἐπιτρέπειν ("he ascended to the city, along with people who were ready, in case anyone should seize him, not to allow it," 19); ἐν δὲ τῇ βουλῇ καὶ τῇ ἐκκλησίᾳ ἀπολογησάμενος ("and after he spoke in the *boulê* and the Assembly on his own behalf," 20); ἀναρρηθεὶς ἁπάντων ἡγεμὼν αὐτοκράτωρ ("he was named high commander with sole authority," 20); ὡς οἷός τε ὢν σῶσαι τὴν προτέραν τῆς πόλεως δύναμιν ("since he was able, in their assessment, to renew the former power of the polis," 20).

implies that Alcibiades is not like other Athenians – and perhaps that he is not to be trusted.[35]

The location then shifts to the Piraeus, where the circumstances and even the language with which Xenophon represents Alcibiades' homecoming recall Thucydides' treatment of the departure of the Sicilian expedition – and the de facto departure of Alcibiades from Athens – years before.[36] But here, a large-scale reversal has taken place: whereas the Athenians in Thucydides dispatched a great expedition to Sicily, only one man in Xenophon has come home again, and he is not a fellow-citizen, but a spectacle.[37]

The conversations amongst Alcibiades' supporters that Xenophon reports also represent the returned exile as being separate and different from his populace. The strikingly undemocratic phrase that opens the indirect discourse, κράτιστος εἴη τῶν πολιτῶν ("he was the most outstanding amongst the citizens," *HG* 1.4.13), calls to mind by contrast Thucydides' depiction of Pericles as Athens' πρῶτος ἀνήρ, "leading citizen" (Thuc. 2.65.9). The power struggles that the speakers believe victimized Alcibiades are vilified as machinations for personal gain (ἴδιον κέρδος), but even when Alcibiades is praised for his efforts on behalf of τὸ κοινόν ("the community"), the supporters recognize *and maintain* that there is a division between his individual assets and those of the city: καὶ ἀπὸ τῶν αὑτοῦ καὶ ἀπὸ τοῦ τῆς πόλεως δυνατοῦ, "both through his personal resources and through those of the polis" (*HG* 1.4.13).

In a further link back to Thucydides' treatment of the Sicilian expedition, the speakers next make reference to the charges against Alcibiades for the profanation of the Eleusinian Mysteries. It was under the cloud of this indictment that Alcibiades set sail for Sicily (Thuc. 6.28.1–29.3), and to avoid trial for it that he fled his homeland (Thuc. 6.53.1–2, 61.1–7). His supporters in Xenophon, however, now choose to read the situation as a tragic one, in which an innocent Alcibiades was unable to come to the rescue of a citizenry and a city desperately in need of his assistance (τοὺς δὲ οἰκειοτάτους πολίτας τε καὶ συγγενεῖς καὶ τὴν πόλιν ἅπασαν ὁρῶν ἐξαμαρτάνουσαν, οὐκ εἶχεν ὅπως ὠφελοίη φυγῇ ἀπειργόμενος, "and although he watched those closest to him, countrymen and relatives and the whole

---

[35] See Nagy 1994 (cited in Pownall 1998: 262 n. 74) on Alcibiades' violation of religious scruples and the potential meaning and consequences of his actions; see also Rood 2004b: 369, who suggests that the unfortunate timing of Alcibiades' arrival "foreshadows [his] downfall."

[36] This connection is widely acknowledged (see note 31, above), and I will therefore confine my analysis to issues of contact between the two ancient historians that are essential to my argument, rather than presenting a complete re-reading of the parallel passages.

[37] See note 34, above.

polis, acting in error, he had no way of assisting them, since he was banned due to his status as an exile," *HG* 1.4.15). These speakers, then, are looking to Alcibiades as an eminent leader with the potential for history-making action, but the depiction is more extreme than it was in Thucydides. In the latter's treatment, Alcibiades' influence was the result of credulous belief rather than reality,[38] and the control of his ability to make history still rested with the *dêmos*, even if the citizen body was not entirely aware of the reach of its authority. In this passage, however, Xenophon shows members of the polis group suggesting that the city is actually unable to pursue the 'right' course without the intervention of the individual.

Even the speakers' memory of Alcibiades' position before Sicily (ὑπάρχειν γὰρ ἐκ τοῦ δήμου αὐτῷ μὲν τῶν τε ἡλικιωτῶν πλέον ἔχειν τῶν τε πρεσβυτέρων μὴ ἐλαττοῦσθαι, "more [esteem] came to him from the *dêmos* than did to his peers, nor was he outranked by those who were his senior," *HG* 1.4.16), suggests his having been unequal even under a democratic system designed to smooth over such differences.[39] Perhaps the most dramatic representation of Alcibiades' isolation from the *dêmos* is the claim by his critics that he alone is to blame (μόνος αἴτιος, *HG* 1.4.17) for the problems of the polis, both past and future. This perspective, while it may appear dramatic, is actually just the mirror image of the supporters' claim that Alcibiades would surely have rescued them if he had not been wrongly exiled (*HG* 1.4.15). In either case, Xenophon's ὄχλος, "common crowd," "mob," or "throng," has no illusions about its ability to make history or even to determine upon and execute good action. It is therefore rather appropriate that Xenophon never actually refers to the crowd in this passage as a δῆμος, or democratic citizenry.[40]

Xenophon's depiction of Alcibiades before the chief Athenian governmental bodies, the *boulê* and the Assembly, carries this concept still further. The individual addresses the groups in his own defense, and, in an atmosphere that discourages all dissent (οὐδενὸς ἀντειπόντος διὰ τὸ μὴ ἀνασχέσθαι ἂν τὴν ἐκκλησίαν, "when no one was expressing disagreement because the Assembly would not have permitted it," *HG* 1.4.20), the only action of the Assembly is to vote Alcibiades into the unique position of "high commander with sole authority," ἁπάντων ἡγεμὼν αὐτοκράτωρ (ibid.).

[38] This is an interpretation that I share generally with Rood 2004b: 369.

[39] Rood 2004b: 368–9 shows that this theme is picked up from one in Thucydides' speech for Alcibiades in book 6, but that there it was used in calls for collaboration, whereas here it is used to emphasize Alcibiades' separateness.

[40] On the shades of meaning associated with such negative terminology, see Chapter 3, above, where it is interpreted as a key to meaning in Herodotus' Persian 'Constitutional Debate.'

Although this phraseology has its roots in fifth-century parlance, its usage here – and the kind of authority that it suggests – represent changes in prior practice.[41]

Pownall has argued that routine αὐτοκράτορες in the late fifth century and beyond tended to be either generals or ambassadors with certain expanded powers assigned ad hoc.[42] The closest prior example to Alcibiades' appointment here comes from Thucydides, where Nicias, Lamachus, and Alcibiades were named στρατηγοὶ αὐτοκράτορες for the expedition to Sicily.[43] Thucydides' other uses of the term, however, are illuminating. Of the sixteen total times he employs αὐτοκράτωρ or its variants, three are associated – on both sides – with the appointment of commanders for the Sicilian expedition,[44] four with powers granted to ambassadors,[45] two with the formation of the government of the Five Thousand,[46] and two with emergencies or secret councils.[47] But the remaining five instances of this term are associated with self-determination that often verges upon the delusional or the destructive.[48] More than half of the usages, therefore, deal with the exceptional, the non-routine, or even the dangerous. The word is also not common in extant fifth-century literature. Before Andocides, there are just three occurrences in Aristophanes and one in Euripides;[49] Thucydides is the earliest known author to use the term more broadly. It is possible that Xenophon was simply deploying accepted but underdocumented vocabulary to describe Alcibiades' new appointment, but the Thucydidean associations imply at the very least quite extraordinary authority.

Schepens has suggested that the sense of the word root *hegemôn-* seems to have taken on increasingly broad implications during the fourth century, moving outward from purely military associations to encompass

---

[41] Domingo Gygax 2006: 489 cites Bloedow 1973: 70 et al. for the description of this position as "unprecedented."

[42] Pownall 1995 esp. 144–6.   [43] Thuc. 6.8.2, 26.1.

[44] Two involve the appointment of the Athenian generals for the Sicilian expedition (Thuc. 6.8.2, 26.1); one more occurs when Hermocrates urges the Syracusans to name generals with this type of power (Thuc. 6.72.5).

[45] In this case, the Spartans authorized to treat for the Peace of Nicias (Thuc. 5.45.1, 45.2, 45.4, 46.1).

[46] With particular regard to the foundation of the lawgiving council and the new '*boulê*' (Thuc. 8.67.1, 3).

[47] One refers to the emergency powers granted to the Athenian archons during the Cylonian coup (Thuc. 1.126.8), and one to the formation of secret oligarchic councils in the Peloponnese against the Spartans (Thuc. 5.27.2).

[48] Thuc. 3.62.4; 4.63.2, 64.1, 108.5, 126.5.

[49] E. *Andr.* 482 (efficacy of centralized authority); Ar. *Pax* 359 (general sense of "leader" or "commander"), *Av.* 1595 (gods as delegates with ambassadorial powers), *Lys.* 1010 (ambassadors with authority to negotiate a peace treaty).

wider political ones, as well.[50] Indeed, the phrase ἡγεμὼν αὐτοκράτωρ itself appears for the first time in extant literature here in Xenophon, but this kind of language in general (though not this explicit phrase) becomes far more common under Philip II of Macedon (ἡγεμών of the League of Corinth), Alexander, and the Hellenistic kings. Domingo Gygax has shown that Plutarch's account of the crowning of Alcibiades during his return to Athens, an incident that does not appear in Xenophon, may well be historical, and suggests that Alcibiades presented himself before the polis as an *euergetês*, or "benefactor."[51] But Xenophon's sustained presentation of the distanced relationship between Alcibiades and the *dêmos*, the language of the return scene, and the theatrical objectification of the leader figure also seem to anticipate the historical and historiographic treatment received by eminent leaders, especially kings, later in the fourth century, and beyond.

5.3 A new way of reading the historical world: Leaders and led in the *Anabasis*

The content of the *Anabasis* invites the consideration of the Ten Thousand as a distinct group in comparison with a few individual leaders, especially Xenophon himself. Two early passages prior to Xenophon's accession to command, however, provide important background: the obituaries of the Persian prince Cyrus (*An.* 1.9.1–31) and of the Greek generals captured by Tissaphernes (*An.* 2.6.1–30).[52] Xenophon's approach to these summaries differs substantially from the work of his historiographic predecessors:[53] the *Anabasis* segments are far more extensive and detailed than, for example, Thucydides' brief (if memorable) notice for Nicias[54] or even his longer

---

[50] Schepens 2007.   [51] Domingo Gygax 2006: 496.

[52] In scholarship on the evolution of biographical writing in ancient Greece, these two extended passages are often considered to be of central importance: on ancient biography and autobiography in general, see the references collected in Chapter 1, above.

[53] See the survey of ancient historiographic obituaries by Pomeroy 1991.

[54] ἥκιστα δὴ ἄξιος ὢν τῶν γε ἐπ' ἐμοῦ Ἑλλήνων ἐς τοῦτο δυστυχίας ἀφικέσθαι διὰ τὴν πᾶσαν ἐς ἀρετὴν νενομισμένην ἐπιτήδευσιν, "Indeed, he was the least worthy of the Greeks of my time to experience such misfortune, because of his consistent dedication to virtue" (Thuc. 7.86.5). Thuc. 7.86.3–5 contains some reflections on the evolution of Spartan and Syracusan attitudes towards Nicias by way of explaining the motives for the latter's execution (καὶ ὁ μὲν τοιαύτῃ ἢ ὅτι ἐγγύτατα τούτων αἰτίᾳ ἐτεθνήκει, "and this, or something very close to it, is why [Nicias] was killed," Thuc. 7.86.5), but it contains no judgment on Nicias' personal qualities and no information on his life experiences that are not directly related to his immediate reception by the enemy.

eulogy for Pericles (Thuc. 2.65.5–9).[55] In particular, more detailed comparison of Xenophon's obituaries with the Pericles passage shows that Xenophon is attempting something quite different from Thucydides.

Thucydides' retrospective of Pericles' career is tightly focused upon the leader's relationship with the *dêmos*, to the exclusion of nearly all other possible themes. The half-sentence that links the *dêmos'* reaction to Pericles' final speech (Thuc. 2.65.1–4) to the eulogy proper (beginning at Thuc. 2.65.5) is particularly telling:

> ὧν μὲν περὶ τὰ οἰκεῖα ἕκαστος ἤλγει ἀμβλύτεροι ἤδη ὄντες, ὧν δὲ ἡ ξύμπασα πόλις προσεδεῖτο πλείστου ἄξιον νομίζοντες εἶναι. (Thuc. 2.65.4)

> They were less susceptible to the personal sorrows that each one felt, thinking that he [Pericles] was of all the best fit for what the entire city needed.

Two separate contrasts appear here. The first, in the μέν-clause, is implicit, but real: the preoccupations of separate citizens are becoming less important to the sentiments of the group as a whole, and that group is growing more tightly unified. The second contrast, in the δέ-clause, again draws attention to the separation between the individual and the group: now, however, the group is the united *dêmos*, and the individual in question is Pericles. Strictly speaking, the grammar of the sentence does not equate the human collective of the *dêmos* (still referenced in the plural) with the polis itself; however, the position of the emphatic phrase ἡ ξύμπασα πόλις, "the entire city," at the beginning of its clause invites a close mental connection between the polis and its people: the citizens have begun to put aside private issues in favor of public concerns, and the public need, ironically, is for the unique service of an eminent private citizen.

The only personal quality explicitly attributed to Pericles in the first half of the eulogy itself is πρόνοια, "prescience," but it is limited in context by the attributive word order (ἡ πρόνοια αὐτοῦ ἡ ἐς τὸν πόλεμον, "his prescience regarding the war," Thuc. 2.65.6): regardless of whether Thucydides' Pericles displays this talent as a consistent personal characteristic, the historian is concerned only with its immediate effects upon the conflict with Sparta. This emphasis on the war continues through Thuc. 2.65.6–7, and resumes again after the eulogy proper concludes (Thuc. 2.65.10–13). Only Thuc. 2.65.8–9, then, discusses Pericles' general conduct, and this account is limited almost exclusively to the leader's ability to guide his

---

[55] On the importance of Pericles to Thucydides' historical and historiographic thought, see Chapter 4, above.

people's collective decisions. Pericles himself is only δυνατὸς . . . τῷ τε ἀξιώματι καὶ τῇ γνώμῃ, "powerful through his reputation and intelligence," and χρημάτων τε διαφανῶς ἀδωρότατος, "eminently immune to corruption by bribery" (Thuc. 2.65.8), neither of which offers significant insight into or judgment of his personality. This 'portrait' by Thucydides is not only extremely limited in its temporal and thematic scope, but also almost entirely external, even practical, in its concerns.

Like Thucydides, Xenophon does link his obituaries back to his larger narrative by highlighting the relationship and the relevance of his subject to the military project at hand.[56] The substance of these passages, however, emphasizes their subjects' personal qualities over their activities. Xenophon's frequent generalizations about character here are ethical in nature and often somewhat moralizing in tone. Rather than being derived from external behavior and from the opinions of others, as in the case of Thucydides' assessment of Pericles, Xenophon's character judgments may be 'proven' by references to particular incidents and anecdotes, such as Cyrus' bravery in wrestling a bear and his generous recompense for the man who rescued him (*An.* 1.9.6). They may be supported by implications of particular life experiences, as when reference is made to Proxenus' gentlemanly ethics affecting his military leadership (*An.* 2.6.19–20). They may even simply be asserted, with unproven motivations assigned by the confident tone of the narrative voice and attached to actions said to be habitual, as in the case of Menon's unscrupulous conduct (*An.* 2.6.21–6), and the cutting rumors about his sexual behavior (*An.* 2.6.28).

Xenophon's combined discussions of personality and leadership imply that individual temperaments and individual choices affect the action of his story.[57] This is further emphasized by the locations of the obituaries within the text: they are presented immediately upon the deaths of their subjects, effectively stopping the narrative in mid course (the Greek mercenaries, for example, do not learn that Cyrus has been killed in battle until *An.* 2.1.3, after his obituary has already been presented in full). By their placement and their length, these excurses elevate the importance of their central figures, and invite critical reflection upon the roles that their characters have now ceased to play in the text. The respective removals of these individuals from the narrative, the obituaries imply, are not only rhetorical or structural turning points, but historical ones as well: almost

[56] E.g. most notably *An.* 1.9.7–10, 14–18, 30–1, on Cyrus; *An.* 2.6.1–4, 7–8, 12–15, on Clearchus; *An.* 2.6.20, on Proxenus; *An.* 2.6.27, on Menon.

[57] Dillery 1995: 71 n. 40, also citing Bruns 1896: 137–44. This is the case whether or not the obituaries should properly be considered 'biographies' in the modern sense, *pace* Dillery 2001: 2.

immediately following the treatment of the executed Greek generals, Xenophon enters his own text as a potential leader for the first time (*An.* 3.1.4).[58]

The timing of Xenophon's appearance as a central character suggests that he is to serve as both a functional and a symbolic replacement for Cyrus. Most of the first book of the *Anabasis* is tightly focused upon Cyrus to the exclusion of nearly all others:[59] he is structurally and verbally represented as the sole personal agent behind nearly all of the action taken by the members of his expedition and the forces under his command. His loss creates a void that is as much rhetorical as it is practical: book 2 of the *Anabasis*, lacking a single central figure to whom most of the significant action may be attached, foregrounds a number of individuals, most notably Tissaphernes, Clearchus, Ariaeus, Proxenus, and Menon. Their shifting relationships with one another underscore the atmosphere of uncertainty amongst the Greek forces, and the deaths of many of them near the conclusion of book 2 (Clearchus, Proxenus, and Menon are amongst the Greek generals executed at *An.* 2.6.1)[60] leave an even more telling gap for Xenophon to fill, both as historiographer and as character.

Xenophon's treatment of the events culminating in his own election as one of the replacement generals for the Ten Thousand (*An.* 3.1.4–47) comprises his first coverage of the relationship between himself and the citizen group from which he comes, and the story is essentially a narrative of physical and symbolic separation. At *An.* 3.1.5–7 the young Xenophon, invited to join Cyrus' expedition by his friend Proxenus, seeks advice from Socrates. Socrates' anticipation of potential problems with the Athenian government, coupled with Proxenus' conviction that Cyrus was κρείττω ἑαυτῷ . . . τῆς πατρίδος, "more valuable for him than [was] his own fatherland" (3.1.4), emphasizes the independent life of the individual in contrast with his citizen group. The character Xenophon is about to enter upon a decision-making process whose results will physically remove him from his polis and estrange him from his *dêmos*.[61]

---

[58] Dillery 1995: 72 correctly notes that although Xenophon is periodically mentioned by name (sometimes with polis, as well) almost as a matter of course in the preceding narrative (specifically at *An.* 1.8.15; add to Dillery's reference 2.4.15, 2.5.37, 2.5.40), the phraseology of *An.* 3.1.4 is that of an introduction.

[59] His obituary begins at 1.9.1.

[60] Ariaeus largely ceases to be a factor shortly thereafter and is mentioned for the last time in the *Anabasis* at *An.* 3.5.1; Tissaphernes, too, nearly vanishes from the narrative at this point, only being mentioned by name later in scattered recollections of the past (*An.* 4.1.1, 4.3.2; 7.1.28) and in conjunction with the campaign that Thibron wishes to conduct against him (*An.* 7.6.1, 6.7, 8.24).

[61] Trouble with the polis, in fact, is something that Socrates fears for Xenophon at *An.* 3.1.5.

At Socrates' advice, Xenophon journeys to Delphi to seek Apollo's opinion of the proposed endeavor; there, by artificially limiting (whether intentionally or unintentionally)[62] his inquiry to the god, he receives what amounts to divine sanction for the expedition to Persia. This passage resonates with at least two other prominent literary descriptions of eminent individuals who act independently of their citizen groups. Firstly, the flawed consultation at Delphi (Socrates upbraids Xenophon for its incompleteness at *An.* 3.1.7) regarding action against Persians seems to recall Herodotus' treatment of Croesus' relationship with the same sanctuary (e.g. Hdt. 1.53.1–3, 71.1, 90.2–91.6). Secondly, the general theme of a major project to be undertaken by an uncertain or reluctant subject, coupled with its conscious promise of future isolation from the *dêmos* and its prominent incorporation of Socrates, recalls the narrative of Socrates' own philosophical 'mission' as assigned by the Delphic oracle. Both Plato's and Xenophon's accounts of that episode and its consequences[63] show Socrates distinguishing himself from the *dêmos* to act as observer and critic: in both situations, the Socrates character demonstrates acute awareness of the gulf between the unusual individual and his citizen group. The Xenophon character in the *Anabasis* is further set apart from his peers by this connection: The story offers both specific and symbolic promise that he will be setting out on his own.

After the death of Cyrus in the battle of Cunaxa and the execution of the Greek generals, Xenophon encamps with the despairing and leaderless Greeks, where he experiences a vision from Zeus (*An.* 3.1.10–12). The dream and the actions to which it spurs him elevate Xenophon the character to a special position within the world of the narrative.[64] The writer, however, maintains an elaborate pose of modesty:[65] the character Xenophon's first speech calling the captains of Proxenus to arms (*An.* 3.1.15–25) concludes with the speaker volunteering to either follow or lead. Even the offer to join the ranks of the officers is couched in polite terms, the positive willingness to function as a subordinate (ἕπεσθαι ὑμῖν βούλομαι, "I am prepared to follow you") contrasted with the negative refusal to assume a more prominent role if asked (οὐδὲν προφασίζομαι τὴν ἡλικίαν, "I do not pretend that my young age [should hinder me]"), and Xenophon's ability as a soldier cast as readiness and aptitude for self-defense (*An.* 3.1.25).

---

[62] I am grateful to E. Baragwanath for advice on the interpretation of this scene that saved me from error.

[63] Pl. *Ap.* 21a–23b, 30e; cf. also X. *Ap.* 1.11–15.   [64] Dillery 1995: 72–4.

[65] A point made in conversation by M. Flower.

These passages and others in the *Anabasis* that present somewhat under-stated representations of Xenophon the leader[66] may help the work as a whole, as has often been suggested, to function in part as an apologia.[67] It might also be argued that Xenophon's preoccupation with analyzing the 'good' commander and developing paradigms for effective leadership[68] differs significantly from interest in historical agency. But the sections that show Xenophon the character self-conscious about his leadership position – or reflecting upon the leadership experiences of others – also betray significant concern on the part of Xenophon the writer with the agency of individuals.[69]

On the other side of the individual–group equation in the *Anabasis* are the Ten Thousand, the closest equivalent that the character Xenophon possesses to a citizen group once the campaign begins. This army, in fact, has often been read as a representation of a displaced polis,[70] and this characterization initially seems to fit the paradigms for historical agency established by Xenophon's predecessors. In Herodotus, the populations of separate Greek poleis functioned as historical agents; in Thucydides, the relationship between eminent individual leaders and the Athenian *dêmos* also had profound consequences for understandings of historical agency. These strong precedents may help to explain the projection in Xenophon of some of the qualities of a polis onto the group of Greek mercenaries.

But this quasi-polis is far from being single-minded or unified.[71] In fact, its 'citizens,' most often referenced in the text as οἱ Ἕλληνες, "the Greeks," or οἱ στρατιῶται, "the soldiers," are fractious (not unlike, in fact, Herodotus' presentation of "the Greeks" as an agent group)[72] and difficult to manage. They cannot make effective group decisions, but neither are they easily led.

---

[66] E.g. *An.* 3.1.45, where Cheirisophus acknowledges that Xenophon was virtually unknown before he emerged from the crisis following the death of Cyrus.

[67] On the *Anabasis* as an apologetic text, e.g. Azoulay 2004 *passim*; Cawkwell 2004: 59–67; Rood 2004a: 322–6; Dillery 1995: 63–4, all with additional references.

[68] This has often been acknowledged in the scholarship, and is treated in wide-ranging detail by Dillery 1995, who applies paradigmatic models to large-scale interpretations of both the *Anabasis* and the *Hellenica*. The most frequently cited general treatment of leadership in Xenophon remains Breitenbach 1967, to whose earlier thoughts on the topic Westlake 1969a (see esp. 206–7) partly responds.

[69] See Dillery, intro. to Brownson 2001: 13–15; see also Ferrario 2012.

[70] See Hornblower 2004: 244–5 for a history of the scholarship on this concept, with references; cf. Dillery 1995: 92 on ancient precedents.

[71] This section of the argument discussing historical agency in the *Anabasis* benefited significantly from criticism and thoughts offered by J. Ober and M. Flower in their evaluations of an original dissertation chapter. I remain grateful to them both for their advice and cite others of their individual suggestions separately as they appear.

[72] I am grateful to J. Ober for this point.

They seem to desire some degree of group autonomy, but simultaneously insist upon strong individual guidance.[73] While some of these paradoxes may simply be due to the essential differences between military and civilian political structures, others of them seem to be deliberately used by Xenophon as loci for the exploration not merely of principles and paradigms for effective leadership, but also for the role of the individual in making – and recording – history.

These issues can be examined most effectively within one of the major type-scenes of the *Anabasis*: military assemblies. It might be argued that these are simply a façade designed to suggest to the soldiers that they have a share in the day-to-day operations of their desperate and highly unusual campaign. While numerous,[74] the assemblies are most often called by the generals. In context, they largely serve as backdrops for exhortations, or as opportunities for the validation of proposals submitted by Xenophon or by other eminent individuals.[75] Only rarely does potential dissent surface: for example, at *An.* 5.1.14, negative sentiment is circumvented by Xenophon's refusal to broach an unpopular motion. *An.* 5.6.11 does present what might seem to be an independent assembly vote on an ambassador's proposal, but the decision is significantly modified by Xenophon, apparently of his own accord, when he presents it to the envoys as the army's spokesman.

An apparent exception, however, occurs in the sequence of assemblies held in book 6, after the soldiers decide to engage in some profit-seeking before traveling home to Greece (*An.* 6.1.17). These meetings, several of which involve rebellion and conflict, center around the choice of a supreme commander who can lead the army to its desired ends. The larger episode begins when the soldiers express their desire for a change in the command structure. The terms they propose, that there should be only a single general in order to avoid the need for consultations amongst a group of *strategoi*, sound as if the military assembly would like to abdicate whatever perceived authority it possesses (*An.* 6.1.18). The captains, acting as representatives

---

[73] See the references in note 82, below, on some of the general qualities of the Ten Thousand as a group.

[74] Dillery 1995: 71, 78 collects the following pan-army assemblies "reported or assumed" after the re-introduction of Xenophon into the narrative at *An.* 3.1.4: 3.2.1, 5.1.2, 5.4.19, 5.6.1, 6.1.25, 6.2.4, 6.4.10, 6.6.11, 6.6.29; to these add at least 6.1.14 (brief notice), 6.4.17, 6.4.21, perhaps 6.6.37, 7.1.24, 7.3.2–3, 7.3.10, 7.6.7.

[75] E.g. *An.* 3.2.33 (Xenophon), 3.3.38 (Xenophon), 5.1.4 (Cheirisophus), 5.1.8–13 (Xenophon, who then proceeds to circumvent objections to another proposal at 5.1.14), 5.4.19–21 (exhortation by Xenophon), 6.6.18 (Agasias), 6.6.30 (Xenophon), 6.6.37 (Cleander), 7.1.32 (Xenophon), 7.1.35 (Coeratadas), 7.3.6 (Xenophon), 7.3.14 (Seuthes, supported by Xenophon).

of their men, then invite Xenophon to assume a position of sole authority (*An.* 6.1.19). At a full assembly meeting (perhaps spontaneous or at any rate not apparently called by the generals, *An.* 6.1.25), he refuses the honor on the grounds of poor auspices, and the men therefore select Cheirisophus instead (*An.* 6.1.31–2). The elevation of a single general to supreme command appears to change the collective climate, at least temporarily: the next military assembly also seems to be initiated by the soldiers themselves, in order to deliberate upon the route for the upcoming portion of their journey (*An.* 6.2.4). At the meeting, a shortage of provisions leads to the determination that money must be extorted from the nearby Heracleots. Xenophon and Cheirisophus, however, both refuse to assist in the oppression of a friendly Hellenic city, and the army's message simply results in their being disbarred from Heraclea and its supply-markets (*An.* 6.2.6–8). The Arcadians and Achaeans, in particular, blame the generals for not supporting the initiative, and initiate a secession, fragmenting the Ten Thousand and deposing Cheirisophus from the high command (*An.* 6.2.10–12; an iteration of the factions appears at *An.* 6.2.14).

The small group of soldiers left with Cheirisophus journeys safely to Calpe Limen, but the large contingent of separatists, led by their own newly elected generals, indulges in a raiding expedition against the Thracians and is ultimately worsted by the defenders (*An.* 6.3.11–12). Xenophon summons his own troops to assist, and their campfires alone frighten off the Thracians (*An.* 6.3.11–25). The separatists are joyfully reunited with Xenophon's troops (*An.* 6.3.24) and all proceed to Calpe Limen together. After an expedition buries the Arcadian dead, the soldiers again call their own assembly (*An.* 6.4.10) – but this time they resolve to subordinate themselves once more to a committee of *strategoi*, and to execute anyone who should propose further separations (*An.* 6.4.11). Regardless of what the authority of this army assembly may actually be, it appears incapable of taking nearly any consequential external action independent of its leaders.[76]

Military maneuvers in the *Anabasis* that are clearly executed by the army are often ascribed to the commanders by name as if the individuals were the main or even the sole physical performers of the action.[77] This 'commander

---

[76] Dillery 1995: 78 iterates some of the army assembly's apparent powers, but these do not translate into independent and efficacious historical agency. Such powers, further, are of less moment if, as Dillery concludes, "the ultimate power of decision rests with the assembly, although the troops are not always aware of this fact and pay considerable attention to the advice of the officers; at an operational level, and especially in crisis situations, the commanders of the army continue to exercise executive control" (79).

[77] Dillery, intro. to Brownson 2001: 13–14, highlighting esp. 4.2.26 and 4.7.10–12.

narrative' was also employed in both Herodotus and Thucydides, but in the case of the former, it was more often used to describe the activities of barbarians, rather than those of Greeks; in the case of the latter, it comprised only one of a number of possible ways of assigning historical agency.[78] In the *Anabasis*, however, this discourse is pervasive during the actual march,[79] and suggests that the most important forces behind the events of the narrative are indeed the leaders of the army.[80] Nevertheless, the troops are never entirely absent. Instead, "Xenophon," for example, is often "accompanied by," "leading," or "bringing" a section of the army, and "the Greeks" are often verbally represented as the collective protagonists or receivers of the action at hand.[81] While Xenophon is certainly not representing historical agency as being shared equally between the commanders and the army, the tandem acknowledgement of leaders and led seems harmonious with the inclusion of the military assemblies throughout the narrative.[82] Both types of narrative represent some limited interaction between the will of the individual leader and the will of the group,[83] even if the nature of military life means that the balance of agency is tilted even more significantly towards the commander than it would be towards the eminent politician in a fourth-century Greek city.[84]

At military assemblies, Xenophon's command decisions are frequently represented as motions laid before the body of the army for its approval or rejection. In reality, however, Xenophon's proposals almost inevitably pass, often unchallenged.[85] The votes of favor are generally noted with

[78] See note 29, above.

[79] In addition to the passages cited by Dillery (note 77, above), see also e.g. 4.3.20–2, 5.2.16.

[80] Dillery 1995: 73–5 views the rhetorical emphasis on individuals over groups as being particularly pronounced during books 3–4 of the *Anabasis*.

[81] E.g. on Xenophon accompanied by troops: 3.3.8, 3.4.38–9, (a refusal), 3.4.42–3, 4.1.6, 4.2.2, 4.2.9, 4.2.16, 4.3.20, 4.3.26, 4.5.7, 4.5.16, 4.5.19, 4.5.21, 4.7.3, 4.7.22, 4.8.16. On "the Greeks" by this name only, e.g.: 3.4.5, 3.4.18, 3.4.27, 3.4.33, 3.4.36–7, 3.5.1, 4.1.8–11, 4.2.12, 4.2.28, 4.3.1, 4.3.5, 4.3.32, 4.6.24–6, 4.7.17, 4.7.18–20, 4.7.27, 4.8.1, 4.8.8–9, 4.8.19. This list is not complete: most notably, it omits the numerous places where the members of the army are called "soldiers," or are recognized only through the use of verbs in the third-person plural.

[82] Dalby 1992, with bibliography, reading the Ten Thousand as a "colonizing expedition" rather than a city. Nussbaum 1967 (cited by Dalby 1992: 16–17 via Marinovich as a strong advocate of the polis model) explores the 'democratic' qualities of the military assemblies in particular at 48–68. Dillery 1995 esp. 92–4 sees the resemblance between the Ten Thousand and a polis as evolving in the course of the *Anabasis*.

[83] See Hornblower 2004. This (im)balance, in the abstract, is not actually so far removed from some of the negotiative behavior that was embedded in fourth-century Athenian political life: see e.g. Ober 1989.

[84] See Ober 1989.

[85] A rare exception is 5.1.14, where Xenophon deliberately withdraws an unpopular idea prior to any discussion. Cf. also the discussions of military assemblies cited in note 82, above.

routine language, and the proceedings as narrated therefore often bear a strongly *pro forma* sense. This maintenance of the illusion of control on the part of the larger group, however, invites closer attention to the relationship between leader and led. The army is allowed, even encouraged, by employing the communication loci that the assemblies represent, to maintain the conviction – or perhaps the shared façade – that it possesses a certain amount of autonomy. The character Xenophon, as a leader, perceives the cognitive value of this balance and works to uphold it by continuing to consult with the Ten Thousand, even as he demonstrates through his disproportionately active engagement in both speech and action that he well understands the practical indispensability of the army's generals. This balance not only adds to the case that the *Anabasis* makes for the value of Xenophon's historical leadership, but also demonstrates Xenophon's active engagement with some of the same questions about historical agency that were posed by Thucydides. The relationship of the eminent leader to his group in the *Anabasis* involves the maintenance of tension between appearances and realities, one very similar in conception to that represented by Thucydides between Pericles and the Athenian *dêmos*.

There is, however, a crucial distinction between Xenophon's depiction of the eminent individual–group relationship and that offered by Thucydides. In Thucydides, although the *dêmos* generally cannot function effectively within the world of the text without its leaders, it does possess significant authority over them. Cleon heeds the Assembly's challenge to take up the conflict at Pylos despite his personal unwillingness to do so; Nicias fears the *dêmos*' retribution for his ineffectiveness in Sicily; Alcibiades must actively work to ingratiate himself and present himself as a desirable leader for the polis. Even Pericles carefully maintains cooperation with the populace in spite of his extraordinary political position. In the *Anabasis*, however, the narrative foregrounding of individual leaders, and particularly of Xenophon himself, strongly implies that the balance between individual and group has shifted, and closer readings bear out this interpretation. The maintenance of perceptions of group authority has become both ritualized and weakened: even when the Ten Thousand elect their officers, the candidates themselves can interfere with the voting processes and exercise significant control over the outcomes (e.g. most notably *An.* 6.1.17–33, where Xenophon refuses to allow himself to be elected to the high command). Finally, at the moment of the break-in to Byzantium, the soldiers themselves are depicted as being consciously *aware* of their inability to act effectively without their commanders:

οἱ δὲ στρατιῶται ὡς εἶδον Ξενοφῶντα, προσπίπτουσι πολλοὶ αὐτῷ καὶ
λέγουσι· Νῦν σοι ἔξεστιν, ὦ Ξενοφῶν, ἀνδρὶ γενέσθαι. ἔχεις πόλιν, ἔχεις
τριήρεις, ἔχεις χρήματα, ἔχεις ἄνδρας τοσούτους. νῦν ἄν, εἰ βούλοιο, σύ τε
ἡμᾶς ὀνήσαις καὶ ἡμεῖς σὲ μέγαν ποιήσαιμεν. (7.1.21)

When the soldiers spotted Xenophon, many of them hurried towards
him and said, "Now, Xenophon, you can become a man. You have a city,
warships, resources, so many troops. Now, if you want to, you could help
us and we would make you great."

The direct admission of the men that their work is really the work of
their general represents a significant turning point in Greek historiographic
thought. Now, even the members of the wider group admit openly that historical agency belongs to the eminent individual, not to them. Here, the soldiers see themselves in a relationship with their commander that is precisely
the opposite of that of Thucydides' Nicias with the Athenian *dêmos*. In Thucydides, Nicias was the unwilling agent of the *dêmos*; here, in the *Anabasis*, the representatives of the army offer themselves as willing agents of
Xenophon. They in effect volunteer to contribute to the further individuation of their general and to support him in history-making achievement.

The assets iterated by the members of the army in *An.* 7.1.21 recall
Xenophon's own thoughts at *An.* 5.6.15–16,[86] where he considers settling
the Ten Thousand in the Pontic region as a colony, and ultimately presents
himself in the guise of another type of individual historical agent, the
ktistês, or "founder."[87] Xenophon the character, then, is considering joining
an eminent company indeed:[88] given the elevation that a *ktistês* typically
received, he seems here to be contemplating his own historical legacy, just as
Herodotus' Leonidas did at Thermopylae.[89] As the historian tells it, the character Xenophon ponders the possibility of the colony and privately makes
sacrifice in search of divine guidance (5.6.15–16). His motivations, however, both with regard to the rites themselves (5.6.22, 27) and with regard
to his goals for the potential colony and its settlers (5.6.17), are misinter-
preted by the army, and Xenophon is accused of secret self-aggrandizement

---

[86] This verbal and conceptual connection between the two passages was pointed out by
Brownson rev. Dillery 2001: 545 n. 7 *ad* 7.1.21.

[87] On the significance of the *ktistês* figure, see Chapter 2, above.

[88] The actual participle in the phrase for "establishing a city" (πόλιν κατοικίσαντας) at 5.6.15 is, as
M. Flower points out, plural, but Xenophon's conduct of advance sacrifices suggests that the
character (and perhaps the historian) views himself as a potential *ktistês*, and the reaction of
the dissenters afterwards (5.6.17–33) implies that they, too, believe that the colony plan rests
centrally in the hands of Xenophon.

[89] See Chapter 3, above.

through a series of escalating rumors (5.6.19–20, 27), to the point where he is forced to discard his plan in a defensive speech before the assembled soldiers (5.6.28–31).[90]

When the colony idea is first introduced in the report of Xenophon's thoughts, it is presented in terms that tend towards the general, the ennobling, and the eternal. However, as it is debated and gradually dismissed, the emphasis moves to immediate benefits and liabilities, and finally to shallow motivations and open distrust. The implication seems to be that Xenophon is able to conceive of himself as a *ktistês*, but that his men are focused on baser, more transient concerns.[91] Xenophon the writer is therefore able to ennoble Xenophon the character in two ways: firstly, through the contemplation of the image of the colonial founder, regardless of whether that image is actually activated, and secondly, through his 'selfless' willingness to yield to the wishes of his men.

Xenophon's careful attention to the eminent individual's ability to construct historical memory through text, explored both here and in Chapter 6 below, finds good parallels in the behaviors of fourth-century elites both inside and outside of Athens. Political and military leaders of this era appear to have enjoyed access to a growing variety of opportunities to present themselves as 'makers of history,' sometimes at the expense of honor and authority being accorded to the collective citizen bodies of their respective poleis. At Athens, where the evidence is most abundant, this development seems to have been comprehensible to the more ordinary members of the population, as well, as witnessed by the decrees proposed and passed by the Assembly, the texts of the orators, and the styles of commemoration employed on tombstones.

5.4 Memory and the polis: Athenian commemorative practices in the earlier fourth century

Although there is a temporary decline in the number of Attic inscriptions preserved from the later years and immediate aftermath of the Peloponnesian War,[92] the first half of the fourth century BC witnesses the most dramatic increase in extant Attic documents of any period in ancient Greek history.[93] While not all typologies peak coincidentally with the corpus as a

---

[90] Indeed, the remainder of book 5 is occupied with the scrutiny of the generals and the reconciliation of Xenophon with the army.
[91] On the men's desire for self-enrichment, see Dillery 1995: 78–83.
[92] Hedrick 1999: 392 fig. 2, 400.   [93] Ibid. 391–5, with references; see esp. 392 fig. 2.

whole,[94] the honorific inscriptions (particularly state decrees), document reliefs, and epitaphs considered here do reflect the trends in the wider epigraphical census.[95] Their contents also display noteworthy changes from the fifth century into the fourth that cannot be fully explained by the challenges of reconstructing historical practices from extant material evidence.[96] Taken together, these three categories of monuments suggest that new ways of thinking about the individual's role in history were at work in fourth-century Athens.

Decrees and document reliefs: The discourse of public honors at Athens, c. 396–350

Official honorific decrees dedicated to Athenian citizens who had benefited the *dêmos* proliferate in the epigraphical record during this period. Votes of commendation are recorded as early as (probably) the 390s.[97] The first firmly dated golden civic crowns for Athenians are attested by *IG* ii/iii² 223 (dated to 343/2),[98] but at least one, albeit from a phratry, rather than from the *dêmos* as a whole, is known from (probably) the second quarter of the century,[99] and crowns of olive for citizens are also documented around that time.[100] A lesser honor, the invitation to a state meal in the *prytaneion*, appears to have been conferred at least as early as the Peloponnesian War upon Athenians who served as envoys, but these offers of δεῖπνον[101] also increase in the epigraphical record during the fourth century.[102]

---

[94] Ibid. 393. Hedrick also maps prytany decrees and ephebic lists in comparison with the entire corpus in order to demonstrate this point: 394 figs. 4–5.

[95] Including the brief falling-off (which may appear as a drop, a plateau, or a slowing of the rate of growth, depending upon the typology) in the late fifth and earliest fourth centuries: e.g. Hedrick 1999: 393–4, fig. 3 (decrees); Lawton 1995: 21–2 (document reliefs); Hedrick 1999: 393 (epitaphs).

[96] E.g. Hedrick 1999: 395–408, on Meritt's correlation of public writing with democratic sentiment.

[97] It is unclear precisely when this practice began. Honorific decrees on behalf of individual Athenian citizens are noted in the literary sources as having been issued during the fifth century, but the documentation of such honors in the epigraphical record commences – and accelerates notably – in the fourth: Whitehead 1983: 66 esp. n. 37, with reference to Osborne 1981: 153–70, esp. 159–68.

[98] Cited in Henry 1983: 23.

[99] *IG* ii/iii² 1238: see Lawton 1995: 129 no. 102, and the discussion of Attic document reliefs, below.

[100] Henry 1983: 13, 23, 39–40.

[101] A "meal"; the word used in the same contexts for the reception of non-Athenians is ξενία, "hospitality" of an outsider or guest: Henry 1983: 271.

[102] Ibid. 262.

This marked increase in known honors to individuals is not confined to the Athenian citizen body. Along with invitations to ξενία,[103] honors awarded to foreigners, including commendations, crowns of gold and of olive, grants of citizenship, decrees of proxeny, offers of "preferential right of access to the *boulê* and *dêmos*," promises of the right of *enktesis* (property-ownership in Attica), and exemptions from taxation all increase or appear for the first time in the epigraphical corpus during the first half of the fourth century BC.[104] It is less remarkable, however, that non-Athenians are receiving an increasingly extravagant range of privileges: meritorious foreigners received special treatment from the Athenian democracy during the fifth century, as well. What is notable is that prominent Athenian citizens now appear more often in the honorific epigraphical record, enjoying elevated status and public acclaim alongside the *xenoi*: in short, during the first half of the fourth century BC the native Athenians are more rapidly closing the acknowledgement gap.[105]

This increased public focus upon the contributions of individuals, both citizens and foreigners, cultivates – and perhaps even reifies – their public importance. The official wording of these honorific decrees as a class, however, remains insistently democratic. The formulaic prescripts[106] continue to make implicit claims to the authority of the *dêmos* and its constituent groups,[107] and the desirable awards that follow are couched in predictable language[108] that demonstrates in its sheer sameness the level of documentary control exercised by the governmental bodies.[109]

Two documents of this period, one dedicated to a foreigner and one to three citizens together, are illustrative. The first inscription, an Athenian state honorific decree for Phanocritus of Parium, is dated with some security to 387/6 BC due to its likely connection to a series of events described in Xenophon (X. *HG* 5.1.25–8).[110] Its text reads as follows:[111]

---

[103] See note 101, above.

[104] Henry 1983 *passim*, the phrase in quotation marks being the title of Henry's chapter 6.

[105] Shear 2007: 99–101 further notes that epigraphical honors for individual citizens seem to appear in the Agora by the early fourth century, emphasizing the relationship between the honorand and the democracy that used the Agora as its governmental center; those for foreigners tended to be erected on the Acropolis, which "had no such democratic connections" (101).

[106] On the prescripts of this period, see Henry 1977: 19–33, esp. 27.

[107] See Chapter 2, above.

[108] The patterns are detailed by Henry 1983, who classifies honorific decrees by the type and date of award.

[109] See note 115, below.   [110] Tod 1948: 47, with references.

[111] Edition from *IG* ii/iii² 29; translation from Rhodes and Osborne 2003: 81 no. 19.

[– – – – – – – – – – – ἀγ]-
[γελί]ας ἕνεκα [παραδοῦ]ναι, ἐὰν κα[ὶ τ]-
[ῶ]ι δήμ[ωι] δοκ[ῆι, καὶ] τὴν εὐεργ[εσίαν]
[ἀ]ναγράψ[αι ἐν στ]ήλει λιθίνει ἐν [ἀ]κ-
[ρ]οπόλει. κ[αλέ]σαι δὲ αὐτὸν ἐπὶ ξέν[ι]-
α εἰς τὸ πρυτανεῖον εἰς αὔριον *vacat*
Κέφαλος εἶπε· τὰ μὲν ἄλλα καθάπερ [τ]-
ῆι βολῆι, ἀναγράψαι δὲ Φανόκριτο[ν]
τὸν Παριανὸν πρόξενον καὶ εὐεργ[έ]-
την αὐτὸν καὶ τὸς ἐκγόνος ἐν στήλ[η]-
ι λιθίνει καὶ στῆσαι ἐν ἀκροπόλε[ι]
[τ]ὸγ γραμματέα τῆς βολῆς, ἐπειδὴ π[α]-
[ρ]ήγγελε τοῖς στρατηγοῖς περὶ [τῶν]
[ν]εῶν τὸ παράπλο, καὶ εἰ οἱ στρατ[ηγο]-
[ὶ] ἐπίθοντο, ἑάλωσαν ἂν α[ἱ] τρ[ι]ήρε[ι]ς
αἱ πολέμιαι· ἀντὶ τούτων ἔναι [κ]αὶ τ-
ὴν προξενίαν καὶ τὴν εὐεργεσί[αν κ]-
αὶ καλέσαι αὐτὸν ἐπὶ ξένια εἰς τ[ὸ π]-
ρυτανεῖον εἰς αὔριον· μερίσαι δὲ τ-
ὸ ἀργύριον τὸ εἰρημένον τὸς ἀποδέ-
κτας ἐκ τῶν καταβαλλομένων χρημά-
[τ]ων, ἐπειδὰν τὰ ἐκ τῶν νόμων μερ[ίσω]-
[σι].

- - - hand over for his message, if it is resolved by the people also, and write up his benefaction on a stone *stele* on the Acropolis.

4 Invite him to hospitality in the *prytaneion* tomorrow.

6 Cephalus proposed:

6 In other respects in accordance with the council; but Phanocritus of Parium shall be written up as a *proxenos* and benefactor, himself and his descendants, on a stone *stele* and it shall be placed on the Acropolis, by the secretary of the council, because he passed over to the generals a message about the passage of the ships, and if the generals had believed him the enemy triremes would have been captured: it is in return for this that he is to receive the status of *proxenos* and benefactor.

16 And invite him to hospitality in the *prytaneion* tomorrow.

18   The said sum of money shall be allocated by the
apodektai from the funds being deposited, when
they make the allocations required by the laws.

Another Athenian state decree, issued for the citizens Antiochus, Stephanus, and Eurypylus, furnishes honors for them at the request of the Phocians, to whom these three individuals had probably served as emissaries or ambassadors.[112] The text is damaged, but sufficient surviving traces of the democratic documentary formulae, coupled with the stoichedon arrangement of the inscription itself, allow its reconstruction with some security:[113]

(vacat unius versus spatium)

      [Ἔδοξεν τῆι β]ολῆι κα[ὶ τῶι δή]-
      [μωι - - -]ς ἐπρυτάνε[υεν]·
      . . . . . ¹⁰ . . . . . ς Δημοφ[ί]λο Φαλ-
      [ηρεὺς ἐγραμ]μάτευε· / . . Υ . .
5   . . . . . ¹⁰ . . . . . ς ἐπεστάτε[ι]· Ο .
      [. . .⁶ . . . εἶπε·] περὶ ὧν Ἀντίο[χ]-
      [ος λέγει ἐψ]ηφίσθαι τῶι δή[μ]-
      [ωι τὸν γραμ]ματέα τῆς [β]ολ[ῆς]
      [ἀναγράψαι ἐν] στή[λ]ηι λιθίν[ηι]
10   [καὶ ἀναθε͂ν]αι ε[ἰς] ἀκρόπ[ολι]-
     [ν τὸ ψήφισμα] Φω[κέων π]ο[λιτε]-
     [ίαν αἰτησ]α[μ]ένων[114] Ἀν[τιόχω]-
     [ι καὶ Στεφ]άνωι καὶ Εὐρυ[πύλ]-
     [ωι· ἐπαινέ]σαι δὲ Ἀντίοχ[ον κ]-
15   [αὶ Στέφαν]ον καὶ Εὐρύ[πυλον]
     [καὶ καλέσ]αι ἐπὶ δε[ῖπνον ἐς]
     [τὸ πρυταν]εῖον ἐς [αὔριον].
     [Τάδε ἠιτ]ήσαντο Φωκ[ῆς Ἀντι]-
     [όχωι καὶ Σ]τ[ε]φάνωι [καὶ Εὐρ]-
20   [υπύλωι· ἔδοξεν] Φωκε[ῦσι . . .]
     . . . . ¹³ . . . . . . I A - - - - -

Resolved by the *boulê* and the *dêmos.* - - - s held the prytany.

[112] See Henry 1983: 262, 271.

[113] *IG* II/III² 70. Restorations are translated but not marked; no argument will be made from the restorations.

[114] *IG ad loc.*: αἰτησ]α[μ]ένων, *de quo supplemento dubitat Wilamowitz.* This is a very important word for the reconstruction of the inscription as a whole, but the interpretation does not depend exclusively upon it.

----------s the son of Demophilus of Phalerum was the secretary...

5   ----------s presided...
          ... proposed it. Concerning those things which
          Antiochus proposes, the *dêmos* has voted
          for the secretary of the *boulê*
          to inscribe this decree on a stone stele

10   and set it up on the Acropolis,
          since the Phocians
          asked for [sc. Phocian] citizenship for Antiochus
          and Stephanus and Eurypylus.
          And to praise Antiochus and

15   Stephanus and Eurypylus
          and to summon them to a meal
          at the *prytaneion* tomorrow.
          The Phocians asked for these things for Antio-
          chus and Stephanus and Euryp-
          ylus. Resolved by the Phocians...

These two decrees, for Phanocritus on the one hand and for Antiochus, Stephanus, and Eurypylus on the other, display both common and separate features. The first, dedicated to a non-native of Athens, records isolated, unique action as well as ongoing, abstract 'benefaction' to the city, and responds with offers of rewards and memorialization, of which the inscription itself is a major part. The second, for citizens, suggests the routine, if apparently highly satisfactory, performance of ceremonial duties and again records the award of honors. The inscriptions have similar phraseology;[115] what differs most significantly is not only the citizenship status of the respective honorands but also the type of service that prompted the honorific response. Phanocritus, probably in addition to being a generally useful friend to the Athenian government, has been the agent of a specific deed that would *potentially* have become meritorious:[116] passing on a critical point of military observation to the Athenian generals. The (likely) Athenian ambassadors, in contrast, are recorded as having done their jobs – so

[115] On the uses of a wide selection of "democratic formulae of disclosure," which Hedrick defines as "statements that explicitly address the political reasons for the writing of inscriptions," see Hedrick 1999: 408–25.

[116] I am grateful to an anonymous reader for directing me to the comments of Osborne 1999: 351–2 on this unusual feature of the inscription: as Osborne puts it, "given that Phanokritos had not actually brought any benefits to the Athenians it was perhaps important, in what may be the only unreal condition in any Attic prose inscription, to emphasize that he would have done but for the generals" (352).

well, in fact, that their hosts apparently honored them with citizenship[117] –
and received their expected dinner-invitation in return.

A well-developed hierarchy of individual public commemoration, then,
appears to have evolved at Athens by the fourth century.[118] Any of the honors recorded in these inscriptions, whether for foreigners or for natives, were
surely desirable. The lesser ones, however, and probably in particular those
voted for minor Athenian democratic officials, were apparently not dependent upon the performance of truly outstanding or high-impact activities.
The Athenian orators of the fourth century comment both directly and
obliquely upon the manneristic outlay of honors to men who may not truly
have deserved them.[119] By 330 BC, Aeschines can suggest that the frequency
of the awards may be making the honors themselves less meaningful:

> ἐν τοίνυν τῷ μητρῴῳ [παρὰ τὸ βουλευτήριον] ἣν ἔδοτε δωρεὰν τοῖς ἀπὸ
> Φυλῆς φεύγοντα τὸν δῆμον καταγαγοῦσιν, ἔστιν ἰδεῖν. ἣν μὲν γὰρ ὁ τὸ
> ψήφισμα γράψας καὶ νικήσας Ἀρχῖνος ὁ ἐκ Κοίλης, εἷς τῶν καταγαγόντων
> τὸν δῆμον, ἔγραψε δὲ πρῶτον μὲν αὐτοῖς εἰς θυσίαν καὶ ἀναθήματα δοῦναι
> χιλίας δραχμάς (καὶ τοῦτ᾽ ἔστιν ἔλαττον ἢ δέκα δραχμαὶ κατ᾽ ἄνδρα), ἔπειτα
> κελεύει στεφανῶσαι θαλλοῦ στεφάνῳ αὐτῶν ἕκαστον, ἀλλ᾽ οὐ χρυσῷ·
> τότε μὲν γὰρ ἦν ὁ τοῦ θαλλοῦ στέφανος τίμιος, νυνὶ δὲ καὶ ὁ χρυσοῦς
> καταπεφρόνηται. καὶ οὐδὲ τοῦτο εἰκῇ πρᾶξαι κελεύει, ἀλλ᾽ ἀκριβῶς τὴν
> βουλὴν σκεψαμένην ὅσοι ἐπὶ Φυλῇ ἐπολιορκήθησαν, ὅτε Λακεδαιμόνιοι καὶ
> οἱ τριάκοντα προσέβαλλον τοῖς καταλαβοῦσι Φυλήν, οὐχ ὅσοι τὴν τάξιν
> ἔλιπον ἐν Χαιρωνείᾳ τῶν πολεμίων ἐπιόντων. ὅτι δ᾽ ἀληθῆ λέγω, ἀναγ-
> νώσεται ὑμῖν τὸ ψήφισμα. (Aeschin. 3.187)

And therefore it is possible to see in the Metroön [next to the Bouleuterion]
the gift that you bestowed upon those from Phyle who conveyed the *dêmos*
home again from exile. Archinus of Coele, one of those who participated
in returning the *dêmos*, was the one who proposed the decree and had it
passed, and he proposed first to present to [the recipients] one thousand
drachmas for sacrifices and offerings (and this is less than ten drachmas
apiece), and then he advocated that each of them be crowned with a crown
of olive – but not of gold. For at that time the olive crown was valued, but
now even the golden one receives contempt. He did not recommend that
this be done carelessly, but rather after the *boulê* investigated thoroughly

---

[117] J. Ober further notes that since the Phocians are said to have requested the honors for the
ambassadors from the Athenians, two different citizen groups have concurred in bestowing
praise upon these individuals.

[118] This hierarchy can be appreciated in detail in e.g. Henry 1983.

[119] See Whitehead 1993: 44 n. 23, who collects e.g. And. 2.23; Isoc. 8.50, 8.88–9; D. 23.196–201;
Aeschin. 3.177–80, and also calls attention to the Aeschines passage (3.187) discussed
immediately below.

which men were besieged at Phyle when the Spartans and the Thirty made their assault on those who held it, and not which men abandoned the battle-line at Chaeronea as the enemy approached. The decree [to be read now] will convince you that I am telling the truth.

Further contribution to the devaluation of which Aeschines complains may have been effected not only by the more frequent award of civic honors to Athenian citizens and foreigners alike, but also by a certain amount of 'trickle-down' effect. During the first half of the fourth century, state honorific iconography and language is increasingly imitated by smaller subdivisions of the democracy, and even by extra-governmental or para-governmental organizations.[120] This trend can also be observed in the Attic document reliefs.[121]

As noted above, the corpus of surviving document reliefs generally parallels the trends observable in the wider epigraphical census: somewhat depressed in the years following the Peloponnesian War, the number of reliefs rises again to peak around the year 350.[122] Relations with other states comprise a major theme in the forty-nine reliefs securely or approximately dated by Lawton to the years between *c.* 396 and 350,[123] but at least fifteen (excluding those too damaged for their content to be identified) were erected to honor individuals.[124] Lawton's nos. 16, 18, 21, 23, 29, 30, 32, 84, 86, 87, 95, and probably 94 were dedicated to foreigners; nos. 102 and likely 91, in contrast, merit particular attention because they were offered for Athenian citizens,[125] a development that marks a change in practices from the

---

[120] Hedrick 1999: 409.

[121] On these reliefs in general, cf. also Chapter 4, above.   [122] Lawton 1995: 22.

[123] Ibid. 90–8, nos. 16–33 (securely), and 122–32, nos. 84–114 (approximately, though nos. 112–14 are dated by Lawton to 'first half fourth century (?)' [*sic*]). Nos. 115–22, dated to approximately the mid fourth century, are conservatively excluded here. Lawton's numbering system for the document reliefs is employed throughout this section, cross-referenced with *IG*.

[124] This represents a slight percentage increase over the fifth-century figures (cf. Chapter 4, above), when of at least thirty-five known reliefs, a minimum of seven, or 20%, were dedicated to individuals; for the first half of the fourth century, at least fifteen of forty-nine examples (cf. note 125, below, on Xennias), or 30.6%, fall into this category. For the second half of the fourth century, in which Lawton's nos. 34–58 and 115–176 are here included, at least thirty-five of eighty-six known or likely document reliefs, or 40.7%, were offered to individuals, and an additional twenty-seven examples provide enough information to suggest that they, too, may possibly be incorporated into this count. In short, the *majority* of surviving document reliefs from the years *c.* 350–300 were likely dedicated to individuals. (Lawton's nos. 177–86, dated only to the 'fourth century,' or 'fourth century (?)' are excluded from these latter statistics, but at least two of these may also have been dedicated to individuals, as well.)

[125] Lawton 1995: 97 no. 33 (= *IG* ii/iii² 138) was also dedicated to an individual, a man named Xennias, possibly along with another male member of his family (two small male figures in the relief portion of the stele suggest the identification of two honorands); however, it is

fifth century, when all identifiable examples of document reliefs honoring individuals appear to have been designated for non-Athenians.[126]

Lawton's no. 102 represents what is likely the earliest document relief securely known to have been presented to an individual Athenian citizen; it may also represent the earliest epigraphical attestation of a citizen receiving a golden crown, if only from a phratry rather than from the state. Although the surviving fragment represents only a small portion of both the relief and the inscription, enough of the wording and decoration are preserved to permit some reconstruction of the contents. One version of the restored text reads as follows:[127]

```
     [ἔδοξεν τοῖς] φράτερσι· Ν[ .... εἶ]
     [πεν· ἐπειδὴ Εὐγ]είτων Εὐ[κλέος ε]
     [ὐηργέτησε τὸ κοιν]ὸν [τῶν] φρατ[έ]
     [ρων ....... 15 ........ ]των καὶ [π]
5    [ράττων διατελεῖ ἀεὶ] τὰ συνφ[έ]ρ
     [οντα τοῖς φράτερσι κ]αὶ νῦν καὶ
     [εν τῶι ἔμπροσθεν χρό]νωι καὶ α[.]
     [ ........ 17 ........ ]μενος τὴν
     [ ....... 15 ....... ] ἔρημον κατα
10   [δικασθεῖσαν ἐν τ]ῶι δικαστ[η]ρί
     [ωι ..... 11 ..... Ε]ὐγείτονος· δ[ε]
     [δόχθαι τοῖς φράτ]ερσι ἐπαινέ[σ]
     [αι Εὐγείτονα Εὐκ]λέος Φαληρέ[α]
     [καὶ στεφανῶσαι αὐ]τὸν χρυσῶ[ι σ]
15   [τεφάνωι ἀπὸ . δραχμ]ῶν ἀρετ[ῆς ἕ]
     [νεκα καὶ δικαιοσύν]ης τῆς [εἰς τ]
     [οὺς φράτερας - - - - - - - - - -]
```

Resolved by the members of the phratry; N .... proposed: since Eugeiton the son of Eucles benefited the collective of phratry
members and in his ac-
5   tion ... always accomplishes beneficial
things for the members of the phratry both now and

impossible to determine from the surviving fragments whether Xennias was an Athenian or a foreigner. Lawton's nos. 26, 90, 106, 111, and possibly 103, 105, and 107 likely also honor individuals, but their state of preservation precludes firm determination.
[126] Cf. Chapter 4, above.
[127] *IG* ii/iii² 1238: edition from Hedrick 1988 (a corrected version of the *IG* edition due to a proposed realignment of the fragments), as adopted by Lambert 1993: 335–7. See Lawton 1995: 129 for additional bibliography and references.

in past time and . . .

. . . by default . . .

10   judged in court[128]

. . . of Eugeiton. It has been determined

by the members of the phratry to praise

Eugeiton, the son of Eucles of Phalerum

and to crown him with a golden

15   crown worth . drachmas for the sake of his virtue

and his justice towards the

members of the phratry - - -]

The language and organization of this decree imitate at the level of the
phratry the wording most frequently observed at the level of the *dêmos*.[129]
The opening formula, which most likely originally read ἔδοξεν τοῖς φράτερσι·
N . . . . εἶπεν,[130] "resolved by the members of the phratry; N. proposed [it],"
is an echo of the now-standardized democratic preamble employed in the
documents of the polis at large; missing are only (naturally) the names of the
national officers of state.[131] Frequent references to the phratry throughout
function not only to emphasize the collective action of the members as a
whole, but also, ironically, to justify the resolution to ἐπαινέ[σαι] ("praise") –
indeed, in this case, to honor quite extravagantly – the individual who stands
out from within the group. This characteristic represents the same verbal
structure as the state honorific inscriptions, which tend to make repeated
mention of the *dêmos* just as this one does of the phratry. More importantly,
however, it also reveals the same uncomfortable duality between group
authority and individual valuation that has characterized Athenian state
documents since the fifth century.[132]

Eugeiton is not alone. In the course of the fourth century, increasing numbers of Athenian citizens are recorded in the document reliefs as receiving
individual honors, both from the state as a whole and from lower-level
civic, religious, and military organizations. Within Lawton's corpus worthy
of note amongst the securely dated examples are nos. 40 (from ephebes
who had themselves received civic honors), 41 (for a naturalized Athenian
citizen), 43 (for a native citizen from his deme), 47 (from a cult for its

---

[128] The translation of these two lines is recommended by Hedrick 1988: 116.

[129] Hedrick 1999: 409 notes that this is a widespread phenomenon under the Athenian
democracy; cf. note 120, above.

[130] Hedrick 1988: 113 notes a misprint in *IG* here and credits Wilhelm with the correction to
[ἔδοξεν τοῖς] φράτερσι.

[131] On the prescript formulae of the earlier fourth century, see Henry 1977: 19–33.

[132] Cf. Chapter 2, above.

two *epimeletai,* "officers" or "managers"), 49 (from the state for an envoy), and probably 53 (from a tribe for its three [?] *epimeletai*).[133] Amongst the approximately dated examples, we find nos. 102 (from a phratry for a native citizen), 125 (possibly from a tribe for its three *epimeletai*), 127 (from a deme for one of its native citizens), 128 (from a tribe for a native citizen), 138 (possibly from a tribe for four recipients), 145 (from a tribe for its priest), 152 (from a deme for its *peripolarchês,* "patrol commander," as Lawton translates), 153 (probably for a religious benefactor or religious official, perhaps a priest), 154–155 (both from demes for pairs of individual citizens), 157 (from the soldiery of a tribe for a taxiarch), 164 (possibly for a priestess of Athena), and 186 (possibly for a phylarch); 57, securely dated to 302/1, is actually for a slave. A significant number of the unidentified or hypothesized reliefs listed in Lawton's catalog might also represent additional examples, but not enough is known about their contents to be certain.

There appears to be in fourth-century Athens, then, a growing tendency to memorialize individuals (sometimes even quite minor ones) active at a variety of levels in the Athenian public sphere. But there is also a debate over the meaning and significance of such honors evident in the discourse of some of the era's most prolific and vocal politicians and advocates: by the mid fourth century the changing commemorative vocabulary of Athens had attracted the attention of the orators. The general pessimistic contrast of the polis of the present with the polis of the past is a well-known rhetorical trope of the period,[134] but the authors also draw attention in more specific detail to perceived differences between the commemorative habits of the earlier years of the democracy and those of their own day. Two of the best examples come from Demosthenes and Aeschines.

Aeschines 3, the speech against Ctesiphon, dates to 330 BC. The case itself, brought over the charge of *graphê paranomôn,* or the proposing of an illegal governmental decree, was essentially an action by Aeschines against the man who advocated the award of a golden crown to Demosthenes. Aeschines, of course, strongly opposed the crown, and it is in this context that he contrasts the honorific habits of the later fourth century with those of the fifth. A large section of the speech (Aeschin. 3.177–91) emphasizes the devaluation of honors awarded by the citizen group: the careless *dêmos* distributes accolades, in Aeschines' words, οὐκ ἐκ προνοίας, "not out of forethought," and as a result its prizes and gestures have lost their meaning

---

[133] This was also the title used of the heads of the respective tribes: see *LSJ ad loc.*
[134] Pearson 1941: 210; see also Nouhaud 1982 *passim.*

(Aeschin. 3.178). Aeschines rhetorically invites the *dêmos* to resume the august governmental, political, and social authority it is supposed to have once enjoyed, presumably during the fifth century. The democratic populace is to conduct a critical examination of its commemorative habits in order to return its honors to their proper and rarified position, and its members are to assume roles as the collective ἀγωνοθέτας πολιτικῆς ἀρετῆς, "overseers of a competition for civic honor" for eminent individuals (Aeschin. 3.180). The Greek phrase itself, however, is heavily loaded, and its messages are mixed. The term ἀγωνοθέται, most notably, bears associations with athletic contests.[135] Here, its usage constructs the members of the *dêmos* essentially as passive observers of the 'real' actions undertaken by their leaders.[136] The *dêmos* itself, this term implies, does not act: it has control only over its own *reaction* to what others actually do. And ideally, these others, cast by the diction of the passage in the role of noble competitors, should be individuals of signal πολιτικῆς ἀρετῆς. The phrase combines an adjective (πολιτική) that, though possessed of a fifth-century pedigree, finds its most frequent deployment in fourth-century literature,[137] with a Homeric noun for valiant, virtuous conduct (ἀρετή), now utterly transformed in its passage from the battlefield to the Agora. The potent combination of archaizing, elitist resonances with apparently democratic terminology may seem on the surface to elevate the authority of the *dêmos*, but actually does it only passing – and in fact rather problematic – service.

Aeschines next calls further attention to changes in Athenian commemorative habits from the fifth century into the fourth (Aeschin. 3.183, 186). By invoking monuments that are physically present in the immediate area (this speech was likely delivered in one of the law-courts in or near the Agora, not far removed from either the Stoa of the Herms or the Stoa

---

[135] See *LSJ ad loc.*, and cf. *Ath. Pol.* 60 on the ἀθλοθέται who oversaw the Panathenaic festival during this same period of time (I am grateful to an anonymous reader for this reference). The term ἀγωνοθέται later also became connected with the annual Athenian dramatic festivals: sometime during (probably) the last quarter of the fourth century, the role of producer at the Dionysia passed from the *choregoi* to an ἀγωνοθέτης; on the date of the introduction of this *agonothesia*, see Wilson 2000: 270–6 and esp. 307–8; Raubitschek 1943: 54–5.

[136] This charge, of course, is not new; it was levied in the literature – with the same vocabulary – at least as early as Thuc. 3.38.4 (during the Mytilenean debate), where Cleon scolded the *dêmos*, saying κακῶς ἀγωνοθετοῦντες, "you do a poor job overseeing the competitions" and calling them θεαταὶ μὲν τῶν λόγων . . . [καὶ] ἀκροαταὶ δὲ τῶν ἔργων, "watchers of speeches and listeners to actions" performed by eminent individuals.

[137] A *TLG* search of extant Greek literature on the adjectival word root πολιτικ-, for example, produces well over ten times as many citations from the fourth century as from the fifth; even if the works of both Plato and Aristotle are wholly excluded, the fourth-century usage still dwarfs the fifth-century one.

Poikilê),[138] Aeschines in effect employs visual aids to argue for the existence of the shifts in aesthetic and political values he described earlier (Aeschin. 3.180).[139] Whether it was grounded in social authority, established tradition, or written law, Aeschines claims, the power of the *dêmos* during the fifth century partially suppressed or rechanneled the commemorative efforts of individuals into claims of history-making authority ventured on behalf of the entire polis.[140] The material evidence from the fifth century, particularly the public monuments and the funerary memorials, appears generally to bear Aeschines out, particularly earlier on.[141] The contrast drawn here is therefore likely to be more than merely a rhetorical trope; indeed, it is reflective of – and simultaneously *conscious of* – discernible shifts in ideological and cultural realities.

That Aeschines, as a politician, should be preoccupied by the contrast between past and present at Athens after Chaeronea is perhaps not surprising. Similar concepts and arguments, however, were also employed by Demosthenes some twenty-two years before. It might be contended that the respective contexts of the two speeches were somewhat similar and thus invited polemic against Athenian commemorative activities, but Demosthenes adduces an additional reference to contemporary Athenian behavior that further implies that his argument, like that of Aeschines, is grounded in realia, rather than merely in rhetoric.

Demosthenes 23, the speech against Aristocrates, was briefly quoted and discussed at the opening of Chapter 1, but the broader passage from which that quotation comes (D. 23.196–9) shows Demosthenes even more clearly criticizing the state of honorific habits at Athens. As discussed in Chapter 2, above, there may have been individual monuments to Miltiades erected after Marathon, and there almost certainly was one to Callimachus. It is at most unclear and at least unlikely, however, that any of these represented an official construction by the state as a whole. In the case of Themistocles, whose behavior later in life seems actually to have been treasonous,[142] there are no

---

[138]   On the law-courts of Athens, see Boegehold 1995; on the topography and monuments of the Athenian city center during the second half of the fourth century BC, see Travlos 1971, updated by Camp 1992 and 2001: 259–61, with references.

[139]   My reading of this situation was developed before Shear 2007 became available: I was glad to see that her analysis of the development of individual-oriented commemoration in the Agora harmonizes with these interpretations (see esp. Shear 2007: 91, 105–6, 113–15).

[140]   This kind of negotiation has been observed elsewhere in Greek culture by e.g. Kurke 1991 on Pindar and Loraux 1986 on the Athenian funeral oration, both of which have influenced my thinking here.

[141]   Cf. Chapters 2 and 4, above.

[142]   On Miltiades' career after Marathon, see Hdt. 6.132.1–136.3, and Chapters 2 and 3, above; on Themistocles' after Salamis, see Hdt. 8.109.1–112.3 (cf. also the international acclaim

major memorials known to have been dedicated to him at Athens proper.[143] This by no means offers objective proof for Demosthenes' assertion that the Athenians of the past οὐ χαλκοῦς ἵστασαν, "did not set up bronzes" (D. 23.196)[144] or make other showy memorial gestures for individuals like these. Perhaps there were comparatively few well-known monuments in the immediate area that would contradict Demosthenes' position?[145] This kind of *ex silentio* argument is difficult, but it comprises only a portion of Demothenes' case.

Demosthenes' second major point in this passage, regarding popular discourse about historical agency (D. 23.198), is striking. If this speech were read in isolation, it might be reasonable to suggest that Demosthenes' depiction of earlier fifth-century diction, particularly given the polemical context of the wider oration, is at best reconstructed, and at worst wholly fabricated. Examination of Herodotus and Thucydides in Chapters 3 and 4 above, however, has already shown that methods for articulating historical agency were under literary debate during the fifth century. The accompanying review of the material evidence has further suggested that the rhetoric of public and popular display was also undergoing changes. Demosthenes' bald assertion that "there is no one who would claim" that a commander was in name the victor of an early fifth-century battle (D. 23.198)[146] is likely exaggerated for effect, but fifth-century evidence suggests that his contention may not be entirely groundless. Phraseology of the kind that Demosthenes cites (e.g. τὴν περὶ Νάξον ἐνίκα ναυμαχίαν Χαβρίας, "Chabrias won the naval battle at Naxos"), for example, becomes more prominent in Greek historiography over time. This way of speaking was comparatively rare in Herodotus, at least as applied to Greeks; nascent in Thucydides, where individuals and

---

Themistocles receives before ultimately going to Persia, at 123.1–125.2); Thuc. 1.135.2–138.6 (a more significant source for Themistocles' disloyalty); and Chapters 3 and 4, above.

[143] Paus. 1.1.2 mentions a tomb of Themistocles at Piraeus, founded by relatives who brought Themistocles' bones back from their burial in Magnesia (the rumor of the secret – and illegitimate – return of the bones, though not the monument, is also reported by Thuc. 1.138.6), and in the same section notes a painted portrait of Themistocles placed in the Parthenon by his children. Neither of these, however, even if contemporary and genuine, would have detracted from Demosthenes' case here. On the 'tomb of Themistocles,' see Wallace 1972; on other images of Themistocles, see Richter rev. Smith 1984: 210–12; Richter 1965: 97–9, both with testimonia.

[144] In fact they may have done so to some extent: see Keesling 2003: 195–6; Krumeich 1997 esp. 51–150, with Dillon 2001.

[145] The first Athenian said to have received a bronze statue in his honor during his own lifetime is Conon (D. 20.68–72, cited in Keesling 2003: 176). As M. Flower points out, this was likely a symptom of the general zeal at Athens for rebuilding an empire: see Seager 1967 esp. 115. For further discussion of Conon, see Chapter 6, below.

[146] Translated at the opening of Chapter 1, above.

groups are often depicted as acting in concert; and far better established in Xenophon, where individuals are verbally responsible for most major activity and comprise the central narrative and ethical focus.[147]

Judicial oratory in fifth- and fourth-century Athens was a highly public form of discourse. Juries were large,[148] significant speeches might be published and circulated after trials were over,[149] and the advocates and speechwriters themselves were often politicians of the highest rank whose well-known agendas might easily follow them into the law-courts.[150] In this context, arguments like those of Aeschines and Demosthenes might have helped to shape contemporary Athenian sentiment and popular discourse about the influence, authority, power, and memorialization of eminent individuals. Even as the orators harangued their audiences about the inferiority of the democracy of the present to the democracy of the past, their examples may have helped to elevate further the memories of the leaders of the previous century, who are often recollected as self-effacing, or at least democratically circumscribed. Individuals such as Themistocles, Miltiades, Aristides, and others repeatedly resurface in oratory as shining examples of leadership and (even if it was a forced and unwilling façade) egalitarian modesty.[151] This increasing reflection upon the lasting contributions of individuals was well in keeping with fourth-century public experience. Even if in a polemical context, it likely helped to perpetuate the conviction that eminent individuals were an essential part of the operation of the democracy – and indeed, had always been so. Public discourse such as this can only have assisted in the construction of perceived social and political divisions, wherein certain individuals were properly situated to take actions worthy of public memory – even history-making actions – and others were not. This attitude also manifests itself in the private sphere, where it likely contributes to some changes in funerary discourse during the first half of the fourth century.

Attic funerary monuments of the earlier fourth century BC

I return now to the quantitative evidence first introduced in Chapter 4, above, regarding the structure and content of Attic epitaphs.[152] Here, I

---

[147] See notes 29, 30, and 57, above.

[148] See Boegehold 1995 on the structures and proceedings of the Athenian law-courts.

[149] E.g. Kennedy 1963: 204–6.   [150] See Ober 1989 esp. 104–48.

[151] See Nouhaud 1982 esp. 165–77, 218–23; Pearson 1941 esp. 226–7.

[152] I am grateful to the general comments of Stears 2000a: 212–14 about some of the dominant features of fourth-century tombstones and epitaphs, which inspired me to study all of this material more closely from both quantitative and qualitative perspectives.

again employ a series of tables that categorize the material in *IG* i³ and *IG* ii/iii², extending from *c.* 396 BC (the approximate terminus of the analysis in Chapter 4) to the mid fourth century.[153] As before, all figures below should best be understood as representing broadly proportionate estimates.[154] The larger-scale relationships between them, from which they derive their interpretive value, will be discussed following the presentation of the data.

A particular challenge in the assembly of this particular set of statistics is the employ by *IG* ii/iii² of several variations on the date label "fourth century BC"[155] for a large number of the inscriptions. While there is no discernible significant difference in style, structure, or content between the epitaphs of the "fourth century BC" and those that have been assigned more specific *IG* dates in the earlier portion of the century,[156] it is naturally difficult to decide how many entries in the former category may actually belong to the earlier portion, say the first half, of the 300s. The epitaphs labeled only "fourth century BC" have therefore been excluded from the figures of Table 5.4.1 below and included in those of Table 5.4.2, in order to provide opportunities for comparison.

---

[153] The following date ranges assigned by *IG* were incorporated into the figures in all tables, below:
- 'before the mid-fourth century' ('ante med. s. IV. a.')
- 'mid-fourth century' ('med. s. IV. a.')
- '*a.* 400–350'
- '*c. a.* [any year or range of years including the years 390–350]'
- '*c. a.* 365–340' (on the grounds that an inscription of this date is more likely than not to fall within the period under investigation here)

Inscriptions bearing the date label 'fourth century BC' ('s. IV a.,' 's. IV. a.?,' and 's. IV a., ut videtur'), as stated in the main text and in the table headings themselves, are eliminated from the figures in the first table and included in those of the second.

The following date ranges assigned by *IG* were excluded from the figures in all tables, below:
- 'fifth/fourth century BC' (this listing is both extremely rare in *IG* ii/iii² and too vague to be of use here)
- 'after the mid-fourth century' ('post. med. s. IV. a.')
- '*c. a.* [any year or range of years beginning after 350]'
- 'after the year 357/6' (referring specifically to *IG* ii/iii² 6635 and 7374, both epitaphs of known individuals who held offices in that year; it is impossible to determine the years of the erections of their monuments)

Although *IG*'s supplements were generally accepted, inscriptions that were so poorly preserved that their contents could not be securely reconstructed were not incorporated into these figures; also eliminated were inscriptions for which *IG* does not suggest any date.

[154] See the more detailed discussion of these problems in Chapter 4, above.

[155] Specifically, 's. IV a.,' 's. IV. a.?,' and 's. IV a., ut videtur'; no distinction was made between these listings in this census.

[156] Save, of course, for the purely practical fact that some of the inscriptions that receive only vague or approximate dates from the editors are amongst the most poorly preserved.

Table 5.4.1 *Approximate census of* IG *ii/iii²* *Attic epitaphs from the first half of the fourth century BC, by type (<u>excluding</u> epitaphs dated by* IG *only to the 'fourth century BC')*

	Category 1: Name(s) only	Category 2: Name(s) + brief extension	Category 3: More extensive epitaphs
Single individuals			
Athenians	213	24	7
Foreigners	95	4	6
Unknowns	299	49	35
SINGLE TOTALS	607	77	48
Multiple individuals			
Athenians	160	37	9
Foreigners	20[a]	3	1
Unknowns	199	5	2
MULTIPLE TOTALS	379[b]	45	12
GRAND TOTALS[c]	986	122	60

[a] Two of these name one of the stated or known ἰσοτελεῖς, i.e. metics (resident foreigners) who were subject to the same fiscal responsibilities as Athenian citizens. There are twenty total entries for ἰσοτελεῖς in *IG* ii/iii², ranging in date from the fourth to the first century BC.

[b] See note a, above.

[c] These sums represent the total number of epitaphs in each of the three categories defined above: they are arrived at by adding together the single and multiple totals for each category.

The categories presented in Tables 5.4.1 and 5.4.2 are more finely divided versions of the divisions first introduced in Chapter 4, above. Epitaphs are initially classified according to their level of detail, content, and length. Those of the first and largest group, "Category 1," merely list the deceased by name, potentially (but by no means always) including patronymic and demotic for Athenians and locality of origin for foreigners. "Category 2" incorporates those epitaphs that carry a short 'extension,' usually only a word or two in length, attached to one or more (if the monument is shared) of the names. During the first half of the fourth century, such an extension is almost inevitably a mention of a familial relationship, most frequently employing the words θυγάτηρ, "daughter," or γυνή, "wife."[157] κεῖται, "lies here," an

[157] These generalizations are also observed by Stears 2000a: 213. Clairmont 1993: vol. V, 11 indexes the uses of these words on sculpted Attic tombstones "outside of epigrams"; the listing nevertheless provides some sense of their frequency. Compare also the fifth-century familial terms referenced at note a to Table 5.4.3, below.

Table 5.4.2 *Approximate census of* IG *ii/iii² Attic epitaphs from the first half of the fourth century BC, by type (*<u>*including*</u> *epitaphs dated by* IG *only to the 'fourth century BC')*

	Category 1: Name(s) only	Category 2: Name(s) + brief extension	Category 3: More extensive epitaphs
Single individuals			
Athenians	328	39	9
Foreigners	172[a]	14	7
Unknowns	473	71	42
SINGLE TOTALS	973[b]	124	58
Multiple individuals			
Athenians	215	54	12
Foreigners	30[c]	9	1
Unknowns	294	8	3
MULTIPLE TOTALS	539[d]	71	16
GRAND TOTALS	1512	195	74

[a] Two of these belong to known or stated *isoteleîs*.

[b] See note a, above.

[c] Four of these belong to known or stated *isoteleîs*.

[d] See notes a and c, above.

extension used in the fifth century, is also known, albeit rarely, in the first half of the fourth. The earlier fourth century further witnesses a rise in the usage of the adjective χρηστός, "good," as a generic reference to the qualities of the deceased.[158] Occasional one-word mentions of occupations are also ventured,[159] and I include these in this category. In "Category 3," finally, are grouped the longest and most extensive epitaphs, those that elaborate for a sentence or more upon the deceased and (often) upon the experience of loss. Within each of these three major epitaph categories, separate counts have been made of monuments classified by *IG* as belonging to Athenians, foreigners, and persons whose origin is unknown; shared epitaphs (those that list two or more names on a single monument) are also separated from those dedicated to single individuals.[160] Finally, Table 5.4.3 is reprinted

[158] This generalization is also observed by Stears 2000a: 213, although she recommends that the word be translated as "useful" and be construed as referring to slaves. Clairmont 1993: vol. V, 12 indexes appearances of this word under the terms observed in note 157, above.

[159] Also observed by Stears 2000a: 212, although Stears sees these as being exceptionally rare in the fourth century.

[160] It should be noted that under most circumstances an epitaph of category 3 (the longest and most extensive type) belongs to and discusses a single individual, even if additional names

Table 5.4.3 *Approximate census of* IG *i³ and* IG *ii/iii² Attic epitaphs from the later fifth century BC (to c. 396), by type (cf. Chapter 4, Table 4.3, above)*

	Category 1: Name(s) only	Category 2: Name(s) + brief extension	Category 3: More extensive epitaphs
GRAND TOTALS	336	24[a]	44

[a] Thirteen epitaphs from *IG* ii/iii² fall into this 'extension' category, and the most common elaboration amongst these is the simple designation of familial relationships with words like θυγάτηρ, μήτηρ, and υἱός (at least six out of the thirteen).

from Chapter 4, above, to facilitate comparison between the fifth- and the fourth-century evidence.[161]

Comparison between Tables 5.4.1 and 5.4.2 on the one hand and Table 5.4.3 on the other shows the recovery of a significantly greater number of Attic inscribed stone funerary monuments dating from the fourth century than from the fifth. This increase in the number of known tombstones from the fifth century to the fourth has often been cited as evidence for increased interest in – and increased practice of – visible funerary memorialization by wider segments of the Athenian population during the fourth century BC.[162] Granted, the 'growth' in the archaeological corpus of monuments from the fifth to the fourth century exceeds proportionally all reasonable demographic estimates of Athenian population increase in the post-Peloponnesian war era,[163] but this particular argument is still somewhat vulnerable due to its inability to accommodate for a variety of unknown factors – most notably, for example, the potential employ of archaeologically 'nonrecoverable' monument forms (e.g. wooden or other perishable markers).[164] Arguments based upon relative proportions of epitaph types within the representative corpora collected by *IG* are therefore likely to be more useful here.

(most commonly of relatives) are included in the same inscription; this situation will be discussed in more detail below.

[161] *IG* i³ and *IG* ii/iii² date ranges included in Table 5.4.3 run from '450–425' (earliest) down to '410–390' and 'beginning of the fourth century' (latest); less specific dates such as 'mid-fifth century' or 'before the mid-fourth century' are not included in the Table 5.4.3 figures, which means that they are likely on the conservative side. Cf. Chapter 4, above, for more detailed information on the dating and categorization of these fifth-century epitaphs.

[162] Morris 1994; Meyer 1993; Morris 1992, all with references.

[163] Meyer 1993: 105 and n. 8, with references.

[164] On the issue of "archaeologically recoverable" Greek burials in general, though emphasizing the earlier periods, e.g. Morris 1987: 93–6, 101–9; cf. Kurtz and Boardman 1971: 56 on the potential use of wooden tombstones during the Geometric era.

During the first half (and perhaps during the whole period before Chaeronea) of the fourth century BC, there appears to have been a discernible tendency on the part of Athenian citizens to employ shared funerary monuments, particularly in the cases of family groups. The excavation of a significant number of family *periboloi* (demarcated burial precincts) from fourth-century contexts in Athens and Attica furnishes qualitative support for this statement,[165] but the figures from Tables 5.4.1 and 5.4.2 provide quantitative data to support it. Funerary inscriptions from the first half of the fourth century at Athens dedicated to multiple individuals by name only (i.e. those of category 1, as defined above) are nearly four times as likely to belong to Athenians as to foreigners, if the ethnicities of the deceased are discernible.[166] Consequently, it may not be unreasonable to suggest that a significant proportion of the 'unknown' multiple-individual epitaphs in category 1 also likely belong to Athenians.

Epitaphs of category 2 (the brief extension type) undergo a relative increase over time as the fifth century transitions into the fourth. Thirteen of the category 2 epitaphs listed in Table 5.4.3 are to be found in *IG* ii/iii^2 (as opposed to *IG* i^3), meaning that they are considered by the editors to date after the archonship of Eucleides (i.e. 403/2 BC). With the *terminus ante quem* established for the material in Table 5.4.3, this means that more than half of the category 2 epitaphs included in the census for this table appear to have been generated in a span of no more than a decade or so, in contrast to the preceding three decades or more. Further, category 2 epitaphs represent 5.94% (24/404) of the total listed in Table 5.4.3; in contrast, they comprise 10.45% (122/1168) of the total listed in Table 5.4.1, and 10.95% (195/1781) of that in Table 5.4.2. Even by the turn from the fifth century into the fourth, the most common extension found in the category 2 epitaphs is a reference to a familial relationship; by the mid fourth century, this extension type is almost invariable.

Comparison between Tables 5.4.1 and 5.4.2 on the one hand and Table 5.4.3 on the other suggests that, at least within the archaeologically recoverable corpus of extant epitaphs, the relative proportion of category 3 epitaphs experiences a notable drop from the fifth century to the first half of the fourth. The proportion of category 1 epitaphs, however, remains

---

[165] See the census of Attic *periboloi* initiated by Garland 1982 and continued by the work of Bergemann 1997 and Closterman 1999.

[166] This rough 4:1 ratio is derived from the fact that known Athenians tend to outnumber known foreigners in the category 1 epitaphs for single individuals at a rate of roughly 2:1. Once this factor is controlled, the general 8:1 ratio of Athenians to foreigners in the multiple-burial section of category 1 falls to roughly 4:1.

Table 5.4.4 *Epitaph types by percentages of* IG *corpus, later fifth (cf.*
Table 5.4.3) and earlier fourth (cf. Tables 5.4.1 and 5.4.2) centuries compared

	Category 1: Name(s) only	Category 2: Name(s) + brief extension	Category 3: More extensive epitaphs
Table 5.4.3 values			
GRAND TOTALS	83.17	5.94	10.89
Table 5.4.1 values (Table 5.4.2 values in parentheses)			
GRAND TOTALS	84.42 (84.90)	10.45 (10.95)	5.14 (4.16)

comparatively constant. A table of relative ratios summarizes the differences most effectively (Table 5.4.4).

The observations above, coupled with these ratios, point towards a notable shift in emphasis in the surviving epitaphs from the later fifth century into the earlier fourth: over a comparatively brief period of time, the relative proportions of the category 3 and category 2 epitaphs have essentially exchanged places, and, if the Table 5.4.2 ratio is taken into consideration, the proportion of category 3 epitaphs has likely dropped still further. This difference is all the more dramatic given that, despite the much larger size of the earlier fourth-century corpus as defined here, the relative proportion of the category 1 epitaphs has remained fairly constant over time: in short, memorialization by name only is far more numerically prevalent in the archaeological record during the later period than it was in the earlier one.

How might these changes be explained? Familial relationships have already been observed to dominate the brief comments made in the category 2 epitaphs in both the fifth and fourth centuries: it remains, therefore, to examine the category 3 examples to see whether any changes in subject matter or content are discernible over time.

If the category 3 epitaphs of the later fifth century demonstrated a comparatively wide degree of diversity in focus and expression (cf. Chapter 4, above), those of the earlier fourth century show significantly greater thematic unity. Within the seventy-four category 3 examples totaled in Table 5.4.2, above, six major topics receive significant emphasis.[167] Their relative

---

[167] These general preoccupations have often been identified by others in various combinations and contexts: see e.g. Stears 2000a: 214; Clairmont 1993: vol. I, 24–5, 27; Humphreys 1980: 113–14; Clairmont 1970: 52–6; Lattimore 1962 *passim*; Friis Johansen 1951: 63; and now in particular the detailed analysis of Tsagalis 2008 esp. 63–213, which appeared too recently to play a role in the development of these arguments.

proportions are represented in Table 5.4.5, below. In the notes accompanying Table 5.4.5, individual examples marked with a * bear the more general *IG* dating of 'fourth century' or its variants; examples without a * carry more specific dates. (Due to the fact that many of the epitaphs incorporate references to more than one of these topics, the sum of the percentages in the table far exceeds 100%.)

The data in Table 5.4.5 suggest the existence of some distinct thematic preferences in the surviving corpus of epitaphs. The 'goodness' of the deceased and the rehearsal of familial relationships are dominant throughout the category 3 collection. The remaining themes, whether or not they may have been considered trite by contemporary audiences, are certainly repetitive. They preference private values over public ones, and betray little concern for the memorialization of historical realities or of the public contributions of the dead. An epitaph dedicated to one Archestrate offers examples of most of the concepts from Table 5.4.5:[168]

πλεῖστομ μὲν καὶ ζῶσα [τ]ρό|πων σῶν ἔσχες ἔπαινον, |
Λυσάνδρου Πιθέως | Ἀρχεστράτη ἔγγονε, καὶ νῦ[ν] |
5 [λ]είπεις σοῖσι φίλοισι μέγαν πόθον, | ἔξοχα δ᾽ αὐτῆς
ἀνδρί, λιποῦσα φάος | μοιριδίωι θανάτωι.

vac. 0.020

εὐσεβῆ ἀσκήσασα βίον | καὶ σώφρονα θνήισκω,
ἡνίκα | 10 μοι βιότου μόρσιμον ἦλθε τέλος. |

vac. 0.020

πένθος μητρὶ λιποῦσα κασιγνή|τωι τε πόσει τε
παιδί τ᾽ ἐμῶι | θνήισκω καί με χθὼν ἥδε καλύ|πτει ⋮
ἥ πᾶσιν κοινὴ τοῖς ἀπογιγνο|15 μένοις·
εἰμὶ δὲ Λυσάνδρου | Πιθέως Ἀρχεστράτη ἥδε.

While you were alive, you received much praise for your ways, O Archestrate, daughter of Lysandros of Pithos, and now you leave for your loved ones great grief, especially for your husband, having left the light for a death allotted by fate.

Having led a pious and prudent life, I die[d], when the fated end of my life came upon me.

Leaving grief for my mother and brother and husband and child, I die, and this earth covers me, earth that is common to all those who have passed away. I am this Archestrate, daughter of Lysandros of Pithos.

---

[168] Edition from *IG* ii/iii² 7227; translation of the last four lines of the inscription as printed here by Stehle 2001: 183, and spelling of names standardized throughout translation.

Table 5.4.5 *Topics mentioned in category 3 epitaphs of the earlier fourth century (cf. Table 5.4.2)*

	Youth or early death[a]	Chronological age[b]	Abstract 'goodness'[c]	Family relationships[d]	Death as universal[e]	Grief or longing[f]
Occurrences (out of 74)	11	10	55	47	18	15
Percentage of total	14.86	13.51	74.32	63.51	24.32	20.27

[a] The following examples from *IG* ii/iii² employ this theme: 5239, 5452, 5847 (likely, from a supplement), 7839a, 8870 (likely), 10108, 11514 (via a reference to a *paidion*, or "little child"), 12335 (not the deceased but the young son whose death caused her in turn to die of grief), 12393, 13100/101, *13113 (likely, from a supplement).

[b] The following examples from *IG* ii/iii² employ this theme: 5239, 5452, 12335 (not the deceased but the young son whose death caused her in turn to die of grief), 12393, 13097, 13098, 13102, 13178, *6214 (a reference to old age, but with no specific number of years mentioned), *10510 (a reference to old age, but with no specific number of years mentioned).

[c] The following examples from *IG* ii/iii² employ this theme: 5239, 5424, 5450, 5452, 5673, 6004, 6857, 6873, 7227, 7711, 7839a, 7965, 8593, 8883, 9112, 10593, 10672, 10864, 11016, 11103, 11169, 11200, 11387, 11438 (likely), 11514, 11812, 11813, 12067, 12151, 12210a, 12254, 12335, 12778, 12839, 13071, 13090/1, 13092, 13096, 13097, 13098, 13099, 13178, 6693a, 5552a, *5501, *6475, *6551, *6858, *10510, *11659, *11701, *12405, *13032, *13113, *13116/19 (likely). It is often expressed in terms of 'grieving no one' or being 'blameless.' Nearly all of these examples employ references to generic positive qualities, but 7393, included in this count, is rather more specific and makes mention of a golden civic crown; similarly, 8883 notes skill in flute-playing, 9112 and *11701 are each dedicated to a nurse, and 11387 refers to a comic. 12254 lists "thriftiness," a character trait not often cited elsewhere in the corpus, amongst the chief virtues of the deceased.

[d] The following examples from *IG* ii/iii² employ this theme: 5239, 5424, 5450, 6857, 7227, 7393, 7711, 7839a, 7965, 8593, 8708, 8870, 8883, 10665, 10864, 11103, 11169, 11514, 11813, 12067, 12151, 12210a, 12335, 12495, 13095, 13097, 13099, 13102, 13102a, 5421a, 6693a, 11614a, 5552a, *6551, *6858, *10510, *12405. The term 'familial relationships' as used here includes the mention of parents, siblings, spouse, or children, by relationship or by name. Nos. 5452, 5673, 5847, 6004, 6873 (likely, from a supplement), 11016, *5501, *6214, *6475, and *13032 make no mention of familial relationships within the surviving epitaphs themselves, but indicate them elsewhere on the same monument (generally by labeling figures in accompanying reliefs or by listing names with patronymics as headers for the remainder of the inscription).

[e] The following examples from *IG* ii/iii² employ this theme: 5450, 5673, 5847, 6004, 7227, 8708, 8870, 11103, 11169, 12151, 13097, 13098, 13102, 13102a, 6693a, *6214, *6551, *11701. Common references that often prompt inclusion in this category include mentions of "fate" (*passim*) and of entering the "gates of Hades/Erebus" (11103) or the "house/chamber of Persephone" (5450, 6004, 8870 (likely), 11169, 12151, 13102a (a reference to the "queen of Hades"), *6551). Despite the specificity of 8708, referring to probable death in a shipwreck ("wandering on the waves"), the same thematic impact is made by the generalizing statement of the epitaph's first line.

[f] The following examples from *IG* ii/iii² employ this theme: 6004, 6873, 7227, 7711, 7839a, 10864, 11103, 11169, 12151, 12335, 12495, 13097 (likely, from a supplement), 13102, *6858, *13032. Epitaphs that refer only to the "memory" or "monument"'of an individual were excluded from this particular category.

This epitaph may display several different (perhaps equally well-liked by the survivors?) versions of the intended epitaph, particularly given the repetition both of the full identification of the deceased and of much of the thematic material (a similarly redundant example is *IG* ii/iii² 12335, discussed below). Despite its fullness, however, it betrays little about Archestrate's life as a member of her polis aside from her familial identification. The epitaph derives its meaning – and Archestrate's life derives its memory – from the statements that Archestrate will be dearly missed by the surviving members of her family.

Touches of originality in concept or expression may occasionally provide surface decoration for these favored themes in the category 3 epitaphs: *IG* ii/iii² 5673, for example, claims that the deceased valued φιλία as much as wealth before sharing in "the fate common to all"; *IG* ii/iii² 8593 refers to a son who dutifully buried his mother and now deserves praise for the monument. Private concerns, however, invariably predominate, and history-making action or even historically grounded references are almost completely absent. The exceptions are largely confined to mention of professions, so few that they can all be iterated here: *IG* ii/iii² 6873 is offered to a woman named Phanostrate who was a μαῖα καὶ ἰατρός ("midwife and healer"), 8883 notes skill in flute-playing, and 9112 and 11701 are each dedicated to a nurse. 12335, unique amongst this group, commemorates a mother said to have died of grief after her child was lost at sea; while the epitaph (a 'pair' of epigrams not dissimilar in their redundancy to *IG* ii/iii² 7227, discussed above) does include a rare reference to real-world events, its focus is firmly on the torture of private loss and its contents are largely derived from the favored themes outlined above in Table 5.4.5.

There are only two category 3 epitaphs in *IG* ii/iii² that probably date to the first half of the fourth century *and* make specific reference to wider historical events or civic life. 11387, dedicated to a comic poet named Euthias, seems to refer to a near-victory in a competition: addressing him, it says, "[you,] being second in order, were first in your wisdom." *IG* ii/iii² 7393, finally, speaks of the award of a golden civic crown. As discussed above, the only known golden crown awarded to an Athenian citizen before *c.* 350 is recorded in a document relief from a phratry, not from the polis as a whole. This epitaph may therefore date near the middle of the fourth century, if not still later. Its unique content, however, represents the culmination of some important trends discussed thus far:[169]

---

[169]   Edition from *IG* ii/iii² 7393.

Ἄρχιππος | Σκαμβωνίδης.

vac.

εἴ τις ἐν ἀνθρώποις ἀρετῆς ἕνεκ᾽ ἐστεφανώθη.

πλεῖστον ἐγὼ μετέχων τῶδ᾽ ἔτυχον στεφάν[ο]

5   χρυσῶ· Ἀθηναίων δὲ ἐστεφάνωσε πόλις·

εὐδαίμων δὲ ἔθανον παίδων παῖδας καταλείπω[ν].

Archippus of the deme Scambonidae.
If anyone amongst men was crowned for his virtue,
then having the greatest share I received this crown
of gold. The city of the Athenians crowned [me].
Blessed, I died, leaving behind the children of my children.

The reference to the crown bestowed by the polis invokes for Archippus the kind of memorialization for individual, historically grounded achievement that is by this period more frequently expressed on public monuments, such as honorific inscriptions and document reliefs.[170] The naming of Archippus' deme and the mention of his descendants, however, serve to 're-privatize' the epitaph and situate it in a more familiar fourth-century context.[171]

But this inscription does not only blur the boundaries between public and private commemoration: despite its date, it also invokes a number of much earlier commemorative paradigms. Its immediate mention of the heroic virtue of ἀρετή in the first line of the epitaph proper creates Homeric associations (cf. Chapter 2, above); by the conclusion of that same line, the completion of the mention of being "crowned for ἀρετή" may suggest connotations of athletic victory. The 'narrative' of Archippus' life experiences, too, recollects, whether independently or intentionally, those of an earlier model: Tellus of Athens, as presented by Herodotus' Solon (Hdt. 1.30.4–5; see Chapter 3, above). The references to being blessed, fortunate, or happy (the semantic fields of the adjectives εὐδαίμων and ὄλβιος overlap in these regards); the uses of superlatives to describe both men's lives; the recollections of honors from the city of Athens; and the mentions of being survived by "children of children" all potentially connect the real individual with the fictional one. The major feature of Tellus' biography that is lacking in Archippus' epitaph is any mention of death in battle or burial at public expense, and this omission may help to explain the unusual and complex content of the inscription. The tombstone appears to be attempting

---

[170] This is a point raised in connection with this epitaph by J. Ober, to whose comments the following observations, including the potential association with Herodotus' Tellus, are also indebted: see now Ober 2008: 257 n. 60.

[171] On the frequency of deme listings in fourth-century citizen epitaphs, see Meyer 1993 and below, *passim*.

to recombine the increasingly divergent public and private commemorative practices of its day, perhaps because Archippus' survivors desired a stronger and more permanent articulation of his historical contributions to the state – an articulation that may in turn have reflected positively upon his family.

Archippus' memorial is unique amongst the examples discussed here. On the whole, epitaphs referring to professions, to the events of an individual life, to historical context, or to history-making action were comparatively rare in the fifth century, but they did comprise a significantly larger portion of the surviving corpus from that time than they do in the fourth century. The fourth-century epitaphs, even the more elaborate ones of category 3, tend to re-echo intimate but general emotional themes whose relevance is almost wholly independent of historical context. These funerary inscriptions also tend to prioritize smaller-scale, localized relationships, such as associations with family members, acquaintances, and demes, rather than emphasizing the polis as a whole.

Two trends in the physical appearances of the fourth-century funerary monuments appear to parallel the tendencies of the epitaphs. Firstly, the surviving figured reliefs from the first half of the fourth century and beyond, as has frequently been noted, prefer scenes from domestic life.[172] Secondly, in an apparently related development, the familial funerary memorials known from Athens tend to increase in size and elaboration in the course of the fourth century.[173] The *naiskos* variety of figured-relief stele, in particular, becomes especially ambitious; by *c.* 350, it can resemble a small building with separate figures inside it.[174] These vast, showy memorials would have contrasted with some of the earlier and flatter figured reliefs (such as that of Dexileus), and also with the state-sponsored funerary monuments: in effect, they claim the family, rather than the polis, as the central context in which the meaning and relevance of an individual life are created.

What became of the *patrios nomos* during the fourth century BC? Although the civic burial ritual continued to exist in some form, at a

---

[172] See the references in note 17, above; more specifically, on males in this context, e.g. Osborne 1998; on females, e.g. Hoffmann 1993.

[173] This is the case not only with individual tombstones (e.g. Clairmont 1993: intro. 38–42, with catalog references), but also with the *periboloi* that often contained them: see Closterman 1999: 57–68. These elaborate memorials are believed to have been arrested by the sumptuary legislation of Demetrius of Phalerum near the end of the century: see O'Sullivan 2009: 47–66.

[174] E.g. Stears 2000a: 209–10; Clairmont 1993: vol. I, 38–41; and esp. Ridgway 1997: 160–2. Richter 1944 discusses two fourth-century figures originally thought to be free-standing sculptures, and demonstrates that they likely became detached from a *naiskos* stele of this type.

minimum for the first three-quarters of the century and likely beyond,[175] evidence and testimonia for the *patrios nomos* decline significantly after the conclusion of the Corinthian War, despite Athens' continuing involvement in a variety of conflicts.[176] This dearth of descriptive and physical material may suggest that the practice evolved into an occasional ceremony to mark especially significant military events, rather than remaining an annual commemoration of all of the war dead.[177] If the *patrios nomos* did indeed become this rarified, many of the war dead of the fourth century would likely have received burial from their own families rather than from the state, and the ongoing ideological and symbolic conflict embodied in the competing commemorative efforts for individuals like Dexileus would therefore have been significantly reduced. Also diminished, however, would have been the symbolic integration of the fallen warrior into his polis; any reduction of the *patrios nomos* would in effect not only have permitted but also validated private funerals and personal expressions of grief. A deceased soldier could therefore have been memorialized primarily as a lost family member, rather than as a lost entry into a homogeneous and largely anonymous collectivity of citizens. Such a personalized aesthetic would fit well with the general priorities of other fourth-century funerary memorials.

The mirror image of this interpretive possibility, however, is also intriguing. For the *patrios nomos* to have become a less frequent and therefore a more selective ceremony could have increased its perceived desirability, and even its prestige. It is possible that it may have functioned as another entry into the increasingly elaborate symbolic 'conversation' in later classical Athens, publicizing the history-making contribution of a smaller – and therefore more 'special' – group of individuals. If all of the war dead did not receive the *patrios nomos*, the ceremony might have in effect elevated some citizens above others, thereby ironically creating stratification where it had once promoted the maintenance of democratic sameness.

A growing division in the commemorative habits of fourth-century Athens, then, seems to have increasingly distinguished those whose activities

---

[175] Loraux 1986: 9 and n. 25, citing D. 18.285–8, notes that "Demosthenes certainly delivered the epitaphios for the dead of Chaeronea, but the [extant funerary] oration to which his name is attached does not satisfy everybody." Clairmont 1983: 22–8 explores the evidence for the holding of *epitaphioi agones* (funeral or memorial games) into the fourth century and beyond.

[176] Lewis 2000–03: 14–15, discussing casualty lists in particular; Clairmont 1983: 21, 209–21, esp. 209.

[177] This may be implied by the comment of Lewis 2000–03: 15, who grants that "there were indeed not many occasions when a *large* number of Athenians died [emphasis mine], but there will nevertheless have continued to be public funerals."

and contributions were qualified (even if in their own eyes) for memorialization as relevant events in the larger history of the polis. Athenians, both citizens and foreigners, who were properly situated by circumstance or by design to 'make history,' or who wanted to appear as if they were so positioned, would have been educated about possible avenues for their contributions by the public monuments proliferating about them. As such, it is likely that the public-honorific discourse of fourth-century Athens became part of a very strong feedback loop: the more individual commemoration that took place, the more intensively individuals were schooled in the types of engagement and self-presentation that could yield public prestige and lasting memory. In turn, the more visible such individuals became, the more strongly they were publicly perceived as being an essential part of the history of the polis itself, and were honored for it.[178]

On the other side of this divide were those whose lives appear to have derived their chief commemorative value from a network of smaller-scale relationships, particularly those of the family. With the development of an increasingly elaborate system for the recording and publicizing of individual contributions to the life of the polis, there may have come a perception that certain individuals – in fact, the *majority* of individuals[179] – were not positioned to be shapers of history as the polis now wrote it, even on a limited scale. They would not be contributing significant political, military, or financial assistance to the city; they would not be officers of its tribes or religious officials in its major cults; they were not likely to perish in major wars whose conflicts could be claimed as heroic. As such, funerary commemoration for these individuals appears to have turned away from deliberately competing with the kinds of memorialization favored by the polis and by its major component bodies and contributing groups. Fourth-century funerary monuments, therefore, perhaps as a partial result of the long-term 'education' of burying populations by the changing habits of public commemoration at Athens, tend against historical grounding and historical context, and towards the relevance of the individual as the member of an *oikos* (familial household) and, for citizens, a deme.[180]

---

[178] See Hedrick 1999: 410.

[179] Including nearly all women, save, perhaps, priestesses: cf. Chapter 4, above, on the monument(s) apparently dedicated to Myrrhine, a priestess of Athena Nike. Lawton 1995: 151–2 no. 164 is a document relief tentatively dated to the second half of the fourth century that may also have been dedicated to a priestess.

[180] See Meyer 1993.

5.5 Conclusion: Agency and its limits

Athenian historical discourse during the earlier fourth century, both literary and public-symbolic, demonstrates a growing focus upon the agency of individuals. Xenophon emphasized the role of the individual in history-making actions; Demosthenes and Aeschines argued that public perceptions of the dependence of the democratic group upon its leaders can give rise to the reality of that dependence. During the same period, a burgeoning of public commemoration for individuals, particularly in the form of honorific decrees, likely contributed to an increasing recognition of categorized or stratified access to historical memory. By the mid century, there appears to have been a general sense that certain individuals were positioned for activities that earned them memorialization as distinct, contributing members (even if minor ones) to the history of the polis. Likely in partial reaction to these developments, funerary discourse of the era moved in a different direction, appealing with increasing frequency to private emotion and the relevance of the individual life to the family unit.

It is not possible to work out these arguments at quite the same level of detail in other major Greek poleis: the evidence, particularly from the earlier fifth century, is simply too limited. However, by the fourth century, monuments and testimonia attached to both Sparta and Thebes suggest that some of the ideas in motion at Athens were also alive in its two greatest antagonists.

6 | Out beyond Athens

Historical agency in Sparta and Thebes

6.1 History's heroes: Expanding the Athenian paradigm

Timber,[1] metals,[2] and a strategic location for shipping near the mouth of the Strymon river made Amphipolis a place worth fighting for, especially in 424 BC. The Athenian colony had only been in existence for about thirteen years: attempts to settle the location had failed twice in the past,[3] and with the Archidamian War escalating, the Athenians desperately needed as much wood as possible for the maintenance of their fleet.[4] But the region was not loyal: Thrace, Macedonia, and the Chalcidice were turning against Athens,[5] and they welcomed the Spartan general Brasidas as an ally and liberator.[6] Although Thucydides may be critical of their credulousness,[7] the northern cities apparently warmed both to Brasidas' conduct and to his personality (Thuc. 4.81.2–3).[8] Brasidas' famed moderation served him well at Amphipolis; when his supporters inside the walls failed to open the gates to him (Thuc. 4.104.4), he captured the surrounding countryside and easily negotiated the city's calm surrender (Thuc. 4.105.1–106.4). Less than two years later, it was again at Amphipolis that he encountered Cleon and the Athenian army (Thuc. 5.6.1–8.4).

The end came quickly: Brasidas attacked; Cleon's hesitation proved fatal. The Athenians fled, and both commanders fell in the slaughter (Thuc. 5.10.1–12). What happened next, however, was extraordinary. The people of Amphipolis not only buried Brasidas in the heart of the city, in front of their agora, δημοσίᾳ ("at public cost"),[9] but they formally heroized him and

---

[1] Borza 1987: 33, 41; Borza 1982b: 1–8; Meiggs 1982: 126–8.   [2] Borza 1982b: 8–12.

[3] Once by Aristagoras of Miletus (Thuc. 4.102.2; Strassler 1996 *ad loc.* also cross-references Hdt. 5.124–6); and once by the Athenians themselves (Thuc. 1.100.3, 4.102.2).

[4] Borza 1987: 41–3.   [5] Thuc. 4.78.1–6, 79.1–2; cf. also 4.80.1–4, 82.1.

[6] I am grateful to S. Saporito for discussion of Brasidas in conversation, in class presentation, and in her undergraduate senior thesis project (Saporito 2009) that called my attention to some of the material that I treat here.

[7] Pearson 1957: 236.

[8] On the admiration Brasidas has attracted from modern commentators, see e.g. Harley 1942.

[9] This is the same word used by Herodotus of Tellus (cf. Chapter 3, above), and by Thucydides himself of the *patrios nomos* (cf. Chapters 2 and 4, above).

named him their *ktistês*, replacing the original colonial founder of their city, Hagnon (Thuc. 5.11.1). Hagnon was still very much alive (he had led out the colony in 437/6: Thuc. 4.102.3), and remained so until at least 413.[10] This would have made Brasidas a sounder choice not only in terms of the ordinary routine of cult (since the heroization of *ktistai* at this time normally followed their deaths),[11] but also, as Thucydides points out (Thuc. 5.11.1), in terms of strategy.[12] Amphipolis had rejected its mother city of Athens in order to defect to the Peloponnesian cause, and it was therefore likely much more appealing for the renegade colony to honor a deceased Spartan than a living Athenian.

Regardless of the extent of any reverence previously shown to Hagnon,[13] the reassignment of the privilege of memorialization here is especially striking in that it happened over such a short period of time. It may have been presaged by the reaction of the inhabitants of Scione to their liberation by Brasidas (Thuc. 4.120.1–121.1). Their award of a public golden crown, likely to be an even scarcer honor at this time than later,[14] to the Spartan general is coupled by Thucydides with a suggestion of heroism, for the historian compares the treatment of Brasidas to that traditionally accorded an athlete (ἰδίᾳ δὲ ἐταινίουν τε καὶ προσήρχοντο ὥσπερ ἀθλητῇ, "individually they placed bands upon his head and presented him accolades as if for an athletic champion," Thuc. 4.121.1).

The paradigm of the athlete-hero seems to have enjoyed especial prominence during the classical era,[15] as a number of individuals who had distinguished themselves in the games acquired heroic status,[16] perhaps in some cases purposely aiming at it through their own behavior.[17] In his

---

[10] See the references collected by McCauley 1993: 241.

[11] McCauley 1993: 241, and see also Chapters 2 and 5, above.

[12] See McCauley 1993: 242–3, and also 250–1, 255–8, on the political nature of hero cult and its changing dynamics in the fifth century.

[13] See Currie 2002: 37–8, esp. n. 134. I do not necessarily agree that the Thucydidean passage implies a wholesale transfer of honors from Hagnon to Brasidas; the emphasis appears to be upon the rituals established for the new *ktistês*, rather than upon those existing for the old one. See also McCauley 1993: 243, who cites other interpretations.

[14] See Chapter 5, above, and cf. Domingo Gygax 2006: 490–6, esp. 495, on the increase of such honors over time.

[15] Note the title of Currie 2002.

[16] See the data collected by Connolly 1998: 16, 21, citing and building upon Farnell 1921: 420–6; see also McCauley 1993: 248.

[17] Currie 2002: 37, asserting that "Historical persons' emulations of heroes (pre-eminently Heracles) constitutes a bid *in those persons' lifetime* and *on their initiative* to be regarded as the equals of established heroes" (emphases *sic*).

examination of the fifth-century athlete-hero Euthymus of Locri, who received heroic honors even during his lifetime, Currie suggests that the process of heroization can be understood as a communicative exchange between the honorand and his audience, i.e. his community. The aspirant hero behaves in a manner that invites others to associate him with an established figure, and then welcomes the assumption that he should be understood – and revered – in the same way as the object of his imitation. Both sides therefore participate in the transaction.[18]

Brasidas, then, was treated by the citizens of both Amphipolis and Scione as the chief agent of the Peloponnesian accomplishments in the north. In life and in death, the public perception of his deeds appears to have been shaped by at least two heroic models dependent upon the recognition of individual pre-eminence: the athlete and the *ktistês*.[19] The historical Brasidas may in fact have chosen, as Euthymus of Locri may also have done, to adapt his specific behaviors to these models in order to invite these kinds of public reactions. Even the historians seem to have considered the possibility: Diodorus, for example, writing centuries later and likely influenced by continuing developments in Greek understandings of historical agency, ascribes performative motivations to some of Brasidas' choices.[20]

The example of Brasidas shows, firstly, that older cultural and religious paradigms could be reinterpreted to confront – or accommodate – the growing ascription of individual historical agency during the classical era.[21] But it also suggests that some of the trends observed thus far at Athens may be represented elsewhere in Greece, as well. This chapter begins near the concluding days of the Peloponnesian War in order to explore how ideas about historical agency were apparently evolving in the earlier fourth century not only at Athens, but also in other city-states, most notably

---

[18] Ibid. 26, 36–8, 43–4; cf. also Currie's discussion at 39 of Connor 1987, an analysis of a somewhat similar pattern from the archaic period.

[19] McCauley 1993 demonstrates the potential of these two models for political impact and political manipulation: see esp. 44–6 (summarizing the hero "categories" of Brelich), 66–7 (on the potential early connection between *ktistês* heroism and politics), 213–23 (on athlete-heroes), 241–4 (on Brasidas in particular), 250–1, 255–7.

[20] D.S. 12.43.3 (fighting style), 68.3 (desire to take Amphipolis). That Brasidas was interpreted as performing to his role is strongly implied, though not stated, by both Thucydides and Diodorus, in (for example) the Homeric qualities they apply to their accounts of his fighting at Pylos (Thuc. 4.11.4–12.1; D.S. 12.62.1–5; on Brasidas compared to Achilles see also Pl. *Symp.* 221c).

[21] I agree here with the developmental view of McCauley 1993 on the political "manipulation" of hero-cult.

Sparta and Thebes. With Athens, these two poleis comprised the major loci of political and military power during the pre-Macedonian fourth century, and their leaders, in particular, seem to have reflected deeply upon the assignment – and the invocation – of responsibility for historically consequent action.

The evidence employed here is again both literary and material. Xenophon's *Hellenica*, in its treatments of Lysander, Agesilaus, and Epaminondas, provides further opportunity (continued from Chapter 5, above) to observe Xenophon's conceptions of historical agency, along with valuable information about the experiences of these eminent individuals. Because there are no surviving historical works from Spartan or Theban authors contemporary to the period between the Decelean War and the battle of Chaeronea, however, additional historical details must be drawn from fragmentary writers like Theopompus, and from later ones like Diodorus Siculus and Plutarch.[22]

The material evidence poses its own particular challenges. The relative magnitude both of ancient Athens and of the archaeological investigations that have taken place across the modern city allow comparatively broad studies to take place there that cannot be reliably duplicated in other poleis. The relevant information is at best scattered across a variety of media, but where Athens might provide scores of examples of a given type of artifact, another polis might yield only a small handful. The material from cities outside of Athens, therefore, generally allows for closer examination of the paradigmatic individual than of his citizen populace. But drawing together some of the archaeological evidence that *does* exist, mainly in the forms of inscriptions, iconography, and honorific statuary (or testimonia thereto), strongly suggests that some of the issues being raised at Athens were also under consideration elsewhere.[23]

---

[22] I avoid using close readings of later writers to construct arguments about fourth-century opinions: on this problem, see both the careful methods and the results of Meadows 1995, who makes the case that much of Pausanias' coverage of latest fifth- and fourth-century Sparta may have been derived from Theopompus, but whose detailed analysis implicitly demonstrates that it is not possible to arrive at a sound understanding of Theopompus' construction of historical agency amongst the Spartans from Pausanias' text alone.

[23] This should not in itself be surprising: some of what we learn from Athens is likely unique to Athens alone, but much else appears to have been shared to varying degrees with other centers of Greek culture: see e.g. Morris 1987 on the development of the polis state, and Kurtz and Boardman 1971 on Greek burial customs. Morris 1992 esp. 145–55 also holds that "cycles of display," meaning general tendencies towards the use of simple vs. lavish grave markers and other visible items (such as houses), can be observed not only at Athens but throughout Greece.

6.2 The Spartans

Lysander

Xenophon's treatment of Lysander in the *Hellenica* maintains a steady focus upon the commander and his personal qualities.[24] It also emphasizes his individuality by establishing deliberate contrasts between Lysander on the one hand and larger groups of Greeks, including his own populace, on the other. These emphases emerge even in the first major scene after Lysander has been elevated to command, a conference between himself and Cyrus, prince of Persia (*HG* 1.5.1–8). The establishment of Persian funding for the new Peloponnesian fleet proves difficult, but Lysander is eventually able to secure the desired pay scale for the sailors by asking for it as a personal favor (*HG* 1.5.6). The sealing of the agreement between Sparta and Persia was a fundamental factor in the conclusion of the Peloponnesian War, allowing Sparta to establish itself as a naval power and challenge Athens in an area in which it had been pre-eminent since the battle of Salamis. Xenophon recalls this situation immediately after reporting the agreement with Cyrus, noting that the Peloponnesians were elated at these developments and the Athenians disheartened (*HG* 1.5.7–8). The implication here is that Lysander's personal negotiations are determinative in the outcome of the war, and the same idea is sustained in the following account of the battle of Notium, which is depicted verbally as a triumph by "Lysander" over "the Athenians" (*HG* 1.5.11–16).[25]

But Xenophon also demonstrates that eminent individuals who seek to construct particular reputations for themselves can have their plans thwarted both by their immediate audiences and by the historians whose commemoration they seek. When Lysander yields the naval command to Callicratidas at the end of his term (*HG* 1.6.1–6), he calls himself θαλαττοκράτωρ, "ruler of the sea" (*HG* 1.6.2), employing a very unusual word-root that both the character and the historian seem to select for striking impact.[26] Callicratidas challenges Lysander's self-presentation, first by

---

[24] I remain very grateful to M. Flower for the recommendation some time since that I incorporate Lysander (particularly his monument at Delphi) and other non-Athenians into this project.

[25] Lysander is named at least once in every section from 10 to 14, and from 10 to the beginning of 13 in every sentence demarcated by modern punctuation. During the combat (13–14), "the Athenians" are named four times; their commanders, Antiochus and Alcibiades, temporarily disappear (save one mention of the former simply as the recipient of Athenian "help" early in 13). The contrast is not nearly so strong as it is in the case of Agesilaus at Coronea (cf. below), but the technique is similar.

[26] Moles 1994: 72.

daring his predecessor to sail to Miletus unharassed before assuming such a
hubristic title, and then by presenting himself, in direct contrast, as a mere
agent of Sparta in the service of his polis who is willing to step aside in
favor of anyone else who feels better qualified for the position (*HG* 1.6.5).[27]
Callicratidas is being disingenuous (as emerges almost immediately when
he admits to his own ambitions, *HG* 1.6.5), and his appointment is in any
case maintained (*HG* 1.6.6). But Xenophon has used Callicratidas here to
demonstrate that public perceptions of historical agency can be negotiated,
that the success of a given leader's 'message' depends upon the receptivity
of his audience, and that the historiographer, by choosing what material to
include and exclude, can under some circumstances be the ultimate arbiter
of an elite individual's historical legacy.

Similar tendencies emerge from Xenophon's narrative of the conclusion
of the Peloponnesian War. The treatment of the battle of Aegospotami
begins with Lysander being given individual control of Cyrus' fortune (*HG*
2.1.14–15), and as preparations for the confrontation take place, Xenophon
sustains a rhetorical contrast between "Lysander" and "the Athenians," in
the same way as he did at Notium (*HG* 2.1.15–24). Lysander is his fleet's
sole agent in the conflict itself (*HG* 2.1.28), takes charge of the settlement
after the fight is over (*HG* 2.1.30–2.2.5, 6), and finally blockades the Piraeus
(*HG* 2.2.9). The character seems poised to assume personal credit for ending the war. But Xenophon's narrative again asserts the primacy of the
historiographer over the self-presentation of the individual. The account
of the peace negotiations (*HG* 2.2.16–23) records in painstaking detail the
assignment of responsibility for each stage of the discussion (*HG* 2.2.16–
18), which culminates in Lysander openly ceding authority to the ephors.
Regardless of why the historical Lysander may have made this choice,[28]
Xenophon's decision to include a description of the entire process essentially
refuses to allow the character Lysander to determine the recollection of the
events.

As plans are made for the Spartan expedition into Asia, Xenophon
explores Lysander's motivations for the campaign: the timing is right and
the resources are in place, but the invasion will also provide a chance for
Lysander to reinstall his decarchies, which the ephors have displaced (*HG*
3.4.1–2). In this case, Lysander's ambition to establish his reputation and

---

[27] Ibid. 74.
[28] Proietti 1987: 38–9 questions Lysander's behavior here, suggesting that Lysander as
vice-admiral may technically have needed to yield privilege to his military superiors or to Agis,
but (given that he was possessed of enormous power at that time) that he might have done so
in an exaggerated fashion to indicate his resentment.

his historical legacy not only outweighs the preferences of his polis, but
also brings him into conflict with his king (*HG* 3.4.7–10). Once arrived in
Asia, Lysander proves to be more popular than Agesilaus, to the degree that
the Greek cities make personal appeals to him when the mechanisms of
their own governments fail them (*HG* 3.4.7). The diagnosis of Agesilaus'
small contingent of Spartiates that Lysander is behaving "more arrogantly
than monarchy" (τῆς βασιλείας ὀγκηρότερον, *HG* 3.4.8) is portrayed by
Xenophon as both a cause and an effect of Lysander's treatment. When
the two leaders finally meet to discuss the problem, Agesilaus addresses
the issue of honorific transactions and suggests that eminent individuals
can affect their own reception: τούς γε βουλομένους ἐμοῦ μείζους φαίνεσθαι·
τοὺς δέ γε αὔξοντας εἰ μὴ ἐπισταίμην ἀντιτιμᾶν, αἰσχυνοίμην ἄν, "[I know
how to disgrace] those who wish to seem better than I am; but I would be
humiliated if I were incapable of reciprocating towards those who increase
my honor" (*HG* 3.4.9). But as Xenophon's own treatment of this and other
episodes shows, it is the author who has final control over the content and
the judgment of history, not his characters.

Xenophon's account of Lysander, then, simultaneously asserts and
demonstrates the power of historiography to assign agency and memory. For Xenophon, the ability of an elite individual to claim authority and script his own recollection depends upon the cooperation of his
audiences, and particularly upon those segments of his audiences who
will not only receive his message favorably but also commit it to permanent form. In Xenophon's view, of course, the most powerful medium
for such commitment is written prose, but the real Lysander seems to
have looked more widely for ways to advertise his position as an agent of
history.

It is said that Samos decreed divine honors for Lysander while he was
still alive;[29] if true, this would be one of the first examples of such deification in the Greek world.[30] Lysander seems to have deliberately invited
such attentions:[31] in particular, the remains of his massive 'Nauarch's Monument' at Delphi, erected at the conclusion of the Peloponnesian War to

---

[29] Flower 1988: 128 and n. 21, citing Plu. *Lys.* 18.3–4 (= 5–6 Ziegler) and noting that Plutarch
claims to have acquired his information from Duris of Samos.

[30] Cf. Flower 1988: 132. There may be others besides Lysander who received such honors around
this time: Currie 2002: 37–8, 43, for example, suggests that Euthymus of Locri may have been
granted divine, as opposed to merely heroic, cult while he was still alive, earlier in the fifth
century. While Lysander may or may not have been the first to be treated in this way, he was
certainly not the last: see the conclusions down to his time summarized by McCauley 1993: 248,
255–60; a full study of deification from Lysander through the Hellenistic era is Habicht 1970.

[31] See the testimonia, bibliography, and narrative collected by McCauley 1993: 245–6.

celebrate his victory at Aegospotami, leave little doubt as to the general message he was sending.[32] Personal dedications had long been a fixture in Greek sanctuaries, but their forms had generally been circumscribed by tradition. Statues, inscriptions, and other items commemorating athletic victories, particularly in the panhellenic competitions, were common;[33] so, at certain sites, were *kouroi* (statues of nude male youths),[34] or gifts of arms and armor.[35] Some particularly wealthy and powerful benefactors also seem to have pursued self-aggrandizement in the form of especially extravagant offerings to the gods.[36] But individual monuments to *historical* accomplishments – "historical" in the ancient Greek sense, meaning in politics or warfare – are less common in the sanctuaries during the earlier classical period, when battle-memorials both in the field and in the sacred precincts tended to celebrate poleis rather than generals.[37] One major exception to these general practices, the statuary monument at Delphi that Pausanias says included Miltiades alongside a number of other Athenian and mythological heroes, was posthumous,[38] which would likely have softened its claims in comparison with those that Lysander was now making.[39]

The overall design of the Nauarch's Monument was showy and venturesome:[40] a large statuary group in bronze (probably over thirty figures), including an image of the god Poseidon crowning Lysander[41] in celebration of his naval victory. An epigram in what may be later

---

[32] McCauley 1993: 245–6; Cartledge 1987: 82–3, with additional secondary references; see also Crane 1996: 177–9.

[33] On sanctuary-dedications by athletes in general, see e.g. Smith 2007. On portrait statues, see Keesling 2003: 175, who holds that athletic victors were part of the narrow class of individuals whose self-representation in sanctuaries was acceptable.

[34] Richter 1960 (1942) is a stylistic study of *kouroi*; on the "context and function" of *kouroi* as dedications, see recently Brüggemann in Meyer and Brüggemann 2007. A particularly important site for these was the sanctuary of Apollo Ptoius, in Boeotia: see Ducat 1971.

[35] For a general discussion, see Jackson 1991.

[36] Famous examples of such benefactors to Delphi as early as the sixth century included e.g. Croesus (Hdt. 1.50.1–55.1) and the Alcmeonids (marble façade of the Temple of Apollo, 514–05 BC: Bommelaer and Laroche 1991: 20, cf. 9–11).

[37] West 1969: 11, 14.

[38] Cartledge 1987: 85. The Callimachus monument to the *polemarch* of Marathon on the Athenian Acropolis, it should be recalled, was also posthumous: on both of these commemorative efforts, see Chapter 2, above.

[39] McCauley 1993: 245; Cartledge 1987: 85.

[40] Testimonia: Plu. *Lys.* 18.1; Paus. 10.9.7–10. Modern summary: Bommelaer and Laroche 1991: 108–9. Problems of reconstruction: Vatin 1991: 103–38. Inscriptions: Meiggs and Lewis 1969: 287–90 no. 95; Tod 1946: 228–31 nos. 94–5. Analysis of the monument in its historical and physical context: e.g. Crane 1996: 177–9.

[41] Paus. 10.9.7.

fourth-century lettering, perhaps the result of recutting, appears on the
base for Lysander's statue:[42]

εἰκόνα ἑὰν ἀνέθηκεν [ἐπ'] ἔργωι τῶιδε ὅτε νικῶν
      ναυσὶ θοαῖς πέρσεν Κε[κ]ροπιδᾶν δύναμιν
Λύσανδρος, Λακεδαίμονα ἀπόρθητον στεφανώσα[ς]
      Ἑλλάδος ἀκρόπολ[ιν, κ]αλλίχορομ πατρίδα.
5   ἐχσάμου ἀμφιρύτ[ου] τεῦξε ἐλεγεῖον ⠆ Ἴων.

Lysander set up his image here on this monument when as conqueror
      with swift ships he destroyed the Cecropidan force,
having crowned Lacedaemon undefeated,
      the acropolis of Greece, homeland of beautiful dancing-grounds.
5   Ion, from sea-girt Samos, created this poem.

Like many of the inscriptions examined in previous chapters, this epigram
emphasizes the historical contributions of its subject and employs elevated,
poetical language. But it is distinguished from similar expressions of praise
in that it reverses some of the traditional expectations with regard to subject
and object. The typical political parlance, represented in honorific decrees
from Athens and also attested elsewhere in the Greek world, has the city
glorifying the individual in return for his service. Here, however, Lysander
verbally crowns Sparta instead, a concept that probably derived, like the
overall tone and style of the monument itself, from the established image of
the outstanding individual who brings honor to his homeland: the victorious athlete.[43]

By Lysander's day, verse had long served as a commemorative medium
for the celebration of athletic achievement, glorifying the poet[44] along with
the victor. Here the poetry, a signed epigram by Ion of Samos,[45] represents a commission to memorialize *historical* deeds, metaphorically transforming Lysander's achievements into the material of heroic legend, just
as the Persian War epigrams had done for their subjects at Athens three

---

[42] Edition from Meiggs and Lewis 1969: 288 no. 95, who date the lettering to "probably . . . the
      second half of the fourth century" and suggest (290) that the epigram may have undergone
      recutting, a possibility that I accept. However, I do not necessarily subscribe to their "sympathy
      with [the] view" that the epigram itself may also be fourth century in date and therefore
      posthumous to Lysander.
[43] Crane 1996: 177; cf. the discussion of the Samian Lysandreia, a festival that included athletics,
      in Flower 1988: 132.
[44] Or at least the poet's artistic persona: on the rhetorical stance of the Pindaric poet, e.g.
      Mackie 2003; Lefkowitz 1991. On the development of *epinikion* as a genre, see R. Thomas
      2007.
[45] A point whose significance is highlighted by Crane 1996: 177.

generations earlier.[46] While the Lysander and Persian War monuments exploit the poetical medium in similar ways, however, their interpretations of historical agency are polar opposites: the Persian War epigrams were probably dedicated by the citizen body to those who fought collectively on behalf of the entire polis, while Lysander's inscription claims honor for himself as victor in battle and depicts him as the individual source of his city's consequent fame.

Plutarch suggests that Lysander may actually have enjoyed an ongoing poetical following for his accomplishments.[47] Even if Lysander's poetical retinue represents a contamination from the historical tradition surrounding Alexander,[48] however, and even if the inscription on the Delphic monument does not represent a commission from Lysander himself, the visual language of the sculptural group also presents a strong statement about individual historical agency. The crowning of the Lysander figure by the image of Poseidon recollects the iconography of, for example, Attic document reliefs (see Chapters 4 and 5, above). There, individuals who had benefited the *dêmos* could be shown being crowned by Athena, patroness of the polis and returner of good deeds in kind.[49] Depicting Poseidon in a similar position here implies that Lysander is both the benefactor of the sea itself and the recipient of cosmic and divine approval.[50]

Lysander portrayed himself in the guise of an athletic victor and placed his own portrait amongst those of the gods (there were apparently images of other divinities gathered around the Poseidon–Lysander pair). There may, therefore, have been only a small cognitive leap remaining for the Samians to name Lysander himself divine, and indeed, the timing of the cult's foundation on Samos does seem to coincide well with the construction of the Nauarch's Monument.[51] Rather than assuming, however, that the sculptural installation itself provoked an offer of deification, it is safer to suggest that the monument embodies themes that the Spartan commander likely also invoked in other contexts.[52] The Samian response to the message

[46] See Derderian 2001: 102–7 and Chapter 2, above.   [47] Plu. *Lys.* 18.5–9.
[48] E.g. Curt. 8.5.7–8; Arr. 4.9.9.   [49] On the iconography of the reliefs, see Lawton 1995: 31–2.
[50] Hornblower 2002: 183; Shur 1931: 31.   [51] Flower 1988: 132–3 and n. 45, with references.
[52] McCauley 1993: 245–8; cf. also Flower 1988: 133, suggesting that the Thasians' offer of divine status to Agesilaus was modeled on the Samian offer to Lysander and represented "another example of how institutions spread amongst the Greeks through imitation." Cartledge 1987: 82 calls attention to Bommelaer's (1981: 7–17 [catalog], 17–19 [epigrams]) survey of the relevant archaeological evidence. Although most of Bommelaer's entries necessarily acknowledge testimonia rather than physical remains, they strongly recommend that Lysander pursued a much broader program of self-promotion.

that Lysander was sending was dramatic,[53] but it was grounded in ways of understanding the position of the individual in human history that had been gradually evolving for decades before the statues of the Nauarch's Monument were raised at Delphi.

The behavior and reception of Lysander contrast with the frequent depiction (in both ancient and modern times) of classical Sparta as a stratified but generally anonymizing society.[54] But Lysander's self-presentation was clearly not intended for Spartans alone: both the scale of his ambitions and the contexts of his 'performances' suggest that he sought the esteem of broader Greek audiences.[55] Particularly in that regard, his accumulation of personal power and his efforts at self-aggrandizement may have been modeled upon the example of Brasidas.[56] Similar responsion, though with very different goals, may also be evident in the case of Agesilaus. The Spartan king, whose reputation amongst the other Greeks seems initially to have suffered in comparison with that of Lysander, may have deliberately scripted some of his decisions, most notably his rejection of cult, in order to *contrast* himself with his ambitious countryman.[57] Xenophon interprets both individuals' behaviors as performative in a variety of contexts, and he therefore uses their experiences in similar ways, claiming for himself in the course of his narrative the rhetorical authority to determine how these men are remembered as agents of history.

Agesilaus

Agesilaus (d. *c.* 360/59) seems to have held a particular fascination for Xenophon. By 394, Xenophon was with Agesilaus on campaign in Asia, and during the summer of that year he fought with the Spartans against his native Athenians at the battle of Coronea. Agesilaus' intervention likely helped to obtain for Xenophon his beloved estate at Scillus (*A.* 5.3.7–13) when the historian was exiled from Athens, and Agesilaus' activities and experiences enjoy the greatest amount of attention of any individual in

---

[53] See McCauley 1993: 248; Flower 1988: 133.   [54] Cartledge 1987: 84–5, and see note 75, below.

[55] McCauley 1993: 248; see also note 52, above, noting in particular the diverse locations of the items listed in the catalog by Bommelaer 1981: 7–8.

[56] McCauley 1993: 247, citing Cartledge 1987: 85, who describes the situation well by suggesting that "in his semi-divine cult, his golden crown, and his personalized remembrance at Delphi Brasidas unmistakeably points forward to Lysander."

[57] Flower 1988: 131–4, examining this possibility with regard to Agesilaus' refusal of an offer of deification from the Thasians; see also Cartledge 1987: 97, suggesting that "following the vicissitudes of his former lover's career . . . had taught Agesilaos what to accept and what to purge from the heritage of Lysander's policies and politics."

Xenophon's corpus, next only to those of Xenophon himself.[58] Given that part of that attention occurs in the form of an eponymous encomium that shares – but often in very different form – some material with the *Hellenica*, it has naturally often been assumed that Xenophon wished to provide a positive treatment in his *Agesilaus* as a potential corrective to the *Hellenica*'s more 'objective' or even negative version of events.[59]

The content of the *Agesilaus*, however, also demonstrates one of Xenophon's dominant interests: the essential qualities of good leadership.[60] This ethical concern is so pervasive throughout Xenophon's works that it can potentially invite the reduction of Xenophon's conception of agency to the summation that individual personalities are what moves the machinery of history. But as introduced in Chapter 5 and in the discussion of Lysander, above, there are two essential characteristics that make Xenophon's views of agency distinctive: firstly, Xenophon, like Herodotus and Thucydides, is interested in the relationships between eminent individuals and their citizen groups, and secondly, even more importantly, Xenophon sees the invocation and acknowledgement of historical agency as a self-conscious process that depends upon both the performer and the recorder of history-making actions. Both of these features can be reviewed in especial detail through Xenophon's treatment of Agesilaus in the *Hellenica* and in the encomium.

In the *Hellenica*, Agesilaus is frequently credited – by internal audiences or by Xenophon – with historically significant activities, either on his own or in partnership with his army or his state.[61] Under these circumstances,

---

[58] It has been suggested that Xenophon appears to have had a blind spot for the strategic, diplomatic, and political shortcomings of his patron and (likely) friend: see in most detail Hamilton 1991, and cf. the different view of Cartledge 1987: 399–412, with a review of selected eulogistic and critical Agesilaus literature at 5–7.

[59] See the review by Tuplin 1993: 193–200. The general interpretation can hold no matter what the priority of the two texts might be.

[60] This has frequently been acknowledged in the scholarship, and is treated in wide-ranging detail recently by Dillery 1995, who applies paradigmatic models to large-scale interpretations of both the *Anabasis* and the *Hellenica*. An influential and frequently cited general study of leadership in Xenophon is Breitenbach 1967.

[61] Having noted that 'historical significance' is, in the eyes of the Greek writers, something that can be assigned by them or by others (see Chapter 1, above), I prefer for current purposes to let Xenophon indicate, as far as possible, what he himself views as historically significant. Rahn 1971: 498–502 has reviewed Xenophon's programmatic statements regarding topics appropriate for historical writing (he summarizes these as "expenditures, dangers and varying strategy of powerful states," 501), and sees the balance of Xenophon's interests as shifting in the course of the *Hellenica* away from the latter, more Thucydidean perspective, towards "the remarkable behavior of individuals and small states" (502). Because this analysis of Xenophon's narratives aims at articulating some of the ways he explores individual historical

however, 'commander narrative' can be deceiving. By this point in Greek literary history it has become an accepted way of describing military movements,[62] but its broad application for this purpose can give the surface impression that Xenophon is assigning far greater prominence to Agesilaus' actions and choices than a closer reading of the text reveals. Indeed, there are some places where 'commander narrative' should not be construed as anything more than a convenient mode of discourse, and other places where Xenophon intends its uses for particular rhetorical purposes.

The first major military act of Agesilaus' reign is the expedition to Asia, and the theme of self-presentation and reception is established by Xenophon at the outset in his coverage of the attempted sacrifice at Aulis (*HG* 3.4.3).[63] Xenophon notes the connection to Agamemnon in neutral language, but the invocation of heroism seems to derive from Agesilaus' own intentions, as he takes personal umbrage (not unlike the Agamemnon of the *Iliad*) at the interruption of his performance by the Boeotians (*HG* 3.4.4).[64] The confrontation seems in its rhetoric to set up an individual conflict between Agesilaus on the one hand and the Boeotarchs on the other (no other parties are mentioned). Shortly thereafter, however, the episode is recalled by the Spartans in very different terms as they make plans to attack Thebes, thereby beginning the Corinthian War:

οἱ μέντοι Λακεδαιμόνιοι ἄσμενοι ἔλαβον πρόφασιν στρατεύειν ἐπὶ τοὺς Θηβαίους, πάλαι ὀργιζόμενοι αὐτοῖς τῆς τε ἀντιλήψεως τῆς τοῦ Ἀπόλλωνος δεκάτης ἐν Δεκελείᾳ καὶ τοῦ ἐπὶ τὸν Πειραιᾶ μὴ ἐθελῆσαι ἀκολουθῆσαι. ᾐτιῶντο δ' αὐτοὺς καὶ Κορινθίους πεῖσαι μὴ συστρατεύειν. ἀνεμιμνήσκοντο δὲ καὶ ὡς θύειν τ' ἐν Αὐλίδι τὸν Ἀγησίλαον οὐκ εἴων καὶ τὰ τεθυμένα ἱερὰ ὡς ἔρριψαν ἀπὸ τοῦ βωμοῦ καὶ ὅτι οὐδ' εἰς τὴν Ἀσίαν Ἀγησιλάῳ συνεστράτευον. ἐλογίζοντο δὲ καὶ καλὸν καιρὸν εἶναι τοῦ ἐξάγειν στρατιὰν ἐπ' αὐτοὺς καὶ παῦσαι τῆς εἰς αὐτοὺς ὕβρεως· τά τε γὰρ ἐν τῇ Ἀσίᾳ καλῶς σφίσιν ἔχειν,

---

agency, I employ examples from both ends of Rahn's spectrum. Xenophon's individuals, including his representation of himself in the *Anabasis*, seem no less concerned with their respective positions in history and memory when their context is 'small' than when it is apparently momentous. Their own behaviors and meditations within the texts point out moments that the historian flags as significant, either crediting them with particular achievements or allowing them to reflect upon unrealized potential. For further thoughts upon political and military affairs as subjects of central concern for the ancient Greek historiographers, see Momigliano 1972: 283–4, 290; cf. Starr 1968: 91–4.

[62] See Dillery 1995: 75 n. 50.   [63] Cf. Dillery 1998: 15, 1995: 107, and note 64, below.

[64] Dillery 1995: 23–4 further suggests that the connection to Agamemnon here may be "drawing attention to the scale of Agesilaus' *unfulfilled* [emphasis *sic*] plans for his campaign in Asia," and that this would help to foreshadow the scale of the disappointment Xenophon represents upon the expedition's withdrawal (cf. below).

κρατοῦντος Ἀγησιλάου, καὶ ἐν τῇ Ἑλλάδι οὐδένα ἄλλον πόλεμον ἐμποδὼν
σφίσιν εἶναι. (*HG* 3.5.5)

The Spartans accepted with pleasure this pretense for attacking the Thebans: they had long since been harboring hostility towards them for their
usurpation of the tithe for Apollo at Decelea, and for their unwillingness
to join in the [attack on] Piraeus. They also blamed them for convincing
the Corinthians not to share in the assault. And they remembered that
when Agesilaus was sacrificing at Aulis they did not allow the offerings
to be burned, but threw them off the altar, and that they did not join
Agesilaus in his expedition against Asia. So they determined that this was
a good time to lead out an army against them and arrest their *hubris*
towards them. For things in Asia were going well for them with Agesilaus
ascendant, and there was no other war active in Greece to be an obstacle
for them.

This passage suggests that the Spartan decision to open hostilities with
Thebes is a collective one, indebted to multiple factors. Agesilaus' experiences at Aulis are cited amongst several other causes, but nearly all of these
are of larger strategic concern (the πρόφασις at the opening of the passage, for
example, is the recent Theban invasion of Phocis, *HG* 3.5.3–4). Xenophon's
choice to describe Spartan thinking in this way assigns responsibility for
the hostilities not to a powerful individual whose symbolic act was slighted,
but to the political and military interests of the poleis involved.[65] Although
Agesilaus himself may have viewed his personal frustrations as an important
motivation, Xenophon refuses to inflate the significance of his character's
original 'performance': after narrating it in detail, he ultimately asserts the
privileged perspective of the historian by offering a more complicated reading of the causes and the agents of the events that follow. This pattern is
repeated elsewhere in both the *Hellenica* and the *Anabasis*: a character acts
in a manner apparently intended to affect his historical reception, but is
'thwarted' thereafter by Xenophon's resumption of the historian's control
over the narrative.[66]

The arrival of Agesilaus' expedition in Asia at the opening of book 4
demonstrates the careful distinction that must be maintained between pure

[65] I am grateful to R. Coons for helpful conversations about individual-vs.-group dynamics in
Spartan politics that took place during the course of his undergraduate senior thesis project in
2008–09. His work demonstrated to me the important tension between Agesilaus (*qua*
individual) and Sparta during the Aulis–Thebes sequence here: Coons 2009: 29–31, esp. 30.

[66] Gray 2011 represents a recent case for – and demonstration of – the utility of reading literary
and conceptual patterns (in this case relating to the issue of leadership) across multiple works
from the Xenophontic corpus (see esp. 179–245).

'commander narrative' and narration that ascribes agency (or the intention thereof):

> Ὁ δὲ Ἀγησίλαος ἐπεὶ ἀφίκετο ἅμα μετοπώρῳ εἰς τὴν τοῦ Φαρναβάζου Φρυγίαν, τὴν μὲν χώραν ἔκαε καὶ ἐπόρθει, πόλεις δὲ τὰς μὲν βίᾳ, τὰς δ' ἑκούσας προσελάμβανε. λέγοντος δὲ τοῦ Σπιθριδάτου ὡς εἰ ἔλθοι πρὸς τὴν Παφλαγονίαν σὺν αὐτῷ, τὸν τῶν Παφλαγόνων βασιλέα καὶ εἰς λόγους ἄξοι καὶ σύμμαχον ποιήσοι, προθύμως ἐπορεύετο, πάλαι τούτου ἐπιθυμῶν, τοῦ ἀφιστάναι τι ἔθνος ἀπὸ βασιλέως. (*HG* 4.1.1–2)

> When Agesilaus arrived at the beginning of fall in Phrygia under the rule of Pharnabazus, he burned and ravaged the countryside, and he took control of the cities, some by force, others by their own will. But when Spithridates said that if [Agesilaus] came to Paphlagonia with him, he would invite the king of the Paphlagonians to talks [with him] and would make him his ally, [Agesilaus] enthusiastically went along, since he had wanted for quite some time to detach a [subject] population from the king.

The first sentence here uses the Spartan king's name as a metonym for his military forces, but the second points to Agesilaus' own personal authority and action. Its indications are borne out by the extended conversational scene that follows, in which Agesilaus negotiates the marriage between Otys and the daughter of Spithridates (*HG* 4.1.3–15). Gray has argued that a central purpose of this section (and of others like it) is to draw attention to certain of Agesilaus' personal qualities,[67] but Agesilaus' desire to provoke defections from the king of Persia is also a genuine political and military strategy. Xenophon's deliberate inclusion of this motivation within the text not only helps to justify the report of the conversation (which may still simultaneously serve moralizing purposes), but also suggests the possibility of individual action leading to genuine historical impact. Agesilaus' particular attempt here, however, fails, and the strong expression of regret that follows (Ἀγησιλάῳ μὲν δὴ τῆς ἀπολείψεως τοῦ Σπιθριδάτου καὶ τοῦ Μεγαβάτου καὶ τῶν Παφλαγόνων οὐδὲν ἐγένετο βαρύτερον ἐν τῇ στρατείᾳ, "Agesilaus bore nothing on the expedition with such grief as the abandonment by Spithridates and Megabates and the Paphlagonians," *HG* 4.1.28) seems to indicate a personal sense of loss.[68]

---

[67] Gray 1989: 46–58, anticipated by Gray 1981: 321–6, 331–2, 334.
[68] M. Flower, referencing X. *Ages.* 5.4–5 and *Hell. Oxy.* 24.4, points out that part of what made this loss personal may also have been Agesilaus' affection for Megabates. The fact, however, that Xenophon does not reiterate this information in the *Hellenica* has the effect of relegating it to the background of the larger picture he is creating.

Agesilaus' disappointment over Spithridates, as Xenophon reports it, may
be connected to the loss of opportunity for historical achievement when the
expedition is suddenly recalled (*HG* 4.2.1):[69] in retrospect, this particular situation represented the last chance for Agesilaus to make significant
political impact in Asia. The tension between individual glory and civic
duty is expressed in particularly high relief in Xenophon's treatment of the
withdrawal (*HG* 4.2.1–5). The image of the weeping allies determined to
follow Agesilaus from their continent to his may show the personal loyalty
that Agesilaus could inspire, but such ties are currently fruitless; even as king,
Agesilaus commands the Spartan army at the authorization of the polis, and
the polis here is depriving – or must deprive – its king of the opportunity
for a history-making campaign. The quasi-heroic prizes awarded during
the mustering of the troops (*HG* 4.2.6–7) are a virtual palindrome with the
invocation of Agamemnon at Aulis, and the individual-centered imagery
culminates in the ironic recollection that Agesilaus conducts his troops back
to Greece in the footsteps of Xerxes (*HG* 4.2.8). Agesilaus' chief accomplishments here take the form of virtue in the exercise of duty, the submission
of the individual to the needs of the state, and the deliberate denial of individual achievement. This is not the conventional way of 'making history'
as an eminent leader in classical Greece,[70] which may help to explain why
Xenophon treats the events in Asia and the withdrawal very differently in
his encomiastic *Agesilaus*.[71]

A variation on the 'commander narrative' technique is used for the battle
of Coronea (*HG* 4.3.15–21). Throughout the passage, fighting contingents
from the various Greek poleis (noted as "Boeotians, Athenians, Argives,
Corinthians, Aenianians, Euboeans," and the like, *HG* 4.3.15 et al.) repeatedly oppose "Agesilaus" (*HG* 4.3.15, 19) or "those with Agesilaus" (*HG*
4.3.15, 16, 17, 18). The parlance creates a substantial rhetorical imbalance,
and Agesilaus therefore occupies a disproportionate position in the recollection of the battle. After the fighting is over, too, the wounded king still
manages to spare the enemy who have sought sanctuary, to have a trophy erected and thank-offerings made, and to journey to Delphi to present
Apollo's share of the spoils (*HG* 4.3.20–1). The passage prefers the role of the
individual to the near-total exclusion of the group: "the Spartans" and the

[69] See note 64, above, and note 71, below.   [70] See esp. Ferrario 2014.
[71] See X. *Ages*. 1.36–8 on the withdrawal, and Dillery 1995: 114–18 on some of the contrasts in
Xenophon's two versions of this period in Spartan history. Dillery further views Xenophon as
being disappointed with Agesilaus' achievements (or lack thereof) in Asia (see 107–8). See now
also Gray 2011: 81–7 on Xenophon's construction of 'greatness' through authorial
interventions in *Ages*.

allies are given little to no attention. The sudden exaggeration feels almost apologetic, as if Agesilaus *must* for some reason be emphasized in deliberate contrast with the other, more 'ordinary' Greeks who contend around him, both on his side and amongst his enemies. Here Xenophon, as historian, may in his manipulation of the 'commander narrative' be metaphorically reclaiming for Agesilaus some of the potential glory and memory that the king lost in Asia – but he may also be calling attention to the rhetorical power that the writer wields over his subjects.

Shortly after Coronea, Agesilaus is once more pulled away from pretensions to individual glory by the pressing needs of the state. In the area of the Isthmus, he almost accidentally gains the surrender of the region of Piraeum. When he sends embers up to those spending the night on high ground, the inhabitants below, seeing the army's new campfires, rush to sanctuary (*HG* 4.5.4–5), and the fort at Oenoe is quickly taken. During the settlement that follows, Agesilaus conducts himself in striking fashion. Surrounded by envoys, he ignores the representatives from Boeotia, and instead, καθήμενος δ' ἐπὶ τοῦ περὶ τὴν λίμνην κυκλοτεροῦς οἰκοδομήματος ἐθεώρει πολλὰ τὰ ἐξαγόμενα, "sitting on the round construction by the lake, he gazed upon all the [spoils] that were being brought out" (*HG* 4.5.6). The refusal to acknowledge the ambassadors, the almost greedy focus upon viewing the fruits of the capture, and even Xenophon's characterization of Agesilaus as behaving μάλα μεγαλοφρόνως ("quite high-mindedly," or "very arrogantly," *HG* 4.5.6; the word-root is otherwise used in fifth-century historiography only by Herodotus, and then only to describe Xerxes)[72] all present Agesilaus as closer to an Eastern despot[73] than to a Spartan king. The scene contrasts effectively with Agesilaus' mustering of the troops for the Asian campaign at Ephesus (*HG* 3.4.16–18). There, Agesilaus was active as both leader and participant; here, however, he is passive, a distanced figure whose power derives not from action, but from deliberate inaction.[74]

---

[72] Hdt. 7.24.1, 7.136.11. Xerxes is frequently invoked as Herodotus' most avid 'spectator': on the historiographic gaze in general e.g. Walker 1993; on Xerxes in particular, see Konstan 1987 esp. 62–7, with references, and cf. Gray 1989: 162, who also connects Agesilaus here with Xerxes but uses different passages to do so. The usage of μεγαλοφρον- here is one of only two places Xenophon employs this word-root in the *Hellenica*. Baragwanath 2008: 254–65 supplies appropriate caution that this term need not be construed as entirely negative in its connotations, but it does label a particular way of thinking that is characteristic of Herodotean tyrants.

[73] See Dewald 2003: 26 and *passim* on what she terms Herodotus' "despotic template." Although Dewald addresses Greeks as well as non-Greeks in her analysis, the Eastern monarchs form the strongest and most detailed paradigms for many of the actions she treats. Cf. also Chapter 3, above.

[74] Xenophon interjects a generalization concluding the description of a spectacle into each of these passages, as well (see *HG* 3.4.18 on Ephesus, and cf. the ending of *HG* 4.5.6 here).

The tension is suddenly broken by word of a Spartan defeat at Lechaeum. Again, as during his expedition to Asia, Agesilaus has been called away from his aspirations to individual glory by the urgent needs of his polis. His demeanor immediately shifts: he leaps to his feet, grasps his spear, and orders the herald to summon his officers for orders: Sparta's reverse has transformed him from despot to general. In what initially appears to be part of the same change, Agesilaus at last agrees to speak with the Boeotian delegates, who request passage into Lechaeum. He promises to accompany them there (*HG* 4.5.9), but his 'escort' takes the form of a ravaging expedition outside the city walls, in order to demonstrate, says Xenophon, "that no one would go out to resist" (*HG* 4.5.10). The contrast between this behavior and that of the relatives of the Spartans killed at Lechaeum, described immediately thereafter, is highlighted by Xenophon: the bereaved families rejoice. Praise of death in war has clear heroic overtones, and seems also to have been part of received ancient traditions about the Spartan way of life.[75] But archaeological evidence also suggests that those who fell in battle may have been granted easier or even exclusive access to grave-markers.[76] They would thus have enjoyed individualized, permanent remembrance not generally accessible to the ordinary population.[77] Agesilaus, in contrast, has not earned such honor here. His behavior at the lake near the Heraeum was problematic; he was unable to save the troops at Lechaeum; and he has vented his anger by deceiving the Boeotian ambassadors and ravaging orchards. Historical memory as measured by traditional Spartan standards – and as selected and reported by Xenophon – here belongs to the fallen soldiers, not to Agesilaus, despite the poses he deliberately assumed.

A similar structure governs the episode of the Acarnanians (*HG* 4.6.1– 7.1). When Sparta is drawn into the conflict between Acarnania and Achaea, "the ephors and the Assembly" (*HG* 4.6.3) send out Agesilaus as leader of the army. He devastates the countryside (*HG* 4.6.5), captures and sells spoils (*HG* 4.6.6), and even defeats the Acarnanians in a skirmish (*HG* 4.6.8–11), then commemorates his actions with a battle-trophy (*HG* 4.6.12). But the

---

[75] A convenient listing of some of the important ancient literary testimonia on this issue is Powell 1988: 233; Cartledge 2002: 51 collects bibliography on the Spartan 'mirage,' as do the papers in Powell and Hodkinson 1994.

[76] See e.g. Low 2006, who collects the evidence, citing Plu. *Lyc.* 27.2 (= 3 Ziegler) and *Mor.* 238D, at 86 and n. 3 (six of the stones in Low's list that mention death *en/em polemô,* "in war" have likely or possible dates in the fourth century). Low's belief that these monuments "do not mark the location of a burial" (90) does not compromise her argument that "these stones provide a medium through which individual Spartans – possibly even individual Laconians – can make a quite personal demonstration of, or even argument for, their relationship to the larger community" (91). Cf. also Cartledge 1978: 35 and n. 71.

[77] See Low 2006: 91, and further discussion below. One might also recall Herodotus' note that he has learned the names of all of the Spartans who perished at Thermopylae (7.224).

Achaeans, Xenophon relates, πεποιηκέναι τε οὐδὲν ἐνόμιζον αὐτόν, ὅτι πόλιν
οὐδεμίαν προσειλήφει, "believed that he had not done anything because he
had not taken a city" (*HG* 4.6.13). Agesilaus' gesture is an invocation of
the importance of the actions that he and his troops have accomplished,
and an inherent bid for their consequence, even their memorialization.[78]
His primary 'audience,' however, refuses to read his accomplishments in
the same way, and asks for a concession: that the Spartans remain to stop
the spring planting. Agesilaus' tactics again change abruptly: now, rather
than looking towards the longer-term reception of his actions, he invokes
τὸ συμφέρον, "the advantageous course," or "expediency," claiming that
it will be more effective to ravage again in the following season after the
crops are already in the ground (*HG* 4.6.13). From an apparent initial goal
of remembrance, then, Agesilaus' justification of his own decisions has
regressed to mere usefulness.[79]

The affair of the Phliasian exiles provides further opportunity to examine
individual and group authority amongst Xenophon's Spartans. The pro-
Spartan party has been expelled from Phlius, and this has severely compromised the two states' relationship (*HG* 5.2.8). The ephors demand that the
exiles be restored (*HG* 5.2.9), but when the returnees' citizen rights are not
renewed, they complain directly to the Spartans (*HG* 5.3.10–12), and the
ephors make plans to dispatch troops under one of the kings. Agesilaus has
friends amongst the partisans and is therefore pleased with the opportunity
to settle Phlius (*HG* 5.3.13), but the shaky negotiations degenerate into an
unpopular siege (*HG* 5.3.16). Agesilaus responds in one of the limited ways
in which he can exercise autonomy: by transforming Phliasian supporters
into soldiers loyal to his command (*HG* 5.3.16–17). In short, he creates a
miniature imitation of Spartan society under his personal control as a solution to what for him is still in large part a personal problem. This, however,
does not guarantee the recognition of his authority at Phlius. Rather than
negotiating with their immediate besieger, the Phliasians seek passage for
an embassy (*HG* 5.3.23). Agesilaus, chafing at this (ὁ δὲ ὀργισθεὶς ὅτι ἄκυρον
αὐτὸν ἐποίουν, "irate at their implication that he was powerless"), negotiates for the privilege of determining the outcome at Phlius, and Xenophon

[78] The trophies that Agesilaus "sets up" both here and at *HG* 4.3.9 need not necessarily be taken
as overt invocations of sole agency on his part, as the parlance for such actions seems to shift
significantly from the fifth century into the fourth (West 1969: 14 and nn. 35–6, with
references; see also Pritchett 1974: 246–75, esp. 273–4, also analyzing the religious and prestige
value of both temporary and permanent trophies).
[79] Coons 2009 argues that expediency is one of the least meaningful historiographic justifications
for Spartan actions.

reports that he does so by arrangement with his personal allies in Sparta, rather than through the popular assembly or the ephors (*HG* 5.3.24). Agesilaus' settlement is comparatively mild, even generous (*HG* 5.3.25), leaving the modern reader (and likely the ancient one, as well) wondering about the extent to which his sentiments were governed by the personal ties with which Xenophon opened the episode. Once again, the individual leader finds himself at odds with the state, not merely over political authority, but over *perceptions* of political authority and therefore of credit for action achieved.

Was Agesilaus as an individual agent finally responsible for Sparta's fall?[80] For Xenophon, the king seems rather to have functioned as a symbol behind which to gather some of the most important political and interpretive problems challenging Sparta in the earlier fourth century.[81] Power, both real and perceived, appears to have been at issue in Sparta, and it is perhaps in partial response to this that Xenophon has depicted agency under dispute between leader and city. He has sketched in his version of Agesilaus an awareness of the potential for advertising oneself as a mover of history, but he has also demonstrated that the permanent assignment of memory rests with the historian. In the end, Xenophon's Agesilaus seems to have had in mind a more substantial historical reputation for himself than events, or even than the historiographer's text, ultimately permitted.[82]

In many ways, then, the experiences and the self-portrayal of Agesilaus contrast with those of Lysander. Lysander, hailed as the victor in the Peloponnesian War, seems to have aspired to the establishment of a Spartan *archê* in the Aegean basin. Founded upon newly established local decarchies, this nascent empire would derive unity from its general subscription to oligarchic *politeiai*, its acknowledgement of Spartan leadership, and perhaps even its revolutionary acclamation of Lysander himself as king.[83] The magnitude of Lysander's aspirations may have helped contribute to the degree of self-promotion in which he seems to have indulged, and his keen

---

[80] See e.g. the varied interpretations of Hamilton 1991 (anticipated in brief by Hamilton 1982); Cartledge 1987 esp. 405–12; Cawkwell 1976.

[81] Dillery 1995 and esp. Cartledge 1987.   [82] See note 69, above.

[83] Cartledge 1987: 81, 86 (on Lysander's early actions to further his personal influence), 87–9 (on Lysander's role in the development of "Spartan imperialism"), 90–4 (on the installation of oligarchic local governments sympathetic to Spartan interests), 94–5 (on Lysander's potential aspiration to become king). Cartledge (96) further recommends that "seen in [the] light [of]" Lysander's ambition for royal power, "the 'Navarch's Monument' of 405/4 and Lysander's deification on Samos acquire a new aura. But if they were part of a concerted plan to prepare the Delphic priesthood to recognize Lysander's regal suitability, they were a failure."

observation of prior experiences and practices seems to have determined the precise forms that the construction of his public persona took.

That Lysander came into both personal and professional conflict with Agesilaus can come as little surprise. While Agesilaus' inheritance of the Spartan throne may have been somewhat unexpected,[84] he was nevertheless a member of the ruling family, and thus entitled to his position by the established constitution. Lysander, on the other hand, was attempting to penetrate the royal ranks as an outsider, an ambition that from a political standpoint would have seemed at least out of keeping with the long stability of the Spartan governmental system and at worst a direct threat to existing power structures.[85] It seems, too, if only from anecdotal evidence, that Lysander's and Agesilaus' personalities as leaders were quite different, the former tending towards the bold and dramatic, the latter rather more deliberate.[86] Agesilaus was able to gradually remove Lysander from the inner circles of power. But he also seems to have purposely distanced himself from Lysander's model of self-presentation.[87] Not only did Agesilaus, as Flower points out,[88] apparently refuse the deification offered him by the Thasians, but he also, according to Xenophon and to other sources, rejected a number of means at his disposal to memorialize himself as the 'owner' of significant historical deeds. Cartledge suggests that Agesilaus' motivations for this pose of modesty were eminently practical, designed to construct a particular political reputation for himself.[89] Xenophon's literary response to this phenomenon, however, offers additional insight into his view of his own position as a historian, and indeed into potential fourth-century understandings of the role of the individual in the motion of history.

Agesilaus laudandus,[90] *Xenophon as Pindar*

Xenophon's Agesilaus character, in both the *Agesilaus* and the *Hellenica*, seems to be possessed of historical insight that reaches beyond the world of the narrative. In the sense that he is aware that his actions will create a

---

[84] On Agesilaus' ascent to the kingship, e.g. Cartledge 1987: 99–115, who contextualizes these events against an outline of the prerogatives of the position.

[85] On Lysander and the kingship e.g. Cartledge 1987: 94–6; on Lysander's earlier background, e.g. Bommelaer 1981: 55–9.

[86] Flower 1988: 127, 133.   [87] See note 57, above.   [88] Flower 1988.

[89] Cartledge 1987: 97–8. Cartledge further offers an analogy between Agesilaus and the Roman emperor Augustus, suggesting that both rulers invoked older political, social, and religious traditions to gradually reconcile their subjects to increasingly "monarchical" rule.

[90] See Currie 2005: 1 n. 1 on the use of this Latin word to refer to the central recipient of the praise in a Pindaric *epinikion*; Currie attributes its "currency" to Bundy 1962 (reprint 1986, digital ed. 2006).

historical legacy and strives for control over it, he has much in common with Herodotus' Leonidas.[91] But changes in the relative breadth of the political sphere and in modes of public communication, even between the time of Herodotus and the accession of Agesilaus to the Spartan throne, now mean that there are comparatively more ways available for eminent individuals to receive memorialization for their historical deeds – and often, as Lysander's experiences showed, more ways for them to court the specific response they desire.[92] The ways in which the historiographic character exploits these avenues in the *Agesilaus* further reveal Xenophon's perception of the relationship between history-making individual and historian.

There are two particular places in Xenophon's eponymous encomium where Agesilaus refuses opportunities for memorialization or for what would widely be perceived as history-making action. These do not suggest that either the literary character or the man was lacking in self-confidence, ambition, or pride. Rather, these examples seem to have been incorporated by Xenophon for a number of reasons. They help to demonstrate that Xenophon's version of Agesilaus is an individual very different from those who enjoy similar status and station both at Sparta and elsewhere (Athens, of course, would have been a natural comparand for Xenophon). And they also offer Xenophon himself a particular opportunity: if Agesilaus will not permit the fullest possible acknowledgement of his historical agency in the media available to him, then Xenophon, as historiographer, may step into the gap.

Two anecdotes from the *Agesilaus* directly confront commemorative practices and behaviors. The first is about statues. Xenophon states that "he forbade the erection of image[s] of his person, although many wanted to present him with such"; Plutarch relates the same anecdote, but has the prohibition extending to after Agesilaus' death, as well.[93] If it was not historical, Plutarch's discussion of the post mortem ban may have derived from observation, whether by him or by others, of a lack of public images of Agesilaus.[94] Xenophon's Agesilaus is here explicitly rejecting a type of commemoration that would probably have been quite unlikely, if not utterly uncharacteristic, in his home polis.[95] It seems to be a dismissal not only

---

[91] See Chapter 3, above.   [92] Cf. Cartledge 1987: 84.

[93] X. *Ages.* 11.7; Plu. *Ages.* 2.2 (= 4 Ziegler), both cited by Flower 1988: 127, who mentions this story.

[94] It may also, like Lysander's poets (see note 48, above), potentially have crossed over from the Alexander literature: on the (spurious) tradition of Alexander's artistic 'edict' upon his own image, see the references collected by Stewart 1993: 360–2; cf. also Stewart 2003: 32.

[95] On the lack of precedent for statues at Sparta commemorating historical deeds, see Cartledge 1987: 82–3. Spartan athletic victors do seem to have set up statues of themselves in panhellenic

of what Lysander did at Delphi,[96] but also of honorific practices that were likely gaining currency elsewhere in the Greek world.[97] While the action may render the Agesilaus character more traditionally (or even just more stereotypically) Spartan to the reading audience of Xenophon's biography, it also shows two other layers of denial at work. Agesilaus will not allow his deeds to be translated into the imagery and poetry associated with honorific statuary; nor will he nominally allow his own audiences, the various publics who would have erected and viewed such statues, to think about him in this manner – which may ironically (and perhaps deliberately) have produced precisely that effect.

The second contrast with contemporary commemorative practices derives from an anecdote in the *Agesilaus*, also noted by Plutarch, in which Agesilaus declines to run horses in the panhellenic games at Olympia. Instead, he encourages his sister Cynisca to race there instead, to show that this activity is not in fact an example of true masculine *aretê* ("virtue").[98] An inscription from Olympia, *IG* V.1 1564a, dated to the early fourth century, testifies to Cynisca's involvement there:[99]

> Σπάρτας μὲν [βασιλῆες ἐμοὶ] 2 πατέρες καὶ ἀδελφοί,
>   ἅ[ρματι δ’ ὠκυπόδων ἵππων] 3 νικῶσα Κυνίσκα
> εἰκόνα τάνδ’ ἔστασε. μόν[αν] 4 δ’ ἐμέ φαμι γυναικῶν
>   Ἑλλάδος ἐκ πάσας τό[ν]5 δε λαβῖν στέφανον.
>   Ἀπελλέας Καλλικλέος ἐπόησε.

[Kings] of Sparta were [my] fathers and brothers.
  Having been victorious with a c[hariot of swift-footed horses], I,
Cynisca, set up this statue. I declare that alone amongst the women
  of all Greece, I took this crown.
    Apelles the son of Callicles made this.

Cynisca seems not to have shared in her brother's reservations. Here, she revels in her position, claiming in this inscription not only her royal

---

sanctuaries, but commemoration for them within Sparta itself was also more limited: see Morgan 2007: 215–16, citing in particular (216 n. 18) Hodkinson 2000: 319–23 and Hodkinson 1999: 156[–7], 175–6 (see also Hodkinson 1999: 152–6 on "dedications by athletic victors," 160–9 on Spartan responses to victories at Olympia, and 170–3 on "the limits on private victory commemorations inside Sparta"); and cf. the "list of victors with statues at Olympia, to 400 BC" by Smith 2007: 137–9.

[96] See notes 40, 57, and 89, above.

[97] While Cartledge 1987: 85 construes the temporal distance between Lysander's Nauarch's Monument at Delphi and Athens' statue of Conon (just over a decade, as the battle of Aegospotami took place in 405 and, as Cartledge notes, Conon's statue was erected in 393) as a long one, I would prefer here to consider this segment of time as being a period of comparatively rapid political, cultural, and social change.

[98] X. *Ages.* 9.6; Plu. *Ages.* 20.1.   [99] Edition from *IG* v.1 1564a.

lineage, but also her unique status as the only Greek woman to have captured such a victory. The inscription was also a base for a particular work of art, a statue by Apelles the son of Callicles.[100] While the very existence of this unique statue could potentially have given rise to the anecdote that Xenophon and Plutarch relate, the Olympia story nevertheless reveals important features of Xenophon's thought. His Agesilaus character here refuses to embrace the paradigm that had helped to make Brasidas and Lysander famous, and that would shortly be used to describe the competition for fame amongst the Thebans, as well: the model of the victorious athlete.[101] It can come as little surprise, then, that Agesilaus refuses the offer of deification from the Thasians: having spurned the path that would render him another Brasidas, he also avoids the one that would make him a second Lysander.[102]

This minimizing of public claims to individual historical agency or even individual achievement also appears in Xenophon's treatment of Agesilaus' Asian expedition both in the *Agesilaus* and in the *Hellenica*. The account from the *Hellenica* (*HG* 4.2.2–3), analyzed above, showed Agesilaus disappointed at the loss of his personal ambitions; the account in the encomium portrays a more deliberate choice of country over self, and duty over prospective honor (*Ages.* 1.36). By Xenophon's account, this prioritization is virtuous.[103] The decision to return to "help Sparta" does therefore garner a certain kind of honor for the Agesilaus character, but one that probably bears little resemblance to what the living king may have been contemplating for his planned campaign. The *kleos* is provided instead not through the successful completion of the military expedition, but through the memorialization of Agesilaus by Xenophon.

Why does the character Agesilaus seem unconcerned in the encomium with the historical memorialization of the great deeds that Xenophon says he wishes to inspire? One possible response may be revealed in a passage from Thucydides, spoken by Pericles during the Funeral Oration:

> μετὰ μεγάλων δὲ σημείων καὶ οὐ δή τοι ἀμάρτυρόν γε τὴν δύναμιν παρασχό-
> μενοι τοῖς τε νῦν καὶ τοῖς ἔπειτα θαυμασθησόμεθα, καὶ οὐδὲν προσδεόμενοι

---

[100] Cf. Crane's reading of the epigram on Lysander's Nauarch's Monument at note 45, above.

[101] In so doing, Xenophon's Agesilaus also implicitly rejects any possibility of heroization that might have become available to such individuals. The examination of this possibility is the central focus of Currie 2005.

[102] Flower 1988 esp. 131–4.

[103] I am grateful to S. Saporito, whose work on her undergraduate senior thesis project (Saporito 2009) prompted me to think more deeply about depictions of virtue in the *Agesilaus* and the *Hellenica*.

οὔτε Ὁμήρου ἐπαινέτου οὔτε ὅστις ἔπεσι μὲν τὸ αὐτίκα τέρψει, τῶν δ'
ἔργων τὴν ὑπόνοιαν ἡ ἀλήθεια βλάψει, ἀλλὰ πᾶσαν μὲν θάλασσαν καὶ
γῆν ἐσβατὸν τῇ ἡμετέρᾳ τόλμῃ καταναγκάσαντες γενέσθαι, πανταχοῦ δὲ
μνημεῖα κακῶν τε κἀγαθῶν ἀίδια ξυγκατοικίσαντες. (Thuc. 2.41.4)

Possessed, then, of a power [attested] by great signs and abundantly witnessed, we are marvelous to people now and will be so to future generations. We have no requirement to be the object of Homer's tribute, nor that
of any other who will provide fleeting pleasure through his words, but to
whose version of events the truth will do injury. We have forced the whole
sea and earth to be open to our boldness, and have sowed everywhere
eternal monuments to both our vengeance and our benefactions.

The Funeral Oration emphasizes throughout, as here, the tension between
logos and *ergon*. But in its surface rejection of Homeric poetry and its
emphasis on the creation of memory through action, this passage also offers
a way of thinking about Xenophon's characterization of Agesilaus. The deeds
of the deceased and the achievements of the polis are here converted into
memory through words, not once, but twice – once by the ostensible speaker,
Pericles, and once by Thucydides, the historian. Encomium is therefore
acknowledged both implicitly and explicitly within the text as one of the
new means of creating lasting historical memory.[104]

In the *Agesilaus*, then, Xenophon himself becomes the crafter of Agesilaus'
historical legacy, playing if not a Homer to Agesilaus' Achilles, then perhaps
at least a kind of Pindar for a king whom he records as deliberately refusing
to take the role of athletic victor. It has long been noted that Xenophon's
encomium is connected in style and thought with Isocrates' *Evagoras*,[105]
and Race has shown that the *Evagoras* in fact employs styles and methods of
praise that owe much to Pindar.[106] In valorizing Agesilaus, a gesture dependent in part upon the character's deliberate rejection of commemoration,
Xenophon the writer casts himself within this particular essay in the role of
memory-maker, in a manner that would have been not only comprehensible to those who respected the poets but also acceptable on the standards
presented by Thucydides' Pericles.

---

[104] My reading here is indebted to the interpretation of the *epitaphios logos* as an agonistic and
historically contextualized genre by Derderian 2001: 163–78; cf. also, as Derderian does,
Loraux 1986 *passim*.

[105] For a summary of the ancient sources, see Marchant 1925: xvii–xx; for more information, see
Flower 1997: 149–50.

[106] See Pownall 2004: 32–5 on the relationship between Xenophon's *Agesilaus* and Isocrates'
Evagoras, referring on this particular topic (32 n. 125) to Race 1987.

The Spartan material evidence

Although there is no reason to assume that the situation must be the result of (for example) pervasive illiteracy or unique governmental structure,[107] a broad supply of state documents is lacking for fifth- and fourth-century Sparta,[108] and no continuous literary works of the classical period survive.[109] Some of the testimonia and the extant public and private inscriptions[110] nevertheless provide evidence of ongoing concern for the relationship between the individual and the citizen body during the classical period.

Pausanias' problematic advertisement of his own achievements on the Serpent Column at Delphi after the Persian Wars was discussed in Chapter 2, above. In contrast, a mode of expression much more acceptable in a pan-hellenic sanctuary during that same period is likely represented by a Spartan inscription from Olympia:[111]

[δέξ]ο ϝάν[α]ξ Κρονίδα{ι} Δεῦ Ὀλύνπιε καλὸν ἄγαλμα
hιλέϝο[ι θυ]μõι τοῖ(λ) Λακεδαιμονίοις.

O lord Olympian Zeus, son of Cronus, accept this beautiful statue
with kindly heart towards the Spartans.

The dates proposed for this community-oriented dedication range roughly between the 490s and the 460s,[112] which would potentially accord well with commemorative trends already observed during this time at Athens and elsewhere, and with the recollection (albeit in polemical contexts) by the Attic orators that group-oriented honors were more common in earlier periods.[113]

In contrast, *IG* v.1 1, a later list of contributions made to "the Spartans" for (most probably) the Peloponnesian War,[114] contains entries from several

---

[107] Cartledge 1978: 36: "on present evidence it is hard to draw a sharp distinction in regard to public documentation between Sparta and, say, Corinth."

[108] Millender 2001: 138–41 (with productive exploration as to why so few inscriptions have been recovered from both Sparta and Corinth); Cartledge 1978: 35–6 (with an iteration of known evidence to date); cf. Tod in Tod and Wace 1906: 4.

[109] Boring 1979: 50–63 (cf. also 73) compiles a list of "minor writers who were Lacedaimonians" ranging from the fourth century BC through the Roman era: all of the authors listed survive only in testimonia or fragments.

[110] Cartledge's (1978: 35–6) list of evidence served as an essential resource checklist for my discussion here in terms of both primary material and secondary bibliography, although I do not treat every example that he mentions.

[111] *SEG* 28.429; Meiggs and Lewis 1969: 47 no. 22. Edition here from Meiggs and Lewis.

[112] Meiggs and Lewis 1969: 47 no. 22 believe that a date earlier in this range is more likely.

[113] See Chapters 4 and 5, above.

[114] See Loomis 1992: 56–60 for a review of possible dates and contexts proposed by previous scholars, 60–76 for Loomis' own argument that the inscription should be placed *c.* 427.

sources that could represent individuals,[115] one of whom may be an affluent Spartan named Molocrus.[116] At issue here would be whether the accumulation of personal fortunes like this was permitted or accepted amongst citizens who were resident *at Sparta* in the time of Lysander.[117] Flower has argued that the testimonia suggest that "in order to acquire precious metals and to live luxuriously, one had to live outside of Sparta on a permanent basis,"[118] but this did not of course eliminate distinctions amongst the Spartan upper classes during the fifth and fourth centuries when opportunities arose for claims to authority and memory in interstate contexts.[119] Privileged Spartans seem to have advertised their status during this time using some of the same symbolic currency employed by elites in Athens and elsewhere, including proxenies and athletic sponsorships,[120] often in highly visible venues such as Olympia and Delphi, where their audiences could quite easily include fellow Spartans as well as other Greeks. While this need not indicate disaffection *per se* with traditional Spartan institutions,[121] it does show the deliberate commemoration of the eminent individual outside of the more equalizing ideologies espoused locally by his citizen group.

Similar contrasts are in evidence in Spartan customs of funeral and burial. The honor of a permanent funeral marker at Sparta bearing an individual's

---

[115] Ibid. 63; cf. also the comments of Hornblower 2002: 154, citing Fornara 1983b: 148–9 no. 132 and Meiggs and Lewis 1969: 181–4 no. 67.

[116] Loomis 1992: 53–4. In Loomis' edition (pl. 17), 'Molocrus' occurs on the side of the stele at ll. 15–19, giving "the Spartans" a talent of silver. I am grateful to an anonymous reader for highlighting that the identity of this individual is not certain; cf. also the references in note 115, above.

[117] Loomis 1992: 54 n. 60 collects the testimonia that suggest that there may have been a ban on the use of coined money enacted by the ephors in the time of Lysander (the most detailed of these testimonia is Plu. *Lys.* 16.1–17.11), but argues that "Molokros' gift suggests, contrary to the widely held view, that individual Spartans *could* own silver in this period" (81; cf. note 114, above, for Loomis' opinion on the date of the inscription). He also, however (54 n. 60), acknowledges a suggestion by Badian that Molocrus may have been resident outside of Sparta: see below.

[118] Flower 1991: 88–94, at 91. Flower also suggests that later authors may in drawing moralizing conclusions have exaggerated the role that the corruption borne by wealth may have played in the 'decline of Sparta.'

[119] I am grateful to E. Baragwanath and N. Sandridge for the reminder in conversation that I should consider here the connections amongst Greek elites, evidenced as early as the archaic era (and witnessed by the Homeric poems), that extended across polis boundaries. On these relationships, see e.g. Mitchell 1997; Herman 1987.

[120] Loomis 1992: 54 n. 60, citing de Ste. Croix 1972: 137–8 on the wealth and prosperity of one Lichas "who was *proxenos* of Argos, victor in the chariot race, and a lavish entertainer" (Loomis). De Ste. Croix also assembles literary testimonia relating to other individuals that help to fill out this picture more broadly. See also the inscription of Cynisca at Olympia, discussed above (for which de Ste. Croix provides additional references), and note 95, above.

[121] The general lack of such disaffection, in fact, is the central argument of Flower 1991.

name was apparently confined to men killed in war[122] and women who perished in childbirth.[123] Low, studying the dedications to fallen soldiers, has noted that they come from a wide variety of locations almost exclusively confined to Laconia, although they are not clustered within the polis itself. Contrasting these scattered, separate stones with the Athenian custom of the *patrios nomos*, Low suggests reading them as "a medium through which individual Spartans . . . can make a quite personal demonstration of, or even argument for, their relationship to the larger community," and "as a focus for mourning and for personal commemoration" by the families of the fallen.[124] But again, the norms for Spartan expression *at Sparta* seem to have been different from those outside of it. Beyond the boundaries of Laconia, Spartan war dead seem generally to have been commemorated collectively,[125] in somewhat the same manner as (for example) Athenians, Megarians, and Boeotians.[126] For Low, these group burials outside of Spartan territory may have served political purposes, advertising particular Spartan messages in other states.[127]

The relationship between individual and group agency as expressed in these monuments to the Spartan war dead is therefore complex. While the individual stones for fallen warriors do invoke separate identities through their use of personal names and record contributions to the state as a whole through their notations of death *em polemô* ("in war"), they are expressly not unique. Rather, their form and content are remarkably consistent over time, their format plain.[128] In this regard they bear some general resemblance to the tombstones recovered at Athens from the periods when funerary commemoration seems to have displayed the least variation: the mid fifth century (cf. Chapter 2, above) and the time following the governorship of Demetrius of Phalerum in the late fourth century.[129] While there does appear to have been room for individual memorialization at

---

[122] See notes 76 and 77, above.

[123] The archaeological evidence currently seems to bear out this rule, although the former provision is certainly more abundantly attested than the latter: on war dead, see Low 2006: 86 (citing Plu. *Lyc.* 27.2 [= 3 Ziegler] and *Mor.* 238D along with the known examples from the excavated corpus); on women in childbirth, see the testimonia and scholarship reviewed by Pomeroy 2002: 52 n. 3.

[124] Low 2006: 85–91, at 91.   [125] Ibid. 92–9.   [126] Ibid. 94 esp. n. 29; Low 2003.

[127] "At the very broadest level . . . all these burials and monuments . . . located well away from Spartan territory . . . function, or can be made to function, as some sort of permanent marker of the relationship between Sparta and the state which hosts the monument" (Low 2006: 93–8, at 98).

[128] Ibid. 86–8, with references.

[129] Demetrius controlled Athens on behalf of the Macedonians *c.* 317–307 BC; on his alleged sumptuary legislation arresting lavish Athenian tombstones, e.g. O'Sullivan 2009: 47–66.

Sparta, the evidence suggests that it was acceptable only within certain enduring parameters.[130]

The Spartan group memorials outside of Laconia may be most effectively contrasted, then, not with the individual war monuments within the boundaries of the state, but with individual commemorative efforts invoked by other Spartans in non-Laconian contexts. The behaviors and experiences of Brasidas, Agesilaus, Cynisca,[131] and (especially) Lysander suggest that tension between individual and group historical agency and memorialization amongst Spartans may best be appreciated away from the immediate area of the polis itself, perhaps because this places the symbolic gestures by individuals beyond the cognitive or legal reach of certain Spartan practices. When the state erects distant monuments, they are put up for collectivities of Spartans, perhaps with their leaders named;[132] individuals, however, may represent themselves in very different ways that may not always have been acceptable either to their polis or to their peers.

That the Spartan experience in this regard may have further elements in common with the Athenian one is suggested, finally, by Low's reading of the Spartan reception of Thermopylae.[133] The specialness of Herodotus' representation of Leonidas in comparison to and contrast with his citizen group was discussed in Chapter 3, above.[134] Low further notes that the commemorative efforts for the battle may have included the following elements: 1. a stele for the Spartans at the battle site, perhaps from the Delphic Amphictyony; 2. possible (perhaps later) stelai at the same site for groups from other participating poleis; 3. a monument for Leonidas at the same site in the form of a lion; 4. a hero-cult for Leonidas at Sparta, founded upon a physical tomb; 5. an inscription explicitly naming the Three Hundred within the polis of Sparta; 6. a possible festival for the Three Hundred and Leonidas (and Pausanias) together.[135] The variety of these symbols and their representations of individual and group historical agency, sometimes agonistic, sometimes blended together, resembles nothing so closely as the treatment of the Athenian dead from Marathon discussed above in Chapter 2.[136] Like the fallen from Marathon, those from Thermopylae were commemorated in multiple locations, both at home and abroad. Both the commanders and

---

[130] Low 2006: 91; cf. also (as Low does elsewhere) Toher 1991: 171.
[131] Cf. also note 120, above, on Lichas.
[132] See Low 2006: 98 on *IG* ii/iii² 11678, the Spartan group monument in the Kerameikos at Athens.
[133] Ibid. 99–101.   [134] See Chapter 3, above.
[135] Low 2006: 100–1 and nn. 43–9, with references.
[136] Clairmont 1983: 116 (cited in Low 2006: 105 n. 43) suggests that the cult accorded to the fallen of Thermopylae may have resembled that for the dead of Marathon.

the fighters were treated as the primary agents of the conflict in different contexts; both the Thermopylae and the Marathon dead received extraordinary representation in inscriptions and later heroization. In short, the same polyvalence that Low sees emerging from Thermopylae ("the dead of Thermopylae are commemorated, individually and as a group, in more than one place, in more than one way, and for more than one purpose")[137] can also be read in the Athenian reception of Marathon.

This is not to suggest that Sparta would have looked to Marathon for inspiration for the commemoration of Thermopylae, but rather to note that both states provide evidence for complicated understandings of – or even debate over – the ascription of historical agency during the earlier fifth century. Toher's analysis of archaic-era funerary regulations in Greek poleis in comparison with Spartan burial practices suggests that this kind of individual–group tension may have been productively harnessed at Sparta, as manifested in the distinctly 'un-Spartan' funerary rites accorded to the kings. For Toher, these practices "served the purpose of affirming the unity of the community,"[138] but, as he points out, they also resembled the veneration given to colonial founders,[139] which would have heroized an individual in return for benefactions to the polis.

As noted in Chapter 2, above, the Athenian radical democracy provided no institutionalized way to reconcile the anonymizing practices of the *patrios nomos* with the special attention accorded even in burial to individuals like Pericles. Outside of the constraints of a democratic system, however, the funerary treatment of the Spartan kings seems to have posed little social difficulty, particularly because the monarchy was hereditary.[140] Competition for agency and commemoration amongst the Spartans, then, seems largely to have taken place outside the city, where eminent Spartan individuals were able to present themselves in terms that were comprensible to and effective throughout the wider Greek world.

6.3 The Thebans

Both Athens and Sparta retained largely consistent governmental systems throughout the classical period. The Athenian Revolution of 507/6 established a form of democracy that, save for the brief oligarchic coup during the Peloponnesian War (411, restoration in 410) and the reign of the Thirty afterwards (404–3), remained generally constant until at least after 322 (the

[137] Low 2006: 99.   [138] Toher 1991: 169–73, at 172.
[139] Ibid. 172, citing (n. 55) Schaefer 1965a: 326.   [140] Toher 1991: 173.

end of the Lamian War). Sparta's unique oligarchic constitution, with its balance between two kings, two assemblies, and an annual panel of ephors, was famed for its stability and longevity.[141] While the specific duties of its various offices and bodies might shift over time, the essential governmental divisions at Sparta remained in place throughout the fifth and fourth centuries, providing a backdrop against which the changes wrought by shifts in political and personal power may be assessed.

In central Greece, however, the case is rather different. The history of Thebes, the Thebans' conceptions of themselves as a functional agent group, and the achievements of Theban leaders are inextricably bound up with the story of Boeotia itself. The Boeotian League[142] (a federation created in the sixth century of the region's cities, whose systems of affiliation provided for common political and military action)[143] witnessed a series of governmental changes during the fifth and fourth centuries (including Medizing with Thessaly during the second Persian War, 480/79, and a ten-year dominance by Athens, 457–47) that repeatedly adjusted the balance of power between populace and leaders, and between the dominant city of Thebes and its neighbors.[144] Such alterations are likely to have had varied effects upon local understandings of historical agency whose detailed rehearsal, at least during the fifth century, may lie out of reach given the current state of the evidence.

In the fourth century, however, the ground becomes somewhat more fertile. While the Peace of 386 broke up the Boeotian League, Thebes quickly returned to prominence again as the leading polis of a renewed federation, and found its greatest triumph at Leuctra[145] (indeed, the years 371–362 are often referred to as the time of the 'Theban hegemony').[146] The period as a whole, between the Corinthian War and the battle of Mantinea, just over twenty years in length, is perhaps better documented (with certain important problems to be noted below) than any other era in Theban history before the late Hellenistic and Roman periods. During this short and eventful time, Thebes achieved pre-eminence not only within the Boeotian League, but also in comparison with other Greek states. This height of accomplishment was ascribed by later writers largely to two outstanding

---

[141] E.g. Cawkwell 1983: 392 n. 28, with ancient references.

[142] Variously in modern scholarship the 'Boeotian Confederacy.'

[143] On the economic and cultic connections that likely also contributed to a sense of common identity and cause amongst the Boeotians and other federated peoples, see Mackil 2013.

[144] A brief history of the changes to Theban and Boeotian organization over time, and of the political structures in operation down to the fourth century, is represented by e.g. Hammond 2000: 81–7.

[145] Hammond 2000: 88–9.   [146] E.g. the title of Buckler 1980. I adopt this terminology, as well.

leaders, Epaminondas and Pelopidas.[147] Given these dynamics, it is possible
to observe during this period in particular the circulation of some Boeotian
ideas about individual and collective historical agency.

It is also important, however, to acknowledge the challenges posed by the
evidence. On the literary side, no contemporary texts by Boeotian writers
survive.[148] Plutarch, himself a Boeotian, composed *Lives* of both Pelopidas and Epaminondas; the former survives and has been characterized
as biased (towards the positive),[149] while the latter is lost.[150] Xenophon
is a contemporary but paid much more significant attention to Athens
and Sparta than he did to Thebes. The third major narrative is that of
Diodorus, who for this period seems to have been using Ephorus.[151] There
can be little access to unaltered fourth-century Theban sentiment from
these authors,[152] and any use of their work therefore needs to proceed with
caution.

In the case of Xenophon, however, it is possible to contextualize his
reception of Epaminondas within his larger views on eminent individuals.
Xenophon's work is often described as being anti-Theban,[153] and while this
may certainly help to explain the reduced coverage of Theban activities in
general and of Thebes' most important commanders in particular,[154] the
treatment of Epaminondas in the *Hellenica* does characterize him as another
self-conscious Greek leader who wishes to be remembered as an agent of
history. The obvious limits placed upon that depiction may also be read as

[147] Shrimpton 1971: 313–14, placing this attribution at least as early as Dinarchus, who was
writing in the 320s.
[148] On the major and minor literary sources for this period and their likely biases, see Buckler
1980: 263–77. Buckler, however, does not discuss there the potential applicability to this later
era of the information about the earlier operations of the League provided by the
Oxyrhynchus Historian: on this, see Hammond 2000: 83–7.
[149] E.g. Westlake 1939: 22 and *passim*.
[150] Whether Pausanias' account of Theban matters from this period derives from Plutarch's lost
Life is debated: for a review of the scholarship and the issues involved, see Tuplin 1984.
[151] Tuplin 1984: 17, with references (nn. 3–4).
[152] See esp. Shrimpton 1971, tracing the evolution of literary traditions about Thebes as they
shifted in the course of the fourth century. For an example of a more detailed problem with
the sources, e.g. Westlake 1939: 17, who describes (with references at n. 5) Momigliano's
reconstruction of Ephorus' attitude towards Thebes and the Boeotian League, namely that
Ephorus, "influenced by Isocratean doctrine . . . attributed the ascendancy of Thebes in the
period from Leuctra to Mantinea not to the Thebans in general, who remained deficient in
intellectual and moral discipline, but wholly to their leaders, who enjoyed the advantages of
παιδεία."
[153] See e.g. Hornblower 1994b: 4–5, 7, citing Tuplin 1993 (in the latter, see the general index s.v.
"Thebes/Theban(s), material damaging to Thebes' reputation," et al.); Buckler 1980: 263–8;
Cawkwell 1972: 256.
[154] See esp. Buckler 1980: 265–7; Shrimpton 1971: 311–12.

another way in which Xenophon demonstrates the authority of his literary genre over the self-presentations of its characters.

Xenophon's Epaminondas

Epaminondas' first introduction into Xenophon's narrative by name (*HG* 7.1.41–3), despite its lateness in the Theban commander's career, compresses into a narrow space many of the ways in which Xenophon discusses other eminent leaders in extraordinary situations. Epaminondas' own motivations are described (a desire for an alliance with the Achaeans); his personal intervention generates the initial action (Peisias takes Oneium because Epaminondas convinces him to do so); he is the only named commander of the expedition against Achaea (στρατεύουσι πάντες οἱ σύμμαχοι ἐπ' Ἀχαΐαν, ἡγουμένου Ἐπαμεινώνδου, "all the allies advanced against Achaea, with Epaminondas in command," *HG* 7.1.42); and when the treaty is finally constituted, Epaminondas receives attentions from the Achaean nobles that are expressed with vocabulary perhaps better befitting an Eastern king. The Achaeans are προσπεσόντων δ' αὐτῷ, and Epaminondas ἐνδυναστεύει over them. The former expression, perhaps to be translated as "falling upon him" or "supplicating him," can mean in other contexts "prostrating themselves before him": it is used elsewhere to reference the bow that is part of the performance of *proskynesis*, a practice traditionally associated by the Greeks with Eastern behaviors, especially the extreme submission shown the king of Persia by his subjects.[155] The verb ἐνδυναστεύω, represented in the *LSJ* as meaning "1. to have power or exercise dominion in or among; 2. [to] procure by one's authority or influence," is used only here in Xenophon's entire corpus. Elsewhere in the classical period, save for two references in the Aesopic and Hippocratic literature,[156] it is employed only by Plato in the *Republic* (7.516d, hypothesizing about individuals who might exercise influence amongst the 'prisoners' in the allegory of the cave) and by Aeschylus in the *Persae* (691, when the ghost of Darius describes the power he wields in the underworld). The phraseology employed here to describe Epaminondas is therefore charged: he is marked out as perhaps presenting himself and being received as something greater than a Greek general.

The very next sentence, however, describes the backlash (*HG* 7.1.43). The Arcadians and some disaffected Achaeans are not pleased with Epaminondas' settlement of Achaean affairs, and "the Thebans" therefore

---

[155] See *LSJ ad loc.* for sample references, adding also the entry for the poetical variant προσπίτνω; cf. also Chapter 8, below.

[156] Aesop. 114.1b line 3; Hp. *VM* 20.34.

replace the existing Achaean governments with harmosts who in turn set up democracies. The results are perhaps predictable given what took place throughout Greece during the Peloponnesian War: conflicts ensue between the entrenched democrats and the exiled oligarchs; in this case, the latter are able to re-establish their power. This system was essentially the one established by Epaminondas, but it is now discredited: his own polis attempted to dismantle it, and in its reconstructed form the Arcadians are left at a disadvantage and the Achaean oligarchic factionalists, who had previously accused Epaminondas of pro-Spartan bias, are now colluding with their former 'enemies.' As Xenophon did with Lysander and with Agesilaus, he has reported this information in a way that suggests that final control of the reception of events rests with the historian, not with an individual who (Xenophon implies) may have carried himself like a king.

Xenophon's fullest coverage of Epaminondas occurs in *HG* 7.5, which treats the expedition into Arcadia and the battle of Mantinea. Given the self-contained nature of this episode, its deliberate placement at the conclusion of Xenophon's longest work, and its treatment of Epaminondas himself, taking the issue of Xenophon's anti-Theban sentiment[157] as a primary guide to the reading of this particular passage would be too limiting.[158] Even if Xenophon interpreted the battle of Mantinea in the longer view as a potentially history-making moment that turned out not to settle the ongoing turbulence in Greek interstate politics, the point at which he chose to conclude the *Hellenica* is nevertheless both deliberate and significant.[159] Here, the death of Epaminondas provides an important demarcation: Epaminondas' leadership, especially his generalship, seems to have been an indispensable ingredient in Thebes' hegemony, and without him, in Xenophon's view, Theban dominance could not be sustained.[160] Whether or not Xenophon admired or even liked anything about Epaminondas, there is nothing in the *Hellenica* whose inclusion is not Xenophon's choice, and the Mantinea episode as a whole further demonstrates this.

The opening of the expedition is treated by Xenophon in 'commander narrative'[161] that foregrounds not only Epaminondas' actions but also the evolution of his rationale (*HG* 7.5.4–7). No other individuals are mentioned

---

[157] See note 153, above.

[158] I am grateful to E. Baragwanath for conversation regarding the Phlius episode that invited my thinking about Epaminondas in this way.

[159] This is the perspective of Dillery 1995: 22–38; see also Shrimpton 1971: 311 and n. 10, noting other historians in antiquity who also observed a 'break' at around the same time.

[160] Buckler and Beck 2008: 132–3, and esp. 139; Shrimpton 1971: 312.

[161] See Chapter 5, above.

in a passage that is otherwise filled with the names of Greek citizen groups. At
HG 7.5.8, Xenophon, in his own authorial voice, commends Epaminondas'
strategy, and then suggests that the decision to decamp from Tegea and
march on Sparta was at least in part a result of Epaminondas' care for his
own historical legacy:

> ὁρῶν δὲ οὔτε πόλιν αὐτῷ προσχωροῦσαν οὐδεμίαν τόν τε χρόνον
> προβαίνοντα, ἐνόμισε πρακτέον τι εἶναι· εἰ δὲ μή, ἀντὶ τῆς πρόσθεν εὐκ-
> λείας πολλὴν ἀδοξίαν προσεδέχετο. (*HG* 7.5.9)

> Seeing that no city was supporting him and that time was going by, he
> thought that something had to be done, or else instead of his past renown
> he would incur great contempt.

Epaminondas is again credited with good planning at *HG* 7.5.11 – just
before he initiates an inconclusive attack on Sparta that results in the loss
of some of his forward troops (*HG* 7.5.12–13). The Theban commander
reflects on his situation and withdraws to Tegea and Mantinea instead;
again, Xenophon analyzes the character's rationale (*HG* 7.5.14). The next
contrast the historian provides is an account of the actions of groups,
the Athenians defending the Mantineans from the Thebans and the Thessalians (*HG* 7.5.15–17), before returning again to an extended treatment of
Epaminondas' concern for his reputation and memory:

> ὁ δ᾽ αὖ Ἐπαμεινώνδας, ἐνθυμούμενος ὅτι ὀλίγων μὲν ἡμερῶν ἀνάγκη ἔσοιτο
> ἀπιέναι διὰ τὸ ἐξήκειν τῇ στρατείᾳ τὸν χρόνον, εἰ δὲ καταλείψοι ἐρήμους
> οἷς ἦλθε σύμμαχος, ἐκεῖνοι πολιορκήσοιντο ὑπὸ τῶν ἀντιπάλων, αὐτὸς
> δὲ λελυμασμένος τῇ ἑαυτοῦ δόξῃ παντάπασιν ἔσοιτο, ἡττημένος μὲν ἐν
> Λακεδαίμονι σὺν πολλῷ ὁπλιτικῷ ὑπ᾽ ὀλίγων, ἡττημένος δὲ ἐν Μαντινείᾳ
> ἱππομαχίᾳ, αἴτιος δὲ γεγενημένος διὰ τὴν εἰς Πελοπόννησον στρατείαν
> τοῦ συνεστάναι Λακεδαιμονίους καὶ Ἀρκάδας καὶ Ἀχαιοὺς καὶ Ἠλείους καὶ
> Ἀθηναίους· ὥστε οὐκ ἐδόκει αὐτῷ δυνατὸν εἶναι ἀμαχεὶ παρελθεῖν, λογι-
> ζομένῳ ὅτι εἰ μὲν νικῴη, πάντα ταῦτα ἀναλύσοιτο· εἰ δὲ ἀποθάνοι, καλὴν
> τὴν τελευτὴν ἡγήσατο ἔσεσθαι πειρωμένῳ τῇ πατρίδι ἀρχὴν Πελοποννή-
> σου καταλιπεῖν. (*HG* 7.5.18)

> Epaminondas, then, reflecting that within a few days he would have to
> withdraw because the time for the expedition was reaching its limit; and
> that if he should leave bereft those to whom he had come as an ally, they
> would be besieged by their opponents and he himself would be utterly
> deprived of his honor – bested in Lacedaemon with a great army by
> a small one, bested in Mantinea in a battle of cavalry, and blamed for
> the alliance of the Spartans and Arcadians and Achaeans and Eleans and
> Athenians because of his invasion of the Peloponnese – did not [believe]

it was possible for him to go away without a fight, calculating that if he
should win, he would free himself from all of these [cares], and if he should
die, he thought it would be a beautiful death for one who was trying to
bequeath to his fatherland the control of the Peloponnese.

Epaminondas sees himself, in Xenophon's sketch, as an individual who
is indisputably capable of making history: indeed, the character views the
outcome of a large battle as determining his own personal *kleos* and the
entire Peloponnese as his potential legacy to his state.

Xenophon's next interjection, at *HG* 7.5.19, suggests that Epaminondas'
interest in his lasting memory and reputation is a predictable corollary of
his *philotimia*, his "love of honor." The historian then praises the courage
and discipline of the Theban troops that Epaminondas has prepared before
describing the battle-tactics that he employs (*HG* 7.5.21–25). The fight itself
is over quickly; Epaminondas is the only individual named amongst the
protagonists, and his death is recorded at *HG* 7.5.25. Xenophon's brief coda
describing the indecisive outcome of the battle of Mantinea (*HG* 7.5.26–7)
finally concludes the *Hellenica* as a whole.

The deliberateness with which Xenophon constructs the entire episode
belies its being a hasty postscript,[162] even if the remainder of the *Hellenica* does shortchange Epaminondas.[163] The interpretive treatment of
Epaminondas' inner thoughts and the commentary on the Theban general's tactics and efficacy as a leader also find good parallels in Xenophon's
accounts of other eminent commanders who seem to present themselves as
agents of history, including Xenophon himself in the *Anabasis*.[164] Regardless
of why Epaminondas may have been exempted from treatment earlier in the
Hellenica, the manner of his coverage in the Mantinea narrative signals that
Xenophon reads him as part of a larger pattern emerging in Greek history.

The Theban material evidence

Although Thebes contributed more and higher-ranking leaders to the college of boeotarchs than did any other city,[165] the function of the Boeotian League itself also depended upon the local governments of smaller
polities.[166] As such, it might be anticipated that inscriptions dealing with

---

[162] See the scholarly interpretations reviewed by Buckler 1980: 265–6.

[163] See note 153, above, and esp. Buckler 1980: 265–6, with references.

[164] See Chapter 5, above, as well as the discussion earlier in this chapter.

[165] Hammond 2000: 84, 86.

[166] On the internal political nature of the League, see e.g. Bakhuizen 1994; Buckler 1980: 15–45;
cf. also Hammond 2000 esp. 91–3.

the small-scale and popular management of the League – the type of
material that might be used to discuss public statements of group agency
amongst the Boeotians – would be available from a variety of sites, particularly from the period of the hegemony. This, however, turns out to be not
quite the case: as a survey of *IG* vii, for example, quickly reveals,[167] there
are very few inscriptions from Boeotia in general that can be securely dated,
and those that can be tend to be placed in the third century BC and later.[168]
As Hammond points out, however, three known proxeny inscriptions do
provide some public articulations of the political dealings of the Theban-
dominated Boeotian League in the early to mid fourth century,[169] and their
language merits brief examination here.

IG vii 2407 and 2408 are proxeny inscriptions dedicated by "the Boeotians" to individuals in the year 364/3 BC; Roesch uses them both as comparands in his initial publication of the third inscription, whose form and
content are very similar to the other two decrees and whose date is likely
365.[170] Given the commonalities in their wording, these three documents
can best be discussed in close comparison with one another.[171]

```
        [Θ]εός. Τύχα. [..]οτέ[λι]-
        ος ἄρχοντος, ἔδοξε
        τοῖ δάμοι πρόξενον
4       εἶμεν Βοιωτῶν καὶ εὐε-
        ργέταν Νώβαν Ἀξι-
        ούβω Καρχαδόνιον, καὶ
        εἶμεν (Ϝ)οι γᾶς καὶ Ϝοικία-
        ς ἔ(π)πασιν καὶ ἀτέλιαν
        καὶ ἀσουλίαν καὶ κατὰ γᾶν
        καὶ κὰτ θάλατταν καὶ πο-
        λέμω καὶ ἰράνας ἰώσας,
12      [β]οιωταρχιόντων Τίμων[ος],
```

167 On the benefits and drawbacks of taking the inscriptions in *IG* as representative samplings,
     see Chapters 4 and 5, above.
168 This is at least in part due to a lack of secure modern knowledge of the sequence of
     governmental officials used in inscriptions for dating local events: on these problems, see
     Barratt 1932. Further, Thebes was sacked by Alexander in 335, an event that created a major
     interruption in the city's chronology until its re-establishment after 316.
169 Hammond 2000: 91, citing Roesch 1984.   170 Roesch 1984: 50–9.
171 Editions from Roesch 1984: 47 (noting that he has used *IG* vii 2407 with Wilhelm's
     corrections), Roesch 1984: 47–8 (Roesch's revision of *IG* vii 2408), and Roesch 1984: 46,
     respectively. Translation from Rhodes and Osborne 2003: 217 no. 43 for *IG* vii 2407 (here
     presented first); the other two translations re-deploy Rhodes' and Osborne's phrases for the
     same or similar words in the Greek to demonstrate the parallels between the inscriptions.
     Cf. also Roesch's French translation of the third inscription (Roesch 1984: 46).

Δαιτώνδαο, Θίωνος, Μέ[λ]-
ωνος, Ἱππίαο, Εὐμαρί[δ]αο,
Πάτρωνος.
       vac.

God; Fortune (*Tycha*)

1 In the archonship of –oteles. Resolved by the
people.

3 Nobas son of Axioubas of Carthage shall be
proxenos and benefactor of the Boeotians; and
he shall have the right to acquire land and a
house, and immunity both by land and by sea,
during both war and peace.

12 The Boeotarchs were: Timon, Daetondas,
Thion, Melon, Hippias, Eumaridas, Patron.

- - - - - - - -

[ἔδοξε] τοῖ δ[άμοι, - -]
[. . . .]λωνος Βυζ[άντιον]
[Βοι]ωτῶν πρόξενον εἶ[μεν]
4   [κ]αὶ εὐεργέταν, καὶ ε[ἴμ]-
[εν] αὐτοῖ ἀτέλε[ιαν] κα[ὶ ἀσ]-
[φά]λιαν καὶ ἀσ[υλίαν]
[καὶ π]ολέμ[ω καὶ ἰράνας]
8   [ἰώ]σας καὶ κατ[ὰ γᾶν καὶ]
[κατ]ὰ θάλασσαν κα[ὶ]
[γ]ᾶς καὶ οἰκίας ἔγκτησι-
[ν] καὶ αὐτῶι καὶ ἐγγόνο-
12   [ι]ς ∶ βοιωταρχιόντων
Ἀσωποδώρω, Μαληκί-
δαο, Διογίτ[ο]νος, Μιξι-
[λ]αο, Ἀμινά[δ]αο, Ἱππίαο,
16   [Δ]αιτώνδαο.
       vac.

[It was decided] . . . by the
people . . .
–lonus of Byzantium
shall be *proxenos*
and benefactor of the Boeotians; and
he shall have immunity
during both war and peace,
both by land and by sea,
and the right to acquire land and a house,
both for himself and his descendants.

The Boeotarchs were:
Asopodorus, Malecidas,
Diogeiton, Mixias,
Aminadas, Hippias,
[D]aetondas.[172]

[Θεός. Τύχα. – *ca. 8* – ἄρ]-
[χοντος, ἔδοξε τοῖ δάμοι]
[πρόξενον εἶμεν Βοιω]-
1   [τῶν κὴ εὐεργέταν] Ἀθ[αν]-
[ῆο]ν Δαμονί[κο]υ Μακεδ-
όνα καὶ εἶμεν αὐτοῖ γᾶς
4   καὶ ϝοικίας ἔππασιν κὴ
ἐνώναν κὴ ἀσυλίαν κ-
ὴ πολέμω κὴ ἰράνας ἰώ-
σας κὴ κατὰ γᾶν κὴ κὰτ θ-
8   άλαττ[α]ν κὴ αὐτοῖ κ[ὴ] γέ-
νι, βο[ιωταρ]χιόντων [Πελο]-
πίδα[ο, Τι]μολάω, Δαμ[οφίλ]ω,
[Π]άτρων[υς], Ἀσωποτέλ[εο]ς,
12   Ἠσχύλω, Παντακλεῖος.
            vac.
God; Fortune (*Tycha*).
In the archonship of –. Resolved by the
people.
Athenaius son of Damonicus[173] of Macedon
shall be *proxenos*
and benefactor of the Boeotians;
and he shall have the right
to acquire land and a
house, and immunity
during both war and peace,
both by land and by sea,
both for himself and his family.
The Boeotarchs were: Pelopidas,
Timolas, Damophilus,
Patron, Asopoteles,
Aischylus, Pantacleus.

The Carthaginian Nobas son of Axioubas (*IG* vii 2407), the unknown citizen
of Byzantium (*IG* vii 2408), and the Macedonian Athenaeus (Roesch's new

---

172 See Rhodes and Osborne 2003: 218 no. 43 on the identity of this individual and on the overlap
of names between the three inscriptions discussed here.

173 Roesch 1984: 58 notes that this individual's name would have been spelled Demonicus in
other contexts.

inscription, presented third in the grouping above) are here all granted the titles of *proxenos* and *euergetês* "of the Boeotians" (Βοιωτῶν) with formulae that sound very much like those of democratic Athens. Most notably, the approval of the decrees is noted with the words ἔδοξε τοῖ δάμοι, "resolved by the people," the implication being that some kind of citizen collective is taking official decisions on behalf of "the Boeotians," the entire body of the confederacy. But this populace is also acknowledging, through the generous[174] honors it confers, not only the pre-eminence of these foreigners, but the perceived need of the Boeotian *damos* for the leadership or benefaction of eminent individuals.

The forms of expression that these decrees employ also make particular statements about the authority, power, and historical agency of "the Boeotians" or "the Thebans" in comparison and contrast with their individual leaders. Although, for example, the phrase "[name in the genitive case] ἄρχοντος," "when N. was ἄρχων," or "in the archonship of N.," found at the head of 2406 (and supplemented for the other inscriptions) also appears at Athens,[175] the decrees themselves are not slavish imitations of Athenian paradigms. Another way in which they differ, in fact, from their Athenian neighbors is in their multiple articulations of governmental authority.[176] Whereas in Athens the public documents tended to demonstrate tension mainly between the acknowledgement of individuals and groups, the decrees of the Boeotian League display different complications: present in these inscriptions are the ἄρχων, the "Boeotian" *damos*, and the boeotarchs. Given the shifting corporate nature of Boeotian government during the period of Theban hegemony, too, these decrees seem to deliberately minimize the question of precisely who constitutes "the Boeotians." A reader utterly unfamiliar with the political history and topography of the region might well assume that these inscriptions had been erected by an oligarchic polis named "Boeotia" – and this may very well be precisely the message that decrees constructed in this manner were intended to send.

To Roesch's three inscriptions may be added a few more that seem to partake in some of the same trends observed in fifth- and fourth-century Athens. These honorific documents and epitaphs further suggest that some

---

[174] At least by contemporary Athenian standards, the only corpus of evidence large enough for comparison: see Chapter 5, above.

[175] See Chapters 2, 4, and 5, above.

[176] Roesch 1984: 50–1, observing this feature in order to diagnose the "federal character" of all three decrees (i.e. the fact that they are regionally, rather than merely locally, binding) and to begin dating the new one. My reading here of the broader implications of this feature, however, is rather different from Roesch's.

of the same questions about individual and group historical agency, and about the memorialization of deeds and individuals, that had surfaced in Attica were likely also circulating in Boeotia. It is not necessary to postulate wholly independent evolution of these ideas. Acceptable terms of memorialization could be worked out on a large scale in a panhellenic sanctuary like Delphi or Olympia just as they could in a polis like Athens, and the received results of this written or unwritten governance might then in turn drift homeward to impact local discourse.[177] Funerary commemorative iconography in neighboring Boeotia has further been acknowledged as occasionally imitating Athenian paradigms,[178] although the epitaphs, few as they are in number, show both similarities with and divergence from the patterns visible in the Athenian examples discussed in Chapters 4 and 5, above.

Some of the inscriptions examined below are certainly or potentially later in date than the period under chief consideration here. However, they do seem to have precedents that I will also mention: in this, they may imply some continuities in attitudes and modes of expression that help to fill in the evidence gaps at Thebes during the second and third quarters of the fourth century. I do not wish to overstate my claims: attitudes towards individuals and groups as agents of history in fourth-century Thebes can scarcely be reconstructed from such a small sample. Rather, I hope to show that the Theban evidence that *does* exist suggests some shared habits of discourse and commemoration amongst the various Greek city-states. Admittedly, different internal belief systems or social convictions may find similar outward expression in entirely separate localities, but some of this expression is made in those most public fora of the Greek world, the panhellenic sanctuaries, where the vocabulary of display had necessarily to be interpretable by a much broader audience.

An epitaph for a citizen of Heraclea Pontica erected at Thebes around the middle of the fourth century shows a number of characteristics also seen in Athenian epitaphs of the same period:[179]

> σοῦ μὲν δὴ πατρὶς δήν, Κερκίνε Φοξίου υἱέ,
>   Ποντιὰς Ἡράκλει᾽ ἕξει ἄχος φθιμένου,
> ἦμ [ποθέ]ων ἐγ χερσὶ φίλων θ[άνες. οὔ]ποτ᾽ ἐπαίνου
>   [λησόμ]εθ᾽· ἦ μάλα γὰρ [σὴν φ]ύσιν ἠγασάμην.
>   . . . . . ανδρος.

> O Cercinus, son of Phoxius, your homeland of
> Heraclea Ponti[c]a will experience destructive grief.
> Longing for it, you died in the arms of your friends. Never
> will we omit/forget our praise. For I marveled greatly at your nature.
> .....andrus.

Of particular interest here are the mention of the loss to the homeland of
the individual citizen and the multiple expressions of personal grief. The
former feature is rather more characteristic of late fifth-century and earliest
fourth-century epitaphs at Athens, especially those that seem to have been
competing with the custom of the *patrios nomos* during or immediately after
the Peloponnesian War.[180] But the latter, the more intimate disclosure of sorrow, finds far more parallels in the fourth-century Athenian corpus.[181] While
these connections may help to support the approximate date for the inscription, they also demonstrate that, again, the Theban-created example is not a
direct imitation of Athenian models. The modes of expression seem familiar, but the way in which they are combined is rather different. Indeed, the
pairing of these two attitudes creates an even stronger claim to the value and
impact of the individual life than would the employment of either one alone.

Dated to the fourth or early third century is an epitaph dedicated to a
Theban, the son of Diogeiton, whose given name is lost. Its contents present
a unique discussion of the complex historical position of the individual in
an increasingly panhellenic world:[182]

> [?ἤλπισεν αὐ]χήσασα πατρὶς Θήβη ποτὲ τῶ[ιδε] |
>   πρωτεύσειμ πάσης Ἑλλάδος εἰς ἀρετήν, |
> πρὶν διάνοιαν τέρμα λαβεῖν, βίον ὧι κε[˘ ‒ ‒] |
>   ὤλε[σσεν] φθονερὰ τ[οῖς ἀ]γαθοῖσι Τύχ[η]. |
> [.]ωι[.. ⁴ʔ. .]οχων ἔθα[ν]εν Διογείτον[ος υἱός], |
>   [.]τ!! [. . . ⁵ʔ. .]εωγ γῆς πατρίας δύναμιν.
> $\begin{bmatrix} 7\text{–}8 \\ nomen \\ - \smile \end{bmatrix}$ οἰκείαι γνώμηι Θηβαῖος ἔτε[υξεν].

> His fatherland of Thebes, exulting in this man, once [hoped?],
>   to hold first place in all of Greece for valor
> until its intention came to an end and
>   fate, cruel to good men, destroyed his? life ...
> ... the son of Diogeiton died
> ... the power of his ancestral land.
> - - -, a Theban, made [this] of his own accord.

---

[180] See Chapters 4 and 5, above.   [181] See Chapter 5, above.
[182] Edition from Hansen 1989: 109 = *CEG* 2.635; cf. also *IG* vii 2536. Hansen's commentary *ad loc.* notes the difficulty of construing the meaning of the first four lines, and I follow his suggestions in my translation here.

The very city of Thebes, then, seems to be acknowledging the pre-eminence of the deceased, whose apparent ability to render his homeland outstanding amongst "all Hellas" for valor (*aretê*) might in some ways be more appropriate for an athletic dedication in a panhellenic sanctuary than for a local tombstone. The fourth-century 'capricious fate' trope reappears, as well. But the grandiose claims to individual impact and relevance reaching beyond the polis are somewhat limited by the final line: this monument was erected by a private Theban citizen. This tombstone, then, may indicate something of the apologetic lengths to which less well-positioned individuals of the fourth century might go in order to invoke the commemorative paradigms established by and for the history-makers of the age.

An example of such a paradigm, though its text is fragmentary, is the Pelopidas statue base from Delphi.[183] Pelopidas has already appeared once, though not been explicitly mentioned, in this discussion of Theban inscriptions: as one of the boeotarchs in the proxeny decree for Athenaeus the Macedonian, above. His routine listing there as part of the governmental life of the Boeotian League is very different from the extraordinary status invoked for him at Delphi by the Thessalians, who erected the monument that bears this inscription:[184]

Σπάρτημ μὲγ χήρ[ωσας – – – – – – – –]
εὐλογίαι πιστ [– – – – – – – – – –]
[πλε]ιστάκι ΔΗ [– – – – – – – – – – –]
4   [στῆ]σαι Βοιω[τ – – – – – – – – –]
Πελοπίδαν Ἱπ[πόκλου Θηβαῖον]
Θεσσαλοὶ ἀνέ[θηκαν Ἀπόλλωνι Πυθίωι]
Λύσιππος Λυσ[– – Σικυώνιος ἐποίησε].

> [*Destroyer*] *of Sparta,* [who came as our helper], / | with praise, with *trust*, [with a statue we crown you]. / | Very often [after this it may be possible for you other trophies too] / | to set up, [glorious leader] of the
> 5   Boeo[tians]. // ‖ (This statue of) Pelopidas, son of Hip[pokles the Theban], | was *dedicated* by the Thessalians [to Apollo Pythios]. | Lysippos, son of Lys[–, the Sikyonian, was the sculptor].

This dedication by the Thessalians to Pelopidas (which the last line suggests took the form of a statue by Lysippus) seems to acknowledge Pelopidas' individual achievement against Sparta. The missing verb-form termination in the first line would likely only confirm the overall message of the monument,

[183] See Shrimpton's comments at note 192, below.
[184] Edition from Bousquet 1963: 206–8 = Delphi inv. 6758 + inv. 7710; translation from Harding 1985: 68 no. 49.

which marks a citizen group's commemoration of a foreign benefactor for actions taken against another group. The invocation of individual historical agency is further strengthened here by the nature and context of the gift itself. Sentiment that might well have been expressed with an honorific state decree is here magnified into an extravagant dedication in a panhellenic sanctuary.

The Pelopidas statue base represents in several ways a change in general Greek commemorative trends from the previous century. It is an honorific gesture from a citizen group to a living foreign benefactor, set up in a sanctuary to record military deeds and marked with a special statue[185] whose subject is explicitly indicated in the dedication.[186] During the fifth century, sanctuary-dedications were frequently (although not exclusively) offered by entire cities if their interests were historical, and were often connected with athletic achievement if they were private.[187] By the fourth century, however, living men are more often acknowledged in the sanctuaries for the performance of historical deeds. Such public advertisements, particularly in panhellenic contexts, of individual political and (especially) military achievements would likely have participated in a number of feedback loops, with groups learning from one another – and perhaps also competing with one another[188] – in their efforts to honor outstanding citizens or foreign benefactors, and well-positioned individuals in turn familiarizing themselves with both the possibilities for such commemoration and the qualities required to earn it. Such individuals would also likely have been spurred, in certain contexts, to competition for honor and memory, not only with one another but also with the poleis that both employed and elevated them.

An inscription from Thebes, probably dating to shortly after the battle of Leuctra in 371, displays deep engagement with this very situation:[189]

---

[185] Cf. Crane's reading of the epigram on Lysander's Nauarch's Monument at note 45, above.
[186] Keesling 2003: 167 examines the significance of such indications, which she notes mark a change in parlance and in meaning from fifth-century usages.
[187] Dillon 2001, citing Hölscher 1998 on civic dedications and Raubitschek 1939 on athletic ones, and noting that Krumeich 1997 recommends that these tendencies be moderated in discussion, since his results suggest that the actual picture was more complicated. Cf. also Smith 2007: 87–8, 94 on statues of athletic victors; and Keesling 2003: 170–85 on the dedications from the Acropolis in Athens.
[188] Lysander's Nauarch's Monument at Delphi, for example (cf. above), has been interpreted as a deliberate contrast to the Athenian monument for Marathon at the same site, since when completed they probably stood across from one another at the bottom of the Sacred Way: see McCauley 1993: 245; Cartledge 1987: 85.
[189] *IG* vii 2462; ed. with commentary Rhodes and Osborne 2003: 150–1 no. 30 and Tod 1948: 92–4 no. 130. Edition and translation here from Rhodes and Osborne.

Ξενοκράτης,

Θεόπομπος,

Μνασίλαος.

ἁνίκα τὸ Σπάρτας ἐκράτει δόρυ, τηνάκις εἷλεν

5   Ξεινοκράτης κλάρωι Ζηνὶ τρόπαια φέρειν,

οὐ τὸν ἀπ᾽ Εὐρώτα δείσας στόλον οὐδὲ Λάκαιναν

ἀσπίδα. "Θηβαῖοι κρείσσονες ἐν πολέμωι",

κάρυσσει Λεύκτροις νικαφόρα δουρὶ τρόπαια,

οὐδ᾽ Ἐπαμεινώνδα δεύτεροι ἐδράμομεν.

Xenocrates, Theopompus, Mnasilaus.

4   When the Spartan spear was dominant, then
Xenocrates took by lot the task of offering a
trophy to Zeus, not fearing the host from the
Eurotas or the Spartan shield. 'Thebans are
superior in war', proclaims the trophy won
through victory/bringing victory by the spear
at Leuctra; nor did we run second to
Epaminondas.

The first two dedicators of the monument (though not the third) are known
figures: Xenocrates was a boeotarch; Theopompus[190] was with Pelopidas
when the Spartans were driven out of the Theban Cadmea.[191] The inscription is of interest here for several reasons: its poetical features, its negotiation
between the agency of individuals and that of the citizen group of Thebans,
and finally its overt attempt to *correct* historical memory.[192]

The meter here, the elegiac couplet, was commonly used for epitaphs
as early as the archaic period,[193] and this private practice seems to have
continued through the fifth century and into the fourth (with a mid fifth

[190] Not the fourth-century historian from Chios.

[191] Tod 1948: 93–4 no. 130, with ancient references; see also Rhodes and Osborne 2003: 150–1.

[192] Tod 1948: 93 suggests that the last line "might be interpreted as a veiled protest against the
undue glorification of [Epaminondas]," although Rhodes and Osborne 2003: 151 disagree
and Tuplin 1987: 105–6 remains neutral. Shrimpton 1971: 313 cites this inscription along
with the Pelopidas statue base from Delphi as "inscriptional proof of the prestige being won
by the Theban heroes in central Greece while they were being ignored in Athens," and
suggests that "very shortly after the actual events there existed glowing stories of Pelopidas
and Epaminondas (whether literary or oral) waiting to enter Athenian literary traditions from
central Greece." I read the Leuctra text as competing over the ascription of agency and
memory more strongly and more openly than Tod recommends, and would therefore suggest
that this inscription not only implies the existence of the "glowing stories" about
Epaminondas that Shrimpton sees immanent in it, but actively attempts to rewrite those
stories (see below).

[193] See e.g. the entries in Pfohl 1967.

century break for elaborate tombstones in Athens, as addressed in Chapters 2 and 4, above). But this inscription need not necessarily have been intended to mark a tomb.[194] Elegiacs were also employed during the classical era for important public monuments to history-making individuals and groups: in Athens, for example, the Agora statue-base for the Tyrannicides bore an epigram in that meter.[195] A common feature of both the epitaphs and the commemorative inscriptions, however, is the use of appropriately heroic language to glorify their content and their agents.[196] Regardless of whether it is making a statement about the living or the dead, this text participates energetically in that tradition. Its poetry, however, rather than sounding Iliadic, as did so many of the offerings from Attica seen in Chapters 2, 4, and 5, resonates instead with Pindar, one of Boeotia's most famous sons.[197] The word root νικαφορ-, "victory-bringing," though not Homeric, occurs a dozen times in Pindar,[198] and the phrase (οὐδ')... δεύτεροι ἐδράμομεν similarly rings of athletic competition. The most important connection here, however, is not merely that of local pride or dialect, but rather the evocation of the essential themes and functions of the Pindaric ode, linking individual achievement simultaneously with the glorification of the 'victor's' homeland and with the world of heroic myth.[199]

Of the three honorands named at the head of the inscription, Xenocrates occupies pride of place in the main anecdote. His position is carefully balanced: he has been chosen by lot from his own citizen group to represent them in setting up a "trophy to Zeus," but in so doing has now been cast as an individual in conflict with the collective Spartans (l. 6). The contrast is explored from the opposite direction, however, when the document moves on to quote either the inscription upon or the essential meaning of that trophy, which memorializes the valor of the entire polis through the glorification of its military victory (l. 7).[200] Now it is the Thebans who have

---

194 *Pace* recently Rhodes and Osborne 2003: 150; for a review of earlier arguments, see Tuplin 1987: 94–5 and nn. 72–4, with references. Tuplin also leans towards identifying this monument as a tombstone.
195 See Chapter 2, above.   196 See note 46, above.
197 The Pindaric quality of the poetry is noted but not explored in detail by Rhodes and Osborne 2003: 150.
198 As evidenced by a *TLG* search.
199 On the social and poetical use of this combination of material to address the problem that "the victor must be reintegrated into his house, his class, *and* his city," see esp. Kurke 1991 (the quotation occurs at 6).
200 On the plurals of the inscription (ll. 5 and 7) likely referring to a single trophy, see Tuplin 1987: 97–8.

successfully opposed the Spartans. The Pindaric victor gains individual *kleos* through his athletic feats – *kleos* that is then both explicitly and metaphorically distributed to the polis through the reconciliation of the victory-ode.[201] Xenocrates, however, this inscription claims, has distinguished himself in service to his city and earned a share in its collective success.

Like the Pindaric athletic victor, too, Xenocrates still requires words to create poetical memory of his deeds,[202] for the Theban battle-trophy, whether implicitly or explicitly, glorifies the populace together, but not the boeotarch himself. In reifying Xenocrates' individual historical achievement in such a laden form as the elegiac poem, this monument is essentially correcting the idea that the victory at Leuctra "belonged" (to borrow the wording of the Demosthenes quotation employed at the opening of Chapter 1, above) to the collectivity of the Thebans alone. Separate ownership and agency is invoked for the three men in its heading, bringing the parlance of the inscription, if the summary by Demosthenes is again to be believed on some level, into line with current trends in fourth-century thought and expression. The resonance between the approach of this document and the orator's argument is particularly important given the differences between the Athenian and the Theban governmental systems: it suggests that interest in group historical agency need not be tied to democratic constitutions.[203]

One final reversal remains in this inscription's treatment of historical agency: the striking last line, at once a boast, an apologia, and an invocation. The phraseology claims equality for Xenocrates, Theopompus, and Mnasilaus with the well-known Theban commander of the battle, defends their achievements and their legacy in comparison with his, and attempts to rearticulate history by both literally and metaphorically rewriting what Shrimpton suggests was already becoming Theban legend.[204] The reader is intended to use the historical account provided by the monument to adjust his understanding of the historical event. Just as the battle-trophy mentioned in l. 8 serves as a metonym for the achievement of the Thebans, so does this monument stand for the accomplishments of the three individuals

---

[201] Kurke 1991 esp. 163–94.

[202] Or simply of his position, if he had no opportunity to act upon his charge to "place a trophy": Rhodes and Osborne 2003: 150–1.

[203] Similar conclusions have been drawn regarding literacy: see Millender 2001: 158, with modern references (citing esp. on Athens Hedrick 1999 and 1994), recommending that "there was no straightforward relationship between political system and public use of the written word in ancient Greece."

[204] See note 192, above.

named upon it. In its description, it re-performs their preferred version of history every time it is read.[205]

Epaminondas as proxenos *and* ktistês

The struggle of this monument to either outstrip or share in the local glory evidently accorded almost immediately to Epaminondas as victor of Leuctra invites reflection upon his public behavior and reception. Epaminondas was clearly understood by later authors, even Athenian ones, as an individual agent of Theban history.[206] He was probably best known for his daring military exploits,[207] and in this both his immediate reputation and his lasting fame would have benefited not only from the growing tendencies of his age to elevate individual generals, but also from the potential associations with the heroic tradition.[208]

Two other roles played by Epaminondas provide further testimony to his reception and help to contextualize him within fourth-century Greek thought: his proxeny at Cnidus and his recollection as the new founder of the city of Messene.[209] An inscription from Cnidus, newly revealed in 1994, records the terms of Epaminondas' *proxenia* there:[210]

> [Ἔδο]ξε [Κνιδί]οις· Ἐ-
> [πα]μειν[ών]δαν Πο-
> [λύ]μμη Θηβαῖον κ-
> [αὶ ἐ]κγόνος προξ-
> [ένο]ς ἦμεν τᾶς πό-
> [λιος] καὶ ὑπάρχεν α-
> [ὐτοῖ]ς ἔσπ[λο]υν ἐ̣-
> [ς Κνίδον καὶ ἔκπλουν]

> Resolved by the Knidians. Epameinondas son of Polymme, the Theban, and his descendants shall be *proxenoi* of the polis, and are to be granted the right to sail into [and to sail out of Knidos].

As Buckler shows, this inscription demonstrates a practical political and military commitment made by the Cnidians in anticipation of receiving

---

205 Cf. the discussion of Derderian 2001: 165–75 on the "agonistic" creation of memory through the spoken performance of funerary oratory.
206 See note 192, above, esp. Shrimpton 1971.   207 E.g. Cawkwell 1972: 254–5.
208 Cf. Chapter 3, above, on Herodotus' 'Homeric' treatment of Leonidas, and this chapter, above, on some of the heroic coloration emerging from Thucydides' depiction of Brasidas.
209 See below on whether Epaminondas may also have been involved in the foundation of Megalopolis.
210 Buckler 1998: 195–6 and nn. 11–12 identifies Blümel 1994: 157–8 as the *editio princeps*; following Buckler, I reprint Blümel's edition here, and Buckler's translation.

similarly favorable treatment from Epaminondas in return. Proxeny would allow them to maintain some level of relationship with Thebes without the entanglements of a formal treaty: instead, they could freely offer what are cast as traditional privileges to an influential individual.[211] But Epaminondas, as a fleet commander being extended rights of free naval passage, seems here to be acknowledged as something more than an average elite citizen.[212] The *proxenia* that the Cnidians extend to Epaminondas is therefore accompanied by explicit consequences for him and implicit consequences for them that are at once politically significant and illustrative of individual power. The issue of the sailing privileges, too, may be productively contrasted with the complaints of the Attic orators addressed in Chapter 5, above: what Demosthenes and Aeschines would probably have presented in a polemical context as an empty escalation of honorific behaviors, the Cnidians would likely have characterized, in Buckler's view, as political prudence.

A final 'monument' to Epaminondas' achievements in war was likely offered in traditional terms that the wider Greek world would have well understood: his re-foundation of Messene. Diodorus suggests that this was partially a strategic decision, due to the location of the site and Thebes' ongoing conflicts with Sparta. But Diodorus also claims that Epaminondas was a man φύσει μεγαλεπίβολος ὢν καὶ δόξης ὀρεγόμενος αἰωνίου, "by his [very] character a planner of great things and grasping for eternal glory" (D.S. 15.66.1). Casting oneself in the role of a colonial founder was by Epaminondas' time a well-known way to leave a permanent mark upon the historical record, and Diodorus' account of Epaminondas' activities at Messene is doubtless influenced by this model. Several pieces of evidence testify to the enduring power of the *ktistês* tradition in the fourth century: *Ath. Pol.* 58.1, the earliest known reference to Harmodius and Aristogeiton receiving sacrifices as "founders" of the Athenian democracy;[213] the reception of Brasidas at Amphipolis, as described by Thucydides (see the opening section of this chapter); and even Xenophon's own thoughts about founding a colony with the remains of the Ten Thousand in the *Anabasis* (see Chapter 5, above). Epaminondas may have deliberately presented himself (or allowed his reception) as a near-*ktistês* of Messene[214] not only because it was a symbolic gesture for the moment, but also because it would have

---

[211]   Buckler 1998: 198–9.   [212]   Ibid. 199–202.

[213]   Taylor 1981: 20–1; see also Kearns 1989: 55, 150.

[214]   Luraghi 2008: 216–17 describes ways in which this foundation may have both borne resemblances to and differed from that of an entirely new colony, even in the eyes of the Messenians, and recommends special caution in evaluating the situation. See also Zizza 2006: 345 n. 6 for additional bibliography.

ensured him lasting remembrance as the liberator of the district's people from Spartan domination and perhaps even earned him accolades in heroic style.[215]

As Hornblower points out, Diodorus does not describe the foundation of Megalopolis (D.S. 15.72.4) in the same terms as he does Messene: most notably, he does not explicitly connect it with Epaminondas.[216] The two cities, however, were certainly manifestations of the same larger strategic goals for those interested in the geopolitical subversion of Spartan power,[217] and later history did link Epaminondas, if not in quite identical ways, with both foundations.[218] Pausanias reports an epigram from a statue at Thebes (Paus. 9.15.6):

> ἡμετέραις βουλαῖς Σπάρτη μὲν ἐκείρατο δόξαν,
> Μεσσήνη δ' ἱερὴ τέκνα χρόνωι δέχεται·
> Θήβης δ' ὅπλοισιν Μεγάλη πόλις ἐστεφάνωται,
> αὐτόνομος δ' Ἑλλὰς πᾶσ' ἐν ἐλευθερίηι.

> Sparta was cut off from its glory through my plans,
> And sacred Messene finally welcomes its children;
> Megalopolis was garlanded with Theban weapons,[219]
> And all of Greece is under its own laws, and free.

Although there is no guarantee that this epigram may be contemporary to the time of Epaminondas' death, Luraghi notes that the concept of *autonomia* here "seems to reflect political slogans and sentiments of the first decades of the fourth century with an accuracy that would be quite surprising in a later fabrication."[220] Like Lysander's inscription on the Nauarch's Monument at Delphi, this epigram emphasizes the impact of an individual agent upon entire cities: it is Epaminondas who is credited with both the arrest of Sparta and the resurgence of Messene, the two concepts joined

---

[215] On the potential to deliberately self-present as a hero, see notes 18, 19, and 20, above.

[216] Hornblower 1990 esp. 73–7. Hornblower's main purpose in his treatment of this particular historian is to argue that Diodorus' chronology is incorrect, and that he has placed the foundation of Megalopolis too late in time by confusing the Tearless Battle with the battle of Leuctra. Whether rectifying this potential error might have changed Diodorus' understanding of Epaminondas' involvement or non-involvement in the city's foundation cannot be proven.

[217] Cawkwell 1972: 266; cf. Hornblower 1990: 76–7.

[218] Hornblower 1990: 76–7, citing Paus. 9.15.6 as discussed here.

[219] Or, with Jones 1935, "By the arms of Thebe was Megalopolis encircled with walls."

[220] Luraghi 2008: 220, citing Rhodes 1999 on *autonomia* and discussing the issue of dating at n. 37. See also Zizza 2006: 345–6 n. 8 (on *autonomia*), 346 esp. n. 9 (on the dating of the monument and the epigram). Ibid. 344–9 no. 46 represents a commentary on the entire epigram.

tightly together in a μέν ... δέ construction that emphasizes the replacement of one power with another. The mention of the "Theban weapons" draws attention to Epaminondas' entire citizen body, but the context in turn provides an inevitable reminder that the subject of the statue was his city's most famous and successful general. Finally, the slogan of the last line claims glory for Epaminondas in the conferral of *autonomia* upon Greece. The concept of 'freedom' for certain of the Greek cities dated back at least to the time of the Persian Wars,[221] and the idea that an individual man might be able to bring about liberating political change was at least as old as the affair of the Athenian Tyrannicides.[222] Thebes, however, had Medized when the Persians came and left no known recollections of a native political myth that might provide an exclusively local inspiration for this line. The poetry seems instead to harness ideas that were comprehensible – and meaningful – to a much broader Greek audience.[223] This statue of Epaminondas may therefore have been anticipating a reception that reached beyond the boundaries of Thebes.

6.4 Conclusion: Self-conscious history

Certain Athenians during this same period also seem to have been exploiting this vocabulary of display to invoke recognition for history-making achievements. Demosthenes states, for example, that the portrait-statue of Conon in the Agora was the first one of a man erected by the state since the Tyrannicides.[224] It would also then have been the first known such example at Athens made for a *living* individual, since a minimum of three to four years must have passed between the deaths even of Harmodius and Aristogeiton and the raising of their statue group by Antenor.[225] To what extent might Conon himself have helped to motivate such an extraordinary gesture?

That Conon was a conscious manipulator of public perception is suggested by the tradition that he advocated "autonomy" for the Greek

---

[221] Raaflaub 2004: 58–89.   [222] See Chapter 2, above.

[223] See Luraghi 2008: 219–20, with references, on the different ways that Messenian independence was interpreted in antiquity. Cf. also Seager and Tuplin 1980, introducing at 141 their argument that "the Greeks of Asia first came to be consistently thought of as a unit, and their freedom to be regularly exploited as a slogan, in the years between 400 and 386."

[224] D. 20.69–70, cited in Keesling 2003: 176. Shear 2007: 107–8 suggests that the placement of Conon's statue in the Agora would have implicitly connected him with the Tyrannicides as a "liberator of Athens and [a] bringer of freedom" (quotation at 107).

[225] See Chapter 2, above.

territories from which he and Pharnabazus expelled the Spartans during the middle years of the 390s.[226] Conon may have been acting in part out of expediency, but his ongoing competition with Thrasybulus was also a likely motivation for his careful attention to his image.[227] His return to Athens from Cnidus, as Strauss observes, was further marked by a series of honorific transactions. Strauss collects the awards that Conon received (an inscription, the Agora statue, an Acropolis statue, and freedom from taxes) and the benefits that he bestowed in kind (reconstructed fortifications, a temple to Cnidian Aphrodite, and a "festival liturgy" for the city), also noting that "the cities of Ionia, ever alert, exchanged statues of Lysander for images of the hero of Cnidus."[228] In a conscious, symbolic gesture, then, Conon had proclaimed to the Ionians the freedom that Athens had failed to win for them a century before, during the great revolt from Persia; in return, the Ionian Greeks had granted Conon himself a series of honors expressed in tangible form.[229] Next, at Athens, Conon engaged in public benefactions that are familiar – in kind if not perhaps in scope and scale – from the fifth century. Like Nicias and even Alcibiades before him, for example, he indulged in grand religious gestures:[230] the Piraeus temple of Cnidian Aphrodite is perhaps his second most significant attempt to construct a historical legacy along with a building.[231] Still more striking, however, would have been his large-scale support, both financial and logistical, for the rebuilding of Athens' Long Walls.[232] The walls themselves would not only memorialize Conon's benefaction, but also in effect portray him as a re-founder of the Athenian Empire,[233] a Themistocles or Pericles reborn in an age that could offer him increased opportunities for memorialization as repayment for his achievements, his leadership, and his philanthropy.

---

[226] Perlman 1968: 261 and nn. 32–3, 262–3 nn. 45–6 (all with references). Perlman further notes that "it is evident that Conon cleverly exploited those same propaganda slogans that had been used by the Spartans in the Peloponnesian War" (261).

[227] Strauss 1984: 38, suggesting that "it is hard to avoid the suspicion that Athens was not big enough for two liberators."

[228] Strauss 1984: 39–40, with references, quotation at 39.

[229] The ironic fact that Conon was essentially under contract to the Persians at the time seems to have posed little or no difficulty: see Perlman 1968: 262 and n. 9, citing X. *HG* 4.8.9 and D.S. 14.85.2.

[230] E.g. Nicias' famous festal benefactions at Delos (Plu. *Nic.* 3.4–8), and Alcibiades' celebration of the procession for the Eleusinian Mysteries upon his return to Athens from exile (X. 1.4.20; Plu. *Alc.* 34.4–6).

[231] On this general concept, e.g. Umholtz 2002: 278–82, esp. 281 n. 78.

[232] See Seager 1967: 103.

[233] This in spite of the fact that the reconstruction was actually begun prior to Conon's intervention: Seager 1967: 103. Cf. also note 224, above.

Chabrias, the acclaimed winner of the battle of Naxos, also received high
honors from the Athenian *dêmos*, most notably a statue in the Agora and
a gold crown.[234] The Agora statue, as Burnett and Edmonson observe,
was probably the next major public dedication after Conon's: its elaborate inscribed base survives, and records a series of honors conferred upon
Chabrias by a variety of foreign and civic entities.[235] A disputed story even
suggests that Chabrias insisted on a particular *pose* for this statue to commemorate the specific battle tactics he had employed against Agesilaus
at Thebes.[236] Regardless of what the specific physical stance might have
been, as Anderson points out, Aristotle's examples in the *Rhetoric* show
that the statue itself could be construed as a testimonial to a specific view
of the deeds of the man.[237] Like Conon, then, Chabrias earned the approbation of his fellow citizens and transformed their approval into a more
permanent form of self-commemoration, in this case through his own
monument to a historical deed: the enshrining of his gold crown on the
Acropolis.[238]

By this point in Greek history, then, a discernible change has taken place.
From a debate over whether individuals or groups are responsible for the
motion of history at the time of the Tyrannicides, the discourse has progressed to a point where, in the mid fourth century, appropriately positioned
individuals are now able to script (in literature and in the epigraphical
record) and stage (in public works of art) their own historical significance.
By making careful choices about their own activities and behaviors, by
demonstrating receptivity to the commemorative efforts of others, and even
by deliberately memorializing themselves, such individuals have learned to
harness public discourse to their advantage, both during their lives and
after their deaths. Private commemoration (save for occasional competitive
statements like the Leuctra inscription treated above), while once engaged
in this debate on a larger scale, has significantly retreated into smaller,
narrower fora. Influential historiographic writing has gradually narrowed
its focus to emphasize not only the history-making individual, but also
his personality and ethical qualities, and even polemical oratory describes
individual leaders in terms that range from public fascination to political
dependence.

The shifting political divisions and near-constant conflicts between the
major poleis of the Greek mainland during the earlier fourth century created

[234] Burnett and Edmonson 1961: 89, with references.
[235] Ibid. and *passim.*   [236] Ibid. 89, citing D.S. 15.33.4; Nep. *Chab.* 1.3.
[237] Anderson 1963: 412–13.   [238] Burnett and Edmonson 1961: 89 and n. 43.

a situation that was ripe for exploitation by any state that could gain a decisive upper hand, but the receptivity of the Greeks to image-making by eminent leaders also set the stage for the notable 'performances' that would follow. Held hostage in Thebes likely from 367–365 BC[239] under the control of Epaminondas and Pelopidas was a foreign adolescent from the north who would have had much opportunity to observe (and later to exploit)[240] these tendencies of the Greeks to lionize those who presented themselves in the appropriate fashion: Philip of Macedon.

[239] On this dating, see Hammond 1997: 356–7.
[240] I am grateful to M. Flower for calling my attention to this connection.

7 | A 'new world order'? Philip II of Macedon

7.1 "Europe has never before produced such a man...")[1]

Not far from the small modern Greek village of Chaeronea, an imposing marble lion of fourth-century sculptural style, found in fragments and now restored to an elevated base, rises over the Boeotian plain. It seems to have served as a funerary marker, since excavations of the monument's precinct yielded a *polyandrion* containing skeletal remains.[2] Although the dating of the excavated material and the number of the dead invited circumstantial association with a famous battle that took place in 338 BC only some 3 km away, modern historians long remained divided as to whether the burials should be linked to the testimony of Pausanias:[3]

> Προσιόντων δὲ τῆι πόλει πολυάνδριον Θηβαίων ἐστὶν ἐν τῶι πρὸς Φίλιπ-
> πον ἀγῶνι ἀποθανόντων. ἐπιγέγραπται μὲν δὴ ἐπίγραμμα οὐδέν, ἐπίθημα
> <δ'> ἔπεστιν αὐτῶι λέων· φέροι δ' ἂν ἐς τῶν ἀνδρῶν μάλιστα τὸν θυμόν·
> ἐπίγραμμα δὲ ἄπεστιν, ἐμοὶ δοκεῖν, ὅτι οὐδὲ ἐοικότα τῆι τόλμηι σφίσι τὰ ἐκ
> τοῦ δαίμονος ἠκολούθησε. (Paus. 9.40.10)

> On the way to the city is the *polyandrion* of the Thebans who died in the battle against Philip. No epitaph has been inscribed upon it, but on top is the figure of a lion. It most likely pertains to the character of the men [within]. An epitaph is lacking, it seems to me, because the fate that conveyed to these men by divine will was no match for their valor.

It has been suggested that the 254 deceased, who were buried in seven lines perhaps reminiscent of military files, may be the members of the Theban

---

[1] "...as Philip, the son of Amyntas" (Theopomp. Hist., preface to the *Philippica*, *FGrH* 115 F 27 = Plb. 8.9.1–4, trans. Flower 1997: 30).

[2] Two of the burials were cremations; the remainder were inhumations. Pritchett 1958: 308 n. 19 collects publications of the earliest excavations at Chaeronea, noting that the first discussion of this project is Soteriades 1902, and the first more extensive report is Soteriades 1903. See also the updated references in Ma 2008.

[3] Pritchett 1958 presents a summary of the arguments to date, with bibliography. Hammond 1938 represented one of the leading earlier voices against interpreting the lion as a Theban memorial (he originally held that the lion was a Macedonian monument), but retreated from this perspective in his 1987 review of Pritchett 1985. Rahe 1981 answers Markle 1978 on a number of topographical and strategic points.

'Sacred Band' of 150 pairs of lovers, a crack fighting unit destroyed in the battle.[4] The lion surmounting their grave was doubtless a somewhat later addition given the prevailing political climate after Chaeronea.[5] But regardless of when it was erected, for contemporary Greek audiences it likely memorialized the destruction of a group at the hands of an individual. Demosthenes' fellow Athenians, for example, by the analysis quoted at the opening of Chapter 1 (D. 23.196–9), would likely have said with Pausanias (above) that "Philip" won the battle, not "the Macedonians."

At Chaeronea in 338, then, Philip II of Macedon defeated an alliance of Greek poleis[6] that included Athens, Thebes and its Boeotian allies, and Corinth, amongst others,[7] and thus opened the path towards Macedonian hegemony in central and southern Greece. But Philip had already, throughout a reign of more than two decades,[8] presented himself as a history-making individual in terms that were broadly comprehensible to the Greeks with whom he negotiated and over whom he ultimately gained power. Was Philip actively trying to win a war of images?[9] From a military and political perspective he had no competitor of similar status: rather, he seems to have been attempting to offer a version of himself whose supremacy the Greeks could recognize, since it was articulated using techniques and symbols that they had long been employing amongst themselves. The Greeks in turn thought deeply about Philip, although their reactions to even his most appealing behaviors were by no means always positive. This fact alone represents an important distinction: an eminent individual in ancient Greece who is understood as making a significant historical impact may quite possibly be construed as an uncomfortable friend, or even as an enemy. This is particularly the case in the analyses of the historiographers, but the acknowledgement that a 'great' man need not always be a good man also

---

[4] Pritchett 1958: 310–11 describes the layout, provides some earlier bibliography for the debate, and offers his support for this interpretation; see also more recently the thoughtful recapitulation and new analysis by Ma 2008 esp. 75–6, 83–5. On the foundation, organization, and massacre of the Sacred Band, see esp. Plu. *Pel.* 18.1–19.5.

[5] Ma 2008: 84.   [6] I am indebted to J. Ober for remarks that encouraged this phraseology.

[7] Worthington 2008: 149 n. 38 recommends for reference the list of the contingents fighting against Philip at D. 18.237.

[8] Philip II ascended the throne of Macedon in 359 upon the death of his brother, Perdiccas III, in battle. Justin alone of the major sources (Just. 7.5.9–10) suggests that Philip may initially have ruled as regent for Perdiccas' young son Amyntas, and then accepted the title of 'king' only under popular pressure. Athens may have supported some of the various early pretenders to Philip's throne, as Philip came to power in the midst of conflict between Athens and Macedon over Amphipolis: a readable account of this period of crisis is Cawkwell 1978: 69–90.

[9] Fredricksmeyer 1982 contends that Philip's long-term projects, though substantially unrealized due to his premature death, may have been every bit as ambitious as Alexander's.

emerges from the material and epigraphical record surrounding Philip. The evidence suggests that Philip's activities invited a variety of responses, but that throughout Philip the *individual* (not "the Macedonians") remained the primary concern for the Greek states and their leaders.

The gap between Philip on the one hand and the Greeks on the other was further affected by ancient understandings of ethnicity: 'Greeks' and 'Macedonians' in the earlier fourth century seem to have been viewed by both groups as distinct peoples. The Greeks already observed a variety of civic and ethnic divisions within their own population. Ionians, such as the Athenians and the coastal populations of Asia Minor, were understood as being separate from Dorians like the Spartans; Theban and Corinthian citizenship, for example, were not mutually interchangeable. And as the discussion in preceding chapters has shown, polis or at best regional identity[10] appears in nearly all situations to have overridden panhellenism. But all of these barriers were nevertheless rather lower than those that the Greeks seem to have believed divided them from the tribal kingdoms to the north, amongst them the Macedonians. The issue was complex. The Macedonians were not precisely foreigners in the most exotic Herodotean sense (indeed, what evidence there is of the Macedonian language as used during the classical period suggests that it was a Greek dialect),[11] but they were not precisely Greeks either.[12]

The Macedonians' hereditary kingship, in particular, set them apart from their neighbors to the south. The archaic period had witnessed Greek tyrannies, including inherited ones, in some numbers. But tyranny had prompted energetic reflection (and often revulsion) in the years that followed,[13] and by the mid fourth century it had become more often something "good to think with," rather than a typical way of running a Greek state.[14] Against this background, the traditional, even archaizing Macedonian dynastic monarchy[15] might well have appeared as an embodiment of many things

---

[10] On unifying factors in the politics of Greek regional *koina*, see Mackil 2013.

[11] For a recent overview of the Macedonian language, see Panayotou 2007. On the Macedonians nevertheless being labeled as 'barbarians' by the Greeks in a variety of contexts, see the references in Worthington 2008: 8; Hammond 1994a: 3.

[12] On the uniqueness and 'separateness' of ancient Macedonians, see Borza 1996, responding to Badian 1982; cf. also Hammond 1995 (against Hammond's subdivisions of the Macedonian people, however, see Rhodes with Lewis 1997: 192–3); Borza 1982a. On modern appropriations of the same problem, see Danforth 2003.

[13] See e.g. the papers in Morgan 2003.   [14] Osborne 2003: 251, with quotation and references.

[15] King 2010: 380 (suggesting that the institution would have seemed "extremely outdated" from a Greek perspective); Worthington 2008: 9; Hammond 1994a: 3. Carney 1996: 21 n. 11 collects references on "the generally Homeric nature of many Macedonian values and institutions" (note amongst her listings Edson 1970 esp. 22–4); see also the references in note 127, below.

that the Greeks believed they had deliberately eliminated from their own civic power structures.[16]

Although much of what is known – and believed – about Macedonian institutions derives from evidence pertaining to Philip and Alexander, some generalizations about the king's position may be carefully ventured. The Macedonian monarch's rule, as King puts it, "seems to have had a strong personal nature."[17] While the king may have gained some legitimacy through the political support of his people,[18] his direct access to natural resources, physical assets, and the army served as important sources for his power.[19] He also derived authority from his military accomplishments, his success in battle, his benefactions to his men, and his participation in the same day-to-day experiences as those under his command.[20] Closer to his inner circle, he tended to cultivate the allegiance of nobles who might occupy positions of trust in the army or the administration, and to cement his bonds with them through further ritualized and performative behaviors. Some of the best known of these, including the Macedonian variants of the *symposion*[21] and the hunt,[22] differed appreciably from contemporary Greek customs, and seem at times to have provoked disapproval from outsiders.[23]

Appearances and performance were important for the king both on the battlefield and at court, but there also remained the issue of his image before the more ordinary peoples of his kingdom. It is not entirely clear how this was constructed before the complex 'programs' of Philip and Alexander, but it seems possible that religious leadership by the royal dynasty played a role,[24] and coinage probably also helped to promulgate the king's messages, especially once it came to include his name.[25] Here, again, practices seem to have differed from those of most Greek poleis: While politics and religious ritual were often closely intertwined amongst the Greeks, authority in the former area did not necessarily guarantee primacy in the latter as it might

---

[16] On Greek "anti-tyranny legislation" during the classical and Hellenistic periods, see Teegarden 2013.

[17] King 2010: 378.

[18] For different perspectives on the authority and activities of an "assembly of Makedones," see Worthington 2008: 11–12; Worthington 2003: 72–3; Hammond 1980: 461–5. A detailed examination of the problem from both sides is King 2010: 384–8.

[19] King 2010: 379.   [20] Carney 1996 esp. 28–9.   [21] See note 179, below.

[22] See Carney 2002; cf. also Bosworth 2002: 275–7; Palagia 2000.   [23] Worthington 2008: 8–11.

[24] Christesen and Murray 2010: 440–1, citing King 2010 (see esp. 380).

[25] See the recent survey by Dahmen 2010, with additional bibliography; on the potential meaning of the earliest Macedonian coinage, see Borza 1990: 126–9; on coinage with the king's name, see ibid. 173.

have done in Macedon,[26] and Greek coins were generally issued by states, not by statesmen.

Even by the mid fourth century BC, then, important distinctions remained between the Greek and Macedonian cultures. During this period, the Macedonian kings who would aspire both to stable reigns at home and to history-making recognition in the wider Greek world faced a particular challenge: They had to present themselves before audiences whose established models for cultural prominence were at times quite different from one another.[27] Here Philip enjoyed something of an advantage, having spent part of his adolescence as a hostage at Thebes[28] during its hegemony over the Boeotian League,[29] and likely having become acquainted with Greek warcraft, politics, and culture thereby.[30] Later in his life, harnessing what he had continued to learn, he controlled his public image with especial care:[31] Indeed, much of the evidence suggests that Philip exploited pre-existing *Greek* models of symbolic and literary discourse in order to cast himself as the new chief agent of Greek history.[32]

Material evidence for Philip's portrayal of himself and for his reception by the Greeks can be classified into three major categories: numismatic, archaeological, and epigraphic.[33] Philip's coins circulated widely,[34] and the repertory of their designs would have served as constant reminders of the image he wished to promulgate. The cities and sacred sites of Macedon advertised themselves to only a limited number of traveling Greeks, but some of these included members of diplomatic delegations[35] whose speeches (most notably those of Demosthenes and Aeschines) about their experiences were powerful public propaganda. As such, the potential impact of places like Pella cannot be discounted. Likely to have been viewed by far more Greeks, however, are the monuments and documents related to Philip that

---

[26] Christesen and Murray 2010: 440–1.

[27] Badian 1982 surveys this situation down the length of the Argead dynasty, concluding with what he views as the most successful (although never completely seamless) efforts at cultural "integration" exerted by Alexander. Stewart 1993: 86–90 reviews the problems facing Alexander in this same regard, not only amongst the Greeks but amongst the Eastern peoples as well; see also Faraguna 2003 (again on Alexander, but with some introductory comments on Philip).

[28] See Hammond 1997; Heskel 1987: 37–8.   [29] See Chapter 6, above.   [30] Hammond 1997.

[31] Roebuck 1948: 74–5, 89–90 is amongst those who refer to Philip's program as "propaganda" (74 and n. 11); see also Sakellariou 1980: 126.

[32] My general thinking about Philip's material program is fundamentally influenced by the scope, content, and methodology of the study of Alexander by Stewart 1993.

[33] Hammond 1994a: 11, ranking these resources as being more useful than the literary evidence for understanding Philip.

[34] Le Rider 1977: 437.

[35] On the size and composition of Athenian (and Spartan) embassies during the classical period, see Mosley 1965.

were set up in the Greek cities and sanctuaries. There are no surviving portrait-statues from Philip's lifetime,[36] but the Philippeum at Olympia, for example, apparently built to display chryselephantine family portraits, is of particular symbolic importance. The epigraphical evidence, while not abundant, comes from a variety of locations and shows Philip's documents employing typical Greek parlance and Greek forms – but alongside unique articulations of the Macedonian king's special role in diplomacy and warfare.

The literary sources are diverse, if scattered.[37] The historiographic corpus on Philip has some works in common with the body of Alexander writings. Two representatives from the 'Vulgate' tradition on the son[38] provide treatment of the father as well: Diodorus (book 16) and Justin (books 7–9).[39] Plutarch's *Lives* of Phocion, Alexander, and (especially) Demosthenes also offer a few pieces of information. These authors, in particular the first two, are valuable not only for the construction of a narrative of Philip's career, but also, despite their difficulties and biases, for an understanding of his longer-term reception. They are all of later date, but *Quellenforschung* has suggested some of their possible fourth-century sources.[40]

Philip is also represented in other literature that was composed during his lifetime. He entered into the speeches and essays of the Attic orators soon after his ascent to the Macedonian throne.[41] Eminent individuals such as Themistocles and Miltiades frequently served the fourth-century orators as rhetorical *topoi* (cf. Chapter 5, above); so, too, did a more recent figure, Alcibiades.[42] But all of these famous men had long since passed from public view. The pervasive and recurring debate over the potential impact of Philip *during* his active career therefore represents a special topic in extant Athenian public discourse. While this development reflects both political realia and strong personal biases, it also shows the extent to which a 'foreign'

---

[36] Prag, Musgrave, and Neave 1984: 70–4 collect bibliography on Philip portraiture; amongst their references, note esp. (70 n. 22) Richter 1965: vol. III, 253.

[37] This overview mentions only the texts – all continuous save for Theopompus – that will be employed in this chapter's discussion. For convenient lists of these and other literary sources on Philip, including the remaining fragmentary authors and the continuous writers who deal with Philip in brief or in passing fashion, see Worthington 2008: 210–15; Hammond 1994a: 11–17.

[38] For an overview of the literary sources on Alexander, see Baynham 2003; cf. also Chapter 8, below.

[39] Justin was in fact epitomizing part of the lost *Historia Philippica* of Pompeius Trogus, a large work composed in the earliest days of the Roman Empire and centering upon the Hellenistic dynasties. On the nature of Trogus' work, see Alonso-Núñez 1987.

[40] Hammond 1937b, 1938a, and 1991, examining Diodorus' and Justin's sources and attempting to recapture attitudes towards Philip expressed in lifetime and near-lifetime (now lost) historiographic literature. The results of this work are summarized in Hammond 1994a: 12–17, but cf. also the review of the latter by Whitby 1995.

[41] See note 37, above.   [42] See Gribble 1999 esp. 90–158.

individual could capture the attention of politicians who believed that he could affect the course of their history.

There are also, finally, comparatively substantial fragmentary remains[43] of the historian Theopompus, who was a contemporary of Philip and dealt in detail with the king's career.[44] As with Xenophon's *Agesilaus*, one of the earliest known biographical encomia,[45] Theopompus' work seems to have innovated upon generic conventions. While his *Hellenica* was apparently a conventional work of history intended to treat the years 411–394 BC,[46] his second and much longer project (for whose composition he may have halted his earlier one)[47] was strikingly titled *Philippica*. Originally fifty-eight books in length, the *Philippica* incorporated a wide variety of historical and non-historical material structured around the reign of Philip, who is said to have figured prominently in approximately sixteen books of the text.[48] Whether Theopompus' overall depiction of his main character was positive or critical,[49] Philip seems to have served him simultaneously as a framework for the narration of history and as a central figure within that narrative, further blurring the generic line between history and biography.

7.2 'Speaking' Greek: Philip's public image in the material evidence

As a monarch aspiring to imperial power, Philip enjoyed vast wealth and a geographic reach that extended far beyond the influence of even the highest-placed leaders of the Greek poleis. He was therefore able to embark upon a diverse publicity campaign involving multiple media. Much of what may have impressed Greeks might also have been designed to impress

---

[43] The difficulties of working with these fragments in detail are outlined by Flower 1997: 1–10, who counts 598 lines of verbatim quotations *in toto* (8).

[44] Theopompus was not the only important historian working during the king's lifetime; on the others, including Ephorus, Anaximenes of Lampsacus, and Callisthenes, see note 37, above; Flower 1997: 2–3. Amongst these, Anaximenes is most likely to have taken specific interest in Philip: see ibid. 40–1, 55.

[45] See Chapter 6, above.   [46] Flower 1997: 27.

[47] See ibid. 29–31 for collected references. Flower (31 n. 26) agrees with Jacoby *FGrH* 115 and Bruce 1987 that the *Hellenica* was interrupted or abandoned rather than completed according to a plan for concluding at Cnidus.

[48] Flower 1997: 29, citing *FGrH* 115 T 31.

[49] The fragments do not permit certain reconstruction of the historian's overall stance on his subject: see the references collected by Flower 1997: 3 n. 8 (esp. Connor 1967); Shrimpton 1977. Flower's own assessment is that Theopompus saw no redeeming value in Philip at all: see Flower 1997: 98–135.

Macedonians, particularly in the cases of circulating items, like coins, or sites located within the borders of Macedon. But inscriptions and monuments erected in Greece proper were probably intended primarily for the Greeks themselves, and therefore 'spoke' a Greek symbolic language. Philip appeared on his artifacts and in his monuments in multiple guises, many of which were already observable in the choices and behaviors of eminent Greeks from the fifth and earlier fourth centuries. He presented himself as a victorious athlete, insurmountable general, and leading statesman; as being favored by the gods; and even as a quasi-divinity.[50]

Known heroizations for victorious athletes seem to have peaked rather earlier than Philip's time,[51] but the discourse of athletic honors remained fertile and active in Greece during the fourth century and beyond.[52] Philip exploited this model in several different ways, most notably on the reverses of his coin issues and through his construction efforts at the heart of the Greek athletic world, in the Altis at Olympia.

Philip's name evoked aristocratic connections with horsemanship,[53] but the image was even more powerful than the word, because it was meaningful both inside and outside of Macedon. A rider could be interpreted as being connected with racing,[54] with the hunt (a potent image amongst the Macedonian nobility),[55] or with the command of cavalry;[56] a charioteer might also be associated with athletic victories or with the divine.[57] One of these two general images, rider or charioteer, manifested in a variety of designs, appears on most of Philip's coin reverses.[58] The equestrian imagery would likely have had greatest potency for the Greek world in recalling the king's victory in the *kelês* (single-horse) race at Olympia, and probably in the chariot-race as well.[59] Philip's entry into the contests there as a

---

[50] See note 32, above.   [51] See Connolly 1998: 16–17, 21.   [52] E.g. van Bremen 2007.

[53] See Head 1911: 224, who suggests that this may have provided an opportunity for punning references in the coin imagery; cf. also Golden 1997: 330–1, 335–6, also offering the reminder (333) that the elite associations of the *hipp-* word-root in Greek are perhaps nowhere more bluntly explored than in the opening scene of Aristophanes' *Clouds* (Ar. *Nub.* esp. 12–125).

[54] See note 58, below.   [55] See note 22, above.

[56] As Spence shows, popular perceptions of cavalry seem to have differed between poleis and regions, but the association of mounted fighters with socio-economic elites seems to be generally constant: see Spence 1993: 164–75 on the ways that ideas about hoplites affected views on cavalry, 176–8 on the role of cavalry in the Macedonian military and elsewhere in the north, and 180–230 on particularly Athenian interpretations of cavalry.

[57] Cf. note 73, below.

[58] Head 1911: 224. On the general iconography of *all* of the reverses, including those of the bronze issues, see ibid. 223–4. In more detail for the gold and silver only, see Le Rider 1977 pls. 1–95, whose chronological and geographical groupings often include iconographic clusters, as well.

[59] Head in note 58, above, and Golden 1997: 335, who registers the event and lists the *kelês* win as having occurred in either the year 383 or 382.

Macedonian was a generally 'Hellenizing' gesture that symbolized shared elite values and appealed to precedents established back in the fifth century.[60] It was probably also a way of invoking Heracles, the paradigmatic athlete-hero[61] who was also a putative ancestor of and a very important symbol for the Macedonian royal house,[62] without Philip's having to participate physically in the sporting events.[63]

Heroic connections alone, however, would not have sufficed if Philip was to establish the positive feedback loop that he needed to consolidate his power. His self-presentation before the Greeks as a victorious general and successful statesman would sketch him as a historical agent for a culture that viewed history as consisting centrally of military and political affairs.[64] If he was able to promulgate the idea that "the Greeks" could accomplish great things with him as their leader, or that he himself could perform history-making actions on their collective behalf, he might be able to inspire and maintain their loyalty.[65] By this point in the fourth century, Philip might follow exempla established by previous eminent Greek leaders in multiple media. Monuments and statuary commemorating political and military achievements would be helpful for his project; so would decrees that reflected positively upon his accomplishments, whether the king was the one conferring benefactions or receiving honors.

No statues or inscribed bases erected by Philip or by others during his lifetime survive. Literary testimonia, however, suggest that Philip did use this particular outlet for self-promotion. As collected by Bieber and by Stewart,[66] the lost statues likely include, conservatively,[67] the chryselephantine statue

---

[60] See Golden 1997: 330–1. On attempts to legitimize the 'Greek' origins of the Argeads, see Borza 1982a; Heskel 1997: 168–9 also offers a summary of the actions taken by Alexander I (d. 452) in order to 'legalize' his participation at Olympia as a Greek and claim Greek ancestry for the Argead dynasty.

[61] E.g. Fontenrose 1968 esp. 86; for a case-study of the invocation of heroism by an athlete employing Heracles imagery, see Currie 2002: 35–41; on broader uses of the Heracles model from Alexander to Augustus, see Anderson 1928.

[62] The Argead dynasty to which Philip belonged traced its family origins back to Heracles (Fredricksmeyer 2003: 254 n. 1 collects ancient references), and Philip's immediate predecessors, like Philip himself, had depicted Heracles on their coins, e.g. the silver coinage of Amyntas III (r. 393–370) and Perdiccas III (r. 365–359): Kraay and Hirmer 1966: nos. 560–1, pl. 169 (a bearded and a youthful Heracles, respectively).

[63] Golden 1997: 333, 336–7. Victory in horse-races or chariot-races in the Greek games was awarded to the owner of the horses, not to the jockey or charioteer; on the evolution of commemorative responses to this inherent ideological challenge during the archaic and earlier classical periods, see Nicholson 2005 passim, esp. the summary of the arguments at 1–18.

[64] See Chapter 1, above.   [65] See esp. Chapters 4–6, above.

[66] Bieber 1949: 377–9; Stewart 1993: 105–6, 171–2, 386–8. Cf. also Richter 1984: 224.

[67] Stewart 1993: 412, using Lucian as an example, rightly cautions against interpreting every literary reference to an artifact or monument as evidence for a lost portrait.

in the Philippeum at Olympia (cf. below); the statue carried in procession at the wedding of Philip's daughter Cleopatra, at which Philip was assassinated (cf. below);[68] bronze statues with Alexander by Chaereas and by Euphranor (the latter probably a chariot depiction);[69] a statue with Alexander in the Athenian Agora, erected by the Athenians following the settlement after Chaeronea;[70] and a statue in the temple of Artemis at Ephesus, erected by the Ephesians.[71] Bieber believes that Philip statues stood in Pella and Philippopolis, as well.[72]

Even though the testimonia on the Chaereas and Euphranor examples are scanty, the chariot imagery of the Euphranor group could have evoked connotations of athletic competition and even of Homeric heroism.[73] But the statues said to have been raised by the Ephesians and the Athenians offer additional insight as to how Philip was received by those who wanted (or needed) his peaceful alliance and support. Stewart calls special attention to the Ephesus testimonium (Paus. 6.3.15–16) and characterizes the statues of Lysander, Conon, and Timotheus set up there as "a series of portraits of victorious liberators," culminating in the images of Philip and Alexander that were later added to the temple.[74] Pausanias, however, is also working here with a larger theme: adulation by the eastern Greeks. For Pausanias, "Samian" and "Ephesian" simply represent subsets of "Ionian," and so he

---

[68] Bieber 1949: 378, citing D.S. 16.92.2.

[69] Stewart 1993: 387–8; Bieber 1949: 378, both citing Plin. *Nat. Hist.* 34.75 and 78, respectively. Stewart 1993: 106 (with references) notes that some interpreters take one of these pairs of statues to be those erected in the Athenian Agora (see note 70, below).

[70] Bieber 1949: 378, citing Paus. 1.9.4 and Clement of Alexandria, *Protrepticus* 4.54.5; Stewart 1993: 387, also citing Pausanias. Stewart 1993: 105–6 notes that some interpreters take these Philip and Alexander statues to be identical with one set of Pliny the Elder's bronzes by Chaereas and by Euphranor (see note 69, above).

[71] Bieber 1949: 378, citing Arr. 1.17.11, believes that this statue was posthumous; Stewart 1993: 171–2 counts it as an image erected during Philip's lifetime. I follow Stewart's interpretation here, as there would have been little specific reason for the addition of Philip to what Stewart characterizes as a "liberator" series after his assassination, unless to please Alexander. That latter goal was surely advanced in any case by the Apelles painting (of Alexander himself) added to the sanctuary during Alexander's visit to Ephesus in 334 BC: Stewart 1993: 171–2, 363–4, with testimonia and references.

[72] Bieber 1949: 378, but without testimonia. Stewart 1993: 105 suggests that another fourth-century dedication mentioned in the literature, a bronze group from Olympia set up by the Eleans that included a statue of Philip (see also ibid. 388), was posthumous to both Philip and Alexander; other possible groups likely posthumous to both kings might include one in Larissa (ibid. 411–12) and a diverse series at Olympia, Delphi, Athens, and Alexandria (ibid. 412–13). There were probably also quite a number of paintings made of Philip, both during and after his lifetime: see ibid. 375, citing Plin. *Nat. Hist.* 35.93–4.

[73] Goh 2004: 7–16 analyzes chariot-driving in Homeric poetry and suggests that "driving a chariot signifies an act of emulation of the heroic past and the divine" (15).

[74] Stewart 1993: 171.

traces their respective dedications throughout the Aegean to argue that they shifted their allegiances from Athens to Sparta and back to Athens again in the course of only a few decades. His examination of the statuary suggests that "the Ionians" took careful account of the internal power structures of the states that they were courting, and that they saw the decision-making power of those states as depending upon eminent individuals.[75] The theme of adulation also emerges from the images of Philip and Alexander in the Athenian Agora, which were probably set up as a thank-offering for Philip's moderation towards Athens after Chaeronea.[76] Even given the proliferation of honorific statues in a variety of locations at Athens during the fourth century,[77] such rapid acknowledgement of a conqueror seems representative of the very issues of agency noted by Demosthenes and discussed above at the opening of Chapter 1.[78]

As the victor of Chaeronea, then, Philip had established himself as pre-eminent in mainland Greece, a political and military position he would shortly reify by having himself named *hegemôn* of the newly founded League of Corinth. Hegemony was quite easily construed by the Greeks as belonging to states that dominated their alliance groups, as Thebes had done between Leuctra and Mantinea. In the case of Philip, however, as Ellis puts it, "for formal purposes, the king himself *was* the state,"[79] and this is, in fact, the articulation that occurs most frequently in Greek inscriptions that mention him.[80] It is not unique to him alone, nor is it new: the use of the ruler's name as a metonym for his people occurs in inscriptions (especially treaties)

---

[75] It is perhaps for reasons like these that proxeny seems to have flourished in the fourth century, both as a form of patronage and as a kind of diplomacy: e.g. Buckler 1998: 198, discussing the extension of *proxenia* to Epaminondas by the Cnidians (on this inscription, see Chapter 6, above), and see more generally Culasso Gastaldi 2004 (on proxenies of Athens granted in Asia).

[76] Stewart 1993: 105–6; Bieber 1949: 377. On the terms of the settlement, see Roebuck 1948: 80–2.

[77] On dedications in the Agora, see the testimonia collected by Wycherley 1957: 207; on the Acropolis in the fourth century, see the general comments of Keesling 2003: 166–8; and on the Acropolis in relationship to other locations as classical habits transition to Hellenistic ones, see Keesling 2007.

[78] These statues, like those in the temple of Artemis at Ephesus discussed above, also provoke contempt from Pausanias: see Paus. 1.9.4 as cited by Stewart 1993: 387.

[79] Ellis 1976: 21; emphasis mine.

[80] Ibid. For examples, see amongst the primary sources the alliance between Philip and the Chalcidians, discussed at note 93, below; *IG* ii² 127 = Tod 1948: 167–70 no. 157 (an alliance between Athens on the one hand and Cetriporis, Lyppeius, and Grabus on the other); Tod 1948: 209–14 no. 172 (an example of the parlance in Delphic inscriptions cited by Ellis 1976: 21, 24); and the creation of the League of Corinth discussed at note 97, below. Further useful commentary, bibliography, and cross-references for all of these examples (save *IG* ii² 127) may be found in Harding 1985, who includes them in his collection of sources, via the concordance at 207–8.

dealing with Thracian and Macedonian leaders as early as the fifth century.[81] But this parlance acquires additional potency at a time when the ascription of historical agency to individuals is becoming increasingly dominant amongst the Greeks, and when honors to individuals, including proxenies, are proliferating.[82]

Although the epigraphical evidence even on Alexander is not so abundant as might be expected,[83] and that on Philip is more limited still, several important inscriptions do suggest the extent to which Philip presented himself before – and was received by – the Greeks as an individual with the means and the position to make history. In particular, a number of documents treating Macedon show a particularly sharp contrast between group and individual as they describe relationships between various Greek poleis on the one hand and "Philip" or his representatives on the other.[84] Surveying them in roughly chronological order, as Hornblower suggests, demonstrates the changing reception of Philip over time.[85]

Hornblower interprets *SEG* 21.246 as "Athenian politeness to envoys *from* Philip at the *beginning* of his reign, no doubt passed in a spirit of condescension towards the new man up there ('how long will he last?')."[86] The document itself is restored by Meritt as follows:[87]

---

[81] Some examples include the following: Thrace, fourth century: *IG* ii² 126, ed. with commentary Rhodes and Osborne 2003: 234–7 no. 47, dated to 357 BC; *IG* ii² 127, ed. with commentary Rhodes and Osborne 2003: 254–9 no. 53, dated to 356/5 BC. Macedon, fifth century: Meiggs and Lewis 1969: 176–80 no. 65; Meiggs and Lewis 1969: 277–80 no. 91. On Thessaly, where the situation was somewhat more complicated due to the presence of both an archon and a *tagos* for the *koinon*, see Rhodes and Osborne 2003: 218–24 no. 44, where the dissolution of an alliance with a *tagos* is part of the terms for forging one with an archon and "the Thessalians." Cf. also the fourth-century inscriptions "in which the king stands for the people as contrahent to a treaty" collected by Perlman 1985: 170 n. 79.

[82] See Chapters 4–6, above, and on proxeny e.g. Henry 1983: 116–62.

[83] See Heisserer 1980, who collects most of the known Alexander evidence into a single volume, with commentary.

[84] Ellis 1976: 21, 24 notes that lists of delegates (*hieromnemones*) to the Delphic Amphictyony include "those from Philip" and later "those from Alexander" alongside (e.g.) "Dorians."

[85] Hornblower 1984: 242 suggests the possibility of studying "the impact of monarchy in . . . fourth century Macedon" through the use of several inscriptions, amongst them two expressly related to Philip that I adopt and analyze in more detail: Tod 1948: 237–8 no. 181 = *SIG* 262; and *SEG* 21.246. Hornblower also points out an important change in attitude from the latter to the former that recommended the chronological treatment here: my slightly broader sampling and closer reading of this material argues strongly that Hornblower is correct.

[86] Hornblower 1984: 242, emphases *sic*.

[87] *SEG* 21.246 = Woodhead 1997: 78, citing Meritt's restorations and offering a tentative date for the inscription of *c.* 364 or 359/8, with a question mark. Edition here from Woodhead. Restorations are translated but not marked; no argument will be made from the restorations.

[- - - - - - - - - - - - - - - - - -]

[- - - - - - - -]ΟΙΣ[- - - - -]

[- - - - εὔ]νοιαν· [ἐπαινέσαι]

[δὲ καὶ τοὺ]ς πρ̣έσβε[ις αὐτοῦ]

[καὶ στε]φανῶσαι θαλ[λοῦ στεφά]

5 [νωι, ἐπ]ε̣[ι]δὴ καὶ κοινεῖ [καὶ ἰδίαι]

[ἀποφαίνουσ]ιν τὴ[ν] εὔν[οιαν τὴν]

[τοῦ βασιλέως] τῶν Μακ[εδόνων..]

[- - - - - - -]Ε[- - - - - - - - - - - - -]

[- -]

... favorable disposition. And to praise
his ambassadors
and to crown them with a crown of olive
because both in common and singly[88]
they demonstrate the favorable disposition
of the king of the Macedonians ...

By the mid fourth century inscriptions offering honors like these, particularly at Athens, have come to feel routine. The language here is of a general type frequently observed during this period,[89] and may therefore show the Athenians simply going through a set of expected motions, as with the honors paid to native Athenian envoys around the same time.[90] The dating of this inscription is admittedly not secure: it may not refer to Philip, but rather to his predecessor in the monarchy, Perdiccas III; conversely, there are also some peculiarities in the specific wording of the honorifics that might recommend a date later by several decades.[91] Assuming that the *presbeis* of the inscription are indeed from Macedon, however, the document still offers insight into the Athenian reception of external delegates: in the performance of a familiar story, they are treated with familiar language to familiar honors that seem to outstrip the significance of their services, at least so far as the generic text can tell.[92]

During the 350s, as Philip began to expand his activities outside of Macedonia, several other inscriptions record his activities. A very careful and

---

[88] Or "both publicly and personally."

[89] Henry 1983: 38–9, correctly noting, however (38), that this particular inscription may represent an early example of the typology.

[90] Ibid. 39–40; cf. Chapter 5, above.

[91] Woodhead 1997: 78–9, with references, also noting that downdating the inscription would pose problems for its historical context that would likely call for a different reading in l. 7.

[92] It is important that a projection of tone not be made based upon whether one wishes to date the inscription before or after Chaeronea.

detailed treaty between Philip and the Chalcidians, dated to 357/6, contains some striking features.[93]

[————————————————————————————] *traces*

ἔχοντε[ς]

[————————————— συμμα]χίην [—————————]ς ᵛ

συμμαχήσω κατ-

[ὰ τὰ ὡμολογημένα. ᵛ Χαλκιδέων] μὲν ὀμνύει[ν] Φιλίπ[πω]ι τὰς [ἀρ]χὰς τὰ<ς>

ξυνὰς καὶ τού-

[ς πρεσβευτάς(?)· τοῖς δὲ Χαλκι]δεῦσι αὐτὸν καὶ οὓς ἂν ἄλλους Χαλκιδεῖς κελεύσω-

5   [σι· ὀμνύειν δ'αὐτοὺς ἀδόλως κ]αὶ ἀτεχνέως, ναὶ μὰ Δία, Γῆν, Ἥλιομ, Ποσει- δῶνα·

εὐορ-

[κέουσι μὲμ πολλὰ καὶ ἀγαθὰ γί]νεσθαι, ἐπιορκέουσι δὲ πολλ[ὰ] καὶ κακά· ὀμνύειν

δὲ τάμνο-

[ντας ὅρκια ἀμφοτέρους. τὰ] δὲ γράμμ[α]τα τάδε γράψαι κη[στή]λην καὶ τὴμ

μαντείην τὴ-

[ν ὑπὸ τοῦ θεοῦ δεδομένην περ]ὶ τῆς συμ[μ]αχίης Χαλκιδέ[ας μ]ὲν ἀναθεῖν ἐς τὸ

ἱε[ρ]ὸν τῆ-

[ς Ἀρτέμιδος ἐν Ὀλύνθοι, Φίλιππον δ' ἐ]ν Δίοι ἐς [τὸ] ἱερὸν τοῦ Διὸς τ[οῦ]

Ὀλυμπίου, καὶ ἐς Δελφοὺς μα-

10   [αντείης τε καὶ στήλης ἀντίγρα]φα θεῖναι. τῶν δὲ γραμμάτ[ω]ν τῶνδ' ἐξεῖν κοινῶι

λόγωι χρό-

[νωι τριῶν μηνῶν (?) διορθοῦσθαι ὅ]τι ἂν δοκῆι Φιλίππωι καὶ [Χαλ]κιδεῦσι. *vacat*

[ἔχρησεν ὁ θεὸς Χαλκιδεῦσι κ]αὶ Φιλίππωι λῶ[ι]όν τε κα[ὶ ἄμει]νον εἴμεμ φίλους τε

καὶ

[συμμάχους γίνεσθαι κατὰ τὰ ὡμο]λογημένα. θῦσαι δὲ καὶ [καλ]λιερῆσαι Διὶ

Τελέοι καὶ

[Ὑπάτωι, Ἀπόλλωνι Προστατηρίωι], Ἀρτέμιδι {⟦ο⟧ρ} Ὀρθ[ω]σίαι, Ἑρμ[ῆι]·

καὶ κατὰ τύχαν ἀγαθὰν ᵛ

---

[93] Edition and translation here from Rhodes and Osborne 2003: 244–8 no. 50.

15   [ἐπεύχεσθαι τὰν συμμαχίαν] ἐσσεῖσθαι· καὶ Πυθ[ῶδ]ε τῶ[ι Ἀ]πόλλωνι

χαριστήρια *vacat*

[ἀποδιδόναι, καὶ μνασιδωρ]εῖν.

vacat

- - - having - - - alliance - - -

2   I shall be an ally in accordance with what has been agreed.

3   Of the Chalcidians there shall swear to Philip the common officials and the envoys; to the Chalcidians, himself and such others as the Chalcidians command. They shall swear without deceit and without craft, by Zeus, Earth, Sun, Poseidon, that to those who keep the oath there shall be much good but to those who break the oath much ill. Both parties shall swear oath-sacrifices.

7   These writings shall be written on a *stele*, and the oracle given by the God about the alliance the Chalcidians shall dedicate in the sanctuary of Artemis at Olynthus, and Philip at Dium in the sanctuary of Olympian Zeus, and copies of the oracle and *stele* shall be placed at Delphi.

10   It shall be permitted to amend these writings by common discussion in a period of three months (?), whatever is resolved by Philip and the Chalcidians.

12   The God responded to the Chalcidians and Philip:

12   It is preferable and better to become friends and allies in accordance with the agreement. Sacrifice and obtain good omens from Zeus Teleos and Hypatos, Apollo Prostaterios, Artemis Orthosia, Hermes; and pray that the alliance will be with good fortune; and give back thank-offerings to Pythian Apollo, and remember your gifts.

Not only does the parlance here represent "Philip" on one side and "the Chalcidians" on the other (especially ll. 3–4), but the formulae of alliance incorporate an abundance of religious assurances: oaths to be taken in the names of "Zeus, Earth, Sun, Poseidon" (l. 5); promises of binding sacrifices (ll. 6–7); reference to a Delphic oracle about the agreement (ll. 7–8) being recorded and publicly erected in multiple sanctuaries (ll. 8–10); and a repetition of what appears to be the text of the oracle itself (ll. 12–16).[94] The extreme degree of caution captured in this treaty, represented by the constant appeals to the divine, may have been prompted by either or both parties, but as has been observed, Philip's forging of a positive connection

---

[94]   Ibid. 248, noting that "universal silence [on this issue] suggests that it was not normal practice to obtain an oracle before agreeing to a treaty." Possible political and propagandistic motivations for the incorporation of the oracle vary (see ibid. 248–9, with references), but they all generally suggest an atmosphere of apprehension and a desire to jockey for the upper hand.

between himself and Delphi (culminating in his involvement in the Third Sacred War) would have served as a powerful propaganda tool,[95] and this inscription might reflect consciousness of that development.[96]

The treaty that followed the battle of Chaeronea and established the League of Corinth shows the same degree of care, although here the energy appears to have been lavished upon providing wording to address as many contingencies as possible. Only the first fragment of the stele (*a*) is quoted and discussed here; the *b* fragment, badly damaged, simply lists signatories in civic and regional groups (as opposed to individual proper names).[97]

[————————— 26 —————————] | [—— 6 ——]

[ὅρκος. ὀμνύω (?) Δία, Γῆν, Ἥλιον, Ποσ]ειδῶ, Ἀ[θηνᾶ]-

[ν, Ἄρη, θεοὺς πάντας καὶ πάσα]ς ἐμμενῶ [ἐν τῆ]-

[ι εἰρήνηι· (?) καὶ οὔτε τὰς σ]υνθήκας τὰ[ς πρ]-

5   [ὸς Φίλιππον καταλύσω, (?)· οὔτ]ε ὅπλα ἐποί[σω ἐ]-

[πὶ πημονῆι ἐπ' οὐθένα τῶν] ἐμμενόντων ἐν τ-

[οῖς ὅρκοις (?) οὔτε κατὰ γῆν] οὔτε κατὰ θάλασ-

[σαν· οὐδὲ πόλιν οὐδὲ φρο]ύριον καταλήψομ-

[αι οὐδὲ λιμένα ἐπὶ πολέ]μωι οὐθενὸς τῶν τ-

10   [ῆς εἰρήνης κοινωνούντ]ων τέχνηι οὐδεμι-

[ᾶι οὐδὲ μηχανῆι· οὐδὲ τ]ὴν βασιλείαν [τ]ὴν Φ-

[ιλίππου καὶ τῶν ἐκγόν]ων καταλύσω, ὀδὲ τὰ-

[ς πολιτείας τὰς οὔσας] παρ' ἑκάστοις ὅτε τ-

[οὺς ὅρκους τοὺς περὶ τῆ]ς εἰρήνης ὤμνυον·

15   [οὐδ' αὐτὸς οὐθὲν ὑπενα]ντίον ταῖσδε ταῖς

[συνθήκαις ποήσω οὐδ' ἄλ]λωι ἐπιτρέψω εἰς

[δύναμιν. ἂν δέ τις ποῆι τι] παράσπονδον πε-

[ρὶ τὰς συνθήκας, βοηθήσω] καθότι ἂν παραγ-

[γέλλωσιν οἱ ἀδικούμενοι (?)], καὶ πολεμήσω τῶ-

20   [ι τὴν κοινὴν εἰρήνην (?) παρ]αβαίνοντι καθότι

[ἂν δοκῆι τῶι κοινῶι συνεδ]ρίωι καὶ ὁ ἡγεμώ-

[ν παραγγέλληι, καὶ οὐκ ἐγκ]αταλείψω το[..]

[————————— 23 —————————]σκ[—— 8 ——]

- - - - - - - - - -

2   Oath. I swear by Zeus, Earth, Sun, Poseidon,
        Athena, Ares, all the gods and goddesses: I shall

---

[95] E.g. Borza 1999: 57, citing (n. 19) Buckler 1989; Perlman 1985: 165, citing (n. 55) Nock 1942: 472 n. 2.

[96] Buckler 1989: 5 (cf. note 139, below).

[97] Edition and translation here from Rhodes and Osborne 2003: 372–5 no. 76.

abide by the peace (?); and I shall neither break
the agreement with Philip (?) nor take up arms for
harm against any of those who abide by the oaths (?),
neither by land nor by sea; nor shall I take any
city or guard-post nor harbour, for war, of any of
those participating in the peace, by any craft or
contrivance; nor shall I overthrow the kingdom
of Philip or his descendants, nor the constitutions
existing in each state when they swore the oaths
concerning the peace; nor shall I myself do anything contrary to those agreements, nor shall I
allow any one else as far as possible.

17   If any one does commit any breach of treaty
concerning the agreements, I shall go in support
as called on by those who are wronged (?), and I
shall make war against the one who transgresses
the common peace (?) as decided by the common
council (*synedrion*) and called on by the *hegemon*; and
I shall not abandon - - -

The most striking usages in this text appear in ll. 11–12 ([τ]ὴν βασιλείαν
[τ]ὴν Φ[ιλίππου καὶ τῶν ἐκγόν]ων καταλύσω) and in ll. 21–22 (ὁ ἡγεμώ[ν]).
Phraseology like "the kingdom of Philip" is not common elsewhere[98] and
the (likely) characterization of Philip himself as *hegemôn*, although neither
the term nor the concept was completely new at this point,[99] nevertheless simultaneously records and creates a situation where Philip is neither
equal nor *primus inter pares* to his co-signatories. Rhodes and Osborne
characterize the situation well:[100]

> What Philip has done in this treaty is combine several recent strands in
> recent Greek diplomacy, to dress up his control of mainland Greece in
> clothes which would be acceptable to the Greeks. A common peace treaty
> settles outstanding disputes and tries to guarantee . . . stability . . . ; the
> apparatus of a *hegemôn* and a *synedrion*, as in such leagues as the Second
> Athenian League, provides a mechanism for enforcing the peace . . . But
> behind this façade lies Philip's supremacy: the Greeks swore to uphold not
> only the constitutions of the member states but also the kingdom of Philip
> and his descendants.

---

[98] Ellis 1976: 21.
[99] Perlman 1985 esp. 169–74, arguing that Philip's terms and language here were grounded in (as
       the article is titled) "Greek diplomatic tradition."
[100] Rhodes and Osborne 2003: 378.

Late in Philip's reign, as Hornblower points out, the reaction of the Athenians to Philip as an individual turned to an attitude of flattery,[101] not only in the form of statuary (cf. above), but also in honorific decrees offered to Philip's officers and courtiers. Two in particular, from shortly before the king's assassination, are of especial interest.[102]

[Θ]ε[οί]. | Ἀλκιμά[χωι προξενία?. | Ἐ]πὶ Φρυνί[χου ἄρχοντος,
5   ἐπὶ τῆς Ἀ|κ]αμαντίδ[ος ἕκτης πρυτανείας, ἧ||1] Χαιρέσ[τρατος
Ἀμεινίου Ἀχαρν|εὐ]ς ἐγρα[μμάτευεν· Γαμηλιῶνος ἑ|βδόμ]ηι [ἱστα-
μένου - - -]

Gods. Proxeny for Alcimachus. In the archonship of Phrynichus, in the sixth prytany, of Acamantis, for which Chaerestratus the son of Ameinias the Acharnian was secretary. On the seventh day of Gamelion . . .

Θεο[ί. | Ἐπ]ὶ Φρυνίχου ἄρχοντος, [ἐπὶ τῆς Πα|νδ]ιονίδος δεκά-
5   της πρυ[τανείας, ἧ|ι Χ]αιρ[έσ]τρατος Ἀ[με]ινίο[υ Ἀχαρνε||ὺ]ς
[ἐγραμμ]άτευεν, τῶν προέ[δρων ἐπ|ε]ψ[ήφιζε]ν [Ἀ]ντιφάνης
Εὐων[υμεύς, ν | Δ]η[μάδης Δη]μέου Παιανιεὺ[ς εἶπεν· | ἀγα]θ[ῆι
τ]ύχηι [τ]οῦ δήμου το[ῦ Ἀθηναί]ων, δεδ]ό[χθ]αι τῶι δήμωι,
10   [ἐ]π[ειδὴ .. ||.....σ.....⌢..νδρον . ν [- 6 - | πρ]ὸ[ς τὸ]ν δῆμον
[τ]ὸν Ἀθην[α]ί[ων....|. κ]α[ὶ] ἐπιμελεῖται Ἀθηναί[ων τῶν ἀ|φικν]-
ο[υμ]ένων ὡς Φίλιππον, [πράττω]ν ἀγ]αθὸν ὅ,τι δύ[νατ]αι Ἀθη-
15   ν[αίοις π||αρ]ὰ [Φ]ιλίππου, ε[ἶνα]ι πρόξε[νον καὶ | εὐ]ε[ρ]γ[έ]την
τ[ο]ῦ [δήμ]ου τοῦ Ἀθ[ηναίω|ν, α]ὐτὸν καὶ ἐκγόνους αὐτο[ῦ, καὶ
ἐπ|ιμε]λεῖσθαι αὐτοῦ τὴμ βου[λὴν καὶ | τοὺ]ς στρατηγοὺς ὅτου ἂν
20   δ[έηται. Ἀ||να]γ[ρ]άψαι δὲ τὴν προξενία[ν εἰς στ|ήλην] λιθίνην,
καὶ στῆσαι [τὸν γραμ|ματέ]α [τ]ὸν κα[τ]ὰ πρυτανείαν ἐν ἀκρο-
πόλ]ει· εἰς [δ]ὲ τὴν ἀναγρ[αφὴν τῆς σ|τή]λης [δό]τω ὁ ταμίας
25   τριά[κοντα δρ||αχμ]ὰ[ς] κατὰ τὸν νόμον.

Gods. In the archonship of Phrynichus, in the tenth prytany, of Pandionis, for which Chaerestratus the son of Ameinias the Acharnian was secretary, and amongst the *proedroi* Antiphanes of Euonymus was putting it to the vote. Demades the son of Demeas of Paeania proposed: With good fortune for the *dêmos* of the Athenians, it has been resolved by the *dêmos*, since . . . towards the *dêmos* of the Athenians . . .

---

[101] See note 85, above, where Hornblower also invites the examination of Tod 1948: 237–8 no. 181 = *SIG* 262. The addition of Tod 1948: 236–7 no. 180 = *IG* ii² 239 is my own.

[102] Editions from Tod 1948: 236–7 no. 180 = *IG* II² 239 and Tod 1948: 237–8 no. 181 = *SIG* 262, respectively. Translations of recurring phraseology are adopted from Rhodes and Osborne 2003.

and he demonstrated care for the Athenians who were approaching
Philip, doing whatever good he was able for the Athenians
[when they were] with Philip, to be *proxenos* and benefactor
of the *dêmos* of the Athenians, him and his descendants, and
for the *boulê* and the generals to give their attention to him whenever
there is need. And for the secretary of the prytany to have the proxeny
inscribed on a stone stele and to set it up on the
Acropolis. And for the engraving of the stele let the treasurer provide
thirty drachmas, in accordance with the law.

The first inscription here, *IG* ii^2 239, (probably) notes only that Alcimachus
was made a *proxenos* of Athens – but this Alcimachus was one of Philip's
officers.[103] For someone of his rank and station to receive the honor of
Athenian proxeny barely a year and a half after Chaeronea[104] suggests that
Athens was making a special effort to court highly placed Macedonians,
surely with an eye on the disposition of their king. For this same
reason, Hornblower characterizes the attitude represented by the second
inscription above as "cowed":[105] The Athenians are seeking every means
at their disposal to gain favor, and the fact that both of these inscriptions
are passed in the same archon year further implies a pattern. The issue
of the proxeny in the second inscription is formulaic,[106] save for the
description of the reason behind it: the recipient of the honor "did
whatever good he was able" for the Athenians when their embassy
approached Philip. It is unlikely that the Athenians could have derived
benefit either from the offers of *proxenia* or from the display of the decrees
if a warmer connection between themselves and Philip was not desired and
intended by both sides, and so these inscriptions should be understood
as part of the same impulse that motivated the erection of the Philip
and Alexander statues in the Agora. They are not merely thank-offerings:
rather, they are gestures towards the establishment of a post-Chaeronea
relationship that is very different from what existed prior to the
battle.[107]

---

[103] Tod 1948: 237 no. 180; see also Heckel 1992: 96, 246–7, both with references.

[104] On the date of this inscription, see Tod 1948: 236–7 no. 180.   [105] See note 85, above.

[106] On the wording of fifth- and fourth-century proxeny decrees, see Henry 1983: 116–62. Useful
collections of examples include Lambert 2006: 127–36 (dealing specifically with the years
352/1–322/1); and by Culasso Gastaldi 2004 (on the fourth century), all with additional
references. On the fifth century, see Walbank 1978.

[107] Cf. Chapter 6, above, on the proxeny decree of the Cnidians for Epaminondas, which seems to
have had similar political purposes (Buckler 1998 esp. 198–202).

Philip's presentation of himself as a statesman is also reflected in his re-foundation of the former Thracian city of Crenides in 356 BC,[108] after it sought his protection from the surrounding peoples.[109] The gesture likely fitted well with Philip's larger plans early in his reign to consolidate his power in Macedonia, strengthen his borders, and take closer control of the rich natural resources of the north.[110] It was also part of the early escalation of his conflict with Athens. Philip's adoption of Crenides formed a strategic sequel and a geographic pairing to his capture of Amphipolis in 357, and *IG* ii² 127, dating to 356/5,[111] whether its decree was passed before or after Philip's intervention,[112] actually shows the Athenians promising to assist the Thracians in the takeover of the town.

But Philip could simply have strengthened the defenses of Crenides and installed a Macedonian garrison there. The formal colonization of the settlement as a 'new' one was a conscious choice and a highly symbolic gesture, particularly given the honors traditionally accorded colonial founders in the Greek world, and the experiences of recent Greek leaders who had imitated those models.[113] The original inhabitants of Crenides were Thasian Greeks,[114] and they were likely to have understood the ramifications of Philip's self-identification as their virtual new *ktistês*. The rapidity with which the Macedonian king literally and symbolically replaced Callistratus, an Athenian exile who had just led out the renewed colony from Thasos to Crenides in 360 BC,[115] exceeds even the then-unprecedented speed of the adoption of Brasidas at Amphipolis.[116] Whether Callistratus had ever been – or intended to be – honored by the colony as its *ktistês* remains unknown, but Philip's aspirations emerge far more strongly than his predecessor's.

The Macedonian king's decision to settle Crenides with Macedonians likely did not reflect so much a desire for cultural integration with Greeks as the need to foster the development of a local population that was loyal to him. Perhaps in part for this reason, Philip, as many have pointed out, took an additional step to remind the Crenidians, both Macedonian and Greek, of his sovereignty: he changed the city's name. From "spring-place," it became "the city of Philip": Philippi. This gesture in particular suggests

---

[108] D.S. 16.3.7, 8.6; see also Koukouli-Chrysanthaki and Bakirtzis 2000: 7, and esp. Sherman 1952: 243 n. 5 *ad* D.S. 16.3.7.

[109] Tod 1948: 170 no. 157, citing Collart 1937.   [110] See Borza 1987 and 1982b.

[111] See Sherman in note 108, above; cf. also note 81, above.

[112] See Phillips 2004: 70, citing Harding 1985; in the latter, see in particular 71 n. 11.

[113] See esp. Chapter 6, above.   [114] D.S. 16.3.7.

[115] See Koukouli-Chrysanthaki and Bakirtzis 2000: 7; Tod 1948: 170 no. 157, citing Collart 1937.

[116] See Chapter 6, above.

that Philip may have been seeking acknowledgement that reached beyond his throne, perhaps even treatment as an eponymous hero.[117]

While the renewal of Crenides as Philippi may have been an early harbinger of the civic foundations of the later Hellenistic monarchs, it was certainly not the last even of Philip's reign. There are at least three other attested cities named or renamed for Philip: Gomphi, in Thessaly, strategically located on the route into Epirus, was probably given new citizens and a new identity as "Philippopolis" or "Philippi";[118] a "Philippopolis" (now Plovdiv, Bulgaria) was founded in Thrace, perhaps from somewhat dispossessed peoples or even from hangers-on to Philip's reorganized Macedonian army;[119] and a "Philippoupolis" was created in the northeastern reaches of Macedonia itself.[120] Still closer to the most populous regions of mainland Greece, Phthiotic Thebes, in Thessaly, may also have been renamed "Philippi," if only temporarily.[121] This is to say nothing of the numerous other municipalities either organized or reorganized by Philip under preexisting local names. These were generally established near his borderlands in remote areas, settled by Macedonians, and probably primarily intended as defensive, rather than cultural, outposts.[122] Though the testimonia are somewhat scanty, they point towards efforts of consolidation and management on a broad scale. The widely scattered towns named for Philip himself would not only have advertised his efforts to unite his territory behind a single dynastic throne, but would also have eloquently demonstrated the kind of attention that he hoped to invite.[123]

Like his efforts to plant colonies and refound cities, Philip's reforms of the Macedonian military probably also helped to increase his personal power

---

[117] Fredricksmeyer 1990: 306–7, citing esp. Malkin 1985: 123–9; see also Fredricksmeyer 1979: 52 n. 40. Habicht 1970: 16, however, is more cautious, and presents the local evidence for a possible heroön of Philip without committing to its interpretation.

[118] Hammond 1994a: 48, 111; Hammond 1994b: 371 n. 25, citing Steph. Byz. s.v. "Gomphi"; Hammond and Griffith 1979: 539–40. On the location, see Peck 1898, s.v. "Gomphi."

[119] Billows 1995: 149–50 n. 14, citing *Suda* s.v. "Poneropolis" (which quotes Theopompus on the derogatory nickname), Plin. *NH* 4.11.41, Plu. *Mor.* 520B; Hammond 1994a: 138–9; cf. Strab. 7.6.2. Later documentary evidence is collected by Jones 1987: 270–3.

[120] Hammond 1994a: 111.

[121] Hammond and Griffith 1979: 540, pointing out that the sole evidence for the name change comes from Steph. Byz. s.v. "Philippi" and speculating that "the city could have paid Philip the compliment of naming itself Philippi" when Philip "liberated" it from Pherae in 352.

[122] Hammond and Griffith 1979: 110–12.

[123] Fredricksmeyer 1979: 52. So potent was the *ktistês* model, apparently, that Alexander imitated Philip's example (whether with or without Philip's encouragement or consent) in 340 BC, while still a very young crown prince: Fredricksmeyer 1990: 306–7, with testimonia and references.

and unify his people.[124] It must be presumed that his involvement with his own population was a central priority: their loyalty would not only have stabilized his reign, but would also have formed the foundation for any large-scale plans of conquest he might be harboring for the future.[125] Some of his efforts, however, may also have been deliberately scripted for his Greek audiences. Certain Macedonian military traditions might naturally have 'played' well before Greeks: that of the king taking the field at the head of his own troops, for example, might be mapped onto the Greek tendency by the fourth century to lionize the commanders of famous or significant conflicts.[126] The elevation of the Macedonian phalanx to the center of Philip's renewed army might also have harmonized well with older Greek traditions about hoplite warfare. While Macedonian culture of the fourth century BC included a number of practices that have been described by modern scholars as "Homeric,"[127] Philip's fighting tactics were not amongst them. His battle strategy involved not chariots and individual *aristeiai*,[128] but disciplined mass infantry, supported by cavalry. Some of the central historical problems concerning the composition and armament of the famed Macedonian phalanx – when and by whom it was equipped with the *sarissa*, exactly what categories of fighters it contained[129] – have arisen precisely because Greek writers construed this formation as a particularly vast and terrifying manifestation of the hoplite phalanx known from the battles of the fifth century BC, perhaps even from before the Peloponnesian War.[130] It is only natural to compare the new with the familiar, but in the case of Philip's military operations amongst the Greeks, the results were potentially polarizing. It has been argued that warfare played a significant role in the maintenance of polis identity, both internal and external, during the later archaic and earlier classical periods.[131] For Philip to lead what the

---

[124] Billows 1995: 16 and n. 55, citing part 1 of Hammond and Griffith 1979; Ellis 1977: 103 and *passim*; cf. also the general discussion of Philip as a commander by Griffith 1980.

[125] Ellis 1977: 114.

[126] Carney 1996: 28 n. 57 (citing Hanson 1989: 107–18, on the roles of Greek commanders during conflict), 29.

[127] E.g. on a selection of subjects Carlier 2000 (on the Macedonian kingship); Carney 1996: 21, 29 (on the Macedonian army); Carney 1992: 176–8 and n. 24 (on issues of honor in the conflict between Philip and Alexander, citing Fredricksmeyer 1990, in which see esp. 304–5); for additional earlier references, see Fredricksmeyer 1966: 181 n. 10 (in the course of a discussion on Macedonian religion).

[128] On the conduct of warfare in Homeric poetry, e.g. van Wees 1996.

[129] On these issues, see Markle 1978.

[130] On hoplite warfare in general during the classical era, see the essays in Hanson 1991; on innovations in traditional hoplite phalanx practices during the Peloponnesian War, see Connor 1988: 27–8.

[131] Connor 1988.

Greeks may have viewed as a larger and better-disciplined version of their own traditional military formation,[132] which for them had at various points comprised a direct reflection of their own political systems,[133] might have painted the Macedonian king as a fearsome enemy, but also might have presented him as a comprehensible commander and even an essential ally.

Philip's many images – heroic athlete, recipient of civic honors, *hegemôn*, *ktistês*, general – all engaged, though on a far broader scale, with guises in which the Greeks were now conditioned to embrace individuals as agents of history. Reaching still further, however, Philip also exercised unprecedented efforts to forge a connection between himself and the divine. Much has been written about where he might fall on the spectrum between presenting himself as a god and simply wanting his many audiences to embrace him as being manifestly superior, perhaps in very new ways.[134] Regardless, Philip would have had to advance cautiously. Would the Greeks accept a Macedonian god as *hegemôn*? Were the Macedonians prepared to worship their king?

It has been argued that the negotiation of this issue may have begun quite close to home, again with Philip's coins. The pervasive equestrian imagery on his reverses, while it could certainly evoke his victories at Olympia and the paradigm of the athlete-hero, might also refer to the 'rider-hero' of the northern Balkans, whose iconography is known from Thrace as early as the Hellenistic period and might represent borrowing from Greek heroic typologies.[135] If so, Philip's reverses could have served multiple rhetorical purposes simultaneously,[136] invoking heroic associations for peoples both near and distant for different reasons while subtly connecting Philip with both. The obverses, too, were potentially rich with symbolism: they concentrated upon superhuman figures, with favorites being Apollo, Heracles,

---

[132] Carney 1996: 21–4.   [133] Connor 1988.

[134] E.g. Carney 2007: 35–9; Baynham 1994; and the references collected by Lott 1996: 29–30 nn. 18–19, adding Fredricksmeyer 2003, 1991 (generally on Philip's desiring recognition as a god); cf. also note 174, below.

[135] Greenwalt 1994: 125–31, with additional references. On the Thracian iconography and its possible sources, see Dimitrova 2002: 223, 226–7; on the cult and imagery of Heracles in Thrace and on Thasos, with possible connections to the rider-hero, see Jesi and Egli 1964, esp. 265 n. 21.

[136] Here and elsewhere, I premise the rhetorical power of circulating coinage, particularly during the periods under discussion in Chapters 7 and 8. Even if its practical purposes were primarily economic (e.g. Martin 1985), coinage (to transform a concept from Ellis 1976: 21) could serve metaphorically as a small piece of the authority of the state or individual in whose name it circulated. Although the coinage of the classical poleis tended towards consistent civic iconography, in the later cases of (for example) Philip, Alexander, and the Hellenistic kings, the coins also bore imagery that suggested more precisely how users and viewers were to interpret, understand, or articulate the authority they embodied.

and Zeus.[137] Heracles, as noted above, was construed as an ancestor of the Macedonian Argead royal house and would have paired well with the athletic-heroic imagery of most of the reverses; Zeus, as Heracles' father, was also a good choice if this dynastic connection was to be invoked, and Zeus' patronage of the festivals at Olympia would also have rendered the imagery meaningful and appropriate. Apollo, too, was a patron of athletes (most notably through the Pythian games at Delphi); however, his appearance on Philip's obverses would have acquired much deeper meaning over time, particularly in light of the king's eventual involvement in the Third Sacred War. Philip does not seem to have assimilated himself to Apollo, but he might well have portrayed himself as being Apollo's rescuer.[138]

In his study of the role of Philip in the Third Sacred War (355–346 BC), Buckler reviews the ancient evidence for Philip's early interest in Apollo, pointing in particular towards two inscriptions: the treaty with the Chalcidians (discussed here in a different context, above) that transcribes a Delphic oracle, and an exile decree from Amphipolis that records payment of a portion of the exiles' estates to the god.[139] But Philip's initial decision to enter into the Sacred War was likely practical, rather than symbolic. The turmoil in central Greece, where the Delphic Amphictyony had yielded in 355 to Theban pressures to declare war on the Phocians, overlapped with Philip's interests in Thessaly.[140] When the Thebans finally approached Philip for help in 347, his decision some months later to enter the Sacred War on their behalf also conveniently placed him on the side of the Amphictyony, so that "he could again enter the fray as the savior of the god."[141] By 346 he had secured the Phocians' surrender.

The large-scale symbolism of Philip's 'protection' of the interests of Apollo (the Phocians, after all, had initially been vilified for their abuse of the resources of the Delphic land and sanctuary)[142] was mirrored on a small scale by the terms of his settlement, which included, most notably,

---

[137] Le Rider 1977 is a comprehensive treatment of Philip's coinage to date (Le Rider 1996 provides a few updates but concentrates centrally upon interpretations of typology and chronology); Head 1911: 222–4 presents a brief overview.

[138] Hornblower 2002 focuses upon the opportunities presented to a prospective *hegemôn* by the geopolitical situation in Greece, and particularly the significance of Philip's involvement in the Sacred War (267–9). This reading suggested my discussion of this conflict here, but with an emphasis upon Philip's potential for self-presentation. See also note 141, below.

[139] Buckler 1989: 5, with testimonia and references. On the Chalcidian treaty (which Buckler cites from Bengtson, *SdA* II[2] no. 308 = Bengtson 1962: 279–81 no. 308), see note 93, above; the second inscription may be found at Tod 1948: 149–51 no. 150.

[140] Buckler 1989: 58, 99, 106, et al. Buckler follows the chronology of Hammond 1937a (the latter also provides a narrative and timeline of the early years of the war at 72–8).

[141] Buckler 1989: 113 (quotation), 126.   [142] Ibid. 15–29.

the return of the precinct and its games.[143] Both gestures would have had useful public meaning: Philip's refusal to avail himself of the concentration of riches in Apollo's shrine was ostentatiously righteous; his renewal of the games, whatever his actual level of involvement, depicted him as both protector and patron. Philip's long associations with athletic-heroic imagery were thus brought to a new kind of fruition: he had now honored the god as victor once again.

But there was also a very meaningful myth that Philip might have had in mind at the conclusion of this conflict, one that took in much of his Olympian imagery under a single narrative and that might have helped to suggest his heroism. This is the story of the struggle between Heracles and Apollo for the Delphic tripod that symbolized control of the sanctuary and the oracle: the fight between the hero and the god was ultimately halted by a thunderbolt from their mutual father, Zeus, and Delphi handed over to Apollo.[144] It has been argued that this myth was taken up in the later sixth century as a symbolic representation of the conflicting interests that gave rise to the First Sacred War.[145] Whether or not that early war itself was actually a historical event, however, Greek 'recollection' of it, in tandem with the mythological narrative, could have proven very useful to Philip.[146]

Robertson points out that the narrative of the First Sacred War as a political struggle seems to surface in the literary record only after the conclusion of the third war, and suggests that this version of the story was deliberately embellished by Speusippus and Callisthenes in support of Philip's agenda.[147] One strand of later tradition[148] about the First Sacred War, in fact, represented most notably by Aeschines and Plutarch, has the conflict motivated by Solon, as the champion of the rights of the Amphictyony over the usurping city of Crisa or Cirrha.[149] The potential mapping of Philip onto the position of Solon could have been quite appealing,[150] especially from the Athenian perspective, and the use of older paradigms to articulate and understand current events was, as has emerged from the discussion thus far, quite familiar in both Athenian literature and Greek symbolic discourse by the fourth century.[151]

---

[143] Ibid. 140.

[144] On the sources and iconography of the myth, see Gantz 1993: 437–9 and note 145, below.

[145] Parke and Boardman 1957; see also Boardman 1978.

[146] See note 147, below.   [147] Robertson 1978 and at 51.

[148] For a division of the literary testimonia into groups that represent different political emphases, see Sordi 1953.

[149] See Robertson 1978: 51 n. 2, 53–5, 73 *et passim*. The ancient testimonia are Aeschin. 3.107–13 and Plu. *Sol.* 11.1–2.

[150] Robertson 1978 esp. 53–4.   [151] See e.g. Thomas 1989; Nouhaud 1982; Pearson 1941.

But what of the older memories of the Delphic conflict, those that might have given rise to the Heracles imagery of the later archaic period? That imagery, too, might have been of great use to Philip. The conflict between Apollo and Heracles, after all, had been peacefully resolved by Zeus, with Apollo returned to his rightful position. Although the analogy, whether it was to be based upon Philip as the restorer of order or as the dynastic descendant of Heracles, would not have been quite perfect, it would have borne the potential for rich meaning, particularly given that the characters of the myth were actually the three major divine figures to appear on Philip's coinage, and all three of them were associated with the kind of athletic heroism that Philip had long espoused. Finally, Philip's gold staters bearing the head of Apollo on the obverse may have just recently begun to be coined at the time that he ended the Third Sacred War:[152] If so, the decision to continue the emblem afterwards would have been still more significant.

Gradual expansion of the cognitive connection between an eminent leader and the gods may be due in part to the reception of that leader's growing achievements,[153] but individuals who wanted to be understood in this way, particularly by the fourth century, could and did help the process along. The Philippeum at Olympia therefore accomplished for Philip, on one level, the same kind of public statement as the Nauarch's Monument at Delphi made for Lysander. But Lysander had been depicted as being *honored* by Poseidon; the Philippeum seemed to invite the contemplation of Philip as something more.[154] Carney has provided meaningful readings of the deliberate liminality of the monument.[155]

Architecturally innovative and visually striking, the small peripteral circular building was prominently located near one of the exits from the sanctuary of Zeus,[156] a god who had long since been appearing on Philip's coinage.[157] Like the temples to the gods around it, the Philippeum housed chryselephantine statues – but the images, sculpted by Leochares, were of Philip, his parents Amyntas and Eurydice, his wife Olympias, and his

---

[152] See Le Rider 1996, esp. 55–9. Le Rider, with others, believes that Philip's Apollo staters began to be issued around 348 BC, but notes (59) that there has been no clear consensus.

[153] See Rose 1957: 340, presenting a new articulation of the findings of Habicht 1956 (= the first ed. of Habicht 1970).

[154] Carney 2000b: 24–5; on the question of Philip's supramortal status, e.g. Fredricksmeyer 2003: 253–6, 1981 esp. 146–7, 154–6, and 1979: 47–61; Borza 1990: 249–50.

[155] Carney 2000b and 2007, to whose interpretations I subscribe here; individual points are acknowledged separately below.

[156] The Philippeum was rediscovered in the third season of the German campaigns at Olympia, in 1877–8. The preliminary publication of the building is Adler et al. 1892: 128–33; the final publication is Schleif and Zschietzschmann 1944.

[157] See note 137, above.

son Alexander.[158] The trappings of divinity were present, but, as Carney observes, "ambiguous" rather than explicit.[159]

Small, ornate buildings constructed by individual states as 'treasuries' to house rich dedications were routine additions to the panhellenic sanctuaries during the later archaic and earlier classical periods, and often featured striking architecture; Philip's offering, however, was not only private and later in time than many of its potential 'models,' but also exceedingly rare in shape.[160] The Philippeum would therefore have looked unusual even from a distance, and once approached, its function was also different.[161] Rather than gathering personal dedications from an entire polis, it was an exclusive, individual repository. An athlete victorious in the games at Olympia (including a horse-owner) would be routinely entitled to erect a statue in the Altis, but these would have been of bronze or stone:[162] in his building, Philip not only changed the materials to gold-and-ivory,[163] but also added other members of his family to the grouping that included his own image. Extravagant personal dedications even from non-athletes, generally in the form of statuary, valuable objects, or arms, were a long tradition in the panhellenic sanctuaries,[164] and some individuals even offered rebuilt or newly decorated temples to the gods,[165] but the Philippeum did not easily fit any of these categories.[166]

---

[158] Paus. 5.17.4, 5.20.9–10, quoted (with modern bibliography) by Stewart 1993: 386–7. On the "special" nature of the materials, see further Carney 2007: 35–6.

[159] Carney 2000b: 25.

[160] Carney 2007: 37–8, with bibliography comparing the architecture of the Philippeum with that of the other treasuries and temples in the Altis; see also Fredricksmeyer 1979: 54. After the Geometric period and down to the time of Philip, Seiler 1986 collects only the *tholoi* in the sanctuary of Athena Pronaia at Delphi and in the sanctuary of Asclepios at Epidaurus; an older *tholos*, likely with civic functions, amongst the governmental buildings along the west side of the Athenian Agora; the round structures in the Theban Kabeireion; a *tholos* in Eretria; and the archaic-era "Old Tholos" at Delphi, parts of which were later disassembled and built into the late archaic Sicyonian Treasury (40) and would therefore not have been visible in Philip's day. On the Athenian *tholos*, see also Thompson 1940: 44–147.

[161] See note 166, below.

[162] See recently Smith 2007: 94–139, covering the years down to 400 BC.

[163] Carney 2000b: 24 notes that "all previous chryselephantine statues were cult images."

[164] E.g. Smith 2007: 95.   [165] E.g. Umholtz 2002.

[166] Carney 2000b: 25: "The Philippeum looked like a temple and was placed where one would expect a temple to be. It contained statues that looked like cult statues, yet there is no evidence for divine cult. It was not a temple. It was not a treasury (the other treasuries contained no cult images and were not placed within the Altis). Its shape resembled that of ἡρῷα (temples or chapels of a hero) but there is no evidence for heroic honors. It was not a ἡρῷον. We know what it was not but cannot be sure what it was, and that is the point." Carney 2007 explores the same problems in greater depth and argues that the building was designed to help establish Philip's intended "dynastic image."

While Philip might not explicitly have declared himself divine, he may have been offered local cult during his lifetime as a 'spontaneous' response to his imagery and his history-making activities. Though it is debated, this is what seems to have happened in the cases of several eminent Greeks, including, for example, Lysander, Agesilaus, and perhaps Brasidas.[167] Possibilities for special attentions being paid to Philip include an Athenian cult at Cynosarges,[168] altars of 'Zeus Philippius' at Eresus,[169] and a cult at Amphipolis.[170] The epithet 'Zeus Philippius' is difficult to interpret, and its ambiguity may be intended, like that of the Philippeum at Olympia, to invite ancient audiences to think of Philip as inhabiting a symbolic range that slid subjectively between the poles of benefactor and divinity.[171] A cult at Amphipolis might perhaps be associated with Philip's reception there as a 'liberator,'[172] just as Brasidas had been welcomed more than fifty years before. In any case, the examples of Brasidas as a newly appointed *ktistês* and of Philip as a city-founder elsewhere in the region might have provided appropriate models for local honors, but whether these may have bordered on the kind accorded to established heroes or (far less likely) the gods is uncertain.[173]

Philip's final gesture connecting himself to the divine was the procession held at the festivities surrounding the wedding of his daughter Cleopatra to Alexander of Epirus in 336 BC.[174] As the display unfolded in the theatre at Aegae, the images of the twelve Olympian gods were carried into the orchestra, followed by a statue of Philip himself. Some members of his mixed Greek and Macedonian audience might well have received Philip as

---

[167] On all of these instances, see Chapter 6, above.

[168] Fredricksmeyer 1979: 49, pointing out that the site was sacred to Heracles and to members of the hero's family; discussion of this potential cult and the evidence for it is one of the major themes of the article.

[169] Lott 1996: 29–30; see also Fredricksmeyer 1981: 146.

[170] Habicht 1970: 12–16 collects and evaluates the ancient evidence for cults at Amphipolis, Athens, Eresus, Ephesus, and Philippi (although on the latter, see note 117, above). I myself do not address Ephesus here, as I think that the evidence does not point towards worship so much as honor.

[171] Lott 1996: 29–30.   [172] See Rose 1957, note 153, above.

[173] Fredricksmeyer 1979: 50–1 is dubious about the Amphipolis cult, as is Badian 1963: 246 n. 16. Hammond and Griffith 1979: 691–5 provide a contrasting view to Fredricksmeyer's general conviction that Philip was possessed of divine aspirations.

[174] D.S. 16.91.4–93.2, 95.1. The secondary bibliography on the procession and its meaning – and on the assassination that happened almost immediately thereafter – is vast: see e.g. Fredricksmeyer 1979: 56–60 (in favor of Philip's leaning towards deification); Hammond and Griffith 1979: 682–4, 695 (*contra*); Borza 1999: 67–8 nn. 37–9, citing both Fredricksmeyer 1979 and Baynham 1994. Fredricksmeyer 1982: 95–6 argues that the wedding itself was already over by the time the procession was held, and that the spectacle was really an opening event for the planned panhellenic attack on Persia.

a "thirteenth Olympian."[175] But for those who might have been wary of the concept, the real, living Philip's conspicuous appearance at the event itself would likely have mitigated some – though likely not all – of the discomfort: Philip was, for that brief moment, both human and more than human at the same time.

7.3 'Reading' Greek: Philip as historical agent in literature

The literary sources that treat Philip do not provide the same kinds of analytical opportunities as do the continuous historiographic projects discussed in Chapters 3–6, above. The contemporary oratorical texts and essays are deeply biased (most notably, Isocrates was an ardent supporter of Athenian *détente* with Macedon, while Demosthenes was Philip's most outspoken opponent); the biographical works of Plutarch are not only explicitly moralizing, but are also focused upon protagonists other than Philip himself; and the historiography includes only works that are either fragmentary or late. Nevertheless, certain details in the literature offer evocative suggestions about Philip's self-presentation and reception before the Greeks. Taken together with the material evidence discussed above, they, too, suggest that Philip deliberately offered himself to the Greeks as an individual agent with the potential to create a new narrative for Greek history – and that the Greeks reacted to him so strongly, at least in part, because they understood the message that he was sending.

It is at this point, however, that a particular problem in the Philip (and Alexander) historiography emerges: the issue of recursivity, or, in this case, the problem of using the historical accounts to argue for the existence of the very historical behaviors that they themselves describe.[176] The larger discussion thus far, however, has suggested that it is this very phenomenon that helps to propel the development of ideas, both specialist and popular, about the 'great man' in classical Greece. Reflections upon the behaviors, achievements, and historical impact of individuals in a variety of media and contexts – literary, material, and even performative[177] – seem to invite the

---

[175] On the "thirteenth Olympian," see Fredricksmeyer 1979: 58–60 (*contra*: e.g. Hammond and Griffith 1979: 682–4).

[176] I remain grateful to J. Ober for encouraging my engagement with this problem – defined in precisely these terms.

[177] Within the boundaries of this particular project, my use of the word "performative" here centrally refers to public behaviors, public ceremonies, and public (or quasi-public) oratory. An expansion into e.g. the texts of the Athenian dramatists, both tragic and (especially)

deliberate scripting of future activities in order to prompt and even control these reflections. The positive feedback loop between commemorative
media and thoughtful, deliberate individual action functions as a kind of
ideological generator, and while its impact is certainly not wholly independent of large-scale historical events, this generator does appear to become
more potent over time. What for the ancient Greeks, then, may have initially
appeared from the inside to be the development of an increasingly sophisticated understanding of the workings of the 'machine' of history (and of the
ways in which an individual could manipulate it) seems to have gradually
emerged, in the political-historical sphere, at least, as an implicit grasp of
the cooperative development of ideology between presenter and audience.

On this reading, the historiography of the Macedonian kings, too, occupies a position along this feedback loop. The situation is somewhat complicated by the temporal remove of much of the evidence (including all
of the continuous narrative history), but in response to this limitation,
my discussion here is structured thematically, rather than examining the
ancient authors in turn. In grouping the evidence in this way, although my
goals are different from his, I am essentially following the methodology of
Hammond,[178] who has suggested through his own work that theme, tone,
and stance can persist through the transmission of content from author to
author. Approached in this manner, even texts that are likely to be biased
can indicate some coherent themes in Philip's diplomatic, military, and
personal choices.

Although the central concern here is Philip's self-presentation and reception amongst the Greeks, the king's interactions with the Macedonians
around him, especially at court, also necessarily affected his reputation
abroad. As noted above, due to his practical need to maintain his social and
political position by participating in established Macedonian cultural practices, Philip seems to have occasionally alienated some members of his Greek
audience. Theopompus and Demosthenes, most notably, are critical of the
king's membership in the extended drinking-bouts that bound together his
inner circle of elites, and the polygamy that was traditional in the Macedonian royal house, too, seems to have attracted Greek contempt.[179] But

---

comic, would likely yield additional material that would be generally supportive of the claims
that I venture here.

[178] See Hammond 1991 and (esp.) 1937b, who uses thematic grouping of content as a central
point of departure to practice *Quellenforschung* upon Justin and Diodorus, respectively.

[179] See Flower 1997: 104–11 on "Philip's private life" (including his drinking), collecting relevant
fragments of Theopompus and comparing them with (106–7) D. 2.17–19. Carney 2003
provides a reading of Macedonian intellectual and cultural life that differentiates between

others of the choices that helped to make Philip successful within Macedon seem to have been cultivated with the simultaneous goal of portraying him before the Greeks as a viable agent of history. Philip's images in the literary testimonia tend to cluster around his deliberate performances as a leader amongst his men (i.e. as a general who shared directly in the experiences of his soldiers, and as a king who maintained an active circle of elite *hetairoi*, or "companions"); as a fearsome military commander; and as a liberator or a merciful conqueror. Running throughout the anecdotes, as well, is a strong suggestion that Philip often depicted himself as being ostentatiously pious. The display of all of these characteristics would not only have contributed to Philip's general reputation, but would also have exploited the models established amongst the Greeks by eminent leaders of previous generations.

This is not to suggest that these were the only possible 'readings' of himself that Philip advertised, nor that the anecdotes preserved in the written accounts are always accurate either in substance or in detail. But the literary evidence does suggest that these general guises may have been important facets of Philip's self-presentation. They seem to have persisted across a variety of source traditions; they are intimately connected with the realia of his immediate imperial activities; and they are coherent with the messages represented in the material evidence. At the same time, it is important to recall that the 'feedback loop' discussed above will have affected the contents of the texts: authors like Diodorus, Plutarch, and Justin are likely to have selected information (from other selections in turn) according to the ideological priorities of their own times. In the end, the literary Philip can at best be viewed as a provocative representation, rather than an objective document – but the literary Philip also represents a set of images to which a living Philip might well have intentionally contributed.

The idea of Philip as a leader amongst (rather than exclusively above) his people was likely intimately linked with Macedonian royal tradition and social structure.[180] Philip seems to have used this image to great effect, as revealed in his apparent behavior as a member of two important groups, his *hetairoi* and his army. Whether judging the Macedonian king favorably or not, the testimonia make repeated reference to the intense, extended evenings he passed in drinking and talking with the Macedonian nobles

---

local and Greek influences, and recommends (49 n. 5) Borza 1995a: 159–71 on the general conditions of Alexander's *symposia*; see also Worthington 2008: 9–11 on the *symposion* and polygamy in Macedonian culture, and on the latter topic, cf. the case study of Carney 1992.

[180] See e.g. Billows 1995: 14, 16–17; Borza 1990: 241–2, 245; Hammond 1989: 140–8. Scholars differ on the degree to which they view Macedonian governmental and cultural norms as being the result of formal institutions.

who served at once as his bodyguards, advisers, and friends; and to the
parties to which he invited visiting dignitaries.[181] These gatherings seem
to have been intended to show Philip to his courtiers as an appropriately
dominant participant in the Macedonian sympotic tradition, and to his
frequent Greek guests as a civilized *bon vivant*.[182] That the two may have
at times, however, been mutually exclusive is suggested not only by the
established differences between the two cultural traditions, but also by the
tone of some of the comments ventured by Diodorus and Plutarch.[183]

As a field commander, Philip seems to have shown little restraint in
putting himself in danger alongside his soldiers, a practice widely recognized
and noted by his Greek audiences.[184] Although the famous arrow wound
to his eye was probably just a fortuitous shot while Philip was reviewing
siege preparations, his collar bone and leg injuries were likely incurred in
combat,[185] showing Philip before his enemies as a formidably self-sacrificing
foe and before his admirers as a quasi-heroic figure. Alexander's Iliadic
behavior in battle has been much appreciated since antiquity (see Chapter 8,
below), but his father seems to have provided an important model for it.[186]

This version of Philip – the leader who shares the luxuries of his court,
the dangers of warfare, and the discomforts of the campaign with an ever-
widening circle of 'colleagues' moving outwards from his closest friends to
his camp-followers – would likely have been comprehensible in its outlines
to Greek audiences, even to those from democratic states. Greek democracy
was in principle (and, more importantly, in the Greek imagination) *direct*
democracy. Especially in its most complex form in fourth-century Athens,
where a careful system of leveling mechanisms had been gradually accruing
since before the Persian Wars, direct democracy relied upon a shared subscription to a concept of equality that likely ranged from nominal to actual
across the various spheres of public life. The image of the citizen-soldier
whose fellow-citizen commander led him into battle was an enduring one

---

[181] E.g. D.S. 16.55.1–2, 87.1, 91.5–6; Plu. *Alex.* 9.5–14; Plu. *Dem.* 16.2–4, cf. also 20.3; Just. 9.8.
On Theopompus, see Flower 1997: 104–7, 122–3.

[182] E.g. D.S. 16.91.5–6.

[183] E.g. D.S. 16.87.1–3 (Philip rebuked for his behavior by Demades at the celebration after
Chaeronea); Plu. *Dem.* 20.3 (Philip drunk and then recalling Demosthenes after Chaeronea).

[184] Riginos 1994 has collected the considerable testimonia on the wounds that Philip suffered in
battle, and notes that (104–5): "In oration 11.22 Philip is described by [Demosthenes] as one
who, enjoying the risks involved, dealt his entire body punishment for the sake of power:
οὕτως εἶναι φιλοκίνδυνον (sc. τὸν Φίλιππον) ὥσθ' ὑπὲρ τοῦ μείζω ποιῆσαι τὴν ἀρχὴν
κατατετρῶσθαι πᾶν τὸ σῶμα τοῖς πολεμίοις μαχόμενον" ("[Philip] is such a lover of danger
that, in order to make his power greater, he has suffered injuries to his entire body while
fighting against his enemies"). See also note 126, above.

[185] Riginos 1994: 106 (eye), 115 (collar bone), 117 (leg).   [186] Fredricksmeyer 1990: 305.

even in an age when mercenaries were playing an increasingly significant role in interstate and (especially) international conflicts.[187] Demosthenes, for example, scripting his words for the larger and more practical world of the Athenian law-courts, still invoked Miltiades at Marathon and imagined him not as a distant, elevated figure, but as an equal member of the polis.[188]

In this context, the slightly archaizing tendency of Macedonian society to draw its king directly and visibly into the *symposion* or onto the battlefield[189] might have provided a natural opportunity for a leader to script his own behavior in the manner of a legend, for the sake of reaching not only his Macedonian audiences, but also his Greek ones. Philip's daring displays of personal valor in combat might have fortuitously invoked the ancient heroes, but his practical skill as a strategist and field commander, coupled with his social and economic position within his own kingdom, permitted him to innovate far beyond the military tactics of his opponents. Philip seems to have harnessed this to his great advantage, frequently allowing his reputation in the field to precede him and thereby using terror itself as a strategem. He also appears to have gone to great lengths not merely to win his battles, but to invite personal credit for the victories.[190] 'Commander narrative' is fully active in much of the extant historical and biographical writing that treats Philip, and as an individual he is frequently contrasted with Greek groups, the latter often mentioned in the now-familiar form of polis collectives even when individual leaders occasionally emerge to speak or act on their behalf.[191]

Philip is further portrayed in the literary evidence as a liberator or a merciful conqueror, as for example in his taking of Thessaly, which was apparently presented in the guise of release from tyranny, or in his pacification of Thrace, where his (likely self-aggrandizing) activities seem to have enabled him to cast himself as a protector of the Greek settlements there.[192] It is possible, too, that more anecdotal material that seems to offer an evaluation of Philip's inner character, such as Justin's statement that Philip offered

---

[187] See Spence 1993: 165–75 on the importance of the "hoplite ethos" even in the fourth century, and Wheeler 1991 on the complexities and tensions inherent in the relationship between leader and phalanx, even over time.

[188] E.g. D. 3.26, 13.21–22, 19.303, 23.196–8, 23.207.

[189] On 'Homeric' aspects of Macedonian culture, see note 127, above.

[190] E.g. D.S. 16.4.3–7, 8.1–2, 53.2–3 (on fear created by Philip's treatment of the conquered at Olynthus); Just. 9.8.

[191] E.g. D.S. 16.1.4–6, 4.1–7, 8.1–5, 14.2, 31.6, 53.2–3, 54.1, 59.5, 69.7–8, 71.1–2, 77.2–3, 86.1–6, 89.1–3, 91.2, 92.1; Plu. *Dem.* 12.7, 16.1, 17.1–6 *passim*, 18.1; Plu. *Phoc.* 12.1, 14.3, 14.7–8, 16.1, 16.5–7; Just. 7.6, 8.1, 8.2, 8.4, 9.1, 9.3, 9.4, 9.5.

[192] D.S. 16.14.2 and D.S. 16.71.1–2.

mild terms to the inhabitants of Methone despite his having lost an eye in the siege,[193] may have been derived from what was originally the careful advertisement of a particular negotiative stance. This possibility emerges most strongly in the description of Philip's behavior after the battle of Chaeronea, which, despite varying surface decoration, is essentially consistent between the accounts of Diodorus (16.86.6–87.3) and Justin (9.4).[194] Philip gives back the fallen to the defeated poleis for burial (although Justin claims that the Thebans were charged money for the privilege),[195] then makes a special alliance with Athens. Both accounts also suggest that Philip refrained from ostentatious celebrations of his conquest (although D.S. 16.87.1–2 has a riotous party stopped in mid course when Philip is shamed by the Athenian rhetor Demades).[196] Such behaviors in general would have been highly appropriate both for a Macedonian attempting to reconcile his supremacy with Greek social values and for an eminent individual attempting to claim his place in history. Philip's victory, while epoch-making, could also be fraught with potential pitfalls. The recollection of Greek leaders of the past would have taught Philip what choices were most likely to enhance his authority, preserve his interstate relationships, and guarantee the reception he desired.

Philip's 'performance' of his own piety, certainly evident in his return of the dead after Chaeronea, also emerges from the historiographic coverage of the earlier events of his reign. He is credited with a festival featuring lavish rituals and games after taking Olynthus (D.S. 16.55.1). During the Third Sacred War, he is said to have presented his army as the defenders of Apollo himself,[197] and to have acquired the Phocian seats in the Delphic Amphictyony διὰ τὴν εἰς τοὺς θεοὺς εὐσέβειαν, "on account of his piety towards the gods."[198] His large-scale plans for his expedition to Asia seemed designed to take in both general religiosity and calls for vengeance that dated back some 150 years: the rationale reported by both Polybius and Diodorus

---

[193] Just. 7.6.

[194] On the sources that may have been employed by Diodorus and by Pompeius Trogus, the latter the source of Justin's *Epitome*, see note 200, below.

[195] This fair treatment of the dead is also suggested, although not stated openly, in Plu. *Dem.* 21.2. Plu. *Dem.* 22.4 also sketches Philip as a merciful conqueror after Chaeronea, although without rehearsing the reasons recognized by Diodorus and Justin.

[196] Plu. *Phoc.* 16.8 has Phocion opposing conspicuous celebrations of Philip's death (perhaps a motif picked up from the tradition and repeated on the other side of the conflict?); similarly, Plu. *Dem.* 20.3 has a drunken Philip reveling immediately after the battle when he looks out at the dead, but then sobering and realizing how fortunate he is to have won; the text also criticizes the Athenians (although explicitly not Demosthenes) for the joy they show upon the death of Philip (22.4).

[197] Just. 8.2; cf. also above.   [198] D.S. 16.1.4 (quotation), 16.59.4–60.2.

is that the Greeks under Philip were to invade Asia to repay the Persian destruction of Greek temples under Darius and Xerxes early in the fifth century, and Diodorus even shows Philip seeking the sanction of Delphi for the mission.[199] It has been argued that moralizing tendencies become increasingly prominent in fourth-century Greek prose writing, including historiography, and so at least some of the detailed attention paid by both Diodorus and Justin to Philip's piety (or lack thereof) might be attributed to their likely use of Ephorus and Theopompus, respectively, amongst their sources.[200] But the archaeological evidence and other testimonia reviewed above also imply that Philip was deeply interested in manipulating public perceptions of his relationship with the heroic and the divine, and Alexander's later imitation of certain of his father's strategies suggests that they were believed to hold some promise.[201]

7.4 Conclusion: Philip's script for a new Greek world

Throughout his reign, Philip harnessed mythology, architecture, coinage, epigraphy, and the foundations of cities to construct his public image, as well as behaving in ways that would guarantee him a particular public reputation and memory. While his larger goals remain disputed,[202] he modeled his self-presentation in significant part upon the paradigms established by eminent *Greek* leaders before him, and it therefore seems that he aspired to be understood as a significant agent of history by Greek standards and on Greek terms. What is of particular interest is that he did so in a manner that might be construed as being broadly panhellenic; that is, he did not commemorate himself or behave in a manner that was indebted to the special cultural norms, language, or practices unique to any one Greek polis. Instead, he used imagery and methods with the broadest possible appeal, including his deep associations with the panhellenic sanctuaries at Olympia and at Delphi, his connections with widely recognized gods and heroes (rather than with more narrowly appreciated local ones), his potential role as a colonial founder, his distinction in warfare, and his capacity for persuasive speech (noted repeatedly by the historians). His free interchange and independent alliances

---

[199] Plb. 3.6.13; D.S. 16.89.2, 91.2–4, respectively.

[200] Pownall 2004, esp. chs. 4–5 on Ephorus and Theopompus, respectively; cf. Flower 1997: 100–1, 130–5. On Diodorus' other sources, see Hammond 1991: 506, 1937b, and 1938a; on Justin's, see Hammond 1991: 506.

[201] On Alexander's imitation of Philip, see e.g. Fredricksmeyer 1990.

[202] E.g. Borza 1999: 60–5 (with basic bibliography), as well as Fredricksmeyer 1982.

with a variety of poleis also guaranteed that Philip's political identity, as with his imagery, had no boundaries. In this regard, the fact that he was a king of a liminal *ethnos* rather than a Greek political leader likely helped, rather than hindered, his aspirations.

When Philip called for a panhellenic expedition against Persia, he was using images from at least as early as the Persian Wars that the Greeks themselves had continued to employ throughout their public rhetoric.[203] He was also pressing upon recollections not only of the 'enslavement' of the Greeks of Asia Minor, who had by this time come to be construed as a single cultural unit,[204] but of the constant interference of the Persians in Greek interstate political affairs since the time of the Peloponnesian War. The Persians were the one enemy that most of the Greek poleis had at some point shared in explicit common, and Philip now presented himself as the ideal leader to defeat them, with the Greeks at his back. The elision was a clever one: the Greeks in Philip's presentation had gradually become one collective 'citizen' group that would now collaborate with Philip to make history.[205] Philip's assassination therefore represented an inconvenient interruption of a trajectory that Alexander, already of age and already a veteran of Chaeronea, was ideally positioned to adopt.

---

[203] See Mitchell 2007.   [204] Seager and Tuplin 1980.
[205] Cf. the final sentence of Ellis 1976 at 234, quoted by Borza 1978: 240: "Towards [Greece] [Philip] turned for security and coalition, but for a continuing source of military objectives and wealth he turned towards Asia."

8 | Alexander 'the Great'

8.1 Alexander in context

The political relationship between individuals and groups in classical Greece was dynamic, as poleis and personalities experimented with articulations of historical agency that explained their relationships in the present and defined their roles for the future. Self-presentation and reception created feedback loops as eminent individuals observed and exploited cultural norms in their attempts to claim history-making agency for themselves, but they were limited in a variety of ways by established expectations for citizen–city cooperation. Though sometimes only in a performative sense,[1] the polis and the will of the citizen group continued to be acknowledged in certain genres of public discourse, even as the commemorative gap between ordinary and eminent individuals continued to grow. Invocations of historical agency and accompanying claims to lasting memory were reflected both in the material evidence and in the historiography as these processes continued.

This is an important reason why Philip, an acute observer of Greek culture, was able to offer himself to the Greek poleis as what may now perhaps be termed a 'great man': the role he played was both old and new. By depicting himself as a maker of history, he was invoking Greek models that reached back at least as far as the Persian Wars. But Philip's role was also innovative in its sheer scope: the 'citizen' group he ultimately aspired to lead reached far beyond his Macedonian army to encompass most of the major states of southern Greece, and his self-presentation invoked a greater number of images on a broader scale than the Greeks had likely experienced before – although the vocabulary of those images was essentially familiar.

Alexander's behavior and reception therefore represent not a sudden explosion, but a logical next step. The Greek world had provided him with paradigms both for the self-advertisement of historical 'greatness' and for the delicate reconciliation of that interest with the entrenched desires of the Greek states for at least nominal autonomy and agency.

---

[1] As perhaps, for example, in the case of the repeated yearly offer to the Athenian *dêmos* to enact an ostracism: see Forsdyke 2000 as discussed in Chapter 2, above.

Philip had already demonstrated that a wide-ranging program, adopting and adapting a variety of established motifs, was likely the most effective path. Alexander's response was larger and more thorough than past attempts, but it was not unique.[2] His public image-making and his reception in historiography share key thematic elements with the behaviors and experiences of other eminent individuals, suggesting that the conceptual repertory of 'greatness' was at this point in Greek history not only appreciated by elites, but even expected by the more ordinary members of their audiences.

Alexander harnessed multiple media for his self-presentation both inside and (especially) outside Macedonia, including statuary and other types of visual art, monuments and public buildings, inscriptions, coinage, literature, and even the foundation of cities. He used these symbolic resources to promulgate a variety of images depending upon his perceived audiences and his goals. Most of these 'versions' of Alexander persisted in various ways throughout his active career, and overlapped with one another to promote the elision between specifically Macedonian and broadly Greek conceptions of what a 'great man' should be. Alexander crafted a version of himself as king of Macedon that emphasized centrally his legitimate descent from Philip and claim to the throne, his membership in the nobility, and his skill as a field commander: this last also helped to advertise him to his Greek audiences. To make further contact with Greek cultural models, Alexander presented himself, at least earlier on in his reign, as an eminent individual who could both collaborate with the Greek poleis and serve as their benefactor; he also ensured that he would be memorialized in appropriate literature that reified his own particular versions of myth and of history. These priorities nearly all in turn supported his self-presentation as a hero, which was designed for both Macedonian and Greek audiences. The cities he created functioned both as tangible memorials of his power and as loci for his recognition as *ktistês*, and to this he added images that assimilated him to both Homeric and athlete-hero paradigms, invoking Achilles and Heracles. Achilles was claimed as an ancestor of Alexander's mother Olympias, and Heracles, a son of Zeus who was traditionally taken up to Olympus after his death, was the putative ancestor of Philip's and Alexander's dynasty. This connection in particular likely helped to inspire Alexander's eventual connnection of himself to the divine, as a competitor of Dionysus and perhaps even as a son of Zeus.

---

[2] Fredricksmeyer 1990, describing how Philip likely served as a paradigm (and in Fredricksmeyer's interpretation also a rival) for Alexander.

Strikingly, none of the individual strategies that Alexander used is explicitly different from those employed by previous eminent Greek leaders, save for the few opportunities that were unique to Alexander's position as the king of an *ethnos* rather than a non-tyrannical leader of a polis (e.g. his personal control over the minting of coins). The popular reaction to him seems to have been predictable, as well. With the Greek world having been gradually acclimated to the appearance of 'greatness' through a long, slow process of negotiation between individuals and groups, Alexander was in effect presented with a tested and trustworthy cultural script to which he only needed to perform. The extant continuous historiography[3] also interprets Alexander's behaviors in accordance with these themes. While this response cannot itself alone testify to Alexander's intentions, it does show the authority of pre-existing cultural models in determining Alexander's later reception, and it also suggests that some of the older (now lost) sources for the extant texts, several of which were contemporary to Alexander, may also have understood him in these ways.[4]

8.2 Alexander's personae

King of the Macedonians

Alexander's ascent to the throne upon Philip's assassination was not entirely unprepared, but it was sudden. He needed to present himself firstly as Philip's legitimate successor, and secondly as an appropriate king for the Macedonians in his own right. Three centrally important elements that would have supported these goals emerge from his larger program: his performance as a member of the social circles of the Macedonian elite; his coinage; and his activities as a military commander. Although all three of these image sets speak early in Alexander's reign to Macedonian social expectations in particular, they are later employed as communicative strategies for the wider Greek world.

Alexander would have been expected by virtue of his status to participate in the social rituals that bound together the noble classes of Macedon, most

---

[3] For an introduction to the diverse literary sources for Alexander, see Baynham 2003 (survey); Hammond 1993 and 1983 (*Quellenforschung* on the five extant historians); the introduction to Stoneman 1991 (*Alexander Romance*); Pédech 1984 (lost and fragmentary eyewitnesses); Pearson 1960 (lost and fragmentary writers); Tarn 1950 (the Vulgate tradition); Robinson 1932 (*Ephemerides*); and cf. Chapter 1, above.

[4] On the "first generation" of Alexander writers, see Baynham 2003: 3–13, with additional references, and cf. also Chapter 1, above.

notably military training,[5] the hunt,[6] and the *symposion*.[7] The other male members of the elite who surrounded him at court and shared in these experiences became the friends of his youth and, as he came of age, his personal inner circle of military officers and courtiers.[8] These *hetairoi*, frequently referred to collectively as Alexander's "Companions," were part of what made him Macedonian, in both the literal and the figurative sense. Even as Alexander's Eastern expedition progressed through the Greek world into the far reaches of the Persian Empire, Macedonian ethnicity remained a point of pride in claiming closeness to Alexander himself. Alexander does seem to have often in practice maintained distinctions between Macedonians and Greeks,[9] but the cities that he and his successors founded in distant lands (and colonized with representatives of both peoples) bore features of a generally Hellenizing culture even as they engaged in various ways with their new environments.[10] Macedonians might also invoke norms that were equally applicable in Greek contexts at moments of cultural crisis, as for example in the debate over whether Alexander should receive *proskynesis* like the king of Persia.[11]

Alexander's coinage followed a similar trajectory: its audience and its meaning seem to have expanded in the course of his reign. Many of Alexander's earliest issues, both gold and silver, that circulated in and around Macedon from the royal mints at Pella and Amphipolis were actually posthumous Philip II types. These were indistinguishable in design from those produced during Philip's lifetime, doubtless replicated not only because of their perceived economic reliability, but also as a firm assertion of continuity in the royal succession.[12] Alongside these issues, however, Alexander also produced his own, newly designed coinage from the same

---

[5] Carney 2003: 48 suggests cavalry experience, to coincide with Macedonian interest in hunting (see note 6, below).

[6] See Carney 2002; Palagia 2000.

[7] Whether the Macedonian *symposion* also involved ritualized song-performance in the manner of some Greek symposia is not clear. On the Macedonian *symposion*, see Chapter 7, above; on the Greek symposium in general, see e.g. Hobden 2009 and the papers in Murray 1990.

[8] On the upbringing of young Macedonian nobles and princes in general, e.g. Carney 2003.

[9] E.g. the discussion by Fraser 1996: 180–4.

[10] Fraser 1996: 184–5; Billows 1995: 146–82. A site frequently invoked in this regard is Aï Khanoum, which revealed upon excavation features of both Hellenic and Bactrian cultures: see Bernard 1967 (esp. 92–3 and n. 4 on whether Aï Khanoum may have been a foundation of Alexander); Bernard et al. 1973–2014 (the series of final publications); Fraser 1996: 153–6.

[11] See note 123, below.

[12] Thompson 1982: 116, citing Le Rider 1977: 400 (silver), 433–8 (gold, and summation), and noting that Alexander continued this imitation down to the year 328. For a brief survey of both Philip's and Alexander's coinage, see Mørkholm 1991: 41–3.

mints:[13] Heracles, Alexander's putative ancestor, appeared on the bronze and silver, likely as "a dynastic message," and Athena and a Nike on the gold.[14] The inscription, ΑΛΕΞΑΝΔΡΟΥ, "of Alexander," shifted in many cases to ΒΑΣΙΛΕΩΣ ΑΛΕΞΑΝΔΡΟΥ, "of Alexander the king," only once Alexander returned from his conquest of India, years later.[15] With the progress of the Eastern campaigns, numerous additional mints for Alexander issues were founded throughout the former Persian Empire. Complex arrangements were sometimes made in order to maintain the delicate balance of Alexander promotion and economic stimulus against potential local resentment: amongst other strategies, local coin-types were sometimes permitted to endure alongside the new ones.[16] In the end, then, Alexander was able to produce a body of what Price has called "panhellenic" coinage, likely designed to promote his larger imperialistic goals.[17]

From Macedon to Greece

Alexander's representation of himself as a strong military commander – in the guises of gifted general, fellow-soldier, and even, at times, Homeric hero – was a model that would likely have spoken equally well to both his Greek and his Macedonian audiences, as witnessed by the varied experiences of Philip, Epaminondas, Lysander, Leonidas, and even Alcibiades. Philip's reform of the Macedonian army, wide-ranging conquests, and refusal to spare himself in battle had solidified the king's role both as a leader and as a fighter in the eyes of the Macedonian citizen-soldiers.[18] Alexander's responsibility was now to perform to these standards while still courting the acknowledgement of his Greek audiences. Homeric imagery proved a valuable bridge.

---

[13] Precisely when Alexander first issued coins on his own authority is disputed; the two dates most favored are 336, shortly after his accession to the throne, and 333/2, after the battle of the Issus (references collected by Stewart 1993: 94 n. 79, 158 n. 1; cf. also Fredricksmeyer 1991: 204 n. 25).

[14] Stewart 1993: 93 (quotation); Stewart interprets the Athena–Nike imagery as symbolizing Alexander's Eastern expedition. Faraguna 2003: 108–9 suggests that the Athena imagery "points to an elaborate attempt . . . to present the expedition in terms acceptable to the Greeks" (109, citing Zahrnt 1996: 146–7). On the new Alexander coin-types, see Price 1991: 29–32 and *passim*, with cross-references to illustrations in vol. II; see also Kraay and Hirmer 1966: no. 569, pl. 172.

[15] Stewart 1993: 93–4, 160, with references. Stewart also believes, with others, that the initial omission of the title "king" was chosen to avoid trouble in Alexander's relationship with the mainland Greeks. The precise date of the titular change is disputed.

[16] Thompson 1982: 119–20, with examples.

[17] Price 1993: 174, and cf. Chapter 7, above, on the political power of coinage.

[18] See Chapter 7, above.

One of Alexander's personal trademarks, according to his remembrance in the literature, was fighting in or near the forefront of his own battles, frequently at great risk to himself. (The sources report much dismay at this amongst the courtiers and high military officers whose own positions depended inextricably upon Alexander's welfare.)[19] His example would potentially not only have intimidated his enemies and inspired his troops, but also proclaimed his unique status in the secondhand reports about him. He is said to have deliberately dressed in spectacular armor, a decision that both recalled the divinely forged armor of his 'ancestor' Achilles[20] and accorded significantly greater prestige to the arms, weapons, and decorations he offered as military rewards.[21] He rode always upon the same famous and pre-eminent horse,[22] and indulged in dangerous solo attacks that recalled the famous *aristeiai* (displays of divinely inspired valor in individual fighting) of the *Iliad*.[23]

The battle of the Granicus, for example, saw Alexander nearly beheaded in single combat with the Persians Rhoesaces and Spithridates, saved only by a dramatic last-minute kill by Cleitus;[24] the battle of Gaugamela is remembered for a furious cavalry charge against the Persian king Darius that is immortalized in the 'Alexander Mosaic' from Pompeii.[25] But the narrative that most thoroughly demonstrates Alexander's personal risk-taking is the Indian campaign against the Malli. The basic outline of events is generally

---

[19] E.g. their responses to an omen that predicted Alexander's wounding at Gaza (Curt. 4.6.10–20; Plu. *Alex.* 25.4–5 [though without any account of the onlookers]; Arr. 2.26.4); and especially their reactions to Alexander's near death amongst the Malli (Curt. 9.6.4–15 [including Craterus' speech]; Arr. 6.13.4); see also Carney 1996: 28–31; Bosworth 1988b: 42–3.

[20] The forging of the arms of Achilles: *Il.* 18.468–613. Alexander's battle attire: e.g. Curt. 4.4.11; Plu. *Alex.* 16.7, 16.10, 32.8–11 (the latter three testimonia cited in Stewart 1993: 351); cf. also the armor ostensibly from the Trojan War that Alexander either wore or carried as a talisman: D.S. 17.18.1, 17.21.2; Arr. 1.11.7, 6.9.3. Plu. *Alex.* 32.8–11, which has Alexander arming for the battle of Gaugamela, is doubtless designed to recall the numerous arming-scenes in the *Iliad* as well, particularly that of Achilles at *Il.* 19.364–403.

[21] E.g. D.S. 17.95.3–5; Curt. 8.5.4, 9.3.21–2; Just. 12.7.4–5.

[22] If the story of Alexander's taming of Bucephalus, whether true or not, was already in circulation during the king's lifetime, his constant use of this horse in battle would have functioned as an endless recollection – and proof – of Philip's ominous declaration that Macedon would not be enough for Alexander (Plu. *Alex.* 6.1–8).

[23] *Il.* 5, 11, and 17 are frequently cited as presenting the *aristeiai* of Diomedes, Agamemnon, and Menelaus, respectively, and it is likely that the origins of these labels are very early, e.g. Hdt. 2.116.3; Cic. *ad Att.* 16.9. This concept is frequently invoked by modern scholars, e.g. Bosworth 1988b: 43, who calls Alexander's operations "a continuing saga of heroic self-exposure."

[24] D.S. 17.20.2–7; Curt. 8.1.20 (a recollection; the Granicus narrative proper is lost with Curtius' missing books 1–2); Plu. *Alex.* 16.8–11; Arr. 1.15.7–8.

[25] D.S. 17.60.1–4; Curt. 4.15.23–33; Plu. *Alex.* 33.4–7; Arr. 3.14.2–3; Just. 11.14.3, 5–7. For a useful analysis of the 'Alexander Mosaic' and collected bibliography, see Stewart 1993: 130–50; cf. also Cohen 1997.

consistent in the major sources.[26] Dissatisfied with the speed at which his Macedonian troops are erecting their siege ladders, Alexander scales the city wall alone. Lingering atop the parapet, he becomes an easy target for enemy fire, then leaps down into the city. There, he is surrounded by enemy fighters. After killing several single-handedly, he is wounded in the chest by an arrow. A number of his nobles arrive but are hard-pressed to defend him until the main body of the Macedonians finally breaks into the city, spurred to frenzy by word that Alexander has fallen. The injured king is carried to safety and, after a dangerous operation to remove the arrow, convalesces for so long that stories of his death begin to spread, either amongst the enemy (Diodorus, Curtius) or amongst his own army (Plutarch, Arrian). To quell the damaging rumors, Alexander makes a public appearance; in Arrian, he summons what little strength he has to appear on foot before his troops and mount and ride a horse. The army is overjoyed, and Alexander retires again to complete his long recovery.

This single anecdote provides numerous examples of 'spectacular' behavior on Alexander's part: the climbing of the wall and the hesitation upon the parapet, posed almost as if upon a stage, drawing the gazes of both armies; the *aristeia* within the city, capped by the appropriately epic fight of his nobles for possession of his still-living body (perhaps recalling the struggle for Leonidas' body in Herodotus)[27]; the draining 'acting job' before the army to suggest his return to health and soundness. It is impossible to ascertain whether the sources preserve accurate impressions of a real performance. But the Homeric coloration that has duly crept into the extant accounts, particularly that of Arrian,[28] suggests that Alexander was comprehended even by some of the lost writers through an epic-heroic lens, perhaps as early as his own lifetime. The result, it appears, was an 'Alexander-in-battle' narrative tradition that could itself be gazed upon as a marvel. The most natural comparand with this version of Alexander, likely by Alexander's own design,[29] was Achilles.

Other features of the literary accounts carry the Achilles connection still further. The major sources describe a series of performative spectacles recalling the Trojan War during the expedition's first landing in Asia:[30] a

---

[26] D.S. 17.98.1–100.1; Curt. 9.4.26–6.2; Plu. *Alex.* 63.2–14; Arr. 6.8.4–13.3; Just. 12.9.3–13. The actual name of the enemy people, however, is unclear: see the outline of the possibilities given by Arr. 6.11.3 and the analysis at Bosworth 1988a: 76–83.

[27] See Chapter 3, above.

[28] On Homeric echoes in Arrian, see Brunt 1976: 464–6, app. 4, with references.

[29] Cohen 1995: 483, citing Pearson 1960: 10.

[30] See e.g. Cohen 1995: 483–6; and esp. Stewart 1993: 78.

sacrifice to Protesilaus, the first of the Greeks to land at Troy; the casting of a symbolic spear into the 'enemy' earth;[31] offerings made at Achilles' tomb; and possibly even running nude with his friends around the hero's burial site, in a re-enactment of an ancient ritual.[32] Alexander is also said to have sacrificed to Priam at the altar where the Trojan ruler was supposed to have been slain by Achilles' son Neoptolemus, and prayed that Achilles' descendants be spared redress.[33] Alexander's visit to the temple of the Trojan Athena and his dedication of his armor there (in return for an antique set said to be from the Trojan War, which he later employed as a battle talisman),[34] also probably invoked the Homeric heroes.[35]

Again like Achilles, Alexander is recalled as indulging in the emotional and physical rituals of grief to an extraordinary, often almost feminine, degree when his close friend Hephaestion died[36] and is said to have planned an elaborate funeral followed by memorial contests and games.[37] The marvelously detailed and tremendously expensive tomb planned for Hephaestion,[38] though never completed, was likely a response to the rustic pyre of Patroclus, with Alexander's symbolic public art and precious materials far exceeding Achilles' ephemeral offerings of oil, honey, animals, and human sacrifices, marked out by an earthen mound (*Il.* 23.161–257). The crowning event in Alexander's competition with his heroic ancestor[39] came in the posthumous honors the king demanded for Hephaestion. Whereas Patroclus was acknowledged in a formal hero-cult only with the passage of historical time,[40] Hephaestion was to receive heroic worship straight away, and if

---

[31] Stewart 1993: 78, citing D.S. 17.17.1–3; Arr. 1.11.5, 7; Just. 11.5.10–12. Curtius' accounts of the arrival in Asia and the visit to Troy, along with the expedition's early conquests in Asia Minor, are lost with his missing books 1 and 2.

[32] D.S. 17.17.3; Plu. *Alex.* 15.7–8; Arr. 1.12.1–2; Just. 11.5.12.

[33] Though this story only occurs in one account, Arr. 1.11.8.   [34] D.S. 17.18.1; Arr. 1.11.7.

[35] For collected references and bibliography on the numerous links between Alexander and Achilles, see, as Stewart 1993: 80 n. 34 recommends, Ameling 1988.

[36] Referenced but not discussed in detail in Stewart 1993: 84. On this issue, see D.S. 17.110.8 (merely a reference to Alexander's bearing his grief with difficulty); Plu. *Alex.* 72.3–4; Arr. 7.14.2–8, esp. 3–4; Just. 12.12.11–12 (Curtius' account of these events is lost in the large lacuna after 10.4.3); cf. *Il.* 18.1–35, 354–5; 19.4–5, 303–37; 23.135–7; 24.3–18. On the central role of women in Greek funerary lamentation rituals, see e.g. Alexiou 1974; Kurtz and Boardman 1971, esp. 142–61; cf. also the prominence of the female mourners surrounding the deaths of both Patroclus and Hector at *Il.* 19.282–302; 22.430–7, 477–514; 24.710–75.

[37] D.S. 17.114.1–115.6; Plu. *Alex.* 72.5; Arr. 7.14.8–10; Just. 12.12.12; cf. *Il.* 23.125–897.

[38] D.S. 17.115.1–5 (the most extensive surviving description); Plu. *Alex.* 72.5; Arr. 7.14.8; Just. 12.12.12. On the 'spectacle' value of the monument, see Kuttner 1999: 101–2.

[39] Stewart 1993: 84, calling attention to Arr. 7.14.4, who suggests the competitive relationship.

[40] On the gradual accord of worship to (first) Bronze Age tombs and (later) established traditional burial sites of Homeric heroes in the course of the Geometric and Archaic periods, see Snodgrass 1980: 38–40; Coldstream 1977: 341–57.

Alexander could have procured the proper permissions he sought from his 'father' Ammon, several of the writers suggest that his beloved friend would have outstripped the Homeric model to become nothing less than a new god.[41]

Were these treatments in the historians the only evidence of Alexander's assimilation of himself to Homeric-heroic paradigms, however, it could be argued that this model was introduced not through Alexander's behaviors and choices, but only on a literary level,[42] a particularly explicable development in a time period when fascination with such connections was accelerating.[43] However, Stewart has shown that certain attributes that Alexander himself may have promulgated in his portraits also invite comparison with Achilles. There are no surviving original portraits of Alexander that can be securely dated to his own lifetime. However, there do exist copies of several typologies that may have originally been developed during the later fourth century.[44] Certain enduring details in these portraits, in Stewart's analysis, suggest that the king likely sought a consistent physical image in both life and art. His clean-shaven face,[45] 'leonine' hair,[46] and *anastolê* (a rising lock or cowlick over the forehead that was an iconographic attribute of divinity)[47] would have connected him visually with the Homeric

---

[41] D.S. 17.115.6 (alone in claiming that Ammon actually granted permission for Hephaestion to be worshiped as a god); Plu. *Alex.* 72.3; Arr. 7.14.7; Just. 12.12.12 (wrongly claiming deification for Hephaestion on the strength of Alexander's orders alone).

[42] Stewart 1993: 82–3 provides a close reading of Achilles resonances in Plu. *Alex.* that are heavily dependent upon Plutarch's literary constructs; see also Mossman 1988.

[43] On interest in Homeric poetry during the Hellenistic period, e.g. Fantuzzi and Hunter 2004 *passim*.

[44] On the general evaluation and identification of later (especially Roman) copies of earlier Greek sculptures, see Richter 1965: 6–20; on the Alexander portrait types that may or may not have originated as lifetime images, see Stewart 1993: 106–21. Bieber 1965 is a convenient, if rather positivistic, summary of the major works of extant Alexander portraiture from the Hellenistic through the Roman periods, but Bieber 1964 is the standard reference and contains more extensive treatments of the same material.

[45] References collected by Stewart 1993: 341–50 *passim*. As noted ibid. 74–5 (with references), this was in an era when most living adult men were bearded and most sculpted gods and heroes, such as Apollo, Hermes, Dionysus, and Achilles, were not. Stewart further calls attention here to the potential negative side of Alexander's beardlessness: amongst *humans* (*contra* gods and heroes), it was associated with softness, lassitude, womanliness, and passive homosexuality.

[46] Stewart 1993: 76–8 (analysis), 341–50 (ancient testimonia). This invocation of the leonine would also have resonated with the cultural traditions of the Macedonians, who had long since associated lion-hunting with the prerogatives of nobility: see Carney 2002, with references; cf. also Bosworth 2002: 275–7; Palagia 2000.

[47] E.g. Stewart 2003: 37; Ridgway 1990: 140 n. 16, 143 n. 28 (with references); Smith 1988: 47–8 (associating the *anastolê* primarily with images of Apollo and Zeus); Schwarzenberg 1975b: 261–3 (on Alexander's *anastolê* as part of a conflation with Zeus, but arguing that the depictions of the man influenced those of the god, rather than vice versa).

hero,[48] and would also have provided easy appearance keys for repeated deployment by sculptors and other artists.

But Homeric heroism, and particularly Achilles' brand of it, was inherently oriented towards individual *kleos* and individual memory. And even though the Homeric world was broadly construed as long-ago history in the classical period,[49] Athenian tragedy, for example, actually used the heroic age as a distancing (or, to use Bowie's parlance, "filtering") mechanism for oblique discourse about contemporary politics.[50] An appeal to the Greek poleis for political ascendancy would therefore also demand behaviors from Alexander that engaged with their current models for historical agency, and demonstrated that he could serve their interests both as collaborator and as benefactor.

The idea that eminent individuals could collaborate with their poleis in order to achieve history-making change was active in Greece at least as early as the Tyrannicides. Over time, as the evidence in Chapters 4–6 showed, the perceptions of this relationship seem to have shifted. Individual leaders increasingly came to be viewed as essential, and the authority accorded to polis groups was in certain situations probably only nominal. There are times and places where both leader and citizenry seem to be performing: the leader acknowledges, at least verbally or symbolically, the ultimate power of the citizen body, which returns his sentiments, provides him with resources, and shares on some level in his achievements.[51] This kind of association is depicted in the evidence (perhaps sometimes rather hopefully) as being mutually productive: in Alexander's case, it emerges with particular clarity in his disposition of the member states of Philip's League of Corinth.

Perhaps the newest concept in Philip's vision of the League was the formation of an entirely new agent group with which he could potentially collaborate as *hegemôn* and *strategos autokratôr*:[52] "the Greeks." "The Greeks" had proven a fractious and ephemeral agent group at nearly every period in their recorded history, and even their 'collective' success during the Persian Wars was indebted to selective recollection rather than objective

---

[48] Stewart 1993: 72–86 (extended analysis).

[49] Most notably, Thucydides treats the Trojan War as 'real' history (Thuc. 1.3.1, 3.4, and esp. 8.4–12.1).

[50] See e.g. Bowie 1997; Easterling 1997 esp. 25–8.

[51] D. 23.198, it will be recalled from the opening of Chapter 1, contends that the Athenians take for themselves all too little of this share.

[52] On the titulature and its possible distinctions, see the references collected by Poddighe 2009: 103 n. 17.

evaluation of the respective contributions of the allied states.[53] But that created memory was very powerful, and still endured strongly in literature, cult, and popular discourse in Philip's day,[54] when he is said to have put forth a vendetta against the Persians as the motivation for an Eastern expedition.[55] Alexander, too, would harness that recollection of Persian enmities in order to propel the League members towards the East. But the League treaty[56] alone was not enough: Alexander still had to strengthen his relationships with the individual states, both inside and outside the League, in order to lay the foundations for his expedition.

Heisserer has collected the limited epigraphical evidence for Alexander's political associations with a number of Greek cities.[57] Like the inscriptions that offer insight into Philip's career, those connected with Alexander represent the king himself, an individual man, as party and signatory to agreements that are struck with entire poleis, represented as collectives known only by their plural names.[58] Heisserer's closing analysis demonstrates that this negotiation process was more prevalent earlier in Alexander's reign, when he seems to have taken greater trouble over the articulation and legitimization of his authority, than later. At a distance from the Greek world and self-sufficient, he did not need to court the Greek poleis any more, and indeed seems to have largely halted his efforts in this regard.[59] But during the period when he apparently needed to promulgate his authority, one way for him to accomplish this was by appealing to well-known models for leader–group interaction that had been employed with increasing frequency in the course of the fourth century.[60]

---

[53] Marincola 2007 esp. 114–23; cf. also Chapter 3, above.

[54] See Marincola 2007 on the reception of the Persian Wars in the fourth century BC; Jung 2006 reviews the evolution of memories of the battles of Marathon and Plataea down through the Roman imperial era.

[55] On the ancient sources, see Chapter 7, above; on Philip's larger goals, see e.g. Fredricksmeyer 1982, and Flower 2000: 98–9 on "panhellenic propaganda" as a foundation for Philip's plans.

[56] See Chapter 7, above.   [57] Heisserer 1980.

[58] Hagemajer Allen 2003 esp. 218–24 has shown that, within the available epigraphical evidence, honors to non-Greeks (amongst whom she includes Macedonians) at Athens between the end of the Peloponnesian War and the death of Philip were more commonly designated for individuals than for states or collectivities.

[59] Heisserer 1980: 233–4, esp. at 234: "The critical change came in 330 when the king, on his way to complete victory over the Persians, dismissed the last (infantry) contingents of the Corinthian League and released the city-states from the *syntaxeis* . . . In theory the League of Corinth was still in existence, for no act is known by which it was dismantled, but its *dogmata* are not heard of again, and for all practical purposes it had ceased to function entirely."

[60] On Philip's modeling of the League of Corinth (and its rhetoric) on established modes of Greek diplomatic interchange, see Perlman 1985. Alexander seems to have continued this technique.

Eminent individuals by Alexander's time could employ, among other tools, media that focused upon one-sided relationships with poleis, typically couched in the form of *euergesia,* or "benefaction." Those who aspired to historical memorialization could perform specific services or present gifts to entire cities: such acts would often be reciprocated with civic honors and commemorated with inscriptions, monuments, or statues. Isocrates, in fact, had broadly recommended this strategy to Philip,[61] and the frequent exploitation of it by other individuals during and after Alexander's lifetime is attested by the vast number of honorific gestures represented in the material evidence and testimonia.[62] Alexander seems to have had less immediate use for such methods than did others during and after his lifetime: spending so much of his reign on the Eastern frontiers limited his relationships with the Greek cities.[63] But a few of his known behaviors fit well with established procedures of benefaction. For example, an inscription attests to his dedication of the temple of Athena Polias at Priene,[64] and there is also evidence that he claimed to be bringing *eleutheria,* or "freedom," to the Greeks of Asia Minor as he drove the Persians from the region.[65]

The literary Alexander

Did Alexander deliberately *behave* in a manner that invited certain literary and cultural reactions? His detailed program of self-promotion, witnessed not only in contemporary and near-contemporary archaeological evidence but in its imitation by his successors,[66] suggests that he was strongly aware of the potential influence of his image. The material metonyms of himself that Alexander created, however, were only potent insofar as they connected their viewers and readers to the *idea* of him,[67] and the construction of that idea, as long as Alexander remained alive, was inherently a work in progress. The extant Alexander historians do narrate the king's life as having been replete with acts of conscious theatre. Whether or not Alexander ever performed

---

[61] Perlman 1985: 172 and n. 92.

[62] Van Minnen 2000: 437–43, an introduction to a more specific treatment of Greco-Roman Egypt, reviews the bibliography on Hellenistic and later euergetism; particularly important from his list for this period is Gauthier 1985.

[63] See note 59, above.   [64] Heisserer 1980: 142–5, 156–8, 164–5.

[65] Seager 1981: 106–7 is less optimistic that this was an important theme for Alexander than is Heisserer 1980: 166–8. On the history of the "freedom of the Greeks" theme, see Seager and Tuplin 1980.

[66] On the imitation of Alexander's image after his death, see Stewart 1993: 229–340.

[67] Stewart 1993, as noted by Samuel 1996.

precisely the deeds they record in precisely those ways (and broader outlines are more likely to reflect reality than are finer points), it is likely that he scripted his own actions with the same attention to detail that he seems to have invested in his campaigns, his literary accounts, and his material program.[68] The historiographers choose to recollect him as if he *did* do these things, suggesting that by the time they (or their sources) were writing, they might expect their audiences to be able to interpret a version of Alexander's character and historical legacy from the ways in which his behavior and his expedition were described.

On a practical level, Alexander did ensure that he was featured in particular types of literature, composed according to established Greek generic expectations, that would guarantee his memorialization and preserve his own version of history. He commissioned geographers, scientists, historiographers, and poets to record his Eastern expedition and his kingship. The works that these writers would produce were likely intended in part to communicate with the intellectual elites of Alexander's empire, and particularly with those whose loyalty and support was most needed: those who spoke Greek. But oral readings of the history and the poetry, in particular, would have had opportunities to reach even broader audiences, and therefore to harness wider popular sympathies.[69]

The 'Bematists,' the surveyors and engineers brought along on the Eastern expedition to document distances, courses, and landscapes along the route, seem to have mingled fanciful ethnographic and zoological accounts with their measurements.[70] In addition to distances between rivers and cities, paths of roads and mountain passes, and seasonal and astrological data, the fragments of the Bematists also introduce a people who love wine so greatly that they bathe in it exclusively, "savages" of Abarimon who have backwards feet and cannot breathe outside of their own land, giant Caspian mice that can gnaw through iron, and Indians so tall they can leap

---

[68] See note 29, above. Carney 2000a represents a test case for the analysis of Alexander's three withdrawals from the company of the army in the course of the Eastern expedition, and argues that the general plots of these episodes are likely factual, that Alexander himself was probably quite aware that he was behaving according to predictable patterns that mirrored those of Achilles, and that Alexander expected others to understand his actions and interpret them along Homeric lines.

[69] I am grateful to M. Flower for recommending this point. On the relationship between prose texts and performance during the classical period, e.g. Thomas 2003.

[70] Baynham 2003: 4, highlighting (n. 4) the translations of Robinson 1953, which collect and treat much of the fragmentary Alexander material. As also noted by Baynham (n. 5), testimonia and fragments of the Bematists may be found at *FGrH* 119 (Baeton), 120 (Diognetus), 121 (Philonides of Crete), 122 (Amyntas), 123 (Archelaus of Cappadocia).

an elephant in a single bound,[71] amongst other imaginative delights. This blending of scientific information with *thaumata* ("marvels")[72] suggests the intellectual context in which the Bematists likely viewed their work as participating: the wide-ranging Ionian logographic tradition of the sixth and fifth centuries BC.[73] The most prominent recent heir to that literary line was Herodotus,[74] whose historical treatment of the Persian Wars incorporated much logographic and ethnographic material, and whose influence on later historiography and other prose literature was undeniable even by Alexander's day.[75] Not only would there likely have been intellectual currency to be gained by the Bematists in invoking such a connection, but they would also have been able to recall the long-standing conflict between Europe and Asia whose origins (in the Trojan War) and climax (in the Persian ones) Herodotus had attempted to explain.[76] Philip and then Alexander, in articulating the 'need' for an Eastern expedition in the first place, had deliberately revived this very conflict.[77] The invocation of the now-mythologized earlier war and its famous chronicler might therefore have lent both legitimacy and the air of legend to Alexander's endeavors.

---

[71] The wine-bathers are the 'Tapyri,' according to both Baeton and Amyntas, *FGrH* 119 F 1 and 122 F 5, respectively, both = Ath. 10.442B; the other examples are from, respectively, Baeton, *FGrH* 119 F 5 = Plin. *Nat. hist.* 7.11; Amyntas, *FGrH* 122 F 3 = Ael. *NA* 17.17; Archaelaus, *FGrH* 123 F 1 = Solin. 52.18–23.

[72] Even given, as Bosworth 1988a: 3–4 points out, the capricious survival of the fragments, which would under the circumstances naturally tend to highlight the bizarre.

[73] Survey: Pearson 1939, with extended chapters on Hecataeus of Miletus, Xanthus of Lydia, Charon of Lampsacus, and Hellanicus of Lesbos; see also the papers in Luraghi 2001. Compact literary-historical summaries: Kurke 2000a: 117–18 (very brief); Lesky 1966: 218–23 (more detailed, with references).

[74] On Herodotus' explicit and implied debts: to the contemporary intellectual milieu, see Thomas 2000; to Hecataeus, see West 1991; to the literary work of his predecessors (via a case study on Herodotus' Persian catalogs), see Armayor 1978a; to the larger scientific trends of his day, see de Ste. Croix 1977. On the transition from Hecataeus to 'true' historiography, see Bertelli 2001 (concentrating on Hecataeus' genealogical, rather than geographical, work). On Herodotus' unique historical and literary approach in contrast to that of his contemporaries, see Fowler 1996.

[75] On the ancient reception of Herodotus over time, see e.g. Hornblower 1992 (on Herodotus' use by Thucydides); Gray 1989 and Keller 1910–11 (on Xenophon); Murray 1972 (on the Hellenistic period).

[76] Flower 2000: 108, discussing the Greeks' association of the Trojan War with the Persian Wars.

[77] Plb. 3.6.8–14; D.S. 16.89.2–3, 91.2; 17.4.9, 24.1; Plu. *Alex.* 14.1 (only a reference to Alexander's being named the leader of the expedition); Arr. 1.1.2 (only a mention of the expedition), 2.14.4; Just. 11.2.5–7; books 1 and 2 of Curtius, where this material would most likely have been included, are lost. On the expedition against Persia (and, ultimately, the burning of Persepolis) as putative vengeance for the Persian sack of Athens in 480/79, see Arr. 1.16.7; 3.16.7–8, 18.11–12 (with Arrian's own criticism at 18.12). On its revival of the Trojan War's conflict between Eastern and Western peoples, e.g. Flower 2000: 108–10.

To Eumenes of Cardia (Alexander's head secretary) and possibly also Diodotus of Erythrae are attributed Alexander's royal *Ephemerides,* the court diaries. The inherently practical purpose of these documents would likely have lent them credibility as repositories of basic facts – which situation has in turn roused scholarly suspicions about the potential for their later falsification.[78] But the converse would also have been possible: the diaries could easily have been shaped, even by the process of simple selection, to show the king's activities in a particular light, and the recorders would have had every incentive to color this documentary 'history' according to Alexander's personal preferences.[79] Expectations like these, in fact, do seem to have been levied upon Callisthenes of Olynthus (*FGrH* 124), a former student of Aristotle who traveled on Alexander's Eastern expedition as historiographer and produced, probably in dispatches, the only known direct eyewitness history of the campaign. He appears from the testimonia and fragments, as many have noted, to have trodden – and occasionally crossed – the line between narrative and encomium. It was, ironically, precisely when he refused to participate in a lived praise-ritual, the *proskynesis* ("prostration") Alexander attempted to urge upon his court, that Callisthenes was accused of conspiracy and killed.[80]

Poets are also attested as members of Alexander's retinue: the list probably included at least Choerilus of Iasos, Agis of Argos, and Cleon of Sicily,[81] if not more. Given Alexander's well-known affinity for the *Iliad,* he and his poets likely construed his journey as the subject of a new epic.[82] If any of the poems proved popular and successful, Alexander would be equipped with a way of promoting his activities and his heroic qualities whose very form would invoke some of the most revered Greek literary traditions. And he would potentially enjoy access to prestige and memory on multiple levels, appearing not only as commissioner and as subject of the poems, but also as actual performer of the deeds that they recorded. This, in turn, would potentially allow him to outstrip even Pindar's victorious kings,

---

[78] See the summary of this problem, with references, in Baynham 2003: 5–6, nn. 8, 10–11.

[79] Eumenes is said to have enjoyed Alexander's high favor: see *FGrH* 117 T 2b–c = Nep. 18.1.4–6 and Plu. *Eum.* 1.4–7, respectively.

[80] Curt. 8.5.10–8.23; Plu. *Alex.* 52.7–55.9; Arr. 4.10.1–12.7; Just. 12.7.1–2. There is a lacuna in Diodorus between 17.83.6 and 17.84.1, where the *proskynesis* debate and the subsequent death of Callisthenes would have been covered. On the possibility of Callisthenes' having lost the king's favor even before his fall, see Borza 1981 esp. 84–5.

[81] Curt. 8.5.7–8, first called to my attention by Stewart 1993: 13.

[82] A concept that apparently increased in popularity after Alexander's death, although none of the works survives: See, on ancient Alexander poems, *FGrH* 153 F 12b, 13, 14a, 15a, and probably 15b and c; on medieval ones, Baynham 1998: 2–4; Cary 1956 *passim.*

who collected poetical praise for owning – but not, of course, for racing themselves – the horses that bore their jockeys and charioteers to victories in the panhellenic games.[83]

Alexander the hero

Likely because it had come to seem such a natural activity for a towering figure, and because of the great success and fame of his first attempt, Alexandria in Egypt,[84] Alexander is traditionally credited with the establishment of many cities. Although only about six *in toto* are secure attributions,[85] they alone would have provided more than enough opportunity for Alexander to seek the heroic attentions due to a *ktistês*, a "founder." (Brasidas, Epaminondas, and Philip, after all, had been honored as founders, too,[86] and might well have served as models for Alexander's choices.) Alexander does, in fact, seem to have received founder-cult at Egyptian Alexandria: the question is the degree to which this was active while he was still alive. The process might have been gradual. An equestrian portrait of Alexander *ktistês* represented in the testimonia may have been erected by its subject, and it has also been suggested that offerings were made at Alexandria in the living Alexander's name.[87] It would therefore have been only a minor step for Ptolemy to create a second, even more important cult of the deified Alexander after the king's death.[88]

Alexander was also able to connect himself with other manifestations of heroism. Alexander's mother, Olympias, claimed descent from Achilles through Neoptolemus, which probably had lent further impetus to Alexander's 'Iliadic' behavior. But the Macedonian Argead dynasty, it will be recalled, also claimed origin from Heracles through Alexander's father

---

[83] Arr. 1.12.2 suggests that none of Alexander's poets was composing lyric poetry (ἀλλ᾽ οὐδὲ ἐν μέλει ᾖσθη Ἀλέξανδρος, ἐν ὅτῳ Ἱέρων τε καὶ Γέλων καὶ Θήρων καὶ πολλοὶ ἄλλοι, "Alexander was not hymned in lyric, as were Hieron and Gelon and Theron and many others"), and may be contrasting Pindar in particular (e.g. Pi. *O.* 9.1, where the poet refers to his own work as a μέλος), who composed several of his odes for these very Sicilian tyrants.

[84] See Fraser 1972: 3.   [85] Fraser 1996, conclusion at 201.

[86] See Chapters 2, 5, 6, and 7, above. Also worth recalling is Xenophon's plan to found a colony of the Ten Thousand – and the negative reaction of the army to the possibility that this would extend enormous privileges to Xenophon: see Chapter 5, above, and Due 1993 on Xenophon as an inspiration for Alexander himself.

[87] A detailed description and analysis of this statue appears as part of a late antique rhetorical exercise (Ps.-Lib. [= Nikol.] *Prog.* 27, *c.* AD 400), cited in Stewart 1993: 397–400. It is possible that the statue was actually erected by Ptolemy, rather than by Alexander himself: Stewart collects modern bibliography on this problem ibid., as well. On the scanty but reasonable evidence for the lifetime cult, see Fraser 1972: 212.

[88] Fraser 1972: 213–28.

Philip,[89] something that Alexander had recalled by placing the head of Heracles upon some of his earliest silver and bronze coinage (cf. above). Despite his elevated status as the son of Zeus, Heracles had also been the son of Alcmena, and therefore half human. In his position as a semi-divine hero, he had accomplished a legendary series of difficult labors that were frequently represented in public art.[90] Further adventure stories told of his wide travels and the other marvelous deeds that he had performed in the course of his wanderings. For the new king of Macedon, already planning to fulfill his father's dream of a massive expedition into Asia, the Heracles tradition, if properly exploited, could be harnessed to justify and even magnify his own achievements.[91]

The Heracles of mythology was a polyvalent hero, and the Macedonian monarchs were therefore able to select the facets they wished to highlight. Philip's panhellenic aspirations as victor in horse and chariot races, for example, were significantly supported by Heracles-athlete imagery.[92] Alexander had additional opportunity to make use of the hero as inspiration for expansion, exploration, struggle, and conquest, but he also continued the associations with Heracles as the traditional founder of the panhellenic games. His expedition not only included athletes, artists, and musicians, but also celebrated its own achievements with festivals that included the customary contests.[93] As patron of these 'games,' then, Alexander became an endlessly renewable image of Heracles, re-enacting the hero's exploits all the way to the edge of the known world.

Close readings of the literary sources also yield numerous possible allusions to the myths of Heracles.[94] A series of individual episodes in the larger narrative of the Eastern expedition are frequently invoked. Upon approaching Tyre, Alexander announces his plans to make sacrifice to Heracles there;

---

[89]   E.g. (amongst numerous testimonia) D.S. 17.1.5; Plu. *Alex.* 2.1; Arr. 2.5.9, 4.11.6; Just. 11.4.5, 12.16.3, and see Chapter 7, above.

[90]   *LIMC* s.v. 'Herakles,' 'IV. Herakles' Labors;' cf. also 'V. Herakles' Expeditions,' and 'VI. Other principal adversaries and locations.'

[91]   Even Alexander's assimilation to Heracles, despite its unprecedented scale, was not a completely new concept: Euthymus of Locri, for example (see Chapter 6, above), seems to have presented himself as Heracles (Currie 2002 *passim*), and later in antiquity, others apparently did so as well (ibid. 37 n. 130).

[92]   See Chapter 7, above.

[93]   Tritle 2009: 122–9; cf. Romano 1990: 74–7 on Alexander's broader association with the culture of the Greek games.

[94]   E.g. Anderson 1928: 19–23, an analysis of the deliberate and detailed portrayal of Alexander as Heracles in Ps.-Call.

the Tyrians' answer, a refusal of admission, is taken by the sources as his provocation to besiege the city.[95] The literary tradition also has Alexander dreaming, during the course of the siege, that Heracles himself is beckoning to Alexander to enter Tyre;[96] once Alexander does take the city, he frees those who have sought sanctuary at Heracles' temple and some envoys who may be on a religious mission to honor the hero.[97] Alexander's journey to the Egyptian oracle of Ammon at Siwah is said to have been undertaken, at least in part, in imitation of an earlier consultation taken by Heracles,[98] and the king's bold capture of the 'Rock of Aornus' is recorded in nearly all of the major sources as an open endeavor to accomplish something that the hero would not – or could not – do.[99]

The idea of not merely worshipping or imitating Heracles, but even surpassing him, becomes in the sources increasingly important to Alexander in the course of the Eastern expedition. Although there are hopeful references to tracing the most distant reaches of Heracles' sway upon the expedition's arrival in India,[100] nowhere, ironically, is this theme more clearly evident than in the accounts of the momentous decision to turn back during the 'mutiny' at the Hyphasis.[101] Arrian's treatment, in particular, has Alexander focusing upon his intense desire to exceed the example and the boundaries set by his famous ancestor. In the West, Alexander plans to reach the Pillars of Heracles (Arr. 5.26.2), which function in the context of his speech both as a known geographic marker and as a powerful (and conveniently eponymous) metaphor. In speaking of the East, he emphasizes how little of Asia

---

[95] D.S. 17.40.2–3; Curt. 4.2.2–5; Arr. 2.15.7–16.7; Just. 11.10.10–11. This 'Tyrian Heracles' (whose precise identity is speculated upon by Arr. *loc. cit.*) is most commonly identified with the Phoenician deity Melkarth.

[96] Curt. 4.2.17; Plu. *Alex.* 24.5; Arr. 2.18.1.

[97] Curt. 4.4.18 (but no mention of Heracles specifically); Arr. 2.24.5. At Arr. 2.24.6, Alexander also celebrates his victory with a sacrifice, a military review, a naval procession, and athletic games in honor of the Tyrian Heracles, and rededicates the Tyrian sacred ship to Heracles, with a new inscription; at Arr. 3.6.1, Alexander holds still another set of sacrifices and games for the Tyrian Heracles after his return from Egypt.

[98] Arr. 2.3.1–2. Arrian also mentions Alexander's additional desire to rival another visit to Ammon by Perseus, another putative ancestor on his father Philip's side via Alcmena, the mother of Heracles.

[99] D.S. 17.85.1–2, cf. 96.2; Curt. 8.11.2; Arr. 4.28.1–4, cf. 30.4 (although Arrian doubts the veracity of the Heracles story and prefers to take it as a metaphor); Just. 12.7.12–13.

[100] Curt. 8.10.1; Arr. 5.3.1–4 (referring to the Heracles stories, but with no commitment to their veracity).

[101] For the most extensive accounts of this mutiny see Curt. 9.2.10–3.19; Arr. 5.25.2–29.3; cf. also D.S. 17.94.1–95.2; Plu. *Alex.* 62.1–8; Just. 12.8.10–17; on Heracles specifically, see Curt. 9.2.29; Arr. 5.26.2, 5.

remains to be conquered, now that the expedition has already outstripped both Heracles and Dionysus by passing Aornus and Nysa (Arr. 5.26.5–6). Arrian's Alexander also repeatedly describes the efforts of his army as πόνοι, "labors" (Arr. 5.25.3–27.4 *passim*). Although this is not the term ordinarily applied to the "Labors of Heracles" (these are conventionally called ἄθλοι, "contests," or "tasks"), it soon becomes clear that this is precisely the context in which Alexander wishes his Macedonians to envision themselves when he redeploys the term πόνοι alongside a reference to Heracles: οὐδὲ Διονύσου, ἁβροτέρου τούτου θεοῦ ἢ καθ᾽ Ἡρακλέα, ὀλίγοι πόνοι ("and there were also more than a few labors for Dionysus, a less sturdy god than Heracles," Arr. 5.26.5).

Smaller references to Alexander's relationship with Heracles are also frequent. Sacrifices are made by Alexander to Heracles (generally alongside other divinities) at significant celebratory moments during the Thracian military campaigns and the Eastern expedition;[102] Alexander also occasionally recalled Heracles' name and dress in his personal life,[103] and apparently incorporated Heracles into dynastic displays.[104] The overriding significance of the king's relationship with the hero, therefore, is surely to be found in the pervasiveness of Heracles in Alexander's imagination, as his self-created links with Heracles are said by the sources to have continued throughout his adult life.

---

[102]   E.g. Curt. 3.12.27 (after the battle of Issus, three altars on the banks of the Pinarus for Jupiter, Hercules, and Minerva); Arr. 1.4.5 (after the subjugation of the Getae, sacrifices for Zeus Soter, Heracles, and the Ister river); Arr. 1.11.7 (after the first landing in Asia, sacrifices for Zeus Apobaterius, Athena, and Heracles); Arr. 6.3.2 (at the point when the army and the navy split up for the journey home, sacrifices for Heracles, Ammon, and other deities); Arr. *Ind.* 36.3 (after the safe return of Nearchus and the fleet, sacrifices for Zeus Soter, Heracles, Apollo Alexicacus, Poseidon, and other deities of the sea).

[103]   See Ephippus, *FGrH* 126 F 5 = Ath. 12.537E, cited and quoted in Stewart 1993: 356 T 48, on Alexander's adoption of Heracles' iconic lion's pelt and club. There is also a tradition that Alexander's relationship with Barsine, the daughter of Artabazus, produced a son whom Alexander named Heracles: e.g. Curt. 10.6.11 (where the boy is unnamed); Just. 13.2.7, and see Brunt 1974, arguing against Tarn 1921, who believes that this son was fictitious.

[104]   A tradition connected with the fictitious 'will' of Alexander has the king commissioning several elaborate statue groups from, variously (examples and testimonia collected by Stewart 1993: 412–13): (H)olkias, a newly appointed client-king of Illyria; Perdiccas; and Ptolemy (Ps. Call. 3.133; Jul. Val. 3.59; *Liber de morte* 122). Inevitably, these groupings include images of Heracles/Hercules, Ammon, Olympias, and Philip, and often representations of Athena/Minerva and Alexander as well, and the various locations proposed for them include not merely Illyria, but also Egypt, Olympia, and Delphi. Although Alexander's 'will,' of course, was a posthumous creation, a case has been made for a fairly early date (Stewart 1993: 413, citing Heckel 1988, who prefers 321 or 315). If this is right, the mere mention of the statue groups (whether or not they were ever actually erected) may legitimately demonstrate others' *perceptions* of Alexander's interest in Heracles.

Alexander the god

While it apparently grew increasingly possible over time for hero-cult to be paid to living persons, in Greek religion a hero was not the same thing as a god.[105] In more recent years, the status of divinity had probably been offered to Agesilaus and Lysander,[106] and was at a minimum implied by Philip, who by the time of his death seems to have been close to presenting himself as divine.[107] But Alexander's systematic connection of himself to Achilles and Heracles may have helped to lay the foundations for his invocation of Dionysus and (especially) for his declaration that he had been revealed as the son of Zeus. No Greek individual had made such venturesome claims before, but again, they were prepared, both before and during Alexander's lifetime.

Alexander's associations of his experiences with those of the god Dionysus become more prominent in the narratives once the Eastern expedition reaches Bactria and India, where the troops and their leaders came to believe that the god had once journeyed.[108] The sighting of ivy in the outer reaches of Bactria was initially taken as evidence of Dionysus' easternmost sway, which observation in turn provided the welcome opportunity for Alexander to 'surpass' a divinity's travels by crossing Dionysus' 'boundaries' (Curt. 7.9.15). The arrival in India, therefore, was cause for great rejoicing, and even the Nysaeans' prudent concoction of Dionysus as the founder of their city[109] – and the concomitant realization on the Macedonians' part that they had to travel still further to win Alexander's 'competition' with the god – could not dampen the spirits of the troops or of their king. The ivy around Nysa was greeted with mass celebrations,[110] and Alexander

[105] On the general characteristics of hero-cult as distinct from other kinds of worship in ancient Greece, e.g. the brief survey by Mikalson 2010; on the development of hero-cult, e.g. Antonaccio 1995.

[106] See Chapter 6, above.   [107] See Chapter 7, above.

[108] Bosworth 1996 argues that there is no extant evidence for Dionysus in India before Alexander, and that Alexander and his advisers may have actually extrapolated the Indian links themselves out of the sighting of some ivy in Bactria (cf. below) and a single reference at E. *Bacc.* 15 (a play that was composed in Macedon and that Alexander and his educated officers surely knew), which refers to Dionysus' having traveled through that region. Arr. 5.3.1–4 reports Eratosthenes' skepticism about the validity of some of the 'mythology' that the members of the Eastern expedition invoked.

[109] Bosworth 1996: 147–53 makes a strong case for this reading: Alexander's recent interest in Dionysus (of which the Nysaeans were probably warned through diplomatic channels) would have virtually guaranteed favorable treatment for their city if they could convince the king that the god had established them there.

[110] For the whole of the Nysa–Dionysus episode, see Curt. 8.10.11–17; Arr. 5.1.1–2.7; Just. 12.7.6–8. There is a large lacuna in the text of Diodorus (after 17.83.9) where this episode would have been covered.

renewed his hopes that in the end he and his men would outstrip Dionysus (Arr. 5.2.1).

Perhaps because the expedition's Indian campaign was cut short by the Hyphasis mutiny, there are few other spectacular invocations of the god transmitted in the literature, save one. After exiting the wastes of the Gedrosian Desert, Alexander and those of his troops who had escaped with their lives entered the comparatively abundant and comfortable environment of Carmania. The story (known to nearly all of the major extant sources) that Alexander celebrated the narrow escape with a lavish Dionysiac triumph, is rejected by Arrian, who prefers a more dignified return heralded by sacrifices and athletic games.[111] The Dionysiac version, however, would have been in much better keeping with the image that Alexander seems to have wanted to project: after conquering parts of the world that the god had never reached, Alexander was returning to his capital literally in the god's place, for he now occupied Dionysus' traditional mythological position as the leader of the procession. And he had also already taken a place in the divine pantheon equal to that of Dionysus, as well, for he had long since been working to identify himself as the son of Zeus.

Alexander's relationship with the Egyptian god Ammon, whom he, with many others, appears to have connected with Zeus,[112] has been debated almost from the time of the king's visit to Ammon's oracle at Siwah in 331/0 BC.[113] Precisely what message he received there remains unknown, but the message he chose to communicate upon his return was that he had been revealed as the god's son. As outrageous as it may have seemed, this was probably a more prudent step along the path to divine status than Philip's final gambit had been, when he interposed a statue of himself into a procession of Olympian gods at his daughter's wedding.[114] Whether or not intended to introduce Philip as a deity,[115] the gesture had furnished a

---

[111] D.S. 17.106.1; Curt. 9.10.22–8; Plu. *Alex.* 67.1–8; Arr. 6.28.1–3 (rejecting the anecdote on the grounds that it is not recorded by Ptolemy, Aristobulus, or any other writers deserving of note).

[112] See e.g. Fredricksmeyer 1991: 200 n. 5; Brunt 1976: vol. I, 467–80 (app. 5), esp. 474–5. The Ammon–Zeus connection was not unique to Alexander, and is evident in Greek literature at least as early as Pindar (Classen 1959 esp. 349–50).

[113] In the extant Alexander historians, see D.S. 17.49.2–51.4; Curt. 4.7.5–32; Plu. *Alex.* 26.11–27.9, cf. also 28.1; Arr. 3.31–4.5; Just. 11.11.2–13. Other ancient testimonia and modern studies about the visit to Ammon in general are collected by Fredricksmeyer 1991: 199 nn. 1–2.

[114] See Chapter 7, above.

[115] D.S. 16.92.5. On this and other possible invocations of divinity by Philip, most notably the chryselephantine statues of himself and his family members that he erected in the Philippeum at Olympia, see Fredricksmeyer 1981: 146–7; cf. also Fredricksmeyer 2003: 254–5; Kuttner 1999: 111; and Carney 2007 and 2000b, as discussed in Chapter 7, above.

cautionary tale for the son and successor, who forged his own links with the heroic and the divine by explicitly connecting them with his *deeds*, rather than merely with his image. There being no established mythological 'script' for the son of Zeus Ammon,[116] however, Alexander was on new ground. As such, his self-portrayal as Ammon's son involved careful negotiation between his own desires for a new and very special type of public recognition on the one hand, and the expectations ingrained in his 'audiences' (friends, advisers, troops, and local peoples) by their cultural and religious backgrounds on the other.

Alexander's new 'divine' parentage was readily honored by Callisthenes,[117] by the court philosopher Anaxarchus,[118] and likely by the court poets as well. Whether or not these individuals actually believed that the physical Alexander had genuinely been sired by a god (a story about Olympias' impregnation by a giant serpent may already have been in circulation),[119] they would doubtless have gained favor from their magnification of the king. Literature, however, was quite a separate case from action, particularly within a Greco-Macedonian culture whose religion was heavily dependent upon orthopraxis rather than orthodoxy. The frequent sacrifices and oaths that Alexander offered to Ammon or to gods 'suggested' by Ammon[120] posed no problems, as the appeasement of local deities of all varieties and origins had long since been an acceptable practice in Greek religion.[121] Alexander's new 'status' also appears to have caused few initial difficulties amongst his friends and advisers – until the debate over possible religious obligations *towards him* began.

Alexander seems to have wanted to be considered a god in his own right, probably while he was still alive. The imitation and 'surpassing' of Achilles, Heracles, and Dionysus strongly implied it, and the claims of

---

[116] Though it might be argued that Heracles, as the son of Zeus, provided some useful paradigms, particularly given that Alexander's journey to Siwah may have been undertaken in imitation of the hero: see note 98, above.

[117] On Callisthenes' role in the spread of Alexander's news, see e.g. Badian 1981: 44–7, 53; Tarn 1950: 347–59 *passim*.

[118] Arr. 4.9.7–9, 10.6–7; Plu. *Alex.* 28.4–6, also strongly implied at 52.5–7.

[119] Selected references to this tale in the major sources include Plu. *Alex.* 2.6, 3.1–4; Arr. 4.10.2 (oblique); Just. 11.11.3, 12.16.2; all imply in various ways that the legend may actually have originated with Olympias.

[120] E.g., in Arrian alone, Arr. 6.3.2, 9.4–5; Arr. *Ind.* 35.8. For an analysis of still other sacrifices that may have been performed by Alexander on Ammon's instructions, see Fredricksmeyer 1991: 209–13.

[121] See e.g. Martin 1987; Burkert 1977 esp. 331–412 (on Greek polytheism); Nilsson 1940. On Alexander's embrace of non-Greek or hybridized deities other than Ammon, see e.g. Bing 1991.

direct descent from the divine pressed his case. Although the precise context and wording of the *proskynesis* debate of 328 BC treated in both Curtius (8.5.5–24) and Arrian (4.10.5–12.7) can have little basis in historical fact, it is likely that the general content reflects some of the concerns held by Alexander's contemporaries, and the ways in which he dealt with them.[122] *Proskynesis*, or obeisance by ritual prostration (frequently accompanied by a kiss), was an act of reverence that had long been required before the Persian king. For Alexander's Greek and Macedonian courtiers and troops, however, *proskynesis* was a religious act, and the Persians' use of this gesture before their ruler therefore appeared fawning, inappropriate, and otiose.[123] Alexander had reached an impasse. Although he had never had himself formally crowned king of Persia,[124] he had defeated Darius and effectively usurped his throne, and could therefore probably safely demand *proskynesis* from the Persians around him, who were accustomed to acknowledging their sovereign in this way. The Greeks and Macedonians, however, were a far different matter, and this may be why Alexander is said to have first broached the possibility of *proskynesis* – and, by extension, the virtual acknowledgement of his divinity – within their private inner circle at the upper echelons of the court.[125]

Alexander's attempt failed. Callisthenes is credited with a dangerous speech that voiced the reservations of many of those present; as noted above, not long afterwards, likely as a result of his opposition, he was accused of involvement in the 'pageboys' conspiracy' and executed.[126] The fact that Alexander would eliminate his chosen historian so abruptly may indicate an evolution in the king's thinking about the methods by which he could both advertise and memorialize himself: even by Greek standards, recollection in text was not so potent as divinity, and Alexander may by now have envisioned himself as existing both inside and outside of history.

---

[122] Badian 1981: 28–30. Arrian says that Alexander's desire to receive *proskynesis* is mentioned widely in the sources (προσκυνεῖσθαι ἐθέλειν Ἀλέξανδρον λόγος κατέχει, "the story is broadly reported that Alexander wanted to be greeted with prostration," Arr. 4.9.9).

[123] E.g. in A. *Ag.* 919–20, 922, 925 Agamemnon's reluctance to receive *proskynesis* upon his return from Troy on the grounds that it is characteristic of "barbarians" (for Aeschylus' audience of 458 BC this term was likely a virtual metonym for "Persians"). The context also strongly suggests that such obeisance is only fitting, in Agamemnon's view, for divinities. See also the analysis by Fredricksmeyer 1979: 48.

[124] On the distinction between the kingship of Persia and Alexander's apparently self-created 'kingship of Asia,' see Fredricksmeyer 2000.

[125] Curt. 8.5.9–10 (where Alexander is decorously 'absent,' but hidden behind a convenient curtain, during the conversation he has requested); Arr. 4.10.5.

[126] See note 80, above.

Amongst other objections, Callisthenes may have reminded Alexander's court that Delphi had declared Heracles immortal, but only posthumously (Arr. 4.11.7). If Alexander had hoped, by extension, for lifetime deification authorized by Ammon's oracle,[127] his hopes were in vain: the Greeks and Macedonians of the court refused at this stage to acknowledge him as divine. So did his Macedonian troops: at the very point of the Eastern expedition's deepest penetration into India, for example, the mutineers on the Hyphasis suggested that Alexander send them home and let his 'father' (Zeus-Ammon) lead him onwards instead.[128] Alexander's desire for divine honors apparently did not fade; by the spring of 323, he is described as receiving Greek emissaries in Babylon who approached him offering golden crowns ὡς θεωροὶ δῆθεν ἐς τιμὴν θεοῦ ἀφιγμένοι, "as if they had really come as oracular envoys, for the worship of a god" (Arr. 7.23.2), and the Athenian Assembly is debating the erection of a statue of Alexander as θεὸς ἀνίκητος ("unconquerable god").[129] Of the extant testimonia, only two say directly that requests for divine treatment came from Alexander himself,[130] but it is probably not wrong to infer that the idea in some form originated with him.[131]

Alexander's efforts to secure divine status during his lifetime were somewhat more successful outside of his immediate surroundings and away from mainland Greece. As the new de facto (but uncoronated) pharaoh of Egypt, he was accorded appropriate position in the complex Egyptian pantheon – and memorialized at the temple at Luxor in reliefs whose inscriptions advertise that he paid for them himself.[132] Alexander may also have succeeded in stimulating the foundation of personal cults in some of the Greek cities of Asia. The evidence for these, however, is all posthumous (third century BC and later), and the literary sources do not mention the cults even at points where they might logically have been expected to do

---

[127] A possibility discussed by Anderson 1928: 16.   [128] D.S. 17.108.3; Arr. 7.8.3; Just. 12.11.6.

[129] Stewart 1993: 381–2 presents testimonia on the statue; Fredricksmeyer 1991: 213 n. 48 collects ancient citations on Alexander's "desire for divine honors" from the Greeks. Cf. Atkinson 1973 and Bickerman 1963 on the Athenian deification debate and the Alexander cult question, respectively; and Worthington 2001: 129–30 on the possibilities that "the envisaged [Athenian] statue was only an honorary one, and . . . that Hyperides [the major literary source for it] is being heavily sarcastic and echoing a popular sentiment that divine honours for the living Alexander, let alone his being recognised as an invincible god, were ridiculed amongst the Athenians."

[130] Fredricksmeyer 1991: 213 n. 48, citing Plu. *Mor.* 219E; Ael. *VH* 2.19.

[131] E.g. Fredricksmeyer 1991: 213. Alexander's relationship with Athens seems to have been difficult. Both sides attempted the expected exchanges of honors, although neither perhaps foresaw truly lasting benefits from the association: see Mitchel 1965: 189–92.

[132] Stewart 1993: 174–8, citing Abd el-Raziq 1984.

so.[133] The major argument in favor of any Asiatic Greek cults having been lifetime honors for Alexander, then, lies in their later comparands: the well-documented divine status and worship accorded to Alexander's successors and the subsequent dynasties of Hellenistic kings.[134]

8.3 Conclusion: Alexander's audiences

There is no need to believe that Alexander was beloved[135] during his lifetime or at the dramatic moment of his death in order to acknowledge the potency of his image. The most powerful 'great men' of classical Greece, in fact, all seem to have in some way provoked both imitation and dissent, and to have both found themselves and made themselves different from the citizen groups from which they came. The most eloquent testimony to the power of Alexander's campaign of imagery is its continuation, in various forms, by the *Diadochoi*. As witnessed by the descriptions of Alexander's death discussed in Chapter 1, above, his 'Successors' quarreled over his authority first with his relics, later through his image, and ultimately by appropriating and adapting his style of kingship for their own. By the year 306, Antigonus and Demetrius, and by 304, Ptolemy, Seleucus, and Lysimachus, felt sufficiently confident in their own claims to authority to take the title of βασιλεύς ("king") and adopt as a permanent symbol the diadem that Alexander had occasionally worn as part of his hybrid Macedonian-Persian royal dress.[136] The claims to legitimacy that these *Diadochoi* constructed between Alexander's death in 323 and the 'Year of the Kings' in 306–304 began with their particular relationships to Alexander the man, but gradually metamorphosed into a more general relationship with Alexander the *concept*.[137] And this association, in turn, determined many of the emblems

---

[133] Evidence collected by Stewart 1993: 98–9, 102, 419–20, app. 3; cf. also Badian 1981: 59–65. Flower 1997: 258–61, however, recalling Lane Fox 1986: 118, highlights two fragments of Theopompus (*FGrH* 115 F 253, 254b), likely from the same letter of advice to Alexander, that may suggest that Alexander was indeed receiving cult – possibly in both Greece and Asia – during his lifetime.

[134] See Habicht 1970, answered by Badian 1981: 33–44, who argues that Alexander's example changed the way the Greek world was prepared to consider the deification of living rulers.

[135] E.g. Heckel 1996. On self-conscious mockery and acknowledgement of ruler-cult as a performance rather than a conviction, at least by elites who claimed to have true understanding of what was really happening, see Scott 1932.

[136] See Gruen 1985; Müller 1973; Ritter 1965. Some would also consider Cassander an entry in this group of self-styled 'kings': those who exclude him are only including the rulers who were able to exercise significant sway outside of Macedon: see Bosworth 2002: 246.

[137] Stewart 1993 esp. 229–340.

of what is now called 'Hellenistic kingship'[138] – several of which emblems, in fact, were part of the symbolic battle for Alexander after his death that was described above in Chapter 1.

In the end, Alexander seems to have done his work so well that he even received substantial credit, both in literature and in popular sentiment, for activities that were not his own. Throughout the Hellenistic and Roman periods, an ever-growing body of literature chronicled his authentic deeds and quickly embellished them with superhuman attitudes, exploits, and accomplishments. Alexander became a rhetorical convention, a romantic hero, an artistic mainstay, a political symbol, and a stable recipient of divine cult far from his first place of worship in Alexandria.[139] The many Alexandrias recorded in later literature, for example, though they cannot all be his,[140] demonstrate that the idea of Alexander as a colonial founder was every bit as potent as the reality. And by the time some of the most fanciful stories about him were stitched together into medieval romances, Alexander could fly.[141]

---

[138] See note 66, above.

[139] A useful survey of Alexander's *Nachleben* in the Hellenistic period is Errington 1975; on the Roman period, see Spencer 2002, Isager 1993, Wirth 1975; on the art works and physical symbolism, see Stewart 1993, Hannestad 1993, Bieber 1964. On the *Alexander Romance* and its effects upon the later literary reception of Alexander, see Cary 1956; on the medieval Alexander, see Aerts, Hermans, and Visser 1978 and now the contributions to Zuwiyya 2011. For a more general survey stretching from the Hellenistic period through medieval Islam, see di Vita and Alfano 1995: 153–91.

[140] See Fraser 1996 and note 85, above.

[141] Lifted up in a kind of basket by birds, first at *Alexander Romance* 2.41. Stoneman 1991 believes that the *Romance* may have found its earliest origins in the third century BC (ibid. 9), but points out that the earliest manuscript is from the third century AD (ibid. 8) and the earliest version of it to contain the flight story is probably late antique in date, AD 300–550 (ibid. 28, citing Bergson). "This [story]," Stoneman further notes, "became one of the most popular pieces of Alexander iconography in the Middle Ages" (ibid. 193, with examples at 194), as now witnessed by its frequent citation in the contributions to Zuwiyya 2011 (see e.g. 400, s.v. "ascent of Alexander," and 402, s.v. "flying machine").

9 | Conclusion

9.1 The 'Themistocles decree'

As Herodotus tells the story, after the Persians destroyed the small Spartan and allied force at Thermopylae in 480 BC,[1] they continued to push southward through central Greece. The stand made by the Greek fleet at Artemisium did not stop the enemy's advance, even though on land the gods, it was said, had protected Delphi by sending an earthquake upon the invaders when they reached the sanctuary of Athena Pronaia. The Persians were closing in on Athens and ravaging Attica as they passed, unencumbered by any real resistance. They arrived, finally, at a city that was largely deserted: the very few who remained had no hope of holding the Acropolis, and Xerxes announced his capture of the ruined town.

The Athenians themselves had escaped before the Persians came, taking refuge on Aegina, on Salamis, in Troizen, hoping to return and rebuild when they could reclaim their land and city. In the meantime, an allied Greek fleet dominated by the Athenian navy would try to turn the Persians back by sea.[2] The ensuing battle of Salamis passed quickly into legend, as did the large-scale plans and preparations that the Athenians, and soon others as well, credited to Themistocles. Numerous references in the ancient texts suggest, in fact, that the evacuation of the city had been ordained through a formal decree proposed by Themistocles to the Athenian Assembly. Although the earliest authors stop short of noting such a decree outright, the later ones actually provide quotations from it.[3]

But was there ever actually a 'Themistocles decree'? The epoch-making nature of Themistocles' leadership was likely appreciated fairly quickly after the battle of Salamis, or at least by the end of the Persian Wars, when he was the recipient of a variety of honors (Hdt. 8.123.1–125.2). His ostracism

---

[1] Cf. also the opening of Chapter 3, above.

[2] The preceding narrative is summarized from Hdt. 8.31.1–64.2 (the issue of whether to make a stand at Salamis is revisited at Hdt. 8.74.2, but after Themistocles' ruse to lock the Greeks into fighting at that location, the battle begins at 8.84.1).

[3] Jameson 1960 esp. 201–2, with collected ancient references, the earliest of which are Hdt. 7.144.3 and Thuc. 1.18.2.

in (probably) 471/0 BC[4] was also a signal of his perceived influence and
acknowledged power both for good and for ill,[5] whether the sentiment
against him was stirred up by an energetic faction[6] or already generally
shared amongst the people. And his role in shaping the political history of
Greece, particularly that of Athens, was certainly recognized in Herodotus'
lifetime.[7] By the fourth century, however, Themistoclean *legislation* seems to
have been acknowledged in retrospect as itself constituting a history-making
act. Demosthenes relates that Aeschines recited part of a 'Themistocles
decree' in 348, and to judge from the context and from Demosthenes' bitter
tone, the purported legislation can only be understood as something of high
consequence and value:

> τίς ὁ συσκευάζεσθαι τὴν Ἑλλάδα καὶ Πελοπόννησον Φίλιππον βοῶν, ὑμᾶς
> δὲ καθεύδειν; τίς ὁ τοὺς μακροὺς καὶ καλοὺς λόγους ἐκείνους δημηγορῶν,
> καὶ τὸ Μιλτιάδου καὶ <τὸ> Θεμιστοκλέους ψήφισμ' ἀναγιγνώσκων καὶ τὸν
> ἐν τῷ τῆς Ἀγλαύρου τῶν ἐφήβων ὅρκον; οὐχ οὗτος; (D. 19.303–4).[8]

> Who shouted that Philip was making his own arrangements for Greece and
> the Peloponnese, but you were lying idle? Who delivered those big, beauti-
> ful speeches, reading the decree<s> of Miltiades and <of> Themistocles,
> and the oath of the ephebes [sworn] in the Aglaurion? Was it not that man
> [Aeschines]?

The ψήφισμα of Themistocles cited here was likely understood as treating
Themistocles' most famous and (arguably) most historically consequent
actions: the evacuation of Athens and Attica and the readying of the Athenian fleet for the battle of Salamis.[9] But what would such a decree actually
have looked like?

A third-century BC inscription found at Troizen presents what clearly
aspires to be a reinscribed version of a legislative act from the early fifth

---

[4] The precise dates of Themistocles' ostracism from Athens and flight to Persia are disputed: see
e.g. Gomme 1945–56: vol. I, 397–401 *ad* Thuc. 1.89.1–118.2, with references, on some of the
major arguments.

[5] On the charges of collusion with the enemy and fiscal corruption that seem to have helped to
topple Themistocles, see Hdt. 8.109.1–112.3; Thuc. 1.135.1–3, 137.4.

[6] The corpus of Themistocles ostraka includes a large number written by the same small group:
on a unique find of some 191 examples lettered in only fourteen different hands, see Broneer
1938: 228–43.

[7] On Themistocles' career, see Hdt. 7.143.1–8.125.2 *passim*, and Chapter 3, above.

[8] Cited by Jameson 1960: 202, with the addition of the <τό> from the scholia, which I have here
moved up to the main text from Dilts' apparatus and have also represented in brackets in my
translation.

[9] Meiggs and Lewis 1969: 50.

century.[10] It may be an idealized or even a fictionalized version of what was *imagined* to have occurred as the Persians approached Athens,[11] but by the date of its carving it was already participating in a tradition that was generations old. The conviction that Themistocles' seminal leadership during the second Persian War was (or should have been) reflected in appropriately worded governmental decrees is more than a testament to the perceived stability of the Athenian democracy and of its rhetorical formulae.[12] It is also a powerful argument that inscriptions had by this time come to be viewed as material reflections of historical realities.[13] So strong did this belief become in the course of the fourth century, in fact, that history-making 'decrees' might actually be retrojected or even forged (at least verbally if not physically) for politically motivated 'redeployment' in Assembly speeches.[14]

Here, then, is another important feedback loop that seems to have contributed to perceptions of agency in classical Greece: as history begets inscriptions (and monuments), so may such memorials beget history.[15] Realia, both physical and written, because of their power to shape memory, can be employed to create versions of the past that will be both palatable in the present and potentially useful in the future. The existence of the 'Themistocles decree' in this particular form, then, suggests that an individual-centered understanding of some of the seminal events of the Persian Wars, even if it might not have been the only preferred perspective at the time, was not only viable but even desirable in succeeding centuries.[16]

---

[10] Edited text of the third-century inscription: Meiggs and Lewis 1969: 48–9 no. 23. As they state at 49, their text is derived primarily from Jameson 1960 and 1962, i.e. the *editio princeps* and a revised version of the same, with only a few changes. The relationship of this document to a potential or purported original has been widely debated: see the extensive bibliography collected by Meiggs and Lewis 1969: 48–52, selectively updated by Dillon and Garland 1994: 200, and esp. by Johansson 2001.

[11] See the moderate perspective of Meiggs and Lewis 1969: 50 on this issue; Robertson 1982 and esp. 1976, in contrast, offer some reasons why fifth-century 'documents' might have been essentially created in the fourth century and beyond. Jameson 1960: 204–6 notes that a particularly interesting feature of the extant inscription is that it shows the flight from Attica being planned *before* the struggles at Thermopylae and Artemisium took place, thereby implying larger strategic thinking on Themistocles' part.

[12] See Hedrick 1999 on the democracy and Henry 1977 on the decree formulae.

[13] Thomas 1989: 86–91 *passim*; cf. Robertson 1976.

[14] Thomas 1989: 84–8, with references. Thomas further notes that "it is at least worth wondering how far the inventors of the fourth-century historical decrees (whoever they were) thought they were merely transferring oral traditions or historical narrative to written documentary form" (92).

[15] And likely especially at Athens: see Hedrick 1999: 410.

[16] Robertson 1982 describes some of the local purposes that the third-century version of the decree might have served; see also Robertson in note 11, above.

Was this view widely accepted? As observed near the opening of Chapter 1, no one piece of literary evidence should be taken to imply on its own the understanding or consent of its purported audience, and no piece of epigraphical evidence should, either. But this particular example again suggests that the interests of the Athenian orators regarding the ascription of agency and memory[17] found representation in other times, places, and media, as well,[18] and that the agency debate continued to find a place in Greek thought down into the Hellenistic era.[19]

9.2 Conclusion: Agency and 'greatness'

I have suggested in this project that the question of "who moves history?" was an active issue during the classical period in Greece. Responses to this inquiry varied not just with time and circumstance, but with the efforts of both the makers and the writers of history to claim or ascribe agency, and thus to shape the creation of memory. Interest in the manufacture of lasting recollection and historical meaning, however, was never exclusively confined to the literary classes, and the efforts of non-elites to participate – to whatever extent they were able – in these processes collectively betray a notable comprehension of what was at stake.

I began my exploration of this situation in Athens in 514 BC with the Tyrannicides, since the special circumstances of their action and its aftermath seem to have provided fertile material for cultural dialogue about historical agency. Public art, popular songs, and later historiography, for example (amongst other forms of evidence), patently do not agree as to who should be credited with having made Athens a democracy – and these disagreements in turn suggest through their pervasiveness and variety that the debate they record was broadly understood. A similar phenomenon is observable surrounding the battle of Marathon (490 BC): the victory in this conflict is variously ascribed through a variety of monuments, located both at Athens and elsewhere, to the specific Athenian commanders (Callimachus and especially Miltiades), to the *Marathonomachoi*, and to the Athenian *dêmos* as a whole.

This tension between the commemoration of the individual and that of the group also emerges from the complex of Athenian rituals known as the

---

[17] See esp. Chapters 1 and 5, above.
[18] Robertson 1976: 22–3 raises the possibility that biographical interests on the part of Craterus of Macedon may have contributed to the accumulation of problematic decree texts like this one.
[19] See Robertson 1982.

patrios nomos, the rites associated with the state burials of the war dead. The *patrios nomos* professed both implicitly and explicitly to honor citizens almost exclusively in terms of their civic tribes, and to determine their 'value' by their service to the state.[20] The rituals in practice, however, both lionized the individual speaker who delivered the funerary oration (the *epitaphios logos*), and created collective tombs that were likely juxtaposed with – and therefore inevitably compared with – elaborate burials of individuals. Similar issues are apparent in private burial practices after the Persian Wars and down nearly to the last quarter of the fifth century, when a general sense of conformity to modest norms seems to have been deliberately violated by a small minority that prioritized display.[21]

The relationship of the individual to the citizen group continues to be explored at Athens during the second half of the fifth century in more elaborate examples of funerary epitaphs that can sometimes contextualize their dedicatees within the state, credit them with historical agency, or claim a specific place for them in memory. Epitaphs like these, although they tend to employ high poetical language and are admittedly a luxury product, are again not confined exclusively to the literary classes. The earliest examples, as in the cases of Pythagoras of Selymbria and Pythion of Megara, are mainly special offerings for foreign benefactors, but over time this type of memorial comes to be used by Athenians, as well – including some who chose, perhaps in a competitive turn that preferenced the valorization of the individual over and above that of the citizen group, to commemorate fallen soldiers outside of the boundaries of the *patrios nomos*.

Herodotus, writing during the later fifth century BC, is also concerned with the assignment of historical agency to individuals and groups. Although he tends to associate the former with 'barbarian' rulers (who generally act on their own authority) and the latter with Greeks (who most often operate in divisions by polis), he also recognizes a third agent category, that of the Greek leader who is challenged to collaborate with his populace in order to take meaningful political or military action. The exploration of these various ways of 'making history' leads Herodotus to examine some of the same issues that emerge from the monuments discussed above, including the invocation of agency and memory on the part of the individual (and the ability of writing, especially in this case historical writing, to confirm or reshape such claims), and the extent to which group action can be construed as determinative of consequential events with or without the involvement of eminent leaders.

[20] Esp. Loraux 1986.   [21] Morris 1994 *passim*; Morris 1992: 108–55.

The association between such leaders and the Athenian citizen body in particular is, in turn, a central preoccupation for Thucydides, whose treatment of historical agency elevates the prominent individual to an essential role. While the disposition of the *dêmos* remains an important part of the picture, Thucydides' Athens is unable to accomplish historically consequent action without the involvement of its political and military leaders, in particular Pericles, Cleon, Nicias, and Alcibiades. The rhetoric of Pericles' speeches demonstrates the ways in which he is able to guide the *dêmos* to see his views as its own. Cleon's success at Pylos in spite of his many personal liabilities reveals the Athenians' need not of him, but of the leadership role that he plays, while Nicias' failure in Sicily is accompanied by a disavowal of agency, constructed both by the character and by Thucydides himself, that shows how dangerous a failed collaboration between leader and *dêmos* can be. The case of Alcibiades is especially striking: he is thought critically necessary by the Athenian populace in large part because this is the image of himself that he purposely constructs for them.

During and after the time that Thucydides is discussing the essential role of individual leaders in the making of history at Athens, the epigraphical record there shows growth in the number of non-funerary inscriptions dedicated to individuals. Honorific decrees, some presented in the form of document reliefs, first appear as offerings for foreigners (just as the more elaborate funerary epitaphs did earlier in the fifth century), but by the fourth century honors for Athenians appear with increasing frequency. Some of these represent recognition for genuinely distinctive service to the state; others of them, however, record transactions that seem quite routine. Overall, however, through its sheer size, this particular corpus provides a useful complement to the staged complaints of the orators that honors at Athens, epigraphical and otherwise, are experiencing devaluation through overuse.

The discourse of Athenian funerary commemoration during the first half of the fourth century appears to have moved in a different direction. Despite a significant increase in the absolute numbers of known funerary inscriptions, a discernibly smaller proportion of the epitaphs (in comparison with those from the later fifth century) address political context, military engagement, civic interest, or even historical specificity. Rather, they tend to emphasize the emotional experience of loss, and to embrace more localized contexts for the creation of meaning, in particular the family. This change may be in part a response to the increasing intensity of public discourse about the 'making of history' during this period: those who could now discern from the monuments proliferating around them that they would not have access to this particular kind of valuation seem to have sought commemoration in the private, domestic sphere instead.

This is the context in which Xenophon's *Hellenica* and *Anabasis* focus intensely upon the figure of the individual leader – not just upon the ethical qualities and professional skills that he might display, but upon how he interprets his (potential) position in history, how he deliberately seeks to be remembered, and how his recollection depends upon the choices made by the historian. The cases of Alcibiades in the *Hellenica*, and of Xenophon himself in the *Anabasis*, show the characters at times seeming to perform on behalf of their respective legacies, and the historian actively determining whether to construct an account that follows those 'invitations' to memorialization.

This rhetorical reflection, at the level both of character and of narrator, upon the authority of historiography continues seamlessly through Xenophon's treatments of non-Athenians, in particular Lysander, Agesilaus, and Epaminondas. But other trends observed at Athens can be traced outside of it, as well. Public Spartan dedications in the major panhellenic sanctuaries tend to be collective in their emphasis, but private ones betray an interest in self-commemoration on the part of political and social elites. Similarly, individual military tombstones located *outside* of the Spartan polis seem to offer a contrast with the famously equalizing ethos of the state that may have dictated acceptable commemoration closer to the city.[22] Finally, Spartan recollection of the battle of Thermopylae seems to have had much in common with the Athenian treatment of Marathon: it took a number of different forms according to which party was to be 'credited' (by the memorial) with the valorous loss.[23]

Analogous behaviors can also be found amongst the Thebans. Epaminondas' colonial foundations of Messene and (likely) Megalopolis may perhaps be viewed in part as a bid to secure his desired place in history.[24] At least three fourth-century proxeny inscriptions show the Thebans honoring important individual benefactors to the civic collective in much the same way as the Athenians did.[25] Themes represented in epitaphs of the period overlap with the generalized expressions of grief observed at Athens – but they also have features in common with the Athenian language of public commemoration. Finally, the Leuctra inscription, *IG* vii 2462, employs high poetical language to elevate its honorees, while its content navigates

---

[22] Low 2006.   [23] Ibid. 99–101.

[24] Diodorus claims that this was one of Epaminondas' general motivations for his activities (D.S. 15.66.1).

[25] Roesch 1984, cited by Hammond 2000: 91.

between the poles of individual and group agency as it 'rewrites' historical recollection in favor of its subjects, whom it claims "did not run second to Epaminondas."[26]

By the time of Philip II of Macedon, the symbolic and literary 'vocabulary' employed to invoke the making of history – and of memory – was highly developed, both at Athens and elsewhere in Greece. The image of Philip transmitted to and by succeeding generations was therefore founded firmly upon precedent. Coinage, monuments, and inscribed documents connected Philip with images that had already proven meaningful: athlete, *ktistês*, general, statesman. The literary testimonia, taken as a whole, suggest that Philip invited interpretation as a leader who worked directly alongside his men, as a formidable fighter and general, and as a liberator. All of these tropes would have been useful in a distinctly Macedonian cultural context, but they also have deep roots in pre-existing Greek models of self-presentation and commemoration. By any standard, Philip seems to have exploited these concepts (or inspired their interpretation) on a far wider scale than had others before him. His effect was further magnified by careful attempts to connect his image with the divine, manifested most clearly, but by no means exclusively, in the Philippeum at Olympia.[27]

The many guises in which Philip's son Alexander ultimately presented himself, and the ways in which he was understood by others, were modeled not only upon Philip's paradigm but upon many decades of experimentation by others who had sought the credit of historical agency and permanent memory, including both groups and individuals. Alexander surpassed all known predecessors in his polyvalence. He was at various times represented in both the material and literary spheres as an ideal Macedonian king, an expert general, a benefactor of the Greek cities, a *ktistês*. His *mimesis* of Achilles and Heracles and his acknowledgement as the 'son' of Zeus Ammon linked him to the gods and heroes even more closely than Philip's highly public displays of piety had done[28] – but Alexander still saw fit to reach beyond his father's efforts and try to control his reception through the written word, as well. The *Ephemerides* and the other royal records, the technical writing of the Bematists, the court poetry generated by a retinue of artists, and the history commissioned from Callisthenes[29] all served to construct a deliberate memory of Alexander whose general shape seems to have endured across successive literary generations.

---

[26] Trans. Rhodes and Osborne 2003: 150–1 no. 30.   [27] Esp. Carney 2000b and 2007.
[28] On the many guises of Alexander, especially his material legacy, see esp. Stewart 1993.
[29] On these items and other literary and material evidence, see esp. Baynham 2003.

The ancient Greek model of the 'great man,' the maker of history, the individual inscribed in permanent memory, was therefore developed over a period of many years that included significant symbolic debates over the historical potential both of the corporate group, especially the polis, and of the ordinary citizen. The individuals whom the ancient Greeks variously construed as historical agents during the earlier classical period were not always successful generals, effective political leaders, or even necessarily Greeks at all. The same modes of commemoration used for eminent leaders were sometimes echoed on a more limited scale by other, less prominent citizens. Groups, in turn, could be understood as being the producers of history-making action – or as collectively abdicating their opportunities to take credit for it. With the passage of time, however, the balance of this symbolic 'conversation' shifted to render fortunately placed political and military leaders the most likely recipients of credit for historical agency. Experimentation and experience together generated a series of feedback loops that simultaneously inspired the 'performers' and the writers of history and educated their audiences. By the lifetime of Alexander, a sophisticated vocabulary of advertisement and commemoration, with important elements likely shared in common across the Greek world, had arisen to depict 'greatness' both in literature and in life. Schooled in this cultural imagery, Alexander was ideally positioned to exploit it. His explosive reception therefore represented not the genesis of the 'great man' concept, but, for the moment, its culmination.

Bibliography

Abd el-Raziq, M., 1984, *Die Darstellungen und Texte des Sanktuars Alexanders des Grossen im Tempel von Luxor* = Archäologische Veröffentlichungen 16 (Mainz).

Adams, Charles Darwin, ed. and trans., 1919, *The Speeches of Aeschines*, Loeb Classical Library (London).

Adams, W. Lindsay, and Eugene N. Borza, eds., 1982, *Philip II, Alexander the Great, and the Macedonian Heritage* (Washington, DC).

Adler, Friedrich, R. Borrmann, W. Dörpfeld, F. Graeber, and P. Graef, 1890–7, *Die baudenkmäler von Olympia*, vol. II (1892) of Ernst Curtius and Friedrich Adler (eds.).

Aerts, W. J., Joseph M. M. Hermans, and Elizabeth Visser, eds., 1978, *Alexander the Great in the Middle Ages: Ten Studies on the Last Days of Alexander in Literary and Historical Writing* = Mediaevalia Groningana 1 (Groningen).

Ajootian, Aileen, 1998, "A Day at the Races: The Tyrannicides in the Fifth-Century Agora," in Kim J. Hartswick and Mary C. Sturgeon (eds.), 1–13.

Alexiou, Margaret, 1974, *The Ritual Lament in Greek Tradition* (Cambridge).

Alonso-Núñez, J. M., 1987, "An Augustan World History: The *Historiae Philippicae* of Pompeius Trogus," *G&R* 34, 56–72.

Ameling, W., 1988, "Alexander und Achilleus: Ein Bestandsaufnahme," in W. Will with G. Heinrichs (ed.), 657–92.

Anderson, A. R., 1928, "Heracles and His Successors: A Study of a Heroic Ideal and the Recurrence of a Heroic Type," *HSCP* 39, 7–58.

Anderson, J. K., 1974, *Xenophon* (London).

  1963, "The Statue of Chabrias," *AJA* 67, 411–13.

Antonaccio, Carla M., 1995, *An Archaeology of Ancestors: Tomb Cult and Hero Cult in Early Greece* (Lanham, MD).

Armayor, O. Kimball, 1985, *Herodotus' Autopsy of the Fayoum: Lake Moeris and the Labyrinth of Egypt* (Amsterdam).

  1978a, "Did Herodotus Ever Go to the Black Sea?" *HSCP* 82, 45–62.

  1978b, "Did Herodotus Ever Go to Egypt?" *Journal of the American Research Center in Egypt* 15, 59–73.

  1978c, "Herodotus' Catalogues of the Persian Empire in the Light of the Monuments and the Greek Literary Tradition," *TAPA* 108, 1–9.

Aron, Raymond, 1958, "Evidence and Inference in History," *Daedalus* 87, 11–39.

Arrington, Nathan T., 2011, "Inscribing Defeat: The Commemorative Dynamics of the Athenian Casualty Lists," *CA* 30, 179–212.

355

2010, "Topographic Semantics: The Location of the Athenian Public Cemetery and Its Significance for the Nascent Democracy," *Hesperia* 79, 499–539.

Atkinson, Kathleen M. T., 1973, "Demosthenes, Alexander, and Asebeia," *Athenaeum* 51, 310–35.

Azoulay, V., 2004, "Exchange as Entrapment: Mercenary Xenophon?" in Robin Lane Fox (ed.), 289–304.

Badian, E., 2004, "Xenophon the Athenian," in Christopher Tuplin (ed.), 33–53.

1993a, *From Plataea to Potidaea: Studies in the History and Historiography of the Pentecontaetia* (Baltimore).

1993b, "Thucydides and the Outbreak of the Peloponnesian War: A Historian's Brief," in E. Badian, 1993a, 125–62.

1982, "Greeks and Macedonians," in Beryl Barr-Sharrar and Eugene N. Borza, (eds.), 33–51.

1981, "The Deification of Alexander the Great," in Harry J. Dell (ed.), 27–71.

1968, "A King's Notebooks," *HSCP* 72, 183–204.

1963, "The Death of Philip II," *Phoenix* 17, 244–50.

Badian, E. (with Denis van Berchem), ed., 1975, *Alexandre le Grand: Image et réalité* = Entretiens Hardt 22 (Geneva).

Bakhuizen, S. C., 1994, "Thebes and Boeotia in the Fourth Century BC," *Phoenix* 48, 307–30.

Bakker, Egbert J., Irene J. F. de Jong, and Hans van Wees, eds., 2002, *Brill's Companion to Herodotus* (Leiden).

Balot, Ryan K., 2001, *Greed and Injustice in Classical Athens* (Princeton).

Baragwanath, Emily, 2008, *Motivation and Narrative in Herodotus* (Oxford).

Barratt, Christina, 1932, "The Chronology of the Eponymous Archons of Boeotia," *JHS* 52, 72–115.

Barron, John, 1990, "All for Salamis," in E. M. Craik (ed.), 133–41.

Barr-Sharrar, Beryl, and Eugene N. Borza, eds., 1982, *Macedonia and Greece in Late Classical and Early Hellenistic Times* = Studies in the History of Art 10, Symposium Series 1, National Gallery of Art, Washington (Washington, DC).

Baumbach, Manuel, Andrej Petrovic, and Ivana Petrovic, eds., 2010, *Archaic and Classical Greek Epigram* (Cambridge).

Baynham, Elizabeth, 2003, "The Ancient Evidence for Alexander the Great," in Joseph Roisman (ed.), 3–29.

1998, *Alexander the Great: The Unique History of Quintus Curtius* (Ann Arbor).

1994, "The Question of Macedonian Divine Honors for Philip II," *MedArch* 7, 35–43.

Bengtson, H., 1962, *Die Staatsverträge des Altertums, II: Die Verträge der griechisch-römischen Welt von 700 bis 338 v. Chr.*, 2nd edn. (Munich).

Bergemann, J., 1997, *Demos und Thanatos. Untersuchungen zum Wertsystem der Polis im Spiegel der attischen Grabreliefs des 4. Jahrhunderts v. Chr. und Funktion der Gleichzeitgen Grabbauten* (Munich).

Bergmann, Bettina, and Christine Kondoleon, eds., 1999, *The Art of Ancient Spectacle* = *Studies in the History of Art* 56, Center for Advanced Study in the Visual Arts Symposium Papers 34 (New Haven).

Bernard, Paul, 1967, *Aï Khanum on the Oxus: A Hellenistic City in Central Asia* (London).

Bernard, Paul, et al., eds., 1973–2014, *Fouilles d'Aï Khanoum*, 9 vols. (Paris).

Bertelli, Lucio, 2001, "Hecataeus: From Genealogy to Historiography," in Nino Luraghi (ed.), 67–94.

Best, J. G. P., 1969, *Thracian Peltasts and Their Influence on Greek Warfare* (Groningen).

Bickerman, E. J., 1963, "Sur un passage d'Hypéride (*Epitaphios*, col. VIII)," *Athenaeum* 41, 70–85.

Bieber, Margarete, 1965, "The Portraits of Alexander," *G&R* 12.2 = *Alexander the Great*, 183–8.

   1964, *Alexander the Great in Greek and Roman Art* (Chicago).

   1949, "The Portraits of Alexander the Great," *PCPS* 93, 373–427.

Billows, Richard A., 1995, *Kings and Colonists: Aspects of Macedonian Imperialism* (Leiden).

Bing, J. D., 1991, "Alexander's Sacrifice *dis praesidibus loci* before the Battle of Issus," *JHS* 111, 161–5.

Blackwell, C. W., ed., 2003, *Dêmos: Classical Athenian Democracy* (A. Mahoney and R. Scaife, eds., *The Stoa: A Consortium for Electronic Publication in the Humanities* [www.stoa.org]), edition of January 18, 2003.

Bloedow, Edmund F., 1973, *Alcibiades Reexamined* = *Historia* Supp. 21 (Wiesbaden).

Blösel, Wolfgang, 2001, "The Herodotean Picture of Themistocles: A Mirror of Fifth-Century Athens," in Nino Luraghi (ed.), 179–97.

Blümel, Wolfgang, 1994, "Two Inscriptions from the Cnidian Peninsula," *EA* 23, 157–8, pl. 17.

Boardman, John, 1978, "Herakles, Delphi, and Kleisthenes of Sicyon," *RA*, 227–34.

   1955, "Painted Funerary Plaques and Some Remarks on Prothesis," *BSA* 50, 51–66.

Boardman, John, N. G. L. Hammond, D. M. Lewis, and M. Ostwald, eds., 1988, *The Cambridge Ancient History*, 2nd edn., vol. IV, *Persia, Greece, and the Western Mediterranean, c. 525 to 479 BC* (Cambridge).

Boardman, John, and C. E. Vaphopoulou-Richardson, eds., 1986, *Chios: A Conference at the Homereion in Chios, 1984* (Oxford).

Boedeker, Deborah, 2002, "Epic Heritage and Mythical Patterns in Herodotus," in Egbert J. Bakker, Irene J. F. de Jong, and Hans van Wees (eds.), 97–116.

   1987, "The Two Faces of Demaratus," *Arethusa* 20.1–2 = *Herodotus and the Invention of History*, 185–201.

Boedeker, Deborah, and Kurt A. Raaflaub, eds., 1998, *Democracy, Empire, and the Arts in Fifth-Century Athens* (Cambridge, MA).

Boegehold, Alan L., 1995, *The Athenian Agora*, vol. XXVIII, *The Lawcourts at Athens: Sites, Buildings, Equipment, Procedure, and Testimonia* (Princeton).

1994, "Perikles' Citizenship Law of 451/0 BC," in Alan L. Boegehold and Adele C. Scafuro (eds.), 57–66.

Boegehold, Alan L., and Adele C. Scafuro, eds., 1994, *Athenian Identity and Civic Ideology* (Baltimore).

Bommelaer, Jean-François, 1981, *Lysandre de Sparte: Histoire et Traditions* (Athens and Paris).

Bommelaer, Jean-François, and Dessins de Didier Laroche, 1991, *Guide de Delphes: Le Site* (Paris).

Bonfante, Larissa, 1989, "Nudity as a Costume in Classical Art," *AJA* 93, 543–70.

Boring, Terrence A., 1979, *Literacy in Ancient Sparta* (Leiden).

Borza, Eugene N., 1999, *Before Alexander: Constructing Early Macedonia* = Publications of the Association of Ancient Historians 6 (Claremont, CA).

1996, "Greeks and Macedonians in the Age of Alexander: The Source Traditions," in Robert W. Wallace and Edward M. Harris (eds.), 122–39.

1995a, *Makedonika*, ed. Carol G. Thomas (Claremont, CA).

1995b, "The Symposium at Alexander's Court," in Eugene N. Borza, 1995a, 159–71, originally published in *Archaia Makedonia* 3 (1983), 45–55.

1990, *In the Shadow of Olympus: The Emergence of Macedon* (Princeton).

1987, "Timber and Politics in the Ancient World: Macedon and the Greeks," *PCPS* 131, 32–52.

1982a, "Athenians, Macedonians, and the Origins of the Macedonian Royal House," in *Studies in Attic Epigraphy, History and Topography Presented to Eugene Vanderpool* = *Hesperia* Supp. 19 (Princeton), 7–13.

1982b, "The Natural Resources of Ancient Macedonia," in W. Lindsay Adams and Eugene N. Borza (eds.), 1982, 1–20.

1981, "Anaxarchus and Callisthenes: Academic Intrigue at Alexander's Court," in Harry J. Dell (ed.), 73–86.

1978, "Philip II and the Greeks," review of J. R. Ellis, *Philip II and Macedonian Imperialism* (London, 1976), *CP* 73, 236–43.

Bosworth, A. B., 2002, *The Legacy of Alexander: Politics, Warfare, and Propaganda under the Successors* (Oxford).

1996, "Alexander, Euripides, and Dionysos: The Motivation for Apotheosis," in Robert W. Wallace and Edward M. Harris (eds.), 140–66.

1993, "Perdiccas and the Kings," *CQ* 43, 420–7.

1988a, *From Arrian to Alexander: Studies in Historical Interpretation* (Oxford).

1988b, *Conquest and Empire: The Reign of Alexander the Great* (Cambridge).

1980, *A Historical Commentary on Arrian's* History of Alexander (Oxford).

1971, "The Death of Alexander the Great: Rumour and Propaganda," *CQ* 21, 112–36.

Bosworth, A. B., and E. J. Baynham, eds., 2000, *Alexander the Great in Fact and Fiction* (Oxford).

Bousquet, Jean, 1963, "Inscriptions de Delphes," *BCH* 87, 188–208.

Bowie, A. M., 1997, "Tragic Filters for History: Euripides' *Supplices* and Sophocles' *Philoctetes*," in Christopher Pelling (ed.), 1997b, 39–62.

Boys-Stones, George, Barbara Graziosi, and Phiroze Vasunia, eds., 2009, *The Oxford Handbook of Hellenic Studies* (Oxford).

Bradeen, Donald W., 1974, *The Athenian Agora*, vol. XVII, *Inscriptions: The Funerary Monuments* (Princeton).

  1969, "The Athenian Casualty Lists," *CQ* 19, 145–59.

  1967, "The Athenian Casualty List of 464 BC," *Hesperia* 36, 321–8.

  1964, "Athenian Casualty Lists," *Hesperia* 33, 16–62.

  1955, "The Trittyes in Cleisthenes' Reforms," *TAPA* 86, 22–30.

Brauer, George C., Jr., 1980, "Alexander in England: The Conqueror's Reputation in the Late Seventeenth and Eighteenth Centuries," *CJ* 76, 34–47.

Breitenbach, H. R., 1967, "Xenophon von Athen," *RE* 9 A 2, 1567–910.

Bremen, Riet van, 2007, "The Entire House is Full of Crowns: Hellenistic Agōnes and the Commemoration of Victory," in Simon Hornblower and Catherine Morgan (eds.), 345–75.

Brenne, Stefan, 1994, "Ostraka and the Process of Ostrakophoria," in W. D. E. Coulson, et al. (eds.), 13–24.

Bridges, Emma, Edith Hall, and P. J. Rhodes, eds., 2007, *Cultural Responses to the Persian Wars: Antiquity to the Third Millennium* (Oxford).

Brock, Roger, and Stephen Hodkinson, eds., 2000, *Alternatives to Athens: Varieties of Political Organization and Community in Ancient Greece* (Oxford).

Broneer, Oscar, 1938, "Excavations on the North Slope of the Acropolis, 1937," *Hesperia* 7, 161–263.

Brownson, Carleton L., 1998 and 2001, ed. and trans., rev. and intro. John Dillery, *Xenophon*, vol. III = *Anabasis*, Loeb Classical Library (Cambridge, MA, 1998; reprint with corrections, 2001).

  1918, 1921, ed. and trans., *Xenophon*, vols. I–II = *Hellenica*, Loeb Classical Library (Cambridge, MA, and London).

Bruce, I. A. F., 1987, "Theopompus, Lysander, and the Spartan Empire," *AHB* 1, 1–5.

  1970, "Theopompus and Classical Greek Historiography," *History and Theory* 9, 86–109.

Brunnsåker, Sture, 1971, *The Tyrant-Slayers of Kritios and Nesiotes: A Critical Study of the Sources and Restorations* (Stockholm).

Bruns, Ivo, 1896, *Das literarische Porträt der Griechen im fünften und vierten Jahrhunderts* (Berlin).

Brunt, P. A., ed. and trans., 1976–1983, *Arrian*, 2 vols., Loeb Classical Library (Cambridge, MA).

1974, "Alexander, Barsine, and Heracles," *RFIC* 103, 22–35.

Buckler, John, 1998, "Epameinondas and the New Inscription from Knidos," *Mnemosyne* 51, 192–205.

1989, *Philip II and the Sacred War* (Leiden).

1980, *The Theban Hegemony, 371–362 BC* (Cambridge, MA).

Buckler, John, and Hans Beck, 2008, *Central Greece and the Politics of Power in the Fourth Century BC* (Cambridge).

Bugh, Glenn R., ed., 2006, *The Cambridge Companion to the Hellenistic World* (Cambridge).

Bulloch, Anthony, Erich S. Gruen, A. A. Long, and Andrew Stewart, eds., 1993, *Images and Ideologies: Self-Definition in the Hellenistic World* (Berkeley).

Bundy, Elroy, 1962, *Studia Pindarica* (Berkeley, 1986 rev. reprint of 1962 edn., digital edn. Berkeley, 2006), http://escholarship.org/uc/item/2g79p68q.

Buraselis, Kostas, and Katerina Meidani, eds., 2010, Μαραθών: η μάχη και ο αρχαίος Δήμος / *Marathon: the Battle and the Ancient Deme* (Athens). *Non vidi.*

Burkert, Walter, 1977, *Griechische Religion der archaischen und klassischen Epoche* = Die Religionen der Menscheit 15, Christel Matthias Schröder, ed. (Stuttgart).

Burnett, Anne Pippin, and Colin N. Edmonson, 1961, "The Chabrias Monument in the Athenian Agora," *Hesperia* 30, 74–91.

Cairns, Francis, 1982, "Cleon and Pericles: A Suggestion," *JHS* 102, 203–4.

Camp, John McK., II, 2001, *The Archaeology of Athens* (New Haven).

1994, "Before Democracy: The Alkmaionidai and Peisistratidai," in W. D. E. Coulson, et al. (eds.), 7–12.

1992, *The Athenian Agora: Excavations in the Heart of Classical Athens,* updated edn. (New York).

Carlier, Pierre, 2000, "Homeric and Macedonian Kingship," in Roger Brock and Stephen Hodkinson, eds., *Alternatives to Athens: Varieties of Political Organization and Community in Ancient Greece* (Oxford), 259–68.

Carlsen, Jesper, Bodil Due, Otto Steen Due, and Birte Poursen, eds., 1993, *Alexander the Great: Reality and Myth* = Analecta Romana Instituti Danici Supp. 20 (Rome).

Carney, Elizabeth, 2007, "The Philippeum, Women, and the Formation of Dynastic Image," in Waldemar Heckel, Lawrence Tritle, and Pat Wheatley (eds.), 27–60.

2003, "Elite Education and High Culture in Macedonia," in Waldemar Heckel and Lawrence A. Tritle (eds.), 47–63.

2002, "Hunting and the Macedonian Elite: Sharing the Rivalry of the Chase," in Daniel Ogden (ed.), 59–80.

2000a, "Artifice and Alexander History," in Bosworth and Baynham (eds.) 2000, 263–85.

2000b, "The Initiation of Cult for Royal Macedonian Women," *CP* 95, 21–43.

1996, "Macedonians and Mutiny: Discipline and Indiscipline in the Army of Philip and Alexander," *CP* 91, 19–44.

1992, "The Politics of Polygamy: Olympias, Alexander, and the Murder of Philip," *Historia* 41, 169–89.

Carr, Edward Hallett, 1969, *What is History? The George Macaulay Trevelyan Lectures Delivered in the University of Cambridge, January–March 1961* (New York).

Carrithers, Michael, Steven Collins, and Steven Lukes, eds., 1985, *The Category of the Person: Anthropology, Philosophy, History* (Cambridge).

Carter, Jane B., and Sarah P. Morris, eds., 1995, *The Ages of Homer: A Tribute to Emily Townsend Vermeule* (Austin).

Cartledge, Paul, 2002, *Sparta and Lakonia: A Regional History, 1300–362 BC,* 2nd edn. (London).

1987, *Agesilaos and the Crisis of Sparta* (Baltimore).

1978, "Literacy in the Spartan Oligarchy," *JHS* 98, 25–37.

Cary, George, 1956, *The Medieval Alexander* (Cambridge).

Castriota, David, 1992, *Myth, Ethos, and Actuality: Official Art in Fifth-Century BC Athens* (Madison).

Cawkwell, George L., 2004, "When, How, and Why did Xenophon Write the Anabasis?" in Robin Lane Fox (ed.), 47–67.

1983, "The Decline of Sparta," *CQ* 33, 385–400.

1978, *Philip of Macedon* (London).

1976, "Agesilaus and Sparta," *CQ* 26, 62–84.

1972, "Epaminondas and Thebes," *CQ* 22, 254–78.

Childs, William A. P., ed., 1978, *Athens Comes of Age: From Solon to Salamis* (Princeton).

Christ, Matthew, 1994, "Herodotean Kings and Historical Inquiry," *CA* 13, 167–202.

1993, "Theopompus and Herodotus: A Reassessment," *CQ* 43, 47–52.

1992, "Ostracism, Sycophancy, and Deception of the Demos: [Arist.] *Ath. Pol.* 43.5," *CQ* 42, 336–46.

Christesen, Paul, and Sarah C. Murray, 2010, "Macedonian Religion," in Joseph Roisman and Ian Worthington (eds.), 428–45.

Christides, A.-F., ed., 2007, *A History of Ancient Greek: From the Beginnings to Late Antiquity* (Cambridge).

Clairmont, Christoph W., 1993, *Classical Attic Tombstones,* 8 vols. (Kilchberg).

1983, Patrios nomos: *Public Burial in Athens during the Fifth and Fourth Centuries BC,* 2 vols. (Oxford).

1979, "The Lekythos of Myrrhine," in Günter Kopcke and Mary B. Moore (eds.), 103–10.

1970, *Gravestone and Epigram* (Mainz).

Clarke, M. J., B. G. F. Currie, and R. O. A. M. Lyne, eds., 2006, *Epic Interactions: Perspectives on Homer, Virgil, and the Epic Tradition Presented to Jasper Griffin by Former Pupils* (Oxford).

Classen, D. J., 1959, "The Libyan God Ammon in Greece Before 331 BC," *Historia* 8, 349–55.

Closterman, W. E., 1999, "The Self-Presentation of the Family: The Function of Classical Attic Peribolos Tombs" (diss., The Johns Hopkins University).

Cohen, Ada, 1997, *The Alexander Mosaic: Stories of Victory and Defeat* (Cambridge).

1995, "Alexander and Achilles – Macedonians and 'Mycenaeans,'" in Jane B. Carter and Sarah P. Morris (eds.), 483–505.

Coldstream, J. N., 1977, *Geometric Greece* (London).

Collart, Paul, 1937, *Philippes, ville de Macédoine, depuis ses origines jusqu'à la fin de l'époque romaine* (Paris). *Non vidi.*

Connolly, Andrew, 1998, "Was Sophocles Heroised as Dexion?" *JHS* 118, 1–21.

Connor, W. R., 1988, "Early Greek Land Warfare as Symbolic Expression," *P&P* 119, 3–29.

1987, "Tribes, Festivals, and Processions: Civic Ceremonial and Political Manipulation in Archaic Greece," *JHS* 107, 40–50.

1984, *Thucydides* (Princeton).

1971, *The New Politicians of Fifth-Century Athens* (Princeton).

1968, *Theopompus and Fifth-Century Athens* (Washington).

1967, "History Without Heroes: Theopompus' Treatment of Philip of Macedon," *GRBS* 8, 33–54.

Connor, W. R., M. H. Hansen, K. A. Raaflaub, and B. S. Strauss, 1990, *Aspects of Athenian Democracy* (Copenhagen).

Conze, Alexander, 1893–1922, *Die attischen Grabreliefs*, 4 vols. (Berlin).

Coons, Robert, 2009, "Spartan Foreign Policy in the Archaic and Classical Periods: From Practicality to Propaganda" (undergraduate senior thesis, Department of Greek and Latin, The Catholic University of America).

Cornford, Francis Macdonald, 1907, *Thucydides Mythistoricus* (London).

Coulson, W. D. E., O. Palagia, T. L. Shear, Jr., H. A. Shapiro, and F. J. Frost, eds., 1994, *The Archaeology of Athens and Attica under the Democracy* (Oxford), 73–81.

Craik, E. M., ed., 1990, *'Owls to Athens': Essays on Classical Subjects Presented to Sir Kenneth Dover* (Oxford).

Crane, Gregory, 1996, *The Blinded Eye: Thucydides and the New Written Word* (Lanham, MD).

Csapo, Eric, and William J. Slater, 1995, *The Context of Ancient Drama* (Ann Arbor).

Culasso Gastaldi, Enrica, 2004, *Le prossenie ateniesi del IV secolo a.C.: Gli onorati asiatici* (Alessandria).

Currie, Bruno, 2005, *Pindar and the Cult of Heroes* (Oxford).

2002, "Euthymos of Locri: A Case Study in Heroization in the Classical Period," *JHS* 122, 24–44.

Curtius, Ernst, and Friedrich Adler, eds., 1890–7, *Olympia: Die Ergebnisse der von dem Deutschen Reich veranstalteten Ausgrabung*, 5 vols. (Berlin).

Dahmen, Karsten, 2010, "The Numismatic Evidence," in Joseph Roisman and Ian Worthington (eds.), 41–62.

Dalby, Andrew, 1992, "Greeks Abroad: Social Organisation and Food among the Ten Thousand," *JHS* 112, 16–30.

Danforth, Loring M., 2003, "Alexander the Great and the Macedonian Conflict," in Joseph Roisman (ed.), 347–64.

Danien, Elin C., ed., 1990, *The World of Philip and Alexander: A Symposium on Greek Life and Times* (Philadelphia).

Day, Joseph W., 1994, "Interactive Offerings: Early Greek Dedicatory Epigrams and Ritual," *HSCP* 96, 37–74.

    1989, "Rituals in Stone: Early Greek Grave Epigrams and Monuments," *JHS* 109, 16–28.

    1985, "Epigrams and History: The Athenian Tyrannicides, A Case in Point," in Laurie Obbink, Dirk Obbink, Virginia Jameson, and Mary Lou Munn (eds.), 25–46.

Dell, Harry J., ed., 1981, *Ancient Macedonian Studies in Honor of Charles F. Edson* = Institute for Balkan Studies 158 (Thessaloniki).

Derderian, Katharine, 2001, *Leaving Words to Remember: Greek Mourning and the Advent of Literacy* (Leiden).

Derow, Peter, and Robert Parker, eds., 2003, *Herodotus and His World: Essays from a Conference in Memory of George Forrest* (Oxford).

Desmond, William, 2004, "Punishments and the Conclusion of Herodotus' *Histories*," *GRBS* 44, 19–40.

Develin, Robert, 1985, "Herodotos and the Alkmeonids," in John W. Eadie and Josiah Ober (eds.), 125–39.

Dewald, Carolyn, 2003, "Form and Content: The Question of Tyranny in Herodotus," in Kathryn A. Morgan (ed.), 25–58.

    1987, "Narrative Surface and Authorial Voice in Herodotus' *Histories*," *Arethusa* 20, 147–70.

Dewald, Carolyn, and John Marincola, eds., 2006, *The Cambridge Companion to Herodotus* (Cambridge).

Dihle, Albrecht, 1956, *Studien zur griechischen Biographie* = Abhandl. Akad. Göttingen 3.37 (Göttingen).

Dillery, John, 1998 and 2001, Introduction to *Xenophon*, vol. III = *Anabasis*, ed. and trans. C. L. Brownson, Loeb Classical Library (Cambridge, MA 1998; corr. repr. 2001).

    1995, *Xenophon and the History of His Times* (London).

Dillon, Matthew, and Lynda Garland, 1994, *Ancient Greece: Social and Historical Documents from Archaic Times to the Death of Socrates (c. 800–399 BC)* (London).

Dillon, Sheila, 2001, review of Ralf Krumeich, *Bildnisse griechischer Herrscher und Staatsmänner im 5. Jahrhundert v. Chr.* (Munich, 1997), *BMCR* 2001.10.02, http://bmcr.brynmawr.edu/2001/2001-10-02.html.

Dimitrova, Nora, 2002, "Inscriptions and Iconography in the Monuments of the Thracian Rider," *Hesperia* 71, 209–29.

Domingo Gygax, M., 2006, "Plutarch on Alcibiades' Return to Athens," *Mnemosyne* 59, 481–500.

Donlan, Walter, 1978, "Social Vocabulary and Its Relationship to Political Propaganda in Fifth-Century Athens," *QUCC* 27, 95–111.

Dougherty, Carol, and Leslie Kurke, eds., 1993, *Cultural Poetics in Archaic Greece: Cult, Performance, Politics* (Cambridge).

Drews, Robert, 1974, "Sargon, Cyrus and Mesopotamian Folk History," *JNES* 33, 387–93.

Ducat, Jean, 1971, *Les kouroi du Ptoion: Le sanctuaire d'Apollon Ptoieus à l'époque archaïque* (Paris).

Due, Bodil, 1993, "Alexander's Inspiration and Ideas," in Jesper Carlsen, Bodil Due, Otto Steen Due, and Birte Poursen (eds.), 53–60.

  1991, "The Return of Alcibiades in Xenophon's *Hellenica* 1.4.8–23," *C&M* 42, 39–53.

Eadie, John W., and Josiah Ober, eds., 1985, *The Craft of the Ancient Historian: Essays in Honor of Chester G. Starr* (Lanham, MD).

Easterling, P. E., 1997, "Constructing the Heroic," in Christopher Pelling (ed.), 1997b, 21–37.

Edson, Charles F., 1970, "Early Macedonia," *Archaia Makedonia* 1, 17–44.

Edwards, Mark, and Simon Swain, eds., 1997, *Portraits: Biographical Representation in the Greek and Latin Literature of the Roman Empire* (Oxford).

Ehrenberg, Victor, 1956, "Das Harmodioslied," *WS* 69, 57–69.

  1938, *Alexander and the Greeks*, trans. Ruth Fraenkel von Velsen (Oxford).

Ekroth, Gunnel, 2007, "Heroes and Hero-Cults," in Daniel Ogden (ed.), 100–14.

Ellis, J. R., 1977, "The Dynamics of Fourth-Century Macedonian Imperialism," in *Ancient Macedonia II: Papers Read at the Second International Symposium held in Thessaloniki, 19–24 August 1973* = Institute for Balkan Studies 155 (Thessaloniki), 103–14.

  1976, *Philip II and Macedonian Imperialism* (London).

Errington, R. M., 1975, "Alexander in the Hellenistic World," in E. Badian (with Denis van Berchem) (ed.), 137–79, discussion 211–21.

  1970, "From Babylon to Triparadeisos: 323–320 BC," *JHS* 90, 49–77.

  1969, "Bias in Ptolemy's History of Alexander," *CQ* 19, 233–42.

Erskine, Andrew, 2002, "Life after Death: Alexandria and the Body of Alexander," *G&R* 49, 163–79.

Evans, J. A. S., 1987, "Herodotus 9.73.3 and the Publication Date of the Histories," *CP* 82, 226–8.

  1981, "Notes on the Debate of the Persian Grandees in Herodotus 3.80–82," *QUCC* 36, 69–84.

Fantuzzi, Marco, and Richard Hunter, 2004, *Tradition and Innovation in Hellenistic Poetry* (Cambridge).

Faraguna, Michele, 2003, "Alexander and the Greeks," in Joseph Roisman (ed.), 99–130.

Farnell, L. R., 1921, *Greek Hero Cults and Ideas of Immortality* (Oxford).

Fehling, Detlev, 1971, *Die Quellenangaben bei Herodot* (Berlin) = *Herodotus and His 'Sources': Citation, Invention, and Narrative Art*, trans. J. G. Howie (Leeds, 1989).

Ferrario, Sarah B., 2014, "The Tools of Memory: Crafting Historical Legacy in Fourth-Century Greece," in Giovanni Parmeggiani, ed., *Between Thucydides and Polybius: The Golden Age of Greek Historiography* (Washington, DC) 263–88.

2012, "Historical Agency and Self-Awareness in Xenophon's *Hellenica* and *Anabasis*," in Fiona Hobden and Christopher Tuplin, eds., *Xenophon: Ethical Principle and Historical Enquiry* (Leiden), 341–76.

2008, "The Isolation of Alcibiades *autokratôr*: Leader and *dêmos* in Xenophon's *Hellenica*," paper delivered at the American Philological Association Annual Meeting (Chicago, IL).

2006a, "Replaying *Antigone*: Changing Patterns of Public and Private Commemoration at Athens *c.* 440–350," in Cynthia B. Patterson, ed., 79–117.

2006b, "Towards the 'Great Man': Individuals and Groups as Agents of Historical Change in Classical Greece" (diss., Princeton University).

Finley, M. I., 1965, "Myth, Memory, and History," *History and Theory* 4, 281–302.

Flory, Stewart, 1987, *The Archaic Smile of Herodotus* (Detroit).

1980, "Who Read Herodotus' Histories?" *AJP* 101, 12–28.

Flower, Michael, 2000, "Alexander the Great and Panhellenism," in A. B. Bosworth and E. J. Baynham (eds.), 96–135.

1997, *Theopompus of Chios: History and Rhetoric in the Fourth Century BC* (Oxford, 1994; rev. edn. 1997).

1991, "Revolutionary Agitation and Social Change in Classical Sparta," in Michael Flower and Mark Toher (eds.), 78–97.

1988, "Agesilaus of Sparta and the Origins of the Ruler Cult," *CQ* 38, 123–34.

Flower, Michael, and John Marincola, eds. and comms., 2002, *Herodotus*: Histories, *Book IX* (Cambridge).

Flower, Michael, and Mark Toher, eds., 1991, *Georgica: Greek Studies in Honour of George Cawkwell* = *BICS* Supp. 58 (London).

Fontenrose, Joseph, 1968, "The Hero as Athlete," *CSCA* 1, 73–104.

Fornara, Charles, 1983a, *The Nature of History in Ancient Greece and Rome* (Berkeley).

1983b, ed. and trans., *Archaic Times to the End of the Peloponnesian War*, 2nd edn. (Cambridge).

1970, "The Cult of Harmodius and Aristogeiton," *Philologus* 114, 155–80.

1968, "The 'Tradition' About the Murder of Hipparchus," *Historia* 17, 400–24.

Forsdyke, Sara, 2001, "Athenian Democratic Ideology and Herodotus' *Histories*," *AJP* 122, 329–58.

2000, "Exile, Ostracism, and the Athenian Democracy," *CA* 19, 232–63.

Fowler, Robert, 2003, "Herodotos and Athens," in Peter Derow and Robert Parker (eds.), 305–18.

1996, "Herodotos and His Contemporaries," *JHS* 116, 62–87.

Foxhall, Lin, and John Salmon, eds., 1998, *Thinking Men: Masculinity and its Self-Representation in the Classical Tradition* (London).

Franko, George Fredric, 2005/2006, "The Trojan Horse at the Close of the *Iliad*," *CJ* 101, 121–3.

Fraser, P. M., 1996, *Cities of Alexander the Great* (Oxford).

1972, *Ptolemaic Alexandria*, 3 vols. (Oxford).

Fredricksmeyer, Ernst (E. A.), 2003, "Alexander's Religion and Divinity," in Joseph Roisman (ed.), 253–78.

2000 "Alexander the Great and the Kingship of Asia," in A. B. Bosworth and E. J. Baynham (eds.), 136–66.

1991, "Alexander, Zeus Ammon, and the Conquest of Asia," *TAPA* 121, 199–214.

1990, "Alexander and Philip: Emulation and Resentment," *CJ* 85, 300–15.

1982, "On the Final Aims of Philip II," in W. Lindsay Adams and Eugene N. Borza (eds.), 85–98.

1981, "On the Background of the Ruler Cult," in Harry J. Dell (ed.), 145–56.

1979, "Divine Honors for Philip II," *TAPA* 109, 39–61.

1966, "The Ancestral Rites of Alexander the Great," *CP* 61, 179–82.

Friedländer, P., and H. B. Hoffleit, 1948, *Epigrammata: Greek Inscriptions in Verse from the Beginnings to the Persian Wars* (Berkeley).

Friis Johansen, K., 1951, *The Attic Grave-Reliefs of the Classical Period: An Essay in Interpretation* (Copenhagen).

Frisch, Peter, 1968, *Die Traüme bei Herodot* (Meisenheim am Glan).

Fritz, Kurt von, 1954, *The Theory of the Mixed Constitution in Antiquity: A Critical Analysis of Polybius' Political Ideas* (New York).

Furtwängler, Adolf, 1895, *Masterpieces of Greek Sculpture: A Series of Essays on the History of Art* (New York).

Gammie, John G., 1986, "Herodotus on Kings and Tyrants: Objective Historiography or Conventional Portraiture?" *JNES* 45, 171–95.

Gantz, Timothy, 1993, *Early Greek Myth: A Guide to Literary and Artistic Sources*, 2 vols. (Baltimore).

Garland, Robert, 1985, *The Greek Way of Death* (Ithaca).

1982, "A First Catalogue of Attic Peribolos Tombs," *BSA* 77, 125–76.

Gauthier, Philippe, 1985, *Les cités grecques et leurs bienfaiteurs* = *BCH* Supp. 12 (Paris).

Geer, Russel M., ed. and trans., 1947, *Diodorus of Sicily*, vol. IX, *Books 18 and 19.1–65*, Loeb Classical Library (Cambridge, MA).

Gentili, Bruno, and Giovanni Cerri, 1988, *History and Biography in Ancient Thought*, trans. Leonard Murray (Amsterdam) = *Storia e biografia nel pensiero antico* (Rome/Bari, 1983).

Gill, Christopher, 1996, *Personality in Greek Epic, Tragedy, and Philosophy: The Self in Dialogue* (Oxford).

Godley, A. D., ed. and trans., 1921, *Herodotus:* The Persian Wars, 4 vols., Loeb Classical Library (Cambridge, MA).

Goh, Madeleine Milim, 2004, "The Poetics of Chariot Driving and Rites of Passage in Ancient Greece" (diss., Harvard University).

Golden, Mark, 1997, "Equestrian Competition in Ancient Greece: Difference, Dissent, Democracy," *Phoenix* 51, 327–44.

Goldhill, Simon, 1990, "The Great Dionysia and Civic Ideology," in John J. Winkler and Froma I. Zeitlin (eds.), 97–129.

Goldhill, Simon, and Robin Osborne, eds., 1999, *Performance Culture and Athenian Democracy* (Cambridge).

Gomme, A. W., 1945–56, *A Historical Commentary on Thucydides,* vols. I–III, books 1–5.24 (Oxford).

Gomme, A. W., A. Andrewes, and K. J. Dover, 1970–81, *A Historical Commentary on Thucydides,* vols. IV–V, books 5.55–8 (Oxford).

Gould, John, 1994, "Herodotus and Religion," in Simon Hornblower (ed.), 1994a, 91–106.

Graham, A. J., 1964, *Colony and Mother City in Ancient Greece* (Manchester).

Gray, Vivienne J., 2011, *Xenophon's Mirror of Princes: Reading the Reflections* (Oxford).

  1998, *The Framing of Socrates: The Literary Interpretation of Xenophon's* Memorabilia = *Hermes* Einzelschriften 79 (Stuttgart).

  1991, "Continuous History and Xenophon, *Hellenica* 1–2.3.10," *AJP* 112, 201–28.

  1989, *The Character of Xenophon's* Hellenica (Baltimore).

  1986, "Xenophon's *Hiero* and the Meeting of the Wise Man and Tyrant in Greek Literature," *CQ* 36, 115–23.

  1981, "Dialogue in Xenophon's *Hellenica,*" *CQ* 31, 321–34.

Green, Peter, 1991, *Alexander of Macedon, 356–323 BC: A Historical Biography* (Berkeley).

  1990, *Alexander to Actium: The Historical Evolution of the Hellenistic Age* (Berkeley).

Greenwalt, W. S., 1994, "The Production of Coinage from Archelaus to Perdiccas III and the Evolution of Argead Macedonia," in Ian Worthington, ed., 105–34.

Gribble, David, 2006, "Individuals in Thucydides," in Antonios Rengakos and Antonis Tsakmakis (eds.), 439–68.

  1999, *Alcibiades and Athens: A Study in Literary Presentation* (Oxford).

  1998, "Narrator Interventions in Thucydides," *JHS* 118, 41–67.

Griffith, G. T., 1980, "Philip as a General and the Macedonian Army," in Miltiades B. Hatzopoulos and Louisa D. Loukopoulos (eds.), 58–77.

Gruen, Erich S., 1985, "The Coronation of the Diadochoi," in John W. Eadie and Josiah Ober (eds.), 253–71.

Habicht, Christian, 1970, *Gottmenschentum und griechischer Städte*, 2nd edn. = Zetemata 22 (Munich).

Hagemajer Allen, Katarzyna, 2003, "Intercultural Exchanges in Fourth-Century Attic Decrees," *CA* 22, 199–246.

Halliwell, Stephen, 1990, "Traditional Greek Conceptions of Character," in Christopher Pelling (ed.), 32–59.

Hamilton, Charles D., 1994, "Plutarch and Xenophon on Agesilaus," *AncW* 25, 205–12.

    1991, *Agesilaus and the Failure of Spartan Hegemony* (Ithaca).

    1982, "Agesilaus and the Failure of Spartan Hegemony," *AncW* 5, 67–78.

Hammond, N. G. L., 2000, "Political Developments in Boeotia," *CQ* 50, 80–93.

    1997, "What May Philip Have Learnt as a Hostage in Thebes?" *GRBS* 38, 355–72.

    1995, "Connotations of 'Macedonia' and of 'Macedones' Until 323 BC," *CQ* 45, 120–8.

    1994a, *Philip of Macedon* (Baltimore).

    1994b, "Philip's Actions in 347 and Early 346 BC," *CQ* 44, 367–74.

    1993, *Sources for Alexander the Great: An Analysis of Plutarch's* Life *and Arrian's* Anabasis Alexandrou (Cambridge).

    1991, "The Sources of Justin on Macedonia to the Death of Philip," *CQ* 41, 496–508.

    1989, "Aspects of Alexander's Journal and Ring in His Last Days," *AJP* 110, 155–60.

    1988, "The King and the Land in the Macedonian Kingdom," *CQ* 38, 382–91.

    1987, "Greek Warfare: Battles and Burials," review of W. Kendrick Pritchett, *The Greek State at War*, Part 4 (Berkeley, 1985), *CR* 37, 236–7.

    1983, *Three Historians of Alexander the Great: The So-Called Vulgate Authors, Diodorus, Justin, and Curtius* (Cambridge).

    1980, "Some Passages in Arrian Concerning Alexander," *CQ* 30, 455–76.

    1968, "The Campaign and the Battle of Marathon," *JHS* 88, 13–57.

    1938a, "The Sources of Diodorus 16, Part 2," *CQ* 32, 137–51.

    1938b, "The Two Battles of Chaeronea (338 and 86 BC)," *Klio* 31, 186–218.

    1937a, "Diodorus' Narrative of the Sacred War and the Chronological Problems of 357–352 BC," *JHS* 57, 44–78.

    1937b, "The Sources of Diodorus 16, Part 1," *CQ* 31, 79–91.

Hammond, N. G. L., and G. T. Griffith, 1979, *A History of Macedonia*, vol. II, *550–336 BC* (Oxford).

Hampton, Timothy, 1990, *Writing From History: The Rhetoric of Exemplarity in Renaissance Literature* (Ithaca).

Hannestad, Niels, 1993, "*Imitatio Alexandri* in Roman Art," in Jesper Carlsen, Bodil Due, Otto Steen Due, and Birte Poursen (eds.), 61–9.

Hansen, Mogens Herman, 1975, Eisangelia: *The Sovereignty of the People's Court in Athens in the Fourth Century BC and the Impeachment of Generals and Politicians* (Odense).

Hansen, Peter Allan, 1983 and 1989, *Carmina epigraphica Graeca*, vols. I–II (Berlin).

Hanson, Victor Davis, ed., 1991, *Hoplites: The Classical Greek Battle Experience* (London).

   1989, *The Western Way of War: Infantry Battle in Classical Greece* (New York).

   1983, *Warfare and Agriculture in Classical Greece* (Pisa).

Harding, Phillip, 2008, *The Story of Athens: The Fragments of the Local Chronicles of Attika* (London).

   1985, ed. and trans., *From the End of the Peloponnesian War to the Battle of Ipsus* (Cambridge).

Harley, T. Rutherford, 1942, "'A Greater than Leonidas,'" *G&R* 11, 68–83.

Harrison, Evelyn B., 1972, "The South Frieze of the Nike Temple and the Marathon Painting in the Painted Stoa," *AJA* 76, 353–78.

Harrison, Thomas, 2000, *Divinity and History: The Religion of Herodotus* (Oxford).

Hartnett, Jeremy, 2010, "The Battle of Marathon," blog entry, *Accents* (Wabash College Classics Department), http://blogs.wabash.edu/accents/2010/10/27/the-battle-of-marathon.

Hartog, François, 1988, *The Mirror of Herodotus: The Representation of the Other in the Writing of History*, trans. Janet Lloyd (Berkeley).

Hartswick, Kim J., and Mary C. Sturgeon, eds., 1998, *ΣΤΕΦΑΝΟΣ: Studies in Honor of Brunilde Sismondo Ridgway* (Philadelphia).

Hatzopoulos, Miltiades B., and Louisa D. Loukopoulos, eds., 1980, *Philip of Macedon* (Athens).

Haubold, Johannes, 2007, "Xerxes' Homer," in Emma Bridges, Edith Hall, and P. J. Rhodes (eds.), 47–63.

Head, Barclay Vincent, assisted by G. F. Hill, George Macdonald, and W. Wroth, 1911, *Historia Numorum: A Manual of Greek Numismatics*, "new and enlarged" edn. (Oxford). Digital edn. by Ed Snible et al. (http://www.snible.org/coins/hn/), edition of July 4, 2008.

Heckel, Waldemar, 1996, "Resistance to Alexander the Great," in Lawrence A. Tritle (ed.), 189–227.

   1992, *The Marshals of Alexander's Empire* (London).

   1988, *The Last Days and Testament of Alexander the Great: A Prosopographic Study* = *Historia* Einzelschriften 56 (Stuttgart).

Heckel, Waldemar, and Lawrence A. Tritle, eds., 2009, *Alexander the Great: A New History* (Malden, MA).

   2003, eds., *Crossroads of History: The Age of Alexander* (Claremont, CA).

Heckel, Waldemar, Lawrence A. Tritle, and Pat Wheatley, eds., 2007, *Alexander's Empire: Formulation to Decay* (Claremont, CA).

Hedrick, Charles W., Jr., 1999, "Democracy and the Athenian Epigraphical Habit," *Hesperia* 68, 387–439.

   1994, "Writing, Reading, and Democracy," in Robin Osborne and Simon Hornblower (eds.), 157–74.

   1988, "An Honorific Phratry Inscription," *AJP* 109, 111–17.

Heisserer, A. J., 1980, *Alexander the Great and the Greeks: The Epigraphic Evidence* (Norman, OK).

Henderson, Jeffrey, 2002, *Aristophanes:* Frogs, Assemblywomen, Wealth (Cambridge, MA, and London).

Henry, Alan S., 1983, *Honours and Privileges in Athenian Decrees: The Principal Formulae of Athenian Honorary Decrees* = Subsidia epigraphica 10 (Hildescheim).

1977, *The Prescripts of Athenian Decrees* = *Mnemosyne* Supp. 49 (Leiden).

Herman, Gabriel, 1987, *Ritualised Friendship and the Greek City* (Cambridge).

Heskel, Julia, 1997, "Macedonia and the North, 400–336," in Lawrence A. Tritle (ed.), 166–88.

1987, "The Foreign Policy of Philip II Down to the Peace of Philocrates" (diss., Harvard University).

Higgins, W. E., 1977, *Xenophon the Athenian: The Problem of the Individual and the Society of the* Polis (Albany).

Hobden, Fiona, 2009, "The Politics of the *Sumposion*," in George Boys-Stones, Barbara Graziosi, and Phiroze Vasunia, (eds.), 271–80.

Hodkinson, Stephen, 2000, *Property and Wealth in Classical Sparta* (London).

1999, "An Agonistic Culture: Athletic Competition in Archaic and Classical Spartan Society," in Stephen Hodkinson and Anton Powell (eds.), 147–87.

Hodkinson, Stephen, and Anton Powell, eds., 2006, *Sparta and War* (Swansea).

1999, eds., *Sparta: New Perspectives* (London).

Hoffmann, Geneviève, 1993, "'Portrait de groupe avec Dame': Etude sociologique des Monuments," in Christoph W. Clairmont, 160–79.

Hohti, Paavo, 1976, *The Interrelation of Speech and Action in the Histories of Herodotus* (Helsinki).

Hölscher, Tonio, 1998, "Images and Political Identity: The Case of Athens," in Deborah Boedeker and Kurt A. Raaflaub (eds.), 153–83.

Holt, Frank L., 2003, *Alexander the Great and the Mystery of the Elephant Medallions* (Berkeley).

Homeyer, Helene, 1962, "Zu den Anfängen der griechischen Biographie," *Philologus* 106, 75–85.

Hornblower, Jane, 1981, *Hieronymus of Cardia* (Oxford).

Hornblower, Simon, 2004, "'This was Decided' (*edoxe tauta*): The Army as polis in Xenophon's *Anabasis* – and Elsewhere," in Robin Lane Fox, (ed.), 243–63.

2002, *The Greek World, 479–323 BC,* 3rd edn. (London).

1995, "The Fourth-Century and Hellenistic Reception of Thucydides," *JHS* 115, 47–68.

1994a, ed., *Greek Historiography* (Oxford).

1994b, "Sources and Their Uses," in D. M. Lewis, John Boardman, Simon Hornblower, and M. Ostwald, eds., *The Cambridge Ancient History,* 2nd edn., vol. VI, *The Fourth Century BC* (Cambridge), 1–23.

1992, "Thucydides' Use of Herodotus," in J. M. Sanders, ed., *ΦΙΛΟΛΑΚΩΝ: Lakonian Studies in Honour of Hector Catling* (London), 141–54.

1991 and 1996, *A Commentary on Thucydides*, vol. I, books 1–3, vol. II, books 4–5.24 (Oxford).

1990, "When Was Megalopolis Founded?" *BSA* 85, 71–7.

1983, "The Raw Materials of Ancient History," review of Michael Crawford, ed., *Sources for Ancient History* (Cambridge), *CR* 34 (1984), 241–2.

Hornblower, Simon, and Catherine Morgan, eds., 2007, *Pindar's Poetry, Patrons, and Festivals From Archaic Greece to the Roman Empire* (Oxford).

Hornblower, Simon, and Antony Spawforth, eds., 1999, *The Oxford Classical Dictionary*, 3rd edn. (Oxford).

How, W. W., and J. Wells, 1912, *A Commentary on Herodotus*, 2 vols. (Oxford).

Humphreys, S. C., 1983, *The Family, Women, and Death: Comparative Studies* (London).

1980, "Family Tombs and Tomb Cult in Ancient Athens: Tradition or Traditionalism?" *JHS* 100, 96–126.

Hurwit, Jeffrey M., 2007, "The Problem with Dexileos: Heroic and Other Nudities in Greek Art," *AJA* 111, 35–60.

Immerwahr, Henry R., 1966, *Form and Thought in Herodotus* (Cleveland).

1954, "Historical Action in Herodotus," *TAPA* 85, 16–45.

Isager, Jacob, 1993, "Alexander the Great in Roman Literature from Pompey to Vespasian," in Jesper Carlsen, Bodil Due, Otto Steen Due, and Birte Poursen (eds.), 75–84.

Jackson, A. H., 1991, "Hoplites and the Gods: The Dedication of Captured Arms and Armour," in Victor Davis Hanson (ed.), 228–49.

Jacoby, Felix, 1949, *Atthis: The Local Chronicles of Ancient Athens* (Oxford).

1945, "Some Athenian Epigrams from the Persian Wars," *Hesperia* 14, 157–211.

1944, "*Patrios nomos*: State Burial in Athens and the Public Cemetery in the Kerameikos," *JHS* 64, 37–66.

1923–6, 1940–58, *Die Fragmente der griechischen Historiker*, 3 vols. (I–II: Berlin, 1923–6; III: Leiden, 1940–58).

1904, *Das Marmor Parium* (Berlin).

Jameson, Michael H., 1962, "A Revised Text of the Decree of Themistokles from Troizen," *Hesperia* 31, 310–15.

1960, "A Decree of Themistokles from Troizen," *Hesperia* 29, 198–223.

Jansen, Joseph Nicholas, 2007, "After Empire: Xenophon's Poroi and the Reorientation of Athens' Political Economy" (diss., University of Texas, Austin).

Jeffery, L. H., 1947, "Some Early Greek Epitaphs," *G&R* 16, 127–32.

Jesi, Furio, and Benjamin Egli, 1964, "The Thracian Herakles," *HR* 3, 261–77.

Johansson, Mikael, 2001, "The Inscription from Troizen: A Decree of Themistocles?" *ZPE* 137, 69–92.

Jones, Horace Leonard, ed. and trans., 1932, *The Geography of Strabo*, vol. VIII, Loeb Classical Library (London).

Jones, Nicholas F., 1987, *Public Organization in Ancient Greece: A Documentary Study* (Philadelphia).

Jones, W. H. S., ed. and trans., 1918, *Pausanias: Description of Greece*, vol. I, *Books 1–2 (Attica and Corinth)*, Loeb Classical Library (London).

    1935, ed. and trans., *Pausanias: Description of Greece*, vol. IV, *Books 8.22–10 (Arcadia, Boeotia, and Phocis and Ozolian Locri)*, Loeb Classical Library (London).

Joost-Gaugier, Christiane L., 1982, "The Early Beginnings of the Notion of 'Uomini Famosi' and the 'De Viris Illustribus' in Greco-Roman Literary Tradition," *Artibus et Historiae* 3, 97–115.

Jordan, Borimir, 1975, *The Athenian Navy in the Classical Period* (Berkeley).

Jung, Michael, 2006, *Marathon und Plataiai: Zwei Perserschlachten als 'lieux de mémoire' im antiken Griechenland* (Göttingen).

Kagan, Donald, 1961, "The Origin and Purposes of Ostracism," *Hesperia* 30, 393–401.

Keaney, J. J., and A. E. Raubitschek, 1972, "A Late Byzantine Account of Ostracism," *AJP* 93.1 = *Studies in Honor of Henry T. Rowell*, 87–91.

Kearns, Emily, 1989, *The Heroes of Attica* = *BICS* Supp. 57 (London).

Keesling, Catherine M., 2010, "The Callimachus Monument on the Athenian Acropolis (*CEG* 256) and Athenian Commemoration of the Persian Wars," in Manuel Baumbach, Andrej Petrovic, and Ivana Petrovic, (eds.), 100–30.

    2007, "Early Hellenistic Portrait Statues on the Athenian Acropolis: Survival, Reuse, Transformation," in Peter Schultz and Ralf von den Hoff (eds.), 141–60.

    2003, *The Votive Statues of the Athenian Acropolis* (Cambridge).

Keller, W. J., 1910–11, "Xenophon's Acquaintance with the *History* of Herodotus," *CJ* 6, 252–9.

Kennedy, George A., 1994, *A New History of Classical Rhetoric* (Princeton).

    1963, *The Art of Persuasion in Greece* (Princeton).

Kerferd, G. B., 1981, *The Sophistic Movement* (Cambridge).

Keyes, Clinton Walker, 1956, *Cicero:* De re publica, De legibus, Loeb Classical Library (Cambridge, MA, and London).

King, Carol J., 2010, "Macedonian Kingship and Other Political Institutions," in Joseph Roisman and Ian Worthington (eds.), 373–91.

Kinzl, K., ed., 1977, *Greece and the Eastern Mediterranean: Studies Presented to Fritz Schachermeyer* (Berlin).

Knigge, Ursula, 1991, *The Athenian Kerameikos: History, Monuments, Excavations*, trans. Judith Binder (Athens).

Konstan, David, 1987, "Persians, Greeks, and Empire," *Arethusa* 20.1–2 = *Herodotus and the Invention of History*, 59–73.

Kopcke, Günter, and Mary B. Moore, eds., 1979, *Studies in Classical Art and Archaeology: A Tribute to Peter Heinrich von Blanckenhagen* (Locust Valley, NY).

Kosmopoulou, Angeliki, 2002, *The Iconography of Sculptured Statue Bases in the Archaic and Classical Periods* (Madison).

Koukouli-Chrysanthaki, C., and C. Bakirtzis, 2000, *Philippi*, 3rd edn. (Athens).

Kraay, Colin M. (text), and Max Hirmer (photographs), 1966, *Greek Coins* (London).

Kraus, C. S., and A. J. Woodman, 1997, *Latin Historians* = *G&R* New Surveys in the Classics 27 (Oxford).

Krentz, Peter M., 2007, "The Oath of Marathon, Not Plataia?" *Hesperia* 76, 731–42.

Krumeich, Ralf, 1997, *Bildnisse griechischer Herrscher und Staatsmänner im 5. Jahrhundert v. Chr.* (Munich).

Kübler, Karl, 1976, *Kerameikos: Ergebnisse der Ausgrabungen*, vol. VII, *Die Nekropole der Mitte des 6. bis Ende des 5. Jhs.*, Teil 1 (Berlin).

Kunze, Emil, and Hans Schleif, eds., 1944, *Olympische Forschungen*, vol. I (Berlin).

Kurke, Leslie, 2000a, "Charting the Poles of History: Herodotos and Thoukydides," in Oliver Taplin (ed.), 2000, 115–37.

   2000b, "The Strangeness of 'Song Culture': Archaic Greek Poetry," in Oliver Taplin (ed.), 2000, 40–69.

   1999, *Coins, Bodies, Games, and Gold: The Politics of Meaning in Archaic Greece* (Princeton).

   1993, "The Economy of Kudos," in Carol Dougherty and Leslie Kurke (eds.), 131–63.

   1992, "The Politics of ἁβροσύνη in Archaic Greece," *CA* 11, 91–120.

   1991, *The Traffic in Praise: Pindar and the Poetics of Social Economy* (Ithaca).

Kurtz, Donna Carol, 1988, "Mistress and Maid," *AION (archeol)* 10, 141–9.

   1975, *Athenian White Lekythoi* (Oxford).

Kurtz, Donna Carol, and John Boardman, 1971, *Greek Burial Customs* (London).

Kuttner, Ann, 1999, "Hellenistic Images of Spectacle from Alexander to Augustus," in Bettina Bergmann and Christine Kondoleon (eds.), 97–123.

La Coste-Messelière, Pierre de, 1957, *Fouilles de Delphes*, vol. IV, *Monuments figurés: Sculpture*, fasc. 4, *Sculptures du Trésor des Athéniens*, 2 vols. (Paris).

Lambert, Stephen D., 2006, "Athenian State Laws and Decrees, 352/1–322/1: III. Decrees Honouring Foreigners. A. Citizenship, Proxeny and Euergesy," *ZPE* 158, 115–58.

   1993, *The Phratries of Attica* (Ann Arbor).

Lane Fox, Robin, ed., 2004, *The Long March: Xenophon and the Ten Thousand* (New Haven).

   1986, "Theopompus of Chios and the Greek World," in John Boardman and C. E. Vaphopoulou-Richardson (eds.), 105–20.

Lang, Mabel, 1990, *The Athenian Agora*, vol. XV, *Ostraka* (Princeton).

   1944, "Biographical Patterns of Folklore and Morality in Herodotus' *History*" (diss., Bryn Mawr College).

Lardinois, André, and Laura McClure, eds., 2001, *Making Silence Speak: Women's Voices in Greek Literature and Society* (Princeton).

Lateiner, Donald, 2002, "Assessing the Nature of Herodotus' Mind and Text," review of Thomas Harrison, *Divinity and History: The Religion of Herodotus* (Oxford,

2000), and Rosalind Thomas, *Herodotus in Context: Ethnography, Science and the Art of Persuasion* (Cambridge, 2000), *CP* 97, 371–82.

1989, *The Historical Method of Herodotus* (Toronto).

Lattimore, Richmond, 1962, *Themes in Greek and Latin Epitaphs* (Urbana).

1939, "The Wise Adviser in Herodotus," *CP* 24, 24–35.

Lawton, Carol L., 1995, *Attic Document Reliefs: Art and Politics in Ancient Athens* (Oxford).

Lefkowitz, Mary R., 1991, *First-Person Fictions: Pindar's Poetic 'I'* (Oxford).

Leo, Friedrich, 1901, *Die griechisch-römische Biographie nach ihrer literarischer Form* (Leipzig, 1901; repr. Hildescheim, 1965).

Le Rider, Georges, 1996, *Monnayage et finances de Philippe II: Un état de la question* (Athens).

1977, *Le monnayage d'argent et d'or de Philippe II frappé en Macédoine de 359 à 294* (Paris).

Lesky, Albin, 1966, *A History of Greek Literature*, trans. Cornelis de Heer and James Willis (London).

Lewis, David M., 2000–3, "Κατάλογοι θανόντων ἐν πολέμωι," *HOPOΣ* 14–16, 9–17.

1992, "The Archidamian War," in D. M. Lewis, John Boardman, J. K. Davies, and M. Ostwald (eds.), 370–432.

Lewis, D. M., John Boardman, J. K. Davies, and M. Ostwald, eds., 1992, *The Cambridge Ancient History*, 2nd edn., vol. V, *The Fifth Century BC* (Cambridge).

Lexicon Iconographicum Mythologiae Classicae = LIMC (Zurich, 1981–99).

Loomis, William T., 1992, *The Spartan War Fund: IG V 1, 1 and a New Fragment = Historia* Einzelschriften 74 (Stuttgart).

1990, "Pausanias, Byzantion and the Formation of the Delian League: A Chronological Note," *Historia* 39, 487–92.

Loraux, Nicole, 1986, *The Invention of Athens: The Funeral Oration and the Classical City*, trans. Alan Sheridan (Cambridge, MA).

Lott, J. Bert, 1996, "Philip II, Alexander, and the Two Tyrannies at Eresos of *IG* XII.2.526," *Phoenix* 50, 26–40.

Lougovaya-Ast, Julia, 2006, "Myrrhine, The First Priestess of Athena Nike," *Phoenix* 60, 211–25.

Low, Polly, ed., 2008, *The Athenian Empire* (Edinburgh).

2006, "Commemorating the Spartan War-Dead," in Stephen Hodkinson and Anton Powell (eds.), 85–109.

2003, "Remembering War in Fifth-Century Greece: Ideologies, Societies, and Commemoration beyond Democratic Athens," *World Archaeology* 35, 98–111.

2002, "Cavalry Identity and Democratic Ideology in Early Fourth-Century Athens," *PCPS* 48, 102–19.

Lucarini, Carlo Martino, ed., 2009, *Q. Curtius Rufus:* Historiae (Berlin and New York).

Luraghi, Nino, 2008, *The Ancient Messenians: Constructions of Ethnicity and Memory* (Cambridge).

2006, "Meta-*historiê*: Method and Genre in the Histories," in Carolyn Dewald and John Marincola (eds.), 76–91.

2001, ed., *The Historian's Craft in the Age of Herodotus* (Oxford).

Ma, John, 2008, "Chaironeia 338: Topographies of Commemoration," *JHS* 128, 72–91.

Macan, Reginald Walter, 1908, *Herodotus: The Seventh, Eighth, and Ninth Books,* vol. I, part 1, *Introduction [and] Book VII, Text and Commentaries* (London).

McCauley, Barbara A., 1993, "Hero Cults and Politics in Fifth Century Greece" (diss., University of Iowa).

MacKay, Pierre, 2011, "The Marathon Stone," blog entry, *Surprised by Time* (Diana Gilliland Wright), 8 April 2011, http://surprisedbytime.blogspot.com/2011/04/marathon-stone.html.

McKechnie, P. R., and S. J. Kern, eds., trans., and comm., 1988, *Hellenica Oxyrhynchia* (Warminster).

Mackie, Hilary Susan, 2003, *Graceful Errors: Pindar and the Performance of Praise* (Ann Arbor).

Mackil, Emily, 2013, *Creating a Common Polity: Religion, Economy, and Politics in the Making of the Greek Koinon* (Berkeley).

MacMullen, Ramsay, 1982, "The Epigraphic Habit in the Roman Empire," *AJP* 103, 233–46.

Malkin, I., 1985, "What's in a Name? The Eponymous Founders of Greek Colonies," *Athenaeum* 63, 114–30.

Marchant, E. C., ed. and trans., 1925, *Xenophon: Scripta Minora*, Loeb Classical Library (London).

Marincola, John, 2007, "The Persian Wars in Fourth-Century Oratory and Historiography," in Emma Bridges, Edith Hall, and P. J. Rhodes (eds.), 105–25.

2006, "Herodotus and the Poetry of the Past," in Carolyn Dewald and John Marincola (eds.), 13–28.

2001, *Greek Historians* = *G&R* New Surveys in the Classics 31 (Oxford).

1997, *Authority and Tradition in Ancient Historiography* (Cambridge).

1987, "Herodotean Narrative and the Narrator's Presence," *Arethusa* 20.1–2 = *Herodotus and the Invention of History*, 121–37.

Markle, Minor M., III, 1978, "Use of the Sarissa by Philip and Alexander of Macedon," *AJA* 82, 486–91.

Martin, Luther H., 1987, *Hellenistic Religions: An Introduction* (Oxford).

Martin, Richard, 1989, *The Language of Heroes: Speech and Performance in the* Iliad (Ithaca).

Martin, Thomas R., 1985, *Sovereignty and Coinage in Classical Greece* (Princeton).

Matthaiou, Angelos P., 2003, "Ἀθηναίοισι δὲ τεταγμένοισι ἐν τεμένεϊ Ἡρακλέος (Hdt. 6.108.1)," in Peter Derow and Robert Parker (eds.), 190–202.

1988, "Νέος λίθος τοῦ μνημείου μὲ τὰ ἐπιγράμματα γιὰ τοὺς Περσικοὺς πολέμους," *HOPOΣ* 6, 118–22, pls. 17–18.

Mattingly, H. B., 1992, "Epigraphy and the Athenian Empire," *Historia* 41, 129–38.

Mattusch, Carol C., 1994, "The Eponymous Heroes: The Idea of Sculptural Groups," in W. D. E. Coulson, et al. (eds.), 73–81.

Meadows, A. R., 1995, "Pausanias and the Historiography of Classical Sparta," *CQ* 45, 92–113.

Meiggs, Russell, 1982, *Trees and Timber in the Ancient Mediterranean World* (Oxford).

1972, *The Athenian Empire* (Oxford).

Meiggs, Russell, and David Lewis, eds., 1969, *A Selection of Greek Historical Inscriptions to the End of the Fifth Century BC*, 1st edn. (Oxford).

Meritt, Benjamin D., 1962, "The Marathon Epigrams Again," *AJP* 83, 294–8.

1956, "Epigrams From the Battle of Marathon," in Saul S. Weinberg (ed.), 268–80, pl. 36.

1945, "Attic Inscriptions of the Fifth Century," *Hesperia* 14.2 = *The American Excavations in the Athenian Agora: Twenty-Sixth Report*, 61–133.

1936, "Greek Inscriptions," *Hesperia* 5.3 = *The American Excavations in the Athenian Agora: Tenth Report*, 355–430.

Meritt, Benjamin Dean, H. T. Wade-Gery, and Malcolm Francis McGregor, 1939–1953, *The Athenian Tribute Lists*, 4 vols. (Cambridge, MA).

Meyer, Elizabeth A., 1993, "Epitaphs and Citizenship in Classical Athens," *JHS* 113, 99–121.

Meyer, Marion, and Nora Brüggemann, 2007, *Kore und Kouros: Weihegaben für die Götter* (Vienna).

Mikalson, Jon D., 2010, *Greek Religion*, 2nd edn. (Malden, MA).

Millender, Ellen G., 2001, "Spartan Literacy Revisited," *CA* 20, 121–64.

Minnen, Peter van, 2000, "Euergetism in Graeco-Roman Egypt," in Léon Mooren (ed.), 437–69.

Misch, G., 1950, *A History of Autobiography in Antiquity*, 2 vols. (London).

Mitchel, Fordyce, 1965, "Athens in the Age of Alexander," *G&R* 12, 189–204.

Mitchell, Lynette [G.], 2007, *Panhellenism and the Barbarian in Archaic and Classical Greece* (Swansea).

1997, *Greeks Bearing Gifts: The Public Use of Private Relationships in the Greek World, 435–323 BC* (Cambridge).

Moles, John, 2002, "Herodotus and Athens," in Egbert J. Bakker, Irene J. F. de Jong, and Hans van Wees (eds.), 33–52.

1994, "Xenophon and Callicratidas," *JHS* 114, 70–84.

Momigliano, Arnaldo, 1985, "Marcel Mauss and the Quest for the Person in Greek Biography and Autobiography," in Michael Carrithers, Steven Collins, and Steven Lukes (eds.), 83–92.

1972, "Tradition and the Classical Historian," *History and Theory* 11, 279–93.

1971, *The Development of Greek Biography*, 1st edn. (Cambridge, MA).

Mooren, Léon, ed., 2000, *Politics, Administration, and Society in the Hellenistic and Roman World: Proceedings of the International Colloquium, Bertinoro 19–24 July 1997* = *Studia Hellenistica* 36 (Leuven).

Morgan, Catherine, 2007, "Debating Patronage: The Cases of Argos and Corinth," in Simon Hornblower and Catherine Morgan (eds.), 213–63.

2003, *Early Greek States Beyond the Polis* (London).

Morgan, Catherine, Robert K. Pitt, and Todd Whitelaw, 2008–9, "Archaeology in Greece, 2008–2009," *AR* 55, 1–101.

Morgan, Kathryn A., ed., 2003, *Popular Tyranny: Sovereignty and Its Discontents in Ancient Greece* (Austin).

Mørkholm, Otto, ed. Philip Grierson and Ulla Westermark, 1991, *Early Hellenistic Coinage: From the Accession of Alexander to the Peace of Apamea (336–188 BC)* (Cambridge).

Morris, Ian, 1996, "The Strong Principle of Equality and the Archaic Origins of Greek Democracy," in Josiah Ober and Charles Hedrick (eds.), 19–48.

1994, "Everyman's Grave," in Alan L. Boegehold and Adele C. Scafuro (eds.), 67–101.

1992, *Death-Ritual and Social Structure in Classical Antiquity* (Cambridge).

1987, *Burial and Ancient Society: The Rise of the Greek City-State* (Cambridge).

Morris, Ian, and Barry Powell, eds., 1996, *A New Companion to Homer* (Leiden).

Morrison, Donald R., 1988, *Bibliography of Editions, Translations, and Commentary on Xenophon's Socratic Writings, 1600–Present* (Pittsburgh).

Mosley, Derek J., 1965, "The Size of Embassies in Ancient Greek Diplomacy," *TAPA* 96, 255–66.

Mossman, J. M., 1988, "Tragedy and Epic in Plutarch's *Alexander*," *JHS* 108, 83–93.

Müller, Olaf, 1973, *Antigonos Monophthalmos und 'Das Jahr der Könige'* (Bonn).

Munn, Mark, 1997, "Thebes and Central Greece," in Lawrence A. Tritle, (ed.), 66–106.

Munson, Rosaria Vignolo, 2001, "*Ananke* in Herodotus," *JHS* 121, 30–50.

1988, "Artemisia in Herodotus," *CA* 7, 91–106.

Murray, A. T., 1966, *Homer*, vols. I–II = *The Odyssey*, Loeb Classical Library (Cambridge, MA, and London).

Murray, Oswyn, 1993, *Early Greece*, 2nd edn. (Cambridge, MA).

1990, ed., *Sympotica: A Symposium on the Symposion* (Oxford).

1972, "Herodotus and Hellenistic Culture," *CQ* 22, 200–13.

Murray, Oswyn, and Manuela Tecuşan, eds., 1995, *In vino veritas* (London).

Mylonas, George E., ed., 1951–3, *Studies Presented to David Moore Robinson on His Seventieth Birthday*, 2 vols. (St. Louis).

1948, "Homeric and Mycenean Burial Customs," *AJA* 52, 56–81.

Nagy, Blaise, 1994, "Alcibiades' Second 'Profanation,'" *Historia* 43, 275–85.

Nagy, Gregory, 1990, *Pindar's Homer: The Lyric Possession of an Epic Past* (Baltimore).

Neer, Richard, 2004, "The Athenian Treasury at Delphi and the Material of Politics," *CA* 23, 63–94.

Nicholson, Nigel James, 2005, *Aristocracy and Athletics in Archaic and Classical Greece* (Cambridge).

Nilsson, Martin, 1940, *Greek Popular Religion* (New York).

Nock, Arthur Darby, 1942, "Religious Attitudes of the Ancient Greeks," *PAPHS* 85, 472–82.

Nouhaud, Michel, 1982, *L'utilisation de l'histoire par les orateurs attiques* (Paris).

Nussbaum, G. B., 1967, *The Ten Thousand: A Study in Social Organization and Action in Xenophon's* Anabasis (Leiden).

Oakley, John H., 2004, *Picturing Death in Classical Athens: The Evidence of the White Lekythoi* (Cambridge).

Obbink, Laurie, Dirk Obbink, Virginia Jameson, and Mary Lou Munn, eds., 1985, *The Greek Historians: Literature and History, Papers Presented to A. E. Raubitschek* (Saratoga, CA).

Ober, Josiah, 2008, *Democracy and Knowledge: Innovation and Learning in Classical Athens* (Princeton).

  1998, *Political Dissent in Democratic Athens: Intellectual Critics of Popular Rule* (Princeton).

  1996a, "The Athenian Revolution of 508/7 BCE: Violence, Authority, and the Origins of Democracy," in Josiah Ober, 1996b, 32–52, originally published in Carol Dougherty and Leslie Kurke (eds.), 1993, 215–32.

  1996b, *The Athenian Revolution: Essays on Ancient Greek Democracy and Political Theory* (Princeton).

  1989, *Mass and Elite in Democratic Athens: Rhetoric, Ideology, and The Power of the People* (Princeton).

Ober, Josiah, and Charles Hedrick, eds., 1996, *Dêmokratia: A Conversation on Democracies, Ancient and Modern* (Princeton).

Ogden, Daniel, ed., 2007, *A Companion to Greek Religion* (Malden, MA).

  2002, ed., *The Hellenistic World: New Perspectives* (Swansea).

Oliver, Graham J., 2006, "History and Rhetoric," in Glenn R. Bugh (ed.), 113–35.

  2000, ed., *The Epigraphy of Death: Studies in the History and Society of Greece and Rome* (Liverpool).

Oliver, James H., 1936, "The Monument with the Marathon Epigrams," *Hesperia* 5, 225–34.

  1935, "The Marathon Epigrams," *AJP* 56, 193–201.

  1933, "Selected Greek Inscriptions," *Hesperia* 2.4 = *The American Excavations in the Athenian Agora: Second Report*, 480–513.

Olson, S. Douglas, 2012, "The New Erechtheid Casualty List Epigram from Marathon: Athens and Herodes Atticus Remember," abstract of paper delivered at the 143rd Annual Meeting of the American Philological Association, Philadelphia, 5–8 January 2012, http://apaclassics.org/index.php/annual_meeting/143rd_annual_meeting_abstracts/17.5.olson/.

Osborne, M. J., 1981, "Entertainment in the Prytaneion at Athens," *ZPE* 41, 153–70.

Osborne, Robin, ed., 2007, *Debating the Athenian Cultural Revolution: Art, Literature, Philosophy, and Politics 430–380 BC* (Cambridge).

  2003, "Changing the Discourse," in Kathryn A. Morgan (ed.), 251–72.

1999, "Inscribing Performance," in Simon Goldhill and Robin Osborne (eds.), 341–58.

1998, "Sculpted Men of Athens: Masculinity and Power in the Field of Vision," in Lin Foxhall and John Salmon (eds.), 23–42.

1997, "Law, The Democratic Citizen, and the Representation of Women in Classical Athens," *P&P* 155, 3–33.

1996, *Greece in the Making, 1200–479 BC* (London).

Osborne, Robin, and Simon Hornblower, eds., 1994, *Ritual, Finance, Politics: Athenian Democratic Accounts Presented to David Lewis* (Oxford).

Osley, A. S., 1946, "Greek Biography before Plutarch," *G&R* 15, 7–20.

Ostwald, Martin, 1991, "Herodotus and Athens," *ICS* 16, 137–48.

O'Sullivan, Lara, 2009, *The Regime of Demetrius of Phalerum in Athens, 317–307 BCE: A Philosopher in Politics = Mnemosyne* Supp. 318 (Leiden).

Pade, Marianne, 2007, *The Reception of Plutarch's Lives in Fifteenth-Century Italy*, 2 vols. (Copenhagen).

Page, D. L., 1981, *Further Greek Epigrams* (Cambridge).

1968, *Lyrica Graeca selecta* (Oxford).

1962, *Poetae melici Graeci* (Oxford).

Palagia, Olga, 2000, "Hephaestion's Pyre and the Royal Hunt of Alexander," in A. B. Bosworth and E. J. Baynham (eds.), 167–206.

Panayotou, A., 2007, "The Position of the Macedonian Dialect," in A.-F. Christides (ed.), 433–43.

Parke, H. W., and John Boardman, 1957, "The Struggle for the Tripod and the First Sacred War," *JHS* 77, 276–82.

Parker, Robert, 1996, *Athenian Religion: A History* (Oxford).

Patterson, Cynthia B., ed., 2006a, *Antigone's Answer: Essays on Death and Burial, Family and State in Classical Athens = Helios* 33 S.

2006b, "'Citizen Cemeteries' in Classical Athens?" *CQ* 56, 48–56.

1998, *The Family in Greek History* (Cambridge, MA).

1981, *Pericles' Citizenship Law of 451–50 BC* (New York).

Pearson, Lionel, 1960, *The Lost Histories of Alexander the Great* (New York).

1957, "Popular Ethics in the World of Thucydides," *CP* 52, 228–44.

1941, "Historical Allusions in the Attic Orators," *CP* 36, 209–29.

1939, *Early Ionian Historians* (Oxford).

Peck, Harry Thurston, 1898, *Harper's Dictionary of Classical Antiquities* (New York).

Pédech, Paul, 1984, *Historiens compagnons d'Alexandre: Callisthène, Onésicrite, Néarque, Ptolémée, Aristobule* (Paris).

Peek, Werner, 1960, "Zu den Perser-Epigrammen," *Hermes* 88, 494–8.

1955, *Griechische Vers-Inschriften*, vol. I, *Grab-Epigramme* (Berlin).

1951–3, "Aus der Werkstatt," in George E. Mylonas (ed.), vol. II, 304–29, pls. 69–70.

Pelling, Christopher, 2006, "Homer and Herodotus," in M. J. Clarke, B. G. F. Currie, and R. O. A. M. Lyne (eds.), 75–104.

2002, "Speech and Action: Herodotus' Debate on the Constitutions," *PCPS* 48, 123–58.

1997a, "Aeschylus' *Persai* and History," in Christopher Pelling (ed.), 1997b, 1–19.

1997b, ed., *Greek Tragedy and the Historian* (Oxford).

1997c, "East is East and West is West – Or Are They? National Stereotypes in Herodotus," *Histos* 1, http://www.dur.ac.uk/Classics/histos/1997/pelling.html.

1990, ed., *Characterization and Individuality in Greek Literature* (Oxford).

Pellizer, Ezio, 1990, "Outlines of a Morphology of Sympotic Entertainment," in Oswyn Murray (ed.), 177–84.

Perlman, S., 1985, "Greek Diplomatic Tradition and the Corinthian League of Philip of Macedon," *Historia* 34, 153–74.

1968, "Athenian Democracy and the Revival of Imperialistic Expansion at the Beginning of the Fourth Century BC," *CP* 63, 257–67.

Perrin, Bernadotte, 1916, *Plutarch: Lives, Pericles and Fabius Maximus, Nicias and Crassus*, Loeb Classical Library (Cambridge, MA, and London).

Petrakos, Basil, 1996, *Marathon*, trans. Alexandra Doumas (Athens).

Petrovic, Andrej, 2010, "True Lies of Athenian Public Epigrams," in Manuel Baumbach, Andrej Petrovic, and Ivana Petrovic (eds.), 202–15.

2007, *Kommentar zu den simonideischen Versinschriften* = *Mnemosyne* Supp. 282 (Leiden).

Pfohl, Gerhard, ed., 1967, *Greek Poems on Stones*, vol. I, *Epitaphs from the Seventh to the Fifth Centuries BC* (Leiden).

Pfuhl, Ernst, 1932, "Zwei Kriegergrabmäler (zu Xenophons hippischen Schriften)," *AA*, 1–7.

Phillips, David, trans. and intro., 2004, *Athenian Political Oratory: 16 Key Speeches* (New York).

Pickard-Cambridge, A. W., 1968, *The Dramatic Festivals of Athens*, 2nd edn., rev. J. Gould and D. M. Lewis (Oxford).

Poddighe, Elizabeth, 2009, "Alexander and the Greeks: The Corinthian League," in Waldemar Heckel and Lawrence A. Tritle (eds.), 99–120.

Podlecki, A[nthony]. J., 1977, "Herodotus in Athens?" in K. Kinzl (ed.), 246–65.

1966, "The Political Significance of the Athenian 'Tyrannicide'-Cult," *Historia* 15, 129–41.

Pomeroy, Arthur J., 1991, *The Appropriate Comment: Death Notices in the Ancient Historians* = Studien zur klassischen Philologie 58 (Frankfurt am Main).

Pomeroy, Sarah B., 2002, *Spartan Women* (Oxford).

Pomper, Philip, 1996, "Historians and Individual Agency," *History and Theory* 35, 281–308.

Poulakos, John, 2008, *Sophistical Rhetoric in Classical Greece* (Columbia, SC).

Powell, Anton, 1988, *Athens and Sparta: Constructing Greek Political and Social History from 478 BC* (Portland).

Powell, Anton, and Stephen Hodkinson, eds., 1994, *The Shadow of Sparta* (London).

Pownall, Frances, 2004, *Lessons from the Past: The Moral Use of History in Fourth-Century Prose* (Ann Arbor).

1998, "Condemnation of the Impious in Xenophon's *Hellenica*," *The Harvard Theological Review* 91, 251–77.

1995 "*Presbeis Autokratores*: Andocides' *De Pace*," *Phoenix* 49, 140–9.

Prag, A. J. N. W., J. H. Musgrave, and R. A. H. Neave, 1984, "The Skull from Tomb II at Vergina: King Philip II of Macedon," *JHS* 104, 60–78.

Price, M. Jessop, 1993, "Alexander's Policy on Coinage," in Jesper Carlsen, Bodil Due, Otto Steen Due, and Birte Poursen (eds.), 171–5.

1991, *The Coinage in the Name of Alexander the Great and Philip Arrhidaeus*, 2 vols. (Zurich).

Pritchett, W. Kendrick, 1993, *The Liar School of Herodotus* (Amsterdam).

1974, *The Greek State at War, Part 2* (Berkeley).

1958, "Observations on Chaironeia," *AJA* 62, 307–11.

1940, "The Term of Office of Attic *Strategoi*," *AJP* 61, 469–74.

Proietti, Gerald, 1987, *Xenophon's Sparta: An Introduction = Mnemosyne* Supp. 98 (Leiden).

Proietti, Giorgia, 2011, review of Kostas Buraselis and Katerina Meidani, eds., *Μαραθών: η μάχη και ο αρχαίος Δήμος / Marathon: the Battle and the Ancient Deme* (Athens, 2010), *BMCR* 2011.09.55, http://bmcr.brynmawr.edu/2011/2011–09–55.html.

Raaflaub, Kurt A., 2004, *The Discovery of Freedom in Ancient Greece* (Chicago).

2003, "Stick and Glue: The Function of Tyranny in Fifth-Century Athenian Democracy," in Kathryn A. Morgan (ed.), 59–93.

1996, "Equalities and Inequalities in Athenian Democracy," in Josiah Ober and Charles Hedrick (eds.), 139–74.

1989, "Contemporary Perceptions of Democracy in Fifth-Century Athens," *C&M* 40, 33–70.

1987, "Herodotus, Political Thought, and the Meaning of History," *Arethusa* 20.1–2 = *Herodotus and the Invention of History*, 221–48.

1983, "Democracy, Oligarchy, and the Concept of the 'Free Citizen' in Late Fifth-Century Athens," *Political Theory* 11, 517–44.

Race, Willam H., 1987, "Pindaric Encomium and Isokrates' *Evagoras*," *TAPA* 117, 131–55.

Rahe, Paul A., 1981, "The Annihilation of the Sacred Band at Chaeronea," *AJA* 85, 84–7.

Rahn, Peter J., 1986, "Funeral Monuments of the First Priestess of Athena Nike," *BSA* 81, 195–207, pls. 11–12.

1971, "Xenophon's Developing Historiography," *TAPA* 102, 497–508.

Raubitschek, A. E., 1943, "Greek Inscriptions," *Hesperia* 12.1 = *The American Excavations in the Athenian Agora: Twenty-Third Report*, 12–88.

1940, "Two Monuments Erected after the Victory of Marathon," *AJA* 44, 53–9.

1939, "Leagros," *Hesperia* 8, 155–64.

Rauscher, Helga, 1971, "Anisokephalie: Ursache und Bedeutung der Grössen-variierung von Figuren in der griechischen Bildkomposition" (diss., Vienna). *Non vidi.*

Ray, J. D., 1988, "Egypt, 525–404 BC," in John Boardman, et al. (eds.), 254–86.

Redfield, James, 1985, "Herodotus the Tourist," *CP* 80, 97–118.

Rengakos, Antonios, and Antonis Tsakmakis, eds., 2006, *Brill's Companion to Thucydides* (Leiden).

Rhodes, P. J., 1999, "Sparta, Thebes, and *autonomia*," *Eirene* 35, 33–40.

    1981, *A Commentary on the Aristotelian* Athenaion Politeia (Oxford).

Rhodes, P. J., and Robin Osborne, eds., intro., trans., and comm., 2003, *Greek Historical Inscriptions, 404–323 BC* (Oxford).

Rhodes, P. J., with David M. Lewis, 1997, *The Decrees of the Greek City-States* (Oxford).

Richter, Gisela M. A., 1984, *The Portraits of the Greeks*, abridged and rev. R. R. R. Smith (Ithaca).

    1965, *The Portraits of the Greeks*, 3 vols. (London, supplement 1972).

    1961, *The Archaic Gravestones of Attica* (London).

    1960, *Kouroi: Archaic Greek Youths: A Study of the Development of the Kouros Type in Greek Sculpture*, 2nd edn. (London) (2nd edn. of Richter 1942).

    1944, "Two Greek Statues," *AJA* 48, 229–39.

    1942, *Kouroi: A Study of the Development of the Greek Kouros from the Late Seventh to the Early Fifth Century BC*, 1st edn. (New York) (1st edn. of Richter 1960).

Ridgway, Brunilde Sismondo, 1997, *Fourth-Century Styles in Greek Sculpture* (Madison).

    1990, *Hellenistic Sculpture 1: The Styles of ca. 331–200 BC* (Bristol).

    1977, *The Archaic Style in Greek Sculpture* (Princeton).

Riginos, Alice Swift, 1994, "The Wounding of Philip II of Macedon: Fact and Fabrication," *JHS* 114, 103–19.

Ritter, Hans-Werner, 1965, *Diadem und Königsherrschaft: Untersuchungen zu Zeremonien und Rechtsgrundlagen des Herrschaftsantritts bei den Persern, bei Alexander dem Grossen und im Hellenismus* (Berlin).

Roberts, Jennifer Tolbert, 1982, *Accountability in Athenian Government* (Madison).

Robertson, Noel, 1982, "The Decree of Themistocles in Its Contemporary Setting," *Phoenix* 36, 1–44.

    1978, "The Myth of the First Sacred War," *CQ* 28, 38–73.

    1976, "False Documents at Athens: Fifth Century History and Fourth Century Publicists," *Historical Reflections* 3, 3–25.

Robinson, Charles Alexander, Jr., 1953, *The History of Alexander the Great*, vol. I = "Part 1: An Index to the Ancient Historians; Part 2: The Fragments" (Providence).

    1932, *The Ephemerides of Alexander's Expedition* (Providence).

Robinson, David Moore, 1934, "Inscriptions from Olynthus, 1934," *TAPA* 65, 103–37.

Robinson, Eric W., 1997, *The First Democracies: Early Popular Government Outside Athens* = *Historia* Einzelschriften 107 (Stuttgart).

Roebuck, Carl, 1948, "The Settlements of Philip II with the Greek States in 338 BC," *CP* 43, 73–92.

Roesch, Paul, 1984, "Un décret inédit de la Ligue thébaine et la flotte d'Épaminondas," *REG* 97, 45–60.

Roisman, Joseph, 2005, *The Rhetoric of Manhood: Masculinity in the Attic Orators* (Berkeley).

    2003, ed., *Brill's Companion to Alexander the Great* (Leiden).

    1984, "Ptolemy and His Rivals in His History of Alexander," *CQ* 34, 373–85.

Roisman, Joseph and Ian Worthington, eds., 2010, *A Companion to Ancient Macedonia* (Malden, MA).

Rolfe, John C., ed. and trans., 1946, *Quintus Curtius*, 2 vols., Loeb Classical Library (Cambridge, MA).

Romano, David Gilman, 1990, "Philip of Macedon, Alexander the Great, and the Ancient Olympic Games," in Elin C. Danien (ed.), 63–79.

Romilly, Jacqueline de, 1992, *The Great Sophists in Periclean Athens*, trans. Janet Lloyd (Oxford).

Romm, James, 2006, "Herodotus and the Natural World," in Carolyn Dewald and John Marincola (eds.), 178–91.

Rood, Tim, 2004a, "Panhellenism and Self-Presentation: Xenophon's Speeches," in Robin Lane Fox (ed.), 2004, 305–29.

    2004b, "Xenophon and Diodorus: Continuing Thucydides," in Christopher Tuplin (ed.), 2004, 341–95.

Roos, A. G., ed., add., and corr. Gerhard Wirth, 2002, *Flavius Arrianus*, vol. II, *Scripta Minora et Fragmenta* (Leipzig).

Rose, H. J., 1956, review of C. Habicht, *Gottmenschentum und griechische Städte* = Zetemata 14 (Munich), *JHS* 77 (1957), 340–1.

Rosivach, V. J., 1987, "Some Fifth and Fourth Century Views on the Purpose of Ostracism," *Tyche* 2, 161–70.

Rösler, Wolfgang, 1995, "Wine and Truth in the Greek Symposion," in Oswyn Murray and Manuela Tecuşan, eds., 106–12.

Rutter, N. Keith, and Brian A. Sparkes, eds., 2000, *Word and Image in Ancient Greece* (Edinburgh).

Ryder, T. T. B., 1965, Koine Eirene: *General Peace and Local Independence in Ancient Greece* (Oxford).

Sagan, Eli, 1991, *The Honey and the Hemlock: Democracy and Paranoia in Ancient Athens and Modern America* (Princeton).

Sakellariou, M. B., 1980, trans. D. Hardy, "Philip and the Southern Greeks: Strength and Weakness," in Miltiades B. Hatzopoulos and Louisa D. Loukopoulos (eds.), 112–27.

Samuel, Alan E., 1996, n.t., review of Andrew Stewart, *Faces of Power: Alexander's Image and Hellenistic Politics* (Berkeley, 1993), *Phoenix* 50, 85–7.

Sancisi-Weerdenburg, Heleen, 2002, "The Personality of Xerxes, King of Kings," in Egbert J. Bakker, Irene J. F. de Jong, and Hans van Wees (eds.), 579–90, originally published in L. de Meyer and E. Haerinck, eds., *Archaeologica Iranica et Orientalis Miscellanea in Honorem Louis Vanden Berghe* (Ghent, 1989), 549–60.

Sanders, J. M., ed., 1992, *ΦΙΛΟΛΑΚΩΝ: Lakonian Studies in Honour of Hector Catling* (London).

Saporito, Samantha, 2009, "Xenophon on Virtue: The *Agesilaus* as an Ethical Model for the *Hellenica*?" (undergraduate senior thesis, Department of Greek and Latin, The Catholic University of America).

Scanlon, Thomas F., 1987, "Thucydides and Tyranny," *CA* 6, 286–301.

Schachermeyr, F., 1970, *Alexander in Babylon und die Reichsordnung nach seinem Tode* (Vienna).

Schachter, Albert, 1986, *Cults of Boeotia*, vol. II, *Herakles to Poseidon* = *BICS* Supp. 38.2 (London).

Schaefer, Hans, 1965a, "Das Eidolon des Leonidas," in Hans Schaefer, 1965b, 323–36.

    1965b, *Probleme der alten Geschichte* (Göttingen).

Schepens, G., 2007, "Hegemony in Fourth-Century Historiography," presentation at "Greek Historiography in the Fourth Century BC: Problems and Perspectives" (conference, Università degli Studi di Bologna, 13–15 December, 2007).

Schleif, Hans, and W. Zschietzschmann, 1944, "Das Philippeion," in Emil Kunze and Hans Schleif (eds.), 1–52.

Schultz, Peter, and Ralf von den Hoff, eds., 2007, *Early Hellenistic Portraiture: Image, Style, Context* (Cambridge).

Schwarzenberg, E., 1975a, "Alexander Rondanini oder Winkelmann und Alexander," in *Wandlungen: Studien zur antiken und neueren Kunst* = *Festschrift E. Homann-Wedeking* (Waldassen-Bayern), 163–88.

    1975b "The Portraiture of Alexander," in E. Badian (with Denis van Berchem) (ed.), 1975, 223–67, discussion 268–78.

Scott, Kenneth, 1932, "Humor at the Expense of the Ruler Cult," *CP* 27, 317–28.

Seager, Robin, 2001, "Xenophon and Athenian Democratic Ideology," *CQ* 51, 385–97.

    1981, "The Freedom of the Greeks of Asia: From Alexander to Antiochus," *CQ* 31, 106–12.

    1967, "Thrasybulus, Conon, and Athenian Imperialism, 396–386 BC," *JHS* 87, 95–115.

Seager, Robin, and Christopher Tuplin, 1980, "The Freedom of the Greeks of Asia: On the Origins of a Concept and the Creation of a Slogan," *JHS* 100, 141–54.

Sealey, Raphael, 1993, *Demosthenes and His Time: A Study in Defeat* (Oxford).

    1977, *A History of the Greek City States, c. 700–338 BC* (Berkeley).

Seiler, Florian, 1986, *Die griechische Tholos: Untersuchungen zur Entwicklung, Typologie, und Funktion kunstmäßiger Rundbauten* (Mainz am Rhein).

Shapiro, H. Alan, 1991, "The Iconography of Mourning in Athenian Art," *AJA* 95, 629–56.

Shapiro, Susan O., 1996, "Herodotus and Solon," *CA* 15, 348–64.

Shear, Julia L., 2007, "Cultural Change, Space, and the Politics of Commemoration in Athens," in Osborne, ed., 91–115.

Sherman Charles L., ed. and trans., 1952, *Diodorus of Sicily*, vol. VII, *Books XV.20–XVI.65*, Loeb Classical Library (Cambridge, MA).

Shrimpton, Gordon, 1997, *History and Memory in Ancient Greece* (Montreal).

    1977, "Theopompus' Treatment of Philip in the *Philippica*," *Phoenix* 31, 123–44.

    1971, "The Theban Supremacy in Fourth-Century Literature," *Phoenix* 25, 310–18.

Shur, Elmer George, 1931, *Sculptured Portraits of Greek Statesmen* (Baltimore).

Slater, Niall, 1985, "Vanished Players: Two Classical Reliefs and Theatre History," *GRBS* 26, 333–44, pls. 1–2.

Smith, Amy C., 2003, "Athenian Political Art from the Fifth and Fourth Centuries BCE: Images of Historical Individuals," in C. W. Blackwell (ed.).

Smith, Charles Forster, ed. and trans., 1919–23, *Thucydides:* History of the Peloponnesian War, 4 vols., Loeb Classical Library (Cambridge, MA, 1919–23, vols. I–II rev. 1928, 1930).

Smith, R. R. R., 2007, "Pindar, Athletes, and the Early Greek Statue Habit," in Simon Hornblower and Catherine Morgan (eds.), 83–139.

    1988, *Hellenistic Royal Portraits* (Oxford).

Smyth, Herbert Weir, 1999, appendix and addendum by Hugh Lloyd-Jones, *Aeschylus:* Agamemnon, Libation-Bearers, Eumenides, Fragments, Loeb Classical Library (Cambridge, MA, and London, 1926; reprint, 1999).

Snell, B., ed., 1971, *Tragicorum Graecorum fragmenta*, vol. I, *Didascaliae tragicae, catalogi tragicorum et tragoediarum, testimonia et fragmenta tragicorum minorum* (Göttingen).

Snodgrass, Anthony M., 1980, *Archaic Greece: The Age of Experiment* (London).

Sobak, Robert Benjamin, 2009, "Skill, Exchange, and Common-Knowledge: Studies on Craftsmen and Craftsmanship in Democratic Athens" (diss., Princeton University).

Solmsen, Lieselotte, 1944, "Speeches in Herodotus' Account of the Battle of Plataea," *CP* 39, 241–53.

    1943, "Speeches in Herodotus' Account of the Ionic [*sic*] Revolt," *AJP* 64, 194–207.

Sommerstein, Alan H., 2008, *Aeschylus:* Persians, Seven Against Thebes, Suppliants, Prometheus Bound, Loeb Classical Library (Cambridge, MA, and London).

Sordi, Marta, 1953, "La prima guerra sacra," *RFIC* 31, 320–46.

Soteriades, G[eorgios]., 1903, "Das Schlachtfeld von Charonea," *AM* 29, 301–30.

    1902, "Ἀνασκαφὴ δύο τύμβων παρὰ τὴν Χαιρώνειαν," *Πρακτικά*: 53–9.

Soulis, E. M., 1972, *Xenophon and Thucydides* (Athens).

Southgate, Beverley C., 2001, *History: What and Why? Ancient, Modern, and Post-modern Perspectives*, 2nd edn. (London).

Spence, I. G., 1993, *The Cavalry of Classical Greece: A Social and Military History with Particular Reference to Athens* (Oxford).

Spencer, Diana, 2002, *The Roman Alexander: Reading a Cultural Myth* (Exeter).

Stadter, Philip, 1980, *Arrian of Nicomedia* (Chapel Hill).

1973, ed., *The Speeches in Thucydides: A Collection of Original Studies with a Bibliography* (Chapel Hill).

Staïs, Valerios, 1893, "Ὁ ἐν Μαραθῶνι τύμβος," *MDAI(A)* 18, 46–63, pls. 2–5.

1890, "Ὁ τύμβος τῶν Μαραθωνομάχων," *Deltion Archaiologikon* 6, 123–32, pl. Δ.

Staïs, Valerios, P. Kavvadias, A. G. Lolling, G. Kaveraou, with K. Metsopoulos, 1890, "Ἀνασκαφαὶ ἐν Ἀττικῇ," *Deltion Archaiologikon* 6, 65–71.

Starr, Chester G., 1968, *The Awakening of the Greek Historical Spirit* (New York).

Stears, Karen, 2000a, "Losing the Picture: Change and Continuity in Athenian Grave Monuments in the Fourth and Third Centuries BC," in N. Keith Rutter and Brian A. Sparkes (eds.), 2000, 206–27.

2000b, "The Times They Are A' Changing: Developments in Fifth-Century Funerary Sculpture," in G. J. Oliver (ed.), 2000, 25–58.

Ste. Croix, G. E. M. de, 1977, "Herodotus," *G&R* 24, 130–48.

1972, *The Origins of the Peloponnesian War* (London).

Stehle, Eva, 2001, "The Good Daughter: Mothers' Tutelage in Erinna's Distaff and Fourth-Century Epitaphs," in André Lardinois and Laura McClure (eds.), 179–200.

1997, *Performance and Gender in Ancient Greece: Nondramatic Poetry in Its Setting* (Princeton).

Steinhauer, Georgios, 2010, "Οι στήλες των Μαραθωνομάχων από την έπαυλη του Ηρώδη Αττικού στη Λουκού Κυνουρίας," in Kostas Buraselis and Katerina Meidani (eds.), 99–108. *Non vidi.*

2004–9, "Στήλη πεσόντων τῆς Ἐρεχθηίδος," *ΗΟΡΟΣ* 17–21, 679–92.

Stern, Jacob, 1991, "Scapegoat Narratives in Herodotus," *Hermes* 119, 304–11.

Stewart, Andrew, 2003, "Alexander in Greek and Roman Art," in Joseph Roisman (ed.), 31–66.

1993, *Faces of Power: Alexander's Image and Hellenistic Politics* (Berkeley).

1990, *Greek Sculpture: An Exploration*, 2 vols. (New Haven).

Stoneman, Richard, 2008, *Alexander the Great: A Life in Legend* (New Haven).

1991, intro. and trans., *The Greek Alexander Romance* (London).

Strassler, Robert B., ed., 2007, *The Landmark Herodotus: The Histories* (New York).

1996, ed., *The Landmark Thucydides: A Comprehensive Guide to the Peloponnesian War* (New York).

Strauss, Barry, 1996, "The Athenian Trireme: School of Democracy," in Josiah Ober and Charles Hedrick (eds.), 313–25.

1984, "Thrasybulus and Conon: A Rivalry in Athens in the 390s BC," *AJP* 105, 37–48.

Stuart, Duane Reed, 1928, *Epochs of Greek and Roman Biography* (Berkeley).

Stupperich, Reinhard, 1994, "The Iconography of Athenian State Burials in the Classical Period," in W. D. E. Coulson, et al. (eds.), 93–103.

1977, "Staatsbegräbnis und Privatgrabmal im Klassischen Athen" (diss., Westfälische Wilhelms-Universität zu Münster).

Szegedy-Maszak, Andrew, 1993, "Thucydides' Solonian Reflections," in Carol Dougherty and Leslie Kurke (eds.), 201–14.

1978, "Legends of the Greek Lawgivers," *GRBS* 19, 199–209.

Taplin, Oliver, ed., 2000, *Literature in the Greek World* (Oxford).

1993, *Comic Angels: And Other Approaches to Greek Drama Through Vase-Paintings* (Oxford).

Tarn, W. W., 1950, *Alexander the Great*, vol. II, *Sources and Studies* (Cambridge).

1921, "Heracles Son of Barsine," *JHS* 41, 18–28.

Taylor, Michael W., 1981, *The Tyrant Slayers: The Heroic Image in Fifth Century BC Athenian Art and Politics* (New York).

Teegarden, David A., 2013, *Death to Tyrants! Ancient Greek Democracy and the Struggle Against Tyranny* (Princeton).

Thomas, Carol G., 2007, *Alexander the Great in His World* (Malden).

Thomas, Rosalind, 2007, "Fame, Memorial, and Choral Poetry: The Origins of Epinikian Poetry – an Historical Study," in Simon Hornblower and Catherine Morgan (eds.), 141–66.

2003, "Prose Performance Texts: Epideixis and Written Publication in the Late Fifth and Early Fourth Centuries," in Harvey Yunis (ed.), 162–88.

2000, *Herodotus in Context: Ethnography, Science, and the Art of Persuasion* (Cambridge).

1992, *Literacy and Orality in Ancient Greece* (Cambridge).

1989, *Oral Tradition and Written Record in Classical Athens* (Cambridge).

Thompson, Homer A., 1978, "Some Hero Shrines in Ancient Athens," in William A. P. Childs, ed., *Athens Comes of Age: From Solon to Salamis* (Princeton), 96–108.

1940, *The Tholos of Athens and Its Predecessors* = *Hesperia* Supp. 4 (Princeton).

Thompson, Homer A., and R. E. Wycherley, 1972, *The Athenian Agora*, vol. XIV, *The Agora of Athens: The History, Shape, and Uses of an Ancient City Center* (Princeton).

Thompson, Margaret, 1982, "The Coinage of Philip II and Alexander III," in Beryl Barr-Sharrar and Eugene N. Borza (eds.), 113–21.

Thomsen, Rudi, 1972, *The Origin of Ostracism: A Synthesis* (Copenhagen).

Threatte, Leslie, 1977, "Unmetrical Spellings in Attic Inscriptions," *CA* 10, 169–94.

Tod, Marcus N., 1948, *A Selection of Greek Historical Inscriptions*, vol. II, *From 403 to 323 BC* (Oxford).

1946, *A Selection of Greek Historical Inscriptions*, vol. I, *To the End of the Fifth Century BC*, 2nd edn. (Oxford).

Tod, M. N., and A. J. B. Wace, 1906, *A Catalogue of the Sparta Museum* (Oxford).

Toher, Mark, 1991, "Greek Funerary Legislation and the Two Spartan Funerals," in Michael Flower and Mark Toher (eds.), 159–75.

Tordi, Anne Wilson, ed. and intro., 2004, Alexandreida in rima: *The Life and Deeds of Alexander the Great in an Anonymous Italian Renaissance Poem* (Lewiston, NY).

Traill, John S., 1975, *The Political Organization of Attica: A Study of the Demes, Trittyes, and Phylai, and Their Representation in the Athenian Council* = Hesperia Supp. 14 (Princeton).

Travlos, John, 1971, *Pictorial Dictionary of Ancient Athens* (New York).

Tritle, Lawrence A., 2009, "Alexander and the Greeks: Artists and Soldiers, Friends and Enemies," in Waldemar Heckel and Lawrence A. Tritle (eds.), 120–40.

1997, ed., *The Greek World in the Fourth Century: From the Fall of the Athenian Empire to the Successors of Alexander* (London).

Tsagalis, Christos, 2008, *Inscribing Sorrow: Fourth-Century Attic Funerary Epigrams* (Berlin).

Tuplin, C. J., ed., 2004, *Xenophon and His World* (Stuttgart).

1993, *The Failings of Empire: A Reading of Xenophon*, Hellenica *2.3.11–7.5.27* (Stuttgart).

1987, "The Leuctra Campaign: Some Outstanding Problems," *Klio* 69, 72–107.

1984, "Pausanias and Plutarch's *Epaminondas*," *CQ* 34, 346–58.

Umholtz, Gretchen, 2002, "Architraval Arrogance? Dedicatory Inscriptions in Greek Architecture of the Classical Period," *Hesperia* 71, 261–93.

Vanderpool, Eugene, 1970, *Ostracism at Athens* (Cincinnati), also published as "Ostracism at Athens," in *Lectures in Memory of Louise Taft Semple*, vol. II, *1968–1970* (Norman, OK, 1972), 217–50.

1966, "A Monument to the Battle of Marathon," *Hesperia* 35, 93–106.

Vatin, Claude, 1991, *Monuments votifs de Delphes* = Archaeologia Perusina 10 (Rome).

Verdin, H., G. Schepens, and E. de Keyser, eds., 1990, *Purposes of History: Studies in Greek Historiography from the 4th to the 2nd Centuries BC* = Studia Hellenistica 30 (Louvain).

Vermeule, E., 1970, "Five Vases from the Grave Precinct of Dexileos," *JDAI* 85, 94–111.

Vince, C. A., and J. H. Vince, eds. and trans., 1926, *Demosthenes:* De corona, De falsa legatione (18–19), Loeb Classical Library (London).

Vince, J. H., ed. and trans., 1935, *Demosthenes:* Against Meidias, Androtion, Aristocrates, Timocrates, Aristogeiton 1 and 2 (21–26), Loeb Classical Library (London).

1926, ed. and trans., *Demosthenes:* Olynthiacs 1–3, Philippic 1, On the Peace, Philippic 2, On Halonnesus, On the Chersonese, Philippics 3 and 4, Answer to Philip's Letter, Philip's Letter, On Organization, On the Navy-Boards, For the Liberty of the Rhodians, For the People of Megalopolis, On the Treaty with Alexander, Against Leptines (1–17 and 20), Loeb Classical Library (London).

Vita, Antonino di, and Carla Alfano, eds., 1995, *Alessandro Magno, Storia e Mito* (Rome).

Vlassopoulos, Kostas, 2007, "Beyond and Below the Polis: Networks, Associations, and the Writing of Greek History," *MHR* 22, 11–22.

Vlastos, Gregory, 1953, "Isonomia," *AJP* 74, 337–66.

Walbank, Michael [B.], 2008, "Proxeny and Proxenos in Fifth-Century Athens," in Polly Low (ed.), 132–9.

   1978, *Athenian Proxenies of the Fifth Century BC* (Toronto).

Walker, Andrew D., 1993, "*Enargeia* and the Spectator in Greek Historiography," *TAPA* 123, 353–77.

Wallace, M. B., 1970, "Early Greek 'Proxenoi,'" *Phoenix* 24, 189–208.

Wallace, Paul W., 1972, "The Tomb of Themistokles in the Peiraieus," *Hesperia* 41, 451–62.

Wallace, Robert W., and Edward M. Harris, eds., 1996, *Transitions to Empire: Essays in Greco-Roman History, 360–146 BC, in Honor of E. Badian* (Norman, OK).

Walsh, John, 1986, "The Date of the Athenian Stoa at Delphi," *AJA* 90, 319–336.

Waters, Kenneth H., 1971, *Herodotos on Tyrants and Despots: A Study in Objectivity* = *Historia* Einzelschriften 15 (Wiesbaden).

Webster, T. B. L., 1969a, *Monuments Illustrating New Comedy* = *BICS* Supp. 50 (London; 3rd edn., 2 vols., rev. and enl. J. R. Green and A. Seeberg, 1995).

   1969b, *Monuments Illustrating Old and Middle Comedy* = *BICS* Supp. 39 (London).

   1967, *Monuments Illustrating Tragedy and Satyr Play*, 2nd edn. = *BICS* Supp. 20 (London).

Wees, Hans van, 1996, "Homeric Warfare," in Ian Morris and Barry Powell (eds.), 668–93.

Weinberg, Saul S., ed., 1956, *The Aegean and the Near East: Studies Presented to Hetty Goldman on the Occasion of Her Seventy-Fifth Birthday* (Locust Valley, NY).

Welles, C. Bradford, ed. and trans., 1963, *Diodorus of Sicily*, vol. VIII, *Books 16.66–95 and 17*, Loeb Classical Library (Cambridge, MA).

West, Stephanie, 2003, "Croesus' Second Reprieve and Other Tales of the Persian Court," *CQ* 53, 416–37.

   1991, "Herodotus' Portrait of Hecataeus," *JHS* 111, 144–60.

West, William C., 1973, "The Speeches in Thucydides: A Description and Listing," in Philip A. Stadter (ed.), 3–15.

   1969, "The Trophies of the Persian Wars," *CP* 64, 7–19.

Westlake, H. D., 1969a, *Essays on the Greek Historians and Greek History* (Manchester).

   1969b, "Individuals in Xenophon, *Hellenica*," in H. D. Westlake, 1969a, 203–25, originally published in *Bulletin of the John Rylands Library* 49 (1966), 246–69.

1968, *Individuals in Thucydides* (Cambridge).

1939, "The Sources of Plutarch's Pelopidas," *CQ* 33, 11–22.

Wheeler, Everett L., 1991, "The General as Hoplite," in Victor Davis Hanson (ed.), 121–70.

Whitby, Michael, 1995, "Philip the Nice," review of N. G. L. Hammond, *Philip of Macedon* (Baltimore, 1994), *CR* 45, 326–8.

Whitehead, David, 1993, "Cardinal Virtues: The Language of Public Approbation in Democratic Athens," *C&M* 44, 37–75.

1986, *The Demes of Attica 508/7–ca. 250 BC: A Social and Political Study* (Princeton).

1983, "Competitive Outlay and Community Profit: φιλοτιμία in Democratic Athens," *C&M* 34, 55–74.

Whitley, James, 1994, "The Monuments that Stood before Marathon: Tomb Cult and Hero Cult in Archaic Attica," *AJA* 98, 213–30.

Will, W., with G. Heinrichs, ed., 1988, *Zu Alexander der Grosse: Festschrift G. Wirth zum 60. Geburtstag am 9.12.86* (Amsterdam).

Wilson, Peter, 2000, *The Athenian Institution of the* Khoregia: *The Chorus, the City, and the Stage* (Cambridge).

Winkler, John J., and Froma I. Zeitlin, eds., 1990, *Nothing to Do with Dionysos? Athenian Drama in its Social Context* (Princeton).

Wirth, Gerhard, 1975, "Alexander und Rom," in E. Badian (with Denis van Berchem) (ed.), 181–210, discussion 211–21.

Woodcock, Eric Charles, 1928, "Demosthenes, Son of Alcisthenes," *HSCP* 39, 93–108.

Woodhead, A. Geoffrey, 1997, *The Athenian Agora,* vol. XVI, *Inscriptions: The Decrees* (Princeton).

Worthington, Ian, 2008, *Philip II of Macedonia* (New Haven).

2003, "Alexander, Philip, and the Macedonian Background," in Joseph Roisman (ed.), 69–98.

2001, "Hyperides 5.32 and Alexander the Great's Statue," *Hermes* 129, 129–31.

1994, ed., *Ventures into Greek History* (Oxford).

Wycherley, R. E., 1957, *The Athenian Agora,* vol. III, *Literary and Epigraphical Testimonia* (Princeton).

Yardley, J. C., 1994, trans., intro. and notes by R. Develin, *Justin: Epitome of the Philippic History of Pompeius Trogus* (Atlanta).

1984, trans., intro., and notes by Waldemar Heckel, *Quintus Curtius Rufus: The History of Alexander* (London).

Young, Rodney, 1951, "*Sepulturae intra urbem,*" *Hesperia* 20, 67–134.

Young, T. Cuyler, 1988, "The Early History of the Medes and the Persians and the Achaemenid Empire to the Death of Cambyses," in John Boardman, et al. (eds.), 1–52.

Yunis, Harvey, ed., 2003, *Written Texts and the Rise of Literate Culture in Ancient Greece* (Cambridge).

1991, "How Do the People Decide? Thucydides on Periclean Rhetoric and Civic Instruction," *AJP* 112, 179–200.

Zahrnt, Michael, 1996, "Alexanders Übergang über den Hellespont," *Chiron* 26, 129–47.

Zizza, Cesare, 2006, *Le iscrizioni nella* Periegesi *di Pausania: Commento ai testi epigrafici* (Pisa).

Zuwiyya, Z. David, ed., 2011, *A Companion to Alexander Literature in the Middle Ages* (Leiden).

Index locorum

Only passages that are subjected to detailed analysis or whose inclusion supports an important part of the argument are listed here. Selected relevant cross-references for editions of the inscriptions are provided at the points of their discussion in the text.

Aeschines
  3.177–91, 213
  3.180, 212
  3.187, 208
Aeschylus
  Ag. 109–12, 172
  Pers. 249–514, 85
Aristophanes
  Ran. 1284–90, 172
Arrian
  1.12.2, 335
  4.10.5–12.7, 342
  5.25.3–27.4, 338
  5.26.2, 337
  7.26.3, 6
Athenaion Politeia
  2.2, 54
  26.4, 176
  58.1, 23

Cicero
  De legibus
    2.59–60, 46
    2.64–5, 46

Demosthenes
  19.303–4, 347
  20.69–70, 280
  20.70, 21
  23.196–9, 215
  23.198, 1–2
Diodorus Siculus
  12.43.3, 232
  12.68.3, 232
  15.66.1, 278
  15.72.4, 279
  16.3.7, 303
  16.8.6, 303
  16.86.6–87.3, 317
  16.91.4–93.2, 311
  16.95.1, 311

  17.117.3–5, 5
  18.26.3–28.1, 8
  18.28.2–6, 8–9

Ephemerides (*FGrH* 117)
  F 3a–b, 5

Herodotus
  Praef., 58
  Praef.-1.5.4, 85–6
  1.6.2–3, 64
  1.26.1–28.1, 65
  1.29.1–2, 66
  1.30.1–3, 66, 68
  1.30.4–5, 68
  1.32.1–9, 68
  1.61.3, 95
  1.95.1, 70
  1.141.1–4, 71
  1.209.1–210.1, 72
  3.39.3–4, 63
  3.40.1–43.2, 64
  3.65.1–66.3, 63
  3.80.1–82.5, 72–5
  3.80.2–6, 74
  3.81.1–3, 74
  3.82.1–5, 74–5
  3.125.2, 64
  3.153–4, 76
  3.155.1–6, 76
  3.160.1–2, 76
  4.87.1–92.1, 76–7
  5.2.2, 77
  5.28.1–6.32.1, 87
  5.55.1–65.5, 24
  5.62.2, 25
  5.97.1–3, 90–1
  5.124.1–2, 96
  6.109.3, 24
  6.109.3–6, 97
  6.121–31, 24

Subject index

Achaea, 247, 262
Achaeans, 197, 247, 262
Achilles, 19, 173, 321, 326–9, 335–9, 341, 353
Acropolis (Athenian), 18, 26, 38, 41, 204, 206, 238, 282, 302, 346
Aegospotami, 235–7
Aeschines, 207–8, 211–13, 229, 278, 288, 308, 347
Aeschylus, 85, 138, 262
Agamemnon, 13, 50, 242, 245
age, 67, 158, 223, 272, 277, 281, 316, 319, 323, 329
agency, 40–1, 45, 56, 60–2, 79–80, 84–9, 97, 159, 241, 348–50
    ascription of, 25, 56, 244, 295, 349
    and greatness, 353–4
    group, 59, 68, 71, 85–6, 105–6, 126, 135, 145, 257, 266
    historical *see* historical agency
    history-making, 58, 320
    limits, 229
agent groups, 195, 260, 329
agents of history, 40–1, 62, 123, 135, 139, 235–6, 240, 243, 261, 265
Agesilaus, 4, 16, 182, 233, 236, 240–54, 258, 263, 339, 352
    Xenophon's, 250–4, 290
Agis of Argos, 334
Agora (Athenian), 21, 26, 31–2, 39–40, 212, 280–2, 302
    statues, 19, 275, 281–2
Alcibiades, 13–14, 15, 124–5, 127–8, 135–43, 184–8, 189–90, 281, 351–2
    Xenophon's, 184–90
Alcmeonids, 2, 23–4, 109, 137
Alexander, 4–11, 19, 190, 287–9, 293–5, 312, 318, 345, 353–4
    audiences, 344–5
    behaviors, 320–2, 328
    coinage, 323
    in context, 320–2
    court, 334, 343
    death, 6, 344

Eastern expedition, 323, 330, 332–9
extant historians, 6, 17, 331
    as god, 339–44
    as hero, 335–8
    as King of the Macedonians, 322–4
    literary, 331–5
    from Macedon to Greece, 324–31
    mother, 321, 335
    personae, 322–44
Alexandria, 9, 335, 345
alliances, 262, 264, 285, 298
allies, 57–8, 77, 92, 96, 230, 244, 245, 262, 264, 298
Altis (Olympia), 291, 310
ambassadors, 189, 205, 206, 246–7, 296
ambition, 54, 75, 235, 240, 250–1
    Lysander, 235
Ammon, 328, 340–1
    Ammon-Zeus connection, 341, 353
    Egyptian oracle of, 8, 337, 340–3
Amphictyony, Delphic, 258, 307–8, 317
Amphipolis, 230–2, 278, 303, 307, 311, 323
Amyntas, 309
Anabasis, 16, 184, 243, 265, 278, 352
    leaders and led in, 190–201
Antiochus, 35, 205, 206
Antiphon, 141
Aornus, 337–8
Apelles, 252–3
Apollo, 34–5, 69, 243, 245, 298, 306–9, 317
Apollodorus, 148
Apollonophanes, 151–2, 154
Arcadia, 33, 57, 263
Arcadians, 197, 262–4
archaic elites, 152, 159
archaic period, 27, 35, 49–50, 67, 173, 274, 286, 309
Archestrate, 222–4
Archippus, 225–6
archonships, 147, 179, 220, 267, 268
Ares, 171–3, 299
aretè, 33, 272
Argives, 245

395